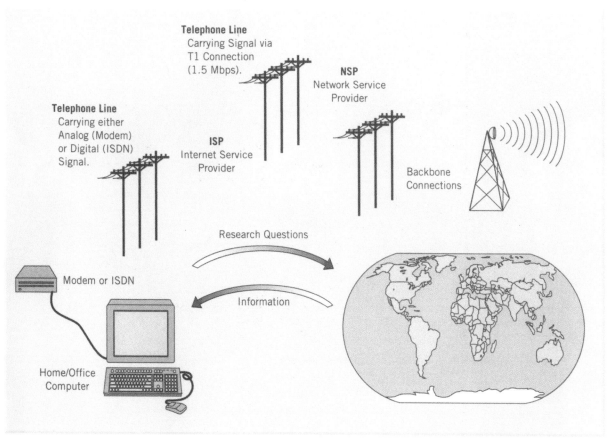

Telephone Line
Carrying Signal via
T1 Connection
(1.5 Mbps).

NSP
Network Service
Provider

Telephone Line
Carrying either
Analog (Modem)
or Digital (ISDN)
Signal.

ISP
Internet Service
Provider

Backbone
Connections

Research Questions

Information

Modem or ISDN

Home/Office
Computer

Accessing the World Wide Web

ESSENTIALS OF MARKETING RESEARCH

SECOND EDITION

V. KUMAR
ING Aetna Chair Professor of Marketing, and
Director, ING Aetna Center for Financial Services
University of Connecticut

DAVID A. AAKER
Gary Shansby Professor of Marketing Strategy
University of California, Berkeley

GEORGE S. DAY
Geoffrey T. Boisi Professor of Marketing, and
Director of the Huntsman Center
For Global Competition and Innovation
Wharton School, University of Pennsylvania

JOHN WILEY & SONS, INC.

ACQUISITIONS EDITOR	Jeff Marshall
EDITORIAL ASSISTANT	Michael Brennan
MARKETING MANAGER	Charity Robey
SENIOR PRODUCTION EDITOR	Norine M. Pigliucci
DESIGN DIRECTOR	Madelyn Lesure
PHOTO RESEARCHER	Elyse Rieder
PHOTO EDITORS	Hilary Newman and Sara Wight
PRODUCTION MANAGEMENT SERVICES	Hermitage Publishing Services

Cover Illustration: © Alexander Barsky/Stock Illustration Source

This book was set in Palatino by Hermitage Publishing Services and printed and bound by Donnelley Willard. The cover was printed by Lehigh Press.

This book is printed on acid-free paper. ∞

To order books please call 1(800)-225-5945.

Library of Congress Cataloging-in-Publication Data
Kumar, V.
   Essentials of marketing research / V. Kumar, David A. Aaker, George S. Day. —2nd ed.
      p.   cm.
   Includes bibliographical references and index.
   ISBN 0-471-41235-X (pbk. : alk. paper)
    1. Marketing research. I. Aaker, David A. II. Day, George S. III. Title.

HF5415.2 .K86 2001
658.8'3—dc21   2001026850

Printed in the United States of America

10 9 8 7 6 5 4 3 2

Dedicated With Love

To My Wife, Aparna and Godmother, Tirupura Mami
To My Wife, Kay
To My Wife, Marilyn

Preface

Managers all over the world make decisions on customer, firm, product, and service related issues on a regular basis. In a highly competitive world, information is the key to success in decision making. Defining, generating, managing, and interpreting information through relevant marketing intelligence becomes an integral part of every organization.

In other words, information is sought after on a continuous basis, and one strategy that can help facilitate this process is marketing intelligence. Since marketing research is an integral part of marketing intelligence, it is necessary to better understand the tools of marketing research.

The scope of marketing research has expanded in this technological era. In the presence of forces such as increased globalization and ever-changing technology, the boundaries of market research have expanded. It has become all the more critical to understand the process of marketing research. With the increase in corporate global competition, the use of marketing intelligence has emerged. Marketing intelligence is a form of business intelligence where legal, ethical collection of data and information is analyzed and transformed for use in strategic planning and problem solving. Tomorrow's managers need to better understand the role of marketing intelligence today. In order to fulfill such a demand, we have created this new edition on the essentials of marketing research. The book clearly focuses on the techniques and steps to marketing intelligence. It also describes the importance of marketing intelligence and its usefulness in strategic marketing decision making.

Readers of this book are presented with a treatise on the major steps in the marketing research process. The book discusses the importance of marketing research and the role it plays in the business world. The use of the Internet is explored in the text along with the global marketing research examples. The computer revolution has increased the power of marketing research and marketing intelligence with respect to sophisticated data – collecting and decision-making opportunities.

The book begins with a macro-level treatment of what marketing research is, where it fits within an organization, and how it helps in managerial decision making. Here, we also discuss the marketing research industry and give a brief treatment of both suppliers and users.

The body of the text takes a micro-level approach, detailing each and every step of the marketing research process. In describing the marketing research process, a decision-oriented perspective has been adopted to help students, who are future managers and researchers, make better decisions. Detailed discussions of the process, with numerous examples from the industry, characterize this micro phase.

Finally, we wrap up with a macro-level treatment of the applications of the marketing research. Here we address the traditional 4P research, as well as contemporary issues such as brand equity, customer satisfaction research, and emerging issues that continue to fascinate marketers, such as direct marketing, database marketing, and relationship marketing.

OBJECTIVES OF THIS TEXT

This book captures the critical elements of *Marketing Research, Seventh Edition,* Aaker, Kumar, and Day. While the *Marketing Research* text offers a comprehensive treatment of all the relevant topics, this book focuses on providing all the necessary ingredients in a concise form.

Our overall objectives in writing this text are:

1. To focus on the techniques and steps that show how a company can gather marketing intelligence and examine its usefulness in strategic marketing decision making.

2. To communicate in an interesting and informative manner the essence of marketing research to future managers and future researchers. Both groups need to know when marketing research can and should be used, what research alternatives exist, how to recognize effective and ineffective research, and how to interpret and apply the results.

3. To illustrate the usefulness of the Internet and other advances in technology for marketing research tasks.

4. To emphasize the current developments in marketing research, such as the distinction between domestic and international market research.

5. To use clear and current examples, applications, and illustrations throughout the book, in an effort to tie the material to the real world and thus provide interest and better understanding to the student.

6. To discuss the fastest-growing applications of marketing research—e-commerce, direct marketing, and database marketing research, and their impact on businesses.

7. To provide a clear and comprehensive treatment of modern data analysis topics. Each chapter includes simple numerical examples to help students get a hands-on feel for the material.

8. To provide a thorough coverage of the most advanced and current marketing research methodologies, pointing out their limitations, as well as their potential for enhancing research results.

HIGHLIGHTS OF THIS BOOK

In line with the trends in the marketplace, the book offers a complete treatment of all of the relevant issues that are necessary. The major offerings of this essentials book are:

1. The use of learning objectives in each chapter to guide the readers of this book.

2. The use of SPSS® software applications along with practice data sets to provide a tool to the understanding of data analysis.

3. Critical definitions are provided in the margin of each chapter.

4. The essential elements in the book are discussed as review points for ease of comprehension and appear at the end of each chapter.

5. The key terms used in the text are presented at the end of each chapter to highlight key points in the chapter.

6. The questions used in each chapter are both practical, challenging, and thought provoking.

7. The end of chapter summary offers a refreshing perspective of the material discussed in the chapter.

8. The practical exercises appearing at the end of each of the five sections in the text offer readers insight into actual experiences in the business world.

9. The end-of-chapter cases and the end-of-section cases offer readers the richness of different perspectives that can be adopted in selling a business problem.

10. The coverage on international marketing research expands the readers' ability to deal with issues that are not encountered in the domestic country research.

11. The use of current and relevant examples enhances the readers' interest and knowledge in marketing research.

12. The internet/web site support with information updates on a regular basis proves to be a "virtual library" in the area of marketing intelligence.

13. The discussion on how to apply marketing intelligence and marketing research in various marketing applications is presented. More importantly, applications include the traditional, contemporary, as well as emerging areas in marketing.

NEW TO THIS EDITION

In line with the above objectives, this revised second edition has undergone some critical changes. The more prominent of these changes are:

1. Incorporation of the important area of marketing intelligence and discusses its usefulness in strategic marketing decision making.

2. The text has been updated with discussions on new topics of interest and methods of practice in marketing research. For example, *Projective Techniques* have been updated to reflect how emphatic interviewing yields insightful results.

3. The new section on *Marketing Research in Practice* in each chapter focuses on the real world applications of marketing research. Several current real-world examples such as *Sprint PCS Wireless web Updates, Hidden Vally, Amazon Marketplace, 3M going Green, Nokia's revival technique* are new to this edition.

4. This text has been shortened and focuses on the necessary elements of core marketing research concepts such as web-based service, modifying questionnaires for cross national research, efficient ways of sampling.

5. Some discussions such as *The Components of the Internet* have been moved to the web to act as an additional source of information for the students.

6. All the cases have been moved to the web site for this book. These cases reflect current and future trends in marketing intelligence.

7. The length of the text has been reduced to enable the coverage of the material in the assigned teaching time period.

8. The chapter on the *Emerging Applications of Marketing Research* focuses on e-commerce, m-commerce, database marketing, and relationship marketing. The growth in e-commerce is phenomenal and the firm's ability to identify individual customers and for tailor marketing messages to them is an important task. Database marketing is on the verge of being the most important tool for businesses facing the challenges at the dawn of the twenty-first century. As firms shift their resources towards targeted marketing, the discussion in this chapter becomes increasingly valuable.

9. There is an incremental shift of attention to the current and future trends in marketing research in lieu of the effects of globalization. Exhibits in the text like *Welcome to the Global Marketplace* and cases showcased on the web such as the *Dell in Latin America* depict the importance of understanding these different yet converging global markets.

10. Firm-specific and data-specific URL's are provided in the book so that the users can access the most recent information.

11. The text has been effectively consolidated from 19 chapters in the previous edition to 16 chapters in this second edition.

12. Spreadsheet illustrations, using *SPSS®*, are provided for many statistical techniques discussed in this book.

13. *SPSS® Student Version 9.0 for Windows* is available with the text. Data sets on the accompanying *SPSS* CD include tables and cases.

SUPPLEMENTS TO THE BOOK

1. An Instructor's Manual with Test Questions accompanies this text. This manual provides solutions to end-of-chapter Questions and Problems, and discusses all the text cases in greater detail. Exam questions are arranged by chapters and include multiple-choice and true/false questions. An example of a course syllabus is presented, and many suggestions for the organization of the course are provided.

2. Web site support: A web site will be updated periodically in order to supplement the text with new up-to-date examples. This site includes the cases and web links cited in the text.

3. A computerized version of the Test Bank is available to instructors for customization of their exams.

4. Downloadable Power Point Presentations are available for all chapters via the text web site.

5. A marketing research video provides a glimpse of marketing research in action.

6. SPSS® software applications along with the practice data-set are available as a CD-ROM.

ORGANIZATION OF THE TEXT

The book is organized to reflect the "macro–micro–macro" approach toward gathering marketing intelligence and imparting marketing research training to the student. The text consists of four parts. Part I and IV deal with the "macro" aspects of marketing research; Parts II and III deal with the micro aspects.

Part I, consisting of four chapters, deals with the nature and scope of marketing research. Since, marketing research is an integral tool of marketing intelligence, the overall framework of marketing intelligence is presented, and where and how marketing research fits in with the other aspects of marketing intelligence is explained. The nature of the research industry and suppliers is also discussed here.

Part II, consisting of Chapters 5 through 11, deals with the fundamental aspects of data collection. This part is further divided into four sections, one section devoted to each of the three fundamental types of marketing research: exploratory, descriptive, and causal. The final section addresses the issue of sampling.

Part III, consisting of Chapter 12 to 14, discusses the fundamental aspects and techniques in data analysis. These include pre-analysis issues such as data editing, coding, and simple techniques such as hypothesis testing, chi-square analysis, and the analysis of variance.

Part IV, exposes the student to traditional, contemporary, and emerging applications of marketing research. Chapter 15 describes how to relay results in written and oral presentations. Chapter 16 covers applications. In a single chapter, these three categories of applications are covered within three sections. The discussion provides the student with a comprehensive picture of marketing research, highlighting where and how the individual units of the research process fit while solving marketing problems.

ACKNOWLEDGMENTS

We wish to thank Rajkumar Venkatesan, Srividya Krishnamurthy, Werner Reinartz, and Suresh Sundaram for their assistance in the preparation of this text. This book could not have been published without the support of our talented Wiley team, which includes our editor, Jeff Marshall, production editor, Norine Pigliucci, marketing manager, Charity Robey, Cindy Rhoads, Michael Brennan, Maddy Lesure, and Elyse Rieder. We would also like to thank our colleagues in various universities for giving us valuable suggestions in developing the first edition as well as constructive feedback in further improving the second edition. Reviewers of the first edition were John Samaras, University of Dallas, Joseph Cangelosi, University of Central Arkansas, Charles Quigley, Bryant College, Mary Wolfenberger, California State University Long Beach, Jeffrey Totten, University of Washington, Catherine Schaffer, Wharton School, University of Pennsylvania, and Pola Gupta, University of Northern Iowa. We would particularly like to thank these reviewers of the second edition:

K. Sivakumar
University of Illinois at Chicago

Sanjay Mehta
Sam Houston State University

Kiran Karande
Old Dominion University

Donald Lichtenstein
University of Colorado, Boulder

Joe K. Ballenger
Stephen F. Austin State University

Jeffrey W. Totten
Bemidji State University

Paul Boughton
St. Louis University

B. Andrew Cudmore
Florida Institute of Technology

Susan Logan Nelson
University of North Dakota

Raj Sethuraman
Southern Methodist University

Finally, we thank our students who have been a constant source of input in developing this text.

Brief Contents

Contents

THE NATURE AND SCOPE OF MARKETING RESEARCH

A Decision-Making Perspective on Marketing Research

Learning Objectives

- Understand the need and use of marketing research in an organization.
- Comprehend how marketing research fits in the bigger scheme of the marketing environment.
- Explain the role of marketing research in decision making.
- Discuss the factors that affect marketing research decisions.
- Understand the implication of ethical issues in conducting research.
- Introduce international marketing research.

◆ INTRODUCTION

Marketing is the process of planning and executing the conception, pricing, promotion, and distribution of ideas, goods, and services to create exchanges that satisfy individual and organizational objectives. The marketing concept requires that customer satisfaction rather than profit maximization be the goal of an organization.[1] In other words, the organization should be consumer oriented and should try to understand consumers' requirements and satisfy them quickly and efficiently, in ways that are beneficial to both the consumer and the organization. Marketing is also often defined as providing products and services that help satisfy the needs of a particular market. To find out what the market's needs are, marketers must learn as much as they can about their customers. In fact, marketers have an insatiable desire to find out more and more about whom they sell to—so much so that it has created an enormous marketing research industry that supports the need for more information. This means that any organization should try to obtain information on consumer needs and gather marketing intelligence to help satisfy these needs efficiently.

Marketing research is a critical part of such a marketing intelligence system; it helps to improve management decision making by providing accurate, relevant, and timely (ART) information. Every decision poses unique needs for information, and relevant strategies can be developed based on the information gathered through marketing research. The process of a research project includes: find a market issue, translate it into a marketing research project, design survey questionnaire, collect

Marketing research is a critical part of a marketing intelligence system; it helps to improve management decision making by providing accurate, relevant, and timely (ART) information.

information from a survey, conduct analyses, and report the findings and marketing implementations.

The Internet has changed the way businesses are conducted today. More and more businesses are going on-line in order to leverage the almost boundless possibilities that the Internet has to offer. The Internet boom has in turn affected the way marketing research is conducted today. Marketing research on the Web requires a thorough understanding of how consumer behavior changes in the cyberworld.

The following examples give the flavor of marketing research in action.

DaimlerChrysler[2]

Market research by DaimlerChrysler showed the increasing demand for small and fuel-efficient cars in European market. So DaimlerChrysler set to work to capitalize on the demand and unveiled a tiny little show car called *Java* in the Frankfurt auto show. A hit in Europe, Java, a Mercedes A-class-sized car, is yet to be introduced in the United States. Java is a powerful four-seater aimed at European, Asian, and South American markets. The ambitious Java project is a sign of the importance the company attaches to its weakness in the small car segment. Cars like these are seen as a way to capitalize on Europe's growing demand for tiny cars.

DaimlerChrysler envisions a three-car plan, with an ultrasmall car at the bottom end. The company also showed convertible and diesel versions of the small car and also displayed a possible sporty roadster model. Java would be the middle-range car and the Mercedes A-class would be at the very top. The company's goal is to produce 500,000 small cars within the next five to six years. This is well above the 200,000 A-class cars it can make now. The company's marketing research indicated that the company had great potential in the growing small car segment for two reasons. First, the growth potential is the strongest in the small car segment. Second, small cars are a way to cut down on pollution. Cars like these will play an important role in the agreement of European carmakers with the European commission on cutting down emission levels.

Gateway Inc.[3]

Marketing research shows that Hispanics are very open to new technology and willingly embrace it. Gateway Inc. decided to capitalize on this aspect of the Hispanic culture and launched the personal computer industry's biggest ethnic-marketing effort. It was an initiative with Spanish language software, PCs, Internet services, and an advertising campaign. The competition of Spanish language Internet portals with Yahoo! Inc. and America Online Inc. is also pushing the Latin pitch. A top executive at Gateway Inc. estimated the PC purchases by Hispanics to be between 1.5 to 2 million machines, which is equivalent to the college student market.

The bulk of Hispanic purchases are equally split between Compaq, IBM, Gateway, and Apple Computer Inc. Gateway wants to get ahead of the pack with a campaign targeting Hispanics. The advertising campaign adds a strong dose of family aspirations to Gateway's folksiness. The ads finish with the theme "Tomarlo Personal" which means taking it personal. The company plans to sponsor various Hispanic events such as Miami's Hispanic Heritage celebration and hold small-scale fiestas at its Gateway Country stores. Gateway is also involved in computer programs at predominantly Hispanic elementary schools in Phoenix and San Gabriel, CA. The company plans to have bilingual staff on the phone and at the stores. Gateway will bundle Spanish versions of popular software with its PCs and will add Spanish pages to its website. The Hispanic campaign is a first not only for Gateway but also for the PC industry. Gateway being a direct-sales company is ideally suited to a Hispanic initiative. This exhibit shows how Gateway successfully used marketing research to configure its product and services to the needs of a particular ethnic group.

Music Samplers on Web Buy CDs in Stores[4]

Research has shown that people who sample music on the Internet via digital downloading and other methods are likely to follow up by purchasing CDs. The results add to the growing pool of conflicting data about the effect of Internet music services on the recording industry. The recording companies are attacking digital entertainment in the courts and Washington over the issue of piracy. Yankelovich Partners, a marketing research firm, surveyed 16,903 people aged 13 through 39 who buy and listen to music and found out that 66 percent of all consumers said that listening to a song online has at least prompted them to later buy a cassette or CD featuring the song.

Services which allow users to download music on their computer, and streaming, which offers radio-style music programming via the Internet, are growing rapidly. Media Metrix found out that the number of visitors on the top 30 Internet music sites grew 19 percent between November 1999 and April 2000, to 22.8 million users. Forrester Research projects that by 2003, paid digital music downloading is expected to hit $1.1 billion in sales. In a recently concluded survey, two-thirds of these users had downloaded music from an on-line source. Ninety-two percent of those who downloaded music or heard streaming music used their desktops to listen to music, just 10 percent used a portable device, and 14 percent used their home stereo. More than 60 percent used the Internet to get music that they couldn't find on the radio.

The survey produced some revealing statistics on the effect of Internet music on music sales. Thirty-three percent of people who stream music said that it made them more likely to purchase CDs in stores, while 61 percent said it didn't affect their buying habits, and only 6 percent said that it made them less likely to purchase CDs. Meanwhile, almost 33 percent of people who downloaded music said that it made them more likely to buy, while 57 percent said their buying patterns were unaffected.

Source: www.gateway.com.

These findings are in contrast to the data used by recording companies in the lawsuit against Napster. The companies used data from surveys by Field Research Corp. and Soundscan. Both of them targeted college consumers. Soundscan found out that music sales near college campuses that had recently banned Napster were down from the first quarter of 1999 through the first quarter of 2000, while overall national sales grew. In a survey by Field Research Corp., 41 percent of Napster users said or implied that the service had replaced some of their CD purchases.

This is an example as to how proper marketing research can be used to establish facts contrary to popular belief. Media Metrix researched the market and concluded that sharing and downloading music on-line *increased the probability* of a consumer buying music CDs.

There are thousands of such examples, because virtually every private- and public-sector organization encounters pressure for more and better information about its markets. Whether the organization serves customers in competitive market environments or clients in a public-sector enterprise it is necessary to understand and satisfy the changing needs of diverse groups of people.

> Marketing research is the function that links the consumer, customer, and public to the marketer through information—information used to identify and define marketing opportunities and problems; generate, refine, and evaluate marketing actions; monitor marketing performance; and improve understanding of marketing as a process. Marketing research specifies the information required to address these issues, designs the method for collecting information, manages and implements the data collection process, analyzes and communicates the findings and their implications.
>
> American Marketing Association
> Official Definition of Marketing Research

This definition highlights the role of marketing research as an aid to decision making. An important feature is the inclusion of the specification and interpretation of needed information. Too often, marketing research is considered narrowly as the gathering and analyzing of data for someone else to use. Firms can achieve and sustain a competitive advantage through the creative use of market information. Hence, marketing research is defined as an information input to decisions, not simply as the evaluation of decisions that have been made. Market research alone, however, does not guarantee success; the intelligent use of market research is the key to business achievement. A competitive edge is more the result of how information is used than of who does or does not have the information.[5]

◆ ROLE OF MARKETING RESEARCH IN MANAGERIAL DECISION MAKING

Marketing decisions involve issues that range from fundamental shifts in the positioning of a business or the decision to enter a new market to narrow tactical questions of how best to stock a grocery shelf. The context for these decisions is the market planning process, which proceeds sequentially through four stages: **situation analysis, strategy development, marketing program development,** and **implementation.** This is a never-ending process, so the evaluation of past strategic decisions serves as an input to the situation assessment. Figure 1-1 suggests some elements of each stage. During each stage, marketing research makes a major contribution to clarifying and resolving issues and then choosing among decision alternatives. The following sections explain these steps in more detail and describe the information needs that marketing research satisfies.

Situation Analysis

Effective marketing strategies are built on an in-depth understanding of the market environment of the business and on the specific characteristics of the market. The depth of this information need can be seen from the list in Table 1-1, which shows the requirements of a major consumer packaged-goods manufacturer.

The macroenvironment includes political and regulatory trends, economic and social trends, and technological trends. Marketing researchers tend to focus on those trends that affect the demand for products and services. For example, the most important influences on the demand for consumer packaged-food products during the 1990s were the following:

- Demographic shifts, including a record number of aging adults who were increasingly affluent and active
- Rapid changes in family structure as a result of delayed marriages, working wives, and a high divorce rate
- Shifts in values as consumers became preoccupied with their own economic and emotional well-being

These trends resulted in increased concerns about the quality of food, nutritional value, personal fitness, and "naturalness." Equally influential were shifts in food, consumption patterns toward "grazing" or snacking, and more away-from-home eating.

The profile of the consumer—as in who they are, how they behave, why they behave as they do, and how they are likely to respond in the future—is at the heart of marketing research. Increasingly, marketing researchers are being asked to turn their

Figure 1-1 Marketing planning process.

TABLE 1-1   Scope of Situation Assessment for a Consumer Goods Manufacturer

1. Market environment
   a. Technologies? How else will customers satisfy their needs?
   b. Economic trends? Disposable income?
   c. Social trends? What are the trends in age, marital status, working women, occupations, location, and shifts away from the center city? What values are becoming fashionable?
   d. Political and regulatory? New labeling and safety requirements.
2. Market characteristics
   a. Market size, potential, and growth rate?
   b. Geographic dispersion of customers?
   c. Segmentation: How many distinct groups are there? Which are growing?
   d. Competition? Who are the direct rivals? How big are they? What is their performance? What are their strategy, intentions, and likely behavior with respect to product launches, promotions, and the like?
   e. Competitive products? Their nature and number?
   f. Channel members? What is the distribution of sales through supermarkets and other outlets? What are the trends? What are they doing to support their own brands?
3. Consumer behavior
   a. What do they buy? A product or service? A convenience, shopping, or specialty good? A satisfaction…?
   b. Who buys? Everybody? Women only? Teenagers (i.e., demographic, geographic, psychographic classification)?
   c. Where do they buy? Will they shop around or not? Outlet types?
   d. Why do they buy? Motivations, perceptions of product and needs, influences of peers, prestige, influence of advertising, media?
   e. How do they buy? On impulse, by shopping (i.e., the process they go through in purchasing)?
   f. When do they buy? Once a week? Everyday? Seasonal changes?
   g. Anticipated change? Incidence of new products, shifts in consumers' preferences, needs?

talents to understanding the behavior and intentions of competitors. Since much data are available from public sources, marketing researchers are well positioned to work with other functions as part of competitor-analysis teams.

A major responsibility of the marketing research function is providing information that will help detect problems and opportunities, and then, if necessary, learning enough to make decisions as to what marketing program would result in the greatest response. An opportunity might be presented by the sense that customers are increasingly dissatisfied with existing products. Marketing research could be asked to detect the dissatisfaction, perhaps determine how many people are dissatisfied, and learn the level and nature of that dissatisfaction. Marketing Research in Practice 1-1 gives an example of how a company overlooked a problem because of improper marketing research.

Various research approaches are used to analyze the market. Perhaps the simplest is to organize information already obtained from prior studies, from published magazine articles, and from customers' comments to a firm's sales representatives. Another approach is to have small groups of customers, called *focus groups*, discuss their use of a product. Such discussion groups can provide many ideas for new marketing programs.

MARKETING RESEARCH IN PRACTICE 1-1

Reebok's Tryst with Mythology

What is in a name after all? Plenty, as Reebok International Ltd. discovered. Reebok committed a marketing blunder when they named a women's shoe after a mythical demon who preyed on sleeping women. The company is considering ways to backtrack after finding that its "Incubus" shoe, released a year ago, shared its name with the medieval creature. This is hard for a company that has built its business on women's footwear.

In-house marketers came up with the name in 1995. It was one of the 1500 names Reebok invented for its 1996 footwear and clothing collections. The company's legal department assured them that nobody else had patented the name. The dictionary definition of the word "incubus" is an evil spirit. A second definition is simply a nightmare.

Source: "Reebok Discovers a Demon on Its Heels," *Houston Chronicle,* February 20, 1997.

When a problem or opportunity has been identified and it is necessary to understand it in greater depth, researchers often use a survey. For example, to understand the competitive position of Quebec in the tourism market, a survey was conducted to determine the benefits sought by visitors and nonvisitors, as well as the risks they perceived. The results identified a large group who felt highly insecure in new and/or foreign environments and who were not attracted by the appeals of uniqueness in culture, traditions, and architecture that Quebec used to differentiate its product. Marketing Research in Practice 1-2 is a classic example of a company changing its product based on the customer's current concerns. Of course, a product has to work before it is "wrapped in green."

Strategy Development

During the strategy development stage the management team of the business decides on answers to three critical questions. Marketing research provides significant help in finding the answers to these questions:

1. What business should we be in?
2. How will we compete?
3. What are our business objectives?

What Business Should We Be In?

Specifically, what products or services should we offer? What technologies will we utilize? Which market segments should we emphasize? What channels should we use to reach the market? A company's choices set the context for all subsequent decisions.

These questions have become especially compelling in markets that are mature and saturated, including most packaged goods, household appliances, automobiles, and services such as banking and air travel. One sure route to growth in this competitive environment is to create highly targeted products that appeal to the tastes of small market segments. Research supports this search for niches with large-scale quantitative market studies that describe buying behavior, consumer beliefs and attitudes, and exposure to communications media. Large samples are needed to delineate the segments, indicate their size, and determine what the people in each segment are seeking in a product.

MARKETING RESEARCH IN PRACTICE 1-2

3M Going Green

3M ranked second in 1999 for its environmental performance among the 50 largest chemical-manufacturing and -using companies worldwide as ranked by Germany's respected, and independent, Hamburg Environmental Institute. Scientists with HIC who conducted the research study noted the company as an environmental "pioneer."

The criteria used to come to the final decision included long-term environmental goals, global standards, environmental management systems, waste management and sustainable product development, and manufacturing processes. In 1994 and 1996, 3M ranked third place in this international study.

These accolades were not earned overnight. 3M has been integrating environmental, health, and safety performance into its daily business routine. The company's "Environmental Policy," adopted in 1975, was among the first of its kind by a major manufacturing company. It calls for 3M to solve its own environmental problems by focusing on preventing pollution, conserving natural resources, and developing products that have minimum effect on the environment.

A couple of decades ago, a voluntary "Pollution Prevention Pays" (3P) program was begun, based on the then-novel concept that pollution prevention is both an environmental and a competitive/financial strategy. Not only has the program been successful beyond expectations, it has also helped keep 3M facilities ahead of many regulatory requirements. In just over two decades, more than 4,600 3P projects initiated by employees worldwide have produced total savings of $810 million while eliminating 1.6 million pounds of releases to air, water, and land. 3P provides much of the philosophical basis for 3M's environmental, health, and safety programs.

So what does the company do next? Maybe work toward being ranked number 1 for its environmental performance.

Source: www.3m.com. For more information on 3M, its products, and its environmental policy visit http://www.3m.com.

How Will We Compete?

Next, the management team has to decide why the business is better than the competition in serving the needs of the target segment, and what has to be done to keep it in front. Competitive superiority is revealed in the market as either differentiation along attributes that are important to target customers, or the lowest delivered cost position. Otis Elevator is able to dominate the elevator business by using information technologies to provide superior service response and preventive maintenance programs that reduce elevator breakdowns—attributes that customers appreciate.

Marketing research is essential for getting answers to three key questions about differentiation: What attributes of the product or service create value for the customer? Which attributes are most important? How do we compare to the competition? For example, every movie has a dozen different story lines, and Joseph Helfgot, a sociologist turned Hollywood market researcher, says he knows which one you want to hear. Helfgot is the one who tells studio executives how to sell their movies and sets sink-or-swim release schedules. Consider *The Silence of the Lambs* (Helfgot won't discuss any of his recent projects). Is it about a gruesome serial murderer? Or a feisty FBI ingenue? Or a brilliant psychotic helping the FBI catch a like-minded fiend? None of the above, Helfgot found out. Audiences were interested in hearing a story about the bizarre relationship between Jodie Foster, an FBI academy graduate, and imprisoned serial killer Hannibal Lecter—played by Anthony Hopkins—who helped her solve the murders. That became the focus of the publicity campaign for what turned out to be a blockbuster hit. With marketing costs accounting for up to a third of movie budgets and with competition for space in movie theaters becoming increasingly fierce, studios have come to rely on whatever information science can provide to help sell their movies.

The attributes of value go well beyond physical characteristics, to encompass the support activities and systems for delivery and service that make up the augmented product. In the lodging market, the key attributes are honoring reservations on time, providing good value for the money, and the quality and amenities of the guest rooms. Each market has unique attributes that customers employ to judge the competitive offerings, which can be understood only through careful analysis of usage patterns and decision processes with that market. This knowledge comes from informed sources and in-depth customer surveys.

An understanding of competitive advantage also requires detailed knowledge of the capabilities, strategies, and intentions of current and prospective competitors. Marketing research contributes here in two ways: identifying the competitive set and collecting detailed information about each competitor. Some ways of undertaking competitive intelligence work are discussed later in the book. Marketing Research in Practice 1-3 talks about how marketing research helped a distributor of graphic arts supplies to be retained by a major supplier.

What Are the Business Objectives?

An objective is a desired performance result that can be quantified and monitored. There are usually objectives for revenue growth, market share, and profitability. Increasingly firms are adopting objectives for service levels (e.g., speed of response to quotations) and customer satisfaction. Marketing research is needed to establish both the market share and the level of customer satisfaction. Sometimes share information—we have x percent of the y market—is readily available from secondary sources, but it may not be if the served market is different from the standard definition or if share is defined in dollar sales terms rather than unit volume.

MARKETING RESEARCH IN PRACTICE 1-3

Understanding a Specialized Industrial Market

A distributor of graphic arts supplies in the Upper Midwest wanted to find out how he was perceived by his customers. He conducted a mail survey and based on the information from the survey, found that he was perceived as a specialist in small print companies and in-plant shops. The man supplier to the distributor was planning to drop this distributor as part of a cost-cutting effort. However, when the distributor shared the research results with the supplier, which clearly positioned the distributor as a specialist in small companies and in-plant shops, the supplier realized that it could reach small end users only through this distributor. Hence, the supplier decided to retain the distributor, a decision that benefited all parties.

Source: Adapted from Dick Gorelick, "Good Research Has Obvious—and Not So Obvious— Benefits." *Marketing News,* September 13, 1993.

Marketing Program Development

Programs embrace specific tasks, such as developing a new product or launching a new advertising campaign. An action program usually focuses on a single objective in support of one element of the overall business strategy. This is where the bulk of ongoing marketing research is directed. You can get an idea of the possibilities of and needs for research from Table 1-2, which describes some of the representative program decisions that utilize information about market characteristics and customer behavior.

To illustrate some possible research approaches, we will focus on the series of market research studies that were conducted to help Johnson Wax Company suc-

TABLE 1-2 Developing the Marketing Program—Representative Decisions That Draw on Marketing Research

1. Segmentation decisions
   Which segment should be the target?
   What benefits are most important for each segment?
   Which geographic area should be entered?
2. Product decisions
   What product features should be included?
   How should the product be positioned?
   What type of package is preferred by the customers?
3. Distribution decisions
   What type of retailer should be used?
   What should be the markup policy?
   Should a few outlets be employed or many?
4. Advertising and promotion decisions
   What appeals should be used in the advertising?
   In which vehicles should the advertising be placed?
   What should the budget be?
   What sales promotion should be used, and when should it be scheduled?
5. Personal selling decisions
   What customer types have the most potential?
   How many salespeople are needed?
6. Price decisions
   What price level should be changed?
   What sales should be offered during the year?
   What response should be made to a competitor's price?
7. Branding decisions
   What should be the name, symbol, logo, and slogan that will be associated with the product?
   What is the position that the brand should adopt vis-à-vis the competition?
   How can brand loyalty be increased?
8. Customer satisfaction decisions
   How should customer satisfaction be measured?
   How often should it be measured?
   How should customer complaints be handled?

cessfully introduce Agree Cream Rinse in 1977 and Agree Shampoo in 1978. The story begins with a major market analysis survey of hair-care practices that was conducted in the early 1970s. The study showed that there was a trend away from hair sprays, but a trend toward shampooing hair more frequently and a growing concern about oily hair. This led to a strategic decision to enter the shampoo and creme rinse market with products targeted toward the oiliness problem. This decision was supported by other studies on competitive activities in the market and on the willingness of the retailers to stock new shampoos.[6]

A total of 50 marketing research studies conducted between 1975 and 1979 supported the development of these two products. A series of focus group discussions was held to understand the oiliness problem and people's perceptions of existing shampoo products. The firm was particularly interested in learning about teenagers, since most of its products were sold to homemakers. One goal of these focus groups was to get ideas for a copy theme. Subsequently, more focus groups were held to get reactions to the selected advertising theme, "Helps Stop the Greasies." Several tests were conducted to gauge customer reaction to different advertisements. In fact, more than 17 television commercials were created and tested.

More than 20 of the studies helped to test and refine the product. Several blind comparison tests were conducted, in which 400 women were asked to use the new product for two weeks and compare it to an existing product. (In a blind test the products are packaged in unlabeled containers and the customers do not know which contains the new product.)

Several tests of the final marketing program were conducted. One was in a simulated supermarket, where customers were asked to shop after they had been exposed to the advertising. The new product, of course, was on the shelf. Another test involved placing the product in an actual supermarket and exposing customers to the advertising. Finally, the product was introduced using the complete marketing plan in a limited test area involving a few selected communities including Fresno, California, and South Bend, Indiana. During the process, the product, the advertising, and the rest of the marketing program were being revised continually. The effort paid handsome dividends: Agree Creme Rinse took a 20 percent share of the market for its category and was number one in unit volume, and Agree Shampoo also was introduced successfully. In the 1980s, Gillette introduced Mink Difference Shampoo, containing mink oil, for the older market, and for the younger segment, Silkience, a self-adjusting shampoo that provided differential conditioning depending on the user's hair type.

Implementation

The beginning of the implementation phase is signaled by a decision to proceed with a new program or strategy and by the related commitments to objectives, budgets, and timetables. At this point the focus of marketing research shifts to such questions as

Did the elements of the marketing program achieve their objectives?
> How did sales compare with objectives?
> In what areas were sales disappointing? Why?
> Were the advertising objectives met?
> Did the product achieve its distribution objectives?
> Are any supermarkets discontinuing the product?

Should the marketing program be continued, revised, or expanded?
> Are customers satisfied with the product?

Should the product be changed?
Should more features be added?
Should the advertising budget be changed?
Is the price appropriate?

For research to be effective at this stage, it is important that specific measurable objectives be set for all elements of the marketing program. Thus, there should be sales goals by geographic area; distribution goals, perhaps in terms of the number of stores carrying the product; and advertising goals, such as achieving certain levels of awareness. The role of marketing research is to provide measures against these objectives and to provide more focused studies to determine why results are below or above expectations.

Sprint PCS Wireless Web Updates[7]

Often underlying this phase of marketing management is uncertainty about the critical judgments and assumptions that preceded the decision. For example, Sprint PCS and Yahoo! have teamed up to bring wireless web updates to a Sprint PCS phone. Users decide which updates they want, including weather reports, stock quotes, and news headlines, and when they want them. Selections can be edited at any time. Every Sprint PCS Phone has the capability to accept wireless web updates and can be easily set up. One fundamental assumption was that the customers would be ready to use the cellular phone for purposes other than traditional cellular phone tasks.

There is overlap among the phases of the marketing process. In particular, the last phase, by identifying problems with the marketing program—and perhaps opportunities, as well—eventually blends into the situation analysis phase of some other follow-up marketing program.

◆ FACTORS THAT INFLUENCE MARKETING RESEARCH DECISIONS

Marketing research is not an immediate or an obvious path to finding solutions to all managerial problems. A manager who is faced with a particular problem should not instinctively resort to conducting marketing research to find a solution to the problem. A manager should consider several factors before ordering marketing research. Sometimes it is best not to conduct marketing research. Hence, the primary decision to be made is whether market research is called for in a particular situation. The factors that influence this initial decision include the following.

Relevance

Research should not be conducted to satisfy curiosity or confirm the wisdom of previous decisions. **Relevance** comes through support of strategic and tactical planning activities—that is, by anticipating the kinds of information that will be required.

Type and Nature of Information Sought

If the information required for decision making already exists within the organization, in the form of results of a study conducted for a different problem, or in the form of managerial experience and talents, marketing research is not called for. Under these circumstances, further research would be redundant and a waste of money. For example, Procter & Gamble, using its prior knowledge of the U.S. coffee market, launched Folger's Instant Coffee nationally, after some preliminary research.

Timing

If a new product is to be launched in the spring season, all the research-based decisions on price, product formulation, name, copy appeals, and other components must be conducted far in advance. One role of the planning system is to schedule needed market research so that it can be conducted in time to influence decisions. The formulation of responses to competitive actions puts the greatest time pressure on researchers, because the results are always wanted "yesterday."

Availability of Resources

Although the need for availability of resources may appear to be obvious, in several instances managers have called for marketing research without properly understanding the amount of resources available—including both financial and human resources. The results of such research often will be inaccurate.

Cost-Benefit Analysis

Willingness to acquire additional decision-making information by conducting marketing research depends on a manager's perception of the incremental quality and value of the information vis-à-vis its cost and the time it would take to conduct the research. Hence, before conducting marketing research, it is necessary to have some estimate of the value of the information being sought. Such an estimate will help determine how much, if anything, should be spent on the research.

◆ USING MARKETING RESEARCH: DOES IT GUARANTEE SUCCESS?

Although research is conducted to generate information, managers do not readily use the information to solve their problems. The factors that influence a manager's decision to use research information are:

1. Research quality
2. Conformity to prior expectations
3. Clarity of presentation
4. Political acceptability within the firm
5. Challenge to the status quo[8]

Some researchers argue that the use of information is a function of the direct and indirect effects of environmental, organizational, informational, and individual factors.[9] However, a researcher should not alter the findings to match a manager's prior notions. Further, managers in consumer organizations are less likely to use research findings than their counterparts in industrial firms.[10] This is due to a greater exploratory objective in information collection, a greater degree of formalization of organizational structure, and a lesser degree of surprise in the information collection.

It can be seen from Marketing Research in Practice 1-4 that the factors that influence market research use are broadly classified as environmental and relationship factors. Environmental factors can be internal and external to the organization. Internal factors include state of the industry and market. Relationship factors are internal to the organization, such as involvement of the decision maker and

MARKETING RESEARCH IN PRACTICE 1-4

Hidden Valley

According to the *Wall Street Journal,* sales of freshly prepared or frozen foods are expected to reach $176 billion a year by 2001. At the same time, takeout and delivered foods currently add up to $460 billion a year. Research shows that almost 100 percent of American families will purchase some sort of pre-prepared food. Also, it has been found that 83 percent of consumers are trying to eat healthier. Hidden Valley has been the first dressing manufacturer to respond to this trend by creating the portable 2.5-ounce single-cup version of its Original Ranch and Light Original Ranch dressings. Sold in six-packs, Hidden Valley has been able to capitalize on the needs of the busy consumer. While responding to consumer demands for healthier more convenient foods, Hidden Valley has developed a product that is perfect for:

- Kids' school lunches
- Desk-side lunches
- After-school snacks
- Picnics
- Road trips
- Parties
- Study breaks
- Camping/hiking

Source: http://www.hiddenvalley.com/single_cups.html.

researcher, communication and trust between the decision maker and researcher, and credibility and perceived usefulness of the research.[11]

It is easier to conduct research and generate information than to understand the consequences of the information. Many companies with excellent marketing research experience have failed in their efforts to capture the actual needs of the consumers.

◆ MARKETING INTELLIGENCE IN AMAZON.COM[12]

Amazon.com opened its virtual doors in July 1995 with a mission to use the Internet to transform book buying into the fastest, easiest, and most enjoyable shopping experience possible. While its customer base and product offerings grew considerably since its early days, it still maintained its founding commitment to customer satisfaction and the delivery of an educational and inspiring shopping experience.

Today, Amazon.com is the place to find and discover anything one wants to buy on-line. Twenty-nine million people in more than 160 countries have made Amazon.com the leading online shopping site. The site includes Earth's biggest selection of products, including free electronic greeting cards, on-line auctions, and millions of books, CDs, videos, DVDs, toys and games, and electronics.

Last year, the company realized that due to heavy competition among the dot(.)com companies, it needed to broaden its marketplace with large range of products with new innovative techniques. Amazon then relied on marketing intelligence to grow and compete effectively amidst strong competition. In November 2000, Amazon.com came up with an open market place called *Amazon Marketplace* that makes it easy for third parties to sell used, rare, and collectible books, music, video, DVD, video games, electronics, tools and hardware, and camera and photo products on the same page where Amazon.com sells the new items. This side-by-side placement ensures that qualified buyers looking for a product are aware of a used, rare, or collectible item at the same time they are looking for the new item.

Amazon Marketplace gives the individual sellers the chance to list items for sale directly on the page where Amazon.com sells the same item new. *Listing is free*—and the seller needs to pay a fee only if his product is sold. Amazon Marketplace sellers ship items directly to their buyers. When a purchase is made, Amazon.com processes payment from the buyer and deposits it in the seller's account. Sellers must ship within two business days of the purchase.

Thus, with the coming of Amazon marketplace, Amazon.com has become the best example of a company that has put in both the business models of B2C and C2C. It now serves as a market exchange, a virtual mall, a distributor, a buy/sell fulfillment model, an auction broker, a search agent, a bounty broker, a virtual merchant, a catalog merchant, and a subscription model. Along with its extensive catalog of products, the site offers a wide variety of other shopping services and partnership opportunities. One big reason that some Amazon customers prefer using Amazon Payments is that, according to Amazon, purchases made using the service are protected by Amazon for up to $2,500 in case the item does not arrive as expected.

Even with its new venture coupled with solid marketing and advertising effort, Amazon.com could not show the much-expected profits due to the economic downturn during the fourth quarter of year 2000. But the hopes are high and future looks brighter.

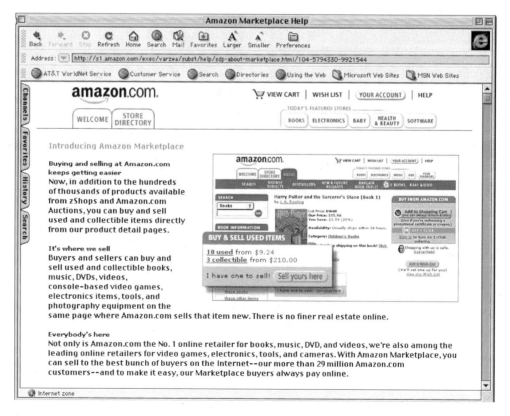

Source: www.amazon.com

◆ ETHICS IN MARKETING RESEARCH

Ethics refers to moral principles or values that generally govern the conduct of an individual or group. Researchers have responsibilities to their profession, clients, and respondents, and must adhere to high ethical standards to ensure that both the function and the information are not brought into disrepute. The Marketing Research Association, Inc. (Chicago, Illinois) has instituted a code of ethics that serves as a guideline for ethical marketing decisions. Marketing Research in Practice 1-5 shows the Code of Professional Ethics and Practices instituted by the Marketing Research

MARKETING RESEARCH IN PRACTICE 1-5

Code of Ethics of Marketing Research Association

The Code of Professional Ethics and Practices

RESPONSIBILITIES TO RESPONDENTS

Data Collection Companies:

1. Will make factually correct statements to secure cooperation and honor promises to respondents, whether oral or written.

2. Will not use information to identify respondents without the permission of the respondent, except to those who check the data or are involved in processing the data. If such permission is given, it must be recorded by the interviewer at the time that the permission is secured.

3. Will respect the respondents' right to withdraw or to refuse to cooperate at any stage of the study and not use any procedure or technique to coerce or imply that cooperation is obligatory.

4. Will obtain and document respondent consent when it is known that the name and addresses or identity of the respondent may be passed to a third party for legal or other purposes, such as audio or video recordings.

5. Will obtain permission and document consent of a parent, legal guardian or responsible guardian before interviewing children 12 years or younger.

6. Will give respondents the opportunity to refuse to participate in the research when there is a possibility they may be identifiable without the use of their name or address (e.g., because of the size of the population being sampled).

Interviewers:

1. Will treat the respondents with respect and not influence him/her through direct or indirect attempts, including the framing of questions, a respondent's opinion or attitudes on any tissue.

2. Will obtain and document permission of a parent, legal guardian or responsible guardian before interviewing children 12 years old or younger. Prior to obtaining permission the interviewer will divulge the subject matter, length of interview and other special tasks that will be required.

For information on Responsibilities to Clients, Data Collectors and the General Public and Business Community, please visit our website.

Source: Reprinted by permission of the Marketing Research Association, Inc., Chicago, IL.

Association.[13] The Council of American Survey Research Organization (CASRO) has also established a detailed code of marketing research ethics to which its members adhere.[14] Normally, three parties are involved in a marketing research project:

1. The client who sponsors the project
2. The supplier who designs and executes the research
3. The respondent who provides the information

The issue of ethics in marketing research involves all three players in a research project.

The Sponsor's Ethics

The sponsor, or the research client, must abide by a number of ethical or moral rules and regulations when conducting a research study. The more common ethical problems in the client establishment stem from the following sources.

Overt and Covert Purposes

Marketing research should not be biased to support a particular decision or to enhance a legal position.

Most researchers have encountered situations where the main purpose of their efforts was to serve someone's organizational goals. Thus, research can be used to postpone an awkward decision or to lend respectability to a decision that has been made already. A related purpose is to avoid responsibility. When there are competing factions, the manager who must make a difficult choice looks to research to guide the decision. This has the further advantage that if the decision is later proven wrong, the manager can find someone else to blame.

Sometimes a covert purpose will open the way to ethical abuses that present difficult dilemmas to researchers. The most serious abuses are created when there is subtle (or not so subtle) pressure to design research to support a particular decision or enhance a legal position.

Dishonesty in Dealing with Suppliers

A few client companies have been known to indulge in "picking the brains" of research suppliers by asking them to submit elaborate bids that detail the research design and methodology the supplier would adopt in conducting the research. Later, the client firm uses these ideas and conducts the research on its own. Another technique that client firms sometimes use is to make a false promise of future contracts in an effort to obtain a low price for the current project.

Misuse of Research Information

The client firm should not misuse information gathered through marketing research projects. For example, databases about consumer preferences are used in target marketing to identify the people who are most likely to buy or use a product. Blockbuster Entertainment Corporation (BEC), a national video rental chain, has a network of more than 1,750 outlets around the United States, renting mostly videos. Using sophisticated computer-matching information technologies, BEC has also formed a massive database of information on the movie videos it rents, and the information can be made available for resale to direct marketers.[15] Even though a federal law prohibits release of the names of video renters, there is no rule against divulging the subject matter of those movies. BEC even made public its intent to sell its renter data,[16] which sparked a debate over consumer privacy. BEC soon came under Federal Trade Commission vigilance, faced a torrent of customer criticism, and received considerable negative publicity. Even though BEC does not rent X-rated movies, the concern and controversy that BEC had infringed on customer privacy rights reached a feverish pitch. The common form of misuse comes from comparative advertisements or product performance claims that stem from data that are statistically not significant. Though puffery in advertisements is a normal practice, gross misuse of research data is ethically unacceptable[17]

Too often, researchers must deal with demands by sales or other personnel for access to results and the names and telephone numbers of respondents. The intention, of course, is to use the research study for the entirely different—and usually unethical—purpose of generating sales leads. The only time this is acceptable is when the interviewer asks specifically whether the respondent will accept a follow-up sales call, or would like more information, and acts precisely on the respondent's answer.

Sadly, in many situations the research study is simply a disguise for a selling pitch. Many people have received phone calls, ostensibly to ask some research questions, that lead to a canned sales message for life insurance, an encyclopedia, or a mutual fund. This is not only unethical behavior because it has no merits on its own, it is also a serious abuse of respondent rights. Not surprisingly, respondents are more suspicious after a few of these encounters and may refuse to participate in any research study.

The Supplier's Ethics

The research supplier faces two common ethical issues:

Confidentiality of research information should be preserved

- Violating **client confidentiality.** Disclosing any information about the client that the supplier has gathered from the research project amounts to a violation of client confidentiality.

- Improper execution of research. Suppliers are required to conduct marketing research projects in an objective manner, free from personal biases and motives. Improper execution also includes using biased sampling, ignoring relevant data, or misusing statistics, all of which lead to erroneous and misleading results.

Abuse of Respondents

Abuse of respondents is perhaps the most frequent and controversial problem that crops up regarding ethics in conducting research. Any form of violation of a respondent's rights amounts to unethical treatment or abuse of the respondent.

The Respondent's Ethics and Rights

A respondent who of his or her own free will agrees to participate in a marketing research project has the ethical obligation to provide the supplier, and hence the client, with honest and truthful answers. The respondent can abstain from answering a sensitive question, but falsifying the answer is ethically improper.

Any respondent who participates in a research project has the following rights:

- The right to privacy
- The right to safety
- The right to know the true purpose of the research

- The right to the research results
- The right to decide which questions to answer

◆ INTERNATIONAL MARKETING RESEARCH

The increase in international trade and the emergence of global corporations resulting from increased globalization of business have had a major impact on all facets of business, including marketing research. The increase in global competition, coupled with the formation of regional trading blocs such as the European Community (EC) and the North American Free Trade Agreement (NAFTA), have spurred the growth of global corporations and the need for international marketing research. The need to collect information relating to international markets, and to monitor trends in these markets, as well as to conduct research to determine the appropriate strategies that will be most effective in international markets, is expanding rapidly. For example, HEB, the largest grocery store chain in Texas, observed that consumers from Mexico crossed the border to shop at HEB stores in Texas. After conducting some marketing research in Mexico, HEB decided to open its first store (and the first American supermarket) in Monterey, Mexico. The stores will be somewhat different from their Texas counterparts, with 70 to 80 percent of the products purchased in Mexico and the remainder in the United States. Research revealed that awareness of HEB is quite high among Mexican consumers and that they place a great deal of emphasis on American products (which are better from the consumers' perspective).[18]

International marketing research can be defined as marketing research conducted either simultaneously or sequentially to facilitate marketing decisions in more than one country.

The marketing research industry in the United States is increasingly growing into an international industry, with more than one-third of its revenues coming from foreign operations. The increase in the importance of global business has caused an increase in awareness of the problems related to international research. **International marketing research** can be defined as marketing research conducted either simultaneously or sequentially to facilitate marketing decisions in more than one country.[19] As such, the basic functions of marketing research and the research process do not differ from domestic and multicountry research; however, the international marketing research process is much more complicated and the international marketing researcher faces problems that are different from those of a domestic researcher.

HEB store in Monterey, Mexico.
Courtesy H.E. Butt Grocery Company.

Throughout this book, we will be discussing the international aspect of the marketing research process, and, when applicable, we will be highlighting the differences between domestic and international research.

The task of marketing research is to find a sizable segment with homogenous tastes. The growing presence of an international market in the United States has been influenced by both domestic and foreign markets. In the domestic arena, ethnic groups range from Chinese to Turkish, each lending a piece of its culture to the U.S. market. Within each ethnic group, the product preference is diverse. These facts present a challenge to marketing research to find a homogenous group among the "melting pot" of international products. Complicating matters is the growing number of foreign manufacturers selling their goods in the United States. Marketing Research in Practice 1-6 describes how the world has become truly a global marketplace and how the average citizen has come to take this for granted.

In order to better address the Canadian market despite the geographic propensity, the U.S. firms would have to conduct independent market research. Marketing Research in Practice 1-7 provides an insight into the nuances that have to be taken into account for the marketing strategies to be effective.

◆ MARKETING INTELLIGENCE

With an ever-increasing rate of global competition in today's business environment, firms nowadays must rely on clear strategic decisions. To propel a successful business and marketing venture and stay on the cutting edge of business, it has become of the utmost importance to collect various information about societies with different cultures, political systems, administrative forms, legal systems, infrastructures, and resource bases. This is a form of business intelligence where legal, ethical collection of data and information will be analyzed and transformed for use in strategic planning and problem solving. The impact of marketing intelligence contributes heavily to tactical and strategic decision making. Intelligence content (actionable knowledge) is used in activities such as identifying internal strengths and weaknesses and external opportunities and threats, preparing business and marketing plans, locating emerging markets, preparing for technological change, and designing risk-reduction strategies.

Increased worldwide marketplace competition tops the list of reasons for initiating the intelligence process. Companies collect intelligence to update strategic and

MARKETING RESEARCH IN PRACTICE 1-6

Welcome to the Global Marketplace

She drives home through the heavy Houston traffic, thinking about her job with a Swiss bank. She listens to music by a Russian composer played by a Canadian orchestra with an Israeli conductor. She loves her German-built car but does not know that it was made using Swedish steel, Argentinean leather, and Japanese electronics. Her tires are from Italy. Her gasoline was refined in Aruba from Venezuelan crude and transported to Texas on a Liberian tanker. Her suit was designed by a French designer and made in Hong Kong from Italian silk. Her shoes are British. Her sweater is New Zealand wool. At home, she steps onto her Persian carpet and sits down at her Danish table. She turns on her Korean television and watches the international news. She starts a load of clothes washing in her new Swedish washing machine. She pours a glass of Australian wine into Irish crystal and prepares to go out to a Thai restaurant to discuss a deal with a Middle East oil company. Through all this, she never thinks about the global supply chains on which her lifestyle is based. Frankly, she could care less!

MARKETING RESEARCH IN PRACTICE 1-7

What Makes Canada Unique Compared to the U.S. Marketplace?

1. Size

   Canada has a bigger land mass than the United States but a population only the size of New York and New Jersey. Some aspects in relation to size are:

   1. The market is heavily concentrated in 3 or 4 cities. Eighty percent of the market is in Toronto, Montreal, Vancouver, and Calgary. These cities are all close to the United States, but thousands of miles apart, so it is important to understand who your customer is before you decide where to locate or how to distribute.

   2. Locating an office or a partner in Canada will depend on what segment of the market you are targeting. Calgary is the center of the oil industry, Toronto for financial services and manufacturing, Vancouver for forestry and resources, and Montreal for all these in the province of Quebec. Do you need representation in just one or all of these centers?

   3. Customers are smaller in size than in the United States. There are just not that many large business customers compared to the United States. As a result, some businesses do not make economic sense (e.g., Canadian on-line legal and commercial databases compared with those available in the United States).

   4. Heavy concentration of people and industry in the cities means that the large Canadian cities are heavily serviced by cable. In times of converging technologies, the availability to serve mass markets in a wired city format is different to most cities in the United States.

2. Culture

   Canada shares many things with the United States, including language, broadcasting, sports, and some common history. Canada also has cultural differences that make it unique. These are:

   1. The Quebec market is a French market with its own culture and way of doing business that is not necessarily the same as the United States or the rest of Canada. Communications must be in French, as must the language of the office. To the outside world this means the need for a French partner.

   2. It used to be said that if you wanted to make a sale to anyone living in the Maritimes, then you had to be a relative or a neighbor. Breakdowns in provincial trade barriers in Canada are attempting to change this, but habits die hard.

   3. Canadians have a reserve or suspicion about suppliers more so than in the United States. The popularity of ordering products by direct mail is less than in the United States. This same reserve may inhibit the growth of ordering and distribution via the Internet.

   4. Canada has a diverse population. In Toronto, for example, 40 percent of the people speak a second language. It is thus a good place from which to develop products for the international market.

3. Regulatory Differences

   Canada is in the process of moving from a regulated marketplace to a deregulated marketplace. Nevertheless, regulation remains endemic to Canadian life and will take a long time to disappear.

   1. Deregulation and competition in telecommunications has come later than in the United States but is proceeding at a fast pace. Telecom players and their equipment providers have strong Canadian ownership and companies such as Bell, NorTel, and Newbridge are global players in their own right.

MARKETING RESEARCH IN PRACTICE 1-7 *(continued)*

What Makes Canada Unique Compared to the U.S. Marketplace?

2. Canada has a regulatory structure supervised by the CRTC (The Canadian Radio and Television Commission). This body makes the rules on telecommunications and broadcasting and understanding how the CRTC works can be critical in some sectors.
3. Cross ownership of telephone companies by cable companies and cable companies by telephone companies is now allowed in Canada, setting the stage for another round of convergence and competition. The battle for who controls what line into the consumer's house still has to be fought in Canada.

4. Industry Structure

   The structure of Canadian industry is one of the major differences between Canada and the United States. In the Information Technology (IT) industry:

   1. Canada has a strong telecommunications sector under the Stentor umbrella. Its computer players are those that have been in Canada for a long time. Some of these have R&D, manufacturing and world service mandates like IBM. Others simply have branch offices in Canada. Software companies thrive in Canada and aim at the U.S. market. You are successful here with sales of $1 million, whereas in the United States it is more likely to be $100 million before you get noticed.
   2. It is generally seen as a "rule of thumb" that what happens in the United States will be followed three to five years later in Canada. This is not always the case, though. Canada has developed leaders in systems integration and the outsourcing of IT by customers to these organizations. Systemhouse and DMR are two such companies, both now owned by U.S. parents.

When conducting research on the market in Canada, one should understand that it is an aging market just like the United States. However, the components of the consumer market are very different.

Source: Remarks made by Roger Briers of TCI Convergence Limited, Management Consultants, to the 1997 Comdex Channels Marketing Forum on "Doing Business in Canada." *http://www.inforamp.net/~tci/keydiff.html*

tactical plans, upgrade products to better suit customer needs, identify internal problems, identify partners, adjust marketing and production schedules, make product-market matches, and prepare for change. Intelligence is a system for collecting and transforming information and content, actionable knowledge that can be used to make business and marketing decisions. Computers are an integral part of most intelligence systems; however, human thought is essential in ensuring that data are transformed into actionable intelligence that is used appropriately, legally, and ethically. Key issues evaluated by Lackman, Saban, and Lanasa in the effective deployment of marketing intelligence system are:

- Activity and value of marketing intelligence in the support of customer/ competitive analysis
- Value of data sources integral to marketing intelligence
- Location of marketing intelligence accountability in the organization
- Level and trend of marketing intelligence resources

Marketing intelligence's highest contributions are to the front-end strategic planning functions such as market targeting, estimation of market potential, and forecasting product demand. The trend to use marketing intelligence will continue to rise and companies that fail to recognize the need for marketing intelligence will lose their strategic and competitive advantage. In support of this trend, a study on Tasty Ice Cream is showcased in this edition as an example of a rigorous marketing intelligence process. The example will illustrate the cyclical process that consists of: (1) framing the question; (2) gathering the data/information; (3) organizing and analyzing data, transforming them into actionable intelligence; and (4) disseminating the outcome to appropriate decision makers.[20]

END OF CHAPTER MATERIAL

SUMMARY

Marketing research links the organization with its market environment. It involves the specification, gathering, analysis, and interpretation of information to help management understand that particular market environment, identify its problems and opportunities, and develop and evaluate courses of marketing action. The marketing management process involves situation analysis, strategy development, and marketing program development and implementation. Each of these areas includes a host of decisions that must be supported by marketing research information. Marketing research, to be effective, should be relevant, timely, efficient, accurate, and ethical.

Video Segment:

Green Marketing—Packaging Choices

L'eggs initially sold its line of hosiery in plastic cases. It later changed the package design to adhere to the wave of "green marketing." The current packaging, as well as a change in distribution, has implied a change in the marketing program. Other companies have also caught on to the "environmental consciousness" movement. X Tree's incorporation of green marketing into its corporate philosophy meant that even if the cost was increased by more than 25 percent, it would continue to position itself as an environment-friendly firm.

Video Segment:

America On-Line (AOL)—Ethics in Maintaining Customer Privacy

AOL's advertising blunder was that it sold customers' phone numbers to commercial users. The issue was not only that it should not have sold these numbers for telemarketing purposes, but that a posted agreement would have helped. The shift to being advertising dependent rather than subscriber-dependent may account for the strategy adopted. This clip addresses the ethical responsibility that firms should have toward keeping customer information private.

KEY TERMS

marketing research

situation analysis

strategy development

marketing program development

relevance

timing

ethics

implementation

sponsor's ethics

supplier's ethics

respondent's ethics

client confidentiality

cost-benefit analysis

international marketing research

MARKETING RESEARCH TOOLBOX
REVIEW POINTS

1. Marketing research is the function that links the consumer, customer, and public to the marketer through information—information used to identify and define marketing opportunities and problems; generate, refine, and evaluate marketing actions; monitor marketing performance; and improve understanding of marketing as a process.

2. Marketing research specifies the information required to address these issues; designs the method for collecting information required to address these issues; designs the method for collecting information; manages and implements the data collection process; and analyzes and communicates the findings and their implications.

3. Marketing research helps to improve management decision making by providing relevant, accurate, and timely (RAT) information.

4. Marketing research is information necessary as input for decision making and *not* just an evaluation of decisions made.

5. The market planning process consists of situation analysis, strategy development, marketing program development, and implementation.

6. Marketing research serves to resolve issues and guides in choosing among decision alternatives in each stage.

7. Marketing research helps detect problems and opportunities in various markets in the situation analysis stage.

8. Marketing research assists in deciding the business to pursue, analyzing the competitive advantage in the market, and setting the objectives for the business.

9. Marketing research helps in developing and evaluating different courses of marketing action.

10. Marketing research can be used to measure the success or failure of the marketing program implemented.

11. Factors that influence marketing research are relevance, type and nature of information, timing, availability of resources, and cost-benefit analysis.

12. The factors that influence a manager's decision to use research information are research quality, conformity to prior expectations, clarity of presentation, political acceptability within the firm, and challenge to the status quo.

13. The three parties involved in a marketing research project are the sponsor, the supplier, and the respondents.

14. The ethical issues involving sponsors are overt and covert purposes, dishonesty in dealing with suppliers, and misuse of research information.

15. The common ethical issues for the supplier are violating client confidentiality and improper execution of research.

16. The respondent is responsible for providing the supplier and hence the client with honest and truthful answers.

17. Any respondent has the following rights: right to privacy, right to safety, right to know the true purpose of research, right to research results, and right to decide which questions to answer.

18. The marketing research industry in the United States is increasingly growing into an international industry, with more than one-third of its revenues coming from foreign operations.

19. International marketing research is marketing research conducted in an international market or research conducted either simultaneously or sequentially to facilitate marketing decisions in more than one country.

QUESTIONS AND PROBLEMS

1. How might the following use marketing research? Be specific.
   a. A small sporting goods store
   b. Continental Airlines
   c. Ohio State University
   d. Houston Astros baseball team
   e. Sears Roebuck
   f. A major television network (CBS, NBC, or ABC)
   g. Compaq Computers
   h. A museum in a major city
   i. A shopping mall in downtown Houston

2. How might marketing research be used to support each of the steps in Figure 1-1 that describes the marketing planning process? For example, how could it help select the served market segment?

3. What are some ethical problems that marketing researchers face in designing and conducting field studies?

4. Most companies have entire marketing research studies, or portions of entire studies, such as interviewing, done by outside suppliers. What factors will determine whether a firm decides to "make versus buy"—that is, to contract out most or all of a study or conduct it themselves?

5. Despite the presence of a written code of ethics, why are some marketing ethical problems hard to cure? Discuss this from the sponsor and supplier point of view.

6. Fred Burton, the owner of a small tennis club in Wichita, Kansas, thinks there is an unmet demand for indoor courts. He is considering employing a marketing research company to study whether a market exists for the indoor facilities.
   a. What factors should Mr. Burton consider before ordering market research to be conducted?
   b. What possible pitfalls must the marketing research company avoid while conducting the study?
   c. After obtaining the market research recommendations, Mr. Burton decides not to use the information generated by the market research study. What factors could have influenced his decision not to use the research information?

7. Linda Phillips, an engineering student, has designed an innovative piece of equipment to help the physically disabled to communicate. The equipment incorporates a system of electronic signals emitted with a slight turn of the head. She feels that this product could have commercial success if marketed to health care organizations, but she has had no past experience in marketing management and does not know how to undertake the market planning and evaluation process. Acting as Ms. Phillips's marketing consultant, suggest a course of action to help her bring this innovative product to its market.

ENDNOTES

1. A. K. Kohli and B. J. Jaworski, "Market Orientation: The Construct, Research Propositions, and Managerial Implications," *Journal of Marketing*, 54 (April 1990), pp. 1–18.

2. Scott Miller, "DaimlerChrysler Synergies Lead to a Show Car," *Wall Street Journal* (September 16, 1999), p. A25.

3. Gary McWilliams, "Gateway Marketing Effort Has a Latin Pitch," *Wall Street Journal* (September 30, 1999), p. B10.

4. Anna Wilde Mathews, "Music Samplers on Web Buy CDs in Stores," *Wall Street Journal* (June 15, 2000).

5. Adapted from P. Vincent Barabba and Gerald Zaltman, *Hearing the Voice of the Market* (Cambridge, MA: Harvard Business School Press, 1991).

6. "Key Role of Research in Agree's Success Is Told," *Marketing News* (January 12, 1979), p. 14.

7. http://www.sprintpcs.com/wireless/wwupdates.asp.

8. Rohit Deshpande and Scott Jeffries, "Attitude Affecting the Use of Marketing Research in Decision Making: An Empirical Investigation," in *Educator's Conference Proceedings*, Series 47, Kenneth L. Bernhardt et al. eds. (Chicago: American Marketing Association, 1981), pp. 1–4.

9. Anil Menon and P. Rajan Varadarajan, "A Model of Marketing Knowledge Use within Firms," *Journal of Marketing*, 56 (October 1992), p. 61.

10. Rohit Deshpande and Gerald Zaltman, "A Comparison of Factors Affecting Use of Marketing Information in Consumer and Industrial Firms," *Journal of Marketing Research*, 24 (February 1987), pp. 114–118.

11. Marketing Science Institute, Sept. 12–13, 1996, p. 6.

12. www.amazon.com.

13. "Code of Ethics of Marketing Research Association" (Chicago, IL: Marketing Research Association, Inc.).

14. "CASRO Code of Standards for Survey Research," Council of American Survey Research Organizations, *Annual Journal* (1992), pp. 19–22.

15. Michael W. Miller, "Coming Soon to Your Local Video Store: Big Brother," *Wall Street Journal* (December 26, 1990), p. 12.

16. "A Blockbuster of a Debate about Privacy: Blockbuster Entertainment May Sell Customer Information from its Database on Film Rentals," *Washington Post* (January 1, 1991), p. E1.

17. Oswald A. J. Mascarenhas, "Exonerating Unethical Marketing Executive Behaviors: A Diagnostic Framework," *Journal of Marketing*, 59 (April 1995), p. 44.

18. "HEB Plans to Open Store in Monterey," *Houston Chronicle* (September 10, 1996), p. C-1.

19. V. Kumar (2000), *International Marketing Research* (Englewood Cliffs, NJ: Prentice-Hall).

20. Adapted from Lackman, Saban, and Lanasa, "The Contribution of Market Intelligence to Tactical and Strategic Business Decisions" *Marketing Intelligence & Planning*, 18, 1 (2000), pp. 6–8.

CASES

For detailed descriptions of the following cases, please visit www.wiley.com/college/kumar.

Case 1-1: Ethical Dilemmas in Marketing Research
Case 1-2: Dell in Latin America?

Marketing Research in Practice

Learning Objectives

- Discuss briefly the practice of marketing research.
- Understand the concept of information systems and decision support systems.
- Explain marketing decision support systems.
- Introduce the various suppliers of marketing research information and the types of services offered by them.
- Talk briefly about the criteria used to select suppliers.
- Introduce the career options available in the marketing research industry.

Good information is critical to the success of any business. But finding *good* information—separating the "wheat" from the "chaff" of the huge volume of available data—is becoming more and more difficult. Indeed, if the old challenge was how to find the *right* information, the new challenge is how to glean the right information from the hundreds of reports, fact sheets, analyses, and so on, that today's industry executives can command at the stroke of a key or the click of a mouse. This constitutes the primary role of *market intelligence*.

In practice, a marketing research department's goal can be grouped into three major categories:[1] programmatic, evaluative, or selective. **Programmatic research** is performed to develop marketing options through market segmentation, market opportunity analysis, or consumer attitude and product usage studies. **Selective research** is done to test different decision alternatives such as new product concept testing, advertising copy testing, pretest marketing, and test marketing. **Evaluative research** is carried out to evaluate performance of programs, including tracking advertising recall, corporate and brand image studies, and measuring customer satisfaction with the quality of the product and service. As the number of products and types of services introduced into the market increase, the need for marketing research explodes. The future of marketing research appears to be both promising and challenging.[2]

Unquestionably, marketing research is a growth industry. In the last decade, real expenditures on marketing research (that is, after adjusting for inflation) more than doubled. This is largely a consequence of economic and social changes that have made better marketing an imperative.

With marketing the new priority, marketing research is the rallying cry. Companies are trying frantically to get their hands on information that identifies and explains the needs of powerful new consumer segments now being formed. Kroger

Programmatic research is performed to develop marketing options through market segmentation, market opportunity analysis, or consumer attitude and product usage studies.

Evaluative research is carried out to evaluate performance of programs, including tracking advertising recall, corporate and brand image studies, and measuring customer satisfaction with the quality of the product and service.

Selective research is done to test different decision alternatives such as new product concept testing, advertising copy testing, pretest marketing, and test marketing.

Co., a U.S. grocery chain store, for example, holds more than 250,000 consumer interviews a year to define consumer wants more precisely. Some companies are pinning their futures on product innovations, others are rejuvenating time-worn but proven brands, and still others are doing both.[3]

Not only are the companies that always did marketing research doing a great deal more, the breadth of research activities also continues to expand.

- Senior management is looking for more support for its strategic decisions; therefore, researchers are doing more acquisition and competitor studies, segmentation and market structure analyses, and basic strategic position assessments.

- Other functions, such as the legal department, now use marketing research evidence routinely. Corporate affairs wants to know shareholders', bankers', analysts', and employees' attitudes toward the company. The service department continuously audits service delivery capability and customer satisfaction.

- Entire industries that used to be protected from the vagaries of competition and changing customer needs by regulatory statutes are learning to cope with a deregulated environment. Airlines, banks, and financial services groups are looking for ways to overcome product proliferation, advertising clutter, and high marketing costs brought on by more sophisticated customers and aggressive competitors.

In this chapter we will look at how companies use the information gathered by marketing research, at the various ways they obtain this marketing research information, and at the career opportunities available in the marketing research industry.

◆ INFORMATION SYSTEMS, DECISION SUPPORT SYSTEMS, AND MARKETING RESEARCH

An **information system (IS)** is a continuing and interacting structure of people, equipment, and procedures designed to gather, sort, analyze, evaluate, and distribute pertinent, timely, and accurate information to decision makers.

An **information system (IS)** is a continuing and interacting structure of people, equipment, and procedures designed to gather, sort, analyze, evaluate, and distribute pertinent, timely, and accurate information to decision makers. Marketing research is concerned mainly with the actual content of the information and how it is to be generated, whereas the information system is concerned with managing the flow of data from many different projects and secondary sources to the managers who will use it. This requires databases to organize and store the information and a decision support system (DSS) to retrieve data, transform it into usable information, and disseminate it to users.

Databases

Information systems contain three types of information. The first is recurring day-to-day information—for example, the market and accounting data that flow into the organization as a result of market analysis research and accounting activities. Automobile firms use government sources for monthly data on new-car sales by brand and geographic area. In addition, surveys are conducted yearly to determine the ages and types of automobiles currently being driven, the lifestyles of the drivers (their activity and interest patterns), their media habits, and their intentions to replace their cars. The accounting department submits sales and inventory data for each of its dealers on a continuing basis, to update and supplement the information system.

A second type of information is intelligence relevant to the future strategy of the business. Automobile firms, for example, collect reports about new sources of fuel to power automobiles. This information might come from scientific meetings, trade organizations, or perhaps from government reports. It also might include information from salespersons or dealers about new-product tests being conducted by competitive firms. Intelligence is difficult to develop, because it usually involves diverse and changing sets of topic and information sources and is rarely collected systematically.

A third input to the information system is research studies that are not of a recurring nature. The potential usefulness of a marketing research study can be enhanced if the information is accessible instead of filed and forgotten. The potential exists that others may use the study, although perhaps not in the way it was originally intended.

Applying Information Systems to Marketing Research

Often the process of developing and using models and information systems reveal gaps in the databank that have to be closed. These emergent needs for information become a marketing research problem. For example:

- Performance (sales, market share, contributions, patronage) may be unsatisfactory relative to objectives. Perhaps the condition can be traced to a specific geographic area, but the underlying reasons still must be sought before action can be taken.

- A competitor may launch a new product or employ a new advertising appeal, with unknown consequences for the firm's competitive position.

- An unavoidable increase in costs puts pressures on profitability (or, in the case of a transit system, for example, increases subsidy requirements to an unacceptable level). Various possible increases in prices (or fares) must be evaluated.

- An upsurge in interest in health and nutrition may suggest to a snack company a new product line directed toward responding to this interest. Concept testing might be a first step in exploring this opportunity.

The information system serves to emphasize that marketing research should not exist in isolation as a single effort to obtain information. Rather, it should be part of a systematic and continuous effort by the organization to improve the decision making process. Marketing Research in Practice 2-1 demonstrates the transition from current ways of viewing and doing things to a new age.

◆ MARKETING DECISION SUPPORT SYSTEMS

Databases have no value if the insights they contain cannot be retrieved. A decision support system not only allows the manager to interact directly with the database to retrieve what is wanted, it also provides a modeling function to help make sense of what has been retrieved. A typical marketing manager regularly receives some or all of the following data: factory shipments or orders; syndicated aggregate (industry) data services; sales reports from the field sales force; consumer panel data; scanner data; demographic data; and internal cost and budget data. These data may also come in various levels of detail and aggregation. Often they use different reporting periods and incompatible computer languages. Add to this, the sales estimates about competing brands and advertising, promotion, and pricing activity, and there is a data explosion.

MARKETING RESEARCH IN PRACTICE 2-1

The Fourth Wave in Marketing Research

The term *Fourth Wave* has come to symbolize the contemporary transition from current ways of viewing and doing things to a new age. The coming changes will shape not only the way information is used, but also our fundamental conception of the role of marketing research in assisting management decisions.

In the *First Wave*, seat-of-the-pants decision making progressed to data-based decisions. Much of the initial interest in marketing research came about during the transition from a sales-oriented to a marketing-oriented business environment. The need to support marketing decisions with data drove much of the initial interest in research. Although a data-based approach makes logical sense, the seeds of dissatisfaction were buried deep within the philosophy. As more data became available, a large problem arose: a handful of data was helpful; a truckload was not necessarily better.

In the *Second Wave*, the progression was from data-based decisions to information-based decision making. Rather than review a multitude of individual facts, the role of marketing research evolved to manipulate data to summarize the underlying patterns. If we could understand the relationships and patterns in the data, so the logic went, this would lead to the insights necessary to drive marketing decisions. Unfortunately, much of the criticism of marketing research today is a result of this excessive focus on methodology and statistics. The problem now with marketing research was not centered on incompetent analysis, but the lack of a decision-maker's perspective and the inability to provide actionable insights consistently once the data were analyzed correctly.

In the *Third Wave*, we progressed from information-based decision making to system-based decisions. The Third Wave involved a number of developments centered on automated decision systems (ADS) that put the power of marketing information directly into the hands of nontechnical decision makers. It was a three-way marriage between marketing analysis, computer and information technologies, and the formal marketing planning process. The team approach, including marketing researchers, systems engineers, and marketing management, provided the synergy needed to build useful computer-based systems that helped managers through the marketing planning and evaluation process. Through pooling expertise and applying information technologies, the full potential of marketing information was realized in the Third Wave.

Finally in the *Fourth Wave*, the emergence of e-commerce and large customer databases have motivated organizations to move from an aggregate-level summarization of data (in order to uncover the underlying patterns as in the Second Wave) to a manipulation of data on an individual-by-individual basis. A majority of organizations currently are leveraging the technology developed during the Third Wave and the rich information they have about each individual customer, to tailor both their product/service and marketing messages on an individual customer basis. Also called *mass-customization*, this strategy develops relations with every customer that an organization possesses and finally allows managers to assess the lifetime value of every individual customer to the organization.

Source: Adapted from "Third Wave of Marketing Research on the Horizon," *Marketing News* (March 1, 1993), p. 6.

Managers don't want data. They want, and need, decision-relevant information in accessible and preferably graphical form for:

1. Routine comparisons of current performance against past trends on each of the key measures of effectiveness

2. Periodic exception reports to assess which sales territories or accounts have not matched previous years' purchases

3. Special analyses to evaluate the sales impact of particular marketing programs and to predict what would happen if changes were made

In addition, managers would like to link different divisions to enable product managers, sales planners, market researchers, financial analysts, and production schedulers to share information.

The purpose of a **marketing decision support system (MDSS)** is to combine marketing data from diverse sources into a single database that line managers can enter interactively to quickly identify problems and obtain standard, periodic reports, as well as answers to analytical questions.

Characteristics of an MDSS

A good MDSS should have the following characteristics.

1. *Interactive:* The process of interaction with the MDSS should be simple and direct. With just a few commands the user should be able to obtain the results immediately. There should be no need for a programmer in between.

2. *Flexible:* A good MDSS should be flexible. It should be able to present the available data in either discrete or aggregate form. It should satisfy the information needs of the managers in different hierarchical levels and functions.

3. *Discovery oriented:* The MDSS should not only assist managers in solving the existing problems, but should also help them to probe for trends and ask new questions. The managers should be able to discover new patterns and be able to act on them using the MDSS.

4. *User friendly:* It should be easy for the managers to learn and use the MDSS. It should not take hours just to figure out what is going on. Most MDSS packages are menu driven and are easy to operate.

A typical MDSS is assembled from four components: a database, display, modeling, and analysis (see Figure 2-1).

MDSS Database

The database contains data from all sources, stored in a sufficiently disaggregated way so that it can be analyzed by product item, sales district, trade account, or time

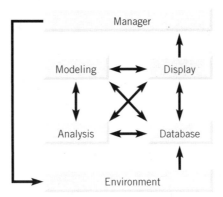

Figure 2-1 The four components of a MDSS.

period. The best systems have easily updated databases and have sufficient flexibility that data can be readily analyzed in new ways. Since most analyses deal with a subset of a larger database, the supporting software should permit random access to any and all data to create appropriate subsets.

Reports and Displays

The capabilities of an MDSS range from simple ad-hoc tables and reports to complex plots, charts, and other graphic displays. Any report or display can include calculations such as variances and running totals, or the results of statistical procedures found in the system. Typical reports produced with an MDSS include status reports that track current trends, exception reports on troubled brands and markets, and variance reports showing budget and actuals for sales and profits.

Analysis Capabilities

Analysis capabilities are used to relate the data to the models, as well as to clarify relationships, identify exceptions, and suggest courses of action. These capabilities should include the ability to make calculations such as averages, lags, and percentage changes versus a previous period, and to conduct seasonal analyses and standard statistical procedures such as regression, correlation, and factor analysis. These procedures will be covered in subsequent chapters of this book.

Models

Models represent assumptions about how the world works, and specifically about how brand sales, shares, and profits respond to changes in elements of the marketing mix. Models are used to test alternative marketing programs, answer "what if" questions, and assist in setting more realistic objectives. For example, managers want help with such questions as: What is the effect on profitability of achieving wider distribution? What is the optimal call level for each sales representative for each account and prospect? What objectives should be set for coupon redemption and the profitability of promotion programs? The models used to address these questions can range from forecasts to complex simulations of relationships among marketing, economic, and other factors.

Using an MDSS offers a number of advantages. It results in substantial cost savings, because it helps the organization make better and quicker decisions. The presence of an MDSS forces the decision maker to view the decision and information environment within which he or she operates; hence, it leads to a better understanding of the decision environment. Since managers can now retrieve and utilize information that was never before accessible, decision making is more effective. Using an MDSS results in better quality and quantity of data being collected and hence increases the value of the information to managers.

Gaining Insights from an MDSS

When an over-the-counter (OTC) drug manufacturer suffered a decline in national unit market share for its drug "Alpha," management turned to an MDSS for insights. They suspected the losses would be traced to actions of the two main competitors. "Beta" was a private-label competitor that was sold at half the price of Alpha. The other competing brand, "Delta," was produced and marketed by another division of the same company, following a similar strategy. Initial data from the decision support system seemed to confirm management's initial suspicions. Alpha's share had dropped from 5.0 percent to 2.5 percent, and Delta's share had more than doubled, from 2.0 percent to 4.5 percent. However, subsequent analysis of the database showed that this information was misleading.

The premise of the further analysis was that any competitive effects should be evident at the regional as well as the national level. To test this possibility, the market-share changes of Alpha were related to share changes of Beta and Delta, by region, for a six-month period.

The results confirmed the adverse effects of Beta on Alpha. In almost every region, a share decrease for Alpha was associated with a share increase for Beta. A different picture emerged, however, when a similar analysis was done with Delta. In the regions where Alpha's share had decreased the least, Delta's share had increased the most. Conversely, Alpha's share had decreased the most in those regions where Delta had gained the least share. Clearly, Delta was not the source of Alpha's problems; more likely, Delta was helping Alpha by combining the two brands' sales force efforts. This analysis prevented a potentially damaging interdivisional dispute and helped focus management's attention on the proper target competitor.

◆ SUPPLIERS OF INFORMATION

In general, managers can acquire the necessary information for decision making from two basic types of sources:

1. The corporate or in-house marketing research department
2. External suppliers

Usually, managers use a mix of in-house and external approaches to solve a problem. Both can feed information directly to their clients, who are users with decision-making needs. More often, the outside suppliers get their direction and provide information to an inside research group. These inside suppliers translate the problems of their clients into specific information requirements, decide how the information will be collected and by whom, and then interpret the findings. Figure 2-2 shows the interaction among the participants in a marketing research activity.

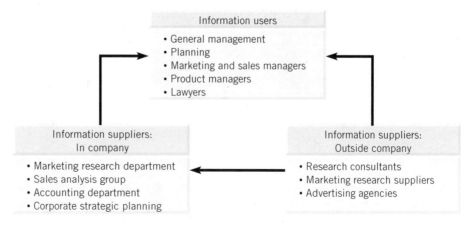

Figure 2-2 Participants in marketing research activities.

The purpose of this section is to discuss briefly the nature and attributes of the providers of marketing research services, the types of services they provide, and the factors that influence the choice of a suitable supplier for a given situation. Figure 2-3 gives a concise summary of the different types of information suppliers within the marketing research industry.

Corporate/In-House Marketing Research

The location of the marketing research department within an organization and the strength of the department vary from firm to firm and to a very great extent depend on the requirements for information and the organizational structure of the firm. Some firms have a single centralized research department, housed in the corporate headquarters, which provides the information required to the various business units scattered geographically and/or functionally.

The other extreme is the completely decentralized operation, wherein each business unit or geographic unit has its own research department. The type of structure adopted depends on the amount of information required, the frequency with which it is required, the uniqueness of the information, and the time available to collect it. In most major organizations, especially in multinational corporations, a mix of both these structures can be found.

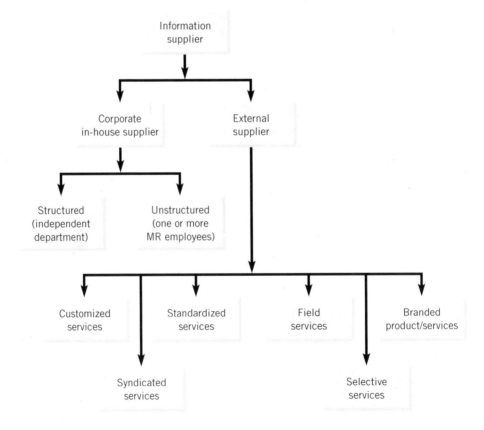

Figure 2-3 Information, suppliers, and services.

Not all organizations (regardless of size) have an in-house research establishment. Even among those that have an in-house research department, it is not unusual to seek the assistance of external suppliers. Virtually all research users at some time use the services of outside research specialists. Depending on the research approach, their role may be limited to raw data collection, questionnaire, or sampling method provided by the client. At the other extreme, the client may assign the entire problem to an outside consultant who is responsible for every step till the completed report and action recommendations. Other possibilities are to bring in outside specialists for special problems (such as a sampling expert to draw a complex sample), or to employ services that have special facilities or data.[4]

Many related considerations influence the decision to go outside:

1. Internal personnel may not have the skills or experience.

2. Outside help may be called in to boost internal capacity in response to an urgent deadline.

3. It may be cheaper to go outside.

4. Shared cost and multiclient studies coordinated by an outside supplier offer considerable savings possibilities.

5. Often, outside suppliers have special facilities or competencies (an established national interviewing field force, conference rooms with one-way mirrors, banks of telephone lines, or test kitchens) that would be costly to duplicate for a single study.

6. Political considerations may dictate the use of an outside research specialist whose credentials are acceptable to all parties in an internal policy dispute.

7. Marketing research is used increasingly in litigation or in proceedings before regulatory or legislative bodies. The credibility of the findings generally will be enhanced if the study is conducted by a respected outsider.

External Suppliers of the Research Industry

The marketing research industry in the United States consists of several hundred research firms, ranging from small, one-person operations to large corporations having operations in multiple countries. Table 2-1 lists the top 25 U.S. research firms, their annual revenues for the year 2000, and the percent change from the previous year.[5] The table also gives an estimate of the total revenue from foreign operations. As can be seen from Table 2-1, the total revenue of the top 25 firms exceeds $7.1 billion and more than one-third of this revenue is estimated to come from foreign operations.

The marketing research industry in the United States is not only huge and profitable, it is also a growing industry. Research spending within the United States showed 5.6 percent real growth (after adjusting for inflation) and 9.0 percent revenue growth over the previous year for the year 1999. Figure 2-4 compares the growth in research spending within the United States for the years 1988 to 2000.[6] According to Jack Honomichl author of the *Annual Industry Review,* the U.S. marketing research industry is becoming more global and cosmopolitan. About $2.6 billion, or 37 percent, of its combined revenues came from work outside the United States.

Honomichl conducted a study of the top 50 research organizations, which had combined revenues of over $7.1 billion. However, when the total industry is taken into account, the revenue level climbs significantly. The industry growth analysis can

TABLE 2-1   Top 25 U.S. Research Organizations

Rank 1999	Rank 1998	Organization	Headquarters	Total Research Revenues (millions)	Percent Change from Outside U.S.
1	1	A.C. Nielsen Corp.	Stamford, Conn.	$1,577.0	2.1%
2	2	IMS Health Inc.	Westport, Conn.	$1,131.2	9.1%
3	3	Information Resources Inc.	Chicago	$531.9	−2.8%
4	—	VNU Inc.	New York	$526.9	15.5%
5	4	NFO World Group	Greenwich, Conn.	$470.5	2.9%
6	6	The Kantar Group Ltd.	Fairfield, Conn.	$270.0	9.4%
7	7	Westat Inc.	Rockville, Md.	$264.4	9.3%
8	8	Arbitron Co.	New York	$206.8	8.8%
9	10	Market Facts Inc.	Arlington Heights, Ill.	$190.3	11.2%
10	9	Maritz Marketing Research Inc.	St. Louis	$172.0	−1.3%
11	11	The NPD Group Inc.	Port Washington, N.Y.	$164.3	14.6%
12	14	Taylor Nelson Sofres Intersearch	Horsham, Pa.	$155.7	10.3%
13	12	United Information Group USA	New York	$139.0	17.0%
14	13	Opinion Research Corp.	Princeton, N.J.	$123.9	10.6%
15	15	J.D. Power and Associates	Agoura Hills, Calif.	$104.0	11.9%
16	17	Ipsos-ASI Inc.	Norwalk, Conn.	$78.8	4.8%
17	16	Roper Starch Worldwide Inc.	Harrison, N.Y.	$73.9	12.0%
18	34	Jupiter Media Metrix Inc.	New York	$69.1	152.6%
19	24	Harris Interactive Inc.	Rochester, N.Y.	$56.0	50.8%
20	21	MORPACE International Inc.	Farmington, Mich.	$54.3	22.3%
21	18	Abt Associates Inc.	Cambridge, Mass.	$53.7	5.7%
22	20	Total Research Corp.	Princeton, N.J.	$51.9	2.3%
23	19	Burke Inc.	Cincinnati	$48.6	−0.4%
24	26	Wirthlin Worldwide	McLean, VA.	$46.5	25.1%
25	23	C&R Research Services Inc.	Chicago	$46.2	20.5%
			Subtotal Top 50	$7,144.7	7.40%

Source: Marketing News (June 4, 2001), p. H4

be extended to include 181 CASRO (Council of American Survey Research Organizations) member firms beyond those listed in the top 10. These 181 firms in CASRO represent more than 85 percent of the survey revenue in the United States.

The Market Research Association (MRA) co-sponsored "How's Your Business Survey" to track trends in marketing research budgets, the staffing of marketing research departments, and the different types of methodologies utilized. Although an increase was projected for budget spending (up 18 percent) and staffing level spending (up 23 percent), research spending has changed slightly. The data collection method of choice is scanner-based sales research, with spending increased by 47 percent for 1995. Among the numerous types of research methods expected to be conducted more frequently in 1995 were sales research (up 34 percent), customer satisfaction research (up 27 percent), promotion testing (up 26 percent), and concept testing and simulated test market sales (up 25 percent).[7]

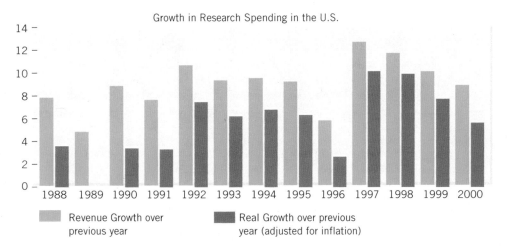

Figure 2-4 Growth in research spending in the United States.

Source: Jack Homonichl, "It Was Another Very Good Year," *Marketing News* (June 5, 2000).

Type and Nature of Services

External suppliers that collectively make up the marketing research industry can be further classified into six different groups, depending on the type and nature of the services they provide. Based on Figure 2-3, the major types of services provided by external suppliers of information are discussed in the paragraphs that follow.

Customized Services. Firms that specialize in customized services work with individual clients to help them develop and implement a marketing research project from top to bottom. They work with management on any given problem and go through the entire research process, including analyzing and presenting the final results.

Syndicated Services. Syndicated services are companies that routinely collect information on several different issues and provide it to firms that subscribe to their services. The Nielsen Television Index, which provides information on audiences viewing different TV programs, is an example of such services. These suppliers also provide information on retail sales, household purchasing patterns, and so on, which they collect through scanner data.

Standardized Services. Standardized services are market research projects conducted in a standard, prespecified manner and supplied to several different clients. The Starch Readership Survey is a typical example of such a service; it provides clients information regarding the effectiveness of print advertisements, in the form of Starch scores.

Field Services. Field services suppliers concentrate on collecting data for research projects. They specialize in various survey techniques such as mail surveys, telephone surveys, or personal surveys. These organizations range from small, one-person establishments to large, multinational, wide-area telephone service (WATS)-line interviewing services, and have extensive facilities for personal interviews in homes and shopping malls. Some of these firms specialize in qualitative data collection methods such as focus group interviews and projection techniques.

Selective Services. Some companies specialize in just one or two aspects of marketing research, mainly concerned with data coding, data editing, or data analysis. These generally are small firms, sometimes referred to as *lab houses,* with expertise in sophisticated data analysis techniques. The proliferation of software for marketing research projects has led to an increase in such lab houses. Any enterprising individual with expertise in computer and sophisticated multivariate analysis techniques can acquire the necessary software packages and establish a firm specializing in data analysis.

Branded Products Services. Some firms have developed specialized data collection and analysis procedures to address specific types of research problems, which they market as branded products. PRIZM, a Claritas Inc. product that forms clusters of the population on the basis of lifestyle and geographic classifications, is an example of one such branded product. Using this technique, the entire U.S. population is divided into 62 clusters. For example the new system contains innovations and discoveries of its own. Among them:

- Dozens of new clusters, including new Latino clusters.
- Clusters with high concentrations of foreign-born and Asian consumers.
- A new way of measuring urbanization and distinguishing between big-city and smaller-city, "edge" city, neighborhoods.
- Finer segmentation among the affluent suburban clusters such as "Blue Blood Estates" and "Winner's circle."

◆ MANAGEMENT OF MARKETING RESEARCH

Initiation of the Research

Marketing research can be initiated by either the operational managers within the organization or the managers of the marketing research department.

Each approach is beneficial in its own way. As operational managers use the results from marketing research to guide their decisions, it is logical to allow operational managers to initiate the research, but certain aspects such as operational managers turnover rate—which results in discontinuity in the marketing information system and the failure of operational managers to identify certain problems that require research—discourage the first approach.

A problem with the second approach is that the marketing research department cannot come up with all the possible situations that require marketing research.

A viable solution that would minimize these problems would be to let marketing research managers give research results on common and recurring topics and to let organizational managers ask for marketing research on specific topics.

Research Design

The specifics about the kind of research and the data sources are the responsibility of the marketing research manager. The norm is to specify the broad perspectives of the research in the first meeting and to decide about the specific details of the research design in a follow-up meeting with operational managers. This helps the researchers in not getting stuck with the first idea that comes to mind. The researcher can then start designing specific data collection procedures and sampling techniques.

Communication between Managers and Researchers

The research purposes specified by the operational managers are often either very narrow or very broad. The research managers have to clarify the research needs of the organization as early as possible. The research manager should acquire information about the research topic. This background information helps the managers articulate their needs, and the additional areas in which the operational managers may require research. Periodic interactions between operational and research managers help accurately identify the research needs of the organization. Managers should also be informed of any limitations of the research as soon as possible.

Managing Expectations about Research

Often, research managers are not able to satisfy operational managers (even if they have done a good job), because of the high expectations of the operational manager. The communication process just described can help set realistic expectations about the project. For example, a research manager who is asked to estimate the number of customers for a home health care organization has to tell the operational managers that marketing research can provide an excellent estimate of the number of referrals from the doctors, but cannot tell how many customers will actually visit the home health care organization, because that decision is influenced by various other aspects, including cost.

It is often advisable to give a realistic completion time for the project, rather than an optimistic completion time.

Recommendation in the Report

There are varied opinions about a research report containing recommendations. The decision of incorporating recommendations in a research report is influenced by two factors. First, the type of research influences the incorporation of recommendations. If the project is a "problem identification" reason, the report need not contain recommendations—for example, if the research is to find why the ticket sales are going down for a local baseball team, it is not necessary to incorporate specific steps that the club should take to boost sales. If the research is a "problem solving" research, it is imperative that the report contain recommendations. For example, if an airline conducts research on whether it should have a telephone service on its flights for a nominal charge, the report should have a "yes" or "no."

Second, the decision to include a recommendation depends on the choice of operational managers. It is always better to ask the manager early in the research whether the recommendations should be given verbally or in writing. However, irrespective of the inclusion or exclusion of recommendations, the research report should have enough details to help managers draw meaningful conclusions.

◆ CRITERIA FOR SELECTING EXTERNAL SUPPLIERS

Once the decision has been made to go outside, there remains the question of which consultant or supplier to retain. What criteria should a firm adopt in selecting an external research supplier? Several academic scholars have conducted research studies to identify the factors that are important in the selection of external suppliers. A crucial factor in the choice is the judgment as to whether the supplier or consultant actually can deliver the promised data, advice, or conclusions. This judgment should be made only after the following steps have been followed:

1. Make a thorough search for names of people and companies who have acknowledged expertise in the area of the study.[8]

2. Select a small number of bidders on the basis of recommendations of colleagues or others who have had similar needs.

3. Personally interview the person who would be responsible for the project, asking for examples of work on similar problems, their procedures for working with clients, and the names of previous clients who could provide references.

4. Check the references of each potential supplier, with special attention to comments on their depth of competence and expertise, their creativity in dealing with problems, and the quality and adequacy of resources available.

Make a selection based on how well the problem and objectives have been understood[9], comments by the references, and whether the quoted price or fee is a good value in light of the research approach that is proposed. Seldom is the lowest quotation the best value. To minimize the problem of comparability, all bidders should respond to the same study specifications.[10]

◆ THE INTERNATIONAL MARKETING RESEARCH INDUSTRY

The growing importance of the international components of the marketing research industry revenue reflects the fact that the United States accounts for only 39 percent of marketing research expenditures worldwide. Western Europe accounts for 40 percent of research expenditures, Japan accounts for nearly 10 percent, and the remainder is accounted for by the rest of the world. Almost all major countries in the world, including the newly industrialized and developing countries, have major marketing research organizations. The leading market research companies in the United States, such as A. C. Nielsen Corp., have subsidiaries in several other countries. The top 10 marketing research firms in the world are listed in Table 2-2.

When a company is entering a new market, it is important not only to understand the consumers but to obtain information from secondary sources. The following list

TABLE 2-2   Top 10 Global Research Organizations

Rank 1999	Rank 1998	Organization	Headquarters	Total Research Revenues (millions)	Percent of Total Revenues Outside Home Country
1	1	A.C. Nielsen Corp.	Stamford, Conn.	$1,525.4	68.1%
2	2	IMS Health Inc.	Westport, Conn.	$1,275.7	60.7%
3	3	The Kantar Group Ltd.	Fairfield, Conn.	$773.5	74.8%
4	4	Taylor Nelson Sofres Plc.	London	$601.3	72.3%
5	5	Information Resources Inc.	Chicago	$546.3	23.7%
6	6	NFO Worldwide Inc.	Greenwich, Conn.	$457.2	61.3%
7	7	Nielsen Media Research	New York	$453.3	2.6%
8	8	GfK Group	Nuremberg	$414.0	55.6%
9	12	United Information Group Ltd.	London	$246.3	63.0%
10	9	Ipsos Group SA	Paris	$245.8	71.3%
			Total	$6,538.8	41.7%

Source: Marketing News (Aug. 14, 2000).

Does Dole fit in?
Kindra Clineff/The Picture Cube.

represents Canadian companies that offer consumer marketing research information for organizations designing strategies to market to the Canadian population.[11]

Canada Inc.

ABM Research Inc.

Butler Research Associates Inc.

Canada Market Research Ltd.

Canadian Facts

Consumer Contact Ltd.

Elliott Research

Thompson Lightstone & Company Ltd.

◆ CAREER OPPORTUNITIES IN MARKETING RESEARCH

Marketing research offers several promising career opportunities,[12] depending on one's level of education, experience, interests, and personality. Interesting and exciting careers are available both within research supplier organizations—typically, external suppliers of marketing research services such as A. C. Nielsen, Information Resources, Inc. (IRI), J. D. Power and Associates, and so on—and within companies that have their own research department. A brief description of marketing research jobs, the required level of education, the real level of experience, and the average annual compensation are provided at www.wiley.com/college/kumar.

END OF CHAPTER MATERIAL

SUMMARY

The focus of marketing research has shifted from ad-hoc methods to collecting data and helping managers make informed, knowledgeable decisions. The marketing decision support system is the latest in a series of developments that help marketing managers use the information they obtain in a more meaningful manner. Marketing research is a key component of the MDSS because it provides one of the main inputs into the system. Marketing research can either be done in-house or bought from outside suppliers. A number of market research companies provide many services, both syndicated and customized.

Video Segment:

Minority Marketing

Given the multiethnic composition of the country as well as a focus on multinational corporations, several companies choose to address and target the minority groups. As mentioned in the 1993 Minority Report, the attitude and findings imply that the differences in shopping behavior and patterns of consumption must be taken into account.

KEY TERMS

programmatic research
selective research
evaluative research
information system
marketing decision support system (MDSS)
MDSS' reports and displays
MDSS' analysis capabilities
MDSS' models

corporate/in-house marketing research
 department
customized services
syndicated services
standardized services
field services
selective services
branded products services

MARKETING RESEARCH TOOLBOX
REVIEW POINTS

1. A marketing research department's goals can be grouped into three major categories: programmatic, selective, or evaluative.

2. Programmatic research is performed to develop marketing actions through market segmentation, market opportunity analysis, consumer attitude, and product usage studies.

3. Selective research is done to test different decision alternatives such as new product concept testing, advertising copy testing, pretest marketing, and test marketing.

4. Evaluative research is carried out to evaluate performance of programs including tracking advertising recall, corporate and brand image studies, and measuring customer satisfaction with the quality of the product and service.

5. An information system is a continuing and interacting structure of people, equipment, and procedures designed to gather, sort, analyze, evaluate, and distribute pertinent, timely, and accurate information to decision makers.

6. Decision support systems retrieve data, transform it into usable information, and disseminate it to users.

7. Types of information required for information systems are recurring day-to-day information, intelligence relevant to the future strategy of the business, and research studies that are not of recurring nature.

8. The information system serves to emphasize that marketing research should not exist in isolation as a single effort to obtain information. Rather, it should be part of a systematic and continuous effort by the organization to improve the decision-making process.

9. The purpose of a marketing decision support system (MDSS) is to combine marketing data from diverse sources into a single interactive database.

10. A good MDSS should be interactive, flexible, discovery oriented, and user friendly.

11. Using an MDSS results in better quality and quantity of data being collected and hence increases the value of the information to managers.

12. Analysis of data using MDSS helps avoid making decisions based on misleading information.

13. Information available for making decisions is from two basic types of sources: corporate or in-house marketing research departments and external suppliers.

14. The type of structure adopted for an in-house marketing research department depends on the frequency with which it is required, the uniqueness of the information, and the time available to collect it.

15. The type and nature of services provided by external marketing research firms include customized services, syndicated services, standardized services, field services, selective services, and branded products services.

16. Selection of external suppliers is made on the basis of how well the problem and objectives have been understood, comments by the references, and whether the quoted price or fee is a good value in light of the research approach that is proposed.

QUESTIONS AND PROBLEMS

1. a. How do marketing information systems aid marketers in their decision making?
   b. What types of information can be obtained from marketing information systems?

2. What are the inherent characteristics of an effective marketing decision support system?

3. A marketing manager needs to find the causes for the decline in market share of his or her company's product. The manager decides to conduct marketing research.
   a. How should the manager go about finding a supplier of research services?
   b. Suppose the manager decides to introduce the product in Europe. A study needs to be conducted to assess the acceptance of the product in various markets. What criteria should the manager use in selecting a research supplier?

4. Suggest three examples of identification of market opportunities or marketing problems from recent secondary data sources.

5. Would the nature of the services provided in an international market approximate to the kind of services provided in the local market? What would be some of the factors that would contribute to the differences that exist?

ENDNOTES

1. Sil Seggev, "Listening Is Key to Providing Useful Marketing Research," *Marketing News* (January 22, 1982), p. 6.
2. Kenneth R. Wade, "The When/What Research Decision Guide," *Marketing Research: A Magazine of Management & Applications*, 5 (Summer 1993), pp. 24–27.
3. "Marketing: The New Priority," *Business Week* (November 21, 1983), p. 96.
4. Paul Boughton, "Marketing Research Partnerships: A Strategy for the 90s," *Marketing Research: A Magazine of Management & Applications*, 4 (December 1992), pp. 8–13.
5. Jack Honomichl, "Top 25 U.S. Research Organizations," *Marketing News* (June 4, 2001), p. 42.
6. Jack Honomichl, "Growth Stunt," *Marketing News* (June 4, 2001).
7. Betsy Peterson, "Trends Turn Around," *Marketing Research: A Magazine of Management & Applications*, 7 (Summer 1995), pp. 40–41.
8. Useful sources are *Greenbook: International Directory of Marketing Research Houses and Services* (New York: American Marketing Association), annual; *Consultants and Consulting Organizations Directory* (Detroit: Gale Research Co.), triennial with annual supplements; and *Bradfords Directory of Marketing Research Agencies in the U.S. and Around the World* (Fairfax, VA: Bradford Publishing, 1984). A list of the top 300 companies that specialize in focus-group interviewing techniques appears in the January issues of *Marketing News*.
9. *Marketing News* provides a directory of software for marketing research applications.
10. Raymond D. Speer, "Follow These Six Steps to Get Most Benefits from Marketing Research Consultant Project," *Marketing News* (September 18, 1981), pp. 12–13. *Marketing News* publishes a directory of international marketing research firms on a regular basis.
11. ESOMAR (http://www.esomer.nl/methserv/57179160.html).
12. Sources: Thomas C. Kinnear and Ann R. Root, *Survey of Marketing Research* (Chicago: American Marketing Association, 1996); Carl McDaniel and Roger Gates, *Contemporary Marketing Research* (Minneapolis: West Publishing), p. 26. *Marketing News* on a regular basis publishes a directory of marketing research firms located within research users such as Coca-Cola, AT&T, etc., in their in-house research departments.

CASES

For a detailed description of the following case, please visit www.wiley.com/college/kumar.

Case 2-1: Philip Morris Enters Turkey

The Marketing Research Process

Learning Objectives

- Be familiar with the various stages of the marketing research process.
- Highlight the importance of the problem/opportunity identification stage of the research process.
- Understand the issues related to hypotheses development.
- Explain the concept of value of information, and its role in deciding when marketing research is beneficial.
- Introduce the international marketing research process.

Honeywell fueled its growth strategy by leaning heavily on market intelligence to pinpoint industries, target market niches, and successfully sell its products. Market intelligence can be used to identify potential market segments for growth and expansion, protect market position against competitors' inroads, discover new product applications, and customize new products. In order to understand this further, one needs to understand how a market research project is conceived, planned, and executed.

The **research process** provides a systematic, planned approach to the research project and ensures that all aspects of the research project are consistent with each other.

The answer in part, is through a **research process,** consisting of stages or steps that guide the project from its conception through the final analysis, recommendation, and ultimate action. The research process provides a systematic, planned approach to the research project and ensures that all aspects of the research project are consistent with each other. It is especially important that the research design and implementation be consistent with the research purpose and objectives. Otherwise, the results will not help the client.

The research process is described in this chapter and in Chapter 4. This chapter provides an overview of the research process, a discussion of the research purpose and research objectives, and a consideration of the value of research information. Chapter 4 gives an overview of the research design and its implementation. Together, these two chapters are the foundation for the rest of the book.

◆ OVERVIEW OF THE MARKETING RESEARCH PROCESS

Research studies evolve through a series of steps, each representing the answer to a key question.

1. *Why should we do research?* This establishes the research purpose as seen by the management team that will be using the results. This step requires understanding the decisions to be made and the problems or opportunities to be diagnosed.

2. *What research should be done?* Here, the management purpose is translated into objectives that tell the researchers exactly what questions need to be answered by the research study or project.

3. *Is it worth doing the research?* The decision has to be made here about whether the value of the information that will likely be obtained is going to be greater than the cost of collecting it.

4. *How should the research be designed to achieve the research objectives?* Design issues include the choice of research approach—reliance on secondary data versus conducting a survey or experiment—and the specifics of how to collect the data. Chapter 4 deals with how to approach these issues.

5. *What will we do with the research?* Once the data have been collected, how will they be analyzed, interpreted, and used to make recommendations for action?

The necessary steps are linked in a sequential process (see Figure 3-1). The development of a research purpose that links the research to decision making, and the formulation of research objectives that serve to guide the research, are unquestionably the most important steps in the research process. If they are correct, the research stands a good chance of being both useful and appropriate. If they are bypassed or wrong, the research will almost surely be wasteful and irrelevant. These aspects of research, too often neglected by researchers, will be discussed in detail in this chapter. Chapter 4 deals with research design; Part II discusses the various methods to collect data; and Part III deals with analysis and interpretation of the data.

◆ THE PRELIMINARY STAGES OF THE MARKETING RESEARCH PROCESS

Step 1: Research Purpose

Seldom will research problems come neatly packaged with obvious information requirements, clear-cut boundaries, and pure motives on the part of the decision makers. Research problems are more likely to be poorly defined, only partially understood, and missing possible decision alternatives that should be analyzed. Launching a research study with such shaky inputs is a recipe for producing unusable findings and unhappy clients. It is in the best interest of both the researcher and the people paying for the research to be sure that the research purpose is fully understood. One of the hallmarks of a competent researcher is the ability to get to the heart of the management problem.

Consider the request by the chairperson of an association of community merchants for a research project to help reduce the propensity of residents in the community to do their shopping in two nearby communities. Clearly, the purpose of the research was to identify and evaluate various ways to increase the local merchants share of shopping by residents.

Further probing, however, revealed that the statement of the problem was a least partially inaccurate. Only late in the research process did the researcher learn that the chairperson was having real difficulty convincing the other local mer-

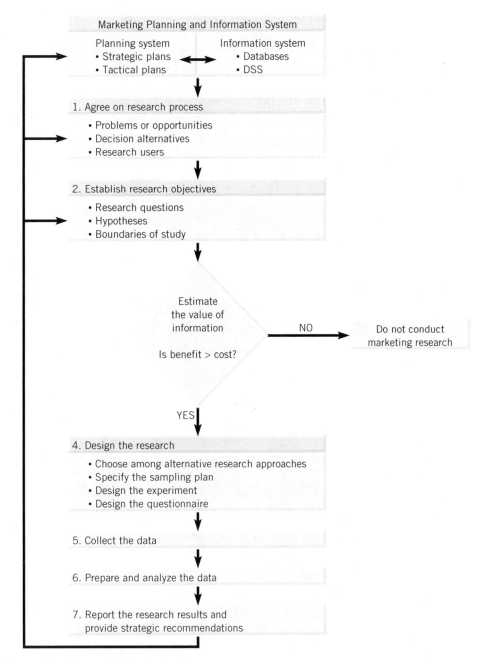

Figure 3-1 The marketing research process.

chants that there was a serious enough outflow of local trade to warrant joint action to reverse the flow. This certainly changed the purpose of the research. Now the researcher would have to measure the level of retail trade outflow, in addition to finding the reasons for the outflow. This required a major change in the research design. Had the change not been made, the results would have been of little value to the client.

The **research purpose** comprises a shared understanding between the manager and the researcher of problems or opportunities to be studied decision alternatives to be evaluated and users of the research results.

The research purpose comprises a shared understanding between the manager and the researcher of the following:

1. Problems or opportunities to be studied
   - Which problems or opportunities are anticipated?
   - What is the scope of the problems and their possible reasons?

2. Decision alternatives to be evaluated
   - What are the alternatives being studied?
   - What are the criteria for choosing among the alternatives?
   - What is the timing or importance of the decision?

3. Users of the research results
   - Who are the decision makers?
   - Are there any covert purposes?

Problem or Opportunity Analysis

A **problem** or **opportunity** often motivates research.

In analyzing problems or opportunities to be studied, constant contact with customers to monitor trends is very important. Marketing Research in Practice 3-1 explains how Reader's Digest Association uses research information to target mailings and measure actual response rates.

Research often is motivated by a problem or opportunity. The fact that sales are below expectations in the East might be a problem requiring research. The fact that people are consuming fewer sweets might be a problem or a potential opportunity for a candy company. In such cases, the research purpose should specify the problem or opportunity to be explored. Identifying and defining the problem or opportunity is a crucial first step in the marketing research process. Especially in situation analysis contexts, exploratory research is needed to identify problems and opportunities. What sales areas are showing weak performance? What segments represent oppor-

MARKETING RESEARCH IN PRACTICE 3-1

Reader's Digest's Direct Mailing Lists

By a large majority, 98 percent, the Reader's Digest Association's business is conducted through direct mail. The company uses research information to target mailings and measures actual response rates and profits when promotions end. Having done this repeatedly in the past, the company now uses a statistical model in advance to plan mailings and forecast profits.

Throughout the year, the company collects and updates customer data through questionnaires placed in bills, shipments, magazines, and self-mailers. It sends mail based on customer's self-reported affinities and established purchasing patterns. When a sales promotion is ready to roll, Reader's Digest finds consumers likely to be interested in the product, then calculates the expected profit value, or EPV, of mailing to individual recipients. Probabilities of purchase, return or cancellation, bad debt, and revenue, go into the equation with cost estimates. If the customer's EPV is positive, his or her name joins millions on the list. Thus, by charting response rates, Reader's Digest mails promotional offers only to a small percentage of customers in its database and elicits better response rates. Analysts at Reader's Digest say that by including more data in the model, they have been able to get a better gains chart. In other words, with a stronger model, by mailing less, the company makes more profit.

Source: Marketing News (March 31, 1997), p. 7.

tunities because they are dissatisfied with current products or because they are underusing the product? Even in exploratory research, however, it will be helpful to identify the nature of the problem or opportunity that is motivating the research. Further, the goal should be to move from exploratory research to research more focused on a decision. Marketing Research in Practice 3-2 describes how Wal-Mart capitalized on an opportunity.

The manager needs to make certain that the real problem is being addressed. Sometimes the recognized problem is only a symptom, or perhaps merely a part of a larger problem. A sobering illustration of this is the plight of Compton Corp.,[1] a manufacturer of capital equipment costing between $10,000 and $25,000. The company was dominant in its market, with a share as large as the next two biggest competitors. All the companies sold their equipment through a network of independent distributors, each of which sold the products of at least two competitors. For several years this market leader had been losing share. In an attempt to reverse the trend, the company changed advertising agencies. When the new agents funded a study of end users, they found to their surprise that the previous agency had done a superb job of creating awareness and favorable attitudes. However, many of the equipment purchasers who favored Compton were actually buying the competing brands. This problem had little to do with the performance of the advertising agency. A new study, oriented toward the distributors, found that Compton's distributor-relations program was very weak relative to its competitors. One competitor emphasized sales contests, another offered cash bonuses to salespeople, and a third was particularly effective with technical sales assistance directed to difficult accounts. Not surprisingly, these factors influenced the distributors when they were asked for advice, or when the prospective purchaser did not have a firm commitment to Compton equipment.

In this case, the real problem ultimately was isolated, but only after much time and energy had been directed toward the wrong problem. When defining the problem, it is important to think broadly about the possible causes or influential vari-

MARKETING RESEARCH IN PRACTICE 3-2

Wal-Mart Starting to Click

Wal-mart, the country's largest retailer, launched a revamped webstore after being chided for its lateness in embracing the Web. The new company will be called WalMart.com and will be a standalone web-retailing company carrying the Wal-Mart brand. It will have its own executive staff separate from the Wal-Mart management. Some experts believe that it is important to catch up with competition before blowing it away; keeping this is in mind, the new website is at par in terms of functionality with the websites of Wal-Mart competitors.

To gain an edge over its competitors, Wal-Mart is using its bricks-and-mortar chain to improve the shopping experience for on-line and off-line customers. It gives buyers the option of returning merchandise at one of its retail stores. After further research it may also offer its bricks-and-mortar shoppers an easy way to buy products at the website. The website offers six times the number of products found at a typical Wal-Mart, with plans of expansion. Customers can browse, then purchase goods at the website in kiosks located in the retail stores.

To help its off-line customers get on-line, Wal-Mart partnered with AOL to create a low-cost, co-branded Internet access. In the future, Wal-Mart plans to collect data on the customers who shop at the site so it can offer a more personalized shopping experience.

Source: Connie Guglielmo, "Wal-Mart Starting to Click," *Inter@ctive week,* 7, 1 (January 10, 2000).

ables. This may justify a separate exploratory research study. Further, what appears to be a genuine problem or opportunity might not be researchable. For example, if a company that manufactures washing machines is interested in determining the replacement rates for all machines sold within the last three years, it might not be worthwhile to pursue the issue. Since most household washing machines have a lifespan ranging from 5 to 10 years, the problem of identifying the replacement rate for working machines sold within the last 3 years may be a nonresearchable problem.

Decision Alternatives

For research to be effective, it must be associated with a decision. Marketing research is committed to the principle of utility. In general, if research is not going to affect decisions, it is an exercise in futility. The researcher should always be sensitive to the possibility that either there are no **decision alternatives**—and therefore no decision—or that the research findings will not affect the decision, usually because of resource or organizational constraints. In such circumstances, the research will have no practical value and probably should not be conducted.

When a decision potential does exist, it is important to identify it explicitly, because the research then can be designed for maximum effectiveness. For example, researchers frequently are asked to assess the potential of a market that is not familiar to the company. But what are the decisions the manager faces? Is the manager thinking of acquiring a company serving that market? Has the lab produced a new product that might be sold as a component to the industry serving that market? The answers will significantly influence the design of the research.

A most useful way to clarify the decision motivating the research is to ask: (1) What alternative actions are being considered? (2) What actions would be taken, given the various feasible outcomes of the research? This line of questioning can be very enlightening for the decision maker, as well as for the researcher, in terms of clarifying exactly what the research can accomplish. The story in Marketing Research in Practice 3-3 illustrates how both can learn from a focus on decisions.

Sometimes the decision involved is highly specific. A *copy test* is used to select a copy alternative. A *concept test* is employed to determine if a concept should be developed further. Sometimes the decision can be very general. What markets should be the primary targets of our organization? Should our marketing program be changed? It is desirable to be as specific as possible, because the research purpose then will be more effective in guiding the development of the research design. However, even if the decision is necessarily general, it needs to be stated clearly.

Criteria for Choosing Among Alternatives. It is essential for the researcher to know how the decision maker will choose among the available alternatives. Suppose a product manager is considering three possible package redesigns for a health care product with declining sales. This would seem to be a straightforward research undertaking, as the decision alternatives are completely specified. However, the product manager could use some or all of the following criteria to choose the best of the three alternative packages:

1. Long-run sales
2. Trial purchases by users of competing brands
3. Amount of shelf space assigned to the brand
4. Differentiation from competitive packages
5. Brand-name recognition

MARKETING RESEARCH IN PRACTICE 3-3

Political Campaign Research

The meeting between Hugh Godfrey and two project directors from Pollsters Anonymous, a well-known survey research company, had taken a surprising turn. Here were two researchers suggesting that no research be undertaken.

Godfrey was campaign manager for John Crombie, a university professor and erstwhile Democratic challenger of the Republican incumbent for the local House of Representatives seat. He and his candidate were anxious to undertake a program of research. They thought it would be a good idea to take surveys in May and September (five months and six weeks prior to the election) of voter awareness of the candidate, attitudes toward him, issue salience, and intentions to vote. The results would be helpful in clarifying the candidate's position and deciding on media expenditures. Positive results would be useful in soliciting campaign contributions, which loomed as a big problem.

During the meeting the researchers had asked what Godfrey expected to find. He was sure that the initial survey would reveal low awareness, and would confirm other information he had that there was a low level of voter registration among Democrats in the area. The next question was whether any foreseeable results would persuade him not to spend all his available resources on a voter registration drive. He had to admit also that the preliminary estimate of $6000 for a May survey was a large chunk of his available funds. In fact, he was thinking, "With the money I would spend on the survey, I could hire enough canvassers to get at least 1500 to 2000 registrations."

The researcher and decision maker need to discuss all possible criteria in advance, and choose those that are appropriate. If the criterion for comparison is long-run sales results, the research approach will be much more elaborate than if the choice is based simply on brand-name recognition.

Timing and Importance. Timing and importance are always pivotal issues in the research process. How crucial is the decision? If the wrong decision is made, what will be the consequences? Obviously, the decision to "go national" with a new government program represents a much larger commitment than the decision to pursue a new program idea a bit further. Other questions concern the timing of the decision. What is the time pressure on the decision? Is information needed quickly, or is there time to develop an optimal research design?

Research Users

Decision Makers When the research results will be used to guide internal problem solving, the researcher must know the objectives and expectations of the actual decision makers. This is very helpful in developing a realistic proposal.

Increasingly, marketing research is entering the public domain, which introduces a new set of users who frequently have very different criteria for evaluating research results. For example:

- A public utility presents a research study to a regulatory body in support of a request for a rate change or the introduction of a change in service level.
- An industry trade association conducts research designed to influence proposed legislation or trade regulations. The Direct Mail Marketing Association has sponsored a study of mail-order buyers in response to a proposed Federal Trade

Commission order that would require sellers to offer a refund if they could not ship the ordered goods within a month.

- A regional transit agency wants to build public support for the continuation of an experimental program involving "dedicated" bus lanes (part of a road or highway on which no automobile traffic is permitted). The research demonstrating the effectiveness of the program is to be presented to various public bodies and citizen groups.

In most cases, the research in these examples will be used to support a decision alternative. However, examination of the results often is conducted in an adversarial setting, which means shortcomings will be more criticized, necessitating a higher quality of research.

Overt and Covert Purposes. It would be naive to presume that research is always conducted to facilitate rational problem-solving activity or that the decision maker always will be willing or able to share reasons for initiating the research. As discussed in Chapter 1, there are times when the main purpose of marketing research is to serve someone's organizational goals or for other unethical purposes. None of these abuses can be condoned. Often, they are specifically prohibited by industry codes of ethics. When they are not, one's moral standards become the compass for deciding what is right.

Step 2: Research Objective

The research objective is a statement, in as precise terminology as possible, of what information is needed. The research objective should be framed, so that obtaining the information will ensure that the research purpose is satisfied.

Research objectives have three components. The first is the research question. It specifies the information the decision maker needs. The second and third elements help the researcher make the research question as specific and precise as possible. The second element is the development of hypotheses that are basically alternative answers to the research question. The research determines which of these alternative answers is correct. It is not always possible to develop hypotheses, but the effort should be made. The third is the scope (or boundaries) of the research. For example, is the interest in current customers only, or in all potential customers?

Research Question

The **research question** specifies the information the decision maker needs.

The research question asks what specific information is required to achieve the research purpose. If the research question is answered by the research, then the information should aid the decision maker.

An illustration comes from a company in the toiletries and cosmetics business, which was interested in acquiring a smaller firm with an apparently complementary product line. One anticipated benefit of the acquisition was the opportunity to eliminate one of the sales forces. The purpose of the research was to assess whether the company could use its existing sales force to distribute the products of the acquired company. The corresponding research objective was to determine how much the retail distribution patterns of the two companies overlapped. Some preliminary evidence suggested (i.e., hypothesized) that distribution coverage would differ by geographic area and store type. The resulting study found that there was very little overlap, because the acquiring company emphasized major metropolitan areas, whereas the other company was represented largely in smaller cities and suburbs.

It is possible to have several research questions for a given research purpose. Thus, if the purpose is to determine if a specific advertisement should be run, the following research questions could be posed:

- Will the advertisement be noticed?
- Will it be interpreted accurately?
- Will it influence attitudes?

These questions correspond to the criteria used to evaluate the advertising alternatives. Similarly, if the purpose is to determine how to improve the services of a bank possible research questions might be:

- With which aspects of the current service are customers most pleased, and with which are they most dissatisfied?
- What types of customers use the various services?
- What benefits do people seek from banks?

Each of these questions should pass the test of being relevant to the purpose. For example, if customer types are identified that use a service such as traveler's checks, it may be possible to modify that service to make it more convenient or attractive to them.

Courtesy Americas Diary Farmers and Milk Processors.
Source: http://www.whymilk.com/famous/raymonds.

The researcher will always try to make the research question as specific as possible. Suppose the research question as to which customer types use the various bank services could be replaced by the following research question: What are the lifestyle and attitude profiles of the users of credit cards, automatic overdraft protection, and traveler's checks? This increase in specificity would aid the researcher in developing the research design by suggesting whom to survey and what questions to include. The role of the research objective is to provide guidance to the research design. The more specific the research question is, the more practical will be the guidance that is provided.

When a research question is set forth, it is sometimes difficult to realize that the question can and should be made more specific. The remaining two elements of the research objective—hypothesis development and the research boundaries—provide exercises to help the researcher make the research question more specific.

Hypothesis Development

*The **development of hypothesis** specifies possible answers to research questions.*

A hypothesis specifies possible answers to a research question. The researcher should always take the time and effort to speculate as to possible research question answers that will emerge from the research. In doing so, the fact that everyone already knows the answer sometimes becomes apparent. More often, the effort will add a considerable degree of specificity to the research question.

A hypothesis could speculate that sales are down in the Northeast because the level of competition has been abnormally high there during the past two months. Such a hypothesis provides considerable detail to a research question that asks what the problem is in the Northeast. It guides the research by ensuring that competitive promotions are included in the research design. One important role of a hypothesis is to suggest variables to be included in the research design—in this case, competitive promotion.

A research problem might be to estimate the demand for a new product. The hypothesis that the product will do well in the North but not in the South adds the concept of geographic location to the problem. It suggests that the sampling plan should include people from both regions. If the hypothesis suggests that the product will not do well in the South because it is not compatible with the southern lifestyle, it becomes evident that the research should measure not only purchase intentions, but also how the product would be used.

Normally, there will be several competing hypotheses, either specified or implied. If all the hypotheses were known in advance to be true, there would be little reason to conduct the research. Thus, one objective of research is to choose among the possible hypotheses. A good illustration of the role of competing hypotheses is the problem faced recently by a satellite television company. A satellite TV company picks up TV and radio signals and pipes the high-quality signals directly into subscribers' homes via satellite. This company provided service to 75 percent of households within its total service area. The problem facing the company was that there were several areas where the penetration rate was far below average. The population in these areas represented about 15 percent of the total service area. Bringing these areas closer to the average would improve profitability significantly. Before remedial action could be taken, however, it was necessary to establish the reasons for the low penetration. Management suggested various reasons:

1. Good television reception is available.
2. There is a very large transient population.
3. Residents have had poor previous experience with satellite service.
4. The price is too high, given the incomes in the area.

5. The sales force coverage has been inadequate.

6. A large percentage of the residents of the area are in age or social class groups that watch little television.

The challenge for the researcher is to devise a research approach that will gather information that can test each of these hypotheses. Hypotheses are not appropriate for all situations. As the upcoming discussions on exploratory research in Chapter 4 will make clear, there may be insufficient information for developing hypotheses. There are also times when the most reasonable hypothesis statement is simply a trivial restatement of the research question. For example:

Question: *Will the advertisement attract attention?*

Hypothesis: It will attract attention.

In such cases the hypothesis will not add anything to the research and should simply be omitted. Hypothesis development should not be viewed as an item on a checklist to be quickly satisfied, but rather, as an opportunity to communicate information and to make the research question more specific.

How does the researcher generate hypotheses? The answer is that whatever information is available, is used to speculate on which answers to the research questions are possible and which are likely. The researcher can use three main sources of information to develop hypotheses, as Figure 3-2 illustrates.

First, the researcher can draw on previous research efforts; in fact, it is not uncommon to conduct exploratory research to generate hypotheses for future large-scale research efforts. The research purpose might be deciding whether to conduct the large-scale studies.

A second source of hypotheses is theory from such disciplines as psychology, sociology, marketing, or economics. Thus, economic theory might suggest the importance of price in explaining a loss of retail sales. Marketing theory could indicate that distribution is important in predicting new-product acceptance. The use of attitude as a measure of advertising impact might be suggested by psychological theory.

A third and perhaps the most important source of hypotheses is the manager's experience with related problems, coupled with a knowledge of the problem situation and the use of judgment. This source is illustrated by the manufacturer who has discovered an unusual increase in selling costs. Past experience with similar prob-

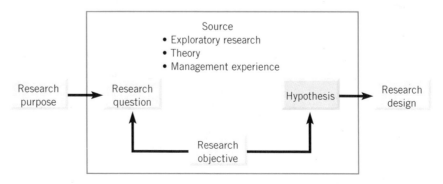

Figure 3-2 Hypothesis development.

lems, plus a preliminary investigation into the reasons for the problem, point to an increase in the proportion and number of small orders received. The tentative hypothesis is: Small orders (suitably defined) have increased in both number and proportion, and this increase, coupled with a higher cost of processing these orders, has raised selling costs. The research could then be directed at the questions of (1) the extent of increase in small orders (and the reasons for the increase) and (2) the additional unit costs involved in processing orders of different sizes.

Research Boundaries

Research boundaries help make the marketing research more precise by indicating the scope of the research.

Hypothesis development helps make the research question more precise. Another approach is to indicate the scope of the research or the **research boundaries.** Is the interest in the total population restricted to men, or to those on the West Coast? Is the research question concerned with the overall attitude toward the proposed new automobile, or is it necessary to learn customer attitudes about trunk space, handling, gas economy, styling, and interior appearance?

Much of the dialogue between the researcher and the decision maker will be about clarifying the boundaries of the study. For example, a manager may wish to study the effects of the 1992 European trade agreement on industry conditions. During the process of hypothesis development, the possible effects may be isolated. This still leaves a number of areas of ambiguity. What is meant by *condition*—profitability, competitive position in world markets, labor relations? How is the *industry* to be defined? What geographic areas are to be considered? What time period is to be appraised?

A final question of research scope regards the desired precision or accuracy of the results. This will, of course, depend on the research purpose. If a multimillion-dollar plant is to be constructed on the basis of the research results, a high degree of accuracy will be required. If, however, the decision involves the investment of a small sum in research and development on a new product idea, then a crude judgment as to the potential of the product would be acceptable.

Step 3: Estimating the Value of Information

Before a research approach can be selected, it is necessary to have an estimate of the value of the information—that is, the value of obtaining answers to the research questions. Such an estimate will help determine how much, if anything, should be spent on the research.

The value will depend on the importance of the decision as noted in the research purpose, the uncertainty that surrounds it, and the influence of the research information on the decision. If the decision is highly significant in terms of the investment required, or in terms of its effect on the long-run success of the organization, then information may have a high value. However, uncertainty that is meaningful to the decision also must exist if the information is to have value. If the outcomes are already known with certainty, or if the decision will not be affected by the research information, the information will have no value.

To illustrate and expand on these concepts, consider the simplified examples in Figure 3-3. In case A, the decision to introduce a new product is shown as a decision tree. The first two branches represent the decision alternatives—to introduce the product or to decide not to introduce it. The second branch represents the uncertainty. Our descriptive model indicates that if the product is successful, a profit of $4 million will result. The indication is that there is a probability of 0.6 (obtained from prior experience) that the product will be successful. However, if the product is not successful, the profit will be only $1 million, an event that will occur with probability 0.4. These subjective probabilities have been calculated based on prior knowledge of the situation. How much should we be willing to pay for perfect information in this case? If someone could tell us, in advance and with certainty, whether the product would be successful, how much would we pay for that information? The correct answer is nothing! The fact is that our decision would be the same regardless of the information. We would introduce the product, for even if the product were not well accepted, we would still make $1 million. In this case, not only is the decision insignificant to the organization, it is nonexistent. There is only one viable alternative. Without alternatives there is no decision contest, even if uncertainty exists; therefore, there is no need for additional information. The **expected value of perfect information** is the value of information under certainty minus the value of information under uncertainty.

In case B, the estimate is that, if the product is not successful, a loss of $2.5 million will occur. Since the expectation of the new product's eventual performance is still, on balance, positive, the product would be introduced.* In this case, however, perfect information now would have value. If we knew in advance that the product would not be accepted, we would decide against introducing it and save $2.5 million. Since our best estimate of the probability of the product not being accepted is .4, the value of the information would be .4 times $2.5 million, or $1 million. Thus, if this decision contest could be repeated many times, perfect information would save us $2.5 million about 40 percent of the time and would save us nothing (since it would not alter our decision) about 60 percent of the time. On average, it would save us $1 million. By spending money on research, we might improve our knowledge of how the product will be accepted. But market research is unlikely to be as good as perfect information, and therefore its value will be less than $1 million. Obviously, if the cost associated with an unsuccessful product were lower, or if the probability of an unsuccessful product were smaller, the value of information would be less.

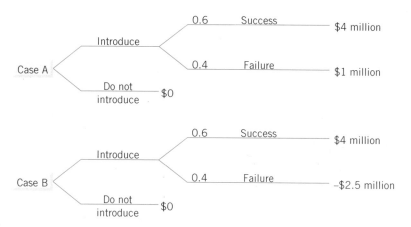

Figure 3-3   Illustrative decision models.

* The expected value of introducing the product would be $0.6(4m) + 0.4(-2.5m) = 1.4m$.

TASTY ICE-CREAM: A CASE EXAMPLE OF MARKETING INTELLIGENCE

Identifying Consumer Preferences

Tasty is a local ice-cream shop with outlets at two locations in the city. Apart from a wide range of gourmet ice creams, it also serves an indigenously brewed espresso coffee: *Aruba*. The managers of Tasty were of the opinion that they could expand their business and increase their profits by understanding their customer's preferences and by establishing a profile of its customers.

Having reached a unanimous decision on hiring an external marketing consultant, the management invited the president of a local marketing firm, Dr. K, to its board meeting. Dr. K was given a briefing on the shop's current operations and about their need to establish a profile of their customers and their preferences. Dr. K suggested that in order to win new customers and, in turn, to expand their customer base, a study had to be conducted on the customers of competition.

Also, the option of converting Tasty into an ice-cream and coffee shop was decided to be explored, laying stress on the Aruba brand.

Prior to his second meeting with the management, Dr. K gathered some background information on the ice-cream industry, current trends, and preferences for various varieties of ice creams. He also talked informally with some of his friends who had visited ice cream shops. With this background, he was ready to discuss preliminary research purposes and objectives, which could be used as a guide to the design of the study.

During the second meeting with the Tasty management, a quick agreement was reached. The primary purpose of the study was to find the preference patterns of Tasty's customers and customers of competition and to establish a profile of a typical customer. The following research objectives consist of a research question and a statement of the study scope:

Research

Question: Study consumption habits of ice cream and coffee by Tasty customers and by customers of competition.

Scope: Customers of Tasty and competition

The customers of competition were included in the study to identify Tasty's strengths and weakness with respect to competition and also to win customers from competition.

Research

Question: Develop demographic and lifestyle profile of the customers of Tasty and customers of competition.

Scope: Customers of Tasty and competition

The demographic and lifestyle activities of the customers help in establishing a typical profile of the customers of Tasty. This helps in direct marketing and changing the atmosphere and décor of its shops to suit its customer's lifestyle.

Research

Question: Identify relevant strategies for growth of Tasty in the city.
Scope: Customers of Tasty

This helps in exploring the possibility of a coffee shop and new locations for Tasty shops in the city.

◆ THE INTERNATIONAL MARKETING RESEARCH PROCESS

As we mentioned in Chapter 1, the basic functions of marketing research and the various stages in the research process do not differ between domestic and international research. The international marketing research process, however, is much more complicated than the domestic research process. This complication stems from operating in different and diverse environmental contexts, ranging from the technologically advanced and stable United States to mature Western European markets, to the fast-changing environments in newly industrialized countries such as Hong Kong and South Korea, to developing economies such as India and Brazil, to transforming economies such as the former Soviet Union and Eastern Europe, and to less-developed countries on the African continent. Marketing Research in Practice 3-4 illustrates some of the differences between the United States and Canada.

Problems may not always be couched in the same terms in different countries or cultural contexts. This may be due to differences in socioeconomic conditions, levels of economic development, or differences in any of the macroenvironmental factors. Several academic scholars have identified and have pointed out the major reason for the failure of businesses and marketing research projects in a foreign environment. The result has been the **self-reference criterion (SRC)** adopted by researchers in defining the problem in a foreign country. SRC assumes that the environmental variables (cultural and others) that are prevalent in the researcher's domestic market are also applicable to the foreign country. This is a major cause for the failure of research projects, since defining the problem is the most crucial step in the marketing research process.

MARKETING RESEARCH IN PRACTICE 3-4

Are Canadians Our Cousins Up North?

The United States and Canada are not only geographically neighbors, but are also each other's largest trading partner. FTA, NAFTA, and interfirm trade explains most of the increasing trade between the two countries. Nearly 90 percent of the total Canadian population lives within 100 miles of the U.S. border. So, can a U.S.-based manufacturer treat the Canadian market as a mere *extension* of the domestic market? Absolutely not! Despite their proximity and close ties, important differences exist between the two countries. These include demographic, economic, and cultural differences. For starters, the Canadian population is about 31,006,347 (July est— *CIA 1999 Factbook*), or roughly about 10 percent of the U.S. population of 272,639,608 (July 1999 est—*CIA 1999 Factbook*), and, interestingly, over 60 percent of the population is accounted for by two major provinces—Ontario and Quebec. Ontario has a socialist government, which is pro-labor and imposes more restrictions on business than the provincial governments or the United States. The costs of doing business are, in general, higher in Canada. Bilingual labeling is required. Personal and corporate income taxes are higher, as are transportation and distri-

MARKETING RESEARCH IN PRACTICE 3-4 *(continued)*

Are Canadians Our Cousins Up North?

bution costs and interest rates. Apart from these macro-level differences, there are differences in the way business is done. For example, offering a sales promotion, like a contest, entails special legal requirements. Furthermore, these legal requirements may vary from province to province.

The cultural differences are as important as the demographic, economic, political, and legal differences. More than 80 percent of the Quebec population uses French as its first language, and Quebec nationals are committed to sovereignty status. Canadians are extremely sensitive to environmental issues, and even municipal governments have strict local environmental ordinances. To make matters worse, Canada uses the metric system.

For more information on Canada check out http://www.cia.gov/cia/publications/factbook.

Source: "Do Your Homework Before You Start Marketing in Canada," *Marketing News* (September 14, 1992), pp. 22, 23; and "Promotions in Canada Have Special Legal Requirements," *Marketing News* (December 7, 1992), p. 14, and adapted from *CIA Factbook 1999* (www.cia.gov).

In foreign market opportunity analysis, when a firm launches international activities, information is accumulated to provide basic guidelines.

One of the most frequent objectives of international marketing research is **foreign market opportunity analysis.**[2] When a firm launches international activities, information can be accumulated to provide basic guidelines. The aim is not to conduct a painstaking and detailed analysis of the world, but to gather information on questions that will help management narrow the possibilities for international marketing activities. To achieve this objective, an international marketing researcher might ask:

- Do opportunities exist in foreign markets for the firm's products and services?
- Which foreign markets warrant detailed investigation?
- What are the major economic, political, legal, and other environmental facts and trends in each of the potential countries?
- What mode of entry does the company plan to adopt to enter the foreign market?
- What is the market potential in these countries?
- Who are the firm's current and potential customers abroad?
- What is the nature of competition in the foreign markets?
- What kind of marketing strategy should the firm adopt?

END OF CHAPTER MATERIAL

SUMMARY

The research process consists of a series of stages or steps that guide the research project from conception through to final recommendations. An overview of the domestic marketing research and the international marketing research processes was presented. This chapter discussed the research purpose and the research objective in detail. Chapter 4 will provide a discussion of the research design and implementation stages. Together, the two chapters will provide a structure for the rest of the book.

The specification of the research purpose includes, first, the identification of the decision involved, its alternatives, and the importance of its timing. Sometimes the decision is as general as: "Should our marketing program be changed?" In such cases it is also useful to specify the problem or opportunity that is motivating the research, or the environmental surveillance objective. The purpose statement also should consider who the research users are. There are times when identifying the research users and understanding their decisions and motives can significantly improve the effectiveness of the research.

The research objective involves the identification of the research questions. The answer to an appropriate research question should be relevant to the research purpose, and the question should be as specific as possible. In particular, hypotheses should be developed whenever possible. The research boundaries specification is also part of the research objective statement.

Even at the early stages of research conceptualization, it is useful to consider what value the resulting information is likely to have. This exercise may lead to a decision to forego the research, or at least make a judgment about the appropriate scale of the research project.

Video Segment:

Fast-Food Industry

Companies have started investing in product development in order to rekindle interest in the customers. As McDonalds and Burger King have done, the best way to boost sales in a market that is not expected to have significant growth is to introduce new items or have product extensions. This not only exhausts the inventory but also reduces cost and, most importantly, boosts consumer interest in the products.

Video Segment:

Positioning Sara Lee in International Markets

Sara Lee is a household name in the United States associated with baked goods. The positioning of the same product in the United Kingdom, Canada, and France reflects how advertising has to be customized in order to meet customer preference. As John Bryan, CEO for Sara Lee Corporation, mentions, the differences in advertising suggest that the company should be aware of the environment code which it is transposing the product.

KEY TERMS

research process	research question
problem/opportunity analysis	research boundaries
decision alternatives	expected value of perfect information
timing and importance of research	scope of the research
decision makers	self-reference criterion (SRC)
overt and covert purposes	foreign market opportunity analysis
development of hypotheses	

MARKETING RESEARCH TOOLBOX
REVIEW POINTS

1. The research process provides a systematic, planned approach to the research project and ensures that all aspects of the research project are consistent with each other.

2. The development of a research purpose that links the research to decision making, and the formulation of the research objectives that serve to guide the research, are the most important steps in the research process.

3. The research purpose comprises a shared understanding between the manager and the researcher of: problems or opportunities to be studied, decision alternatives to be evaluated, and users of the research results.

4. A problem or opportunity often motivates research.

5. For research to be effective it must be associated with a decision. If the research is not going to have an effect on decisions, it is an exercise in futility.

6. Knowledge of the objectives and expectations of the actual decision makers help in constructing the research purpose accurately.

7. The research objective is a statement, in as precise terminology as possible, of what information is needed.

8. The research objective has three components: research question, development of hypothesis, and scope or boundaries of the research.

9. The research question asks what specific information is required to achieve the research purpose.

10. The research question is often made as specific as possible.

11. A hypothesis is a possible answer to the research question.

12. Research boundaries aid in making the research question more precise. The research scope determines the desired precision or accuracy of the results.

13. The value of information will depend on the importance of the decision as noted in the research purpose, the uncertainty that surrounds it, and the influence of the research information on the decision.

14. International marketing research is more complicated than the domestic research process. This complication stems from operating in different and diverse environmental contexts.

15. Foreign market opportunity analysis implies that information should be accumulated to provide basic guidelines and not make a detailed and painstaking analysis of the world.

16. Expected value of perfect information is the value of information under certainty minus the value of information under uncertainty.

QUESTIONS AND PROBLEMS

1. Jim Mitchell, a high-profile businessperson, is considering running for state governor against a two-term incumbent. Mitchell and his backers do not want to enter the race unless there is a reasonable chance of winning. What are some research questions and hypotheses that, if answered, could help him make the decision?

2. At the beginning of Chapter 1 there are three examples of management information needs: DaimlerChrysler, Gateway Inc., and Music Samplers on Web Buy CDs in Stores. Review each of these situations and develop an appropriate set of research purposes and objectives.

3. In the United Kingdom, cars are polished more frequently when the owners do not have garages. Is the lack of a garage a good variable for predicting sales of car polish? Are there other hypotheses that might explain this finding?

4. Can you think of additional research objectives for Tasty's study?

5. You have been retained by a manufacturer of major appliances to investigate the probable color preferences for stoves and refrigerators in the coming year. What is the purpose of the research? Are there different purposes that might require different research approaches?

6. The president of a small chain of women's clothing stores was concerned about a four-year trend of decreasing profits. The stores have been characterized as being rather conservative over the years with respect to their product line, store decor, and advertising. They have consistently avoided trendy clothes, for example. Their market is now becoming extremely competitive because several aggressive fashion stores are expanding and are aiming at the young, fashion-conscious buyer. As a result of this competition and the disappointing profit trend, the president is considering making the product line appear less conservative and more oriented toward the young buyer. Before making such a risky change, the president thinks it is prudent to conduct some marketing research to learn the exact status of his chain. What should be the research purpose? Compose a set of research questions that would be helpful.

7. Consider the example in Figure 3-3. What would be the expected value of perfect information if the loss would be $1 million instead of $2.5 million? How about if the loss would be $10 million instead of $2.5 million? What would it be if the probability of failure would be .2 instead of .4? Explain in words what is meant by the expected value of perfect information and what its implication is.

8. ExoArt, Inc., a small U.S.-based manufacturer of exotic jewelry, feels that a market exists for its product in foreign markets. However, the company's managers have no experience in the international environment, and do not know how to proceed in forming a marketing strategy for international markets. They have decided to contact a marketing research firm to help with the process. The researchers recommend a "foreign market opportunity analysis" as a starting point for the company's internationalization.
   a. What is the aim of a foreign market opportunity analysis?
   b. Which questions might a researcher ask to gather information for the analysis?
   c. What is the most probable cause of failure for a business or marketing research project in a foreign environment?

9. Crystal-Clear Lens, Inc., a newly formed mail-order contact lens company, has struggled to obtain break-even sales after five years in the eyewear market. The company's founders thought that a high demand would exist for mail-order supply as a low-cost alternative to purchasing lenses at optical outlets. These retail outlets usually are within close geographic proximity to an affiliated optician. This allows customers to have their eyesight examined by the optician and then take the prescription to the optical outlet to purchase their eyeglasses or contact lenses. Many retail outlets offer coupons that refund the cost of the eye examination upon the purchase of contact lenses, and offer several free follow-up visits after the sale to check that the prescription has been made up correctly. The mail-order process requires customers to send in their prescription after the eye examination, whereupon the contact lenses will be supplied within two weeks of receipt of the order. The managers at Crystal-Clear Lens, Inc., have employed you as their marketing research consultant, to determine the reasons for the low sales.
   a. What would be the research purpose of this study?
   b. How does the research purpose differ from the research objective? Illustrate this difference in terms of the Crystal-Clear Lens example.
   c. What specific information would be required to achieve the research purpose? (That is, state the research question.)
   d. State some preliminary hypotheses to answer the research question.

10. a. Are there any differences between the basic functions of marketing research in a domestic environment and those of an international environment?

    b. Why is the international research process considered more complicated than the domestic research process?

ENDNOTES

1. Adapted from Irving D. Canton, "Do You Know Who Your Customer Is?" *Journal of Marketing* (April 1976), p. 83.
2. Adapted from R. Michael Czinkota and Ilkka A. Ronkainen, *International Marketing,* 3rd ed. (Orlando, FL: Dryden Press, 1993).

CASES

For detailed descriptions of the following cases, please visit www.wiley.com/college/kumar.

Case 3-1: A Videocart Test for Bestway Stores
Case 3-2: Philips Electronics NV

Research Design and Implementation

Learning Objectives

- Understand the definition and purpose of research design.
- Be familiar with the different types of research designs.
- Identify the appropriate data collection method for a given research design.
- Describe and briefly discuss the various sources of errors in a design.
- Be introduced to the concepts of budgeting and scheduling a project.
- Describe the elements of a research proposal.
- Be introduced to the issues in international marketing research design.

A **research design** is the detailed blueprint used to guide research study towards its objectives.

The choice of **research approach** is significant because it determines how the information will be obtained.

A **research design** is the detailed blueprint used to guide a research study toward its objectives. The process of designing a research study involves many interrelated decisions. The most significant decision is the choice of **research approach,** because it determines how the information will be obtained. Typical questions at this stage are: Should we rely on secondary sources, such as the Census? Which is more appropriate, an exploratory approach with group discussions or a survey? Is a mail, telephone, fax, or personal interview survey better for this problem?

To design something also means to ensure that the pieces fit together. The achievement of this fit among objectives, research approach, and research tactics is inherently an iterative process in which earlier decisions are constantly reconsidered in light of subsequent decisions. This may mean a revision of the research objectives as new insights are gained into the complexities of the population to be sampled, or a reassessment of the research approach in light of realistic cost estimates. Consequently, few researchers find they have designed their research studies in the neat and linear fashion that is implied by Figure 4-1; however, this figure is a useful overview of major research design topics to be introduced in this chapter. Also, in this chapter we will discuss the research proposal as a vehicle for summarizing significant decisions made during the research design process.

◆ RESEARCH APPROACH

The choice of a research approach depends on the nature of the research that one wants to do. In this section the various types of research approaches, data collection methods, and the factors affecting their choice are discussed.

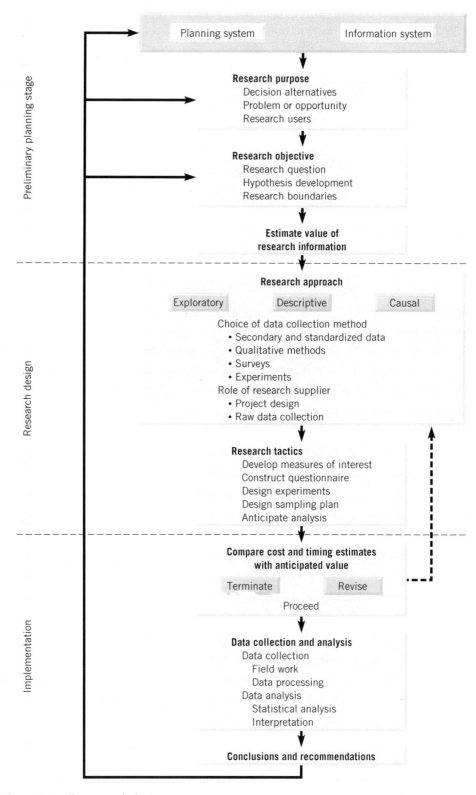

Figure 4-1 The research design process.

Types of Research

All research approaches can be classified into one of three general categories of research: exploratory, descriptive, or causal. These categories differ significantly in terms of research purpose, research questions, the precision of the hypotheses that are formed, and the data collection methods that are used.

Exploratory Research

Exploratory research is used when one is seeking insights into the general nature of a problem, the possible decision alternatives, and relevant variables that need to be considered. Typically, there is little prior knowledge on which to build. The research methods are highly flexible, unstructured, and qualitative, for the researcher begins without firm preconceptions as to what will be found. The absence of structure permits a thorough pursuit of interesting ideas and clues about the problem situation.

Exploratory research hypotheses are either vague and ill defined, or they do not exist at all. Table 4-1 illustrates this point with three examples. In the first example, the research question asks what alternative ways there are to provide lunches for school children. It was precipitated by information suggesting that there are problems with existing school lunch programs. In this case, no information suggests even the most tentative of hypotheses. In the second example, the research question is to determine what benefits people seek from the product. Since no previous research considered consumer benefits, it is difficult even to provide a list of them. In the third example, the hypothesis is advanced that a root cause of customer dissatisfaction is an image of impersonalization. However, this hypothesis is extremely tentative and provides at best only a partial answer to the research question.

Exploratory research is also useful for establishing priorities among research questions and for learning about the practical problems of carrying out the research. What kinds of questions will respondents be able to answer? What are the barriers to contacting the appropriate respondents? When should the study be conducted? An example of exploratory research is given in Marketing Research in Practice 4-1.

> **Exploratory research** is used when one is seeking insights into the general nature of a problem, the possible decision alternatives, and relevant variables that need to be considered.

MARKETING RESEARCH IN PRACTICE 4-1

Marketing Research Goes Undercover

More Americans are eschewing material wealth for the simpler life, and Foote Cone & Belding (FCB), a leading marketing research agency, figures the best way to research this "down-shifting" trend is to examine back-to-basics consumers in their natural habitat: the small town. In 1989, the company targeted a small Illinois town code-named "Laskerville" (named for FCB founder Albert Lasker), where the research unit could go undercover to observe and interact with everyday citizens. At Laskerville, researchers conduct sophisticated marketing research that includes eavesdropping, reading local newspapers, and even attending funerals. The birth of Laskerville was motivated by the need for better ways to research trends and values among consumers. There are no notes, tape recorders, or surveys allowed. The basic gist of the research is to simply chat with the locals and be on the lookout for clues as to what they are thinking and feeling. Popular hangouts for folks in Laskerville include town meetings, church meetings, barber shops, funerals, and car dealerships. Though the methodology was "messy," FCB apparently has gotten valuable results from the research.

Source: "Researchers Go Undercover to Learn about 'Laskerville,'" *Marketing News* (May 11, 1992), p. 11.

A variety of productive exploratory approaches will be discussed in Chapters 5 and 7, including literature reviews, individual and group unstructured interviews, and case studies.

Descriptive Research

Descriptive research embraces a large proportion of marketing research. The purpose is to provide an accurate snapshot of some aspect of the market environment, such as:

Descriptive research embraces a large proportion of marketing research. The purpose is to provide an accurate snapshot of some aspect of the market environment.

- The proportion of the adult population that supports the United Fund
- Consumer evaluation of the attributes of our product versus competing products
- The socioeconomic and demographic characteristics of the readership of a magazine
- The proportion of all possible outlets that are carrying, displaying, or merchandising our products

In descriptive research, hypotheses often will exist, but they may be tentative and speculative. In general, the relationships studied will not be causal in nature. However, they may still have utility in prediction.

In number 4 in Table 4-1, the research question concerns where people buy a particular type of product. One hypothesis is that upper-class families buy this type of product in specialty stores and middle-class families use department stores. There is no explicit cause–effect relationship. The question is simply to describe where people buy. With this hypothesis it is clear that if data are gathered, it will be important to include indicators of social class and to be prepared to analyze the data with respect to stores classified as specialty and department stores. Thus, the development of the hypothesis provides guidance to the researcher by introducing more detail to the research question. Similarly, in the sixth example, the hypothesis suggests that when image is being measured, it is necessary to include measures of innovativeness. Marketing Research in Practice 4-2 provides an example of the outcome of descriptive research.

MARKETING RESEARCH IN PRACTICE 4-2

Nokia Targets the Right Segments

After gaining first-mover advantage in the European market, Nokia, the Finnish cellular telephone manufacturing giant, suddenly hit a speed bump in late 1995. Its stock plummeted, and calls for executive firings echoed from Wall Street to Helsinki. Nokia did not fire anyone, but instead redesigned their manufacturing plan and soon had the company back on track.

Today, Nokia has an impressive product line that includes the 6100, which is the focal point of an AT&T nationwide campaign. Other cellular telephone manufacturers like Motorola and Ericsson are not far behind with new products of their own. These include Ericsson's multiband "world phone" that would make roaming services across oceans possible and Motorola's newly designed digital phones. Realizing the threat to their market share, Nokia decided to follow a strategy perfected by Nike Inc., which turns one product into dozens of niche offerings, each one targeted to different moods, occasions, and age groups. To achieve this Nokia surveyed its target market about their preferences on cell phones. It divided its target market into segments such as executives, teenagers, and college students. Descriptive research was done to find out the target market's preferences for features such as color, weight, and functions. Nokia then incorporated the findings in its business strategy and now Nokia produces a

TABLE 4-1   Three Research Approaches

Research Purpose	Research Question	Hypothesis
Exploratory research		
1. What new product should be developed?	What alternative ways are there to provide lunches for school children?	Boxed lunches are better than other forms.
2. What product appeal will be effective in advertising?	What benefits do people seek from the product?	Constructs unknown.
3. How can our service be improved?	What is the nature of any customer dissatisfaction?	Suspect that an image of impersonalization is a problem.
Descriptive research		
4. How should a new product be distributed?	Where do people now buy similar products?	Upper-class buyers use specialty stores, and middle-class buyers use department stores.
5. What should be the target segment?	What kinds of people now buy the product, and who buys our brand?	Older people buy our brand, whereas the young married are heavy users of competitors'.
6. How should our product be changed?	What is our current image?	We are regarded as being conservative and behind the times.
Causal research		
7. Will an increase in the service staff be profitable?	What is the relationship between size of service staff and revenue?	For small organizations, an increase of 50 percent or less will generate marginal revenue in excess of marginal costs.
8. Which advertising program for public transit should be run?	What would get people out of cars and into public transit?	Advertising program A generates more new riders than program B.
9. Should a new budget or "no frills" class of airfare be introduced?	Will the "no frills" airfare generate sufficient new passengers to offset the loss revenue from existing passengers who switch from economy class?	The new airfare will attract revenue from new passengers.

Nokia Targets the Right Segments

new model phone every 35 days, each one targeted to different moods, occasions, and age groups. New phones targeted to executives include a small $950 steel-encased phone that looks and feels like a Zippo lighter. For teenagers, Nokia offers "chameleon phones": a small panel on the phone allows a person to match the color of the phone to their outfit or whatever their preference may be. Finally, for the tech community, Nokia plans to release a second version of its $995 Communicator, a phone that allows you to surf the Web. Nokia is counting on the Communicator to carry it into the third generation.

Source: http://www.businessweek.com. For more information on Nokia and its marketing efforts, visit www.nokia.com.

Causal Research

When it is necessary to show that one variable causes or determines the values of other variables, a **causal research** approach must be used. Descriptive research is not sufficient, for all it can show is that two variables are related or associated. Of course, evidence of a relationship or an association is useful; otherwise, we would have no basis for even inferring that causality might be present. To go beyond this inference, we must have reasonable proof that one variable preceded the other and that there were no other causal factors that could have accounted for the relationship.

Suppose we had evidence that territories with extensive sales coverage, as measured by the number of accounts per salesperson, had higher per-capita sales. Are there sufficient grounds for a decision to increase sales coverage in areas where sales are currently weak? The answer would depend first on whether past increases in sales coverage had led to increases in sales. Perhaps the allocation of the sales force's annual budget was based on the previous year's sales. Then we might conclude that past sales increases led to an increase in sales coverage—a conclusion with dramatically different implications. Second, we would have to be sure that there were no other reasons for differences in sales between territories. Perhaps the weak sales territories had special requirements because of climate differences, and our product was at a disadvantage; or perhaps the weak territories were served by competitors with local advantages. In either case, adding more salespeople to weak sales territories would not improve sales, for the basic problems still would be present.

Because the requirements for proof of causality are so demanding, the research questions and relevant hypotheses are very specific. The examples in Table 4-1 show the level of detail that is desirable. Marketing Research in Practice 4-3 describes an application of causal research.

Detective Funnel

Each of the three types of research—exploratory, descriptive, and causal—has a distinct and complementary role to play in many research studies. This is most evident in studies that are initiated with this question: Why are our sales (share, patronage, contributions) below our objectives or below last year's performance? The first step is to use exploratory techniques to generate all possible reasons for the problem. Thereafter, a combination of descriptive and causal approaches is used to narrow the possible causes. Hence, the research is used in exactly the same way that a detective

MARKETING RESEARCH IN PRACTICE 4-3

Is Everyday Low Pricing Leading to Everyday Low Profits?

Over the past six months, Procter & Gamble has announced that 50 percent of its volume was on "value pricing"—its name for everyday low prices—and that it expects to save $175 million from the shift. But a new report from Salomon Brothers offers a more sobering picture of P&G's trendline at the checkout stand. In 10 of 11 household product categories it tracked, P&G's dollar market share in supermarkets fell in 1992. The million-dollar question now facing the retail industry is, "Should supermarkets adopt the everyday low prices (EDLP) strategy? Does the EDLP strategy provide greater profits over traditional pricing strategies?"

A group of researchers from the University of Chicago conducted an experiment to find answers to these questions. The researchers manipulated prices in 19 product categories in 88 stores of Dominick's Finer Foods, Inc., based in Chicago and patronized by an estimated 1 million people each week. Some stores used the standard pricing approach, called "high-low" in the industry. Others were converted to everyday low pricing, in which prices were reduced and kept low. In their analysis of everyday low pricing, the researchers moved prices up and down 10 percent in the key categories—which included beer, cereals, cigarettes, detergents, frozen entrees, juices, and soft drinks—and accounted for 30 percent of an average store's sales. In stores with everyday low pricing in those categories, prices were dropped an additional 10 percent. In stores with a high–low strategy, prices were raised 10 percent to test consumer response.

The result: Stores featuring everyday low pricing rang up slightly more sales but much less profit than the high–low stores. Overall, profits in the categories that used everyday low pricing were about 17 percent below what grocers would have made with the traditional high–low approach, the researchers calculate. They attribute the difference to the higher profit margins on items that aren't on sale.

Source: Adapted from Jon Berry, "So How Is P&G's Share? Lagging, New Study Says," *Brandweek* (April 19, 1993), p. 16; Richard Gibson, "Broad Grocery Price Cuts May Not Pay," *The Wall Street Journal* (May 7, 1993), pp. B1, B8.

proceeds to eliminate unlikely suspects. Descriptive research evidence is often sufficient to filter out many of the possible causes.

For example, a municipal transit company, seeking to understand why ridership has declined suddenly, can quickly dispose of weather-related factors by examining weather records to see if the recent weather pattern has been unusual. Similarly, evidence from customer records can be used to determine if telephone complaints about the quality of service have increased. Also, customer surveys might reveal that service, frequency and fares are the two most important factors in evaluating transit service, whereas riders are indifferent to the amount and type of advertising inside buses. If fares have not risen or the costs of competitive transportation modes such as car parking or operating costs have not declined, then attention can be focused on service frequency. Whether this is the causal factor depends on whether there was a reduction in frequency that preceded the decline in ridership.

Data Collection Methods

The research designer has a wide variety of methods to consider, either singly or in combination. They can be grouped first according to whether they use secondary or

TABLE 4-2   Relationship between Data Collection Method and Category of Research

Data Collection Method	Category of Research		
	Exploratory	Descriptive	Causal
Secondary sources			
information system	a	b	
databanks of other organizations	a	b	
syndicated services	a	b	b
Primary sources			
qualitative research	a	b	
surveys	b	a	b
experiments		b	a

a = Very appropriate method b = Somewhat appropriate method

Secondary data are collected for some purpose other than solving the present problem.

Primary data are collected especially to address specific research objective. A variety of methods, ranging from Qualitative Research to Surveys, to Experiments may be employed.

primary sources of data. **Secondary data** are already available, because they were collected for some purpose other than solving the current problem. Included here are (1) the existing company information system; (2) databanks of other organizations, including government sources such as the Census Bureau or trade association studies and reports; and (3) syndicated data sources, such as consumer purchase panels, where one organization collects reasonably standardized data for use by client companies. **Primary data** are collected especially to address a specific research objective. A variety of methods, ranging from qualitative research to surveys to experiments, may be employed. These methods are described in more detail in Table 4-2. Some methods are better suited to one category of research than another.

MARKETING RESEARCH IN PRACTICE 4-4

A Decade of Surveys in Germany

After the fall of the Berlin Wall on November 9, 1989, data collection in Germany experienced a dramatic turn of events. Since the reunification of the country, citizens in Germany have opened more doors and accepted more phone calls for the sake of survey research. Before the collapse of the Berlin Wall, only one in five West German citizens had ever participated in any survey-based study. By 1996, that number had increased to 29 percent of West Germans participating in surveys, as well as a significant increase in survey response by citizens of the former East Germany. In 1988, written surveys were the preferred method of surveying, but by 1996 telephone surveys had become the preferred choice of data collection. In 1986, nearly half of all interviews in West Germany were done at the subject's home, but by 1996 nearly 40 percent of all interviews were being done over the telephone. Researchers in the former East Germany have also switched to telephone interviews as the preferred method of data collection; nearly 35 percent of all interviews are being done over the telephone. West Germans also stated that they would be more likely to accept calls from marketing and opinion research firms or government statistical offices than they would calls requesting charity contributions. Germans in general are becoming more comfortable with the survey process, and more willing to answer sensitive questions. Almost 52 percent of the German population in 1996 reported being comfortable in an interview situation. Another drastic change in the seven years after the fall of the Berlin Wall has been the number of subjects willing to respond about political opinions, increasing from 35 percent to 59 percent.

Source: www.ama.org/pubs/articles. For more information on Germany go to www.cia.gov.

Because different methods serve different purposes, a researcher often will use several in sequence, so the results from one method can be used by another. For example, in investigating the potential for a new frozen dessert product, a researcher may begin by consulting secondary sources, such as Census statistics or industry trade association statistics, or by studying the performance of similar products that have been launched into the same market. Then qualitative research would be used to gain insights into the benefits sought by customers and into sources of dissatisfaction with the existing products. These tentative insights could be confirmed by telephone survey interviews of a representative sample of potential buyers. Finally, a controlled-store experiment might be used to test the appeal of different packages. Data collection methods also vary depending on the managerial style and the culture of the organization. Marketing Research in Practice 4-4 describes survey methods used in Germany.

TASTY ICE-CREAM: A CASE EXAMPLE OF MARKETING INTELLIGENCE (*continued*)

Choosing a Research Approach for the Tasty Study

Seldom is a data collection method perfectly suited to a research objective. A successful choice is one that has the greatest number of strengths and the fewest weaknesses relative to the alternatives. Often this is achieved by combining several methods to take advantage of their best features and minimize their limitations. This was what Dr. K had to do to get the amount of information required by the research objectives and still remain within the budget.

From the beginning it was clear that the overall research approach would involve preliminary qualitative research, followed by a survey, to understand the current trends in ice cream and coffee consumption and test the specific hypotheses. Dr. K proposed to use magazines such as *Ice Cream Reporter* and financial reports of leading ice cream companies to identify the current trends in the industry. An executive summary was then prepared based on this secondary research. The problem was to decide the method of data collection.

The principal survey options were to mail questionnaires, use personal or telephone interviews, or use focus-group discussions. Each, however, had a serious drawback. Personal interviews using trained interviewers were simply too costly and would have been feasible only with a sample that was too small. Focus-group discussions would have provided only qualitative information. The questionnaire could have been administered by mail, but experience suggested that the response rates would be low unless substantial incentives and follow-ups were used.

The solution was a Purchase Intercept Technique, in which customers who visited the Tasty shop were asked to fill out a questionnaire. An incentive was used to boost the response rate of the respondents. The advantage of the telephone in reaching large samples economically was utilized to establish contact with the customers of competition in areas surrounding the locations of competing ice cream shops in that city.

The research approach was successful in achieving a high response rate at a low cost per completed interview. The key to success was in matching the approach to the study objectives and the characteristics of the population, notably, the presence of an up-to-date listing, the limited geographic area to be covered, and the participants' inherent interest in the subject of the survey.

◆ RESEARCH TACTICS AND IMPLEMENTATION

Once the research approach has been chosen, research tactics and implementation follow: the specifics of the measurements, the plan for choosing the sample, and the methods of analyses must be developed.

Measurement

The first step is to translate the research objective into information requirements and then into questions that anticipated respondents can answer. For example, one of the objectives in the Tasty study is to estimate demand for the proposed clientele. This means that information will be needed on respondents':

1. Overall evaluation of the shop
2. Current taste preferences
3. Likelihood of switching to new flavors

As we will see in Chapters 9 through 11, there are many ways to ask questions to obtain this kind of attitudinal information.

Once the individual questions have been decided, the measuring instrument has to be developed. Usually this instrument is a questionnaire, but it also may be a plan for observing behavior or recording data. The researcher designing an effective questionnaire must be concerned with how questions on sensitive topics such as income can be asked, what the order of the questions should be, and how misinterpretations can be avoided.

Sampling Plan

Most marketing research studies are limited to a sample or subgroup of the total population relevant to the research question, rather than a census of the entire group. The sampling plan describes how the subgroup is to be selected. One approach is to use probability sampling, in which all population members have a known probability of being in the sample. This choice is indicated whenever it is important to be able to show how representative the sample is of the population. The sample size must be decided at this stage, as this has direct implications for the project budget. Another critical decision is how to minimize the effect on the results of sample members who cannot be reached or who refuse to cooperate.

Anticipating the Analysis

When one is bogged down in the details of tactical research problems, it is easy to lose sight of the research objectives. Before actual data collection begins, the researcher must be alert to the possibility that the data will be inadequate for testing the hypotheses, or will be interesting but incapable of supporting action recommendations. Once the data have been collected, it is too late to lament, "Why didn't we collect data on that variable?" or "Why didn't we foresee that there wouldn't be enough respondents to test that hypothesis?"

With these concerns in mind, the researcher should plan how each of the data items is to be analyzed. One useful device is to generate fictional (dummy) data from the questions in the measurement instrument. These dummy data can be analyzed to ensure that the results address the objectives. For example, a great deal of preliminary data analysis consists of cross-tabulating one question with a second question.

Each of the anticipated tables should be reviewed in terms of its relevance to the research question. Any shortcomings identified now will help guide the changes to the questionnaire before it is sent into the field.

Analysis of Value versus Cost and Time Involved

At this stage of the design, most of the cost has yet to be expended, but the research is now completely specified and a reliable cost estimate should be available. Thus, a more detailed cost-benefit analysis should be possible to determine if the research should be conducted as designed or if it should be conducted at all.

One component of cost to be considered is the time involved. A research study can take six months or more. It may be that such a time period will delay a decision, thus creating the risk that a set of attractive conditions will be missed. For example, if the research designed to test a new product takes too long, a competitor may pre-empt the market with its own version of the product.

The analysis can conclude that either the research design is cost-effective and should proceed or that it is not and should be terminated. Usually, instead of termination, consideration will be given to a revised research design that will be less costly. Perhaps a smaller sample could be used, or a laboratory experiment could be substituted for a field experiment. Throughout the whole research process, new information is uncovered that may make it useful to alter the purpose, the research question, the research approach, or some aspect of tactics. Indeed, it is much more accurate to think of the research process as a series of iterations and reconsideration, rather than an ordered sequence of well-defined steps. Marketing Research in Practice 4-5 illustrates an example of how one firm allocates its budget for marketing research.

Errors in Research Design

The usefulness of a research project depends on the overall quality of the research design and on the data collected and analyzed based on the design. Several potential

MARKETING RESEARCH IN PRACTICE 4-5

Fisher Price: Counting Every Penny

Fisher Price, a $1 billion toy company, allocates a different percent of sales revenue to market research each year, depending on company performance. The director of marketing research at Fisher Price, Shelly Glick-Gryfe, believes in "spending its precious marketing dollars wisely" and employs various strategies to do so.

The marketing department steers its efforts toward testing only large, big-selling items and supplements their results with similar products, trade reaction, and price points. Smaller research firms are hired for the personal attention received by Fisher Price, and outside firms are used to write and conduct the surveys. In the quest to improve the image of their products, the department conducts focus groups that can act as general indicators for the market and may help to reveal problems or opportunities. When faced with a tight budget, the department concentrates on constant customer feedback. It may also cut back on strategic research and try a more general approach by reviewing advertisements. The development of new research methodologies also helps to streamline costs. Gryfe emphasizes the importance of making sure that the research to be done is actionable, preventing unnecessary work.

Source: Allison Lucas, "When Every Penny Counts," *Sales and Marketing* (February 1996), p. 74–76.

sources of error can affect the quality of a research process. The errors can influence the various stages of the research process and result in inaccurate or useless research findings. Errors specific to each stage of the research process are mentioned in subsequent chapters. In Figure 4-2, we present an overview of the various types of errors that can affect a research design, with a brief description of each type. For a detailed description of the different types of errors, refer to the appendix at the end of this chapter.

◆ BUDGETING AND SCHEDULING THE RESEARCH PROJECT

Two common approaches to budgeting for a marketing research project are estimating the dollar costs associated with each research activity or determining the activities to be performed, in hours, and then applying standard cost estimates to these hours. The former approach is typically used when a marketing research project is relatively unusual or expensive. The latter approach is used for routine marketing research projects or when the researcher has considerable knowledge of research activity costs.

Since certain research activities (most notably, data analysis) cannot be initiated before other activities (data collection) are completed, research activities must be closely coordinated for a research project to be completed on time and within budget. Scheduling makes certain that appropriate personnel and resources are available to carry out the necessary research activities, so that the entire research process is com-

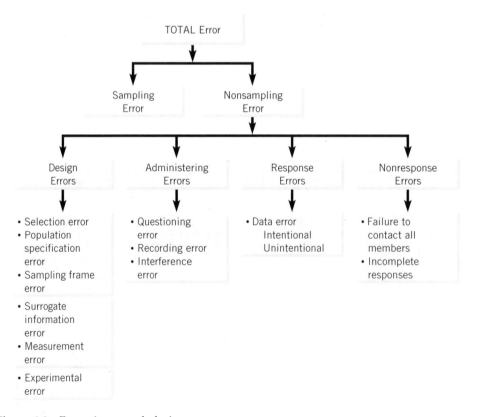

Figure 4-2   Errors in research design.

pleted as economically and efficiently as possible. One approach to scheduling is to use an activity flowchart, a schematic representation or diagram that sequences the required research activities.

Scheduling helps marketing researchers answer a vital question: Who is responsible for accomplishing what research activity within what time period? This is a critical question for any marketing research project, for it not only allocates a person to a task but also provides a time frame within which the task is to be accomplished. Essentially, it identifies the personnel accountable for a particular task.

Several creative managerial techniques can be used for scheduling a research project, most notably:

1. The critical path method
2. The program evaluation and review technique
3. GANTT charts
4. Graphical evaluation and review techniques

The **critical path method** (CPM) is a network approach that involves dividing the marketing research project into multiple components and estimating the time required to complete each component. The **program evaluation and review technique (PERT)** is a probability-based scheduling approach that recognizes and measures the uncertainty of project completion times.

GANTT charts are a form of activity flowchart that provide a schematic representation incorporating the activity, time, and personnel requirements for a given research project. An illustration of the use of a GANTT chart for a marketing research project is given in Figure 4-3. **Graphical evaluation and review techniques (GERT)** are essentially a second-generation PERT approach to scheduling, in which both the completion probabilities and activity costs to be built into a network representation are considered.

The **critical path method (CPM)** is a network approach that involves dividing the marketing research project into multiple components and estimating the time required to complete each component.

The **program evaluation and review technique (PERT)** is a probability-based scheduling approach that recognizes and measures the uncertainty of project completion times.

GANTT charts are a form of activity flowchart that provide a schematic representation incorporating the activity, time, and personnel requirements for a given research project.

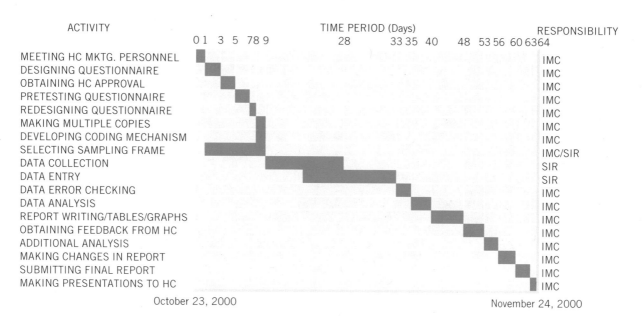

Figure 4-3 GANTT chart for the 2000 Houston Cellular Study.

◆ RESEARCH PROPOSAL

A **research proposal**
describes a plan for con-
ducting and controlling a
research project.

A **research proposal** describes a plan for conducting and controlling a research project. Although it has an important function as a summary of the major decisions in the research process, it is useful for a number of other reasons as well. Administratively, it is the basis for a written agreement or contract between the manager and researcher, as well as a record of what was agreed upon. As such, it provides a vehicle for reviewing important decisions, providing a check that all parties still agree on the scope and purpose of the research, and reducing later misunderstandings. Frequently, proposals are used to make a choice among competing suppliers and to influence positively the decision to fund the proposed study. For these latter purposes, a proposal should be viewed as a persuasive device that demonstrates the researcher's grasp of the problem and ability to conduct the research, and that also highlights the benefits of the study.

Like other communications, the structure and coverage of a proposal must be tailored to the situation. However, the following content outline has been used widely, as it ensures that likely questions will be anticipated.

Basic Contents of a Proposal

Executive summary: A brief overview of the contents of the proposal. This may be the only part some people read, so it should be sufficient to give them a basic understanding of the proposal.

Research purpose and objective: A description of the management problem, defining the information to be obtained in terms of research questions to be answered. This information must be related explicitly to the management problem.

Research design: Presents the important features of the research methods to be used, with justification of the strengths and limitations of the chosen method relative to the alternatives. All aspects of the research that might be elements of a contract should be discussed, such as sample size, quality control procedure, data collection method, and statistical analysis. Details of questionnaire format, sample selection procedures, and so forth, should be confined to an appendix.

Time and cost estimates: All negotiated aspects, including total fees, payments, provisions, treatment of contingencies such as the clients' decision to expand or cancel the study, and the schedule for submission of interim, draft, and final reports.

Appendixes: Any technical matters of interest to a small minority of readers should be put at the back end of the proposal.

An example of a research proposal is given in Marketing Research in Practice 4-6.

◆ DESIGNING INTERNATIONAL MARKETING RESEARCH

As we explained in earlier chapters, international marketing research is conducted to aid in marketing decisions typically in more than one country. Designing a research process for international marketing decision making is considerably more complex than designing it for a single country. Conducting research in different countries implies much greater attention to issues such as:

1. Understanding the nature and type of information sought
2. Defining the relevant unit of analysis
3. Formulating problems, variable specifications, and categories

MARKETING RESEARCH IN PRACTICE 4-6

A Research Proposal to Crystal Bank

Research Purpose

The purpose of the study is to analyze various issues pertaining to the credit needs of consumers living in certain areas of Austin that have branches of Crystal Bank. Specifically, the research objectives are to

- Gauge consumer sentiment on the services provided by various financial institutions;
- Identify areas of improvement among the services provided by the financial institutions;
- Determine the type of loans most requested for/needed by the consumers;
- Identify the important and attractive attributes of the different types of loans;
- Determine the types of lending institutions most popular with the consumers;
- Identify the important characteristics that make a lending institution attractive to the consumers; and
- Provide a demographic profile of the consumers.

Research Design

The survey research will be conducted by mailing a questionnaire to a total of 300 consumers living in the areas served by each of the 15 Austin area branches of Crystal Bank. The questions cover a wide range of issues including

- Identifying the types of accounts operated by the consumer, whether he or she is happy with the services;
- Obtaining likelihood of the respondent applying for a specific type of loan in the next 12 months;
- Determining the characteristics of the loan application and loan repayment that are important to the respondent; and
- Identifying characteristics of the lending institutions which influence the respondent's choice.
- Finally, it will seek demographic and lifestyle information about the respondents.

Sample Research Questions

Do you currently deal with a financial institution?
____ Yes ____ No

If Yes, what type of financial institutions do you deal with?
(Check all that apply)
____ Savings and Loan ____ Bank
____ Credit union ____ Other (Please specify _____)

Have you applied for any loan in the past five years?
____ Yes ____ No

MARKETING RESEARCH IN PRACTICE 4-6 (continued)

A Research Proposal to Crystal Bank

If Yes, where did you apply for the loan? (Check all that apply)
____ Savings and Loan   ____ Credit Union
____ Mortgage Company   ____ Bank
____ Other (Please specify _____)

What type of loans did you apply for? (Check all that apply)
____ Home purchase   ____ Automobile
____ Home repair/remodeling ____ Educational
____ Major appliance purchase ____ Personal
____ Other (Please specify _____)

Rank the following factors in decreasing order of importance, which will influence your choice of lending institution in applying for any loan. (1—Most important; 2—Second most important, and so on)
____ Institution reputation
____ Location of the institution
____ Present relationship with the institution
____ Level of service provided
____ Other (Please specify _____)

4. Identifying and selecting sources of information
5. Determining availability and comparability of data
6. Achieving equivalence of samples and measures across countries and cultures
7. Identifying the degree of centralization of the research
8. Coordinating research across countries
9. Finding errors in the research design
10. Learning the cost of conducting research in multiple countries

Marketing Research in Practice 4-7 gives a brief synopsis of the pitfalls a researcher can encounter while conducting international marketing research.

◆ ISSUES IN INTERNATIONAL RESEARCH DESIGN

Regardless of the basic research design selected (exploratory, descriptive, or causal), researchers must be familiar with and experienced in handling several issues or problems unique to the conduct of marketing research within and across countries and cultural groups. Three issues critical to international research design are (1) determining information requirements, (2) determining the unit of analysis, and (3) achieving equivalence of construct, measurement, sample and analysis.[1]

Determining Information Requirements

In determining the information required for international marketing research, a primary consideration is the specific level and type of decision for which the research is

MARKETING RESEARCH IN PRACTICE 4-7

A Practitioner's View of the Key Pitfalls in Conducting International Research

The key pitfalls to avoid when conducting an international marketing research project are

1. **Selecting a domestic research company to do your international research:** Only a handful of domestic research companies are both dedicated to and expert in international research. It is important that international projects be coordinated by a team whose sensitivity and knowledge of foreign markets will ensure a well-executed study. Emphasis should be placed on selecting a research company with a solid reputation and extensive experience in the design, coordination, and analysis of global research.

2. **Rigidly standardizing methodologies across countries:** Attempting to be consistent with a methodological approach across countries is desirable but, among other things, two key questions need to be asked in order to determine whether a particular methodology will yield the best results: (a) Does the culture lend itself to that methodology? For example, relationships in Latin America are based on personal contact. Hence, when conducting business-to-business surveys, personal interviews, though expensive, are more efficient than telephone interviews. (b) Does the local infrastructure hinder the use of that methodology? For example, telephone surveys are very common in the United States, but in Russia the telephone system is notoriously inefficient. For example, the Moscow office for the *Economist* conducted an informal study to determine how ineffective the phone system is. The office kept a log of international calls made in a 30-day period. A total of 786 calls were attempted, of which 754 resulted in no connection, 6 calls were cut off halfway through, and 2 were wrong numbers. Also, the cost of using this inefficient system is exorbitant. To install the phone costs $1,050, telephones cost $15 each, and a one-minute call from Moscow to the United States costs $3.[2]

3. **Interviewing in English around the world:** When conducting business-to-business research, even if the executives in the foreign country speak English, interviewing in English might result in inaccurate responses. Are the subjects comprehending the questions accurately and fully, or are there nuances to the question that are not being understood? Are their answers to open-ended questions without detail and richness due to their apprehension about responding in a non-native language? Moreover, has their attention been diverted to a consideration of accents (their and/or the interviewer's) rather than the research questions at hand? Hence, even though translating the questionnaire may be costly and time consuming, it results in more accurate responses.

4. **Setting inappropriate sampling requirements:** Several country-specific variables influence the selection of appropriate sampling procedures in multicountry marketing research. For example, although random sampling is statistically the most reliable technique to use, it may be impractical in a given foreign market. Reasons may include the fact that in many of the less developed countries the literacy rate is very low. Hence, when sampling for surveys that require the respondent to be literate, random sampling might not work.

5. **Lack of consideration given to language:** Translations into the appropriate local languages need to be checked carefully. When possible, a quality control procedure of "back-translation" should be followed. The prime consideration is to ensure translation of the questionnaire so that there is equivalent meaning and relevance in all the countries where the project is being conducted.

6. **Lack of systematic international communication procedures:** One of the biggest problems of international research is communicating clearly with the local research companies. Do they understand the objectives of the study? Do they understand the sampling criteria? And do they understand what is expected from them? All too often, assumptions are made concerning the above issues that lead to major problems in the study's execution.

MARKETING RESEARCH IN PRACTICE 4-7 (*continued*)

A Practitioner's View of the Key Pitfalls in Conducting International Research

7. **Misinterpreting multicountry data across countries:** Analysis of the study's data must focus on the international market from which the data were gathered. Survey comparisons across countries should be made with the understanding of how the particular countries may differ on many key factors, including local market conditions, the maturity of the market, and the local competitive framework for the study category.

8. **Not understanding international differences in conducting qualitative research:** When conducting qualitative research such as focus groups, group discussions, and in-depth interviews, the researcher must be aware of the importance of culture in the discussion process. Not all societies encourage frank and open exchange and disagreement among individuals. Status consciousness may result in situations in which the opinion of one is reflected by all other participants. Disagreement may be seen as impolite, or certain topics may be taboo.[3] Also, in some countries, such as parts of Asia, mixed-sex and -age groups do not yield good information in a consumer group discussion. Younger people, for example, often defer to the opinions of older people. If groups cannot be separated by age and sex, one-to-one interviews should be done.

Source: Adapted from Daphne Chandler, "8 Common Pitfalls of International Research," *The Council of American Survey Research Organizations Journal* (1992), p. 81.

being conducted. In general, the types of decisions fall into two broad categories—strategic decisions and tactical decisions. These two types differ significantly in their information requirements and the level in the organization structure where the decision making is done.

Global strategic decisions involve decisions at the macrolevel.

Global strategic decisions are made mostly at corporate headquarters, and they normally concern issues pertaining to foreign market selection, market entry, mode of entry, market expansion strategies, and decisions related to global standardization versus local adaptation of marketing-six strategies. Such decisions involve the entire organization and determine the overall allocation of company resources across country markets. If a firm is involved in more than one product category, the decisions involve not only country markets but also product markets within countries. The information required for global strategic decisions is governed by the company's overall objectives and has implications pertaining to the company's long-term survival.

Global tactical decisions involve decisions at the microlevel.

Global tactical decisions, on the other hand, are concerned with microlevel implementation issues, and the information required for tactical decision making is obtained mostly from primary data. These decisions are concerned primarily with marketing-mix strategies in country/product markets—for example, what type of advertising copy would be effective in a given culture. The decisions are made at the functional or subsidiary level rather than at the corporate level.

Unit of Analysis

In conducting marketing research in more than one country, another major issue to be sorted out is at what level the analysis is to be done. Should it be done at (1) the global level, considering all countries simultaneously (a very complicated and seldom undertaken unit of analysis); (2) the regional level, considering groups of countries as being relatively homogeneous in terms of macroenvironmental factors (e.g., the European Union and the North American Free Trade Agreement countries can be considered regional trading blocs); (3) the country level, where each country is taken as a separate unit; or (4) similar segments across countries (a recent trend that is gaining popularity)? In this last type of analysis, the researcher targets homogeneous segments having similar tastes and preferences across countries.

Construct, Measurement, Sample, and Analysis Equivalence

Construct equivalence deals with how both the researcher and the subjects of the research see, understand, and code a particular phenomenon. The problem confronting the international researcher is that, because of sociocultural, economic, and political differences, perspectives may be neither identical nor equivalent. The international researcher is constantly faced with the self-reference criterion problem and its implications in formulating a research design. Construct equivalence is concerned with the question: "Are we studying the same phenomenon in countries X and Y?" For example, in the United States, bicycles are used predominantly for recreation; in the Netherlands and various developing countries, they provide a basic mode of transportation. This implies that the relevant competing product set must be defined differently. In the United States it will include other recreational products, whereas in the Netherlands it will include alternative modes of transportation.

Measurement equivalence deals with the methods and procedures the researcher uses to collect and categorize essential data and information. Construct and measurement equivalence are highly interrelated. Measurement is the operationalization of the constructs to be used. Measurement equivalence is concerned with the question: "Are the phenomena in countries X and Y measured the same way?" For example, while Americans measure distance in miles, citizens in most of the other countries of the world measure it in kilometers.

Because of sociocultural, economic, and political differences among or between countries, the international researcher faces two problems not encountered by the domestic researcher: (1) identifying and operationalizing comparable populations, and (2) selecting samples that are simultaneously representative of other populations and comparable across countries. **Sampling equivalence** is concerned with the question: "Are the samples used in countries X and Y equivalent?" For example, children in the United States are legitimate respondents, because they exercise substantial influence in the purchase of cereals, toys, desserts, and other items, whereas in Oriental cultures, it is the parent who decides most of these issues.

Construct equivalence deals with how both the researcher and the subjects of the research see, understand, and code a particular phenomenon.

Measurement equivalence deals with the methods and procedures the researcher uses to collect and categorize essential data and information.

Sampling equivalence deals with the problems faced by the international researcher in identifying and operationalizing comparable populations and selecting samples that are simultaneously reresentative of other populations and comparable across countries.

An extended Asian family.
Carol Wolinsky/Stock, Boston.

An American family.
©Corbis Stock Market.

Analysis equivalence deals with adjustments to be made in the analysis techniques in different countries with repect to the cultural habits that affect the respondents tendencies.

Regarding **analysis equivalence,** respondents from different countries have a tendency to choose either extreme scale points or middle values based on their cultural habits. Therefore, it may not be appropriate to compare the means of different scale items across countries; rather, some measure of deviation from the norm should be established. In other words, standard deviations may be better measures for comparison purposes.

Apart from these issues, other aspects of the research process, such as identifying sources of data, availability, and comparability of data from different countries, problems associated with primary data collection across countries, and so forth, add to the complexity of the international research process. Also, these issues add to the nonrandom error component of the research process. These issues will be dealt with in greater detail in subsequent chapters.

END OF CHAPTER MATERIAL

SUMMARY

In this chapter the focus has shifted from the manager's problems and information needs—as expressed in the research purpose and objectives—to the strategic and tactical decisions that will achieve the objectives of the research approach. The various research approaches include qualitative research, surveys, observation, and experimentation. Tactical research design decisions include the choice of a research supplier, questionnaire development, the design of the experiment, the sampling plan, and the anticipation of data analysis. Implementation involves a final cost–benefit check, plus data collection, data analysis, and the development of conclusions and recommendations. Also, issues relevant to the design of international marketing research projects are discussed in this chapter.

An important distinction can be made among exploratory, descriptive, and causal research. Exploratory research, which tends to involve qualitative approaches such as group interviews, is usually characterized by ill-defined or nonexistent hypotheses. Descriptive research, which tends to use survey data, is characterized by tentative hypotheses that fall short of specifying causal relationships. Causal research, which tends to rely on experimentation, involves more specific hypotheses involving causal relationships. Possible sources of errors in research designs are presented, and the concepts of budgeting and scheduling a research project are discussed in some detail.

The major decisions during the research process are summarized in the research proposal. This step is essential to ensuring that the manager's problems have been translated into a research study that will help obtain relevant, timely, and accurate information—and will not cost more than the information is worth.

Video Segment

Consumer Confidence Index

The accuracy in using consumer spending as a gauge to measure the health of the economy is the focus of this study. The problem is that it is not a very effective means to forecast the state of the economy but rather, a reasonable indicator of the sub-cycles. The consumers' spending patterns and perceptions are often extrapolated to be indicative of the level of confidence in the economy, but the onus is to measure the reliability of such an index.

Video Segment

The New Coke

The Beverage Digest refers to Coke Classic as the success story of the 1980's. However, this belies the story of the New Coke strategy, which was based entirely on the taste tests and almost ignored the association that consumers made with the brand. This case reflects the need for companies to understand the image as well as intangible merits that they attach to brands that often complements (and in this case supercedes) the tangible aspects.

KEY TERMS

research approach
research design
exploratory research
descriptive research
causal research
research proposal
secondary data
primary data
critical path method (CPM)
program evaluation and
    review technique (PERT)

graphical evaluation and review technique
    (GERT)
GANTT charts
global strategic decisions
global tactical decisions
construct equivalence
measurement equivalence
sampling equivalence
analysis equivalence

MARKETING RESEARCH TOOLBOX REVIEW POINTS

1. A research design is the detailed blueprint used to guide a research study toward its objectives.

2. The choice of a research approach is significant because it determines how the information will be obtained.

3. All research approaches can be classified into one of the three general categories of research: exploratory, descriptive, and causal.

4. Exploratory research is used when one is seeking insights into the general nature of a problem, the possible alternatives, and relevant variables that need to be considered.

5. Exploratory research is also useful for establishing priorities among research questions and for learning about the practical problems in carrying out the research.

6. Descriptive research embraces a large proportion of marketing research. It is used to provide an accurate snapshot of some aspect of the market environment.

7. In descriptive research, the development of the hypothesis provides guidance to the researcher by introducing more detail to the research question.

8. When it is necessary to show that one variable causes or determines the values of other variables, a causal research approach must be used.

9. Descriptive research can show that two variables are related or associated. Causal research is used to determine whether one variable preceded the other and that there were no other causal factors that could have accounted for the relationship.

10. Secondary data are data collected for some purpose other than solving the current problem.

11. Primary data are collected especially to address a specific research objective. A variety of methods, including qualitative research, surveys, and experiments, may be employed.

12. Once the research approach has been chosen, research tactics and implementation follow: the specifics of the measurements, the plan for choosing the sample, and the methods of analysis must be developed.

13. Once the questions for the respondents have been decided, the measuring instrument has to be developed. Usually this instrument is a questionnaire, but it also may be a plan for observing behavior or recording data.

14. The sampling plan describes how the respondents are to be selected.

15. Several potential sources of error can affect the quality of a research process.

16. Given the constraints on the availability of and use of resources, budgeting and scheduling activities ensure that the resources are used effectively and efficiently.

17. The most often-used scheduling techniques are the critical path method (CPM), the program evaluation and review technique (PERT), GANTT charts, and graphical evaluation and review techniques (GERT).

18. The CPM is a network approach that involves dividing the marketing research project into multiple components and estimating the time required in completing each component activity.

19. The PERT is a probability-based scheduling approach that recognizes and measures the uncertainty of project completion times.

20. GANTT charts are a form of activity flowchart that provide a schematic representation incorporating the activity, time, and personnel requirements for a given research project.

21. A research proposal describes a plan for conducting and controlling a research project.

22. The basic contents of a proposal are executive summary, research purpose and objective, research design, time and cost estimates, and appendixes.

23. Three critical issues in international marketing research design are determining information requirements, determining the unit of analysis, and achieving equivalence of construct, measurement, sample, and analysis.

24. Global strategic decisions involve decisions at the macrolevel, while global tactical decisions involve decisions at the microlevel.

25. Construct equivalence deals with how both the researcher and the subjects of the research see, understand, and code a particular phenomenon.

26. Measurement equivalence deals with the scaling methods and procedures the researcher uses to collect and categorize essential data and information.

27. Sample equivalence deals with the problems faced by the international researcher in identifying and operationalizing comparable populations and selecting samples that are simultaneously representative of other populations and comparable across countries.

28. Analysis equivalence deals with adjustments to be made in the analysis techniques in different countries with respect to the cultural habits that affect the respondents' tendencies.

QUESTIONS AND PROBLEMS

1. Is a research design always necessary before a research study can be conducted?

2. In what ways do exploratory, descriptive, and causal research designs differ? How will these differences influence the relative importance of each research approach at each phase of the marketing program development process described in Chapter 1?

3. A manufacturer of hand tools uses industrial supply houses to reach its major markets. The company is considering a new, automatic inventory-control procedure. How would

you proceed with an exploratory study in advance of a larger study of the dealers' reactions to this new procedure?

4. What problems can you foresee in a test of the hypothesis that federal food stamps issued to low-income individuals are being used to supplement food budgets rather than replace former spending on food?

5. The problem of a large Canadian satellite TV company was described in Chapter 3. A number of hypotheses were offered by management to account for the poor penetration in several areas comprising 15 percent of the population of the total service area. If you were the researcher assigned to study this problem, how would you proceed? Specifically, is the statement of purpose of the research adequate? What alternative research designs should be considered? Will one design be adequate to test all the hypotheses?

6. Smith Computers, Inc., a U.S.-based manufacturer of personal computers, has developed a microcomputer using the Pentium microchip technology, but at a fraction of the cost of its competitors. The company has an in-house marketing research department, and a study has been ordered to assist in developing the marketing program for this product.
   a. Which type of research would be most appropriate for this study?
   b. What are the possible errors that could be made in designing the research project?
   c. Scott Peters, the head of the marketing research department, must prepare a research proposal. Suggest a content outline that will ensure that all likely questions will be addressed.
   d. Peters has also been given the task of identifying foreign market opportunities for this product. What critical issues must be considered in formulating the research design?

7. a. How is a cost–benefit analysis useful to the management in deciding whether to conduct a marketing research study?
   b. What are the two approaches to budgeting for a market research project?
   c. For what situation is each approach most suitable?

8. Sugar Land Creamery is planning to launch a new flavor of ice cream and wants to get a "snapshot" of the potential market. The ice cream has a coconut–white-chocolate flavor with mixed-in pistachios and is aimed at the premium market. What type of research design is appropriate? Develop the research purpose, research questions, and hypothesis.

9. What possible problems might be encountered by a domestic research company in conducting an international research study?

ENDNOTES

1. V. Kumar, *International Marketing Research* (Englewood Cliffs, NJ: Prentice-Hall, 2000).
2. http://www.kreml.nnov.ru/comrepe/part4.htm.
3. R. Michael Czinkota and A. Ronkainen Ilkka, *International Marketing*, 3rd ed. (Orlando, FL: Dryden Press, 1993), pp. 550, 551.

CASES

For detailed descriptions of the following cases please visit www.wiley.com/college/kumar.

Case 4-1: Reynold's Tobacco's Slide-Box Cigarettes
Case 4-2: California Foods Corporation

CASES AND PRACTICAL EXERCISES FOR PART I

CASE STUDY

I-1

Jones Inc.

In the fall of 1997, Dana Shawn, General Manager of Jones Inc., was considering whether a newly developed pull-up variety of diapers with adjustable straps was ready for market testing and, if so, how it should be tested.

Since 1995, Jones Inc. had sold, under the trade name Cuddly, disposable diapers with velcro straps, as well as conventional stick-ons from its base in Camden, New Jersey. The company received its supply of raw materials from nearby manufacturers (which included plastics and tissue paper as well as velcro and adhesive straps). These raw materials were, in turn, processed and assembled at the plant in Camden.

Jones Inc.'s sales had grown steadily from 1990 until 1993 to an annual level of $3.75 million. In the spring of 1990, a panel investigated the diaper market. Since then, prices had risen so that the company had a profit for the year to date. However, between 1993 and 1997, a series of price wars cut the company's sales to $3.6 million by 1997. Due to the price wars, the price for a pack of 24 diapers was close to $5.00—the lowest ever.

Jones Inc. served approximately 130 grocery store accounts, which were primarily members of a cooperative buying group or belonged to a 10-store chain that operated in the immediate area. Jones Inc. no longer had any major chain accounts, although in the past it had sold to several such retailers. All three of the major chains operating in the area had developed exclusive supply arrangements with national and regional manufacturers, so Jones Inc. was limited to 25 percent of the overall market.

Although Jones Inc. had a permit to sell its products in Boston, a market six times the size of Camden, management decided not to enter that market and instead concentrated on strengthening their dealer relationships. In addition, it was felt that if a price war were to ensue, it might extend from Boston into the Camden area.

Although there was a change within each household, in terms of income levels, number of working members,

number of children, the market and profit situation in early 1997, Jones Inc. began to look for ways to increase sales volume. During the previous three years, management had felt that this product could help to reverse Jones Inc.'s downward sales trend, if given the correct marketing effort. However, the financial problems caused by the loss of the national grocery chains and the price war limited the firm's efforts. Ms. Shawn thought those factors had caused Jones Inc. to suffer a loss of share of diaper sales in the stores they served.

Since 1995, Ms. Shawn had been experimenting with the packaging with the hope that a new package would boost sales quickly. They could change the size of the packages being offered, the diaper sizes to reach different age groups of the infants, and the diaper design to accommodate the differences in gender. One of the main design changes was to gradually increase the diapers size range. This would be to start from the infant and lead up to the toddler stage—and, given the changes in weight and mobility, design the diaper with better straps and better-fitting side elastics. Initially, the company released its pull-up trainer diapers and waited to see whether the product would be accepted in the market.

By 1996, Ms. Shawn had already implemented the pull-ups in the market with an aggressive marketing strategy. The pull-ups addressed the toddlers who were to be trained to get over the diaper. The pull-up diapers replaced the larger diaper sizes to parents who chose to use the pull-ups as a training tool. The packaging of the pull-ups would also have to facilitate the involvement of the toddlers—the designs on the pull-ups were to especially stimulate the use of this product.

The rest of the product line, however, was left unchanged. There were no special promotional efforts undertaken by Jones Inc., but unit sales of the new pull-up diapers were more than triple the unit sales of the old large diapers (see Exhibit I-1). Although the increased sales volume was welcomed, unit packaging costs rose from 7.2 cents to 12.0 cents. This more than offset the

This case is also available on the website www.wiley.com/college/kumar

CASE STUDY

I-1

Jones Inc.

saving of 4 cents created by decreasing the number of pull-up diapers per package. Retail prices were reduced from 41 cents per pull-up to 20 cents for the new product, while the price for the 24-pack remained at 25 cents. The increased sales then increased the total dollar contribution to fixed costs by only 5 percent. (All manufacturers priced their diapers to give retailers a 10 percent margin on the retail selling price. Competitors' retail prices for their product remained at 43 cents.)

Ms. Shawn thought that the new concept of disposable training pants was responsible for the increased sales. However, there were high packaging costs, and the entry into the diaper market was difficult unless the cost was reduced without affecting product quality and size of the package.

The problem would have been solved if the package size were to be altered, but that sudden change in the market would be unsettling to the consumers who were gradually adopting the usage of the product. Because economies of scale came into play when producing pull-ups' stronger lining, costs could be reduced if more units were produced and sold. Ms. Shawn thought that packaging would have to be made more convenient. Large packs were more economically feasible, but they would also have to be easy for the parent to carry home. Also, storage would have to be considered. Parents would not want to purchase large quantities of pull-ups because research showed that most toddlers outgrow this stage within three to four months.

Part of the promotion through advertising was that children should be seen as participants in the process. Not only would there have to be consideration of the kind of print on the pull-ups (graphics and pictures that would appeal to the kids), but also there would need to be accommodations for differences in the tastes of boys and girls.

EXHIBIT I-1

Jones Inc.

	1994	1995	1996	1997	1998
		Unit Sales of Old Large Diapers (Pull-Ups after May 1997)			
January		1,203	3,531	7,899	18,594
February		996	3,651	7,629	20,187
March		960	3,258	6,677	20,676
April		853	3,888	6,081	20,199
May		861	4,425	5,814	18,420
June		915	4,044	12,726	14,424
July		978	3,546	13,422	16,716
August		1,254	3,696	15,105	16,716
September		1,212	3,561	23,601	18,657
October	1,740	1,485	4,731	23,214	
November	1,437	2,928	4,499	22,146	
December	1,347	3,528	6,177	17,916	

CASES AND PRACTICAL EXERCISES FOR PART I *(continued)*

CASE STUDY

I-1

Jones Inc.

By 1997, work had begun on developing a multipack that would contain different prints of pull-ups. One of the possible promotions could be the sale of diaper rash cream with the purchase of the pull-ups (or a coupon to redeem $0.75 off the price of the cream). The increase in sales would be possible if there were to be a reduction in the price or if the packaging of the product were to be changed.

Several problems soon became apparent. The size of the pull-ups was often too large or too small for the toddler, and most parents chose to continue with tried-and-tested diapers. Second, it was exceedingly difficult to maintain the margin while replacing the gathers used in diapers with elastic band. This was initially done in order to make the pull-ups more leak-proof. Since the usage rate as compared to diapers (per day) was less, this made it even more difficult to sell large packs—and given that the sizes might not be applicable over a long period of time, it did not seem feasible to sell in large packs of 48.

The multipack was redesigned and again tested in the plant and by employee families. The packaging was updated and the pull-ups were adjusted in terms of quality as well as the appearance (in terms of prints and the design of the pull-ups). It appeared that the new package was performing satisfactorily.

Negotiations with Jones Inc.'s supplier resulted in an estimated price of 18.5 cents for the first 100,000 units. Thereafter, unit costs would drop to 17.5 cents.

Ms. Shawn decided that the best multipack carrier possible had been designed. Her attention then turned to methods of testing the new packs for consumer acceptance. Mr. Charles Krieger, president of Jones Inc., sent the following letter concerning market testing:

Dear Ms. Dana,

Concerning the market test of new diapers and pull-ups, I have a few suggestions that may be helpful, although the final decision is yours. I think we should look for a few outlets where we are not com-

peting with the other manufacturers, perhaps Bill's Market. Actually, if we use Bill's, then the test could be conducted as follows:

1. Give Bill a special deal on the multipacks for this weekend.
2. In the next two weeks, we'll only deliver the multipacks and not the single packs at all.
3. In the third week we'll deliver both the multipacks and the single packs.
4. During the third weekend we'll have someone make a survey at the store to determine its acceptance.
5. Here is how it could be conducted:
   a. Station someone at the aisle.
   b. After the shoppers have chosen either the single or the multipacks, question them.
   c. If they chose the multipacks, ask them why.
   d. If they chose the single packs, ask them why they didn't buy the multipacks.
   e. Thank them for their help and time.

Yours,

Charles Krieger

(signed)

Questions for Discussion

1. Should the new multipack carrier be tested?
2. If a test is judged necessary, what should be the criteria for success or failure?
3. How useful is the proposed test in addressing the management problem? What changes, if any, would you recommend?
4. What kind of criteria do you think will affect the results of the testing? What kinds of markets would you think are appropriate for such a product?

◆ PRACTICAL EXERCISES

Section 1

Q1.   Your objective is to assess the range of opinions about the introduction of toy guns for kids over five years of age. Form groups of four and use the following as a guide to your research.

1.   *Situation Analysis:* What is the environment within which you are operating? What would be some of the aspects you would consider to be important to your understanding of the applicability of the research?

2.   *Strategy Development:* What is the scope of your opinion? What are the objectives you would set as a team toward achieving a specific target? What market segments would you be targeting as part of your research?

3.   *Marketing Program Development:* Referring to Table 1-2, assess whether your analysis meets the decision that could be made.

4.   *Implementation:* Would you be able to apply the results of the research you have conducted? What factors influence the marketing program you would implement?

In conducting the research, suggest an appropriate research method. Rationalize why you chose this method as the means to obtain more information. (*Hint:* Would you choose causal, descriptive, or exploratory research method?) What measures would you take in order to minimize error in research design and application?

What are some of the ethical questions you would address in conducting this research? What is the group's opinion on respondent privacy? What measures would you take in order to minimize violation?

Q2.   A local store selling oriental foods plans to expand its operations by opening branches in other parts of the city. Conduct an environmental analysis and determine what would be some of the specific details you would take into consideration prior to opening a store. What kind of research would you conduct in order to estimate the demand for oriental foods? Would lifestyle variables be key factors in your decision?

Q3.   Campbell Soup wants to introduce a soup kit that has a dried soup mix, a packet of croutons, and seasonings. Provide a report on the marketing research process you would take when you are introducing a new product into the market. What do you think are the perils in product innovation? What would be the kind of research you would undertake? Given the three research approaches, which would be most appropriate to the product you are trying to sell? When designing a product, would you consider testing to be a vital component?

Q4.   Provide an example of a newly introduced product and assess whether the research undertaken was adequate to its success.

Errors in Research Design

The total error in a research study is the difference between the true mean value (within the population) of the variable being studied and the observed mean value obtained through the research study. This error has two main components, sampling error and nonsampling error.

◆ SAMPLING ERROR

Sampling error is the difference between a measure obtained from a sample representing the population and the true measure that can be obtained only from the entire population. This error occurs because no sample is a perfect representation of a given population, unless the sample size equals the population. This issue will be dealt with in greater detail in Chapters 11 and 13.

◆ NONSAMPLING ERROR

Nonsampling error includes all other errors associated with a research project. There may be several different reasons for these errors, which can be broadly classified into four groups: (1) design errors, (2) administering errors, (3) response errors, and (4) nonresponse errors.

Design Error

Design errors, also called researcher-induced errors, are due mainly to flaws in the research design. There are several different types of design errors.

Selection error: Selection error occurs when a sample obtained through a non-probability sampling method is not representative of the population. For example, if a mall interviewer interested in the shopping habits of visitors to the mall avoids interviewing people with children, he or she is inducing a selection error into the research study.

Population specification error: Population specification error occurs when an inappropriate population is chosen from which to obtain data for the research study. For example, if the objective of a research study is to determine what brand of dog food people buy for their pets, and the research draws a sample from a population that consists predominantly of cat owners, a population specification error is induced into the study.

Sampling frame error: A sampling frame is a directory of population members from which a sample is selected. A sampling frame error occurs when the sample is drawn from an inaccurate sampling frame. For example, if a researcher interested in finding the reasons why some people have personal computers in their homes selects the sample from a list of subscribers to *PC World*, he or she is inducing a sample frame error into the study.

Surrogate information error: Surrogate information error is the difference or variation between the information required for a marketing research study and the information being sought by the researcher. The famous (or rather infamous) New Coke taste tests are a classic example of surrogate information error. The researchers in that case were seeking information regarding the taste of New Coke versus Old Coke, but the study should have determined consumers' attitudes toward a change in the product and not just their taste preferences.

Measurement error: Measurement error is the difference or the variation between the information sought by a researcher for a study and the information generated by a particular measurement procedure employed by the reseacher. Measurement error can occur at any stage of the measurement process, from the development of an instrument to the data analysis and interpretation stage. For example, if a researcher interested in the individual income of the respondent words the question as annual household income, a measurement error is being induced into the research study.

Experimental error: An experiment is designed to determine the existence of any causal relationship between two variables. Any error caused by the improper design of the experiment induces an experimental error into the study.

Data analysis error: Data analysis error can occur when the data from the questionnaires are coded, edited, analyzed, or interpreted. For example, uncorrected coding of data or a wrong use of a statistical analysis procedure can induce a data analysis error into the study.

Administering Error

All errors that occur during the administration of a survey instrument to the respondents are classified as administering errors. They are caused by mistakes committed by the person administering the questionnaire. They may be caused by three major factors:

Questioning error arises while addressing questions to the respondents. If the interviewer does not word the question exactly as designed by the researcher, a questioning error is induced.

Recording error arises from improperly recording the respondent's answers. If the interviewer misinterprets the response or hears it inaccurately, this induces a recording error into the study.

Interference error occurs when an interviewer interferes with or fails to follow the exact procedure while collecting data. For example, if the interviewer fabricates the responses to a survey, it induces an interference error.

Response Error

Response errors, also called data errors, occur when the respondent—intentionally or unintentionally—provides inaccurate answers to the survey questions. This might be due to the respondent's failing to comprehend the question or it may be due to fatigue, boredom, or misinterpretation of the question. Response errors can also occur when a respondent who is unwilling or embarrassed to answer a sensitive question provides an inaccurate or false response.

Nonresponse Error

Nonresponse errors occur if (1) some members of a sample were not contacted, and hence their responses were not included in the study; or (2) some of the members contacted provide an incomplete or no response to the survey instrument. The primary reasons for this error occurring include the unwillingness of respondents to participate in the study and the inability of the interviewer to contact the respondents.

Experimental Research

◆ WHAT CONSTITUTES CAUSALITY?

Causation, strictly speaking, means that a change in one variable will produce a change in another. In this context, the definition will be broadened somewhat to include the concept of a precondition influencing a variable of interest. For example, we could conceive that credit card usage is determined partly by a person's sex. In this case, sex could be conceptualized as causal in nature, despite the fact that it would be impossible to take a group of people and change their sex to observe whether if a change in credit card usage was produced. The weaker term *influence* often will be used when it is more appropriate than the term *cause* but the logic of the analysis normally will remain the same.

Given the causation concept, that a change in one variable will produce a change in another, it is reasonable to conclude that if two variables are causally linked, they should be associated. If association provides evidence of causation, then, conversely, the lack of association suggests the absence of cessation. Thus, an association between attitude and behavior is evidence of a causal relationship:

> If association provides evidence of causation, then, conversely, the lack of association suggests the absence of cessation. Thus, an association between attitude and behavior is evidence of a **causal relationship**.

$$\text{Attitude} \rightarrow \text{behavior}$$

Conditions for Valid Causal Inferences

As the preceding discussion on competing explanations indicates, the concept of causality is complex. The scientific notion of causality is very different from the commonsense, everyday notion.[1] The following table summarizes the difference between the commonsense and the scientific notions of causality:

Commonsense Notion	Scientific Notion
• There is a single cause of an event; i.e., X is the only cause of Y.	• There can be more than one cause; i.e., X may be only one of the multiple causes of Y.
• There is a deterministic relationship between X and Y.	• There is only a probabilistic relationship between X and Y.
• The causal relationship between X and Y can be proved.	• The causal relationship can never be proved; we can only infer that X is a cause of Y.

Thus, the scientific notion holds that causality is inferred; it is never demonstrated conclusively.[2] Then what kind of evidence can be used to support causal inferences? The following types of evidence are relevant to evaluating causal relationships:

- *Condition of concomitant variation*—evidence that a strong association exists between an action and an observed outcome
- *Condition of time order of occurrence*—evidence that the action preceded the outcome
- *Absence of competing causal explanations*—evidence that there is no strong competing explanation for the relationship and that a high level of internal validity exists

In addition, if the resulting causal inference is to be useful to management, it should be:

- Generalizable beyond the particular setting in which it was found; that is, it should have a high level of external validity
- Persistent in that it will hold long enough to make management action worthwhile

As discussed earlier, even if the above-mentioned conditions are fulfilled—that is, there is evidence of concomitant variation, time order of occurrence, and absence of competing explanations—the presence of a causal relationship can never be scientifically proved. The presence of strong evidence only increases our confidence in inferring the presence of a causal relationship. The results from controlled experimental research studies, conducted in different environmental settings, increase the reliability of our inference.

◆ ISSUES IN EXPERIMENTAL RESEARCH

Experimental research involves decision making on three major issues:

1. What type of experimental design should be used?
2. Should the experiment be performed in a laboratory setting or in the field?
3. What are the internal and external threats to the validity of the experiment, and how can we control for the various threats to the experiment's internal and external validity?

We will discuss the various types of experimental designs and how these designs take care of the threats to experimental validity. In the next section we will discuss the difference between laboratory and field experiments and the conditions that dictate the choice of one over the other. We will also discuss the threats to the internal and external validity of the experiment.

Basic Symbols and Notations[3]

We introduce six notations that are commonly used while conducting experiments. First are observation *(O)* and exposure *(X)*.

> *O* denotes a formal *observation* or measurement of the dependent variable that is made as part of the experimental study. Symbols O_1, O_2, and so on, will be used when two or more measurements of the dependent variable are involved during the experiment.
>
> *X* denotes *exposure* of test units participating in the study to the experimental manipulation or treatment. Symbols X_1, X_2, and so forth, will be used when the test units are exposed to two or more experimental treatments.

Note: The ordering of *O*'s and *X*'s from left to right will represent the time sequence in which they occur.

EG denotes an *experimental group* of test units that are exposed to the experimental treatment. Symbols EG_1, EG_2, and so on, will be used when the experiment has more than one experimental group.

CG denotes a *control group* of test units participating in the experiment but not exposed to the experimental treatment. Symbols CG_1, CG_2, and so on, will be used when the experiment involves more than one control group.

R denotes random assignment of test units and experimental treatments to groups. Randomization ensures control over extraneous variables and increases the reliability of the experiment.

M denotes that both the experimental group and the control group are matched on the basis of some relevant characteristics. Matching helps reduce the experimental error that arises out of selection bias.

◆ TYPES OF EXPERIMENTAL DESIGNS

Experimental designs can be broadly categorized into two groups: classical designs and statistical designs. The basic difference between these two types of experimental designs is that classical designs consider the impact of only one treatment level of an independent variable at a time, whereas statistical designs allow for examining the impact of different treatment levels of an independent variable and also the impact of two or more independent variables.[4] For the purpose of this book we will discuss only classical designs. The designs are discussed in Table A-1.

Validity

Internal validity refers to the ability of the experiment to show relationships unambiguously. For example, a large response to the Omaha advertisement might be caused by the number of people in Omaha, the weather when the advertisement was run, or the scheduling of civic activities. Although it is possible, by improving the experimental design, to reduce the number of competing explanations of the results of field experiments, they still tend to have less internal validity than laboratory experiments.

Threats to Internal Validity[5]

The major source of threat to internal validity comes from eight different classes of extraneous variables, which if not controlled might produce effects confounded with the effects of the experimental stimulus.

1. *History:* Events external to the experiment that affect the responses of the people involved in the experiment.
2. *Maturation:* Changes in the respondents that are a consequence of time, such as aging, getting hungry, or getting tired.
3. *Testing:* The effects of taking a test on the results of a subsequent test.
4. *Instrumentation:* The measuring instrument may change, as when different interviewers are used.
5. *Statistical regression:* Operates where groups have been selected on the basis of their extreme scores.

TABLE A-1 Classical Designs Used in Experimental Research

Name of Design	Actual Design	Inference
Preexperimental Designs		
One-Group After-Only Design	$EG\ X\ O$	An observation is made after an experimental group has been exposed to an experimental treatment.
Nonmatched Control Group Design	$EG\ X\ O_1$ $CG\ O_2$	The results of the stimulus would then be O_1–O_2.
Matched Control Group Design	$EG\ M\ X\ O_1$	M indicates that the two groups are matched with respect to some variable of interest.
One-Group Before-After Design	$EG\ O_1\ X\ O_2$	The interest changes from O_1 to control O_2 to control O_1 from being large due to large cities.
True Experimental Designs		
Two-Group After-Only Design	$EG\ R\ X\ O_1$ $CG\ R\ O_2$	R indicates that the test units are randomly assigned to the test and control groups.
Two-Group Before-After Design	$EG\ R\ O_1\ X\ O_2$ $CG\ R\ O_3\ O_4$	The output of interest is the difference obtained by subtracting O_2 from O_1 and O_4 from O_3.
Solomon Four-Group Design	$EG\ R\ O_1\ X\ O_2$ $CG\ R\ O_3\ O_4$ $EG\ R\ X\ O_5$ $CG\ R\ O_6$	This design provides several measures of the experimental effect [i.e., $(O_2 - O_4)$, $(O_2 - O_1)$ – $(O_4 - O_3)$, $(O_6 - O_5)$].
Quasi-Experimental Designs		
Time Series Designs	$EG O_1 O_2 O_3 O_4\ X O_5 O_6 O_7 O_8$	There are variants to this design, depending on whether the measurements are all from the same sample or from separate samples.
Continuous Panel Studies	These collect a series of measurements on the same sample of tests units, over an extended period of time	They offer insights into choice behavior that cannot be obtained from any other source.

6. *Selection bias:* An experimental group is systematically different in some relevant way from the population being studied.

7. *Mortality:* Respondents dropping out of the experiment while the experimental research is in progress.

8. *Selection-maturation interaction:* In certain experimental designs, the selection-maturation interaction effect might be mistaken for the effect of the experimental variable.

External validity refers to the applicability of the experimental results to situations external to the actual experimental context. Field experiments tend to have much greater external validity than laboratory experiments. Laboratory experiments, however, tend to be much less costly and allow the experimenter greater control over the experiment, thus reducing alternative explanations of the results and increasing internal validity.

Threats to External Validity[6]

The exposure to an experimental treatment, such as a mockup of a new product in a laboratory, can be so different from conditions in the real world that projections become very difficult and risky.

In addition to the problem of artificiality in laboratory experiments, most of the previous list of eight internal validity threats also apply to external validity. In particular, selection bias can be very serious.

Guidelines for Conducting Experimental Research

For a complete list of guidelines for conducting experimental research please visit http://www.wiley.com/college/kumar.

Common Misuses of Experimental Research in Marketing[7]

Experimental and quasi-experimental design approaches have their own uses, methodological sets, benefits, and pitfalls. Each family of techniques is highly appropriate for specific uses, but neither is amenable to slavish application for all marketing purposes. Some examples of the most common misuses include:

- Concluding from a test of two media spending levels that sales are inelastic with regard to media and that advertising can be turned off entirely
- Observing that a 10 percent price increase has no impact, so sales are not responding to price, and the price can be increased by 25 percent
- Deciding that an umbrella display for a number of brands won't work because a similar display that was tested for a single brand didn't pay off

ENDNOTES

1. David A. Kenny, *Correlation and Causality* (New York: Wiley, 1979).
2. Gilbert A. Churchill, Jr., *Marketing Research: Methodological Foundations,* 5th ed. (New York: Dryden, 1991), pp. 167–168.
3. This system of notation was introduced by Donald T. Campbell and Julian C. Stanley, *Experimental and Quasi Experimental Designs for Research* (Chicago: Rand McNally, 1963).
4. E. Paul Green, S. Donald Tull, and Gerald Albaum, *Research for Marketing Decisions,* 5th ed. (Englewood Cliffs, NJ: Prentice-Hall, 1988).
5. Ibid.
6. Seymour Banks, *Experimentation in Marketing,* (New York: McGraw-Hill, 1965), p. 33.
7. John L. Carefoot, "Modeling and Experimental Designs in Marketing Research: Uses and Misuses," *Marketing News* (June 7, 1993), p. H19.

DATA COLLECTION

Secondary and Standardized Sources of Marketing Data

Learning Objectives

- Define and introduce the various secondary data sources.
- Discuss the uses, benefits, and limitations of secondary data.
- Describe the various sources and forms of secondary data.
- Provide a brief overview of the sources of secondary data used in international marketing research.
- Get a feel for the applications of secondary data in domestic and international marketing research.
- Introduce the various standardized sources of marketing data.
- Provide a description of each of the well-known sources of standardized marketing data.
- Discuss the sources and applications of scanner data.
- Develop a framework for the various applications of standardized data sources.

In this chapter we begin the task of identifying and assessing the data that answer the decision maker's specific questions.

One of the hallmarks of market intelligence is familiarity with the basic sources pertaining to the market being studied, coupled with sensitivity to their respective strengths and weaknesses. This means that time will not be lost in an aimless search for nonexistent data, and neither time nor money will be wasted on a premature decision to go into the field to obtain the data.

Figure 5-1 shows the principal sources available to a researcher who is responding to a research question or considering what data to collect in order to anticipate future information needs. This chapter is concerned primarily with externally available **secondary data sources,** for which the specification, collection, and recording of the data are done by someone other than the user. We will take a particularly close look at census data, because it is so fundamental to understanding all aspects of a market economy. This becomes evident when census data are used to analyze market demand. We will also look at **standardized data** which are collected especially for a set of information users with a common need. Standardized data are both purpose-

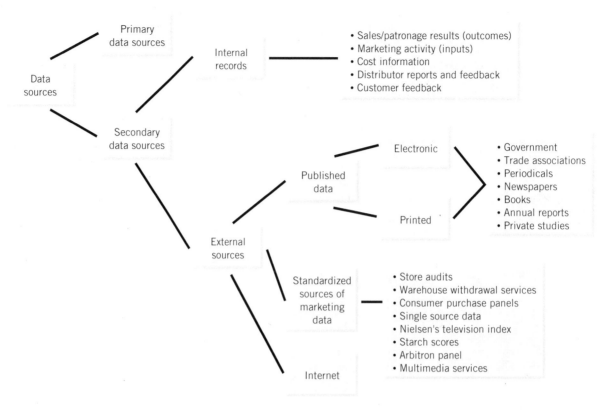

Figure 5–1 Sources of secondary data.

specific and expensive, but still much cheaper than having each user do it singly. Often, the immediate and unique needs of a decision maker require collecting original, or **primary data,** which is the topic of the rest of the book.

◆ INTRODUCTION TO SECONDARY DATA

Secondary data are data that were collected by persons or agencies for purposes other than solving the problem at hand.

Secondary data are data that were collected by persons or agencies for purposes other than solving the problem at hand. They are one of the cheapest and easiest means of access to information. Hence, the first thing a researcher should do is search for secondary data available on the topic. The amount of secondary data available is overwhelming, and researchers have to locate and utilize the data that are relevant to their research. Most search procedures follow a distinctive pattern, which begins with the most available and least costly sources. Figure 5-1 shows the various sources of secondary data. The order, from top to bottom, corresponds roughly to the order in which the alternative sources should be considered, or to the likelihood of that type of data being incorporated into the marketing information system. That is, almost all information systems initially are based on routinely collected internal data, and expand through the inclusion of data from published and standardized sources.

Uses of Secondary Data

Secondary data can be used by researchers in many ways:

1. Secondary data may actually provide enough information to resolve the problem being investigated. Suppose a marketing researcher needs to know the income of households in a particular market area. All the researcher has to do is to look into the appropriate Census Bureau report.

2. Secondary data can be a valuable source of new ideas that can be explored later through primary research.

3. Examining available secondary data is a prerequisite to collecting primary data.

4. It helps to define the problem and formulate hypotheses about its solution. It will almost always provide a better understanding of the problem, and its context frequently will suggest solutions not considered previously.

5. Secondary data is of use in the collection of primary data. Examining the methodology and techniques employed by other investigators in similar studies may be useful in planning the current one. It may also suggest better methods.

6. Secondary data also helps to define the population, select the sample in primary information collection, and define the parameters of primary research.

7. Secondary data can serve as a reference base against which to compare the validity or accuracy of primary data. It may also be of value in establishing classifications that are compatible with past studies so that trends may be more readily analyzed.

The benefits and limitations of secondary data are summarized in Table 5-1.

◆ INTERNAL SOURCES OF SECONDARY DATA

Internal Records

A company's **internal records** on accounting and control systems provide the most basic data on marketing inputs and the resulting outcomes.

A company's **internal records** on accounting and control systems provide the most basic data on marketing inputs and the resulting outcomes. The principal virtues of these data are ready availability, reasonable accessibility on a continuing basis, and relevance to the organization's situation.

Data on inputs—marketing effort expended—can range from budgets and schedules of expenditures to salespeople's call reports describing the number of calls per day, who was visited, problems and applications discussed, and the results of the visit.

TABLE 5-1 Benefits and Limitations of Secondary Data

Benefits	Limitations
1. Low cost	1. Collected for some other purpose
2. Less effort expended	2. No control over the data collection
3. Less time taken	3. May not be very accurate
4. Sometimes more accurate than primary data	4. May not be reported in the required form
5. Some information can be obtained only from secondary data	5. May be outdated
	6. May not meet data requirements
	7. A number of assumptions have to be made

Extensive data on outcomes can be obtained from the billing records on shipments maintained in the accounting system. In many industries the resulting sales reports are the single most important items of data used by marketing managers, because they can be related (via exception reporting methods) to plans and budgets to determine whether performance is meeting expectations. Also, they may be compared with costs in order to assess profitability.

New developments in information technology that tie customers more tightly to suppliers are improving the timeliness and depth of the sales information available to managers. For example, American Hospital Supply has supplied hospitals with computers so that hospital order entries go directly to the sales department, where they are stored in a computer and can be immediately accessed and analyzed for trends and transaction details. Salespeople at Wrangler Womenswear can connect their portable computers to the corporate computer to send and retrieve messages, enter orders, and receive up-to-date sales information.

Using Internal Data Effectively

Many diagnostic studies potentially can be undertaken with various combinations of internal and external data, to address such questions as the following:

- What is the effect of marketing inputs (number of sales calls or types of distribution channels) on outcomes such as profitability and unit sales within regions or sales territories?
- Is our sales performance within key market segments or types of retailers improving or deteriorating?
- Are current sales and marketing expenditures above or below the levels set in the annual budget and sales plan?

Such insightful analyses, however, often are thwarted because of limitations in the accounting system (the reporting formats frequently are rigid and inappropriate for marketing decisions) and distortions in the data.

Customer Feedback

Increasingly, companies are augmenting their internal records with systematic compilations of product returns, service records, and customer correspondence, in a manner that permits easy retrieval. Responding to the voice of the customer has become critical in order to maintain or increase market share in today's competitive environment.[1] Complaint letters are being used as sources of data on product quality and service problems. One reason is the insight they can provide into the problems of small groups with unusual requirements, reactions, or problems. For example, a premarket skin abrasion test of a new talc-based bath powder uncovered no problems, but the complaint letters that poured in shortly after the reformulated product was introduced revealed serious problems among a small group with sensitive skin.

A letter of complaint is actually a rather infrequently used method of resolving dissatisfaction; instead, people are more likely to switch brands, shop in a different store, or complain to their friends. Manufacturers are almost completely cut off from knowledge of customer unhappiness, because most complaints are voiced to retailers and there is little systematic feedback from retailers to manufacturers.

Customer returning a product to a store.
Frank Siteman/Monkmeyer Press Photo.

Customer Database

Many companies have started to build customer databases on their own. A customer database is raw information on the customer that can be sorted and enhanced to produce useful information. Records of frequent customers and their transactions are maintained, and the companies use this data to find out what is common among its customers. This data can also be used to find out about customers' product preferences, form of payment, and so on. Holiday Inn has created a customer database for its Priority Club members in order to track their activities and transactions with regard to the company.[2] These customer databases are now being used extensively by marketing managers for formulating relationship marketing strategies. This is discussed in greater detail in the final chapter of the book.

◆ EXTERNAL SOURCES OF SECONDARY DATA

Published Data Sources

Published data are by far the most popular source of marketing information. Not only are the data readily available, often they are sufficient to answer the research question. For example:

- A marketing manager studying developments in the wine industry will use trade association data to learn how the total consumption of wine is broken down, by type of customers, geographic area, type of wine, brand name, and distribution client. These data are available annually and sometimes quarterly, so significant trends can be isolated readily.

- A person starting a new specialty shop will use census data on family character-istics and income, to support a likely location for the shop.
- Local housing planners rely on census data dealing with the characteristics of housing and households in their locality to judge the need for new housing con-struction or housing rehabilitation.

The prospective user of published data is also confronted with the problem of matching a specific need for information with a bewildering array of secondary data sources of variable and often indeterminate quality. What is needed first is a flexible search procedure that will ensure that no pertinent source is overlooked. Second, the user needs some general criteria for evaluating quality. These issues will be dealt with in the next two sections.

The major published sources are the various government publications (federal, state, provincial, and local), periodicals and journals, and publicly available reports from such private groups as foundations, publishers, trade associations, unions, and companies. Of all these sources, the most valuable data for the marketing researcher come from government census information and various registration requirements. The latter encompass births, deaths, marriages, income tax returns, unemployment records, export declarations, automobile registrations, and so on.

How should someone who is unfamiliar with a market or research topic pro-ceed? In general, two basic rules are suggested to guide the search effort: (1) Start with the general and go to the specific, and (2) make use of all available expertise.[3] The four main categories are: authorities, general guides and indices, compilations, and directories.

Authorities

Knowledge of pertinent sources—and of their limitations—comes from continued experience. Thus, the best starting point is someone else who has been doing research on the same subject. Trade associations and specialized trade publications are particularly useful, for they often compile government data and collect addi-tional information from their subscribers or members.[4] If information about a spe-cific geographic area is sought, the local Chamber of Commerce is a good place to begin. When the problem or topic is too large or ill defined, there is no substitute for a well-informed reference librarian.

General Guides and Indices

Within the category of **guides and indices** there is a hierarchy of generality. At the top are the "guides to the guides," such as Constance Winchell's *Guide to Reference Books* (Chicago: American Library Association), *The Bibliographic Index: A Cumulative Bibliog-raphy of Bibliographies* (New York: H. W. Wilson Co.), *The Cumulative Book Index* (New York: H. W. Wilson Co.), and *Guide to Special Issues and Indexes of Periodicals* (New York: Special Libraries Association).

At the next level of reference materials are guides to general business informa-tion sources. Several important bibliographies are: the *Encyclopedia of Business Infor-mation Sources*, the *Encyclopedia of Geographic Information Sources* (Detroit: National Gale Research Co.), and the *Statistical Reference Index* (Washington, D.C.: Congres-sional Information Service). At a third level of generality, business periodical indices (e.g., *Psychological Abstracts*, Washington, D.C.: American Psychological Association; *The Wall Street Journal*) contain references to a large number of journals, periodicals, and newspapers.

For studies of international markets there is the *International Bibliography of Marketing and Distribution* (Munchen-Pullach: Verlag Dokumentation). Each country has its own reference guides to domestic periodicals. For example, in Canada there is the (Annual) Statistics *Canada Catalogue* and the *Canadian Business Index*, and in the United Kingdom there is the *Annual Abstract of Statistics* (London: H. M. Stationery Office). Most countries have reference guides to state and provincial jurisdictions. For example, *Canadiana* (Ottawa: National Library of Canada) includes a regular listing of provincial and municipal government publications.

Marketing researchers often overlook valuable information on trends and conditions in specific markets, which is produced by firms such as Frost and Sullivan, Predicasts, Euromonitor, Economist Intelligence Unit, Stanford Research Institute, and A. D. Little. Although these reports may be expensive, they usually are much cheaper than primary research. These reports are indexed and described in:

- Findex (Find/SVP), with over 15,000 reports on file from over 600 publishers worldwide
- Off-the-Shelf-Publications (Commack, NY), which provides a monthly catalog of market reports
- Research Alert Direct, a new line of Internet-delivered alerting services; reports deal with trends in consumer markets, attitudes, and lifestyles

Compilations

Compilations are intermediate sources in that they facilitate access to the original sources. This is particularly desirable with statistical information. The standard work in this area is the *Statistical Abstract of the United States* (Washington, D.C.: U.S. Bureau of the Census), which contains selections from the various censuses as well as data collected by other agencies. For example, data on the number of industrial robots installed worldwide, by country, are compiled by the U.S. International Trade Commission. General-purpose marketing statistics are published in volumes such as: *Market Guide* (New York: The Editor and Publisher), *Marketing Economics Guide* (New York: Marketing Economies Institute), and the *Rand McNally Commercial Atlas and Marketing Guide*. Other valuable compilations are the *Sales and Marketing Management* annual statistical issues detailing the "Survey of Buying Power," which includes industrial incomes, sales of six types of retail stores, market potential indices for states, countries, and metropolitan areas, and similar statistics for Canada.

Directories

Directories are useful for locating people or companies that could provide information. Trade directories supply a wealth of information on individual companies, including addresses, names of executives, product range, and brand names. Information on parent companies and subsidiaries often is provided. The *Thomas Register of American Manufacturers* (New York: Thomas Publishing Co.) lists such data on more than 156,914 manufacturing firms. There is now a Thomas Register for Europe, which is the first pan-European buying guide for manufacturers. *Who Owns Whom* (North American Ed.) lists about 180,000 domestic and foreign subsidiaries and associated companies classified by 100,000 products and categories. Some directories are narrowly focused, such as *McKitrick's Directory of Advertisers*, or the *Pulp and Paper Directory of Canada*. A number of directories, such as *World Who's Who in Finance and Industry* (Detroit: National Cole Research Co.), and *Standard & Poor's Register of Corporations, Directors and Executives* (covering the United States and Canada), provide general biographical information on individuals.

It is important to realize that only a few of the better-known sources have been described or mentioned here. Almost all of these guides, compilations, and directories are now available either on-line or on CD-ROM. You are always best advised to seek the assistance of a qualified reference librarian whenever a new area or topic is being studied.

Computer-Retrievable Databases

Even with the array of printed bibliographies, directories, and indices, a search can be very time-consuming. Recent advances in computer technology have resulted in more efficient methods of cataloging, storing, and retrieving published data. The growth in the number of electronic databases has been dramatic. It is estimated that more than 4,750 on-line databases are available to researchers and analysts working in almost every area of business, science, law, education, and the social sciences. Many of these databases are now accessible from personal computers, as well as terminals equipped with an appropriate telephone linkage. Increasingly, the software developed for the user's communication with the database system is designed to be user friendly. As a result, use of these electronic information sources has expanded rapidly to facilitate almost any search for information; it is no longer limited to computer specialists.

The large number of **computer-retrievable databases** can be overwhelming. Databases can be classified by type of information contained or by the method of storage and retrieval. Figure 5-2 gives a comprehensive view of the classification.

Databases Classified by Type of Information

Reference Databases. Reference databases refer users to articles and news contained in other sources. They provide on-line indices and abstracts and are therefore

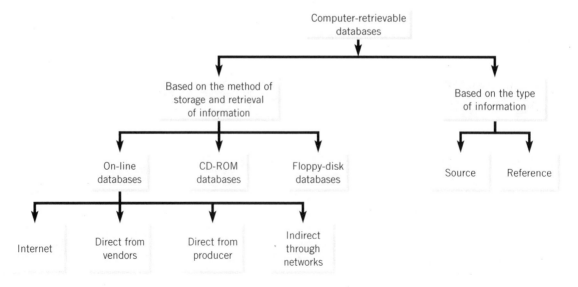

Figure 5-2 Classifying computer-retrievable databases.

referred to as **bibliographic databases.** These databases are quick and efficient. Use them to get an overview of a subject before obtaining a large amount of detailed information. Reference databases provide three distinct search features:

1. They are up-to-date summaries or references to a wide assortment of articles appearing in thousands of business magazines, trade journals, government reports, and newspapers throughout the world.

2. The information is accessed by using natural-language key words, rather than author or title. For example, the word *steel* will cause the computer to retrieve all abstracts that contain that word.

3. Key words can be combined in a search for articles that cover a number of related topics.

Source Databases.   Source databases provide numerical data, a complete text, or a combination of both. These include the many economic and financial databases and textual source databases that contain the complete texts of newspaper or journal articles.

As opposed to the indices and summaries in the reference database, source databases provide complete textual or numerical information. They can be classified into

1. Full-text information sources
2. Economic and financial statistical databases
3. On-line data and descriptive information on companies

Lexis–Nexis has introduced three new services. Tracker scans thousands of publications daily and delivers relevant news for only those topics designated by the customer. PubWatch allows users to scan a particular publication table of contents and select only the stories they want to read. AM News Brief provides the news summary every day. Market research reports from more than a dozen brand names such as Data Monitor Find/SVP, and Nielsen are also available.

In addition to the various major databases that provide financial information about companies and stocks, such as Standard & Poor's Compustat Services and the *Value Line Database,* a number of on-line sources provide nonfinancial information about companies. Examples include the following:

Dun and Bradstreet Identifier: More than 57 million public and private companies, government agencies, and contractors, schools and universities with five or more employees, listing addresses, products, sales executives, corporate organization, subsidiaries, industry information, and sales prospects worldwide.

Disclosure: 12,500 U.S. public companies with at least $5 million in assets. Information includes description of the business, balance sheet, cash flow, income statement, financial ratios, president's letter, and management discussion.

American Business Directory: Over 10 million companies, mainly private. Also lists government offices and professionals, such as physicians and attorneys. Includes estimates of sales and market share.

Standard & Poor's Corporate Description Plus News: 12,000 public companies, with strategic and financial information plus news. Includes business description, incorporation history, earnings and finances, capitalization summary, stocks and bond data.

Invested Group MarkIntel: Comprises two databases, MarkIntel, which features reports authored by top-rated business publishing firms, and MarkIntel Master, which features exclusive on-line primary research from leading consulting and market research firms.

Data-Star: Has several individual files with full-text market research reports. Also provides a Focus Market Research that includes Data Monitor, Euromonitor, ICC Keynote Report, Investext, Frost and Sullivan, European Pharmaceutical Market Research, and Freedonia Industry and Business Report.

NTIS: The National Technical Information Service is the official source for government-sponsored U.S. and worldwide scientific, technical, engineering, and business-related information. The NTIS collection includes business and management studies, and international marketing reports. The information is available in CD-ROMs, computer tapes and diskettes, and on-line.

Databases Classified by Storage and Retrieval Methods

Another useful way of classifying databases is based on their method of storage and retrieval. They can be classified as on-line databases, CD-ROM databases, or floppy-disk databases.

On-line Databases. On-line databases can be accessed in real time directly from the producers of the database or through a vendor. In order to access on-line databases, all one needs is a personal computer, a modem, and a telephone line. On-line databases drastically reduce the time required for a search and bring data right to the desk. Use of the Internet to obtain useful marketing research information is discussed in Chapter 6.

Courtesy Barnes and Noble.

Cyber shopping.
Gilles Mingasson/Gamma Liaison.

CD-ROM Databases.[5] Compact disk read-only memory (CD-ROM) technology has revolutionized the way information is stored and retrieved. Storage and retrieval is no longer restricted to large, mainframe machines accessed by modems. Now, large amounts of information can be stored on compact disks and can be read by personal computers. A single CD-ROM can hold approximately 650–700 megabytes of information (as much as 500 floppy disks), or 250,000-plus pages of text. The main advantage of CD-ROM over on-line access is that there are no on-line connect-time charges or long-distance telephone charges. The most powerful CD-ROM applications usually are sold by annual subscription or one-time fee for unlimited data access. Typically, the user receives a disk with updated information each week, month, or quarter. Almost all the reference and source databases that are available on-line are also available on CD-ROM.

Floppy-disk Databases. As the name suggests, floppy-disk databases store information on floppy disks. These are the least popular of the databases, and with the prices of CD-ROM technology coming down at a rapid rate, these types of databases may be totally replaced by the CD-ROM databases. The *Current Contents on Diskette* series is an example of a floppy-disk database.

Accessing Computer-Retrievable Databases

On-line databases are accessible both from their producers and increasingly from on-line information services. Most on-line services charge a fee for access to each database, a charge for the amount of information retrieved, and possibly supplemental charges, depending on the nature of the information or the contract arrangements.

Advantages of Computer-Retrievable Methods

The main advantage of computer-retrievable methods is the scope of the information available on databases. They now cover several thousand U.S. and worldwide information sources. A second advantage is the speed of information access and retrieval. Often, much of the information is available from a computer before it is available in published form, because of the time required for printing and mailing printed material. Third, commercially available search procedures provide considerable flexibility and efficiency in cross-referenced searching. For example, by using the EIS Industrial Plants database, it is possible to locate plants that simultaneously meet several criteria, such as geographic location, industry code, and market share. The future of computer-retrievable databases is exciting. Marketing Research in Practice 5-1 gives us an idea about mobile databases and how they are predicted to affect the future.

MARKETING RESEARCH IN PRACTICE 5-1

Databases Going Mobile

Mobile databases are no longer a novelty now that they are not only benefiting corporate road warriors, but are also driving the sale of major database and replication service systems and the bulking line of major database vendors.

To avoid being left out in the cold, database companies are pouring resources into mobile database systems to beat the competition. Sybase produced an MS-DOS version of Adaptive Server in 1992 and that decision is paying off now with more than double the revenue of its closest competitor.

MARKETING RESEARCH IN PRACTICE 5-1 *(continued)*

Databases Going Mobile

Experts believe that the overall mobile systems market is growing at a 20 percent rate, but the embedded database market will grow considerably faster. In the past, end users worked on client-server systems to download data from a server and work with the data on their desktops, but with mobile databases a user can work in a single environment or work on the database server itself. It is also possible to collect data from information in the field and update the corporate database. In today's workplace, where people like technicians, floor managers, and even telecommuters are carrying devices such as laptops, a mobile database system can coordinate a central business database to their mobile devices.

Oracle 8 *i* Lite can be put on a Palm hand-held computer with an ability to handle Structured Query Language and act like a database. The prices have been drastically reduced, making it affordable for companies to extend applications to mobile devices that were previously available only in-house. In the majority of the cases, the user gets SQL function in a mobile application, rather than doing any extensive database querying or data analysis. But what remains to be seen is how much functionality will appear on the mobile devices of tomorrow. Some experts are confident that we will be walking around with a database on a mobile phone.

Source: Charles Babcock, "Databases are going mobile," *Inter@ctive Week 7,5* (February 7, 2000).

Limitations of Computer-Retrievable Methods

The main limitations of the reference databases are their reliance on the accuracy of the abstract author, the dependence on the journal and article selection policy of the database producer, and the idiosyncrasies of the search procedures of the different databases, as well as the different database network vendors.[6]

Because the computer search is based on finding certain key words within the abstract, there is the possibility that some important information will be missed if an abstract is missing a key word. On the other hand, a lot of irrelevant data may be generated if certain key words used to limit a search are not cited in an abstract. For example, a manufacturer of minicomputers who is interested only in developments pertaining to minicomputers may not want to retrieve the entire database on computers. However, the abstract may contain the word *computer* and accessing information on minicomputers would also yield general computer information.

Another limitation arises from the enormous amount of information now available on-line. It is often quite difficult to know which of the myriad sources has the correct information most readily accessible. Finally, the researcher using on-line database retrieval services must weigh the benefits of the research procedure—including timeliness, speed, and scope of information retrieval—against the costs of searching and accessing computer-retrievable databases.

◆ CENSUS DATA

The demographic, economic, and social statistics contained in great detail in **census data** are key aspects of many marketing studies; for example:

The parent corporation of Toys 'Я Us, Kids 'Я Us, and Babies 'Я Us must decide where to locate stores as well as the kind of stores to open. These decisions will require (1) census of population information about the populations with access to the proposed locations, (2) census of retail trade information about likely competitors and local wage levels, and (3) census of construction industries information about land development, contractors, and construction costs, available by state and metropolitan area.

All countries conduct a mandatory enumeration of important facts about their population and the economic and social environment. The major national and international census data collection agencies and some of their major publications are the U.S. Bureau of the Census, Statistics Canada, Statistical Office of the European Communities (Social Statistics, Industrial Statistics), Great Britain Central Statistical Office *(Annual Abstract of Statistics)*, Japan Bureau of Statistics *(Japan Statistical Yearbook)*, and the United Nations *(Statistical Yearbook)*.

The U.S. Bureau of the Census is illustrative of the scope of these undertakings. There are actually eight regular **economic censuses,** taken in the years ending with the numbers 2 and 7, and **censuses of population** and **housing,** which are taken every 10 years in the year ending with 0. The eight economic censuses compile detailed statistics on the structure and functioning of the major economic sectors: agriculture, construction industries, manufacturers, mineral industries, retail trade, service industries, transportation, and wholesale trade.

Two major innovations were introduced in the 2000 Census. One is the availability of census data on CD-ROM. For a fee, the Census Bureau provides detailed summaries of the information it obtains on CD-ROM. The bureau also sells computer software that may be used for accessing and tabulating data on the CD-ROM. The second major innovation in the 2000 Census was the introduction of the Topologically Integrated Geographic Coding and Referencing (TIGER) system. The TIGER system gives the user the ability to generate a digitized street map of the entire 3.6-million-square-mile map of the United States. Specifically, with use of the TIGER system, one can literally chart every block in every county in the United States, both

Toys ' Я Us and Kids ' Я Us.
Beringer/Draten/The Image Works.

topographically and demographically. Five versions of the TIGER maps are available from the federal government. These include the prototype and precensus versions, both issued in 1989; the Initial Voting Codes version, released in October 1990, which blankets the United States by election districts; and the initial and final postcensus versions, the latter released in the early part of 1991. TIGER covers 3,286 counties in the United States, including addresses from the most populated urban areas to the most rural areas. One of TIGER's most popular uses is to plot store locations.

To use census data effectively, one must be able to locate quickly the specific information relevant to the research topic. The *Index to Selected 2000 Census Reports* and the *Index to 2000 Census Summary Tapes* list all the titles of tables available from the 2000 Census in either printed or tape form. Each table is described in terms of the variable and the level of aggregation used. For example, one table may be described as "education by sex," with an indication of the level of aggregation available.

Census data can be obtained at many levels of aggregation (see Figure 5-3). The smallest identifiable unit is the **city block** bounded by four streets and some other physical boundaries. City blocks then are combined arbitrarily to form **block groups.** The block groups then are collected together to make up **census tracts,** which are generally used to approximate neighborhoods. Census tracts have populations of more than 4,000 and are defined by local communities. In urban areas, census tracts are combined to form **metropolitan statistical areas (MSAs),** which are counties containing a central city with populations of at least 50,000.

The general concept of a metropolitan area is one of a large population nucleus, together with adjacent communities that are determined to have a high degree of economic and social integration with that central nucleus. In June 1983 the federal government replaced the old **standard metropolitan statistical area (SMSA)** designation with new definitions. To maintain comparability, data for an earlier period are revised where possible to reflect the MSA boundaries of the more recent period. In addition to the new standard MSAs, the largest defined areas are **consolidated met-**

> **Census data** can be obtained at many levels of aggregation: city block, block groups, census tracts, and metropolitan statistical areas (MSAs).

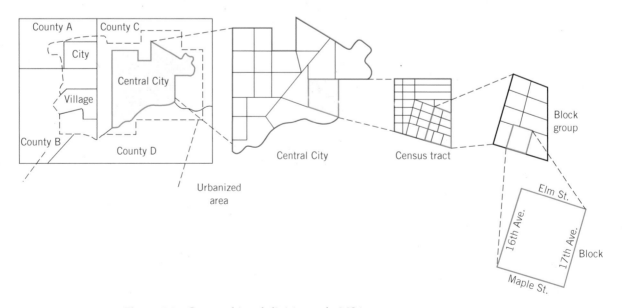

Figure 5-3 Geographic subdivisions of a MSA.

ropolitan statistical areas (CMSAs), which are metropolitan complexes containing separate component areas. (There are 335 MSAs and 68,000 census tracts and 254,000 block groups in the United States, including Puerto Rico.)

Finally, the whole country is divided into four large regions (Northeast, Midwest, South, and West). In addition, census data are available by civil divisions, such as states, counties, cities, and wards. The data from the latest census can be obtained from the Census Bureau's on-line database called Cendata. Cendata has an efficient measuring system that leads you to the data you need.

◆ NORTH AMERICAN INDUSTRY CLASSIFICATION SYSTEM

The **North American Industry Classification System** is a new system for classifying establishments based on their production processes.

The **North American Industry Classification System (NAICS)** is the new standard code system to describe business establishments and industries, replacing the Standard Industrial Classification (SIC) codes. It is the first industry classification system developed in accordance with a single principle of aggregation: the principle that producing units that use similar production processes should be grouped together in the classification. (See Table 5.2.)

The North American Industry Classification System (NAICS) is scheduled to go into effect for reference year 1997 in Canada and the United States, and 1998 in Mexico. It was developed to provide a consistent framework for the collection, analysis, and dissemination of industrial statistics. Designed by the U.S., Mexican, and Canadian Governments, NAICS has implications for economists, regulators, marketers, publishers, and anyone else who uses industry-based data. The most obvious use of the codes are in the 1997 Economic Census. Of the 1,170 NAICS codes, 358 are new industries, 390 are revised from SIC, and 422 can be compared to the older SIC codes.

The system was developed by the United States, Canada, and Mexico to provide comparable statistics across the three countries. For the first time, government and business analysts will be able to directly compare industrial production statistics collected and published in the three North American Free Trade Agreement countries. NAICS also provides for increased comparability with the International Standard Industrial Classification System (ISIC, Revision 3), developed and maintained by the United Nations.

NAICS industries are identified by a 6-digit code, in contrast to the 4-digit SIC code. The longer code accommodates the larger number of sectors and allows more flexibility in designating subsectors. It also provides for additional detail not necessarily appropriate for all three NAICS countries. The international NAICS agreement fixes only the first five digits of the code. The sixth digit, where used, identifies subdivisions of NAICS industries that accommodate user needs in individual countries. There are 20 broad sectors in the NAIC system, up from the 10 divisions of the SIC system.[7]

TABLE 5-2   North American Industrial Classification System

NAICS level	NAICS code	Description
Sector	51	Information
Subsector	513	Broadcasting and telecommunications
Industry group	5133	Telecommunications
Industry	51332	Wireless telecommunications carriers, except satellite
U.S. Industry	513321	Paging

Source: http://www.census.gov/epcd/www/naics.html.

◆ APPRAISING SECONDARY SOURCES

Users of secondary sources rapidly develop a healthy skepticism. Unfortunately, there are many reasons why a forecast, historical statistic, or estimate may be found to be irrelevant or too inaccurate to be useful. Before such a judgment can be made, the researcher should have answers to the following questions:

1. *Who?* This question applies especially to the reputation of the collecting agency commerce, or the government agency may be unwilling to report the true state of affairs or to take the time to collect the data, which may result in a biased guess.

2. *Why?* Data that are collected to further the interests of a particular group are especially suspect. Media buyers, for example, soon learn to be wary of studies of media. It is easy to choose unconsciously those methods, questions, analysis procedures, and so forth, that favor the interests of the study sponsor, and it is unlikely that unfavorable results will be shown to the public.

3. *How?* It is impossible to appraise the quality of secondary data without knowledge of the methodology used to collect them. Therefore, one should immediately be suspicious of any source that does not describe the procedures used—including a copy of the questionnaire (if any), the nature and size of the sample, the response rate, the results of field validation efforts, and any other procedural decisions that could influence the results. The crucial question is whether any of these decisions could bias the results systematically.

4. *What?* Even if the available data are of acceptable quality, they may prove difficult to use or may be inadequate to the need. One irritating and prevalent problem is the classifications that are used. Wide variations in geographic, age, and income groupings across studies are common; for example, there is no accepted definition for the minimum number of stores in a supermarket chain.

5. *When?* There are few things less interesting than last month's newspaper. Sooner or later, the pace of change in the world in general, and in markets in particular, renders all secondary data equally obsolete and uninteresting except to the historian. The rate of obsolescence varies with the types of data, but in all cases the researcher should know when the data were collected. There may be a substantial lag between the time of collection and the publication of the results.

6. *Consistency?* With all the possible pitfalls in secondary data, and the difficulty in identifying them fully, the best defense is to find another source that can be used as a basis for comparison. Ideally, the two sources should use different methodologies to arrive at the same kind of data. In the likely event that there is some disagreement between the two sets of data, the process of reconciliation should first identify the respective biases in order to narrow the differences and determine which set is the most credible.

◆ APPLICATIONS OF SECONDARY DATA

Secondary data are widely used for a number of marketing research problems. We have already discussed the various sources of secondary data and how to appraise them. In this section we will look at the various applications of secondary data. Table 5-3 gives a comprehensive framework of the types of sources to be used for different applications.

Demand Estimation

Most marketing resources—especially sales effort, service coverage, and communication activity—are allocated by region, segment, or territory. The key to efficient allocation is knowledge of the potential of each segment relative to other segments. Hence, **demand estimation** is a key determinant of resource allocation. Demand can be estimated from secondary data by direct data methods or corollary data methods.

Direct Data Methods

Direct data methods are based on a desegregation of total industry data. The sales information may come from government sources, industry surveys, or trade associations. For example, the National Electrical Manufacturers Association reports shipments of refrigerators to retailers. Such data are useful for establishing relative market potential only if the sales can be broken down by the organization's sales or operating territories. Fortunately, industry refrigerator shipment data are available by trading area. This permits a direct comparison of the share of company sales and industry sales in each territory.

Corollary Data Methods

One solution to the absence of industry sales data for each territory is to use another variable that is (1) available for each sales territory or region and (2) correlated highly with the sales of the product. For example, the territory demand for child-care services or baby food is correlated highly with the number of births in the area during the previous three years. Thus, the share of births in all geographic areas within the territory of interest would be a good proxy for the relative market potential within that territory.

Companies use·other methods that are peculiar to their product and sales environment to forecast sales. An example of such a method is given in Marketing Research in Practice 5-2. In the example, Hansen Company, a manufacturer of quick

Table 5-3   Applications of Secondary Data

Demand Estimation	Monitoring the Environment
1. Census data	1. Press releases
2. Standard industrial classification (SIC)	2. Legislation and laws
3. Trade association data	3. Industry news
4. Experts and authorities	4. Business and practitioner literature, such as magazines
Segmentation and Targeting	Developing a Business Intelligence System
1. PRIZM	1. Competitor's annual reports
2. CLUSTER PLUS	2. Press releases
3. ACORN	
4. DMI	
5. SIC	
6. TIGER	

MARKETING RESEARCH IN PRACTICE 5-2

Relative Sales Potentials

What can be done if a reliable estimate of total industry sales is unavailable, the customers cannot provide a good estimate of their purchases of the product, and the product is used in many industries, so that there are no obvious corollary variables? This was the situation confronting the Hansen Company, a manufacturer of quick connective couplings for air and fluid power transmission systems, which distributed these products through a national network of 31 industrial distributors. To be able to evaluate and control their activity, the company badly needed data on the relative performance of their distributors. Its approach was based on the only reliable data that were available to it—sales of company products. To utilize these data, it made the assumption that it should be possible for Hansen distributors to attain the same sales-per-employee ratio in noncustomer establishments as in customer establishments. To establish the sales-per-employee ratio that would serve as a performance standard, the following steps were taken:

1. A random sample of 178 accounts was drawn from a census of all customer accounts buying $2,000 or more from the seven best distributors (where "best" was defined in terms of perceived effectiveness of management and utilization of an up-to-date data processing system).

2. Each account was assigned to a two-digit NAIC group on the basis of its principal output or activity.

3. Data on the number of employees in each account were obtained primarily from industrial directories.

4. Sales-per-employee ratios were computed for each NAIC group within the set of seven distributors.

5. Sales-per-employee ratios for each NAIC group were multiplied by the total employment in all establishments in each of the 31 distributor territories. The employment data came from the current edition of the *County Business Patterns* publication of the U.S. Census.

The output of these five steps was a table for each distributor, patterned after the following table, which gives the results for distributor A.

Distributor A—2001 Sales Potential

Two-Digit NAIC	2000 Hansen Sales per Employee	Total Employees	Sales Potential
33	$1.61	4,213	11,416
34	2.48	14,892	58,424
35	3.23	15,707	83,175
36	1.98	32,477	93,067
37	1.76	2,124	9,461
38	3.43	509	7,423
Total		69,922	262,966

The resulting sales potential was compared with actual sales, which for distributor A amounted to $164,237 in 2001. That is, actual sales performance was 60 percent of sales potential. The sales performance for all distributors ranged from 23.0 percent to 69.0 percent, with an average of 52.6 percent. It is not surprising that the distributor with sales of only 23.5 percent of potential was subjected to a very careful review, which revealed that the salespeople did not really know how to sell the product to major accounts in the area.

connective couplings for air and fluid power transmission systems, uses a "sales-per-employee ratio" to forecast sales.

Monitoring the Environment

One of the most important uses of secondary data is to monitor the environment in which the company is functioning. **Monitoring the environment** is crucial these days, because it is highly volatile and because attitudes, fashions, and fads change so often. To keep abreast of all the latest developments, a company must be in constant touch with newspapers, general magazines, and periodicals. It has to know all the latest legislation and laws that may affect it. To know about the most recent trends in the industry, a firm must keep up on the latest journals in the field.

Segmentation and Targeting

Market **segmentation** is common among businesses seeking to improve their marketing efforts. Effective segmentation demands that firms group their customers into relatively homogeneous groups. Sellers of industrial goods segment their markets using the North American Industrial Classification System (NAICS) and Dun's Market Identifiers (DMI).

One of the latest developments with regard to segmentation for consumer products is **geocoding,** or a cluster demographic system, which identifies groups of consumers who share demographic and lifestyle characteristics. Several services now can link U.S. Census data on a ZIP code-basis to lifestyles, helping marketing researchers identify the best areas in which to concentrate their efforts. Among the services are PRIZM (by Claritas), CLUSTER PLUS (by Donnelly Marketing Information Services), and ACORN (CACI, Inc.).

About 1,000 consumer characteristics can be used to build clusters of homogeneous groups. Demographic variables include age, marital status, size of household, and income. Behavioral characteristics include amount of TV watched, amount of white bread consumed, types of magazines read, and so on. Geographic areas range from cities and countries to ZIP Codes, census tracts, and block groups.

The **Potential Rating Index Zip Markets (PRIZM)** system is based on evidence that people with similar cultural backgrounds and circumstances will gravitate naturally toward one another. Each of the 35,600 zip markets was first described according to 34 key demographic factors. These zip markets were originally clustered into 40 distinct groups, which were each very homogeneous within themselves and very different from other groups. Subsequently, 22 new consumer groups were added, bringing the total number of clusters to 62. The larger number of clusters reflect the increasing ethnic and economic complexity of the nation's population.[8] Claritas has also introduced workplace PRIZM, which accurately profiles a market's working population and demonstrates the difference between the area's daytime and nighttime demographics.

Since every market is composed of ZIP Code areas, it is possible to estimate the sales potential of a market by zip market clusters. As an example, a power tool manufacturer was able to create a PRIZM profile of product warranty cards mailed by recent buyers. This told the manufacturer which ZIP Code areas should be chosen as targets markets and helped to allocate media spending and sales force effort.

The ACORN system ("A Classification of Residential Neighborhoods") assigns 256,000 block groups or neighborhoods to 44 clusters with less colorful descriptions. Within the larger group of "Wealthy Areas" there are three clusters: "Established

The **Potential Rating Index Zip Markets (PRIZM)** system is based on evidence that people with similar cultural backgrounds and circumstances will gravitate naturally toward one another.

Suburbs," "Newer Suburbs," and "Mixed-Housing Inner Suburbs." Both ACORN and Donnelly rejected colorful descriptions, because they tend to focus on a single tendency that is not shared by all residents in the cluster. They also contend that ZIP Codes are too heterogeneous to classify properly. On average, 68 percent are apparently misclassified using ZIP Codes rather than block groups. They further argue that block groups are better because they do not shift from year to year, unlike ZIP Code boundaries. ACORN has also teamed with ICD, which collects information on lifestyle variables, and has launched a new product called Life Style Plus, which uses ICD lifestyle information to enhance Acorn-based data.

Developing a Business Intelligence System

A **business intelligence system** is a system that contains data on the environment and the competitors.

A **business intelligence system** is basically a system that contains data on the environment and the competitors. It forms an integral part of the marketing decision support system. Both primary and secondary data form a part of the business intelligence system. As has already been said, data on the environment can be obtained from a variety of sources. Data on competitors can be obtained from their annual reports, press releases, patents, and so on.

◆ SOURCES OF SECONDARY DATA FOR INTERNATIONAL MARKETING RESEARCH[9]

Secondary data are a key source of information for conducting international marketing research. This is, in part, due to their ready availability, the high cost of collecting primary data versus the relatively low cost of secondary data, and the usefulness of secondary data in assessing whether specific problems need to be investigated, and if so, how. Further, secondary data sources are particularly valuable in assessing opportunities in countries with which management has little familiarity, and in product markets at an early stage of market development.

A wide variety of secondary data sources are available for international marketing research. These range from sources that provide general economic, social, and demographic data for almost all countries in the world, to sources that focus on specific industries worldwide.

A host of sources of macroeconomic data are to be found, ranging widely in the number of countries or regions covered. Many of these are based on or derived from United Nations and World Bank data. The Business International, Euromonitor, and Worldcasts divisions of Predicasts also publish annual information on macroeconomic variables.

The preceding macroeconomic data sources, with the exception of Euromonitor, relate to the general business environment. They therefore do not provide much indication as to market potential for specific industries. A number of sources of industry-specific data are available. They are United Nations *Yearbooks*, publications of the U.S. Department of Commerce, *The Economist*, and the Worldcasts.

The following sources provide valid information on market research in Canada as well as an insight into the business climate. These present a review of the statistical data that is valuable when collecting secondary data.

- Canadiana—The Canadian Resource Page
- Canadian Business InfoWorld

Nickname	**Blue Blood Estates**	**Winner's Circle**	**Executive Suites**	**Pool & Patios**	**Kids & Cul-de-Sacs**
Demographic Caption	Elite Super-Rich Families	Executive Suburban Families	Upscale White-Collar Couples	Established Empty Nesters	Upscale Suburban Families
Cluster Number	01	02	03	04	05
Percent of U.S. Households	1.18%	2.15%	1.32%	1.85%	2.93%
Predominant Adult Age Range	45–64	45–64	45–64	45+	Under 18, 35–54
Key Education Level	College Grads	College Grads	College Grads	College Grads	College Grads
Predominant Employment	Professional	Professional	Professional	Professional	White-Collar/ Professional
Household Income	$135,900	$90,700	$68,500	$67,100	$68,900
Lifestyle Preferences	Belong to a healthclub Visit Eastern Europe Buy classical music Watch "Wall Street Week" Read *Architecural Digest*	Have a passport Shop at Ann Taylor Have Keogh plan Watch "NYPD Blue" Read cooking magazines	Belong to a healthclub Visit Japan/Asia Have an airline card Watch "Friends" Read *Entrepeneur*	Shop at Lord & Taylor Travel by train Buy $250+ blinds Watch the British Open Read *Business Week*	Shop on-line Visit Disney World Use a debit card Watch "The X-Files" Read boat magazines
Socioeconomic Rank	Elite (1)	Wealthy (2)	Affluent (8)	Affluent (9)	Affluent (10)
Race/Ethnicity	W (A)	W (A)	W (A)	W (A)	W (A)

PRIZM lifestyle segmentation example.
http://yawl.claritas.com.

- Statistics Canada Sites
  - Statistics Canada Catalogue
  - Statistics Canada Daily Publication
  - Statistics Canada 1991 Census Summary
- Canadian Industry Profiles—by Industry Canada
- Queen's University—Center for the Study of Public Opinion—Decima Quarterly Reports
- Supreme Court of Canada[10]
- Statistics Canada (http://www.stancan.ca/start.htm)

You can also find numerous other sources specific to individual countries or product markets. The U.S. Department of Commerce, for example, publishes *International Marketing Handbook,* which provides profiles and special information about doing business in various countries. Information regarding regulations, customs, distribution channels, transportation, advertising and marketing research, credit, taxation, guidance for business travelers abroad, and so forth, are compiled in their "Overseas Business Reports." Governments or other bodies frequently publish national yearbooks or statistical data books. Various private sources also publish regional and country handbooks. The World of Information publishes the *African Guide* and the *Middle East Review,* for example.

◆ PROBLEMS ASSOCIATED WITH SECONDARY DATA IN INTERNATIONAL RESEARCH

Two major problems are associated with secondary data in international marketing research: **data accuracy** and the **data comparability** across countries.

Data Accuracy

Different sources often report different values for the same macroeconomic factor, such as gross national product, per-capita income, or the number of television sets in use. This casts some doubt on the accuracy of the data. This may be due to different definitions followed for each of those statistics in different countries. The accuracy of data also varies from one country to another. Data from highly industrialized nations are likely to have a higher level of accuracy than data from developing countries, because of the difference in the sophistication of the procedures adopted. The level of literacy in a country also plays a role in the accuracy of the macroeconomic data collected in that country.

Comparability of Data

Business statistics and income data vary from country to country because different countries have different tax structures and different levels of taxation. Hence, it may not be useful to compare these statistics across countries. Population censuses may not only be inaccurate, they also may vary in frequency and the year in which they are collected. Although in the United States they are collected once every 10 years, in Bolivia there was a 25-year gap between two censuses. So most population figures are based on estimates of growth that may not be accurate and comparable. Measurement units are not necessarily equivalent from country to country. For example, in Germany the expense incurred on buying a television would be classified as entertainment expense, whereas in the United States it would be classified as furniture expense.

◆ APPLICATIONS OF SECONDARY DATA IN INTERNATIONAL RESEARCH

Secondary data are particularly useful in evaluating country or market environments, whether in making initial market-entry decisions or in attempting to assess future trends and developments. They thus form an integral part of the international marketing research process. More specifically, three major uses of secondary data are in:

1. Selecting countries or markets that merit in-depth investigation
2. Making an initial estimate of demand potential in a given country or a set of countries
3. Monitoring environmental changes

Secondary data can be used systematically to screen market potential, risks, and likely costs of operating in different countries throughout the world. Two types of generalized procedures are used. The first procedure classifies countries on two dimensions: the degree of demographic and economic mobility, and the country's domestic stability and cohesion. The second procedure calculates multiple factor indices for different countries. For example, *Business International* publishes information each year on three indices showing (1) *market growth,* (2) *market intensity,* and (3) *market size* for countries in Western and Eastern Europe, the Middle East, Latin

America, Asia, Africa, and Australia. Customized models, which are geared to specific company objectives and industry characteristics, can also be developed using secondary data.

Once you determine the appropriate countries and markets to be investigated in depth, the next step is to make an explicit evaluation of demand in those countries or markets.[11] This is important when considering initial market entry, because of the high costs and uncertainty associated with entering new markets. Management has to make an initial estimate of demand potential, and also has to project future market trends.

Four types of data analyses are unique to demand estimation in an international context. The first and the most simplistic is lead-lag analysis. This uses time-series (yearly) data from a country to project sales in other countries. A second procedure is the use of surrogate indicators. This is similar to the use of general macroindicators, but develops the macroindicators relative to a specific industry or product market. An example of a surrogate indicator is the number of childbirths in the country as an indicator of the demand potential for diapers. A third technique, which relies on the use of cross-sectional data (data from different countries), is analogous to the use of barometric procedures in domestic sales forecasting. One assumes that if there is a direct relationship between the consumption of a product, service, or commodity and an indicator in one country, the same relationship will hold in other countries for purposes of estimating the demand. The fourth and most complex forecasting model is the econometric forecasting model. This model uses cross-sectional and time-series data on factors underlying sales for a given product market for a number of countries to estimate certain parameters. Later, these models can be used to project the market demand.

A third use of secondary data in an international context is to monitor environmental changes. Monitoring environmental changes requires surveillance of a number of key indicators. These should be carefully selected and tailored to the specific product or range of products with which management is concerned. Two types of indicators are required. The first monitors the general health and growth of a country and its economy and society; the second monitors those of a specific industry or product market. A variety of procedures can be used to analyze the effect of environmental factors on world trends or industrial countries, and on product markets, as well as to analyze the implications for market growth and appropriate marketing strategies. These range from simple trend projections or tracking studies and the use of leading indicators to the more complex scenario evaluation studies.

◆ INTRODUCTION TO STANDARDIZED SOURCES OF MARKETING DATA

The more specific and topical the need for information, the smaller is the likelihood that relevant secondary data will be found. The researcher then has the choice of designing a special study or taking advantage of standardized data collection and analysis procedures. The latter alternative generally exists whenever several information users have common information needs and when the cost of satisfying an individual user's need is prohibitive. These conditions are most often encountered with consumer goods that are sold to large, diffuse markets and are repurchased at frequent intervals. A further condition—especially important for data sources such as store audits and continuous consumer panels—is that the information needs are recurrent and can be anticipated. Thus, the data supplier can enter into long-term relationships with clients and be sure of covering the heavy fixed costs. The clients get continuity of data series, which is essential for monitoring and evaluation purposes.

This section describes and evaluates the major syndicated sources of marketing data, including store audits, consumer purchase panels, scanner-based systems, and media-related standardized sources. Each source has a distinctive profile of strengths and weaknesses that reflects differences in orientation, types of measures, and their location in the distribution channel. To get a full picture of the market situation of a product category or brand, it is usually necessary to use several sources in combination. Unfortunately, when this is done the result is more often confusion rather than clarity of insight, because of information overload. This is such a prevalent problem that the last section of this chapter is devoted to recently developed decision support systems that help reduce the confusion.

The use of standardized data sources has been revolutionized by so-called **single-source data** from scanner systems. This means that all data on product purchases and causal factors—such as media exposure, promotion influence, and consumer characteristics—come from the same households. These data are being made possible through advances in information technology whose full impact is only slowly being understood. At the moment it does not appear that single-source data will fully displace other standardized sources, but it will be used in conjunction with them to generate important new insights.

To understand the basic motivation for using standardized sources, consider the problems of a manufacturer of cold remedies who has to rely on factory shipment data for sales information. Management is especially interested in the reaction to a new convenience package that was introduced at the beginning of the cold season in December. By the end of January, the following information had been received from the accounting department:

Week Ending	Factory Shipments
December 28	12,700 cases
January 4	19,800 cases
January 11	18,200 cases
January 18	14,100 cases
January 25	11,050 cases

All the usual problems of interpreting time-series data are compounded in this example by the ambiguities in the data. The peak in factory shipments during the week ending January 4 represents a substantial amount of "pipeline filling," and an unknown amount of product sold for pipeline filling still remains on the shelves. Also unknown is competitive performance during this period: Did the new package gain sales at the expense of competition, or was there a loss of market share? Shipment data provide no diagnostic information, so these questions remain: How many retail stores used the special displays of the new product? Were competitors making similar or more effective offers? Was there a carryover of last year's stock in the old package? Without answers to these questions, the manager is in no position either to correct problems or continue the strong points of the campaign.

◆ RETAIL STORE AUDITS

Every two months a team of auditors from a research firm visits a sample of stores to count the inventory on hand and record deliveries to the store since the last visit.

Sales during the two-month period, for any desired classification of product category (including brands, sizes, package types, flavors, etc.), are computed as follows:

$$\text{Beginning inventory} + \text{Deliveries} - \text{Ending inventory} = \text{Sales for the period}$$

These **retail store audit** results are projected—to arrive at nationwide and regional estimates of total sales, inventories, and so forth—and reported to the client six to eight weeks after the end of the period. During each store visit, the auditor also may collect such observable information as shelf prices, display space, the presence of special displays, and in-store promotion activities.

A. C. Nielsen Co. and Audits and Surveys provide auditing services. Nielsen's auditing services cover four major reporting groups:

1. Grocery products
2. Drugs
3. Other merchandise
4. Alcoholic beverage

Audits and Surveys deals with products, regardless of the type of retail outlet carrying the product. The data provided by these two companies are incredibly rich. Table 5-4 summaries the information that is provided in the bimonthly report of Nielsen.

TABLE 5-4   Contents of a Nielsen Store Audit Report

Each of the following variables can be subdivided as follows:
  a   Sales districts
  b.   Size of country (A, B, C, or D)
  c.   Type of store (e.g., chain versus large-medium-small independents)
  d.   Thirty-two largest metropolitan markets

1. **Sales** (volume, trend, and share) on the basis of retail dollars and units, pounds or equivalent cases for total market, and major brands by sizes, flavors, types, etc., as appropriate to the category
2. **Distribution**
   a.   Percentage of all stores, and all commodity sales, carrying each brand, and size
   b.   Out-of-stock conditions
   c.   Retail inventories
   d.   Stock cover (the length of time the stocks will last, assuming current rates of sales)
   e.   Source of delivery (wholesaler, rack jobbers, manufacturer, chain warehouse, or interstore transfers)
3. **Selling prices** and volume sold at each price or deal
4. **Retailer support** in terms of shelf facings, special displays, in-store advertising, and newspaper advertising
5. **Media advertising** for total market and major brands
6. **Special analyses** (illustrative)
   a.   Analyses of combinations of brands stocked to determine the extent to which individual brands compete together
   b.   Cumulative distribution of new products

◆ CONSUMER PURCHASE PANELS

From store audits and warehouse withdrawal services, we can learn how much product is moving through the distribution channel. Because this information is one step removed from the actual purchase transaction, we still don't know who bought, how frequently they bought, or whether the seeming stability of market shares reflects stable purchasing patterns, or a great deal of switching back and forth between brands and stores in response to short-term promotional efforts. To answer these questions, we need detailed records of purchasing activity by the same people over an extended period of time. Here are two methods for collecting this data:

1. In the **home audit** approach, the panel member agrees to permit an auditor to check the household stocks of certain product categories at regular intervals. A secondary condition is that the panel member save all used cartons, wrappers, and so on, so the auditor can record them.

2. In the **mail diary** method, the panel member records the details of each purchase in certain categories and returns the completed diary by mail at regular intervals (biweekly or monthly).

Both types of panels are used extensively in Europe, whereas in the United States and Canada, the mail diary method is dominant. When comparisons have been possible, the two methods have produced equally accurate market share and trend data.[12]

Market Research Corporation of America (MRCA), National Family Opinion (NFO), and the National Purchase Diary Panel (NPD) all operated mail diary panels.

The National Purchase Diary Panel maintains the largest diary panel in the United States. More than 600,000 households record their monthly purchases in about 50 product categories. National Family Opinion also maintains special-purpose diary panels. For example, NFO has a baby panel consisting of 2,000 few mothers and 2,000 expecting mothers that provides quarterly information on baby-related products and services.

Advantages of Consumer Panels

*The biggest advantage of a **consumer panel** is the ability to measure changes in the behavior of individuals.*

The data from a **consumer panel** can be analyzed as a series of snapshots—providing information on aggregate sales activity, brand shares, and shifts in buyer characteristics and types of retail outlets from one month to the next. However, just as a motion picture is more revealing than a snapshot, the ability to measure changes in the behavior of individuals is the real advantage of a panel. Knowledge of the sequence of purchases makes it possible to analyze:

- Heavy buyers and their associated characteristics
- Brand-switching rates and the extent of loyal buying (Evidence of stable purchase activity in the aggregate usually masks a great deal of individual movement.)
- Cumulative market penetration and repeat purchase rates for new products (The success of new products depends jointly on the proportion who have tried them once and then purchased them a second, third, or fourth time.)

A **continuous purchase panel** is an excellent vehicle for conducting quasiexperiments. A change in price, advertising copy, or package can be implemented in one region, and the results can be compared with those of other regions where no change

Consumer panel interview.
Photo courtesy of 21st Sensory, Inc., Bartlesville, Oklahoma.

was made. Also, because of the lengthy relationship with members of continuous panels, there is much more opportunity to collect classification and attitudinal information to help understand the observed changes in behavior.

Compared with interview methods, although not with audits, the continuous purchase panel is more accurate. Several studies have found that interview respondents will exaggerate their rate of purchasing (an effect that is most pronounced for infrequently purchased products) and dramatically oversimplify brand-switching behavior. Apparently, survey respondents tend to equate their most recent brand buying behavior with their "normal" behavior—whether or not this is accurate.

Limitations of Consumer Panels

The limitations of consumer panels include **selection bias, mortality effect**, and **testing effects**.

The limitations all relate to the vulnerability of panels to various biases. The first problem encountered is **selection bias,** because of the high rates of refusal and the resulting lack of representativeness. It is estimated that panel recruitment rates may vary from 10 to 15 percent when the initial contact is made by mail in the United States, to 50 percent or more for personal contacts made on behalf of panels in Great Britain.

A related problem is **mortality effect,** which may mean a dropout rate in excess of 20 percent a year. Some of this is unavoidable, because it is attributable to moves and illness. To reduce both the refusal and mortality rates, all panels offer some incentive for continuing participation; these include direct money payments and stamp schemes in exchange for gifts.

There is little doubt that those who refuse or drop out, differ from those who participate and remain. In particular, those who are not interested in the topic are the most likely to drop out. These losses are replaced by new members with similar characteristics. This amounts to a matching procedure, but of course, it is not possible to match on all important characteristics. In a subsequent chapter we will examine the problem of refusals, which afflicts all forms of survey work. As a consequence, however, all panels underrepresent the very rich, the very poor, and the transitory.

Panels also are subject to a variety of **testing effects.** There is a definite tendency for new panel members to report unusual levels of purchasing because of the novelty of the reporting responsibility. This effect is so pronounced that the first month's results usually are discarded. Surprisingly, there is little evidence to suggest that there is any long-run conditioning behavior that would lead to great brand loyalty or price consciousness that would produce systematically biased data.

Finally, keep in mind that usually one person records the purchases. Whenever a product, such as cigarettes or toothpaste, is purchased by several members of the household, there is a good chance that some purchases will be missed. These products are also troublesome to analyze, for what appears to be brand switching simply may be the purchasing of different brands for (or by) different members of the household.

◆ SCANNER SERVICES AND SINGLE-SOURCE SYSTEMS

It is no understatement to say that standardized sources of marketing data for consumer goods are being revolutionized by the **universal product code (UPC)** scanner. By the end of 1992, 80 percent of the commodity value of groceries, 85 percent of the commodity value of mass merchandises, and 40 percent of the commodity value for drugs came through scanner-equipped retail stores.[13]

Within markets equipped with scanner checkouts, purchases are recorded by passing them over a laser scanner, which automatically reads the bar-coded description (the universal product code) printed on each package. This, in turn, activates the cash register, which relates the product code to its current price—held in computer memory—and calculates the amount due. All the pertinent **scanner data** on the purchase are then stored in the computer and can be accessed instantly for analysis. In addition to price, the memory stores information on coupon use, so marketers can quickly measure consumer response to using coupons across product categories. Information about shelf space, end-of-aisle displays, use of cooperative advertising, and the like can be retained on these scanners and then measured with respect to impact on sales, item movement, and net contribution.

As mentioned earlier, the effect of scanners is being felt in the conduct of retail audits, where in-person audits will soon be obsolete, and in the growth of single-source services that track the behavior of individual households, from the TV set to the checkout counter. In 1986, manufacturers spent about $10 million for these services; by 1987, it had grown to $50 million; and in 1991 they spent more than $200 million. By the end of 1999, this figure had grown to more than $700 million.

Scanner-Based Audit Services

The immediate benefits of **scanner data** are a high degree of accuracy, time savings and the ability to study very short time periods of sales activity.

The most immediate benefits of scanner data are a high degree of accuracy, time savings, and the ability to study very short time periods of sales activity. To appreciate these benefits, consider the introduction of a new food product into a test market monitored by a scanner-based audit service.

According to the standard bimonthly reports from the store audit service, there was steady progress in building the market share. During the second bimonthly period (see the graph), share more than doubled, as retailer advertising and coupon promotions were stepped up.

The results from the third period normally would not be available for six to eight weeks. With scanning data, however, weekly reports on this product were available within two to three weeks of the period's end. These weekly reports were also far more revealing, as we see from the data shown in Figure 5-4 for the same time period following the launch. The first 11 weeks followed a fairly typical new-brand cycle, with share by week 10 only half of the initial peak. Back-to-back price and coupon

Hand-held scanner.
Charles Gupton/Stock, Boston.

promotion in weeks 12 and 13 boosted shares to twice the introductory level. Shares then declined, until a further promotion in week 18. Fortunately, postpromotion shares were always higher than prepromotion shares through week 22. The sharp decline in week 23 was traced to a shortage of the most popular size of package, which was rectified during the next week.

Three scanner-based audit services provide nationally, or locally, representative results within two weeks of the end of the reporting period. Each service provides

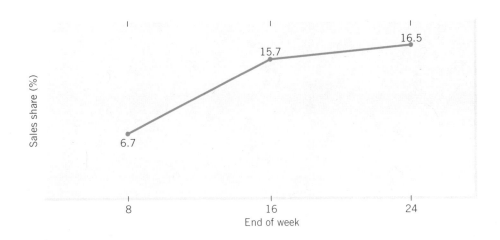

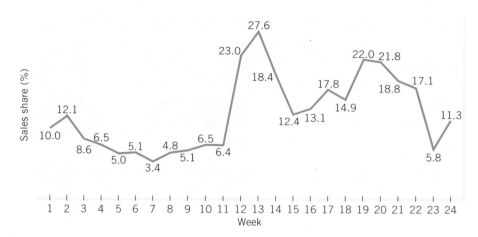

Figure 5-4   Weekly results from scanner service.

full detail on each UPC in a product category: product description, size, price, unit movement and unit share, and dollar sales and share, as well as availability in stores, shelf-space allocation, and coupon usage. These data can be made available in virtually any combination of stores, to look at sales by chain, geographic area, or even individual store.

Super SCANTRACK is A. C. Nielsen's new retail measurement service that integrates supercenter grocery information into the grocery channel. Consumer grocery-buying habits are changing. More and more shoppers are going to supercenters—stores that combine a full-line grocery store with a full-line mass-merchandiser store in the same building with the same checkout lanes. Previously, supercenters were classified within the mass merchandiser category. This classification created several issues, such as:

- Channel misalignment when comparing food-buying behavior
- No clear way to distinguish the environment between traditional "discount" mass stores and supercenter mass stores

Additionally, adding a grocery store to a mass merchandising store fundamentally changes that store due to the uniqueness of the grocery-shopping occasion. The fast growth of this store format and industry needs led to the development of A. C. Nielsen Super SCANTRACK.

Applying Scanner Data

Scanner data are used mainly to study the behavior of the consumer when different elements of the marketing mix are varied. They are also used to study and forecast the sales of a new product. For example, in 1991 Frito Lay, Pepsico's $4.2-billion-a-year snack-food division, tested its new multigrain snack called Sun Chips for 10 months in the Minneapolis area. The company experimented with 50 ridges and a salty, nutty flavor, and introduced the product on supermarket shelves. Using scanner data from consumer panels, the company discovered how many shoppers actually took home their first bag of Sun Chips in a given week and who went back a second and third time. This "depth of repeat" gives the company a much clearer sense of the product's potential.[14]

Even retailers are using scanner data. They not only purchase scanner data, they also conduct their own tests.[15] They conduct a number of experiments to analyze historical demand at various pricing levels and determine the prices at which they can maximize their total contribution.

Single-Source Systems

Single-source systems are usually set up in reasonably self-contained communities, with their own newspaper and cable TV, that are roughly representative of the country's demographics.[16]

After recruiting a test panel of community households, with small payments or coupons as inducements, the researcher monitors each home's TV sets and quizzes household members periodically on what newspapers and magazines they have read. This provides detailed records of exposure to programming and specific commercials.

Each panel member presents an identification card at a scanner-equipped grocery store each time a purchase is made. This card alerts the checkout terminal to send an item-by-item record of those purchases to a computer file. Then researchers can relate the details of a household's purchase of each product to previously collected classification information about the household and any promotional stimuli to which the household members were exposed.

These panel households can also be individually targeted for newspaper advertising, so a marketer can experiment with different combinations of advertising copy and/or exposure, discount coupons, and in-store price discounts and promotions. The effects of these different programs can be monitored unobtrusively in the supermarket, and each purchase can be compared with what the panel member had purchased before the test. To control for competitive activity, the service also tracks the amount of feature, display, and couponing activity in each supermarket.

Television advertising exposure also can be controlled through the cable system. For example, it is possible to transmit a Duncan Hines cake mix commercial only to Betty Crocker customers to find out if they can be induced to switch. The process of collecting data and providing it to manufacturers and retailers is shown in Figure 5-5.

A typical application of single-source systems is an experiment by the Campbell's Soup Company. Using an index of 100 for the average household's V8 consumption, Campbell's found that demographically similar TV audiences were consuming vastly different quantities of V8. In early 1987, for example, *General Hospital* audiences had a below-average 80 index, while *Guiding Light* audiences had an above-average 120 index. The results were surprising because *General Hospital* had a slightly higher representation of 25- to 54-year-old women, who were known from other research to be heavier buyers of V8. With this sort of information at hand, it becomes possible to rearrange media schedules to raise the average index.[17]

The advantages of single-source data for this kind of market response study—compared with conventional market tests—are (1) availability of extensive pretest records, (2) immediate availability of test results, and (3) ability to compare the purchases of households receiving a specific ad during the test with their own purchases prior to the test, as well as with purchases of those who were not exposed to the new product ad.

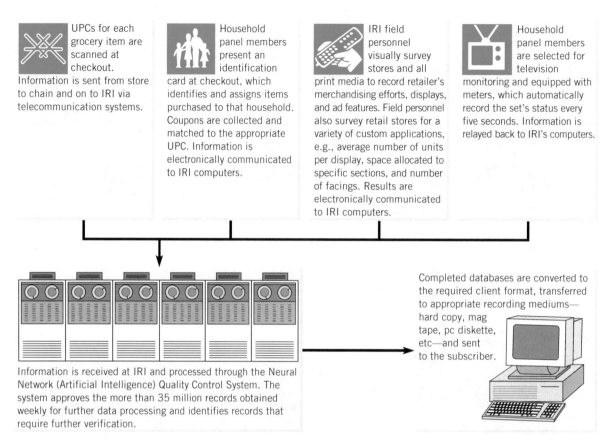

UPCs for each grocery item are scanned at checkout. Information is sent from store to chain and on to IRI via telecommunication systems.

Household panel members present an identification card at checkout, which identifies and assigns items purchased to that household. Coupons are collected and matched to the appropriate UPC. Information is electronically communicated to IRI computers.

IRI field personnel visually survey stores and all print media to record retailer's merchandising efforts, displays, and ad features. Field personnel also survey retail stores for a variety of custom applications, e.g., average number of units per display, space allocated to specific sections, and number of facings. Results are electronically communicated to IRI computers.

Household panel members are selected for television monitoring and equipped with meters, which automatically record the set's status every five seconds. Information is relayed back to IRI's computers.

Information is received at IRI and processed through the Neural Network (Artificial Intelligence) Quality Control System. The system approves the more than 35 million records obtained weekly for further data processing and identifies records that require further verification.

Completed databases are converted to the required client format, transferred to appropriate recording mediums—hard copy, mag tape, pc diskette, etc—and sent to the subscriber.

Figure 5-5   The process of scanner data collection by IRI.

Source: Information Resources, Inc.

The disadvantage is that single-source systems can track purchases only at grocery stores and drugstores that are equipped with scanners. Furthermore, the test services do not know whether viewers actually are watching a television commercial when it is on, or whether they leave the room during the commercial break. Test participants who are paid volunteers might also unconsciously bias the results, because they know they are sending a message to advertisers. An unresolved question is whether tests conducted in small, self-contained markets can predict nationwide results. Finally, there are significant differences in results among competing single-source services that raise questions about the quality of the findings.

Comparing Single-Source Services

One of the most advanced services is BehaviorScan, by Information Resources, Inc. (IRI).[18] It has 3,000 households wired in each of various minimarkets across the United States, from Pittsfield, Massachusetts, to Visalia, California. BehaviorScan, an electronic test marketing service, allows marketers to test new products or new marketing programs. BehaviorScan targets TV commercials in a controlled environment to specific households and tracks the effectiveness of those ads in six smaller markets. It pioneered the service and has had the most experience in conducting tests. IRI's system uses the identification card described earlier, so that details of transactions can be recorded, by household, upon presentation of the card to cashiers at participating stores. IRI also has another product called InfoScan. InfoScan is a syndicated market tracking service that provides weekly sales, price, and store-condition information on products sold in a sample of 19,800 food, drug, and mass-merchandise stores. The InfoScan service also includes a national sample of 125,000 households, whose purchases are recorded by checkout or hand-held scanners. BehaviorScan provides data about different markets, whereas InfoScan provides data on different products. Retail sales, detailed consumer purchasing information, and promotional activity are monitored and evaluated for all UPC products.

For several years A. C. Nielsen had been testing a single-source service—Consumer Panel Services—and had 15,000 homes by 1989. By 2000, Nielsen would have increased its panel size to 125,000 households. Nielsen, along with another new entrant, Scan America (a joint venture of Control Data and Selling Areas Marketing, Inc., a subsidiary of Time, Inc.), offers a very different technology. Unlike BehaviorScan participants, Nielsen families record their purchases at home by passing a penlike wand over goods bearing bar codes, keying in other information about coupons at the same time. The information is transmitted daily through a device attached to participants' television sets. Because Nielsen's system is not dependent on retailers who cooperate, it allows tracking of purchases from a wider range of stores, but it has been criticized for requiring that participants be actively involved in entering the data. Another important difference is that Nielsen can send test commercials over the air, so members of the sample do not have to be cable subscribers.[19]

Retail Measurement Services provides product movements data through food, drug, and other retail outlets in 79 countries. Flagship service is U.S.-based Scan Track, which provides weekly data on packaged-goods sales, market shares, and retail prices from 4,800 UPC scanner-equipped supermarkets. Another service, Precision, tracks health and beauty aids product sales through 7,800 drug and mass merchandiser stores. In other countries, either scanning or audit-based methods are used to collect retail data. Marketing Research in Practice 5-3 provides an illustration of the gain in power by retailers when acquiring information.

Expert Systems Based on Single-Source Services

The rapid increase in the use of scanner technology has brought a peculiar problem to the marketing analyst. Although about a decade ago researchers were struggling to obtain data to conduct research, they now are faced with exactly the opposite problem. Users of scanner data have been overwhelmed with the data. Therefore, suppliers of scanner data have created expert systems to give the data more utility for the managers. These expert systems are designed to cut the mass of scanner data down to actionable pieces of information. There are many expert systems that give solutions to specific problems. Both IRI and A. C. Nielsen have developed expert systems to make the decision process easier. A partial list is provided here.

Information Resources, Inc.[20]

- **Apollo Space Management Software** provides suggestions for optimizing shelf allocations for each item in the section of a retail store. It analyzes scanner data from the InfoScan database to review the amount of shelf space, price, and profit components of product category shelf sets, such as dishwashing soaps or cereals. Apollo can also produce photo-quality schematics using its library of 120,000 product images and dimensions. Thus, the retailer gets a visual picture of what the shelf reallocation will look like.

MARKETING RESEARCH IN PRACTICE 5-3

"Goodbye" to Total Market Audits: Hello to Problems

By withdrawing its scanning data from the Nielson Retail Index, Safeway has not just dealt a potentially fatal blow to the market researcher's retail audits. It has also triggered a train of events that could alter the entire shape of the market for information on consumer spending. The move was due to a disagreement on the value of information that Nielsen pays to include Safeway in its audits.

Leaving Nielsen's retail audit business crippled, Safeway introduced its own information management company that sells data from its 365 outlets directly to suppliers. Nielsen's changed price policy has led other retailers to consider following Safeway's strategy and therefore avoid negotiating price. This potential move could spell the end for syndicated data, and mark the "birth of a new data revolution." Furthermore, as more retailers gain control over the release of data, the use of scanning data by manufacturers might turn to abuse. Before, the focus was on marketing, research, and long-range planning, but will now be needed for streetfighting, defending against delisting, and negotiating.

If Sainsbury's, a UK-based big grocery chain, joins Safeway and other big chains (non-Nielsen Collaborators), nearly half the market will be closed to brand marketers. Manufacturers are facing the challenge of acquiring information from scratch due to the high price retailers tack on their own data, especially the deep dependency manufacturers had on Nielsen for consumer information. One alternative is to increase the volume of consumer panels with existence data that they would own.

The growing tension between manufacturers and retailers has given rise to "pack mentalities" for both retailers carving out their own information business and manufacturers, hunting for information, and protecting their own self-interests.

Source: Alan Mitchell and David Benady, "Retailers Push Data into a New Ice Age," *Marketing Week* (January 12, 1996): 20–21.

- **CoverStory** provides a cover memo, like the one a marketing researcher would write, to describe the key events reflected in a database. The system locates the important "news" and writes a memo for managers, complete with charts, tables, and graphs.
- **Sales Partner** is designed to help manufacturers sell to retailers, by using the retailers' own scanner data. It sorts through the data to provide the most convincing arguments a sales representative can direct to the retailer.

A. C. Nielsen[21]

- **Promotion Simulator** is an easy-to-use software application that automatically simulates future promotion strategies. It uses historical Nielsen data to calculate the effect of the promotional plans on manufacturer and retailer profitability, given the price points and retail conditions in the plan.
- **Spotlight** is an expert system that runs through the database, calculating volume and share changes and searching for the key merchandising and competitive factors that influence those factors. Then it summarizes the findings in a presentation-quality report.
- **Sales Advisor** automatically highlights need-to-know information and enables the sales force to add personal insights to presentation-quality output. Sales

Shelf spacing in a retail store.
Chuck Keeler/Stone

Advisor produces finished summaries and presentations of sales and marketing data.

◆ MEDIA-RELATED STANDARDIZED SOURCES

Another area in which there is a great deal of commercial information available for marketers relates to advertising and media. A number of services have evolved to measure consumer exposure to the various media and advertisements. A few of them are described here.

Nielsen Television Index (NTI)

The **Nielsen Television Index (NTI)** is probably the best known of all the commercial services available in this category. As a system for estimating national television audiences, NTI produces a "rating" and corresponding share estimate. A **rating** is the percent of all households that have at least one television set tuned to a program for at least 6 minutes of every 15 minutes that the program is telecast. **Share** is the percent of households that have a television set tuned to a specific program at a specific time.

The **people meter** which is attached to the television set, continuously monitors and records television viewing in terms of when the set was turned on what channels were viewed how long the channels were tuned in and who in the household was watching that channel.

From 1987 onward, Nielsen has been using "people meters" instead of the traditional diary to obtain this information. The **people meter,** which is attached to the television set, continuously monitors and records television viewing in terms of when the set was turned on, what channels were viewed, and how long the channels were tuned in.[22] The data are stored in the people meter and later are transmitted via telephone lines to a central processing facility.

Nielsen National Television Index (NTI) is based on a national 5,000-household sample equipped with people meters, and reporting TV, cable, and home video viewing. At the market level, Nielsen Media Research (NMR) provides Nielsen Station Index (NSI), which uses set meters to measure TV audiences through weekly mail diary surveys in 211 local markets among 100,000-plus households. Nielsen Home video Index (NHI) measures cable and VCR audiences using a combination of NTI, NSI, and custom diaries. Data on syndicated programs in the Nielsen Syndication Service (NSS) come from the same sources. Two services, through people meters, measure Hispanic audiences for Spanish-language media across the United States (800 households) and in the Los Angeles market (200 households).

The Nielsen NTI-NAD data are used by media planners to analyze alternative network programs. Next, the cost efficiency of each program is calculated. Cost efficiency represents a television program's ability to deliver the largest target audience at the smallest cost. A cost per thousand (CPM) calculation is computed as

$$\frac{\text{Cost of a commercial}}{\text{Number of target audience delivered}} = \text{CPM}$$

Arbitron Diary Panel

There has been a lot of recent controversy over Nielsen television ratings. The networks claim that since Nielsen became a monopoly—all the other rivals dropped

A. C. Nielsen's people meter.
Courtesy Nielsen Media Research.

out—service has been unprofessional. The networks also have problems with Nielsen's sampling methodology. The networks charged that Nielsen bases its ratings on too few diaries, making its data less representative of what viewers watch. In response to this, Nielsen decided to send out 10 percent more paper diaries for viewers to note what they watch. By October 1998 the number of diaries had increased by 50 percent, which Nielsen claims is the largest increase in sample size in the history of TV audience measurement.

Arbitron, a subsidiary of Control Data, maintains both national and regional radio and TV panels. The panel members are chosen by randomly generated telephone numbers, to ensure that households with unlisted numbers are reached. Those household members who agree to participate when called are sent diaries in which they are asked to record their radio listening behavior over a short duration. Most radio markets are rated only once or twice a year; however, some larger ones are rated four times a year. The TV diary panel is supplemented with a sample of households that have agreed to attach an electronic meter to their television sets. Arbitron produces custom reports for clients. Typically, these are based on an interactive computer-based system called Arbitron Information on Demand (AID).

Starch Scores

The previous two sources of marketing data involve radio and television ratings, whereas **Starch scores** cover print media. The Starch Readership Service measures the readership of advertisements in magazines and newspapers.[23] Some 75,000 advertisements in 1,000 issues of consumer and farm magazines, business publications, and newspapers are assessed each year, using 100,000 personal interviews.

The Starch surveys employ the **recognition method** to assess a particular ad's effectiveness. Four degrees of reading are recorded:

1. *Nonreader:* A person who does not remember having seen the advertisement in the issue

2. *Noted:* A person who remembers seeing the advertisement in the issue

3. *Associated:* A person who not only "noted" the advertisement, but who also saw or read some part of it that clearly indicated the brand or advertiser

4. *Read Most:* A person who read 50 percent or more of the written material in the ad

Because newspaper and magazine space cost data are also available, a "readers per dollar" variable can be calculated. The final summary report from Starch shows each ad's (one-half page or larger) overall readership percentages, readers per dollar, and rank when grouped by product category.

Multimedia Services

Multimedia services are research services conducted in multiple media, such as television, print, and radio. Simmons Media/Marketing Services uses a national probability sample of some 19,000 respondents and serves as a comprehensive data source, allowing the cross-referencing of product usage and media exposure. Four different interviews are conducted with each respondent, so that magazine, television, newspaper, and radio can all be covered by the Simmons Services. Information is reported for total adults and also for males and females separately.

Media-mark Research also makes available information on exposure to various media and on household consumption of various products and services. Its annual survey of 20,000 adult respondents covers more than 250 magazines, newspapers, radio stations, and television channels, and more than 450 products and services.

◆ APPLICATIONS OF STANDARDIZED SOURCES OF DATA

Standardized data sources are used widely in a number of marketing research problems. We have already discussed the various sources of standardized data. In this section we will look at some of the applications of standardized data. Table 5-5 gives a comprehensive framework of the types of sources used for different applications.

Measuring Product Sales and Market Share

A critical need in today's increasingly competitive environment is for firms to have an accurate assessment of their performance. Marketing performance typically is measured by the company's sales and market share. Firms can track their own sales through analyses of their sales invoices. An alternative source that can be used is the on-line bibliographic data source. The measurement of sales to final customers historically has been done by the use of diary panels and retail store audits. Scanner data is now being widely used for this purpose.[24]

Measuring Advertisement Exposure and Effectiveness

With media costs rising exponentially, and the options for advertising increasing dramatically with the advent of cable television, measurement of advertising exposure and effectiveness and program ratings has become critical. Advertising exposure and effectiveness in the print media are tested by Starch scores[25] and in the audiovisual media by Nielsen Television Services and Arbitron. Ratings of the various network and cable programs can be found in the Nielsen Television Index, and those of the radio programs in the Arbitron panels. Multimedia services such as the Simmons Media/Marketing Services and Media-mark Research conduct research on overall media exposure and effectiveness. Scanner data also have been used extensively for modeling ad exposure and measuring ad effectiveness.[26]

Table 5-5 Applications of Standardized Data Sources

Measuring Promotion Effectiveness	Measuring Ad Exposure and Effectiveness
1. Scanner data	1. Starch scores
2. Diary panels	2. NTI
	3. Arbitron
	4. Multimedia services
Measuring Product Sales and Market Share	**Estimation and Evaluation of Models**
1. Diary panels	1. Scanner data
2. Retail audits	2. Starch scores
3. Scanner data	3. Diary panels
4. Internal records	4. Internal records
5. SIC	

Measuring Promotion Effectiveness

Only since the advent of scanner data have marketers begun to fathom the power of promotion in increasing product sales and market share. This is evident from the fact that the number of coupons, samples, displays, and features at the retail outlets have increased tremendously over the past few years. Before scanner data was introduced in a big way, promotion effectiveness was measured by diary panels of the NPD group. Since store-level scanner data and scanner panels were introduced by IRI and Nielsen, measurement of promotion effectiveness has been revolutionized. The effect of promotions now can be observed directly through scanner data.[27,28]

Estimation and Evaluation of Models

Models are essentially explanations of complex phenomena, expressed by symbols. They can be mathematical, verbal, graphical, or a figure. Marketing researchers build models to explain the various marketing phenomena and to draw managerial implications from them. The models can either be at the aggregate level or at the individual level. Scanner data are used to evaluate the efficacy of the model and estimate the response of the market to changes in the marketing-mix elements.[28] Standard industrial classifications (SICs) and diary panels are used for this purpose.

END OF CHAPTER MATERIAL

SUMMARY

The theme of this chapter is the wealth of published data available to marketing researchers. Many management problems can be resolved by recourse to the firm's internal records or to secondary sources such as government statistics, trade association reports, periodicals, books, and private studies. With the growing power of computers, these data are increasingly easy to access in databases. The low cost and convenience of these database sources leave no excuse for not starting a marketing research study with a thorough scan of what is already available. Invariably, the researcher will be surprised at the extent of what is already available without any effort. Even if it is not entirely suitable, the secondary data sources can provide useful pointers on how to design a good research study.

Between the generally available secondary sources (which are economical and quickly found but perhaps not relevant) and primary data (which are designed to be directly relevant but consume considerable time and money), there are various standardized information services. These exist whenever there are economies of scale in collecting data for a number of users with similar information needs. The most widely used services are still retail store audits and consumer panels. With recent developments in information technology, and especially the widespread adoption of store checkout scanners, the use of these services is quickly shifting to scanner audits. New capabilities for understanding consumer response by integrating measures of purchase behavior and communications exposure in single-source data are also changing the conduct of research very rapidly.

The remainder of this book will emphasize the collection and analysis of primary data, for it is here that the greatest problems and opportunities are found. Knowledge of the methods of primary data collection is also essential to informed usage of secondary sources.

Video Segment:

Catalina

Coupon generation based on consumer purchases forms the focus of this company. Using the scanner system installed in most check-out counters, this monitors the consumer buying patterns for certain categories. The problem with this system, however, has been the privacy issue, with customers showing discomfort with scanners collecting and collating information on products that they consider personal. The fact that this company is at the heart of the micromarketing movement suggests that scanner data applications are entering the dimension of effective database management.

KEY TERMS

secondary data sources
standardized data
primary data
internal records
published data sources
general guides and indices
compilations
directories
computer-retrievable databases
reference databases
bibliographic databases
source databases
on-line databases
CD-ROM databases
floppy-disk databases
census data
economic censuses
censuses of population and housing
city block
block groups
census tracts
metropolitan statistical areas
standard metropolitan statistical areas
consolidated metropolitan statistical areas
North American Industrial Classification
   System

demand estimation
monitoring the environment
segmentation
geocoding
potential rating index zip markets
business intelligence system
data accuracy
data comparability
single-source data
universal product code
retail store audit
Nielsen Television Index
home audit
rating estimate
mail dairy
share estimate
continuous purchase panel
people meter
selection bias
arbitron diary panel
mortality effect
starch scores
testing effects
recognition method
scanner data
multimedia services

MARKETING RESEARCH TOOLBOX
REVIEW POINTS

1. Secondary data are data that were collected by persons or agencies for purposes other than solving the problem at hand.

2. The most significant benefits secondary data offer a researcher are savings in cost and time.

3. The limitations of secondary data are: problems of fit, lack of knowledge of how the data was initially collected, and the data may be outdated.

4. A company's internal records: accounting and control systems provide the most basic data on marketing inputs and the resulting outcomes.

5. Two major external sources of secondary data are published data sources and computer-retrievable data sources.

6. The various tools that help in finding published sources of secondary data are talking to experts, general guides and indices, and compilations and directories.

7. Based on the content of information, computer-retrievable databases are classified as reference databases and source databases.

8. Computer-retrievable databases are classified based on storage and retrieval methods as on-line databases, CD-ROM databases, and floppy-disk databases.

9. On-line databases are accessible both from their producers and increasingly from on-line information services.

10. The main advantages of computer-retrievable methods are scope of information available on databases, speed of information access, and considerable flexibility and efficiency in cross-referenced searching.

11. The main limitations of the reference databases are their reliance on the accuracy of the abstract author, the dependence of the journal and article selection policy of the database producer, and the idiosyncrasies of the search procedures of the different databases.

12. Census data can be obtained at many levels of aggregation: city block, block groups, census tracts, and metropolitan statistical areas (MSAs).

13. The key to obtaining census data in the industrial and services market is the North American Industrial Classification System (NAICS). This is a uniform numbering system for classifying establishments according to their activities.

14. The Potential Rating Index Zip Markets (PRIZM) system is based on evidence that people with similar cultural backgrounds and circumstances will gravitate naturally toward one another.

15. Before secondary data are used for research, the researcher should have answers to *who* provided the data, *why* the data were collected, *how* the data were collected, *what* is in the data, *when* the data was collected, and the *consistency* of the data when compared with other data sources.

16. The applications of secondary data include demand estimation, monitoring the environment, segmentation and targeting, and developing a business information system.

17. The major problems associated with secondary data in international research are data accuracy and comparability of data.

18. Secondary data are particularly useful in evaluating country or market environments, whether in making initial market entry decisions or in attempting to assess future trends and developments, screen market potential, risks, and likely costs of operating in different countries, and to monitor environmental changes in an international context.

19. Retail store audits calculate sales over a period as follows:

Beginning inventory + Deliveries – Ending inventory = Sales for the period

20. Consumer purchase panels are recorded using home audits and mail diaries.

21. In the home audit approach the panel member agrees to permit an auditor to check the household stocks of certain product categories at regular intervals. A secondary condition is that the panel members save all used cartons, wrappers, and so on, so that the auditor can record them.

22. In the mail diary method, the panel member records the details of each purchase in certain categories and returns the completed diary by mail at regular intervals.

23. The biggest advantage of a panel is the ability to measure changes in the behavior of individuals.

24. The limitations of consumer panels include selection bias, mortality effect, and testing effects.

25. The immediate benefits of scanner data are a high degree of accuracy, time savings, and the ability to study very short time periods of sales activity.

26. Scanner data are used mainly to study the behavior of the consumer when different elements of the marketing mix are varied.

27. The advantages of single-source systems are availability of extensive pretest records, immediate availability of test results, and ability to compare the purchases prior to the test as well as with purchases of those who were not exposed to the new product advertisement.

28. Expert systems are designed to cut the mass of scanner data down to actionable pieces of information.

29. The Nielson Television Index (NTI) is a system for estimating national television audiences. NTI produces a rating and a corresponding share estimate.

30. The Starch surveys employ the recognition method to assess a particular advertisement's effectiveness. Four degrees of reading are noted: nonreader, noted, associated, and read most.

31. Applications of standardized sources of data include measuring product sales and market share, measuring advertising exposure and effectiveness, measuring promotion effectiveness, and estimation and evaluation of models.

QUESTIONS AND PROBLEMS

1. You are opening a new retail store that will sell personal computers and software. What secondary data are available in your area to help you decide where to locate the store? Would the same data be relevant to someone opening a convenience copying center?

2. A large chain of building supply yards was aiming to grow at a rate of three new yards per year. From past experience, this meant carefully reviewing as many as 20 or 30 possible locations. You have been assigned the task of making this process more systematic. The first step is to specify the types of secondary information that should be available for the market area of each location. The second step is to identify the possible sources of this information and appraise their usefulness. From studies of the patrons of the present yards, you know that 60 percent of the dollar volume is accounted for by building contractors and tradesmen. The rest of the volume is sold to farmers, householders, and hobbyists. However, the sales to do-it-yourselfers have been noticeably increasing. About 75 percent of the sales were lumber and building materials, although appliances, garden supplies, and home entertainment systems are expected to grow in importance.

3. For each of the following products, which industry associations would you contact for secondary data? (a) foreign convenience dinners, (b) numerically controlled machine tools, (c) irrigation pipe, (d) imported wine, (e) compact disc players, and (f) children's shoes.

4. Obtain data on beer consumption in your state or province for the latest available year. Calculate the per-capita consumption for this area and compare it with that for the country as a whole. What accounts for the difference?

5. Educational Edge, a small company with limited resources, is interested in segmenting potential markets for its erasable transparencies.
   a. Which type of data would be best suited to obtain the required information?
   b. What are the possible sources of information to aid in the segmentation decision?
   c. What are the benefits and limitations of using secondary data for this purpose?

6. Howard Enterprises, a small family-owned manufacturer of unique lamps, has begun to receive unsolicited inquiries about its product from foreign countries. The company has been operating exclusively in the domestic environment, but these inquiries have become numerous enough to suggest that a market for these specialty lamps may exist abroad. J. P. Howard, the company head, decided to contact Peter Franks, an old college friend of his, who is now the head of marketing research for a multinational company, to ask for his advice on how to proceed in evaluating foreign country markets. Mr. Franks recommends that Howard Enterprises should select countries that merit in-depth investigation and proceed to make an initial estimate of the demand potential in these countries.
   a. Considering the limited resources that are available to Mr. Howard's company, explain how secondary data can be used to help Mr. Howard follow his friend's recommendation.
   b. What are the possible limitations of secondary data of which Mr. Howard must be aware when conducting the marketing research?

7. From secondary data sources, obtain sales for an entire industry and the sales of the major firms in that industry for any year. Compute the market shares of each major firm. Using another source, obtain information on the market shares of these same firms. Are there differences? If so, why?

8. Which of these two, a product audit (such as the Audits and Surveys National Market Audit) or a store audit (such as the Nielsen Retail index), would be more suitable for the following products: (a) peanut butter; (b) cameras; (c) engine oil additives; (d) chewing gum. Why?

9. The manager of a supermarket in Hoboken, New Jersey, has two local newspapers competing for weekly ads. The salesperson for newspaper A claims that although A's rates are significantly higher than newspaper B's, paper A has the best circulation in the market. Also, readership studies show that area residents really scrutinize the paper's pages. The salesperson for newspaper B concedes that the publication does not have the widest circulation, but points to readership studies showing that its ads are equally effective. "Why pay twice as much for an ad, when my paper can do as strong a job for less money?" This problem has been unresolved for some time. Recently, the store had nine scanner checkouts installed. The manager would like your advice on how to use the store's scanner sales data to compare the effectiveness of the two newspapers.

10. What combination of standardized services would you use to monitor the effects of your existing cereal brands when a new cereal brand is being introduced? Why? Would you use the different services to monitor trial and repeat purchases of the new cereal product in a test market?

11. Campbell's Soup used BehaviorScan data to discover that viewers of two daytime serials had very good appetites. *Search for Tomorrow* viewers bought 27 percent more spaghetti sauce than average, but 22 percent less V8 vegetable juice. Viewers of *All My Children* bought 10 percent less spaghetti sauce than average, but purchased 46 percent more V8 than the norm for all viewers. How would you go about explaining the differences between these two programs that led to the consumption differences? What action would you recommend to the Campbell's Soup management? Would concepts of different targeted markets be one of the areas to discuss? What would be the next strategy to be adopted?

12. Wash O'Well, a leading detergent company in Canada, is unable to explain the reason why its new zeolite-based detergent has not captured the anticipated market share since its launch in Minneapolis, Minnesota, in 1992. The company has decided to focus on point-of-sale activities: for example, which brands have distribution in which stores, what shelf location each brand occupies, the kinds of displays in effect, and so forth. The marketing manager has been instructed to recommend a suitable source of standardized data.
   a. What are the various data source alternatives available to Wash O'Well?
   b. Discuss the advantages and limitations of each of them and recommend the data source most suitable for Wash O'Well's needs.

13. a. What are the two types of consumer panels used for gathering marketing research data?
    b. Which type of panel is most frequently used in the United States?
    c. What are the advantages and disadvantages of using a consumer panel?
    d. What do you think are some of the precautionary measures you would take when using consumer panels? Do you think they would be an effective means of reflecting purchase behavior?

ENDNOTES

1. Ellen R. Kidd, "Establishing Quality Focus in a Multi-Cultural Organization," presented at the *Third Congress on Competitive Strategies.*

2. Paula A. Francese and Leo M. Renaghan, "Finding the Customer," *American Demographics* (January 1991), pp. 48–51.

3. More extensive discussion of data sources and how to locate them can be found in Lorna Daniels, *Business Information Sources* (Berkeley, CA: University of California Press, 1985); Lorna Daniels, "Notes on Sources of External Marketing Data," in B. Shapiro, R. Dolan, and J. Quelch (eds.), *Marketing Management Vol. II* (Homewood, IL: Richard D. Irwin, 1985), Appendix; Barbara E. Brown, *Canadian Business and Economics: A Guide to Sources of Information* (Ottawa: Canadian Library Association, 1984); and Leonard M. Fuld, *Competitor Intelligence* (New York: Wiley, 1985).

4. A comprehensive listing of these associations can be found in the *Encyclopedia of Associations* (Detroit: National Gale Research Co., 1984); and in Leonard M. Fuld, *Competitor Intelligence* (New York: Wiley, 1985).

5. For more information, see Jennifer Langlois, *CD-ROM 1992: An Annotated Bibliography of Resources* (Westport, CT: Meckler, 1992).

6. An interesting compilation of reasons why a database search might not meet with success is provided in Jeff Pemberton, "Faults and Failures—25 Ways that Online Searching Can Let You Down," *Online* (September 1983).

7. http://www.census.gov/epcd/www/naics.html.

8. Christina Del Valle, "They Know Where You Live—And How You Buy," *Business Week* (February 7, 1994).

9. For a more detailed discussion, see Susan P. Douglas and C. Samuel Craig, *International Marketing Research* (Englewood Cliffs, NJ: Prentice-Hall, 1983).

10. Canadian Academic Marketing Page—School of Library and Information Science, University of Alberta, March 27, 1995 (http://gpu2.srv.ualberta.ca/~slis/guides/market/guide.htm).

11. V. Kumar, A. Stam, and E. A. Joachimsthaler, "An Interactive Multicriteria Approach to Identifying Potential Foreign Markets," *Journal of International Marketing,* 2, 1 (1994), p. 29–52.

12. Seymour Sudman and Robert Ferber, *Consumer Panels* (Chicago: American Marketing Association, 1979).

13. Source: A. C. Nielsen; http://acnielsen.com/products/reports/scantrack/.

14. Susan Caminiti, "What the Scanner Knows about You," *Fortune* (December 3, 1990).

15. James Sinkula, "Status of Company Usage of Scanner-based Research," *Journal of the Academy of Marketing Science* (Spring 1986, p. 17).

16. The following articles give a good overview of the single-source systems: David Curry, "Single Source Systems: Retail Management Present and Future," *Journal of Retailing* (Spring 1989), pp. 1–20; Melvin Prince, "Some Uses and Abuses of Single-Source Data for Promotional Decision Making," *Marketing Research* (December 1989), pp. 18–22; "Futuristic Weaponary," *Advertising Age* (June 11, 1990), pp. 5–12.

17. Joanne Lipman, "Single Source Ad Research Heralds Detailed Look at Household Habits," *Wall Street Journal* (February 16, 1988), p. 35.

18. The information on BehaviorScan is drawn from a pamphlet from Information Resources Incorporated.

19. A good article that compares the two single-source suppliers is Leon Winters, "Home Scan vs. Store Scan Panels: Single Source Options for the 1990s," *Marketing Research* (December 1989), pp. 61–65. Also see "Now It's Down to Two Equal Competitors," *Superbrands 1991: A Supplement to Adweek's Marketing Week*, p. 28; and "IRI, Nielsen Slug it Out in Scanning Wars," *Marketing News* (September 2, 1991), p. 1.

20. Source: Information Resources Incorporated.

21. Source: A. C. Nielsen.

22. William R. Dillon, Thomas J. Madden, and Neil H. Firtle, *Marketing Research in a Marketing Environment* (Boston: Irwin, 1990); and Soong Roland, "The Statistical Reliability of People Meter Readings," *Journal of Advertising Research* (February–March 1988), pp. 50–56.

23. *Starch Readership Report: Scope, Method and Use* (Mamaroneck, NY: Starch INRA Hooper, undated).

24. V. Kumar, and T. Heath, "A Comparative Study of Market Share Models Using Disaggregate Data," *International Journal of Forecasting* (July 1990), pp. 163–174; Francis J. Mulhern and Robert P. Leone, "Implicit Price Bundling of Retail Products: A Multiproduct Approach to Maximizing Store Profitability," *Journal of Marketing* (October 1991), pp. 63–76.

25. George M. Zinkhan and Betsy D. Gelb, "What Starch Scores Predict," *Journal of Advertising Research* (August–September 1986), pp. 45–50.

26. Gerald J. Tellis, "Advertising Exposure, Loyalty, and Brand Purchase: A Two-State Model of Choice," *Journal of Marketing Research* (May 1988), pp. 134–144; V. Kumar and R. T. Rust, "Market Segmentation by Visual Inspection," *Journal of Advertising Research* (1989), pp. 23–29.

27. Sunil Gupta, "Impact of Sales Promotions on When, What, and How Much to Buy," *Journal of Marketing Research* (November 1988), pp. 342–355; V. Kumar and R. Leone, "Measuring the Effect of Retail Store Promotions on Brand and Store Substitution," *Journal of Marketing Research* (May 1988), pp. 178–185; Robert C. Blattberg and Scott A. Neslin, *Sales Promotion: Concepts, Methods, and Strategies* (Englewood Cliffs, NJ: Prentice Hall, 1990).

28. V. Kumar, A. Ghosh, and G. Tellis, "A Decomposition of Repeat Buying," Marketing Letters, 3, 4 (1992), pp. 407–417; Peters S. Fader, James M. Lattin, and John D. C. Little, "Estimating Nonlinear Parameters in the Multinomial Logit Model," *Marketing Science* (Fall 1992), pp. 372–385.

CASES

For detailed descriptions of the following cases please visit www.wiley.com/college/kumar.

Case 5-1: Barkley Foods
Case 5-2: Kerry Gold Products, Ltd.

Marketing Research on the Internet[1]

Learning Objectives

- Give a brief overview of the past and current developments of the Internet.
- Describe the components of the Internet.
- Illustrate current commercial research applications.
- Demonstrate the current use of the Internet as a marketing research tool.
- Provide an outlook of future developments.

Companies are selling cars (www.kbb.com), groceries (www.peapod.com), and just about everything else on-line. It is fast and easy. And we don't have to sully our hands with cash, or rub elbows at the mall. At the start of the new century, 55 million of us are shopping to our hearts' content at home. Internet commerce is expected to soar to $64 billion by 2003. Projected at $336 billion as of June 2000, the value of goods and services traded between companies on-line is expected to reach $6 trillion by 2005. According to estimates, the market for products sold through on-line services has grown from about $518 million in 1996 to more than $6.6 billion by 2000.[2] A breakdown of projected on-line revenues for various products is given in Table 6-1. The fourth quarter of 2000 saw close to $1 billion in purchases of new brand names that were able to electronically reach their consumers. This has brought the overall purchasing level for 1997 to nearly $2 billion. According to the research conducted by Forrester Research Inc., consumers will be spending close to $64 billion for products and services on the Web by 2003.[3]

About 50 percent of U.S. homes have personal computers and almost all have modems, but four trends indicate that this will increase in the near future. First, the prices of personal computers are decreasing and will continue to drop. Additionally, a modem is a basic component of any new system sold today. Second, although current home connections to the Internet are slow, the technology in this area is changing rapidly. Cable TV companies are offering cable modems, which provide very-high speed connections to the Internet. Further, local telephone companies are beginning to market DSL (Digital Subscriber Line) services to homes and businesses, which also offer higher-speed connections compared to modems. Third, some companies are spending large sums of money on T1 and T3 dedicated lines that are projected to

TABLE 6-1   Projected On-line Shopping Revenues (in millions)

	2000	2001	2002
Travel (air, hotel, car)	$4,590	$6,301	$8,606
PC hardware & consumer electronics	$4,290	$5,959	$8,219
Grocery	$1,872	$3,889	$6,557
PC software	$730	$1,341	$2,315
Books	$725	$1,265	$2,199
Clothing and accessories	$443	$893	$1,926
Tickets (e.g., concert)	$568	$1,071	$1,753
Specialty gifts (e.g., flowers)	$587	$913	$1,381
Music (e.g., CDs)	$354	$670	$1,148
Other	$1,416	$2,230	$3,409
Total	$15,574	$24,533	$37,496
Growth rate	57%	58%	53%

Source: Jupiter Communications, http://www.internetworld.com/daily/stats.

retail between $700 and $1,000/month. Fourth, WebTV, a fast, easy, and affordable way to explore the exciting world of the Internet through television, was recently introduced. A WebTV receiver costing around $199 is connected to a TV and a phone line. The Internet is the market intelligence medium. One can scan published data from around the world on all types of products and services. This information can then be downloaded for further analysis. By creating dynamic links to this information (adding it as a bookmark or favorite), the Internet becomes a market intelligence tool for the organization.

All these factors will increase the number of people with access to the Internet and will obviously increase the potential to gather information about consumers, access secondary data sources, advertise, and sell products. Marketing Research in Practice 6-1 provides a typical profile of the Internet user base.

MARKETING RESEARCH IN PRACTICE 6-1

Profile of Internet Users

According to a survey conducted by the Pew Research Center for the People and the Press, there is now a more mainstream audience present on the Internet. Today, web users are less computer savvy, less affluent, and include more women compared to early Internet devotees. The survey discovered that the users are more middlebrow and mainly send or receive e-mail as a primary activity on the Internet. There is a very different demographic pattern from that of early Internet users. Presently, women have overtaken men among newcomers. In 1998, women made up 48 percent of the web users and 52 percent were men. Overall, 80 percent of Internet users are under age 50, compared with 63 percent of all Americans, and 39 percent of Internet users are college graduates, compared with 22 percent of the nation at large. The most significant change of the development of the Internet is the growing amount of non–college graduates that go on-line.

Source: www.people-press.org.

The Internet offers real advantages to all firms, including small ones. Since the cost of constructing a website is reasonably low, a firm with less than a million dollars in sales is as accessible to potential customers worldwide as Nestle or French Telecom. The Internet can "level the playing field" for marketing to potential customers through efficient use of the medium. Examples abound of companies that have made it big through the use of the Internet.[4]

Marketing Research in Practice 6-2 illustrates the use of Internet for marketing research. The rest of this chapter focuses on explaining the power of the Internet in marketing research applications.

◆ WHAT IS THE INTERNET?

The Internet is a worldwide network of computers that was originally designed by the U.S. Department of Defense to provide an alternative communications network. It started small, as **ARPAnet** (Advanced Research Project Agency Network) in 1969. ARPAnet supported government needs and research laboratories. The infrastructure of the network was designed to be nonhierarchical. If any one node was destroyed (it was the middle of the Cold War), the rest of the network could continue to operate. In the 1970s the Internet began to be interconnected with large universities. Finally, in April 1995, control over the Internet backbone was granted to commercial carriers and the public got access to the network. It has grown dramatically since then, and today it is a major force in the information world. The Internet is a network of home and business computer users, libraries, universities, organizations, and so on, using a common protocol. This common protocol is called **TCP/IP.** TCP stands for **Transmission**

MARKETING RESEARCH IN PRACTICE 6-2

The Power of the Internet

GroceryWorks is an on-line grocery service offering all of the products available in traditional supermarkets. This Dallas-based company offers shoppers the convenience of shopping on-line for all items, including meat, fish, produce, prepared meals, and refrigerated and frozen foods, with the convenience of same-day delivery for free. There is no minimum order and no service charges such as sign-up fees or monthly charges. The service is available 24 hours a day. GroceryWorks features a state-of-the-art website (user friendly, quick to use, rich with information). Grocery orders are filled using a highly automated distribution center for staples. GroceryWorks was founded in 1999. The virtual aisles of GroceryWorks were the brain-child of Kelby D. Hagar, a fifth-generation Texan who is bringing his pioneer spirit to the Internet. He began to study various industries and realized that the grocery business was ideal for on-line service. In traditional grocery stores, fixed costs are high—"virtual stores" can be more efficient for less. And many people simply don't want to spend their free time going to the grocery store—they are ready for the convenience of home delivery and being able to shop on-line. GroceryWorks' goal is to change lifestyles of people to make their daily routine easier. The company chose to debut its innovative on-line service in Dallas, currently serving an area that stretches from downtown Dallas north to San Francisco, from Richardson/Plano on the East, to Coppell/Irving on the West. These are areas within an 8-mile radius of the company's first distribution center.

Source: www.groceryworks.com.

Control Protocol and IP stands for **Internet Protocol.** Simply stated, TCP breaks down information into packets for transfer and reassembles them at the destination point. IP ensures proper delivery of data to the right address.

Numerous communication services are available for exploring the Internet, some of which are explained here.

- **World Wide Web (WWW)**—the most visible portion of the Internet, which supports text, graphics, video, and audio. The WWW is an environment within the Internet that was originally developed by the European Particle Physics Laboratory (CERN). It is also called a hypermedia environment because it supports the use of hyperlinks. Hyperlinks lie at the very heart of the WWW because they allow user-friendly navigation among the offerings of the Internet by simply using "point and click." Any hyperlink (text or image) can point to virtually any document anywhere on the WWW.

- **E-mail**—a major communication path that allows you to send and receive mail around the world.

- **File Transfer Protocol (FTP)**—sends and retrieves files to other locations. For instance, software is most often downloaded via FTP.

- **TELNET**—a program that enables a user to "log in" to a remote host site. For example, a file can be edited on a remote computer via Telnet.

◆ CHARACTERISTICS OF THE INTERNET

In 1995 and 1996, the Internet emerged as a fundamental information medium and created much enthusiasm in all walks of life. Our sociological and economic structure is being rewritten, the corporate world is dramatically realigning its strategies, and individuals are showing a long-inhibited eagerness to explore. However, the new medium has so far created more questions than answers. If 1995 could be called the year of the Internet, then 1996 was the year of exploring, surveying, and structuring the activities. Numerous companies and research institutions started projects in order to answer a whole array of burning questions. The following list shows some of their objectives:

- Assess the dimension of the Internet in terms of access and usage patterns.
- Develop demographic and psychographic user profiles.
- Understand why consumers and businesses try to use the Internet.
- Assess opportunities, attributes, and benefits of interactive programs.
- Develop methodologies to track consumer and corporate behaviors and actions.

Prominent marketing research firms started projects to find answers to these questions. Naturally, the answer to any of these questions is highly dynamic at this point, because the medium itself is still evolving. Nevertheless, decision makers crave more hard information in order to utilize this medium to its maximum. Some of the most prominent projects or ventures that seek information in these areas at this point in time are shown in Table 6-2.

Brief results from commercial projects are usually posted on the Internet, whereas the full report can be purchased from the particular research company. These reports are usually directed toward business managers who try to improve their decision making with regard to the use of the Internet.

TABLE 6-2   Projects in Internet User Profile

Commercial	
CommerceNet	CommerceNet/Nielsen Internet Demographics Survey
I/PRO	I/PRO, Cyberatlas
Forrester	New Media Research

Academic	
University of Michigan	HERMES
Vanderbilt University	Project 2000
Georgia Institute of Technology	GVU WWW User Surveys

CommerceNet is an industry association for Internet commerce. Launched in Silicon Valley, California, in April 1994, membership had grown to over 600 companies and organizations worldwide by 2000. Members include banks, telecommunication companies, Internet service providers, on-line services, and software and service companies, which are together transforming the NTE into a global electronic marketplace.

The CommerceNet/Nielsen Internet Demographics Survey had been conducted for the sixth time by April 1999. This prominent study is designed to assess the dimension of the new medium in terms of personal access and usage patterns and to identify behavioral changes over time. Each Internet demographics study in the series is based on telephone interviews with randomly selected respondents aged 16 and over, and each set of results is statistically representative of the overall U.S. and Canadian populations. More than 7,200 persons were interviewed for the April 1999 study.[5] Access to the Internet jumped to 112.5 percent in the United States and in Canada from 16 percent of the population in August 1995 to 34 percent by June 2000.

I/PRO is a San Francisco–based provider of services and software for the independent measurement and analysis of website usage. Their products enable website operators to analyze site usage, while advertisers and media buyers rely on I/PRO for optimal site selection.

Web Trends is a traffic auditing software. It can tell the times and dates a site was accessed, the region or country of visitors, and the path the visitor took through the website. This helps in understanding as much as possible about the traffic a website generates, who is visiting the site, how long they are staying, which pages they are viewing, and most important, which pages they are not viewing.

Experts estimate that business-to-business (B2B) electronic commerce will grow to $7.29 trillion in 2004.[6] The B2B revolution will end up being about a lot more than e-commerce. A *B2B e-market maker* is defined as an enterprise that brings together buyers and sellers within a particular industry, geographic region, or affinity group for the purpose of commerce. It provides content, value-added services, and, at times, commerce transaction capabilities. Companies like Ford and General Motors have announced that they would each set up an Internet exchange for the buying and selling of parts and other materials. This intermediary market is quickly evolving to a highly competitive market that includes a variety of players with previously disparate business models, including software, portals, distributors, ASPs, and business service providers.

It seems likely that it will become one of the powers that move the macroeconomic levers. Supply chain automation is supposed to reduce costs and if it works out to be anything like the scale predicted then the resulting gains in productivity

CommerceNet is an industry association for Internet commerce.

Internet Demographics Survey is a prominent study that is designed to assess the dimension of the new medium in terms of personal access and usage patterns and to identify behavioral changes over time.

I/PRO is a San Francisco–based provider of services and software for the independent measurement and analysis of website usage. Their products enable website operators to analyze site usage while advertisers and media buyers rely on I/PRO for optimal site selection.

should provide a needed counterweight to inflationary pressures for years to come. The efficiencies provided by Internet-based project management and supply-chain services could give margins a big lift in huge, mature industries like construction. Marketplace sites that rationalize pricing via dynamic commerce should pump up the bottom line for companies in smokestack sectors, such as automobiles and chemicals. Entire companies will disappear if they cannot keep up with the demands of their supply-chain partners.

However, some changes brought about by this revolution will be unpleasant. People will be forced out of jobs that computers can do more effectively. The Internet is shifting the division of labor from man to machine, allowing the computers to do the stuff they are good at. If the human capital freed up by technology can be leveraged in any sort of meaningful way, the B2B boom could result in a revenue growth undreamed of.

◆ PROFILE OF WEB USERS

The demographic composition of the Internet is perhaps the most valuable tool for the market researcher who will be able to use the specific information in subsequent targeting as well as in evaluating the effectiveness of the medium. In terms of the gender differences, approximately 48 percent women access the Web, as compared to 52 percent of the men as per the 1998 survey. The growth in the number of women using the Internet has been close to 7 percent over the past two years.

Table 6-3 refers to the age composition of the users on the Web. As the greater portion of the users are from the 31–40 year old age group, the positioning of the information as well as the reach of the advertising and retailing efforts can then be altered. This insight helps in structuring the websites in order to address this group. Income levels are also crucial in determining the kind of products and services to market on the Web (Table 6-4)

The users of the Web tend to be multifaceted. The reasons for which the Web is being used would be information pertinent to the market researcher. Figure 6-1 refers to the different reasons for which the Web is used, as well as the frequency with which users access information.

When conducting market research, data on the shopping habits of the users will provide some understanding of the role of the Web in pushing products as compared to retail stores off-line. The habits of the "surfers" also provide an insight into the degree to which there is some loyalty and continued exposure of information or advertising on a website.

TABLE 6-3   Age Distribution of Users of the Internet

Age	Percent Users
16–25	17.5
26–30	16.1
31–40	25
41–50	22.1
51–65	12.1
66+	2.7

Source: http://www.gvu.gatech.edu.

TABLE 6-4   Income Distribution of Users of the Internet

Income	Percent Users
Would not say	17.3%
Below $10,000	2.7%
$10,000–$19,000	4.8%
$20,000–$29,000	7.3%
$30,000–$39,000	11.5%
$40,000–$49,000	11.2%
$50,000–$74,000	21.0%
$75,000–$99,000	11.8%
Over $100,000	12.4%

Source: http://www.gvu.gatech.edu.

Since its beginning in 1994, the GVU WWW User Survey has accumulated a unique store of historical and up-to-date information on the growth and trends in Internet usage. It is valued as an independent, objective view of developing web demographics, culture, user attitudes, and usage patterns. Recently the focus of the survey has been expanded to include commercial uses of the Web, including advertising, electronic commerce, intranet web usage, and business-to-business transactions. Table 6-5 outlines the items purchased on-line in 1998. (For more information

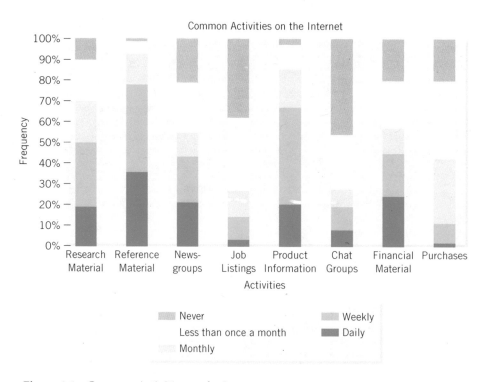

Figure 6-1   Common Activities on the Internet

Source: http://www.gvu.gatech.edu/user_surveys/survey-1998-10/.

TABLE 6-5 Items Purchased On-line

Computer hardware	48.5%
Generic grocery items	2.5%
Video/movies	15.8%
Travel arrangements	30.2%
Music CDs/tapes/albums	41.4%
Home electronics	14.0%
Books	52.6%
Concerts/plays	9.9%
Investment choices	11.8%
Insurance services	2.5%
E-zines	14.9%
Flowers	13.3%
Apparel	13.6%

Source: http://www.gvu.gatech.edu.

on distribution on Internet users based on household income across regions in the world, go to http://www.wiley.com/college/kumar.)

Perhaps the most significant aspect is that we are able to collect information on the users and chart a demographic profile, and in that attempt we also arrive at a psychographic preference list of what can be placed on these sites in order to better serve their needs. The Internet reaches consumers and retailers without the geographic limitation, giving it a more universal appeal. This is good, but it challenges marketers who are trying to target a specific group of people and effectively convey information.[7]

◆ WWW INFORMATION FOR MARKETING DECISIONS

Cyberatlas, a division of I/PRO, compiles and publishes public-domain information about Internet market size, growth, forecast, and demographics.

Cyberatlas, a division of I/PRO, compiles and publishes public-domain information about Internet market size, growth, forecast, and demographics. In addition, Cyberatlas provides news on WWW markets such as advertising, finance, and search services, as well as normative data and industry benchmarking studies.

Forrester Research from Cambridge, Massachusetts, offers a service called **New Media Research.** One component of this project is Media & Technology Strategies, which focuses on new business media models for publishers, broadcasters, and information service providers. Research topics include, for example, how information will be priced in the electronic marketplace. This is critical information for corporations that do heavy advertising on the Web (such as Ebay or Amazon) because they want an adequate return on their advertising spending. Many different proposals have been made for pricing ads on the Internet. Forrester found out that advertisers complain about pricing schemes based on cost per thousand and would rather see click-through (based on the number of clicks for the ads) pricing. Table 6-6 shows the 10-largest on-line advertisers from November 1999 to April 2000.

Web-advertising expenditure forecasts are difficult to specify, but the average projections of a consensus forecast estimates around $3 billion for the year 2000. As estimated by the International Data Corporation, the projected overall ad revenue in millions of dollars has been progressively increasing. Although the growth of the

TABLE 6-6   On-line Advertisers*

	Advertiser	Impressions (millions)	Spending (millions)	Unique Creatives
1	WingspanBank	1,800	$38	200
2	Lowestfare	1,500	$28	150
3	LifeMinders	1,500	$42	1,200
4	Amazon	1,400	$34	570
5	oneandonly	1,200	$27	140
6	AmeriDebt	1,100	$26	230
7	HealthQuick	1,100	$23	100
8	NextCard	1,000	$32	340
9	Capital One	1,000	$23	290
10	eBay	930	$28	360

* The ranking is based on banner impressions, i.e., the number of times a particular ad is rendered for viewing by a user.

Source: David Butcher, *Revolution* (August 2000).

Web is tremendous, it would be advantageous to obtain specific information on on-line advertising efforts.[8]

The advantages of advertising on the Internet cannot be understated. First, a targeted audience can be reached. Many websites request personal information about the visitor, which can be used not only to define the site's audience but also to produce customized ads to be shown on the next visit. Many sites are, in fact, a mechanism for delivering an audience rather than selling a product or a service. Second, Internet advertising is very much like direct-response advertising in that customers can link directly to an advertiser's home page and request information, browse a catalog, buy a product, or order a service. Webmasters are increasingly being advised to involve customers in such things as new product development and product naming exercises. Many of the most popular Internet and computer-related products have been exposed to customers in experimental form, and then changed significantly due to user feedback.[9]

One problem in Web advertising is audience measurement. A firm would like to measure "eyeballs"—that is, how many total exposures an ad receives. However, on a given site visit, customers often go back and forth rapidly between hypertext pages. Measuring the number of times a particular page is on the screen may not be the appropriate measure of exposure, as the screen time may have been very brief. A minimum amount of time might be necessary before it can count as a *hit*. Or the viewer may not scroll all the way down the screen. These issues confront the large number of companies interested in measuring site audiences.[10] To address these problems, some new services are being developed.

AdCount by NetCount is a tracking service of Web users that attempts to measure the effect of web ads. It promises not only to monitor how many web cruisers see an ad but whether they click on it to be connected to the advertiser's own website. Such "click-through" rates are the true measure of whether an ad placement had an effect. For this purpose special software is installed on the host computer. The software sends frequent updates of ad activity on the sites to a central computer from which the reports are generated. These reports usually comprise daily and weekly totals of ad impressions and click-throughs, daily and weekly totals of ad transfers

AdCount is a tracking service of web users that attempts to measure the effect of web ads. It promises not only to monitor how many web cruisers see an ad but whether they click on it to be connected to the advertiser's own website.

(clicks on ads that successfully deliver the user to the advertiser's website), and advertiser summary reports with comparable statistics on each ad tracked.

HERMES (University of Michigan) and **Project 2000** (Vanderbilt University) are two academic research endeavors on the activities of the Internet. While HERMES looks at the commercial uses of the World Wide Web, such as predicting consumer and corporate trends, Project 2000 tries to enrich and stimulate generation of knowledge on the role of marketing in the new hypermedia environment.

Media Metrix is an Internet tracking service launched in January 1996. They set the standard for Internet and digital media measurement worldwide, focused on measuring all people in all places on all media platforms. They provide accurate, reliable, and timely behavioral data to web marketers, advertising agencies, web publishers, and research agencies, and are at the core of clients' critical strategic business decisions. Media Metrix utilizes its patented metering methodology to measure actual Internet and Digital Media audience usage behavior in real time—click-by-click, page-by-page, and minute-by-minute. They offer monthly, weekly, and daily data collection and reporting, and a sample of over 100,000 people under measurement worldwide. Media Metrix captures in-depth demographics for each sample member including age, gender, household size and composition, income, education level, geographic location, and more, allowing them to link user behavior with important demographic characteristics (http://www.mediametrix.com/products/methodologies.jsp).

Nielsen Media Research has enlisted the participation of 9,000 home-Internet surfers from the United States for its on-line audience measurement service. The venture allows Nielsen to follow their activities on the Web to find out how much time they spend on individual sites and basic demographic details such as age, gender, and income. With this service web publishers and ad agencies receive competitive information about what companies are advertising on-line, which sites are getting most advertising, along with the size and demographics of the audience that saw the ad (http://www.zdnet.com/zdnn/stories/news/0,4586,2229197,00.html).

Table 6-7 illustrates the extent of the use of web resources for various activities.

Some good examples of how companies are using the Internet and the World Wide Web are the following:

- Half.com is regarded as the premier site for fixed-price person-to-person e-commerce. Previously owned items such as books, CDs, videocassettes, and video games are offered on-line through an organized virtual marketplace. Half.com overcomes the inefficiencies between the supply and demand for used mass-

HERMES is an academic research project that looks at the commercial uses of the World Wide Web, such as predicting consumer and corporate trends.

Project 2000 tries to enrich and stimulate generation of knowledge on the role of marketing in the new hypermedia environment.

TABLE 6-7   Primary Uses of the Web

Education	15.6%
Shopping	13.3%
Entertainment	15.2%
Work	16.6%
Communication	9.0%
Personal information	18.7%
Killing time	9.4%
Other	2.2%

Source: www.gvu.gatech.edu/user_surveys/survey-1998-10/graphs/use/q30.htm.

market items, streamlining the entire process of connecting people to buy and sell over the Internet.

- OnlineChoice.com provides a service where buyers register together in "buying pools" to receive discounted prices on various products such as wireless service, electricity, and gasoline from companies willing to supply that demand. Based on the principle of "group buying power," suppliers save money on marketing costs if they sell to a single-pooled large group of people.

- Autotrader.com offers on-line solutions for trading used cars. The site lists used vehicles for sale by private owners, dealers, and manufacturers. It enables prospective buyers to decide on the cars that meet their needs, and allows sellers to place classified ads and get *Kelly Blue Book* values to determine their asking price.

- The Kelly Kar Company (www.kbb.com) was founded in 1918 by Les Kelly. The first *Blue Book of Motor Car Values* was published in 1926, and the *Blue Book* quickly became the reference publication on used car prices. In 1993, *Kelly Blue Book* made its initial venture into the consumer publication area by publishing a *Consumer Edition* of the *Blue Book*. It features 15 years of used car values on over 10,000 models of cars, trucks, and vans. It is available in bookstores as well as on the Web. In 1995, the *Kelly Blue Book* made its move to the Web and has become the standard in used car values.

Studies done by A. C. Nielsen Corp. found that fewer shoppers are going to the grocery store (down from 94 percent in 1997 to 91 percent in 1999). Also, according to A. C. Nielsen, most people do not like their grocery shopping experience. On-line shopping is obviously a good option for these consumers. In some major cities, consumers can use computer software to order groceries at home from WinDixie, Safeway, or Jewel stores and have them delivered. Consumers enjoy real-time savings and weekly specials. They can shop at any hour and sort by attributes such as calories or fat content; the groceries are selected by specially trained Peapod buyers and delivered at an agreed time for a fee. In addition, retailers are also experimenting with their suppliers electronically linking up.

◆ THE INTERNET AND MARKETING RESEARCH TODAY

People disagree about the value of the Internet as a marketing research tool. Many think that quality information is hard to find and that the Internet is too slow. Although there is some truth to these statements, they need some qualification. Like any traditional information resource, the Internet has certain advantages and disadvantages. Some information can be searched well on the Internet when other information sources are not available at all. Besides this, the Internet is characterized by dynamic technological developments, which influence the information search process. This section looks at a variety of ways the Internet can be used for marketing research.

Primary Research

Collection of primary information over the Internet is still in its incubation stage. Although there exist some promising starts, the Internet is being used in mainstream marketing research with caution. One such start is the use of electronic mail for survey research. This technique uses e-mail for the entire process of receiving, completing, and returning questionnaires. Marketing Research in Practice 6-3 explains how

MARKETING RESEARCH IN PRACTICE 6-3

Software for E-mail Surveys

E-mail has become the latest tool for conducting surveys. Decisive Survey lets researchers use e-mail to conduct polls, surveys, and similar assessments. Questions and choices can be typed in or cán be selected from a built-in-library of questions and text blocks. The user can also customize the templates that are available and the final version can be printed.

The software then converts the survey into an e-mail text message that can be read and responded to from anywhere. It works across campus LANs, intranets, the Internet, AOL, CompuServe, and with any computer. A click on "Collect Responses" automatically gathers results. There are hundreds of ways to view data. These include 2D and 3D charts, standard rating statistics, cross tables and cross charts, by respondent, through custom filters, and more. Data can also be exported to other applications, including statistical analysis packages like SPSS and SAS.

Decisive survey's ease of use leads itself to a wide array of assessment or polling needs. Recipients can be imported from a file, taken from an address book and/or enforced manually. Survey management tools are also included.

Source: The Internet in Education, p. 28.

e-mail surveys can be used in primary research. This type of survey technique has a number of advantages:

- Questionnaires are delivered, or redelivered if lost, in a matter of seconds.
- Responses and feedback are delivered faster.
- E-mail surveys are less expensive than regular mail surveys.
- E-mail messages are usually read only by the recipient.
- Unlike telephone surveys, messages can be sent, read, and replied to at the convenience of the user.

Some of the less desirable properties of e-mail surveys are that the security of electronic mail is low in comparison to traditional media. Also, it is impossible to guarantee the anonymity of e-mail responses, because every e-mail includes the respondent's name and network address. When market researchers opt for this method, they must include a disclaimer in the survey that explains this shortcoming to the participants.

Other forms of primary data collection are performed primarily through interactive forms that are filled out on the screen. Marketing Research in Practice 6-4 gives an example of an Internet survey. The key issue is to provide a disclaimer that the firm seeks only composite data, and that names and addresses will not be used for solicitation or sold to another vendor. This kind of survey can also be conducted by announcing it on appropriate lists and groups, and then sending respondents the survey via e-mail.[11]

As the population of on-line users increases, new research issues have arisen concerning the demographics and psychographics of the on-line user and the opportunities for a product or service. On-line focus groups are conducted entirely on-line—everything from recruitment and screening (which the recruiter does via

MARKETING RESEARCH IN PRACTICE 6-4

Enter to Win "Spend it your way" Indonesia.com's Sweepstakes

What would you do with a $10,000 windfall? Travel? Renovate? Shopping Spree? Enter now for your chance at $10,000!

You must be eighteen (18) or older to play. Please read the "Create Your Dream" Sweepstakes Official Rules and Privacy Statement before entering the sweepstakes.

Already a member of Indonesia.com and the Communicate.com Network? Enter this sweepstakes by logging in here:

Member name:

Password:

Forgot Your Password?

Log in to enter

Interested in becoming a member?

As a member of the Communicate.com Network, you get a free email account, simplified entry into sweepstakes and contests and participation in discussion forums.
Sign up now and we'll enter you in the sweepstakes too!

To enter without becoming a member, please fill in the form below.

All fields are required for entry.

First name:

MARKETING RESEARCH IN PRACTICE 6-4 *(continued)*

Enter to Win "Spend it your way" Indonesia.com's Sweepstakes

Last name:

Email address:

Age range: | 18-24 ▼ |

Gender: | Female ▼ |

Zip or Postal code:

Country of residence: | USA ▼ |

Yes! Send me news about exclusive benefits, special offers and giveaways offered by these web sites:

☐ **Select All Domains**

☐ **sports**	☐ **health & beauty**	☐ **country portals**
☐ hockey.com	☐ makeup.com	☐ brazil.com
☐ rugby.com	☐ perfume.com	☐ indonesia.com
☐ cricket.com	☐ cologne.com	☐ malaysia.com
☐ wrestling.com	☐ body.com	☐ vietnam.com
☐ boxing.com	☐ exercise.com	☐ vancouver.com
☐ karate.com	☐ vegetarian.com	☐ yen.com
☐ rodeo.com		☐ canadian.com
☐ automobile.com		☐ leisure.com

☐ **telecom**	☐ **electronic music**	☐ **miscellaneous**
☐ call.com	☐ dance.com	☐ burnaby.com
☐ number.com	☐ electronic.com	☐ endracism.com
☐ overseas.com	☐ trance.com	☐ focus-groups.com
☐ mouse.com	☐ keyboard.com	☐ importers.com
	☐ techno-music.com	☐ surrey.com

[Enter me!]

Source: http://www.communicate.com.

e-mail) to moderation of the discussion itself. This method allows researchers to reach target segments more effectively.

As the on-line population increases, the demographics broaden, enabling remote global segments to be reached, something not possible via traditional methods. One of the limitations of on-line research is that the results cannot be projected to the general population because not everyone has access to a computer, modem, and on-line service.

Another difference between on-line and traditional qualitative research is that cyberspace is populated by trend leaders. Commonly targeted by marketers, advertisers, and product manufacturers, trend leaders are early adopters who try out new ideas, products, services, and technologies before these innovations reach popularity in the mass market.

On-line focus groups, while lacking the dynamics of a face-to-face discussion, provide a unique alternative to the traditional method. An on-line environment allows respondents to interact voluntarily "behind their computer screens," and therefore encourages them to respond with honest and spontaneous answers. Furthermore, all respondents, extroverted and introverted, get a fair chance to express their views, and "instant messaging" allows the key focus-group players to interact privately with each other.

Although on-line respondents do not "hear" each others' answers, they can see them. Thanks to "emoticons"—the use of certain keys that, typed in combination, look like sideways facial expressions, like a smile :-)—on-line focus group participants and moderators can express themselves.[12]

Companies are increasingly collecting information from their website visitors. Especially for companies that sell over the Web, collecting information about potential customers who have Internet access is critical. This type of data collection can serve a number of purposes:

- Counting and describing website visitors in order to customize website content to suit their needs
- Collecting additional information for customer databases, which then may be used by product development, sales, marketing, or service departments
- Receiving questions or suggestions regarding the use of a product
- Receiving and answering complaints

It is surprising to see how many website visitors are willing to leave personal information (such as address, phone number, e-mail address). In many cases, companies offer a small reward as a token for the complying visitor. For example, during a promotional compaign upon completing a questionnaire at the Campbell Soup website (http://www.campbellsoup.com), the company mails a number of coupons for their products to the customer.

I/PRO has launched a service called I/CODE that lets users submit information about themselves once; it then makes the data available to sites participating in the I/CODE scheme. The advantage to the user is being able to skip answering the same questions repeatedly, and I/CODE offers prizes as an incentive to register. Publishers and advertisers pay for the information, and in return can build a database of users and track their behavior. CNET gathers information about users without asking questions. Its servers can recognize each visitor's browser and computer type as well as the domain (.com, .edu, .org, etc.). It uses this information to deliver a "banner" (e.g., advertising) tailored to different types of users—for example, a Mac warehouse banner for a Mac user and a PC warehouse ad for a PC user.

Secondary Research

The Internet's forte is probably its advantages in researching secondary information. As the 1998 *GVU WWW User Survey* pointed out, nearly 50 percent of the respondents use the Internet on a weekly basis for gathering information. Another 78 percent of Internet users search for competitor information.

The Internet competes with several other on-line resources to satisfy the information need of businesses and consumers. Businesses typically rely on professional databases such as Lexis/Nexis or Knight-Ridder. Consumers most often utilize commercial on-line services such as America Online or CompuServe. Although the latter also provide Internet access, they represent a comprehensive information resource in themselves. Table 6-8 depicts how the Internet compares against other on-line information sources.

The main advantages of the Internet at this point are its very broad scope, covering virtually every topic, and its comparably low cost. These characteristics make it a very appealing medium for both consumers and businesses. Also, it is expected that the technical constraints of the Internet, such as low bandwidth, will be gradually resolved in the future, making it less cumbersome to use in terms of downloading times.

Finding out information about competitor activities is an important task for businesses. The Internet is a prime tool for this task, since it reduces the time spent and may increase substantially the quality of the information collected. Product and financial information are probably suited best for competitive tracking. Especially larger corporations display this information most often in their websites. On the other hand, pricing information might not be amenable to tracking readily, since it is not common for businesses to display product prices (unless they actually sell over the Internet). Competitive promotion and distribution information is probably the least suited to tracking via the Internet. Information about products or companies can be obtained using search engines on the Web. (For an exposition on search engines, refer to the appendix to this chapter.) However, search engines have certain limitations and hence, do not guarantee that all relevant information will be obtained. For this purpose, there are providers of custom search services, who search for information for a fee.

TABLE 6-8 Comparison of Information Sources

	Internet (WWW, Usenet)	Professional Databases (e.g., Lexis/Nexis)	Commercial On-line Services (e.g., CompuServe)
Speed[a]	Low to high	High	Low to high
Information structure	Not well structured	Very well structured	Well structured
Information scope	Very broad	Depends on the database, mostly narrow	Medium to broad
Overall information quality	Low to high	High to very high	Medium to high
Search tools	Limited, not complete	Extensive, accurate	Mostly accurate
User support	Limited	Very good	Good
Cost	Low	High to very high	Medium

[a] Depending on modem, server, and database structure.

Custom Search Service

A growing number of **custom search services** are becoming available. These offer information tracking and forwarding for a fee. These services range from one-time custom searches to regular news deliveries. These services commonly specialize in a particular area such as global telecommunication or food processing and then offer their search results in a regular electronic newsletter to subscribers. Depending on the service, the charges can be based on usage (one time or for the whole project), time frame (weekly, monthly, yearly), object (document fee, fee per researched publication), amount of text (number of characters), or any combination of these. For example, Dow Jones News/Retrieval Service provides customized business and financial news and information. Its service scans more than 10 million companies from around the world, and the user can search 55 million business articles. The user retrieves the headlines of the articles for free and pays $2.95 for each article viewed. Also, the customer can select "topic folders" from a list of 1,200 preconfigured folders tracking information relevant to a user's particular needs.

Agents

The use of intelligent **agents** in monitoring information is increasing rapidly. For illustrative purposes, let us consider a competitive analyst for a TV producer. The analyst needs constant information on the pricing of competitors' products. An intelligent agent would monitor websites of TV manufacturers and TV retailers, collect price and availability information, and deliver easy-to-skim summaries. According to a study by Coopers & Lybrand, companies that place a premium on competitive intelligence grew 200 percent faster than firms that didn't.

Agents function in many different ways. Some are available on the Internet and preprogrammed for particular search tasks, such as Bargain Finders. This commercial application will most likely gain tremendous significance in the near future. Other types of agents are software that is purchased by the user, who then has to specify downloading criteria. Most often, searches are scheduled at night so the users do not have to wait to download documents. Agent technology is on the verge of entering the mainstream of Web search, and the future is likely to bring many innovations in this area.

Free Information Providers

Besides the customized fee-based information delivery services, a number of news organizations have set up websites that offer access to current and archived information. **Free information providers** include news agencies such as Reuters, newspapers such as *The New York Times,* and news services such as CNN. Normally, these services are similar to but not an exact replica of the original counterpart. A new breed of virtual information sources, such as NEWS (by ClariNet), is published exclusively on the WWW. Overall, these information sources offer high-quality and extensive resources for day-to-day news and business information.

In terms of obtaining customized news on the Internet, one can subscribe through a source called EntryPoint. It is a free toolbar that delivers personalized news, customized content, and alerting functionality directly to a user's desktop without disturbing daily computer tasks. Users can retrieve news, monitor stock activity, obtain sports scores, shop at their favorite on-line store, view personal financial information, and more. EntryPoint is completely customizable to the web surfer's preferences where selected topics are delivered instantly. The greatest advantage of this streamlined, all-encompassing e-commerce and information source is that it is absolutely free!

To help you avoid the common pitfalls in information searching, Marketing Research in Practice 6-5 highlights the seven deadly sins of the on-line search process.

TASTY ICE-CREAM: A CASE EXAMPLE OF MARKETING INTELLIGENCE (*continued*)

It was just another pleasant spring afternoon in Houston, Texas. Raj, president of Tasty Ice-Cream, a local ice cream shop with two outlets in the city, had closed his shop early, as his employees were long requesting a half-day off to do some Easter shopping. On his way back home, Raj was giving a cursory look to the financial report of his shop over the past six months. It was business as usual, but the growth rate had fallen and the profits were stagnant during the last two years. Houston's tropical weather and multicultural demographics had attracted Raj to set up a couple of ice-cream shops in Houston five years earlier. Tasty's exquisite European Flavor helped it differentiate itself in a highly competitive market. Tasty's business picked up at a steady pace and Raj was able to break even in the first two years. But after that, entry of new players in the market and changing consumer preferences stymied the growth rate, and profits have remained the same for the past two years. Raj felt the urgent need to make some changes in the shop's atmospherics and menu to bring the growth rate back to a steady pace.

Raj decided to consult a local marketing firm, Innovative Marketing Consultants (IMC), to find the consumer's preferences and trends in the ice-cream industry and to get a clear idea of his consumer base. He also wanted to explore the option of having a coffee shop inside Tasty. Raj had observed that when families came to his shop, the parents preferred to drink coffee, while their kids were busy eating ice-cream. Raj also wanted to implement changes by summer, the time when the ice-cream business is at its peak.

Taking into consideration Raj's urgency, Dr. K, the president of IMC, decided to use the Internet for his secondary data search. He used different search engines—Infoseek, Lycos, and AltaVista—to get a wide coverage of the net. The Internet was very useful in gathering information about the current trends and preferences in the ice-cream industry. He used customized search services to get financial reports of ice-cream firms. This gave him an estimate of the size of the market. Several periodicals' (e.g., *Ice-Cream Reporter*) on-line versions allowed Dr. K to search for articles on specific topics. This helped him save time, compared to the laborious process of scanning the periodicals manually. The Internet was also used to gather information about the trends in the coffee industry. Census data on retail trade came in very handy in giving an estimate of the coffee market in Houston.

Using his information from the Internet, Dr. K was able to prepare an executive summary on the ice-cream industry in a couple of days. He divided the summary into subcategories that included size of the market, trends, and future estimates. The executive summary formed the basis for formulating the issues to be addressed specific to Tasty during primary data collection. The usage of the Internet for secondary data collection helped Dr. K save time and complete the research before summer, in spite of his busy schedule.

MARKETING RESEARCH IN PRACTICE 6-5

The Seven Deadly Sins of On-line Searching

Pride	Assuming one does not need to read the manual or other material for the search process
Haste	Rushing into a search before thinking through your search goals
Avarice	Trying to perform an extensive search when only a few good pieces of information are necessary
Apathy	Not thinking creatively about what sources would best cover the subject
Sloth	Using the same old sources for every search
Narrow-mindedness	Trying only one formulation of the search
Ignorance	Not knowing the on-line system's tricks and tools

Source: Mary Ellen Bates, "The Seven Deadly Sins of Online Searching," *Online User* (November/December 1996), pp. 21–27.

◆ HOW TO SEARCH FOR INFORMATION ON THE WEB

When searching for information in the Internet, several search engines can be used. Yahoo, AltaVista, Excite, Google, and Infoseek are some of the commonly used search engines. An important aspect in using these search engines is to know how to search for information within a search engine. For example, if you want to use AltaVista to search for information, then the following hints may be useful:[13]

- Type a few words; more is usually better, since you never know how documents are written. Use synonyms: England, Great Britain, United Kingdom.
- Do not worry about the number of results to query. The Web is very large; many documents will contain at least one word from the query. What matters is that the search engine returns them in the right order with the most relevant first.
- What you are looking for should be listed in the first couple of pages. If it is not, try rephrasing the query.
- To make sure a word is in a document, put a plus sign in front of it. For example, recipe + chicken rice. This will return sites that definitely have the word "chicken" in them, whereas "rice" and "recipe" would be optional. Similarly a minus sign (–) ensures that a word does not appear: enter recipe chicken – broccoli, if you don't like this vegetable.
- If you are not sure whether to use uppercase or lowercase, use all lowercase. The query *Paris* will match only this exact spelling, whereas the query *paris* matches "Paris," "PARIS," and "paris."
- To find a phrase, put double quotes around the words. For example "to be or not to be" is a phrase, and so is "chicken soup." But you have to be sure that the words are exactly in this order with nothing in between.

According to an NPD on-line survey, users of search engines value ease of use, speed of response, reliability and accuracy of results, and organized, up-to-date information. The survey also found that once people have selected a search engine, they are likely to stay with it, even if their search is unsuccessful. Users tend to try the same search engine using different words to reach their intended destination.[13]

International Marketing Research

The Internet, as a global medium, increases the scope of communication tremendously. Even though the globe-shrinking experience is already prevalent, the Internet's ability to communicate across borders will have a dramatic effect. Market researchers will be able to tap into foreign information sources as easily as they use the ones at home. Marketing Research in Practice 6-6 gives an illustration on the power of the Internet for international marketing research.

MARKETING RESEARCH IN PRACTICE 6-6

International Marketing Research on the Internet

Reeno, Inc., a chemical company based in Minneapolis, Minnesota, operates worldwide in the area of agricultural inputs such as fertilizer, pesticides, and seeds. In the early 1990s the company developed a new product line of agricultural seeds for improved cotton, rice, and corn varieties. After these products became an initial success in the home market, Reeno saw a tremendous potential for these products in countries such as India and China. These countries have a large and growing population, and they have to satisfy a constantly growing demand for food. Therefore, making agricultural output more efficient is a high priority in these countries.

However, Reeno knew from its past operations that introducing a new product in a country with a completely different culture is not an easy task. They felt a need for more information regarding the purchase behavior and decision making of rural farmers in these countries. Reeno's new line of seeds differed considerably from existing products, but the advantages of the new seed varieties had to be communicated properly. They appointed Innovative Marketing Consultants (IMC), a Houston-based marketing research company, to do this research project. The task for IMC was to conduct secondary research on the agricultural commodity markets in India and China. Also, IMC was to provide a report on the decision-making behavior of Indian and Chinese farmers.

The Internet was the natural first stop for Dr. Werner, the project supervisor at IMC. He started with a very broad search utilizing a number of different search engines of the World Wide Web, such as Alta Vista and Lycos. The search input was a number of different word combinations, such as "farmer + India," "India + cotton," "corn + production + China," or "rural + China." The use of different search engines is important because no single engine indexes the whole WWW. These searches led mostly to an extensive list of documents containing these search terms. Upon reviewing the preliminary results and bookmarking the promising sites, Dr. Werner refined his search terms. After a few hours he already had a fairly good idea regarding which websites contained relevant information. The next step was to examine the short list of promising websites. Here, the real advantages of the Internet came into play, because many of the websites contained hyperlinks to related websites. Because he was dealing with a narrow topic, he found himself several times linked to a website which he had already visited: a true effect of the networked information structure. After half a day of intensive search he had a very good idea of the existing information resources on the Web with respect to his topic, and he had collected an impressive volume of useful information. Among other things, he obtained detailed information on agricultural crop harvests and production areas for both countries for consecutive years from Cornell University in New York. Furthermore, the same resource supplied information on seed and fertilizer imports and exports. In fact, he downloaded a spreadsheet file that contained all the data so that he could continue working with the file. The Internet archive of *The Hindu*, India's national newspaper (Chennai), offered all farming-related

MARKETING RESEARCH IN PRACTICE 6-6 *(continued)*

International Marketing Research on the Internet

stories within the last 5 years. General country information about India and China was abundantly present. A rural sociology discussion list from the University of Kentucky gave him a number of interesting facts about farmers' practices in developing countries. From Lund University in Sweden he obtained an article written by an agricultural sociologist about farming developments in India.

All in all, within less than a day Dr. Werner was able to gather an impressive amount of qualified information on the subject. Even more impressive was the fact that he did this without even leaving his office desk. He collected useful information in a fraction of the time he would have spent in libraries or collecting other secondary resources. Also, he was able to pinpoint his search much more quickly than he used to with printed resources.

Source: Prepared by V. Kumar and Werner Reinartz for classroom discussion.

Particularly for businesses that are involved in international activities, the collection of intelligence from international resources will become natural. Also, some databases, such as STAT-USA, are built and maintained by U.S. government agencies. These offer information to companies entering the growing international trade market at no cost. Further, the most common Internet language is English. Figures 6-2 and 6-3 give you an idea of the way the World Wide Web has penetrated the entire world and where the major users are located.

Recent survey conducted in Canada revealed that 37 percent of Canadian homes have a PC, of which 50 percent have a modem, another 19 percent plan to buy a modem in the near future. Fifty percent of the people with modems (8 percent of the total Canadian population) have used their computer and modem to access some type of on-line information service or database.[14]

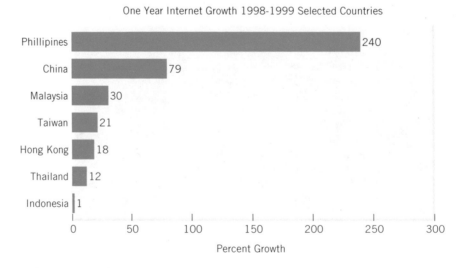

Figure 6-2 One-year Internet growth 1998–1999, selected countries.

Source: http://acnielsen.com/services/media.

Applications of International Market Research—E-Commerce

Electronic commerce or **e-commerce** (also known as e-trade) describes the exchange of hard currencies as well as goods and services over the World Wide Web. The wired or wireless means of communication has been extremely successful as an avenue in promoting the exchange of information as well as commodity trade between countries otherwise separated by geographic stipulations.

The market value of the Canadian business-to-consumer Internet commerce was in the $50 million to $70 million range in 1997. This rose to $600 million to $800 million by 2000. E-commerce in the United States is expected to grow from $1.2 trillion in 2000 to $4.8 trillion in transaction value by 2004. Although this commerce is soaring, several countries in Asia mention the discrepancy in the trade levels. Only 1 percent of Asian households are linked to the Web. By 2004, this will be equal to that in the United States. The suggestion of an electronic trade imbalance in favor of the United States seems to be the scenario unless Europe has more to offer.[15]

◆ THE ETHICAL STANDPOINT FOR THE INTERNET

In order to target consumers more effectively, the most important strategy would be to understand them more intimately and create a marketplace of precisely targeted advertising, promotion, and selling. The benefit of the Internet would be to accumulate data, and develop a database that would provide a profile of the consumer beyond what is possible by traditional survey research.

The problem with this access to consumer databases is that there are no defined or legal limits that curtail the abuse of information sharing. The shroud of secrecy that promotes sharing of such information, a boon for the market researcher, strikes hard at the consumer. Perhaps the biggest threat of all is that several businesses exploit the consumer profile information and develop strategies based on them. Often this information is exchanged without the consent of the individual.

One of the problems with information gathering over the Web is that many of the customers falsify their preferences (40 percent, according to the seventh User Survey of the Graphic, Visualization & Usability Center at the Georgia Institute of Technology, falsify data when asked to register at websites).

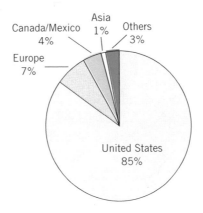

Figure 6-3 Where the users are.

Source: http://cyberatlas.internet.com.

As in the surveys conducted off-line, the information collected about individuals is not bound by any laws or policies unless stated by the company, and therefore, companies do share data. Consumers have the option of informing Web merchants that they want their identity to be kept anonymous and that information about their purchases should not be used. However, these "opt-out" lists often are not effective in excluding consumers in direct marketing efforts. So the onus often falls on the consumer to prevent information about them from being given and to take action regarding identity "exploitation."

ESOMAR, the World Association of Opinion and Marketing Research Professionals, has issued a guideline on conducting marketing and opinion research using the Internet to protect the interests of the general public and to uphold performance standards in market research. It gives the marketing and opinion researchers a guideline, which they must respect in accordance with national and international self-regulation. In 1998, ESOMAR issued a first guideline on Internet research. The latest version is endorsed by both the ICC (International Chamber of Commerce) and the WFA (World Federation of Advisors). The ethical and professional standards to be observed by all on-line researchers are outlined in Marketing Research in Practice 6–7.

Several companies have addressed this problem and have taken steps not only to state that they will not violate customer information, but also to disclose how they plan to use this collected information. These include Hotmail and Amazon.com.

The Electronic Frontier Foundation *(www.eff.org)* and the Electronic Commerce Knowledge Center *(www.commerce.org)* created Etrust, which evaluates sites and privacy practices. Furthermore, it serves as a guard dog and awards its logo to sites that "pass" its test to gain the seal of approval. However, the effectiveness of this system rests on the watchfulness of the consumers and depends on whether they read through the disclosure.[16]

MARKETING RESEARCH IN PRACTICE 6-7

New Guidelines on Conducting Marketing and Opinion Research Using the Internet

The ESOMAR/ARF Guideline on Conducting Marketing and Opinion Research using the Internet is designed to protect the interests of the general public and to uphold performance standards in market research. The Guideline spells out the principles that marketing and opinion researchers must respect in accordance with national and international self-regulation.

Specifically, the Guideline sets out the following ethical and professional standards to be observed by all those conducting on-line research:

- Respondents' cooperation is voluntary and no personal information should be sought from or about respondents without their prior knowledge and agreement.
- The researcher's identity must be disclosed to respondents.
- Respondents' rights to anonymity and adequate security of data must be safeguarded.
- Survey reports should describe the methods used.
- Special care must be taken when interviewing children and young people.
- Researchers should not send unsolicited messages on-line to respondents who have indicated that they do not wish to receive such messages relating to that specific research project.

Source: http://www.esomar.nl/press/Internetguideline2000A.htm. For more information on ESOMAR visit www.esomar.nl.

◆ THE INTERNET AND MARKETING RESEARCH DEVELOPMENTS

The time when one could keep up with the information on the World Wide Web is already ancient history. With the Web growing dramatically, it becomes impossible to track even a small and well-defined segment of the Web. This makes it harder for market researchers to find the information they seek. The purpose of this section is to point out some developments of the Internet that are most likely to happen in the near future, and that will affect the way a market researcher utilizes the Web.

Intranets

Intranets are internal company networks. The utilization of intranets will aid in the communication and distribution of information inside large corporations.

Intranets are internal company networks. Although corporations are looking for ways and means of communicating to consumers through the World Wide Web, it is apparent that intranets are the building blocks for successful commercial activity. These internal networks start off as ways for employees to connect to company information. Intranets may also incorporate connections to the company's various suppliers. According to many industry experts, the advent of total commerical integration is fairly close—employees, suppliers, and customers will soon operate in a totally seamless environment. The advantage for an intranet user is that he or she can connect to the Internet easily, whereas Internet users cannot access intranets without appropriate security codes.

Intranets aid in the communication and distribution of information inside large corporations. This is especially crucial to people for whom information and know-how are mission-critical, such as management consultants or software developers. Once information is gathered, it is stored in internal databases so that it can be accessed from any company location in the world. By researching internal databases in the first place, the danger of duplicating information search procedures in separate locations is minimized and therefore, the return on information is maximized. For example, Arthur Andersen maintains a large internal database to which every consultant worldwide has access. When starting on a new project, the associate can research the database to find out if a similar project has been worked on before (by Arthur Andersen consultants) and what types of information are already available.

Thus, the Web can become an integral part of the information system of a corporation. **Firewalls** (merarchical layers of software protected by passwords) can protect from outside intrusion into the intranet. Sales, marketing, and communication applications can combine internal and external information resources smoothly. **Extranets** are networks set up between two companies to access information from both firms.

Extranets are networks set up between two companies to access information from both firms.

Speed

There are a number of promising technologies on the horizon, all of which have a common objective: **to increase the bandwidth of the Internet**. The demand for high speed connections is huge since more and more large data files such as multimedia applications are sent over the Internet.

There are a number of promising technologies on the horizon that have a common objective: to increase the bandwidth of the Internet. The demand for high-speed connections is huge, since more and more large data files such as multimedia applications are sent over the Internet. The ability to send and receive large amounts of data, such as a full motion picture, was still very limited in the last decade. However, this constraint is likely to disappear in the near future as cable companies venture into this new medium. Backbone operators such as MCI and Sprint are using fiber-optic networks that can accommodate transmission of full-screen motion pictures. Marketing researchers will gain tremendously from this development. For example, focus groups can be conducted from remote locations, and participants who are thousands of miles apart can participate effectively. This will allow market researchers to

TABLE 6-9   Which Way to the Internet?

Connection	Speed[a]	Cost[b]
Dial-Up	56 kbps	$
ISDN	128 kbps	$$$
DSL	1 mbps	$$
T-1	1.5 mbps	$$$
ARC Fiber	10 mbps	$$

[a] Speeds representative of average downloads per second.
[b] $ = 10.00–25.00/mo., $$ = 40.00–70.00/mo., $$$ = 200.00–1,000.00/mo.

discuss special topics with professionals or researchers who otherwise could not be brought together due to time and travel constraints.

Work is currently being done in the area of *photonic switching*—switching light waves without converting light to electrical energy. This work eventually will enable networks to take the next leap to speeds not even dreamed of today.

Table 6-9 compares speeds and costs of various Internet connection lines.

The Future of the Internet

Some say the Internet is broken. The evidence is everywhere. Outages drop millions of people off-line for hours, sometimes days. The number of users has been doubling every year since 1988, and traffic on some long-distance routes doubles every four months. World Wide Web pages take a long time to load because data pipes are clogged.

On the other hand, others say the Internet is doing just fine. Audio and video applications formerly only dreamed of are now commonplace. Messages zip along 350 times faster than they did in 1998. The major providers are increasing their capacity at a prodigious rate. The growth of the Internet worldwide has been phenomenal. The expansion of the Internet in Europe in 1996 nearly overwhelmed the continent's Internet links and posed challenges for its governments.[17] In 1997 there were 3 million Internet users in Asia, and the total is growing at about 5 percent per month. At the end of this decade, Asia grew to have about 50 million users.[18] Marketing Research in Practice 6-8 discusses how emerging Internet technologies are helping television commercials get new web venues.

MARKETING RESEARCH IN PRACTICE 6-8

Television Commercials get new Web Venues

A string of startup companies is experimenting with new ways to deliver video marketing messages to consumers. Several companies are setting into motion plans to use fresh techniques in presenting video commercials. Later this year TiVo plans to offer viewers the option of watching extended commercials stored on the TiVo system. Viewers watching a commercial could click on an icon appearing on-screen during a live broadcast to start a longer two-minute commercial that gives more information on the product.

At NetZero, the free Internet access service is taking a different approach to storing ads for later viewing. It plans to offer video commercials that users watch as they are dialing into access service. The key will be to present entertaining commercial messages that engage—rather than annoy—users during the dial-in process.

Source: S.V.H. *Inter@ctive Week 7,5* (February 7, 2000).

Both of these outlooks are correct; the truth lies somewhere in between. Engineers have been predicting the collapse of computer networks since before there even was an Internet, and the scare reemerges every few years.[19]

END OF CHAPTER MATERIAL

SUMMARY

The Internet is a worldwide network of computers originally designed by the U.S. government to provide an alternative communications network. Today, the Internet is a network of home and business users, libraries, universities, organizations, and others. The Internet uses a common computer language, and there are numerous communication services (e.g., the World Wide Web) available for exploring the Internet. The Internet can level the playing field for marketing to potential customers through efficient use of the medium. Both commercial and academic ventures have explored the characteristics of users of the Internet as well as uses for the Internet.

Collection of primary information on the Internet is increasing, as evidenced by the use of e-mail for survey research. Other forms of primary data collection are performed primarily through interactive forms, which are filled out on the screen. On-line focus groups are conducted entirely on-line—everything from recruitment and screening to moderation of the discussion itself. Secondary information about products or companies can be obtained using search engines on the Web. The power of the Internet for international marketing research cannot be underestimated.

KEY TERMS

Advanced Research Project Agency
    Network (ARPAnet)
World Wide Web (WWW)
e-mail
File Transfer Protocol (FTP)
Transmission ControlProtocol/Internet
    Protocol (TCP/IP)
TELNET
CommerceNet
ESOMAR
Media Metrix
Cyberatlas
I/PRO

Web Trends
New Media Research
AdCount
HERMES
Project 2000
custom search service
agents
free information providers
e-commerce
intranets
extranets
firewalls

MARKETING RESEARCH TOOLBOX
REVIEW POINTS

1. The Internet is a network of home and business computer users, libraries, universities, organizations, and so on that use a common computer language. This common "computer language" is called TCP/IP. TCP stands for Transmission Control Protocol and IP stands for Internet Protocol.

2. CommerceNet is an industry association for Internet commerce.

3. Net Views is an ongoing study that allows consumer packaged-goods and other marketers to quantify Internet's potential as a marketing tool across categories and brands.

4. Internet Demographics Survey is a prominent study designed to assess the dimension of the new medium in terms of personal access and usage patterns and to identify behavioral changes over time.

5. I/PRO is a San Francisco-based provider of services and software for the independent measurement and analysis of website usage. Their products enable website operators to analyze site usage, while advertisers and media buyers rely on I/PRO for optimal site selection.

6. Cyberatlas, a division of I/PRO, compiles and publishes public-domain information about Internet market size, growth, forecast, and demographics.

7. The advantages of advertising on the Internet include ease of reaching a target audience and direct response advertising.

8. One problem associated with web advertising is audience measurement.

9. Media Metrix is an Internet tracking service that measures actual Internet and digital media audience usage behavior in real-time.

10. HERMES (University of Michigan) is an academic research project that looks at the commercial uses of the World Wide Web, such as predicting consumer and corporate trends.

11. Project 2000 (Vanderbilt University) tries to enrich and stimulate generation of knowledge on the role of marketing in the new hypermedia environment.

12. Collection of primary information over the Internet is still in its incubation stage. Although some promising starts exist, the Internet is being used in mainstream marketing research with caution.

13. The main forte of the Internet is probably its advantages in researching secondary information.

14. The various service providers that overcome the limitation of conventional search engines are custom search services, agents, and free information providers.

15. The Internet, as a global medium, increases the scope of communication tremendously. Even though the globe-shrinking experience is already prevalent, the Internet's ability to communicate across borders will have a dramatic impact.

16. Intranets are internal company networks. The utilization of intranets will aid in the communication and distribution of information inside large corporations.

17. Extranets are networks set up between two companies to access information from both firms.

18. There are a number of promising technologies on the horizon, all of which have a common objective: to increase the bandwidth of the Internet. The demand for high-speed connections is huge, since more and more large data files such as multimedia applications are sent over the Internet.

QUESTIONS AND PROBLEMS

1. Alex Houston has to make an unscheduled trip this coming weekend to New York from his home town, Paris, Texas. He searched on the Internet for the lowest-price offering and bought his ticket. Demonstrate the search process that Alex used to get his ticket. Do you think that different search engines will provide varied results?

2. Assume that your family is interested in visiting the NASA Space Center in Houston. They would like to gather more facts about the place before they embark on a trip. How can you assist them in this process? What kind of information would they be requiring to get to NASA?

3. Design a customer satisfaction questionnaire and e-mail it to your friends. Ask them to respond to your survey by filling out the questionnaire and e-mailing it back to you. How do you think this differs from the paper questionnaire in terms of design and response rate?

4. You are hired as an intern in the marketing research department of a large hotel chain in the United States. The firm is interested in expanding its worldwide operations and is interested in country-specific information regarding real estate and labor laws. How will you obtain this information on the Internet?

5. Pick any company of your choice, and
   a. Identify its website.
   b. Browse through the website.
   c. List the type of information that is available through the website.
   d. In order to better understand the industry the company is functioning in, run a search and review the results. Are there sites that provide industry-wide values?

ENDNOTES

1. Note that the Internet sites listed in this chapter were compiled around October 1996. However, rapid change is one of the genuine properties of the Internet. Therefore, these sites may have been changed or linked with another site by the time you read this. You should go through the search procedure (e.g., Net Search in Netscape) for current information on relevant websites or visit http://www.wiley.com for an index of updated links.

2. CommerceNet, http://www.commerce.net/news/press/ann061699.html.

3. Forrester Research, http://www.forrester.com/ER/Press/Forrfind.

4. Jim Carlton, "Think Big," *Wall Street Journal,* June 17, 1996, p. R27.

5. Women shoppers head to the Web in force as the number of Internet buyers jumps 40 percent in nine months CommerceNet, http://www.commerce.net/news/press (April 2000).

6. Edward Cone, "Net Markets: Set to Rock the World," *Inter@ctive Week* 7,5 (February 7, 2000), p. 34.

7. Amy Cortese, "A Census in Cyberspace," *Business Week* (May 5, 1997), p. 84.

8. Thomas E. Weber, "Red Flags from Leading Web-Ad Sellers," *Wall Street Journal* (December 18, 1997), p. 1.

9. Bob Lamons, "Is Your Website Living Up to Its Potential?" *Marketing News* (October 27 1997), p. 8.

10. Donald R. Lehman and Russell S. Winer, *Product Management* (Chicago, IL: Irwin, 1997).

11. J. H. Ellsworth and M. V. Ellsworth, *The Internet Business Book* (New York: Wiley, 1996).

12. *Marketing Report* (July 22, 1996), p. 4.

13. J. Zilber and J. Papageorge, "Simple Search Secrets," *Net,* 2 (1997), pp. 37–41.

14. *Computing Canada* (November 9, 1997); NSTN (Canada's Internet Navigator) at http://www.i-m.com/.

15. (i) Charles Whaley, "Electronic Commerce Explodes on the Internet Despite Safety Concerns," *Computing Canada,* Netscope—Electronic Commerce Supplement, (September 29, 1997). (ii) IMRG (U.K. electronic trade organization), *Inter@ctive Week* (November 24, 1997).

16. Connie Guglielmo, "Sacred Trust: Personal Data Up for Grabs," *Inter@ctive Week* (December 8, 1997), pp. 72–74.

17. Brent Gregston, "The European Picture: The Net Is Conquering the Old World," *Internet World* (December 1996), pp. 52–55.

18. Gene Mesher, "The Internet in Asia," *Internet World* (December 1996), pp. 56–57.

19. Elizabeth Weise, "Growing Pains Entangle Internet," *Houston Chronicle* (October 27, 1996). Section E, p. 5.

CASES

For detailed descriptions of the below case and appendix please visit www.wiley.com/college/kumar.

Case 6-1: Caring Children's Hospital
Appendix: The Components of the Internet

Information Collection: Qualitative and Observational Methods

Learning Objectives

- Explain the need for qualitative research.
- Introduce the different types of qualitative research methods.
- Discuss in-depth interviews, focus-group, and projective techniques in detail.
- Be familiar with the various observational methods.

This chapter shifts the focus from the utilization of already-available secondary data to the collection of primary data for a specific purpose. Seldom is enough known about a marketing problem or situation for the researcher to be able to proceed directly to the design of a structured study that would yield representative and quantifiable results. Hence, qualitative data collection is done to obtain a basic feel for the problem before proceeding to the more analytical portion of the study.

A variety of qualitative methods can be used for such exploratory purposes. Specifically, we will discuss individual and group interviews, and case studies. The category of qualitative methods includes projective techniques that are used when self-reports are likely to be misleading. Although projective techniques are utilized during exploratory research, they are also used as a primary data collection method.

Observational methods are also discussed in this chapter. The observation of ongoing behavior is a widely used exploratory method, as well as an effective way to collect quantitative information when direct questioning is not possible.

◆ NEED FOR QUALITATIVE RESEARCH

The purpose of **qualitative research** is to find out what is in a consumer's mind. It is done to access and also get a rough idea about the person's perspective. It helps the researcher to become oriented to the range and complexity of consumer activity and concerns. Qualitative data are collected so researchers can know more about things that cannot be directly observed and measured. Feelings, thoughts, intentions, and behavior that took place in the past are a few examples of those things that can be obtained only through qualitative data collection methods.

The basic assumption behind qualitative methods is that an individual's organization of a relatively unstructured stimulus indicates the person's basic perceptions of the phenomenon and his or her reaction to it.[1] The more unstructured and ambiguous a stimulus is, the more subjects can and will project their emotions, needs, motives, attitudes, and values. The structure of a stimulus is the degree of choice available to the subject. A highly structured stimulus leaves very little choice: The subject has unambiguous choice among clear alternatives. A stimulus of low structure has a wide range of alternative choices. If it is ambiguous, the subjects can "choose" their own interpretations.

◆ QUALITATIVE RESEARCH METHODS

Collectively, these methods are less structured and more intensive than standardized questionnaire-based interviews. There is a longer, more flexible relationship with the respondent, so the resulting data have more depth and greater richness of context—which also means a greater potential for new insights and perspectives. The numbers of respondents are small and only partially representative of any target population, making them preludes to, but not substitutes for, carefully structured, large-scale field studies.

There are three major categories of acceptable uses of qualitative research methods:

1. Exploratory
   - Defining problems in more detail.
   - Suggesting hypotheses to be tested in subsequent research.
   - Generating new product or service concepts, problem solutions, lists of product features, and so forth.
   - Getting preliminary reactions to new product concepts.
   - Pretesting structured questionnaires.

2. Orientation
   - Learning the consumer's vantage point and vocabulary.
   - Educating the researcher to an unfamiliar environment: needs, satisfactions, usage situations, and problems.

3. Clinical
   - Gaining insights into topics that otherwise might be impossible to pursue with structured research methods.

The range of possible applications of these methods can be seen from the following examples:

1. A telephone equipment supplier wanted to know what features to incorporate in an answering device located in a telephone substation (rather than in the home or office). From several group discussions came ideas for many features such as variable-length messages and accessibility from any telephone. Specific features and price expectations were tested in a subsequent survey.

2. Before Beckman Instruments entered the process-control equipment market, it conducted four separate group interviews with instrumentation engineers. Participants came to the three-hour sessions in part because of the opportunity to talk with others in the field. Their complaints and comments about lack of readability of scales and unreliability of recording equipment were very influential in subsequent design decisions.[2]

Among the heaviest users of qualitative data are Japanese firms. They prefer "soft data" collected by managers during visits to dealers and customers, because such data give them a much better feel for a market's nuances. Talks with dealers who know their customers result in realistic, context-specific information. These talks relate directly to consumer attitudes, or the way the product has been or will be used, rather than being remote from actual behavior.[3] If Japanese firms do conduct surveys, they interview only people who have actually experienced the product or service, rather than asking a random sample about general attitudes. When Toyota wanted to learn what Americans preferred in small, imported cars, they asked groups of Volkswagen Beetle owners what they liked and disliked about that particular car.

Use of Computers in Qualitative Research

Four major perceived constraints have traditionally mitigated the use of qualitative research:

1. Volume of data
2. Complexity of analysis
3. Detail of clarification record
4. Time-consuming nature of the clerical efforts required

Computer technology has helped alleviate most of these problems and has helped to increase the use of qualitative research. The role of computer applications in the various tasks of qualitative data analysis is briefly described in the following paragraphs.

Transmitting

Data has to be transmitted into text using a word processor and then it has to be converted into ASCII. Only then can the data be imported into the program. Some popular programs used for qualitative analysis are Hyper Research, Atlas/Ti, NUD.IST, and Hypher Qual.

Storing

With the use of computer data, storage becomes very easy. It also brings more sophistication in the organization of data. The researcher can access the material quickly and precisely.

Coding

Codes have to be assigned by the researcher. Codes are labels assigned to data segments to enable taxonomic organization of the data. Once codes have been assigned, the computer can recall and print out all material belonging to a specific code. Each extracted piece is logged with its source, so that the researcher can easily see from where it was extracted. The software can be used for complex, multiple coding. Coding systems can be reused much more easily, and researchers can collaborate directly with each other by working in parallel on the data analysis of one text, as some programs (e.g., Atlas/Ti and NUD.IST) support the concept of multiauthoring for code systems.

Searching and Retrieving

Researchers use not only standard Boolean operations (and, or, not), but also various kinds of more complex search requests. For example, it is possible to request the computer to perform a search such as "produce a list of quotations relating to code 'acceleration of a car' as described by single men."

Building Relationships

The computer can be used to assist in the complex tasks of building relationships between the data segments as part of the theory development process. In some programs (e.g., Atlas/Ti, Infination, and NUD.IST), the relationship between data segments can then be visualized as a network with annotated lines linking codes, memos, or quotations.

Matrix Building

Matrixes are cross-tabulations of variables, codes, or dimensions of the data that help the researcher see how certain elements of the data interact. Many programs (e.g., NUD.IST) feature a special matrix-building function that speeds up this task.

Individual In-Depth Interviews

Individual in-depth interviews are conducted face to face with the respondent to explore the subject matter of the interview in detail. There are two basic types of indepth interviews. They are **nondirective** and **semistructured,** and their differences lie in the amount of guidance the interviewer provides.

Nondirective Interviews

In **nondirective interviews** the respondent is given maximum freedom to respond, within the bounds of topics of interest to the interviewer.

In nondirective interviews the respondent is given maximum freedom to respond, within the bounds of topics of interest to the interviewer. Success depends on (1) establishing a relaxed and sympathetic relationship; (2) the ability to probe in order to clarify and elaborate on interesting responses, without biasing the content of the responses; and (3) the skill of guiding the discussion back to the topic outline when digressions are unfruitful, always pursuing reasons behind the comments and answers. Such sessions normally are one to two hours long and may be tape recorded (always with the permission of the respondent) for later interpretation.

Semistructured or Focused Individual Interviews

In **semistructured** or **focused individual interviews** the interviewer attempts to cover a specific list of topics or subareas.

In semistructured or focused individual interviews the interviewer attempts to cover a specific list of topics or subareas. The timing, exact wording, and time allocated to each question area are left to the interviewer's discretion.

This mode of interviewing is especially effective with busy executives, technical experts, and thought leaders. Basic market intelligence, such as trends in technology, market demand, legislation, competitive activity, and similar information are amenable to such interviews. The open structure ensures that unexpected facts or attitudes can be pursued easily.

This type of interview is extremely demanding, and much depends on the interviewer's skill. First, the interviewer must be sufficiently persuasive to get through the shield of secretaries and receptionists around many executives, in order to get an appointment. The major challenge is to establish rapport and credibility in the early moments of the interview, and then maintain that atmosphere. For this, there is no substitute for an informed, authoritative person who can relate to respondents on their own terms. This can be achieved by asking the respondent to react to specific information provided by the interviewer. Care should be taken to avoid threatening questions. A good opener might be, "If you had to pick one critical problem affecting your industry, what would it be?" Cooperation sometimes can be improved by offering a quid pro quo, such as a summary of some of the study findings.

A difficult problem with these interviews is the matter of record keeping. Some executives dislike tape recorders, so it may be necessary to use a team of interviewers who alternate between asking questions and recording responses. To keep the interview as short as possible, it is usually best to leave behind a structured questionnaire for any specific data that are wanted, because this can be assigned to staff for answering. Finally, since the appropriate respondents for these studies are often difficult to identify, and may represent many parts of an organization, it is always advisable to ask for recommendations about which other people it might be useful to interview.

Individual in-depth interviews are also used in consumer markets to identify key product benefits and trigger creative insights. Three techniques are being widely used now. In the first technique, **laddering,**[4] questioning progresses from product characteristics to user characteristics. A good starting point is with a repertory (sometimes called Kelly's triad). If the topic were airlines, respondents might be asked to compare one airline in a set of three to the other two: How do airlines A and B differ from C? How do A and C differ from B? And so on. Each attribute, such as "a softer seat," is then probed to see why it is important to the respondent; then that reason is probed, and so on. The result might be the following kind of dialogue:

> In **laddering,** questioning progresses from product characteristics to user characteristics. In hidden-issue questioning, the focus is not on socially shared values but rather on personal "sore spots"—not on general lifestyles but on deeply felt personal concerns.

Interviewer: "Why do you like wide bodies?"

Respondent: "They're more comfortable."

Interviewer: "Why is that important?"

Respondent: "I can accomplish more."

Interviewer: "Why is that important?"

Respondent: "I will feel good about myself."

Notice that the dialogue has moved from a very tangible aspect of an airline to its contribution to self-esteem.

The second technique is called **hidden-issue questioning.** In hidden-issue questioning, the focus is not on socially shared values but rather on personal "sore spots"—not on general lifestyles but on deeply felt personal concerns. The third technique, **symbolic analysis,** attempts to analyze the symbolic meaning of objects by comparing them with their opposites. For example, the following question could be asked: "What would it be like if you could no longer use airlines?" Responses such as "Without planes, I would have to rely on long-distance calls and letters" may be received. This would suggest that one of the attributes that can be highlighted in an ad campaign for an airline could be face-to-face communication. Sometimes an interviewer may have to go outside a country to interview people or may have to design questionnaires that are to be administered in other parts of the world. Issues that an interviewer commonly faces when interviewing in another culture are described in Marketing Research in Practice 7–1.[5]

> **Symbolic analysis** attempts to analyze the symbolic meaning of objects by comparing them with their opposites.

Telephone depth interviewing is starting to gain greater acceptance among consumers, and has proven to be more beneficial than focus groups. More telephoning is being used in qualitative research because of the following factors: The telephone has become a standard medium of communications, clients are more receptive to saving time and therefore money, and studies can be conducted in remote areas that other qualitative methods, such as focus groups, cannot access.

MARKETING RESEARCH IN PRACTICE 7–1

Qualitative Interviewing in the International Context

Evaluation has become an international activity. International and cross-cultural short-term evaluation site visits are much more subject to misinterpretations and miscommunications than traditional, long-term anthropological fieldwork. The data from interviews are words. It is tricky enough to be sure what a person means when using a common language, but words can take on a very different meaning in other cultures. In Sweden, I participated in an international conference discussing policy evaluations. The conference was conducted in English, but I was there for two days, much of the time confused, before I came to understand that their use of the term *policy* corresponded to my American use of the term *program.* I interpreted policies, from an American context, to be fairly general directives, often very difficult to evaluate because of their vagueness. In Sweden, however, policies are very specific programs.

The situation becomes more precarious when a translator or interpreter must be used because of language differences. Using an interpreter for conducting interviews is fraught with difficulty. Special and very precise training of translators is critical. It is important that questions be asked precisely as you want them asked, and that full and complete answers be translated. Interpreters often want to be helpful by summarizing and explaining responses. This contaminates the interviewee's actual response with the interpreter's explanation to such an extent that you can no longer be sure whose perceptions you have—the interpreter's or the interviewee's.

There are also words and ideas that simply can't be translated. People who regularly use the language come to know the unique cultural meaning of special terms, but they don't translate well. One of my favorites from the Caribbean is "liming." It means something like hanging out, just being, doing nothing—guilt free. In conducting interviews for a program evaluation, a number of participants said they were just "liming" in the program. But that was not meant as a criticism. Liming is a highly desirable state of being, at least to participants. Funders might view the situation differently.

The high esteem in which science is held has made it culturally acceptable in Western countries to conduct interviews on virtually any subject in the name of science. Such is not the case worldwide. Evaluation researchers cannot simply presume that they have the right to ask intrusive questions. Many topics may be taboo. I have experienced cultures where it is simply inappropriate to ask questions to a subordinate about a superordinate. Any number of topics may be taboo, or at least indelicate, for strangers—family matters, political views, who owns what, how people came to be in certain positions, and sources of income.

There are also different norms governing interactions. I remember with great embarrassment going to an African village to interview the chief. The whole village was assembled. Following a brief welcoming ceremony, I asked if we could begin the interview. I expected a private, one-on-one interview. He expected to perform in front of and involve the whole village. It took me a while to understand this, during which I kept asking to go somewhere else so we could begin the interview. He did not share my concern about preference for privacy. What I expected to be an individual interview soon turned out to be a whole village focus group interview! In many cultures it is a breach of etiquette for an unknown man to ask to meet alone with a woman. Even a female interviewer may need the permission of a husband, brother, or a parent to interview a village woman.

Source: Michael Quinn Patton, *Qualitative Evaluation and Research Methods,* Second Edition (Thousand Oaks, CA: Sage Publications, 1990).

Focus-Group Discussions

A focus-group discussion is the process of obtaining possible ideas or solutions to a marketing problem from a group of respondents by discussing it. The emphasis in this method is on the results of group interaction when focused on a series of topics a discussion leader introduces. Each participant in a group of five to nine or more persons is encouraged to express views on each topic, and to elaborate on or react to the views of the other participants. The objectives are similar to unstructured in-depth interviews, but the moderator plays a more passive role than an interviewer does.

The **focus-group discussion** offers participants more stimulation than an interview; presumably, this makes new ideas and meaningful comments more likely.[6] Among other advantages, it is claimed that discussions often provoke more spontaneity and candor than can be expected in an interview. Some proponents think that the security of being in a crowd encourages some participants to speak out. Marketing Research in Practice 7-2 illustrates two scenarios of focus-group discussions.

Focus-group discussion offers participants more stimulation than an interview; presumably this makes new ideas and meaningful comments more likely.

Focus-group facility.
Courtesy Sofres Intersearch.

MARKETING RESEARCH IN PRACTICE 7-2

A Tale of Two Focus Groups

It's Wednesday evening, and the first focus group of the night at a New Jersey facility is winding up a session paid for by a mid-sized Eastern city that wants nothing more than to become a bonafide tourist destination. This group, composed entirely of people over 50 who already have visited the destination, seems reluctant to have the session end. The city in question is an important site in African-American history, and several well-informed black women are relishing their reminiscences of it. One very animated woman seems pleased that she knows a number of facts that the moderator doesn't.

She mentions that the city is also the site of an annual basketball playoff for African-American colleges. A white man wonders whether people who are not African American would hesitate to visit the city were it to advertise its connection to that event. A heated discussion breaks out, and the other participants agree that the man is off the mark.

After the moderator ends the session—which went 10 minutes past its 90-minute time slot—several of the members of this well-informed group shake hands and say how much they've enjoyed meeting each other.

Now it's time for the 6:00–7:30 p.m. session. A decidedly tired-looking group of men and women, all parents between the ages of 30 and 45, plop down in their chairs. Maybe it's because the participants haven't had dinner yet, or miss their kids, or had tough days, or intimidate each other, or have lackluster personalities, but this crowd is much less expressive. They also don't seem as well-informed. Several seem as if they'd probably criticize just about anything on general principle.

A mother of two, friendly and eager to please, says she found the city's history fascinating and she believes others would, too. The man next to her—a naysayer if ever there were one—says he ended up in the city by accident and found nothing much of interest there. Several minutes later, the woman unaccountably switches her mind and says that she doesn't think the city's history would interest many people. A heavy atmosphere settles over the room. Everyone looks drained and no one ventures a strong view.

Interestingly, given the differences in the two panels, both groups were chosen through random phone surveys conducted by the facility personnel. The panelists were asked their ages, number of children and familiarity with the city. They also were asked if they had participated in similar sessions. In recent years the industry has been plagued by "focus-group junkies" who show up repeatedly. Recently, annoyed sponsors have begun demanding fresh blood.

Both panels were asked to give reactions to eight possible slogans for the city. Surprisingly, both groups chose the same three slogans, each of which underscored the city's diverse attractions, such as restaurants, shopping, and children's amusements. The participants' consensus was that a broad-based pitch would attract the largest number of tourists. Similarly, they rejected several slogans playing up the city's role in history, concluding that such a focus would be too narrow.

Client John Boatwright, who owns a Virginia tourism consulting group called Boatwright & Co., says it is occurrences like very different groups arriving at identical results that gives him confidence in focus groups. Clients tend to conclude they are on the right track when such coincidences take place, he says. "If you do four to six groups and get a consensus, you can conclude that if you did exponentially more groups, you would get the same results," he explains.

Source: Leslie Wines, "A Tale of Two Focus Groups," *Forecast Magazine* (July/August 1995), p. 27.

Carmen Sandoes, marketing manager for the Bronx Zoo, says the nonprofit institution used focus groups to test various appeals to increase the number of zoo visitors. Participants were divided evenly between those who had and had not been to the zoo. They were asked to pick animal concepts—such as "Great Snakes Day" and

"Big Bears Week"—which could be used as special-events themes. These themes—promotional tools—would feature exotic snakes for a day or display grizzly polar bears for a week. Using the focus group helped Sanders and her staff to find which animals aroused the most interest and to implement their discovery in the form of future special events.

In conducting focus groups, it is very important to position focus group observers by spending time briefing them before the groups start and debriefing them afterward. Positioning client observers can avoid problems of misinterpretation of results in the future, and prepare observers to gain a better understanding of what they will be seeing and hearing. Observers are less prone to assume that the opinions of one or two participants are somehow representative of any group of people other than the focus-group participants themselves. Some of the issues that need to be addressed in the briefing session are:

1. Outlining the intended direction of the group
2. Explaining how participants were recruited
3. Reeducating observers on the concepts of random selection, statistical reliability, and projectability of research results

There are no hard-and-fast rules for choosing focus groups rather than individual in-depth interviews for qualitative studies. The comparison in Table 7-1 can help you to make the choice.[7]

Key Factors for Focus-Group Success

As a rule, three or four group sessions usually are sufficient. The analyst invariably learns a great deal from the first discussion. The second interview produces much more, but less is new. Usually, by the third or fourth session, much of what is said has been heard before, and there is little to be gained from additional focus groups. Exceptions to this rule occur if there are distinct segments to cover, such as regional differences in tastes, the differences between women working in the home and outside the home, or the differences between married or unmarried women.

A focus group is not an easy technique to employ. Further, a poorly conducted or analyzed focus group can yield misleading results and waste a good deal of money.[8] In 2001 the recruitment costs, payments to participants, space rental, moderation, and analyst fees easily ranged from $4,000 to $6,000 per focus group for consumer studies.[9] The typical cost for an industrial focus group was approximately $5,000. The key success factors are:

1. Planning the agenda
2. Recruiting participants
3. Effective moderation
4. Analysis and interpretation of the results

For more information on running successful focus group, go to http://www.wiley.com/college/kumar.

Planning the Agenda

Planning starts by translating the research purpose into a set of managerially relevant questions, which ensures that client and moderator agree on specific objectives before the study begins. From these questions, the group moderator can prepare a discussion guide to serve as a checklist of the specific issues and topics to be covered.

TABLE 7-1 Comparison of Focus Groups and Individual In-Depth Interviews

	Focus Groups	Individual In-Depth Interviews
Group interactions	Group interaction is present. This may stimulate new thoughts from respondents.	There is no group interaction. Therefore, stimulation for new ideas from respondents comes from the interviewer.
Group/peer pressure	Group pressure and stimulation may clarify and challenge thinking.	In the absence of group pressure, the thinking of respondents is not challenged.
	Peer pressure and role playing may occur and may be confusing to interpret.	With one respondent, role playing is minimized and there is no peer pressure.
Respondent competition	Respondents compete with one another for time to talk. There is less time to obtain in-depth details from each participant.	The individual is alone with the interviewer and can express thoughts in a noncompetitive environment. There is more time to obtain detailed information.
Influence	Responses in a group may be "contaminated" by opinions of other group members.	With one respondent, there is no potential for influence from other respondents.
Subject sensitivity	If the subject is sensitive, respondents may be hesitant to talk freely in the presence of several other people.	If the subject is sensitive, respondents may be more likely to talk.
Interviewer fatigue	One interviewer can easily conduct several group sessions on one topic without becoming fatigued or bored.	Interviewer fatigue and boredom are problems when many individual interviews are needed.
Amount of information	A relatively large amount of information can be obtained in a short period of time with relatively small cost.	A large amount of information can be obtained, but it takes time to obtain it and to analyze the results. Thus, costs are relatively high.
Stimuli	The volume of stimulus materials that can be used is somewhat limited.	A fairly large amount of stimulus material can be used.
Interviewer schedule	It may be difficult to assemble eight or ten respondents if they are a difficult type to recruit (such as very busy executives).	Individual interviews are easier to schedule.

Source: James Cowley, "Anyone Can Run Research Focus Groups, Right?" *Marketing News,* 33, 6 (March 1, 1999).

However, this list is strictly for general guidance; it is not desirable to read formal questions to the group.

An important issue is the order in which the moderator introduces topics. Usually, it is best to proceed from a general discussion to increasingly specific questions, for if the specific issue is addressed first it will influence the general discussion. It is also easier for respondents to relate to a specific issue when it has been preceded by a general discussion. For example, Mother's Cookies was interested in concept-testing a new fruit-filled cookie, and a proposed introductory promotion involved tickets to a circus performance. The moderator started with a general discussion about snacks and then moved to the use of cookies as snacks and the question of buying versus making cookies. Only after this general discussion was the more specific topic addressed.

The set of topics covered may change after each focus-group experience. The moderator and client might decide that a question is not generating useful, nonrepetitive information, and might drop it from the remaining focus groups. Or a new, interesting idea might emerge, and reactions might be sought from subsequent groups.[10]

Recruitment

When recruiting participants, it is necessary to provide for both similarity and contrast within a group. As a rule, it is undesirable to combine participants from different social classes or stages in the life cycle, because of differences in their perceptions, experiences, and verbal skills.[11]

Within an otherwise homogeneous group, it may be helpful to provide for a spark to be struck occasionally, by introducing contrasting opinions. One way to do this is to include both users and nonusers of the product or service or brand. If the product carries social connotations, however, this mixing may suppress divergent opinions; for example, buyers of large life insurance policies may believe that nonbuyers are irresponsible. Some moderators believe that having conflicting opinions within a group may invite either a "rational" defense or a "withdrawal" of those who think their opinions are in a minority.

One controversial source of participants is the "experienced" panel, whose members have been trained in ways that contribute to the dialogue in the group. Those who oppose this practice think that "professional" respondents who show up repeatedly are so sensitized by the interview experience that they are no longer representative of the population.[12]

Although groups of 8 to 12 have become customary, smaller groups may be more productive.[13] With 12 panelists, for example, after subtracting the time it takes to warm up (usually about 3 minutes) and the time for the moderator's questions and probes, the average panelist in a 90-minute focus group has 3 minutes of actual talking time. The experience becomes more like a group survey than an exploration of experiences, feelings, and beliefs. It is also a very expensive form of survey, so cutting group size makes sound economic sense.

The Moderator

Effective moderating encourages all participants to discuss their feelings, anxieties, and frustrations, as well as the depth of their convictions on issues relevant to the topic, without being biased or pressured by the situation.[14] It is often difficult to prevent opinionated participants from starting the conversation in a focus group. To avoid this problem, the moderator can have every member of the focus group write down his or her initial response to the product or service before the start of the discussion. Then if the group gets off track, participants can refer back to the original statement.[15] The following are critical moderating skills:

* Ability to establish rapport quickly by listening carefully, demonstrating a genuine interest in each participant's views, dressing like the participants, and avoiding the use of jargon or sophisticated terminology that may turn off the group.
* Flexibility, observed by implementing the interview agenda in a way the group finds comfortable. Slavish adherence to an agenda means the discussion loses spontaneity and degenerates into a question-and-answer session.
* Ability to sense when a topic has been exhausted or is becoming threatening, and to know which new topic to introduce to maintain a smooth flow in the discussion.
* Ability to control group influences to avoid having a dominant individual or subgroup that might suppress the total contribution.

Common techniques for conducting successful focus-group interviews include the chain reaction, devil's advocate, and false termination. In the **chain reaction technique,** the moderator builds a cumulative effect by encouraging each member of the focus group to comment on a prior idea suggested by someone else in the group, by adding to or expanding on it. When playing *devil's advocate*, the moderator expresses extreme viewpoints; this usually provokes reactions from focus-group members and keeps the discussion moving forward in a lively manner. In *false termination*, the moderator falsely concludes a focus-group interview, thanks group members for participating, and inquires whether there are any final comments. These "final comments" frequently lead to new discussion avenues and often result in the most useful data obtained.

Analysis and Interpretation of the Results

Analysis and interpretation of the results are complicated by the wealth of disparate comments usually obtained, which means that any analyst can find something that agrees with his or her view of the problem. A useful report of a group session is one that captures the range of impressions and observations on each topic, and interprets them in the light of possible hypotheses for further testing. When reporting comments, it is not sufficient merely to repeat what was said without putting it into a context, so that the implications are more evident.

The moderator must keep several features of group interactions in mind during the analysis. An evaluation of a new concept by a group tends to be conservative; that is, it favors ideas that are easy to explain and not necessarily very new. There are further problems with the order of presentation when several concepts, products, or advertisements are being evaluated. If group participants have been highly critical of one thing, they may compensate by being uncritical of the next.

Trends in Focus Groups

Focus groups represent 10 percent to 15 percent of market research and the number of focus groups being conducted is growing at a rapid pace. There may be more than 50,000 focus groups conducted annually. The quality of focus-group facilities has also become better. Instead of tiny viewing rooms with small one-way mirrors, plush two-tiered observation areas now wrap around the conference room to provide an unobstructed view of all the respondents. Telephone focus groups have emerged recently. This technique has been developed for respondents who are difficult to recruit, such as doctors. These focus groups use the conference calling facility to conduct the discussion. In cities where focus-group facilities are not available, focus-group discussions can be conducted in church basements, in restaurants, and in a variety of hotel meeting rooms. The cost structure for a typical focus group is given in Marketing Research in Practice 7-3.

Two-way focus groups involve allowing one target group to listen and learn from a related group.

Another emerging trend is in **two-way focus groups.**[16] This allows one target group to listen and learn from a related group. In one application, physicians viewed a focus group of arthritis patients discussing the treatment they desired. A focus group of these physicians was then held to determine their reactions. A new focus-group television network called the Focus Vision Network may represent a third trend. Instead of flying from city to city; clients can view the focus groups in their offices. Live focus groups are broadcast by video transmission from a nationwide network of independently owned focus facilities. The cost of this option is, of course, quite high.[17] Focus Vision also plans to unveil an international network of focus facilities. Thus, global focus groups will be possible in the near future.[18]

The Internet is the latest way to obtaining time-compressed information from on-line surveys and focus groups, information that arrives "just in time" to help companies make quality decisions.

On-line surveys sample public and employee opinions and give immediate statistics. On-line focus groups offer a more personal approach. Participants can interact with one another and a facilitator. They can click to background information or a variety of images to clarify their understanding of issues or questions. They can see the immediate results of their discussions and change their mind if they like. All is recorded and becomes a part of new data.

One major advantage of on-line focus groups is real-time results; another is cost. On-line focus groups typically run one-fifth to one-half the cost of a traditional market research project. They also help overcome state and national boundaries.

MARKETING RESEARCH IN PRACTICE 7-3

Cost Factors in a Focus Group

For business-to-business groups, budget for $4,000 to $9,000 per group and a three-group minimum. It is a rare project that includes more than six groups, so you can assume that most focus group projects will cost between $15,000 and $50,000. The breakdown of costs is roughly as follows:

Facility: $300 to $500 per group

Recruitment: Depends on difficulty of finding people—generally the single biggest cost factor

Moderator: $1,000 per group and up, depending on type of report

Participant fees: About $50 per participant for an ordinary professional (e.g., engineer), $100 for managers and people in high demand (e.g., MIS directors), greater than $100 for executives, doctors, and the like

Videotaping: $500 per group

Food: $5 to $15 per participant

Vendor overhead: Varies

Today, on-line focus groups are used to test new products, evaluate the perform-ance of existing ones, brainstorm hot ideas, and test traditional market research to see if any questions need to be reworded or expanded. They are used for crisis, diver-sity, and morale management. They tap the creative thinking of employees and shape corporate policies. On-line groups also promise a faster turnaround, and the respondent pool can stretch across the city. However, on-line qualitative research has its limitations, and for studies in which intense conversations or body language is important, the traditional focus group still is the tool of choice.[19]

Projective Techniques

The central feature of all projective techniques is the presentation of an ambiguous, unstructured object, activity, or person that a respondent is asked to interpret and explain.[20] The more ambiguous the stimulus, the more respondents have to project themselves into the task, thereby revealing hidden feelings and opinions. These tech-niques often are used in conjunction with individual nondirective interviews.

Projective techniques are used when it is believed that respondents will not or cannot respond meaningfully to direct questions about (1) the reasons for certain behaviors or attitudes, or (2) what the act of buying, owning, or using a product or service means to them. People may be unaware of their own feelings and opinions, unwilling to make admissions that reflect badly on their self-image (in which case they will offer rationalizations or socially acceptable responses), or too polite to be critical to an interviewer.

The following categories of projective techniques will be discussed: (1) word association, (2) completion tests, (3) picture interpretation, (4) third-person tech-niques, (5) role playing, and (6) case studies.

Word Association

The **word-association technique** asks the respondent to give the first word or phrase that comes to mind after the researcher presents a word or phrase. The word association technique has been useful for obtaining reactions to potential brand names.

The **word-association technique** asks respondents to give the first word or phrase that comes to mind after the researcher presents a word or phrase. The list of items used as stimuli should include a random mix of such neutral items such as *chair, sky,* and *water,* interspersed with the items of interest, such as *shopping downtown, vaca-tioning in Greece,* or *Hamburger Helper.* An interviewer reads the word to the respon-dents and asks them to mention the first thing that comes to mind. The list is read quickly to avoid allowing time for defense mechanisms to come into play. Responses are analyzed by calculating:

1. The frequency with which any word is given as a response
2. The amount of time that elapses before a response is given
3. The number of respondents who do not respond at all to a test word within a reasonable period of time

The result of a word-association task often is hundreds of words and ideas. To evaluate quantitatively the relative importance of each, a representative set of the tar-get segment can be asked to rate, on a five-point scale, how well the word fits the brand, from "fits extremely well" to "fits not well at all." It is also useful to conduct the same associative research on competitive brands. When such a scaling task was performed for McDonald's on words generated from a word-association task, the strongest associations were with the words *Big Macs, Golden Arches, Ronald, Chicken McNugget, Egg McMuffin, everywhere, familiar, greasy, clean, food, cheap, kids, well-known, French fries, fast, hamburgers,* and *fat.* In the same study, Jack-in-the-Box had much lower associations with the words *everywhere, familiar, greasy,* and *clean,* and much higher associations with *tacos, variety, fun,* and *nutritious.*[21]

The word-association technique has also been particularly useful for obtaining reactions to potential brand names. Consumers associate a brand with (1) product attributes, (2) intangibles, (3) customer benefits, (4) relative price, (5) use/application, (6) user/customer, (7) celebrity/person, (8) lifestyle personality, (9) product class, (10) competitors, and (11) country/geographic area.[22] This technique is being used extensively to explore these associations. Word association has also been used to obtain reactions to and opinions about advertising slogans. For example, Bell Telephone found that one theme for advertising, "The System Is the Solution," triggered negative, "Big Brother is watching you" reactions among some people. According to a recent study, word association can be used for finding consumer wants for products that do not exist. In this study consumers were asked to rate novel verb–object combinations, which generated a number of interesting "really new" function ideas and allowed researchers to assess buyer responses. Using the method, they elicited potential new functions for food-processing technology. Top scores included "spend less money on food," "alert to spoiling food," "learn more about food," and "calculate calories of food."[23]

Completion Tests

Completion tests involve giving a respondent an incomplete and ambiguous sentence, which is to be completed with a phrase.

The simplest **completion test** involves giving a respondent an incomplete and ambiguous sentence, which is to be completed with a phrase. The respondent is encouraged to respond with the first thought that comes to mind. Sentences are usually in the third person ("The average person considers television…" "People drawing unemployment compensation are…"), but may refer directly to the object or activity ("Insurance of all kinds is…") The completion test can be expanded readily to involve the completion of a story presented as an incomplete narrative or simply as a cartoon. In one such study, people were shown a crude picture of two women shopping in a supermarket (Figure 7-1). When told that one woman is purchasing dry soup mix, they were asked to tell a story about her and to describe what she is

"I think shopping is aerobic."

Figure 7-1   Two women shopping. ©1998 William Hamilton, The Cartoon Bank.

Source: From "Dreams, Fairy Tales, Animals, and Cars," by Sidney J. Levy, in *Psychology and Marketing* 2, Summer 1985, pp. 67–81, copyright ©1985 by John Wiley & Sons, Inc.

saying to the second woman. They were also asked to tell what the second woman is like. Based on this, user profiles for the soup mix were developed.[24]

Picture Interpretation

Picture interpretation technique is based on the Thematic Apperception Test (TAT). The respondent is shown an ambiguous picture in the form of a line drawing, illustration, or photograph and asked to describe it.

The **picture interpretation technique** is based on the Thematic Apperception Test (TAT). The respondent is shown an ambiguous picture in the form of a line drawing, illustration, or photograph, and asked to describe it. This is a very flexible technique, for the pictures can be adapted readily to many kinds of marketing problems. An example of picture interpretation was a study that showed the respondents two scenes.[25] One involved a break after a daytime hike on a mountain; the other showed a small evening barbecue with close friends. During the scene the beer served was either Coors or Lowenbrau. Respondents were asked to project themselves into the scene and indicate, on a five-point scale, the extent to which they would feel *warm, friendly, healthy,* and *wholesome.* The study was designed to test whether the advertising of Coors and Lowenbrau had established associations with their use-contexts— Coors with hiking, wholesomeness, and health, and Lowenbrau with a barbecue-type setting, friends, and warmth. The results showed that Coors was evaluated higher in the mountain setting and Lowenbrau in the barbecue setting, as expected, but that the other word associations were not sensitive (related) to the setting. For example, in the hiking context, Coors was higher on the *warm* and *friendly* dimensions, as well as on *healthy* and *wholesome.*

Third-Person Techniques

By asking how friends, neighbors, or the average person would think or react in the situation, the researcher can observe, to some extent, the respondents projecting their own attitudes onto this **third person,** thus revealing more of their own feelings.

By asking how friends, neighbors, or the average person would think or react in the situation, the researcher can observe, to some extent, the respondents projecting their own attitudes onto this **third person,** thus revealing more of their own true feelings. Magazines use this technique to identify which articles to feature on the cover, to stimulate newsstand sales. Direct questioning as to the articles of greatest interest to the respondent tends to be confounded by socially desirable responses.

Another variant of this technique provides a shopping list or a description of a person's activities, and asks respondents to describe the person. The respondents' attitudes toward the activities or items on the list will be reflected in their descriptions of the person. Usually, two lists are prepared and presented to matched sets of respondents; these could be grocery shopping lists, in which all items are identical except that Nescafe instant coffee on the first list is replaced by Maxwell House (drip grind) coffee on the second list.[26] Differences in the descriptions attributed to the two lists can reveal the respondents' underlying attitudes toward the product or activity that is being studied.

Role Playing

In **role playing** a respondent assumes the role or behavior of another person, such as salesperson in a store. This person then can be asked to try to sell a product to consumers who raise objections.

In **role playing,** a respondent assumes the role or behavior of another person, such as a salesperson in a store. This person then can be asked to try to sell a product to consumers, who raise objections. The method of coping with objections may reveal the respondents' attitudes, if they project themselves fully into the role playing without feeling uncomfortable or embarrassed.

Another technique with similar expressive objectives is the *role rehearsal* procedure used as part of a focus-group discussion. The participants in a focus group are encouraged, by offering them an incentive, to alter their behavior pattern in some extreme way.

Case Studies

A **case study**, in the research sense, is a comprehensive description and analysis of a single situation. The data for a case study usually are obtained from a series of lengthy, unstructured interviews with a number of people involved in the situation, perhaps combined with available secondary and internal data sources.

Case studies are very productive sources of research hypotheses. This approach was used by a food company to suggest the attributes that might characterize successful district sales managers. A successful and an unsuccessful manager from otherwise similar territories (i.e., the territories had similar market structure, potential, and competitive situations) were studied closely for two weeks. They were interviewed, observed during sales calls and trips with their salespeople, and given a series of personality tests. The differences were used to develop a series of surveys that were administered to all the managers.

In some circumstances, a case study may be the only way to understand a complex situation. For example, the decision-making processes in large organizations may be imperfectly understood by a single participant. This problem makes it difficult to understand the sequence of decisions leading to, for example, the choice of a telephone service that customers use to call for reservations, get information, or place purchase orders. A telecommunications manager may simply be a technical consultant on the telephone system for the using company, without knowing how the system is used in the business. The functional managers in marketing or operations actually may make the decision to offer the service to customers but not know the intricacies of the switching network. To get a picture of the company's use of the service, all parties must be interviewed. Marketing Research in Practice 7-4 makes a case for case studies.

*A **case study** is a comprehensive description and analysis of a single situation. Case studies are very productive sources of research hypotheses.*

MARKETING RESEARCH IN PRACTICE 7-4

A Case for Case Studies

Which would you rather bet your company's strategy on: what consumers say or what they do? Surveys, focus groups, and mall intercepts attempt to develop an understanding of customers' motivations by collecting reactions to researchers' questions. The major criticism of these methods is that what they gather are mere opinion statements that don't reveal actual behavior. Instead of gathering poorly considered opinion statements, the case-study approach builds insight into marketing behavior by pursuing—and verifying—the stories behind specific recent purchases in a given product category. It builds the full stories of how 50 supermarket shoppers selected their peanut butter last Tuesday, or how 25 companies replaced their PBX systems last month.

Key arguments for the case-study approach are

- Case studies uncover motivations through demonstrated actions, not through statements of opinions.
- They're conducted in the surroundings where a product is bought or used to achieve greater immediacy (and accuracy) of response.
- They use observation and documentation to stimulate questions and corroborate responses.
- They access multiple decision makers.
- They require the talents of "marketing detectives" rather than "census takers."

Source: "Study What People Do, Not What They Say," *Marketing News* (January 6, 1992), pp. 15, 32.

Empathic Interviewing[27]

Empathic interviewing is a form of **exploratory research** that draws from the wisdom of sociology, psychology, market research, and anthropology to help researchers probe beneath generalizations and identify the social factors that influence consumer behavior. In understanding how complex decisions and behaviors emerge, empathic interviewing can supplement or replace traditional research methods. Some guidelines in conducting empathic interviews include:

1. Imagine yourself in the person's situation.
2. Avoid self-referencing.
3. Gently challenge generalizations by asking for specific examples.
4. Ask open-ended, nonleading questions that start with *how, what,* and *why.*

Other Projective Techniques

Many other projective techniques have been developed and used in recent years. BBDO Worldwide has developed a trademarked technique called Photo Sort. Consumers express their feelings about brands through a specially developed photo deck showing pictures of different types of people, from business executives to college students. Respondents connect the people with the brands they think they use. Another photo-sort technique called the Pictured Aspirations Technique (PAT) has been created by Grey Advertising. This device attempts to uncover how a product fits into consumers' aspirations. Consumer drawings are used to unlock motivations or express perceptions. Researchers ask consumers to draw what they are feeling or how they perceive an object. Marketing Research in Practice 7-5 discusses how qualitative research has focused on women in the last three decades.

MARKETING RESEARCH IN PRACTICE 7-5

Focus on Women: Three Decades of Qualitative Research

There are three identifiable periods for qualitative research of women:

1. The early 1970s—the end of the traditional era
   * Focus groups were done during the day (assuming all women were housewives).
   * Women were paid less than men for attending ($7.50 vs. $10.00).
2. The late 1970s through late 1980s—the discovery of the new working women
   * Market researchers started including women in studies for nontraditional products (e.g. air travel, investments, cars).
3. The late 1980s to the present—the end-of-the-century women
   * Researchers now routinely include women in what previously had been all-male groups.
   * Women hold their own mixed-gender focus groups on such nontraditional categories such as technology, financial management, and sports.

For other interesting articles on marketing research visit http://www.ama.org/mn.

Source: Judith Langer, *Marketing News* (September 14, 1998), p. 21.

Most people make rational, conscious, purchase decisions and can accurately report the reasons for their decisions when asked. However, many decisions appear to result from preconscious drives that can be either expressed or repressed. When a drive is repressed, a consumer may not be able to access the reason for a particular purchase decision. A technique called the *implicit model* provides a solution to this type of a problem.

In one study, a respondent, discussing the brand of interest, had only positive comments regarding the brand. Then a set of animal photographs was presented and the respondent was asked to select the animal that best represented this brand. The respondent chose a photo that described a sly, wily, cunning, and even sneaky animal. This animal was a pretty, nice, neat-looking animal that was really a fairly mean, predatory creature stealing its prey in the night.[28]

Ways to Get More Out of Qualitative Research[29]

To get extraordinary value from research dollars, one must develop a team of exceptionally good listeners in the backroom. Listening is hard work, especially to group after group. It's tempting to go numb with munchies, criticize the participants' every *faux pas,* and dismiss whatever they say that doesn't agree with our agenda. We pay attention to "the mistakes," to what we disagree with, or we listen for agreement, noticing comments that support our ideas or beliefs. Listening with a beginner's mind provides us an opportunity to hear something really new, to listen for knowledge and even discovery. How do we get through the veils of our own perceptions that can cloud our listening?

- *Acknowledge that biased listening is likely and begin by "downloading" your expectations.* Have each member of the backroom to write down what they expect to hear on flipcharts and post them. This will help get prejudice out on the table, enabling us to be more receptive to what actually transpires.
- *Maximize the inputs from your internal voice and the external ones.* Mind mapping is one good way to actively listen to oneself as well as the outside world using a free-form, graphic note-taking process. Another way to pay attention to the customer is to keep a notepad with columns headed "Observations," "Quotes," "Insights," "Possibilities," "Challenges," and "Ideas." Keep a running commentary throughout the focus group in each of these columns, and there will be a wealth of useful material for debriefs and action.
- *Keep an eye and ear out for disconnects.* When we look and listen closely, we may notice that consumers' words seem out of sync with what they present. Studies demonstrate that a larger part of the message is transmitted through tone of voice, pitch/rhythm, gestures, facial expressions, and body language. When we observe a lack of congruency, it's good to ask ourselves why this might be happening from the subject's view.
- *Listen empathetically.* The backroom listener should spend the first portion of the group on only one individual so that he can feel as if he's inside the participant's head. After a while, broaden the listening and observing to encompass all panelists.
- *Capture the teams' observations, insights, connections, surprises, confirmations, and implications while they are fresh.* Immediately after each group, take time to share

this information with the whole listening team to avoid losing important observations and also to free the mind to listen to subsequent groups.

Good listening in the backroom is active, involved, open-minded, flexible, creative, and courageous. When practiced, it leads to more intimate understanding of the consumer and better-quality products and services.

Limitations of Qualitative Methods

Most of the limitations of these qualitative methods stem from the susceptibility of the results to misuse, rather than their inherent shortcomings. There is a great temptation among many managers to accept small-sample exploratory results as sufficient for their purposes, because they are so compelling in their reality. The dangers of accepting the unstructured output of a focus group or a brief series of informal interviews are twofold. First, the results are not necessarily representative of what would be found in the population, and hence, cannot be projected. Second, there is typically a great deal of ambiguity in the results. The flexibility that is the hallmark of these methods, gives the moderator or interviewer great latitude in directing the questions; similarly, an analyst with a particular point of view may interpret the thoughts and comments selectively to support that view. In view of these pitfalls, these methods should be used strictly for insights into the reality of the consumer perspective and to suggest hypotheses for further research.

◆ OBSERVATIONAL METHODS[30]

The third research approach, *observational studies* (sometimes referred to as *ethnography*), is popular in some companies. A small number of consumers are monitored to see what they actually do when performing the targeted tasks, such as preparing, serving, or eating dinner. Observational studies can offer new insights because consumers are not even aware of all of their behaviors, and looking at consumers in new ways can spark new product ideas and creative advertising. There are strong arguments for considering the observation of ongoing behavior as an integral part of the research design. Some of these are the following:

- **Casual observation** is an important exploratory method. Managers continually monitor such variables as competitive prices and advertising activity, the length of lines of customers waiting for service, and the trade journals on executives' desks to help to identify problems and opportunities.

- **Systematic observation** can be a useful supplement to other methods. During a personal interview, the interviewer has the opportunity to note the type, condition, and size of the residence, the respondent's race, and the type of neighborhood with regard to mixed types and qualities of homes and apartments. Seldom is this data source adequately exploited in surveys.

- Observation may be the least expensive and most accurate method of collecting purely behavioral data such as in-store traffic patterns or traffic passing a certain point on a highway system. Thus, people's adherence to pedestrian safety rules before and after a safety campaign can be measured most easily by counting the number of people who cross against the light or outside the sidewalks.

- Sometimes observation is the only research alternative. This is the case with physiological phenomena or with young children who cannot articulate their preferences or motives. Thus, the Fisher Price Company operates a nursery school in a residential area as a means of field-testing potential new toys.

Direct Observation

Direct observation is frequently used to obtain insights into research behavior and related issues.

Direct observation is frequently used to obtain insights into research behavior and related issues, such as packaging effectiveness. One firm uses an observer, disguised as a shopper, to watch grocery store shoppers approach a product category. The observer measures how long shoppers spend in the display area and watches to see whether they have difficulty finding the product, whether the package is read, and whether the information seemed hard to find. This kind of direct observation can be highly structured, with a detailed recording form prepared in advance, or can be unstructured. When making an unstructured observation, the observer may be sent to mingle with customers in the store and look for activities that suggest service problems. This is a highly subjective task, because the observer must select a few things to note and record in varying amounts of detail. This inevitably will draw subjective inferences from the observed behavior. For example, just what was meant by the frown on the face of the shopper waiting at a cash register?

Regardless of how the observation is structured, it is desirable that the respondents not be aware of the observer.[31] Once conscious of being observed, people may alter their behavior, but in very unpredictable ways. One-way mirrors, disguises, and cameras are some of the common solutions. Care should be taken, however, that there is not an invasion of privacy.

Contrived Observation

Contrived observation can be thought of as behavioral projective tests; that is, the response of people placed in a contrived observation situation will reveal some aspects of their underlying beliefs, attitudes, and motives.

Contrived observation can be thought of as behavioral projective tests; that is, the response of people placed in a contrived observation situation will reveal some aspects of their underlying beliefs, attitudes, and motives. Many direct-mail offers of new products or various kinds of books fall into this category, as do tests of variations in shelf space, product flavors, and display locations. The ethics of such offers can be very dubious, as in the example where a manufacturer decides to produce a product only after receiving an acceptable number of orders from a direct-mail advertisement.

A variant of this method uses buying teams, disguised as customers, to find out what happens during the normal interaction between the customer and the retailer, bank, service department, or complaint department. This method has provided useful insights into the discriminatory treatment of minorities by retailers and the quality of public performance by employees of government agencies, banks, and airlines. One is hard pressed to think of other ways of finding out about the knowledgeability, helpfulness in meeting customers' needs, and efficiency of the staff. Clouding this picture are some serious, unresolved questions of ethics.

Content Analysis

Content analysis is an observation technique used to analyze written material into meaningful units, using carefully applied rules.[32] It is defined as the objective, systematic, and quantitative description of the manifest content of communication. It includes observation as well as analysis. The unit of analysis may be words, charac-

Content analysis is an observation technique used to analyze written material into meaningful units, using carefully applied rules. It is defined as the objective, systematic, and quantitative description of the manifest content of communication.

ters, themes, space and time measures, or topics. Analytical categories for classifying the units are developed, and the communication is broken down according to prescribed rules. Marketing research applications involve observing and analyzing the content or message of advertisements, newspaper articles, television and radio programs, and the like. For example, a study hypothesized that because of the growing number of elderly Americans, advertisers would use more elderly models in their promotions. After a content analysis of all the advertisements, the researchers found that the use of elderly people in advertisements has indeed increased.

Physical Trace Measures

Physical trace measures involve recording the natural "residue" of behavior. These measures are rarely used, because they require a good deal of ingenuity and do not usually yield a very good measure.

Physical trace measures involve recording the natural "residue" of behavior. These measures are rarely used, because they require a good deal of ingenuity and usually yield a very gross measure. When they work, however, they can be very useful.[33] For instance, (1) the consumption of alcohol in a town without liquor stores has been estimated from the number of empty bottles in the garbage,[34] (2) an automobile dealer selected radio stations to carry his advertising by observing the most popular dial settings on the radios of cars brought in for servicing; (3) one magazine readership research method employs small glue spots in the gutter of each page spread of a magazine, so broken glue spots are used as evidence of exposure; and (4) a museum gauges the popularity of individual exhibits by measuring the rate of wear on the floor tiles in front of the exhibit and by the number of nose smudges on the glass of the case around the exhibit.

The home audit approach to purchase panels is another type of physical trace measure. The auditor describes the inventory in several pre-specified categories.

The *home-audit approach* to purchase panels (described in Chapter 5) is yet another type of physical trace measure. The auditor describes the inventory in several prespecified categories. This method is not very useful if used on a one-shot basis, for it then requires a very tenuous assumption that possession indicates purchase and usage. However, if the inventory is made over an extended period and is supplemented with a record of cartons and wrappers, an indication of the rate of purchase is possible.

Humanistic Inquiry

Humanistic inquiry is a controversial research method that relies heavily on observation, but it is being used in marketing with increasing frequency.[35] The humanistic approach advocates immersing the researcher in the system under study rather than as in the traditional scientific method, in which the researcher is a dispassionate observer. Throughout the immersion process, the humanistic researcher maintains two diaries, or logs. One is a theory-construction diary that records in detail the thoughts, premises, hypotheses, and revisions in the researcher's thinking. The second set of notes the researcher maintains is a methodological log. Detailed and time-sequenced notes are kept on the investigative techniques used during the inquiry, with special attention to biases and distortions a given technique may have introduced. To access whether the interpretation is drawn in a logical and unprejudiced manner from the data gathered and the rationale employed, humanistic inquiry relies on the judgment of an outside auditor or auditors.

Behavior-Recording Devices

Various **behavior-recording devices** have been developed to overcome particular deficiencies in human observers. The most obvious example is the traffic counter, which

Behavior-recording devices have been developed to overcome particular deficiencies in human observers.

operates continuously without getting tired, and consequently is cheaper and probably more accurate than humans. For the same reasons, as well as for unobtrusiveness, cameras may be used in place of human observers. Someone still has to interpret what is recorded on the film, but the options exist of sampling segments of the film, slowing the speed, or having another observer view it for an independent judgment.

Of the mechanical devices that do not require respondents' direct participation, the A. C. Nielsen *people meter* is best known. The people meter is attached to a television set to record continually to which channel the set is tuned. It also records who is watching. Arbitron recently developed a pocket people meter that is no larger than an electronic pager and can recognize the unique code that broadcasters embed in the soundtrack of radio or television programs.[36] The latest trend is to develop "passive people meters." These meters will record an individual's broadcast viewing and listening without his or her intervention. Mediacheck has introduced one such system. It has two units: a set-top meter that detects audio codes to identify programming being watched or listened to, and a device such as a pendant or a wristwatch worn by the person being measured. The main drawback of this system is that it requires that all programming carry a nonintrusive audio code that can be recorded by the meter system. Neilsen is also developing its own passive people meter. It will recognize a person entering the room and will also keep track of the person's activities while watching TV. SMART's methodology differs from Nielsen's approach in a few key ways. Nielsen wires its meters directly to the tuners in the TVs and VCRs of each sample household, and makes a telephone connection to gather return data. SMART's people meters have sensors that can pluck the signals from the air, requiring no wire connection. Existing household electrical wiring is used to transmit return data. SMART is also designed to read Universal Television Program Codes (UTPCs), which are embedded in some program signals.[37] Technological advances such as the Universal Product Code (UPC) have had a major impact on mechanical observation. The UPC system, together with optical scanners, allows for mechanical information collection regarding consumer purchases, by product category, brand, store type, price paid, and quantity.

Some types of observation are beyond human capabilities. All physiological reactions fall into this category. Therefore, devices are available to measure changes in the rate of perspiration as a guide to emotional response to stimuli (the psychogalvanometer), and changes in the size of the pupils of subjects' eyes, which are presumed to indicate the degree of interest in the stimulus being viewed (the pupilometer). These devices can be used only in laboratory environments, and often yield ambiguous results.

Eye-movement recorders record the experience of viewing pictures of advertisements, packages, signs, or shelf displays, at a rate of 30 readings per second.

Experience with **eye-movement recorders** has been more successful. This device records the experience of viewing pictures of advertisements, packages, signs, or shelf displays, at a rate of 30 readings per second. The recorded eye movements show when the subject starts to view a picture, the order in which the elements of the image were examined and reexamined, and the amount of viewing time given each element. One application is for testing the visual impact of alternative package designs.

Voice-pitch analysis examines changes in the relative vibration frequency of the human voice to measure emotion.

Voice-pitch analysis examines changes in the relative vibration frequency of the human voice to measure emotion.[38] In voice analysis, the normal or baseline pitch of an individual's speaking voice is charted by engaging the subject in an unemotional conversation. The greater the deviation from the baseline, the greater voice-pitch analysis has been used in package research, to predict consumer brand preference for dog food.[39] For example, MindTrack, a brainwave-to-computer interface, measures direct emotional response to virtually any communication medium and does not require a verbal response from the participant. While participants are exposed to a 10-second advertisement or a TV show, MindTrack detects brainwaves through sensors attached to a headband, similar to an electroencephalogram, and registers quantitative, digital results. The intensity changes in emotional responses are traced while the consumer is exposed to the target medium.

Limitations of Observational Methods

The vast majority of research studies use some form of questionnaire. Observation methods, despite their many advantages, have one crucial limitation: They cannot observe motives, attitudes, or intentions, which sharply reduces their diagnostic usefulness. To be sure, these cognitive factors are manifested in the observed behavior, but so are many other confounding factors. For example, the Zippo Lighter Company seemingly has a valuable measure of advertising effectiveness in the volume of its lighters sent in for repair. Despite the mention of the free repair privilege in the advertising, it is questionable whether such a measure can unambiguously test for impact.

Observational methods suffer other limitations as well. They are often more costly and time consuming, and may yield biased results if there are sampling problems or if significant observer subjectivity is involved. However, these biases usually are very different in character from those that affect obtrusive, questionnaire methods. This is one of the underexploited strengths of observation methods: They help to increase our confidence in questionnaire measures if they yield similar results when used as a supplement.

◆ RECENT APPLICATIONS OF QUALITATIVE AND OBSERVATIONAL METHODS

Qualitative and observational methods have been applied by many organizations. The following are a representative sample.

- **On-site observation** is an underutilized method that has tremendous potential for helping marketers understand consumers' thinking. It is as valuable as traditional qualitative techniques such as focus group and in-depth interviews. On-site observation gives researchers the chance to observe and learn about consumer purchasing decisions as they are being made. Observing consumers decisions as they choose products from a shelf or casually asking them to explain their preferences can lead to a wealth of qualitative information. The best approach in conducting on-site observation is by placing researchers in a supermarket and presenting them as shoppers who need advice from another shopper in making a purchasing decision. The shopper in question will give spontaneous responses on the product noteworthy for marketing analysis.

  A skilled researcher can do about 35 interviews a day in several supermarkets with minimal overhead costs and an excellent yield for qualitative work. It requires individuals who are outgoing and are able to listen—not just hear what people say. A person with these traits can then be taught how to obtain relevant answers, absorb information, evaluate responses, and avoid asking leading questions. Field observation also requires tremendous patience, discipline, and enthusiasm.

- A new method for identifying new consumer or industrial product functions involves asking consumers to rate "miniconcepts," novel verb-object combinations that describe possible new functions for products. (A new function for a vaccum cleaner, for example, might be "deodorize rug."). Whether the technology is available to perform these functions is immaterial. The aim of the miniconcepts method is simply to generate interesting, "really new" function ideas and assess buyer responses.

The miniconcept method was tested among 30 middle-aged mothers regarding needs and opportunities for new food-related products. Their results indicated latent needs for products that would educate them about food, enhance their enjoyment of food, and enable them to prepare foods that have healing and energizing properties. Using this method, marketing researchers can identify opportunities for really new functions in any product category. Current technologies can then be applied—or new technologies developed—to address and fulfill these needs. Thus, the new method makes marketing research efficient and effective.

END OF CHAPTER MATERIAL

SUMMARY

Exploratory research is an essential step in the development of a successful research study. In essence, this kind of research is insurance that major elements of the problem or important competing hypotheses will not be overlooked. It further ensures that both the manager and the researcher will see the market through the consumer's eyes. Fortunately, research design is an iterative and not a sequential process, so major initial oversights are not necessarily irreversible. In particular, the exploratory technique of semistructured interviews should be reemployed later when the structured study is pretested. Properly handled, a pretest should provide opportunities for respondents to express their frustrations with the specific questions, as well as to identify deficiencies in the scope of the questions.

In this chapter we also discussed observational methods. These are useful during the exploratory stage of the research design but are even more valuable as a data collection method. The advantages of observational methods will become even more apparent in Chapter 8, as we examine the errors that are inherent when an interviewer starts to interact with a respondent.

Video Segment:

Targeting the Youth

Stretchy and *yummy* are two associations made with candy by children at a creative development group test. In the early stages of product development, a growing number of companies are looking to children and teenagers for strategies to be developed for candy and toys. In order to instill brand loyalty early in children, companies strive to optimize the shift in role of children as active participants in the decision-making process.

KEY TERMS

qualitative research	role playing
exploratory research	case studies
nondirective interviews	causal observation
semistructured interviews	systematic observation
laddering	direct observation
hidden-issue questioning	contrived observation
symbolic analysis	content analysis
focus-group discussion	physical trace measures
chain reaction technique	humanistic inquiry
two-way focus groups	behavior-recording devices
word-association technique	eye-movement recorders
completion tests	voice-pitch analysis
picture interpretation technique	empathic interviewing
third-person techniques	on-site observation

MARKETING RESEARCH WORKSHOP REVIEW POINTS

1. The purpose of qualitative research is to find out what is in a consumer's mind. It is done in order to access and also get a rough idea about the person's perspective.

2. The basic assumption behind qualitative methods is that an individual's organization of a relatively unstructured stimulus indicates the person's basic perceptions of the phenomenon and his or her reaction to it.

3. The three major categories of qualitative research methods are exploratory research, learning about the consumers' vantage point and vocabulary, and clinical research.

4. The major advantages of computers in qualitative research are ease of transmission, storage, coding, searching and retrieving, building relationships, and matrix building.

5. The two types of individual in-depth interviews are nondirective interviews and semistructured interviews.

6. In nondirective interviews the respondent is given maximum freedom to respond, within the bounds of topics of interest to the interviewer.

7. In semistructured or focused individual interviews the interviewer attempts to cover a specific list of topics or subareas.

8. The three methods of using individual in-depth interviews in consumer markets are laddering, hidden-issue, and symbolic analysis.

9. In laddering, questioning progresses from product characteristics to user characteristics. In hidden-issue questioning, the focus is not on socially shared values but rather on personal "sore spots"—not on general lifestyles but on deeply felt personal concerns. Symbolic analysis attempts to analyze the symbolic meaning of objects by comparing them with their opposites.

10. Focus-group discussion offers participants more stimulation than an interview; presumably this makes new ideas and meaningful comments more likely. Among other advantages, it is claimed that discussions often provoke more spontaneity and candor than can be expected in an interview.

11. The key success factors for a focus group are planning the agenda, recruiting participants, effective moderation, and analysis and interpretation of the results.

12. Two-way focus groups involve allowing one target group to listen to and learn from a related group.

13. The central feature of projective techniques is the presentation of an ambiguous, unstructured object, activity, or person that a respondent is asked to interpret and explain. Projective techniques are used when it is believed that respondents will not or cannot respond meaningfully to direct questions: the reasons for certain behaviors or attitudes; what the act of buying, owning, or using a product or service means to them.

14. The word-association technique asks the respondent to give the first word or phrase that comes to mind after the researcher presents a word or phrase. The word association technique has been useful for obtaining reactions to potential brand names.

15. Completion test involves giving a respondent an incomplete and ambiguous sentence, which is to be completed with a phrase.

16. Picture interpretation technique is based on the Thematic Apperception Test (TAT). The respondent is shown an ambiguous picture in the form of a line drawing, illustration, or photograph, and asked to describe it.

17. By asking how friends, neighbors, or the average person would react in the situation, the researcher can observe, to some extent, the respondents projecting their own attitudes onto this third person, thus revealing more of their own feelings.

18. In role playing, a respondent assumes the role or behavior of another person, such as salesperson in a store. This person then can be asked to try to sell a product to consumers who raise objections.

19. A case study is a comprehensive description and analysis of a single situation. Case studies are very productive sources of research hypotheses.

20. Direct observation is frequently used to obtain insights into research behavior and related issues, such as packaging effectiveness. Regardless of how the observation is structured, it is desirable that the respondents not be aware of the observer.

21. Contrived observation can be thought of as behavioral projective tests; that is, the response of people placed in a contrived observation situation will reveal some aspects of their underlying beliefs, attitudes, and motives.

22. Content analysis is an observation technique used to analyze written material into meaningful units, using carefully applied rules. It is defined as the objective, systematic, and quantitative description of the manifest content of communication.

23. Physical trace measures involve recording the natural "residue" of behavior. These measures are rarely used, because they require a good deal of ingenuity and do not usually yield a very accurate measure.

24. The home audit approach to purchase panels is a type of physical trace measure. The auditor describes the inventory in several prespecified categories.

25. Behavior-recording devices have been developed to overcome particular deficiencies in human observers.

26. Eye-movement recorders record the experience of viewing pictures of advertisements, packages, signs, or shelf displays, at a rate of 30 readings per second.

27. Voice-pitch analysis examines changes in the relative vibration frequency of the human voice to measure emotion.

28. Observational methods cannot observe motives, attitudes, or intentions, which sharply reduces their diagnostic usefulness. Observational methods are often more costly and time consuming, and may yield biased results if there are sampling problems or if significant observer subjectivity is involved.

29. On-site observation gives researchers the chance to observe and learn about consumer purchasing decisions as they are being made.

QUESTIONS AND PROBLEMS

1. What are the significant differences between nondirective and semistructured individual interviews? In what circumstances would a nondirective interview be more useful than a semistructured interview?

2. You have conducted two group meetings on the subject of telephone answering devices. In each group there were seven prospective users of such devices, and in the two groups there were four users of telephone answering services. (These services use an operator to intercept calls and record messages.) When the client's new-product development manager heard the tapes and read the transcripts of the two meetings, the first reaction was, "I knew all along that the features I wanted to add to our existing model would be winners, and these people are just as enthusiastic. Let's not waste any more research effort on the question of which features are wanted." What do you say?

3. There have been a number of complaints in your city that minorities are discriminated against by local major appliance retailers (with respect to prices, trade-ins, sales assistance, and credit). How would you use the techniques described in this chapter to study this question?

4. A local consumer organization is interested in the differences in food prices among major stores in the area. How should it proceed in order to obtain meaningful comparisons?

5. Toothpaste manufacturers have found consistently that if they ask for detailed information on the frequency with which people brush their teeth, and then make minimal assumptions as to the quantity of toothpaste used on each occasion, as well as spillage and failure to squeeze the tube empty, the result is a serious overstatement of toothpaste consumption. How would you explain this phenomenon? Would it be possible to design a study to overcome these problems and obtain more accurate estimates of consumption? Describe how such a study could be conducted.

6. The school board of St. Patrick's High School is concerned about the rise of student violence involving guns during the past two months. During an emergency meeting, Father Hennessy, the school's principal, insisted that steps be taken to return student behavior to its traditionally exemplary level. He suggested that this rise in the level of violence was for reasons beyond the experience of most of the school board members, and recommended that they needed to gather some background information on the situation in order to address the problem knowledgeably. The school board agreed with his proposal and decided to commission a market research study to question students on whether they carried guns and their underlying motivation for doing so. The research firm, Church and Associates, has decided to use focus groups or individual in-depth interviews to obtain the required information.
   a. Which of these mentioned techniques is suitable for this purpose? Give reasons.
   b. Church and Associates has recommended separate focus-group discussions involving the faculty. How can the moderator effectively encourage all the participants to discuss their feelings on the topic?
   c. What possible questions could be asked in an in-depth interview?

7. How can a pretest add to the quality of a marketing research study?

8. For each of the following scenarios, indicate whether qualitative or quantitative research is more appropriate. Also, recommend a specific technique for each and justify your answer.
   a. A manufacturer of herbal teas wants to know how often and for what purposes consumers use herbal tea products.
   b. A political campaign manager wants to identify ways of sharply increasing the amount of contributions from the population.
   c. An amusement park is nearing the final stages of designing two new rides. It wants to measure the reactions of the public and their potential enthusiasm for the new rides.
   d. A company that manufactures potato chips has two alternative package designs for the product and wants to determine which design will yield higher sales.

9. What difficulties might be encountered when conducting a qualitative interview in an international context?

10. What would be some of the exploratory research methods that you would look into when you are planning on selling toothpastes in an international market, such as China? If you are marketing packaged goods such as Koolaid, what would be your main concern in terms of pretesting and exploratory research?

ENDNOTES

1. Fred N. Kerlinger, *Foundations of Behavioral Research,* 3rd ed. (New York: Holt, Rinehart and Winston, 1986).

2. "Beckman Gets Customers to Design its Products," *Business Week* (August 17, 1974), p. 52.

3. Johny K. Johansson and Ikujiro Nonaka, "Market Research the Japanese Way," *Harvard Business Review* (May–June 1987), pp. 16–22.

4. Jeffrey F. Durgee, "Depth-Interview Techniques for Creative Advertising," *Journal of Advertising Research* (January 1986), pp. 29–37.

5. For additional discussion of cross-cultural research and evaluation, see Michael Quinn Patton, *Culture and Evaluation: New Directions for Program Evaluation* (San Francisco: Jossey-Bass, 1985); Walter J. Lonner, and John W. Berry, *Field Methods in Cross Cultural Research* (Newbury Park, CA: Sage, 1986).

6. Martin Lautman, "Focus Groups: Theory and Method," *Advances in Consumer Research* 9 (October 1981), p. 54.

7. See Thomas Greenbaum, "Focus Groups vs. One-on-Ones: The Controversy Continues," *Marketing News* (September 2, 1991), p. 16.

8. Peter Tuckel, Elaine Leppo, and Barbara Kaplan, "Focus Groups under Scrutiny: Why People Go and How It Affects Their Attitudes Towards Participation," *Marketing Research,* 12 (June 1992).

9. For a comprehensive listing of the providers of focus-group facilities, see "1997 Marketing News Directory of Focus Group Facilities and Moderators," *Marketing News* (January 6, 1992).

10. David W. Stewart and Prem N. Shamdasani, *FocusGroups: Theory and Practice* (Newbury Park, CA: Sage, 1990).

11. Nelson E. James and Nancy Frontczak, "How Acquaintanceship and Analyst Can Influence Focus Group Results," *Journal of Advertising* 17, (1988), pp. 41–48.

12. Wendy Hayward and John Rose, "We'll Meet Again … Repeat Attendance at Group Discussions—Does it Matter?" *Journal of the Advertising Research Society* (July 1990), pp. 377–407.

13. For more discussion, see Edward F. Fern, "The Use of Focus Groups for Idea Generation: The Effects of Group Size, Acquaintanceship, and Moderator on Response Quantity and Quality," *Journal of Marketing Research,* 19 (February 1982), pp. 1–13.

14. Naomi R. Henderson, "Trained Moderators Boost the Value of Qualitative Research," *Marketing Research* (June 1992), p. 20.

15. "Marketing Research," *Marketing Report* (October 28, 1996), p. 3.

16. Michael Silverstein, "Two Way Focus Groups Can Provide Startling Information," *Marketing News* (January 4, 1988), p. 31.

17. "Network to Broadcast Live Focus Groups," *Marketing News* (September 3, 1990), pp. 10, 47.

18. Cindy Miller, "Anybody Ever Hear of Global Focus Groups?" *Marketing News* (May 27, 1991), p. 14.

19. Heckman James, "Turning the Focus Online: Web Snares Ever-more Qualitative Research," *Marketing News* (February 28, 2000), p. 15.

20. Harold H. Kassarjian, "Projective Methods," in Robert Ferber, ed., *Handbook of Marketing Research* (New York: McGraw-Hill, 1974), pp. 3–87; Sidney J. Levy, "Dreams, Fairy Tales, Animals, and Cars," *Psychology and Marketing*, 2 (Summer 1985), pp. 67–82.

21. David A. Aaker, *Managing Brand Equity: Capitalizing on the Value of a Brand Name* (New York: Macmillan, 1991).

22. David A. Aaker, *Managing Brand Equity: Capitalizing on the Value of a Brand Name* (New York: Macmillan, 1991).

23. Insights from Marketing Science Institute, Fall 1997.

24. Sidney J. Levy, "Dreams, Fairy Tales, Animals, and Cars," *Psychology and Marketing*, 2 (Summer 1985), pp. 67–81.

25. David A. Aaker and Douglas M. Stayman, "Implementing the Concept of Transformational Advertising," *Psychology and Marketing* (May–June 1992), pp. 237–253.

26. This was the design of the classic study by Mason Haire, "Projective Techniques in Marketing Research," *Journal of Marketing*, 14 (1950), pp. 649–656. However, recent validation studies have found that differences in the two descriptions also are influenced by the relationship of the two test products to the items in the shopping list, so the interpretation is anything but straightforward. See also James C. Andersen, "The Validity of Haire's Shopping List Projective Technique," *Journal of Marketing*, 15 (November 1978), pp. 644–649.

27. Peggy Lawless, *Marketing News* (January 4, 1999).

28. Carol B. Raffel, "Vague Notions," *Marketing Research* (Summer 1996), pp. 21–23.

29. Laurie Tema-Lyn, "Five Ways to Get More Out of Qualitative Research," *Marketing News* (June 7, 1999), p. H38.

30. Barbara L. Watts, "Mixed Methods Make Research Better" *Marketing News* (February 28, 2000), p. 16.

31. Cliff Scott, David M. Klien, and Jennings Bryant, "Consumer Response to Humor in Advertising: A Series of Field Studies Using Behavioral Observation," *Journal of Consumer Research*, 16 (March 1990), pp. 498–501.

32. An excellent summary article of content analysis is Richard Kolbe and Melissa Burnett, "Content Analysis Research: An Examination of Applications with Directives for Improving Research Reliability and Objectivity," *Journal of Consumer Research* (September 1991), pp. 243–250. Other examples of content analysis are Mary Zimmer and Linda Golden, "Impressions of Retail Stores: A Content Analysis of Consumer Images," *Journal of Retailing* (Fall 1988), pp. 265–293; and Terence Shimp, Joel Urbany, and Sakeh Camlin, "The Use of Framing and Characterization for Magazine Advertising of Mass Marketed Products," *Journal of Advertising* (January 1988), pp. 23–30.

33. For a fuller discussion, see Sechrest Lee, *New Directions for Methodology of Behavior Science: Unobtrusive Measurement Today* (San Francisco: Jossey Bass, 1979).

34. Joseph A. Cote, James McCullough, and Michael Reilly, "Effects of Unexpected Situations on Behavior-Intention Differences: A Garbology Analysis," *Journal of Consumer Research*, 12 (September 1985), pp. 188–194.

35. Elizabeth Hirschman, "Humanistic Inquiry in Marketing Research: Philosophy, Method and Criteria," *Journal of Marketing Research* (August 1986), pp. 237–249. For more detailed information, see Yvonna Lincoln and Edward Guba, *Naturalistic Inquiry* (Beverly Hills, CA: Sage, 1985).

36. "Arbitron to Develop 'Pocket People Meter,'" *Marketing News* (January 4, 1993).

37. Tim Triplet, "Nielsen May Face SMART Competitor," *Marketing News* (September 15 1997), p. 12.

38. Nancy Nighswonger and Claude Martin, Jr., "On Voice Analysis in Marketing Research," *Journal of Marketing Research* (August 1981), pp. 350–355.

39. Glen Brickman, "Uses of Voice Pitch Analysis," *Journal of Advertising Research* (April 1980), pp. 69–73.

CASES

For detailed descriptions of the below cases please visit www.wiley.com/college/kumar.

Case 7-1: Mountain Bell Telephone Company
Case 7-2: Acura

Information from Respondents: Issues in Data Collection

Learning Objectives

- Briefly mention the different kinds of information that are collected through surveys.
- Introduce the various errors that occur while conducting a survey.
- Introduce the different kinds of survey methods.
- Discuss the survey methods and describe the process involved using each method.
- Enumerate the advantages and disadvantages of the survey method.
- Discuss future trends in survey methods.
- Elucidate the problems that the researcher faces in conducting international surveys.
- Briefly mention the various factors that influence the selection of the various survey methods.
- Discuss the ethical issues involved in collecting data from respondents.

There is a transition of market research into market intelligence whereby the former emphasis on data collection is shifting to translating information into action. However, to translate data into useful information, one needs to collect the relevant data. The survey is the overwhelming choice of researchers for collecting primary data. The methods already discussed—qualitative and observational research, secondary data analysis, and secondary data research on the Internet—are more likely to be used to improve or supplement the survey method than to take its place.

The principal advantage of a survey is that it can collect a great deal of data about an individual respondent at one time. It is perhaps only stating the obvious to say that for most kinds of data the respondent is the only, or the best, source. The second advantage of this method is versatility. Surveys can be employed in virtually any setting—whether among teenagers, old-age pensioners, or sailboat owners—and are adaptable to research objectives that necessitate either a descriptive or causal design.

There are as many survey methods as there are different forms of communication technology. As the technology for communication progresses, the number of survey methods also proliferates. Recent advances in fax technology and in electronic mail have introduced many new possibilities for conducting error-free surveys. Hence, a researcher has to know the mechanics of each method clearly, and also how it performs compared to the other methods. The choice among different survey methods is never an easy one. In this chapter, the three most prevalent methods of conducting surveys—personal interviews, telephone interviews, and mail surveys—are discussed in detail. The latest trends in survey methods are also discussed. Conducting international surveys leads to a number of new problems that are not encountered in domestic research. These problems and possible solutions are also discussed briefly.

◆ INFORMATION FROM SURVEYS

Surveys can be designed to capture a wide variety of information on many diverse topics and subjects. Attitudes are often the subject of surveys. Information on attitudes frequently is obtained in the form of consumers' awareness, knowledge, or perceptions about the product; its features, availability, and pricing; and various aspects of the marketing effort. Surveys can also capture the respondent's overall assessment and the extent to which the object is rated as favorable or unfavorable. Information can be obtained about a person's image of something. Each person tends to see things a little differently from others, so no two images are apt to be exactly alike. Decisions are also the topic of research, but the focus is not so much on the results of past decisions but more on the process by which respondents evaluate things. Those seeking survey information are often interested in those aspects of the decision process that people use to choose actions. Marketers are often concerned with why people behave as they do. Most behavior is directed toward satisfying one or more human needs. Thus, the answer to the question of "why" is often obtained by measuring the relationship between actions and needs, desires, preferences, motives, and goals.

Measuring behavior usually involves four related concepts: what the respondents did or did not do; where the action takes place; the timing, including past, present, and future; and the frequency or persistence of behavior. In other words, it often means assessing what, where, when, and how often. Surveys can also be conducted to determine respondents' lifestyles. Grouping the population by lifestyle can be used to identify an audience, constituency, target market, or other collections of interest to the sponsor. Social contact and interaction are often the focus of survey research or bear heavily on other issues relevant to the survey.

◆ SOURCES OF SURVEY ERROR

The process by which respondents are questioned appears deceptively simple. The reality, however, is closer to Oppenheim's opinion that "questioning people is more like trying to catch a particularly elusive fish, by hopefully casting different kinds of bait at different depths, without knowing what is going on beneath the surface."[1]

The problem of getting meaningful results from the interview process stems from the need to satisfy reasonably the following conditions:

- Population has been defined correctly
- Sample is representative of the population
- Respondents selected to be interviewed are available and willing to cooperate
- Respondents understand the questions

- Respondents have the knowledge, opinions, attitudes, or facts required
- Respondents are willing and able to respond
- Interviewer understands and records the responses correctly

These conditions often are not satisfied because of interviewer error, ambiguous interpretation of both questions and answers, and errors in formulating responses. These **survey errors** are shown in Figure 8-1 as filters or screens that distort both the question and response. Ambiguity, usually a consequence of poor question wording, is covered in Chapter 10. In this section, we will deal with the factors that influence prospective respondents' willingness to cooperate and provide accurate answers to whatever questions are asked.

Nonresponse Errors Due to Refusals

Refusal rates are highly variable. They can be as low as 3 to 5 percent of those contacted for a short interview on a street corner or at a bus stop, to 30 or 35 percent and higher for lengthy personal and telephone interviews or mail questionnaires, which are of little interest to most subjects. High refusal rates are a major source of error, for those who refuse to be interviewed are likely to be very different from those who cooperate. People cooperate for a number of reasons, such as trying to be friendly and helpful, to interact socially when they are lonely or bored, to know more about the subject, or to experience something novel. Many people also cooperate when they expect a reward or a direct benefit.

People refuse to answer survey questions for a number of reasons. Fear is the main reason for refusal.[2] Other reasons might be that some may think of surveys as an invasion of privacy; the subject matter may be sensitive (such as death, sexual habits, etc.); or there may be hostility toward the sponsor.[3] Refusal rates can be reduced if the reason for refusals is related to a phenotypic source. A **phenotypic source of refusal** refers to characteristics of the data collection procedure (which questions are asked, how they are asked, the length of the interview, and so on). These elements vary from study to study and can be controlled to a certain extent. But if the source of refusals is

A **phenotypic source of refusal** refers to characteristics of data collection procedure (which questions are asked, how they are asked, the length of the interview, and so on). These elements vary from study to study and can be controlled to a certain extent.

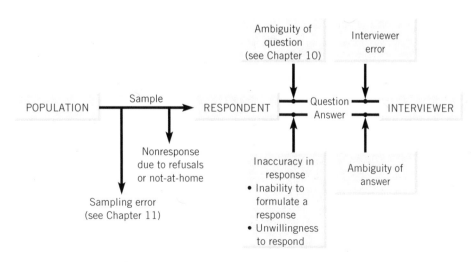

Figure 8-1 Sources of error in information from respondents.

A **genotypic source of refusal** refers to the indigenous characteristics of respondents (such as age, sex and occupation).

genotypic, then it is difficult to control for them. A **genotypic source of refusal** refers to the indigenous characteristics of respondents (such as age, sex, and occupation). One avenue to reducing this type of refusal is to try to interview respondents in ways that are less intrusive in their lives.[4] Other methods, such as multiple callbacks (mailings), guarantee of anonymity, increasing surveyor credibility, incentives for completed responses, randomized responses, and shortening the survey through matrix designs, can increase response rates.[5] An example of the effect of nonresponse errors is given in Marketing Research in Practice 8-1.

Inaccuracy in Response

Respondents may be unable to give any response, or unwilling to give a complete and accurate response.

Inability to Respond

Inaccuracy in response occurs due to **inability of the respondents to respond**, and **unwillingness of the respondents** to respond.

Respondents may not know the answer to a question because of ignorance or forgetting, or may be unable to articulate it. All three problems create further errors when respondents contrive an answer, because they do not want to admit that they don't know the answer or because they want to please the interviewer. Respondents are likely to be ignorant when asked some questions. Sometimes, for example, only one partner in the marriage may be aware of the financial status of the family (such as insurance, investments, and benefits).

The likelihood of forgetting an episode such as a visit to a doctor, a purchase, and so forth, depends on both the recency of the occurrence and the importance of the event, as well as on what else was happening at the same time.[6] Ideally, questions should be asked only about recent behavior. If retrospective questions are required, the accuracy of recall can be improved by questioning the respondent about the context in which an event occurred. Memories may be sharpened by **aided-recall techniques.** These attempt to stimulate recall with specific cues, such as copies of magazines, pictures, or lists. It is always preferable to ask about specific occasions of an activity.

Aided-recall techniques attempt to stimulate recall with specific cues, such as copies of magazines, pictures, or lists.

It is essential to keep in mind that most respondents want to be cooperative; when in doubt, they prefer to give too much rather than too little information. Memory

MARKETING RESEARCH IN PRACTICE 8-1

Nonresponse Bias Leads to Wrong Prediction in Presidential Opinion Poll

An example of significant bias as a result of low response to mail questionnaires is the often cited *Literary Digest* presidential poll in 1936. The two candidates were Alfred E. Landon of the Republican Party and Franklin D. Roosevelt of the Democratic Party. The *Literary Digest* conducted a mail survey and predicted a victory for Landon in the election. But Roosevelt won by a big margin in a landslide victory for the Democrats. The story is told that the sample was drawn from telephone books, and the Republicans (Landon's party) were more likely to have telephones in 1936. Hence, this biased the sample toward Republicans. In addition, the failure of the poll to predict correctly was attributed to nonresponse; only a minority of those asked to return questionnaires did so. As is typical of mail surveys, those who returned the questionnaire wanted the underdog Landon to win. The Landon supporters were particularly likely to want to express their views, whereas the Roosevelt supporters, since they were the majority, did not bother to respond to the survey.

Source: www.ama.org.pubs/articles.

Telescoping occurs when an event is remembered to have occurred more recently than it actually did.

Averaging occurs when something is reported as more like the usual, the expected, or the norm.

Omission occurs when a respondent leaves out an error or some aspect of an experience.

Response bias factors subvert positive motivations that were present when the respondent agreed to participate.

distortions compound this source of error by **telescoping** time, so that an event is remembered as occurring more recently than it actually did.[7] Another common memory error is **averaging,** whereby something is reported as more like the usual, the expected, or the norm. This is a particular problem for researchers trying to study the exceptions to the ordinary. General Foods' researchers interested in homemaker's variations in evening meals found it very difficult to overcome the respondent's tendency to say, "It was Sunday, so it must have been roast beef." In studies of evening meals at General Foods, researchers reduced the averaging problem by asking respondents a series of questions that helped them to reconstruct the event. A third memory pitfall is called **omission,** where a respondent leaves out an event or some aspect of an experience. Respondent fatigue and poor interviewer rapport are demotivating, and result in increased omitting. The use of graphic aids or recognition measures will help to reduce omission.

Unwillingness to Respond Accurately

During the interview a number of **response bias** factors may come into play to subvert the positive motivations that were present when the respondent agreed to participate. Questionnaires that are lengthy and boring are especially vulnerable to these biases.

1. *Concern about invasion of privacy.* Although most respondents don't regard a survey, per se, as an invasion of privacy, their tolerance may not extend to detailed personal questions.

2. *Time pressure and fatigue.* As a lengthy interview proceeds, the accuracy of responses is bound to decline.

3. *Prestige seeking and social desirability response bias.* Questions that have implications for prestige—such as income, education, time spent reading newspapers, tastes in food, or even place of residence—may be biased subtly in ways that reflect well on the respondent.

4. *Courtesy bias.* There is a general tendency to limit answers to pleasantries that will cause little discomfort or embarrassment to the interviewer, or to avoid appearing uncooperative.

5. *Uninformed response error.* Simply asking someone a question implies that the interviewer expects the respondent to have an answer. This expectation, plus a desire to appear cooperative, may induce respondents to answer a question despite a complete lack of knowledge about the topic.

6. *Response style.* Evaluative questions requiring a good-bad, positive-negative judgment are afflicted by systematic tendencies of certain respondents to select particular styles or categories of response regardless of the content of the question. For example, Wells found that yea-sayers consistently gave higher ratings to favorably evaluated advertisements and were more likely to exaggerate self-reports of product purchases.[8]

Interviewer Error

Interviewers vary enormously in personal characteristics, amount of previous experience, style of interviewing, and motivation to do a thorough job. The differences among interviewers also mean a great deal of variability in the way interviews are conducted.

Respondent's Impression of the Interviewer

For most respondents a personal interview is a sufficiently novel experience that the interviewer becomes a major source of clues to appropriate behavior. The interviewer must be seen as a person who is capable of understanding the respondent's point of view, and of doing so without rejecting his or her opinion. This kind of rapport is most likely to be established quickly when respondent and interviewer share basic characteristics such as sex, age, race, and social class.

The attitudes the interviewer reveals to the respondent during the interview can greatly affect their level of interest and willingness to answer openly. Especially important is a sense of assurance and ease with the task. Communication will be inhibited further if the interviewer appears flippant or bored, constantly interrupts the person when speaking, or is too immersed in note taking to look up.[9] Obviously, proper selection of interviewers, coupled with good training, can reduce many of these problems.

Questioning, Probing, and Recording

The way an interviewer asks a question and follows up by probing for further details and clarification will be colored by (1) the interviewer's own feelings about the "appropriate" answer to the questions and (2) expectations about the kind of answers that "fit" the respondent. For example, when interviewing a person with limited education, the interviewer might shift unconsciously from a question worded, "Have any of your children attended college?" to, "I don't imagine any of your children have gone to college. Have they?" In one study it was found that one interviewer obtained 8 percent response rate while another interviewer obtained 92 percent response rate choosing the same option.[10]

Perhaps the most common interviewer error is insufficient probing. The respondents may not be expected to have much to say about the subject or may have given an answer that the interviewer thinks is "right."

Fraud and Deceit

Modest interviewer compensation and the problem of monitoring the activities of personal interviewers out in the field, or telephone interviewers calling from their home, provide ample incentive for cheating. This may be as serious as outright fabrication of an entire interview or judicious filling in of certain information that was not obtained during the interview. Because it is such a serious potential source of error, most commercial research firms validate 10 to 15 percent of the completed interviews. This entails interviewing a sample of those who were reported to have been interviewed, to verify that an interview actually took place and that the questions were asked.

Improving Interviewer Quality

New approaches to improving data collection quality are being constantly tried in order to overcome some of the interview problems that have been mentioned. Field briefings can be improved by preparing videotaped briefings to show to interviewers, to ensure a consistent message to all interviewers prior to data collection. Actual interviews can be recorded by camera at a particular site, and all interviewers can be rotated through that site to check on the quality of interviewing. Finally, if electronic quality checks are too expensive, research firms can hire independent field personnel to check quality.

The array of problems and sources of error, summarized in Table 8-1 have the greatest effect on the personal interview method. By far the best way to minimize the problems is by proper recruitment, selection, training, motivation, and control of

TABLE 8-1 Sources of Error in Interview Surveys

1. Nonresponse errors due to refusals
   a. Fear of the consequences of participation
   b. Resentment of an invasion of privacy
   c. Anxiety about the subject

2. Inaccuracy in responses
   a. Inability to give a response
      i. Ignorance of the answer
      ii. Memory problems
      iii. Problems in formulating an answer
   b. Unwillingness to respond accurately
      i. Concern about invasion of privacy
      ii. Time pressure and fatigue
      iii. Desire to enhance prestige
      iv. Desire to appear cooperative
      v. Biased response style
      vi. Interviewer expecting the respondent to have an answer

3. Errors caused by interviews
   a. Provision of clues to "appropriate" responses
   b. Inadequate questioning and probing
   c. Fraud and deceit

interviewers. Yet the potential for poor-quality interviews is enormous.[11] Although other methods of data collection are less prone to interview error, they have offsetting problems, as we will see later in this chapter.

◆ METHODS OF DATA COLLECTION

The choice of data collection method is a critical point in the research process. The decision is seldom easy, for there are many factors to be considered and many variables of the six basic **survey methods:**

1. Personal interview

2. Telephone interview

3. Mail survey

4. Fax survey

5. E-mail survey

6. Web-based survey

In this section, we will look briefly at the different methods of data collection and the factors affecting the choice of method.

Because each research problem will have a different ranking of importance, and no data collection method is consistently superior, few generalizations can be made. Much depends on the researcher's skill in adapting the method to the circumstances. Overall, however, the telephone and the mail survey methods are the dominant methods for conducting surveys. In the 1990 Walker Industry Image Study, it was found that 69 percent of the respondents had participated in mail surveys, 68 percent had participated in telephone surveys, 32 percent in mall-intercept surveys, and 15 percent in door-to-door interviews. However, both in academic and business environment, fax services are being used increasingly. The characteristics of each survey method are explained briefly in Table 8-2.

"That's the worst set of opinions I've heard in my entire life."

Robert Weber. ©1975 from the *New Yorker* Collection.

TABLE 8-2   Basic Survey Methods and Their Characteristics

Survey Methods	Characteristics
Personal interviews	The interviewer interviews the respondent in person.
	There is direct contact between the interviewer and the respondent.
	The environment (mood of the respondent and the interviewer, the time and place of the interview, etc.) affects the data collection process to a large extent.
	It is the costliest and the most time-consuming form of data collection.
Telephone interviews	The interviewer interviews the respondent over the telephone.
	The interviewer has only verbal contact with the respondent.
	The environment plays a relatively minor role in the data collection process.
	Data collection cost is in between that of a personal interview and a mail survey.
Mail surveys	The questionnaire is administered through the mail.
	The interviewer has no contact with the respondent.
	The environment plays no role in the data collection process.
Fax surveys	The questionnaire is administered via fax.
	The interviewer has no contact with the respondent.
	Respondents have time to give thoughtful answers, look up records, or consult with others.
	It is fast and the administrative costs are fixed.
E-mail surveys	The questionnaire is administered via e-mail.
	The interviewer has no contact with the respondent.
	Setup time and expertise required are minimal.
	It is difficult to determine the sampling variables and their target proportions.
Web surveys	The questionnaire is administered via the World Wide Web.
	The interviewer has no contact with the respondent.
	Administrative cost is the lowest.
	It offers design flexibility and data control.

◆ COLLECTING DATA

Personal Interviewing

The different methods of conducting **personal interviews** can be classified based on the respondents to be contacted and on the means of contacting them. In this section the different types of personal interview methods are discussed, as well as their advantages and limitations. Marketing Research in Practice 8-2 tells how a form of personal interviewing helped a firm identify opportunities.

Process

The personal interviewing process is characterized by the interaction of four entities: the researcher, the interviewer, the interviewee, and the interview environment. Each of the three participants has certain basic characteristics, both inherent and acquired. Each also has general research knowledge and experience, which vary a great deal. Collectively, these characteristics influence the interviewing process and, ultimately, the interview itself. During a personal interview, the interviewer and the interviewee interact and simultaneously influence one another in an interview environment. The choice of an interview environment is made by the researcher, depending on the type of data to be collected. A brief discussion of the various personal interview methods, classified according to interview environment, follows.

Door-to-Door Interviewing

The **door-to-door interview,** in which consumers are interviewed in person in their homes, has traditionally been considered the best survey method. This conclusion

MARKETING RESEARCH IN PRACTICE 8-2

Storytelling: A New Way to Get Closer to the Customer

Surveys and focus groups cannot always help you understand what drives consumer behavior. Traditional market research no longer works with an increasingly diverse and fickle customer base. Researchers are now onto a new method called storytelling, eliciting real-life stories from customers about how they behave and what they truly feel. At the heart of this new brand of customer research is a search for subtle insights into human behavior. This is important because 80 percent of all human communication is nonverbal.

Unlike traditional market research, it may not cost a lot to gather the right kind of stories from customers. If done right, as few as 25 interviews can deliver the insight media.

Kimberly-Clarke worked through deep-rooted emotions when it attempted to reinvent the diaper business some years back. Every time another kid graduated to underpants, the company lost a customer for life. The company then assigned a team to probe the parents who were in the throes of toilet-training their children. The research team met customers at their homes to hear real-life stories and made a few important discoveries. The stories in toilet-training come from parents' feelings of failure, which they would never admit in a focus group. The team realized that parents viewed diapers as clothing that signifies a particular stage of child development, not as a waste-disposal fodder. Clothing has meaning, and the message of diapers sent to toilet trainees was disastrous. So the company rolled up to Huggies Pull-ups Training Pants, a transition product that looked like underwear and fit like it too, yet still kept accidents on the inside. By the time competitors caught up, the company was selling $400 million of Pull-ups a year.

Source: Fortune, February 3, 1997.

Door-to-door interviewing.
Jeff Dunn/The Picture Cube.

was based on a number of factors. First, the door-to-door interview is a personal, face-to-face interview with all the attendant advantages—feedback from the respondent, the ability to explain complicated tasks, the ability to use special questionnaire techniques that require visual contact to speed up the interview or improve data quality, the ability to show the respondent product concepts and other stimuli for evaluation, and so on. Second, the consumer is seen as being at ease in a familiar, comfortable, secure environment.

Executive Interviewing

Executive interviewing refers to the industrial equivalent of door-to-door interviewing. This type of survey involves interviewing business people at their offices concerning industrial products or services.

The term **executive interviewing** is used by marketing researchers to refer to the industrial equivalent of door-to-door interviewing. This type of survey involves interviewing business people at their offices concerning industrial products or services.

This type of interviewing is very expensive. First, individuals involved in the purchase decision for the product in question must be identified and located. Once a qualified person is located, the next step is to get that person to agree to be interviewed and to set a time for the interview.

Finally, an interviewer must go to the particular place at the appointed time. Long waits are frequently encountered; cancellations are not uncommon. This type of survey requires the very best interviewers, because frequently they must conduct interviews on topics about which they know very little.

Mall-Intercept Surveys

Shopping-center interviews are a popular solution when funds are limited and the respondent must see, feel, or taste something. Often, they are called **mall-intercept surveys,** in recognition of the interviewing procedures. Interviewers, stationed at

Mall intercept interview.
Alan Oddie/PhotoEdit.

entrances or selected locations in a mall, randomly approach respondents and either question them at that location or invite them to be interviewed at a special facility in the mall. These facilities have equipment that is adaptable to virtually any demonstration requirement, including interview rooms and booths, kitchens with food-preparation areas, conference rooms for focus groups, closed-circuit television and sound systems, monitoring systems with one-way mirrors, and online video-screen interviewing terminals.

Since interviewers don't travel and respondents are plentiful, survey costs are low. However, shopping center users, who are not representative of the general population, visit the center with different frequencies, and shop at different stores within the center.[12] These problems can be minimized with the special sampling procedures described in Chapter 11. The number of people who agree to be interviewed in the mall will increase with incentives.[13]

Self-Administered Questionnaires

In the **self-administered interview** method, no interviewer is involved. Even though this reduces the cost of the interview process, this technique has one major disadvantage: There is no one present to explain things to the respondent and clarify responses to open-ended questions. This results in the answers to most of the open-ended questions being totally useless. Some have argued, however, that the absence of an interviewer results in the elimination of interviewer bias.

Self-administered interviews are often used in malls or other central locations where the researcher has access to a captive audience. Airlines frequently use this technique to get information about their services; the questionnaires are administered in flight. Many hotels, restaurants, and other service businesses provide brief questionnaires to patrons to find out how they feel about the quality of service provided.

Purchase Intercept Technique[14]

The **purchase intercept technique (PIT)** is different from but related to the mall-intercept approach. This technique combines both in-store observation and in-store interviewing to assess shopping behavior and the reasons behind that behavior. Like a mall intercept, the PIT involves intercepting consumers while they are in a shopping environment; however, the PIT is administered at the time of an observable,

In the self-administered interview method, no interviewer is involved. Even though this reduces the cost of the interview process, this technique has one major disadvantage: there is no one present to explain things to the respondent and clarify responses to open-ended questions.

The **purchase intercept technique (PIT)** is different from but related to the mall-intercept approach. Like a mall intercept, the PIT involves intercepting consumers while they are in a shopping environment; however, the PIT is administered at the time of an observable, specific product selection, as compared to consumers in a mall location.

specific product selection, as compared to consumers in a mall location. The researcher unobtrusively observes the customer make a purchase in a particular product category; then the researcher intercepts the customer for an interview as soon as the purchase has been made.

The major advantage of the PIT is that it aids buyer recall. Interviewing at the point of purchase minimizes the time lapse between the purchase and data collection, and can provide a neutral set of memory cues for the respondent while the purchase is still salient. Apart from difficulties in gaining access to stores, the principal disadvantage of the PIT is that it samples only purchasers and not anyone else who might be influencing the decision on what to buy or where to shop.

Omnibus Surveys

Omnibus surveys are regularly scheduled personal interview surveys with questions provided by a number of separate clients. The questionnaires, based on which interviews are conducted, will contain sequences of questions on different topics.

Omnibus surveys are regularly scheduled (weekly, monthly, or quarterly) personal interview surveys with questions provided by a number of separate clients. The questionnaires, based on which interviews are conducted, will contain sequences of questions on different topics. Each sequence of questions is provided by one client, and the whole questionnaire is made up of such sequences of questions, on diverse topics, from different clients.

There are impressive advantages to the omnibus approach whenever only a limited number of personal interview questions is needed. The total costs are minimized, since the rates are based on the number of questions asked and tabulated, and the cost of the survey is shared by the clients. The results are available quickly, because all the steps are standardized and scheduled in advance. The regularity of the interview schedule and the assurance that the independent samples are matched make this a suitable base for continuous "tracking" studies and before–after studies.

Table 8-3 provides some approximate indices of the direct cost of a completed interview, to help compare data collection methods. In 1998, an index value of 1.0 corresponded to a cost of $30.00. Thus, in 1998, one could expect a 40- to 60-minute personal interview on a national basis, with one call-back and 10 percent validation, to cost between $75 ($2.5 \times \$30.00$) and $105.00 ($3.5 \times \$30.00$). This cost assumes that

TABLE 8-3 Comparative Indices of Direct Costs per Completed Interview in 2001 (including travel and telephone charges, interviewer compensation training, and direct supervision expenses)

Data Collection Method	Index of Cost[a]
1. *Mail survey* (costs depend on return rate, incentives, and follow-up procedure)	0.3–0.8
2. *Fax survey* (costs depend on return rate, incentives, and follow-up procedure)	0.3–0.8
3. *On-line interviewing*	0.08–0.15[15]
4. *Telephone interviews*	
a. 7-minute interview with head of household in metropolitan area	0.5–0.8
b. 15-minute interview with small segment of national population from a central station	1.3–1.7
5. *Personal interviews*	
a. 10-minute personal interview in middle-class suburban area (1 callback and 10 percent validation)	1.5–1.8
b. 40- to 60-minute interview of national probability sample (1 callback and 10 percent validation)	2.5–3.5
c. Executive (VIP) interviews	4.0–15.0 +

[a] In 2001 an index value of 1.0 corresponded to an average cost of $35.00.

the study is conducted by a commercial research supplier and a general population is interviewed. If the sample to be interviewed consists of a particular segment, such as physicians, then a 40- to 60-minute interview would cost close to $200 per interview.

Until recently, it was thought that the personal interview method was always the best way to reduce nonresponse bias. Interviewers can track down hard-to-find respondents and minimize refusals by being physically present at the door. Unfortunately, the costs of the call-backs needed to achieve high response rates are becoming excessive. This is especially a problem in inner-city areas; interviewers are reluctant to visit them and may refuse to enter the areas at night even when they work in teams.

Telephone Interviewing

The **telephone interview** gradually has become the dominant method for obtaining information from large samples, as the cost and nonresponse problems of personal interviews have become more acute. At the same time, many of the accepted limitations of telephone interviewing have been shown to be of little significance for a large class of marketing problems.

Process

The telephone interviewing process generally is very similar to personal interviewing. Several unique aspects of telephone interviewing, such as selecting the telephone numbers, the call outcomes, the introduction, when to call, and call reports, are described here.

Selecting Telephone Numbers

There are three basic approaches to obtaining telephone numbers when selecting study participants for telephone interviews. A researcher can use a prespecified list, a directory, or a random dialing procedure. Prespecified lists—membership rosters, customer lists, or lists purchased from commercial suppliers of telephone numbers—are sometimes used for selected groups of people. This use, however, is not widespread in marketing research.

The traditional approach to obtaining numbers has been to use a directory, one provided by either a telephone company or a commercial firm (for instance, the Polk

Computer-assisted telephone interviewing.
Index Stock.

crisscross directory). However, a directory may be inadequate for obtaining a representative sample of consumers or households. On the average, about 40 million U.S. households have unlisted telephone numbers. People who are voluntarily not listed in a telephone directory tend to have characteristics somewhat different from those listed.

To overcome telephone directory nonrepresentativeness, many researchers now use **random-digit dialing** when they interview consumers by telephone. In its most general form, complete random-digit dialing is a nondirectory procedure for selecting all 10 (area code, prefix or exchange, suffix) telephone number digits at random. Although this approach gives all households with telephones an approximately equal chance of being called, it has severe limitations. It is costly to implement, both in dollars and time, since not all possible telephone numbers are in service, and therefore many telephoning attempts are to nonexistent numbers. Additionally, complete random-digit dialing does not discriminate between telephone numbers in which a researcher is interested and those of no interest (numbers outside the geographic study area and those of business or government). Further, all the prefixes in the United States are distributed across the regular land lines (78 percent), cellular (10.5 percent), paging (4.6 percent), shared wireless (3.3 percent), and other (4 percent).[16]

A variation of random-digit dialing is **systematic random-digit dialing (SRDD).** In SRDD, a researcher specifies those telephone area codes and exchanges, or prefixes, from which numbers are to be selected. Thus, government, university, business, or exchanges not of interest (outside the geographic study area) are avoided. The researcher determines a starting number (seed point) plus a sampling interval—a constant number added systematically to the starting number and subsequent numbers generated, to obtain the list of telephone numbers to be called. **Plus-one dialing** is a directory assisted, random-digit-dialing telephone number selection procedure. Plus-one dialing consists of selecting a random sample of telephone numbers from one or more telephone directories, then adding the constant "1" to the last four digits of each number selected. For metropolitan areas, it is necessary to generate approximately four times as many telephone numbers as completed interviews desired, because of not-in-service numbers and the like. An illustration of the SRDD process is described in Marketing Research in Practice 8-3.

SRDD has several advantages. Because there is a random starting point, each telephone number has an equal chance of being called. Second, since telephone exchanges tend to cover specific geographic areas, a spatial focus is possible. Third, if the same number of telephone calls is attempted from each exchange

> A variation of random-digit dialing is **systematic random-digit dialing (SRDD).** In SRDD, a researcher specifies those telephone are codes and exchanges, or prefixes, from which numbers are to be selected.

MARKETING RESEARCH IN PRACTICE 8-3

An Illustration of the SRDD Process

Suppose an interviewer wants to poll a thousand ($n = 1,000$) respondents on the eve of the presidential election in a particular area (with the area code prefix as 743). There are a total of ten thousand ($k = 10,000$) numbers with the prefix 743, that is, 743–0000 to 743–9999. The first step in the SRDD process is to compute the sampling interval (I) given by k/n, which in this case is equal to 10. The interviewer then randomly chooses a telephone number in the interval 743–0000 to 743–0010. Once a number is chosen (say, 743–0005), then, to generate additional numbers, the value of I is added to each of the previously selected numbers. In other words, the telephone numbers to call would be 743–0005, 743-(0005 + I), 743-(0005 + 2I),…, 743-[0005 + (n − 1)I].

studied, the resulting sample tends to have the same geographic dispersion as the original population. Finally, SRDD can be incorporated into a standard computer program.

Call Outcomes

Once the telephone numbers have been selected, a call is made. Once a call has been attempted, eight possible **call outcomes** can occur. Table 8-4 lists the eight call outcomes and the method to handle each outcome.

The Introduction

One of the most important aspects of telephone interviewing, and the key to a successfully completed interview, is the introduction. For the interview to be completed successfully, the interviewer must gain immediate rapport with potential study participants. Gaining rapport requires a pleasant telephone voice (being male or female does not seem to matter) and a good introduction. It is important that the introduction state the topic of study clearly but in brief. An overly long introduction tends to decrease cooperation and elicit refusals to participate.

When to Call

To efficiently obtain a representative sample of study participants, telephone interviews should be attempted at times when prospective interviewees will most likely be available. For consumer interviews, telephone interviews should probably be attempted between 6 P.M. and 9 P.M. on weekdays, and 10 A.M. to 8 P.M. on weekends. Calling before 6 P.M. on weekdays decreases the chances of reaching working individuals, and calling after 9 P.M. incurs the wrath of those who are early to bed. On the other hand, the best time to reach homemakers or contact individuals at work is between 9 A.M. and 4:30 P.M.

TABLE 8-4 **Call Outcomes and Recommendations to Deal with Them**

Call Outcome	Recommendation
The telephone is not in service.	Eliminate the number from further consideration.
The number dialed is busy.	Call the number again later, because the characteristics of the people whose lines are busy will be different from those whose lines are not.
No one answers the call.	Call the number back later, because the characteristics of the people who are not at home will be different from those who are at home.
The number called is a fax number.	Send a fax to the respondent requesting his time to conduct the interview, and get his or her telephone number.
An answering machine comes on.	Leave a message in the answering machine saying who you are and the purpose of your call. Call the number again after some time.
The call is answered by someone other than the respondent.	Find out when the respondent will be available and call back at that time.
The person contacted is not in the sampling frame.	Eliminate the number from further consideration.
The call is answered by the person to be contacted.	Conduct the interview.

Call Reports

A **call report** is a form that has telephone numbers to be called and columns for interviewers to document their telephoning attempts—what day and time the call was made, the outcome, the length of the call, and so forth. Call reports provide records of calling experiences and are useful for managing data collection.

Other Issues

Overall, the telephone method dominates the personal interview with respect to speed, absence of administrative problems, and cost per completed interview. As we saw in Table 8-3 the costs of a telephone survey will seldom exceed two-thirds of the comparable costs of a personal interview.[17] Costs can be reduced further with omnibus surveys. The key to the low costs for the latter surveys is the **wide area telephone service (WATS),** which provides unlimited calls to a given zone in Canada or the United States for a fixed monthly charge.

For better or worse, the telephone is an "irresistible intruder." A ringing telephone compels us to answer. Long-distance calling brings a further dimension of urgency and importance to reaching the desired respondent. (This tends to counteract the fact that it is easier for a person to terminate midway through a telephone interview.)

Mail Surveys

The third major survey method is the **mail survey.** In this survey mode, questionnaires traditionally are mailed to potential study participants, who complete and return them by mail.

The Process

Superficially, interviewing by mail consists of identifying and locating potential study participants, mailing them questionnaires, and waiting for completed questionnaires to be returned. Substantively, the process is a series of distinct and often difficult decisions regarding the identification of study participants and the mail interview package—outgoing envelope, cover letter, questionnaire, return envelope, and the incentives, if any, to be used.

Unlike personal and telephone interviews, mail interviews require at least broad identification of the individuals to be sampled before data collection begins. Without such an identification and an associated mailing address, mail interviews are not feasible. Therefore, an initial task is to obtain a valid mailing list of potential study participants. Mailing lists can be obtained from customer lists, association or organization membership rosters, telephone directories, publication subscription lists, or commercial "list houses." Regardless of its source, the mailing list must be current and relate closely to the group being studied. As might be expected, obtaining a useful mailing list is especially difficult when a list that is representative of the general population is desired.

Decisions must also be made about the various elements to be contained in a mail survey. Although many of these decisions involve relatively mechanical elements, each decision influences both the response rate and the response quality. Some decisions that are to be considered are

> Type of return envelope
> Postage
> Method of addressing

> Cover letter
>
> Questionnaire length, content, layout, color, and format
>
> Method of notification (should there be a follow-up?)
>
> Incentive to be given

One decision area is method of notification. In both preliminary and follow-up notification, a researcher communicates with potential mail interview respondents more than once. Preliminary notification may also be used to *screen*, or qualify, individuals for study inclusion. This communication may be by postcard, letter, or telephone. Follow-up communication methods include sending potential study participants postcards or letters, or telephoning them a few days after they receive the questionnaire to remind them to complete and return it as soon as possible.

Other Issues

The most likely reason for choosing a mail survey is cost, but there are other reasons also, as illustrated by the decision of the Census Bureau to switch from a personal interview to a census by mail to gain "better results, including a shortening of the period for collecting the data and more reliable answers supplied directly by respondents, instead of through a more-or-less inhibiting intermediary, the enumerator."[18] This approach worked well for the 1970 census, when forms were mailed to 60 percent of American households, of which 87 percent were completed voluntarily. More recent tests, to larger segments of the population, have not been so encouraging. Mail surveys generally are superior when sensitive or potentially embarrassing topics, such as sexual behavior and finances, are covered (as long as the respondent is convinced that the answers will be kept in confidence). The absence of an interviewer means that a large number of variables are controlled inadequately, including:

- The identity of the respondent (Was it the addressee who answered, or an assistant or a spouse?)
- Whom the respondent consults for help in answering questions
- The speed of the response (The usual time lag before receipt of a questionnaire delays the study and makes the responses vulnerable to external events taking place during the study.)[19]
- The order in which the questions are exposed and answered (The respondent can look ahead to see where the questions are leading, so it is not possible to funnel questions from the general to the specific, for example.)
- Respondent understanding of the questions (There is no opportunity to seek clarification of confusing questions or terms, so many respondents return their questionnaire partially completed.)
- Range of responses (The mail-out methodology only provides snapshots of the extremes because those with outstandingly positive or similarly negative experiences are the ones most likely to respond.)
- The opportunity to probe for further information.[20]

One consequence of these problems is that long questionnaires with complicated questions cannot be used without diminishing the response rate. As a rule of thumb, six to eight pages is the upper limit on topics of average interest to respondents.[21]

Mail surveys are limited to situations where a mailing list is available and the cost of the list is not prohibitive. Unfortunately, there are a number of possible flaws in all such lists: obsolescence, omissions, duplications, and so forth. This makes it difficult to find the ideal list, which consists entirely of the type of person to be contacted, and also represents all of those who exist. Great care must be taken at this stage to ensure that the study objectives can be achieved without excessive compromise.

If the boon of mail surveys is cost, then the bane is response rates. The **response rate** to mail surveys gives an indication of the number of questionnaires that have been returned. The Council of American Survey Research Organizations defines response rates as the ratio of the number of completed interviews with responding units to number of eligible responding units in the sample.[22] Implementing the definition may be simple or complex, depending on the methods used to select the sample.[23] The problem is not that acceptable response rates cannot be achieved, but rather, that the rate is hard to forecast and there is substantial risk that an acceptable rate may not be achieved.

Many factors combine to influence the response rate, including (1) the perceived amount of work required, which in turn depends on the length of the questionnaire and the apparent ease with which it can be completed; (2) the intrinsic interest of the topic; (3) the characteristics of the sample; (4) the credibility of the sponsoring organization; (5) the level of induced motivation; and (6) increased unethical use of marketing research to sell products (see Marketing Research in Practice 8-4). A poorly planned mail survey on a low-interest topic may achieve only a 10 to 15 percent response rate. Under the right circumstances, 90 percent response rates are possible. Based on response rates, mail-out surveys are more expensive than phone surveys.

Coping with Nonresponse to Mail Surveys

Nonresponse is a problem, because those who respond are likely to differ substantially from those who do not respond. Surveyers can show some respect for correspondents'

MARKETING RESEARCH IN PRACTICE 8-4

Ethics in Surveys

Millions of Americans find in the welter of junk mail they receive items labeled "survey," usually in oversized envelopes, sent by political or other advocacy groups. They usually include a brief questionnaire, perhaps half a dozen questions worded to encourage "yes" answers if the group is for something or "no" answers if it is against. Most consumers can detect the manipulative nature of these surveys and do not respond. Consumer nonresponse represents a threat to legitimate marketing research.

Though many marketing groups have spoken out against the unethical behavior of the causes and candidates, public relations (PR) is most effective in stopping the distribution of advocacy surveys. After authorizing a sound PR budget, mass media should be used to send the message about how surveys are fooling the public by misrepresenting responses and asking for contributions under false pretenses. Clients, the users of survey research information, should be made aware that discouraging the phony-survey practice is crucial to them. These "surveys" are likely to undermine the reliability of the marketing research data they depend on by further discouraging consumer response. Their support will be useful for the campaign against advocacy surveys.

Source: Thomas T. Semon, "Advocacy Surveys Threaten Marketing Research," *Marketing News,* April 24, 1995, p. 9.

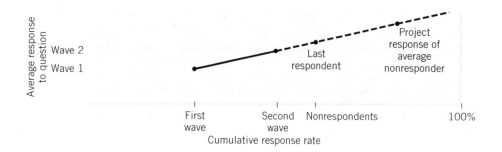

convenience and the value of their time, most importantly. Calling during dinner time is convenient for the researcher, but an obvious nuisance for the respondent. Long, repetitive questionnaires demonstrate contempt for the value of respondents' time. Introductory statements meant to provide a rationale for the interview are often disingenuous, dishonest, or even fradulent.[24] The best way to protect against this bias is to improve the response rate. The most consistently effective methods for achieving high response rates involve some combination of monetary incentives and follow-ups or reminders.[25] Table 8-5 lists the various common methods for coping with nonresponse to mail surveys. The inclusion of a dollar bill in the mailing, which is the usual reward, has been found to improve response rates by increments of 18 to 27 percent when compared to returns when no incentive is used. Although other incentives increase response, the dollar may be the least expensive incentive with the most positive results.[26] Comparable improvements have been obtained from the single or multiple follow-up letter. Although each follow-up brings additional responses, the optimum number seems to be two. In summary, the only proven techniques to increase response rates are follow-up techniques and monetary incentives.

TABLE 8-5   Common Methods Used for Coping with Nonresponse to Mail Surveys

Inducement	Examples
Anonymity	Assurance of anonymity
Appeals	Social utility, egoistic
Foot-in-the-door	Use of initial request and then a subsequent request to those who comply with the initial request
Follow-ups	Postcard, letter, replacement questionnaire
Incentives	Nonmonetary, monetary
Personalization	Hand-addressed envelope, personal signature
Preliminary notification	Advanced letter, telephone prenotification
Questionnaire length	Printing on both sides of sheet
Response deadline	Request for immediate reply
Sponsorship	Company, trade association, university researcher
Type of postage (outgoing)	Commemorative stamp, first class
Type of postage (return envelopes)	Business reply envelope, metered postage

Source: Adapted from Jeffrey Connant, Denise Smart, and Bruce Walker, "Mail Survey Facilitation Techniques: An Assessment and Proposal Regarding Reporting Practices," *Journal of the Market Research Society,* vol. 32, no.4 (1990), 569–580.

Mail Panels

A **mail panel** is a representative national sample of people who have agreed to participate in a limited number of mail surveys each year. A number of these panels are operated by firms such as Market Facts, Home Testing Institute, and National Family Opinion, Inc. The latter firm, for example, offers a number of panels that contain 130,000 people. The major advantage is the high response rate, which averages 75 to 85 percent.

A typical mail panel is the Conference Board Survey of Consumer Confidence. This card is sent with cards from as many as 10 other studies, which spreads the costs of the survey. Since the questions and the sampling procedures are the same every quarter, the Conference Board has a standard measuring stick for tracking fluctuations in consumer attitudes and buying intentions.

Panels are recruited to match the general population with respect to geographic location, city size, age of homemaker, family income, and so on. Hence, it is possible to draw special samples of particular occupation groups (such as lawyers), age categories (such as teenagers), and geographic areas. Large samples can be obtained quickly in test-market areas, for example. Inevitably, those people who agree to serve on such panels will be different from the rest of the population—perhaps because they are more interested in such research, have more time available, and so forth. Little is known about the effect of such differences on questionnaire responses.

Fax Surveys[27]

As a consequence of their deep penetration of some markets, fax machines have become feasible tools for use by marketing researchers in addressing certain research questions. **Fax surveys** can provide faster and higher response rates without reducing data quality. Fax and telephone communication technology continue to improve rapidly in comparison to mail, so the variable cost per contact is going in opposite directions for the two modes of transmission. However, it is not anticipated that the image quality possible with fax transmission will match that of mail (especially with colors and graphics) any time in the foreseeable future, nor will fax machines soon be a realistic mode of survey administration to ultimate households. Although it is probably premature to consider fax as a practical means of collecting data from consumer households, it can be used now for research with industrial, commercial, or institutional respondents. Under certain conditions, marketing researchers may prefer faxes over mail surveys.

Fax surveys are appropriate when:

1. The study has an organization population with universal or nearly universal ownership of fax machines.
2. The questionnaire does not require high image quality or color.
3. Respondents can give the questionnaire to a subordinate for faxing or mailing and/or can mail the response back through an office metering system so the inconvenience of addressing a response and applying postage is minimized.
4. The study does not benefit greatly from enclosing incentives.
5. Faxed returns go to a line that is not too busy.
6. Respondents are not concerned about junk faxes.
7. The return cost does not matter to respondents.
8. The survey does not contain sensitive questions.

Although many surveys do not have urgent deadlines, if fax provides quicker responses than mail, then faxes should be considered in place of mail, in situations where rapid response is desirable. For instance, a firm needing immediate feedback on a product recall, a proposed price change, or a last-minute ad campaign decision would be pleased to save three to five days of survey time by resorting to fax rather than mail contact. Fax correspondence, by its nature, appears to have a greater urgency, and people may actually take the time to respond sooner to fax correspondence than to mail correspondence.

Unless each questionnaire is unique, only one cover letter and questionnaire needs to be printed for fax transmittal. This results in savings in paper and printing costs. In some cases a hard copy of the questionnaire material need not be printed, because a computer can transfer the document to the fax machine. This capability eliminates the need to print labels or type addresses, purchase envelopes, and so on, all of which can add considerable cost in terms of time, labor, and materials. Using monetary incentives to encourage response is not as easy with fax as it is with mail surveys, and it is not possible to provide self-addressed, postage-paid return envelopes with fax questionnaires (except for a toll-free phone number for return faxes).

Electronic Mail (e-Mail) Surveys

The rapid proliferation of pagers and answering machines, coupled with negative consumer attitudes toward phone surveys, are making phone surveys less representative and more expensive. Fax surveys are an option, but their use is limited in general to consumer response research because fax machines are not a standard household item. However, e-mail is a flexible alternative as PCs outnumber fax machines in households two to one.[28] With the arrival of fiber-optics technology and interactive multimedia computing, paper-and-pencil methods of data collection may well become obsolete in the near future. Researchers will be able to e-mail the questionnaires into the respondents' computers and get their responses back into their own computers without any human interference at all. This will drastically reduce the errors committed in the surveys. E-mail surveys can become one of the most effective and popular survey methods of the future. With the use of the Internet becoming more prevalent globally, e-mail surveys can be used for international surveys. Fax and e-mail surveys will increase as other countries become more industrialized. They are bound to become important data collection methods in the future. Marketing Research in Practice 8-5 illustrates the use of multimedia facilities for data collection.

Figure 8-2 and Table 8-6 illustrate previously described data collection methods with new computerized methods.

The survey by Times Mirror Center revealed significant differences among various groups. College graduates were 2.5 times as likely to have a home PC than were high school graduates; households with an income of more than $50,000 were five times as often equipped with a PC than were those earning below $20,000. Even among PC owners, there are large variations with respect to modem ownership. Computer-user households with an income of more than $50,000 were nine times as likely to have a modem-equipped PC than were those earning below $20,000.

Advantages

Apart from the speed of response the advantages of e-mail surveys include:

- Clients' response to a "teaser" as, where interested parties can ask to have more information sent by mail.

- Changes to follow-up questionnaire can be made easily.
- Easy identification of respondents who return their questionnaire through the e-mail leader makes editing of the mailing list very easy.
- Undelivered messages are returned immediately.
- It is a semi-interactive medium, so respondents can clarify doubts.

MARKETING RESEARCH IN PRACTICE 8-5

Multimedia Research

The importance of timely information, especially for product development, has spurred the growth of data collection techniques via the computer. Due to multimedia interviewing systems, interviewer mistakes and biases can be avoided and analytical designs such as skip patterns and conjoint/discrete choice studies are easily handled. As for the consumer, the systems offers an extremely user-friendly interface. Respondents can work at their own pace as they interact with a virtual TV, responding to different types of stimuli, from color concept descriptions to full-motion, stereo-sound commercials or product demonstrations. Other advantages include lower research costs and enhanced security because concepts are scanned into the system, which eliminates paper.

Some applications of multimedia interviewing include concept optimization studies, concept screening studies, and pricing studies, all used during the product development cycle.

Source: Todd Kaiser, "Multimedia Research Can Improve New Product Development Today," *Marketing News* (June 3, 1996), p. 24.

TABLE 8-6   Eight Methods of Computerized Data Collection Available to Marketing Researchers

Survey Methods	Characteristics
Computer-assisted personal interviewing	A method in which the researcher conducts in-person interviews, reads questions to the respondent off a computer screen, and keys the respondent's answers directly into the computer.
Computer-assisted self-interviewing	An on-site member of the research team intercepts and directs willing respondents to nearby computers. Each respondent reads questions off a computer screen and keys his or her answers directly into a computer.
Fully automated self-interviewing	Respondents independently approach a centrally located computer station or kiosk, read questions off a screen, and key their answers directly into the station's computer.
Computer-assisted telephone interviewing	Members of the research team telephone potential respondents, ask questions of respondents from a computer screen, and key the answers directly into a computer.
Fully automated telephone interviewing	An automated voice asks questions over the telephone, and respondents use keys on their touch-tone telephones to enter their replies.
Computer disks by mail	The researcher mails potential respondents computer disks containing a survey to be completed by respondents on their own computers. They mail the disks back to the researcher when done.
Electronic mail survey	Using batch-type electronic mail, researchers send e-mail surveys to potential respondents who use electronic mail. Respondents key in their answers and send an e-mail reply. Alternatively, using interactive e-mail, researchers can send potential respondents e-mail prompting them to access an address that contains an interactive survey. Respondents access the survey and enter their answers.
Computer-general fax survey	The researcher uses a computer to automatically dial the telephone numbers of potential respondent's fax machines and send a survey electronically. Respondents provide written responses on the paper copies, then fax or mail the completed survey back to the researcher.

Computer-Assisted Data Collection Methods

BENEFITS	Personal	On-site		Telephone		Mail	E-mail	Fax
	Computer-Assisted Personal Interviewing	Computer-Assisted Self Interviewing	Fully-Automated Self-Interviewing	Computer-Assisted Telephone Interviewing	Fully Automated Telephone Interviewing	Computer Disks by Mail	Electronic Mail Survey	Computer Generated Fax Survey
Respondents need not have any computer-related skills	✓			✓	✓			✓
Allows respondent to choose own schedule for completing survey		✓	✓			✓	✓	✓
Can easily incorporate complex branching questions into survey	✓	✓	✓	✓	✓	✓	✓ ✗	
Can easily use respondent-generated words in questions throughout the survey	✓	✓	✓	✓		✓	✓ ✗	
Can accurately measure response times of respondents to key questions	✓	✓	✓	✓	✓	✓	✓ ✗	
Can easily display a variety of graphics and directly relate them to questions	✓	✓	✓	✓	✓	✓	✓ ✗	
Eliminates need to encode data from paper surveys	✓	✓	✓	✓	✓	✓	✓	
Errors in data less likely, compared to equivalent manual method	✓	✓	✓	✓	✓	✓	✓	
Speedier data collection and encoding, compared to equivalent manual method	✓	✓	✓	✓	✓	✓	✓	✓

x = interactive e-mail only

Figure 8-2 Computer-assisted data collection methods.

Source: Marketing Research, Seventh Edition, Aaker, Kumar, and Day.

231

Limitations

- Limited number of Internet subscribers causes bias.
- Incompatibility exists between different systems.
- Questionnaires are easy to ignore and delete.
- There are a large number of incorrect addresses.
- Rigid typing requirements make clear, simple, and correct directions a necessity.
- Human factor—fear of competitors, inexperience with e-mail—may constitute a response bias.

Combinations of Survey Methods

Since each of the basic methods of data collection has different strengths and weaknesses, it is sometimes desirable to combine them and retain the best features of each while minimizing the limitations. Some of the feasible combinations (or sequences) are illustrated here:

1. Telephone → appointment	Personal interview →	Leave behind a self-administered questionnaire to be mailed later
2. Telephone → request	Mail survey → for permission to mail a questionnaire	Telephone follow-up (optional)
3. Personal → interview	Telephone pre-interview (as part of a panel study or verification)	
4. Mail survey →	Telephone follow-up	
5. Telephone or → personal interview	Self-administered → questionnaire	To be either picked up or delivered by mail to "interviewer"
6. Telephone request → for permission to fax questionnaire	Fax survey →	Follow-up telephone (optional)

With the exception of the reinterview panel design of sequence 3, each of these combinations has proven effective in increasing the response rate. Indeed, sequence 1 is virtually mandatory for personal interviews with executives, as we noted in the previous chapter. The virtues of the other sequences are not quite so obvious.

The **telephone prenotification approach** is essentially a phone call to ask permission to mail or fax a questionnaire. The key is the telephone presentation; if the return rate is not acceptable, a follow-up phone call can be made.

The **lockbox approach** is designed to circumvent the screens that receptionists and secretaries set around busy executives. The mail is used to deliver a small locked box that contains a letter telling the respondent that the combination to the lock will not be provided until the time of the interview. This serves to stimulate the respondent's curiosity and increases the response rate.

The drop-off approach is an illustration of sequence 5, which is particularly well suited to studies within compact geographic areas. Some of the advantages are that

The **telephone prenotification approach** is essentially a phone call to ask permission to mail or fax a questionnaire. The key is the telephone presentation, which must not only gain agreement to participate but also make sure the prospective respondent is serious about cooperating.

In the **lockbox approach**, the mail is used to deliver a small locked metal box containing a questionnaire and other interviewing materials such as flashcards, exhibits, and pictures. A cover letter, attached to the box, explains the purpose of the survey and tells the prospective respondent that the interviewer will conduct a telephone interview in a few days.

(1) only lightly trained interviewers are required; (2) response rates are high; (3) lengthy questionnaires can be used without affecting response rates; and (4) it is a very cost-effective method.[29]

Table 8-7 presents a comprehensive set of advantages and disadvantages of the various survey methods just discussed.

Trends in Survey Research

Surveys will continue to dominate as a method of data collection for marketing research, at least for the next few decades. Rapid advancement in technology, however, is changing the very nature of data collection and survey methods. Computers and interactive technology are revolutionizing the way surveys are conducted. This section will look into some survey methods that have become popular in the last few years, and also the future of survey research.

Computer-Assisted Telephone Interviewing (CATI)

In **computer-assisted telephone interviewing (CATI)**, computers are being used increasingly to control the administration and sequence of questions asked by an interviewer seated at a terminal. This use of computers provides researchers with a way to prevent many interviewer errors.

Computers are being used increasingly to control the administration and sequence of questions asked by an interviewer seated at a terminal. In **CATI**, the computer dials the respondent's number automatically, and the questionnaire scrolls down in front of the interviewer as the survey is conducted. This use of computers provides researchers with a way to prevent many interviewer errors, such as choosing the wrong respondent in a household, failing to ask a question that should be asked, or asking a series of questions that is not appropriate for a particular respondent.

The primary advantage of the CATI approach is that it eliminates the need for editing completed questionnaires and creating computer data files by later manually entering every response with a keyboard. There is no checking for errors in completed questionnaires because there is no physical questionnaire. Data entry for completed questionnaires is eliminated because data are entered directly into a computer file as the interview is completed.

This second operation brings to light another advantage of computer-assisted interviewing. Instantaneous results available with computerized telephone interviewing provide some real advantages. Based on preliminary tabulations, certain questions may be dropped, saving time and money in subsequent interviewing[30], for example, more than 90 percent of those interviewed answered a particular question in the same manner, there may be no need to continue asking the question.

Tabulations may also suggest the addition of questions to the survey. If an unexpected pattern of product use is uncovered in the early interviewing stages, questions can be added to further delve into this behavior. Finally, managers may find the early reporting of survey results useful in preliminary planning and strategy development.

There are some limitations to computer-controlled telephone interviewing. It is generally more expensive to use the computer than to administer the traditional paper-and-pencil questionnaire. For that reason, use of a computer-controlled system is recommended when a large number of surveys must be done or when the questionnaire will be used many times in a tracking study.

A second limitation relates to the problems involved in using a mechanical system and to human error in its programming and operation. A program must be written and carefully debugged for each questionnaire. The computer system must be able to handle the demands of a large number of interviewers. At the worst, several days of interviewing may pass before someone notices that a mistake has been made.

At its best, CATI can produce faster, more complete data to the researcher.

TABLE 8-7 Advantages and Disadvantages of Survey Methods

Type of Survey Method	Advantages	Disadvantages
Personal interviewing	• There are sample designs that can be implemented best by personal interview (e.g., area probability samples). • Personal interview procedures are probably the most effective way of enlisting cooperation. • Advantages of interview questions—probing for adequate answers, accurately following complex instructions or sequences—are realized. • Multimethod data collection, including observation, visual cues, and self-administered sections, are feasible. • Rapport and confidence building are possible (including any written reassurances that may be needed for reporting very sensitive material). • Probably longer interviews can be done in person.	• It is likely to be more costly than alternatives. • A trained staff of interviewers that is geographically near the sample is needed. • The total data collection period is likely to be longer than for most procedures. • Some samples (those in high-rise buildings or high-crime areas, elites, employees, students) may be more accessible by some other mode.
Telephone interviewing	• Costs are lower than personal interviews. • Random-digit-dialing (RDD) allows sampling of general population. • There is better access to certain populations, especially as compared to personal interviews. • Data collection periods are shorter. • There are advantages of interviewer administration (in contrast to mail surveys). • Interviewer staffing and management are easier than in personal interviews—smaller staff needed, not necessary to be near sample, supervision and quality control potential is better. • Response rate is likely to be better from a list sample than from mail.	• There are sampling limitations, especially as a result of omitting those without a telephone. • Nonresponse associated with RDD sampling is higher than with interviews. • There are questionnaires or measurement constraints, including limits on response alternatives, use of visual aids, and interviewer observations. • It is possibly less appropriate for personal or sensitive questions if no prior contact.
Self-administration	• Presenting questions requiring visual aids is easier (in contrast to telephone interviews). • Asking questions with long or complex response categories is facilitated. • Asking batteries of similar questions is possible. The respondent does not have to share answers with an interviewer.	• Especially careful questionnaire design is needed. • Open questions usually are not useful. • Good reading and writing skills are needed by respondents. • The interviewer is not present to exercise quality control with respect to answering all questions, meeting questions' objective, or the quality of answers provided. • They are ineffective as a way of enlisting cooperation (depending on group to be studied).
Mail procedures	• Cost is relatively low. • They can be accomplished with minimal staff and facilities. • They provide access to widely dispersed samples and samples that for other reasons are difficult to reach by telephone or in person.	• Interviewer is not involved in data collection. • Good mailing addresses for sample are needed.

Method		
Drop-off questionnaire	• Respondents have time to give thoughtful answers, look up records, or consult with others. • The interviewer can explain the study, answer questions, and designate a household respondent. • Response rates tend to be like those of personal interview studies. • There is more opportunity to give thoughtful answers and consult records or other family members than in personal or telephone interview surveys.	• They cost about as much as personal interviews. • A field staff is required (albeit perhaps a less thoroughly trained one than would be needed for personal interviews).
Fax surveys	• Cost is relatively low. • They can be accomplished with minimal staff and facilities. • They provide access to widely dispersed samples, and samples that for other reasons are difficult to reach by telephone or in person. • Respondents have time to give thoughtful answers, look up records, or consult with others. • Telephone charges are decreasing. • Local faxes are free. • Administrative costs are fixed. • It is fast. • Technology is improving. • List management is easy. • Faxes can be sent and received by computer. • Faxes are more reliable than mail in some countries.	• Fixed costs for computer/fax equipment, multiple phone lines are higher. • Costs increase with minutes. • Cost varies by time on-line, time of day, distance, and telephone carrier. • Faxes are currently limited to organizational populations. • Anonymity is lost. • Confidentiality cannot be guaranteed.
E-mail-based surveys	• They require little setup time and even a novice can easily use this method to gather and analyze data. • Millions of e-mail addresses can be purchased very cheaply. • Benchmarks can often be established from information known about respondents ahead of time. • Respondents have time to formulate answers. • Turnaround time is very low.	• It is limited to flat-text format; questionnaires cannot typically do skip pattern logic, randomization, or thorough error checking. • They are suited for internal audience only. • The practice of spamming can easily backfire and cause problems later on. • It is difficult to determine the sampling variables and their target population.
Web-based surveys	• It offers the flexibility to create more complicated surveys with skip patterns and randomizations and may even include complex graphics and sound. • Speed of recruitment is very fast and travel costs and time are eliminated. • Web-based surveys tend to collect broad-based data from individuals all over the world who voluntarily respond to surveys that are posted on websites.	• Web-based surveys must attract respondents to the web page—as a result, all segments of a web population may not be represented in the sample. • Internet users use different browsers, which may present images and text on web pages in different ways.

TASTY ICE-CREAM: A CASE EXAMPLE OF MARKETING INTELLIGENCE (*continued*)

Choice of Survey Methods for Tasty's Study

A market intelligence effort to gather information through surveys was undertaken over a five-week period in each store. The customers who visited Tasty over a period of time (Purchase Intercept Technique) formed a sample for the survey. This sample was a good prospect for accurate information. Sample sizes of 200 and 100 consumers were selected from the two locations A and B, respectively. To obtain information about customers of the competition, a telephone survey was conducted in the city. Random samples of respondents having different prefixes were selected. The sample targeted residents in and around locations of competing ice cream shops in the city. A sample of 400 respondents was selected at random from the pre-selected prefixes. The respondents were asked about their frequency of visits to ice cream shops, the factors influencing their choice of ice cream shops, the services they expect at the ice cream shop, demographics, and lifestyle activities. A copy of the questionnaire used for customers of Tasty and customers of competition along with a coding sheet is available in the diskette accompanying the book.

◆ SURVEYS IN THE INTERNATIONAL CONTEXT

While conducting surveys for international research, researchers must take into account a number of differences between the domestic and the international environment. In this section the differences between domestic and international research and the problems faced by the researcher in conducting international research are discussed briefly for the three major survey methods.

Personal Interviews

Personal interviewing tends to be the dominant mode of data collection outside the United States.[31] Lower wage costs imply that personal procedures are cheaper than in the United States. On the other hand, use of personal interviewing requires the availability of field staff fluent in the relevant language.

Often, however, given the lack of a pool of trained interviewers in other countries, companies with local research units or international research organizations may train and develop their own field staffs. This provides greater control over the quality of the interviewing conducted in different countries. This is in marked contrast to the practice of "buying field and tab services" from an outside organization, which is common in the United States. These interviewers are not necessarily required to work exclusively for a given research supplier, though often they may do so of their own choice.

Gaining the cooperation of respondents is more difficult in some countries than in others. In Latin countries, and particularly in the Middle East, interviewers are regarded with considerable suspicion. In Latin countries, where tax evasion is more prevalent, interviewers are often suspected of being tax inspectors. In the Middle East, where interviewers are invariably male, interviews with housewives often have to be conducted in the evenings when husbands are at home.

Telephone Interviews

In international marketing research, the advantages of telephone interviews are not always as evident. Low levels of telephone ownership and poor communications in many countries limit the coverage provided by telephone surveys. In addition, telephone costs are often high, and volume rates may not be available. Again, this depends on the specific country and the target population. Consequently, the desirability of conducting a telephone survey will depend to a large extent on the nature and purpose of the survey.

In industrial international marketing research, the use of telephone surveys may be quite effective. Most businesses, other than some small or itinerant retailers or craftspersons, are likely to have telephones.

With the decline of international telephone costs, multicountry studies can also be conducted from a single location. This significantly reduces the time and costs associated with negotiating and organizing a research project in each country, establishing quality controls, and so on. Although the additional costs of making international telephone calls are incurred, these may not be highly significant when a centralized location is used.[32]

International calls also obtain a higher response rate. Results obtained using this technique have been found to be highly stable. Interviewer and client control is considerably greater. The questionnaire can be changed and modified in the course of the survey, and interviewing can be extended or stopped to meet the client's requirements. It is necessary to find interviewers fluent in the relevant languages, but in most European countries this is not a problem.

In consumer research, the feasibility of using telephone surveys depends on the level of private telephone ownership in a country, and the specific target population. In countries such as India, which is predominantly rural, the telephone penetration is only 1 percent, and hence telephone surveys may not be the ideal method to adopt.[33] Even in relatively affluent societies such as Great Britain, telephone penetration is only 80 percent, and telephone interviewing is not widely used because many practitioners are still skeptical about it. In Britain and France, there are substantial declines in telephone response rates in large cities. However, these declines are not observed in Germany and Switzerland. The Eastern European countries and countries in the newly formed Commonwealth of Independent States have a poor telecommunication system. In such countries, conducting telephone surveys may not be a good idea.

Mail Surveys

As in the case of telephone interviews, the advantages and limitations of mail surveys in international marketing research are not always clear, because of the absence of mailing lists, poor mail services, and high levels of illiteracy. In many markets the efficacy of mail surveys depends on the specific product market being investigated (that is, industrial versus consumer), and also on the nature of the survey. Response rates are also a problem in international mail surveys. When international mail surveys are conducted, the response rates vary depending on the country to which the questionnaires are mailed.

Mail surveys typically can be used effectively in industrial international marketing research. Mailing lists such as those from Bottin International, or directories for specific industries, are generally available. In consumer research, and particularly in developing countries, the use of mail surveys may give rise to some problems. Mailing lists comparable to those in the domestic market may not be available, or not sold, and public sources such as telephone directories may not provide adequate coverage. Lists that are available—that is, magazine subscription lists or membership association lists—may be skewed to better-educated segments of the population. In addition, in some countries, the effectiveness of mail surveys is limited not only by low literacy levels, but also by the reluctance of respondents to respond to them.[34] Levels of literacy are often less than 40 or 50 percent in some Asian and African markets, thus limiting the population that can be reached by mail. Mail surveys are also hazardous in countries such as Brazil, where it has been reckoned that 30 percent of the domestic mail is never delivered, or Nicaragua, where all the mail has to be delivered to the post office. Even in countries where literacy levels and mail services make the use of mail surveys feasible, a tendency to regard surveys as an invasion of privacy may limit their effectiveness.

Thus, while mail surveys may be used effectively in industrial marketing research, in consumer research they may be appropriate only in industrialized countries where levels of literacy are high and mailing lists are generally available.

E-mail Surveys

E-mail surveys are the easiest and the fastest of the three methods of on-line research (HTML [downloadable], interactive survey, and e-mail). It requires relatively little setup time. Even a novice can easily use this method to gather data and then analyze it. It is, however, limited to flat-text-format questionnaires and cannot typically include skip pattern logic, randomization, or thorough error checking. They are more suited for internal audiences. Millions of e-mail addresses can be purchased or acquired very cheaply, but the practice of spamming can easily backfire and create a lot of other problems. Researchers should be encouraged to evaluate the adequacy of any test for on-line surveying. Because it is a new and rapidly changing environment, it is difficult to determine the sampling variables and their target proportions.

◆ FACTORS AFFECTING THE CHOICE OF A SURVEY METHOD

One of the important decisions a researcher must make is the way in which the data will be collected. The decision to choose among the various survey methods already discussed is affected by a number of factors. Some of them are described below.

Factors	Description
Sampling	If one is sampling from a list, the information on the list matters. If a list lacks either good mailing addresses or good telephone numbers, trying to collect data by mail, phone, or fax is complicated. Random digit dialing has improved the potential of telephone data collection strategies by giving every household with a telephone a chance to be selected.
Type of population	The reading and writing skills of the population and its motivation to cooperate are two salient considerations in choosing a mode of data collection. Self-administered approaches to data collection place more of a burden on the respondent's reading and writing skills than do interviewer procedures.
Question form	If one is going to have a self-administered questionnaire, one must reconcile oneself to close-ended questions, that is, questions that can be answered by simply checking a box or circling the proper response from a set provided by the researcher. Self-administered open answers often do not produce useful data.
Question content	Researchers have argued that one or another of the strategies should have an advantage when dealing with sensitive topics. Self-administered procedures are thought to be best, because the respondent does not have to admit directly to an interviewer a socially undesirable or negatively valued characteristic or behavior.

Response rates	The rate of response is likely to be much more salient than other considerations in the selection of data collection procedure. Obviously, one of the strengths of group-administered surveys is the high rate of response. In mail surveys there is no doubt that the problem of nonresponse is central. The effectiveness of telephone strategies in producing high response rates depends in part on the sampling scheme.
Costs	The great appeal of mail or fax and telephone survey procedures is that in most cases they cost less than personal interviews. Survey costs depend on many factors, such as questionnaire length, geographic dispersion of the sample, availability and interest of the sample, call-back procedures, respondent selection, and the availability of trained staff.
Availability facilities	The facilities and staff availability should be considered in choosing a data collection mode. Developing an interviewing staff is costly and effective. Attrition rates are generally high for newly trained interviewers. Many new interviewers are not very good at enlisting the cooperation of respondents, producing high refusal rates at the start. One practical consideration about doing an interviewer-conducted survey is the ability to execute a professional data collection effort.
Duration of data collection	The time involved in data collection varies by mode. Surveys done in a very short period of time pay a cost in nonresponse, because some people cannot be reached during any short period. However, telephone surveys routinely can be done more quickly than mail or personal interview surveys of comparable sizes.

◆ ETHICAL ISSUES IN DATA COLLECTION

Even companies that practice legitimate research can violate the rights of respondents by deliberately engaging in a number of practices such as:

- Disguising the purpose of a particular measurement, such as a free draw or free product choice question
- Deceiving the prospective respondent as to the true duration of the interview
- Invading the privacy of the respondent
- Misrepresenting the compensation in order to gain cooperation
- Not mentioning to the respondent that a follow-up interview will be made
- Using projective tests and unobtrusive measures to circumvent the need for a respondent's consent
- Using hidden tape recorders to record personal interviews (or recording phone conversations without the respondent's permission)
- Conducting simulated product tests in which the identical product is tried by the respondent except for variations in characteristics, such as color, that have no influence in the quality of a product
- Not debriefing the respondent[35]

Many of these practices cannot be condoned under any circumstances, and others present the conscientious researcher with a serious dilemma. Under certain circumstances, disguising the nature of the research hypotheses may be the only feasible method by which to collect the necessary data. Yet these practices have the potential to create biased data and suspicion or resentment that later may be manifested in a refusal to participate in subsequent studies.

END OF CHAPTER MATERIAL

SUMMARY

There is bound to be a number of errors when surveys are conducted, some of which can be controlled and others of which cannot be controlled. A researcher should know all the potential sources of errors and should try to reduce their impact on the survey findings. This is a good research practice and will lead to more robust results.

The choice of a survey method—that is, whether to use mail, or telephone or personal interviews—is determined by a number of factors. A knowledge of these factors will make it easier for the researcher to decide among the various methods. The most important factors are the sampling plan to be employed, the type of population to be surveyed, the response rates required, the budget for the survey, and the available resources. A number of factors may be important for the choice of survey method other than those discussed here. It depends on the particular study, but the factors listed in the text are the most common ones.

All data collection methods are susceptible to misrepresentation by the researchers. Two principal sources of this misrepresentation are disguising the true purpose of a marketing activity, such as selling, by calling it marketing research, or abusing respondents' rights during a legitimate data collection process. Both of these practices involve a disregard of professional business ethics. Maintaining high standards of business ethics while collecting data is the obligation of all responsible researchers.

Video Segment:

Precision

Teleservicing—that is the name by which the Precision Company differentiates itself from its competition. By collecting information from consumers regarding the products or services, this firm is geared toward providing a database for use on a real-time basis. The role of such a company is to provide telemarketing and information-gathering services for companies interested in gaining a more thorough consumer profile.

Video Segment:

1-800 Numbers

Several companies have set up 1-800 lines in order to obtain complaints and comments on the products and services offered. As Precision Response Compnay (in the previous Video Segment) tries to outreach to the consumers, the benefit of establishing such a system would be to find out the grievances of the customers and to make amends. Along with serving as a warning mechanism of product problems, companies hope these 1-800 numbers will provide a quick overview of the manner in which the company is being perceived by the customers.

KEY TERMS

information from surveys
survey errors
phenotypic source of refusal
genotypic source of refusal
inability to respond
aided-recall techniques
telescoping
averaging
omission
response bias
interviewer error
survey methods
personal interview
door-to-door interview
executive interviewing
mall-intercept surveys
self-administered interview
purchase intercept technique (PIT)
omnibus surveys
telephone interviewing
selecting telephone numbers
random-digit dialing

systematic random-digit dialing
call outcomes
call reports
wide area telephone service (WATS)
mail surveys
nonresponse to mail surveys
mail panels
e-mail surveys
fax surveys
telephone prenotification approach
lockbox approach
computer-assisted telephone interviewing
(CATI)
sampling
population type
question form
question content
response rates
costs of survey
duration of data collection
web-based surveys

MARKETING RESEARCH TOOLBOX
REVIEW POINTS

1. The survey is the overwhelming choice of researchers for collecting primary data. The principle advantage of a survey is that it can collect a great deal of data about an individual respondent at one time.

2. The various types of information collected using surveys include respondents' attitudes toward an object, image of a certain thing, behavior patterns, and demographics.

3. High refusal rates are a major source of error, for those who refuse to be interviewed are likely to be very different from those who cooperate.

4. A phenotypic source of refusal refers to characteristics of data collection procedure (which questions are asked, how they are asked, the length of the interview, and so on). These elements vary from study and can be controlled to a certain extent.

5. A genotypic source refers to the indigenous characteristics of respondents (such as age, sex and occupation).

6. Inaccuracy in response occurs due to inability or unwillingness of the respondent to respond.

7. Respondents may not know the answer to a question because of ignorance or forgetting, or may be unable to articulate it.

8. The various causes for the inability of respondents are telescoping, averaging, and omission.

9. The various factors that influence response bias are concern about invasion of privacy, time pressure and fatigue, prestige seeking and social desirability response bias, courtesy bias, uninformed response error, and response style.

10. Interviewers vary enormously in personal characteristics, amount of previous experience, style of interviewing, and motivation to do a thorough job.

11. The four basic survey methods are personal interview, telephone interview, mail survey, and fax survey.

12. The personal interviewing process is characterized by the interaction of four entities: the researcher, the interviewer, the interviewee, and the interview environment.

13. Door-to-door interviewing is considered the best survey method. It is the only viable way to do long, in-depth, or detailed interviews and certain in-home product tests.

14. Executive interviewing is used by marketing researchers to refer to the industrial equivalent of door-to-door interviewing. This type of survey involves interviewing businesspeople at their offices concerning industrial products or services.

15. In shopping mall intercept surveys, interviewers are stationed at entrances or selected locations in a mall, randomly approach respondents, and either question them at that location or invite them to be interviewed at a special facility in the mall.

16. In the self-administered interview method, no interviewer is involved. Even though this reduces the cost of the interview process, this technique has one major disadvantage: there is no one present to explain things to the respondent and clarify responses to open-ended questions.

17. The purchase-intercept technique (PIT) is different from but related to the mall-intercept approach. Like a mall intercept, the PIT involves intercepting consumers while they are in a shopping environment; however, the PIT is administered at the time of an observable, specific product selection, as compared to consumers in a mall location.

18. Omnibus surveys are regularly scheduled personal interview surveys with questions provided by a number of separate clients. The questionnaires, based on which the interviews are conducted, will contain sequences of questions on different topics. Each sequence of questions is provided by one client and the whole questionnaire is made up of such sequences of questions, on diverse topics, from different clients.

19. Personal interviews are usually preferred when a large amount of information is required and the questions are complex or involve tasks such as sorting cards into ordered piles or evaluating visual cues. Personal interviewing has a high degree of flexibility and is advantageous when an explicit or current list of households or individuals is not available.

20. Personal interviews are time consuming, administratively difficult, and costly.

21. There are three basic approaches to obtaining telephone members when selecting study participants for telephone interviews. A researcher can use a prespecified list, a directory, or a random-dialing procedure.

22. A variation of random-digit dialing is systematic random-digit dialing (SRDD). In SRDD, a researcher specifies those telephone area codes and exchanges, or prefixes, from which numbers are to be selected.

23. Plus-one dialing is a directory-assisted, random-digit-dialing telephone number selection procedure. Plus-one dialing consists of selecting a random sample of telephone numbers from one or more telephone directories, then adding the constant "1" to the last four digits of each number selected.

24. To efficiently obtain a representative sample of study participants, telephone interviews should be attempted at times when prospective interviewees will most likely be available.

25. Call reports provide records of calling experiences and are useful for managing data collection.

26. The advantages of telephone interviews are: more interviews can be conducted in a given time period because no time is lost in traveling and locating respondents, more hours of the day are productive, especially the evening hours when working women and singles

are likely to be at home and apartment doors are locked, and repeated call-backs at different times of the day can be made at very low cost.

27. The limitations of telephone interviews include inability to employ visual aids or complex tasks, and potential for sample bias is high.

28. In mail surveys, questionnaires are mailed to potential study participants, who complete and return them by mail.

29. The most likely reason for choosing a mail survey is cost; the other advantages include reduction in the number of intermediaries involved, and mail surveys are superior when sensitive issues are covered.

30. The limitations of surveys include low response rates, inability to establish the identity of the respondent, inability to establish the speed of the response, and the inability to explain the question to the respondent.

31. A mail panel means a representative national sample of people who have agreed to participate in a limited number of mail surveys each year.

32. Fax surveys are appropriate when the study has an organization population with universal or nearly universal ownership of fax machines, and the questionnaire does not require high image quality or color.

33. The telephone prenotification approach is essentially a phone call to ask permission to mail or fax a questionnaire. The key is the telephone presentation, which must not only gain agreement to participate but also make sure the prospective respondent is serious about cooperating.

34. In the lockbox approach, the mail is used to deliver a small locked metal box containing a questionnaire and other interviewing materials such as flashcards, exhibits, and pictures. A cover letter, attached to the box, explains the purpose of the survey and tells the prospective respondent that the interviewer will conduct a telephone interview in a few days.

35. In computer-assisted telephone interviewing (CATI), computers are being used increasingly to control the administration and sequence of questions asked by an interviewer seated at a terminal. This use of computers provides researchers with a way to prevent many interviewer errors.

36. Personal interviewing tends to be the dominant mode of data collection outside the United States. Lower wage costs imply that personal procedures are cheaper than in the United States.

37. In international marketing research, the advantages of telephone interviews are not always evident. Low levels of telephone ownership and poor communications in many countries limit the coverage provided by telephone surveys.

38. Mail surveys typically can be used effectively in industrial international marketing research. Mailing lists such as those from directories for specific industries are generally available. In consumer research, and particularly in developing countries, the use of mail surveys may give rise to mailing lists and coverage problems.

39. Factors influencing choice of a survey method include sampling, type of population, question form, question form, question content, response rates, costs, available facilities, and duration of data collection.

40. Web-based surveys tend to collect broad-based data from individuals all over the world who voluntarily respond to surveys on the Web. The web surveys can collect demographic information, as well as other types of purchase, psychographic, and opinion data.

41. E-mail surveys require relatively less setup time. They are limited to flat text format; questionnaire cannot typically include skip pattern logic, randomization, or thorough error checking.

42. Misinterpretation of data collection stems from two principal sources: representing marketing activity other than research as research; abuse of respondents' rights during the data collection process under the rationale of providing better-quality research.

QUESTIONS AND PROBLEMS

1. How would you overcome some of the problems you might anticipate in designing a survey to establish the kind of paint used by the "do-it-yourself" market when the members of this sample last redecorated a room?

2. How would you balance the requirements of improving the quality of interviews against any ethical considerations that may arise?

3. Is the biasing effect of an interviewer more serious in a personal or telephone interview? What steps can be taken to minimize this biasing effect in these two types of interviews?

4. People tend to respond to surveys dealing with topics that interest them. How would you exploit this fact to increase the response rate in a survey of attitudes toward the local urban transit system, in a city where the vast majority of people drive to work or to shop?

5. If you were a marketing research manager, would you permit the following if they were important to the usefulness of a study?
   a. Telling the respondent the interview would take only two or three minutes when it usually took four minutes and a follow-up ten-minute interview was employed.
   b. Telling the respondent the questionnaire would be anonymous but coding it so that the respondent could be identified (so that additional available information about the respondent's neighborhood could be used).
   c. Secretly recording (or videotaping) a focus-group interview.
   d. Saying the research was being conducted by a research firm instead of your own company.

6. You are product manager for Brand M butter, a nationally known brand. Brand M has been declining in absolute level of sales for the last four consecutive months. What information, if any, that could be obtained from respondents would be useful for determining the cause or causes of this decline?

7. What are the general advantages and disadvantages associated with obtaining information by questioning and by observation? Which method provides more control over the sample?

8. Innovative Marketing Consultants Inc. has been contracted to conduct a job-satisfaction survey among the 2,470 employees of United Machine Tools, Inc., Dayton, Ohio. The management insists that the questionnaire be comprehensive and incorporate all the views of the respondent in order to improve the work environment.
   a. What factors should Innovative Marketing Consultants consider in choosing the survey method to be used?
   b. Which question form would be most likely to supply management with the information it has requested?
   c. Design a sample questionnaire that Innovative Marketing Consultants will use in conducting the job-satisfaction survey.
   d. What possible sources of survey error might be encountered?
   e. United Machine Tools, Inc., has a wholly owned subsidiary at Madras, India. What additional factors must Innovative Marketing Consultant consider in choosing the survey method to assess the job-satisfaction levels of the employees at the Madras plant?
   f. What ethical problems might you encounter in obtaining the data from the employees? Would disclosure of the employee profile be an important issue to consider?

9. Mark Hirst, a high school student in Sydney, Australia, developed an innovatively shaped surfboard that radically increased the number of maneuvers a surfer could per-

form in low surf. In his enthusiasm to research the market, he developed a comprehensive seven-page questionnaire to be completed by customers and distributed it among surf supply stores.

a. How will the length of the questionnaire affect the response rate?

b. What possible biases could arise from Mark's sampling method?

10. Families for the Future, a nonprofit organization formed to promote a return to the family values of the 1950s in the United States, is conducting a mail survey to determine the level of domestic violence and its causes. The organization plans to survey families in urban areas in four cities across the United States.

a. What are the possible sources of survey error in this study?

b. How might the study be redesigned to eliminate these errors?

ENDNOTES

1. A. N. Oppenheim, *Questionnaire Design and Attitude Measurement* (New York: Basic Books, 1966).

2. George S. Day, "The Threats to Marketing Research," *Journal of Marketing Research*, 12 (November 1975), pp. 462–467.

3. Frederick Wiseman and Mariane Schafer, "If Respondents Won't Respond, Ask Nonrespondents Why," *Marketing News* (September 9, 1977), pp. 8–9; Susan Kraft, "Who Slams the Door on Research?" *American Demographics* (September 1991), p. 14.

4. A. Ossip, "Likely Improvements in Data Collection Methods—What Do They Mean for Day-to-Day Research Management?" *Journal of Advertising Research, Research Currents* (October–November 1986), pp. RC9–RC12.

5. Arthur Saltzman, "Improving Response Rates in Disk-by-Mail Surveys," *Marketing Research*, 5 (Summer 1993), pp. 32–39.

6. Charles F. Cannel, Lois Oksenberg, and Jean M. Converse, "Striving for Response Accuracy: Experiments in New Interviewing Techniques," *Journal of Marketing Research*, 14 (August 1977), pp. 306–315.

7. W. Cook, "Telescoping and Memory's Other Tricks," *Journal of Advertising Research*, 87 (February–March 1987), pp. 5–8.

8. William D. Wells, "The Influence of Yea-Saying Response Style," *Journal of Advertising Research*, 1 (June 1963), pp. 8–18.

9. Donald P. Warwick and Charles A. Lininger, *The Sample Survey: Theory and Practice* (New York: McGraw-Hill, 1975), pp. 198, 203.

10. J. Freeman and E. W. Butler, "Some Sources of Interviewer Variance in Surveys," *Public Opinion Quarterly* (Spring 1976), pp. 84–85.

11. Good discussions of what can be found in Warwick and Lininger are in Robert Ferber, ed., *Handbook of Marketing Research* (New York: McGraw-Hill, 1974), pp. 2.124–2.132, 2.147–2.159.

12. Seymour Sudman, "Improving the Quality of Shopping Center Sampling," *Journal of Marketing Research*, 17 (November 1980), pp. 423–431.

13. Frederick Wiseman, Marianne Schafer, and Richard Schafer, "An Experimental Test of the Effects of a Monetary Incentive on Cooperation Rates and Data Collection Costs in Central-Location Interviewing," *Journal of Marketing Research* (November 1983), pp. 439–442.

14. Ellen Gregory, "Cost/Quality Issues Plague Mall Intercepts," *Marketing Research* (Summer 1996), pp. 46–47.

15. http://www.euroleaders.com.

16. "The Frame," published by Survey Sampling, Inc. (September 1996).

17. Stanley L. Payne. "Data Collection Methods," in Robert Ferber, ed., *Handbook of Marketing Research* (New York: McGraw Hill, 1974), pp. 2.105–2.123.

18. Quoted from Census Bureau sources by Paul L. Erdos, "Data Collection Methods: Mail Surveys," in Robert Ferber, ed., *Handbook of Marketing Research* (New York: McGraw Hill, 1974).

19. Michael J. Houston and Neil M. Ford, "Broadening the Scope of Methodological Research on Mail Surveys," *Journal of Marketing Research*, 13 (November 1976), pp. 397–403.

20. Joe Inguanzo, "Based on Response Rates, Phone Surveys Are Cheaper than Mail," *Marketing News* (Jan. 6, 1997), p. 15.

21. Quoted from Census Bureau by Paul L. Erdos, "Data Collection Methods: Mail Surveys," in Robert Ferber, ed., *Handbook of Marketing Research* (New York: McGraw Hill, 1974), pp. 2–91.

22. Council of American Survey Research Organizations, "On the Definition of Response Rates," Special Report (Port Jefferson, NY: CASRO, 1982).

23. Frederick Wiseman and Maryann Billington, "Comment on a Standard Definition of Response Rates," *Journal of Marketing Research* (August 1984), pp. 336–338.

24. Thomas T. Semon, "Treat Your Respondents Well: You Need Them," *Marketing News* (Nov. 24, 1997), p. 12.

25. Leslie Kanuk and Conrad Berenson, "Mail Surveys and Response Rates: A Literature Review," *Journal of Marketing Research*, 12 (November 1975), pp. 440–453; Jeanine M. James and Richard Bolstein, "The Effect of Monetary Incentives and Follow-up Mailings on the Response Rate and Response Quality in Mail Surveys," *Public Opinion Quarterly*, 54 (Fall 1990), pp. 346–361.

26. Sheldon Wayman, "The Buck Stops When it Comes to Dollar Incentives," *Marketing News* (Jan. 6, 1997), p. 9.

27. John P. Dickson and Douglas L. MacLachlan, "Fax Surveys?" *Marketing Research* (September 1992), pp. 26–30.

28. Lewis C. Winters, "Questionnaires in the 1990s: Wands and Scannable Forms Are 'In,'" *Marketing Research* (June 1992), p. 46.

29. David Schwartz, "Locked Box Contains Survey Methods, Helps End Some Woes of Probing Industrial Field," *Marketing News* (January 27, 1978), p. 18.

30. For more details on cost savings, refer to John P. Liefeld, "Response Effects in Computer Administered Questioning," *Journal of Marketing Research*, 25 (November 1988), pp. 405–409.

31. D. Monk, "Marketing Research in Canada," *European Research* (November 1987), p. 274; J. J. Honomichl, "Survey Results Positive," *Advertising Age* (November 1984), p. 23.

32. M. De Houd. "International Computerized Telephone Research: Is It Fiction?" *Marketing Research Society Newsletter* (January 1982), pp. 14–15.

33. D. Sopariwala, "India: Election Polling in the World's Largest Democracy," *European Research* (August 1987), pp. 174–177.

34. George S. Day, "The Threats to Marketing Research," *Journal of Marketing Research*, 12 (November 1975), pp. 462–467.

35. Ibid.

CASES

For detailed descriptions of the below cases please visit www.wiley.com/college/kumar.

Case 8-1: Essex Markets (A)
Case 8-2: More Ethical Dilemmas in Marketing Research

Attitude Measurement

Learning Objectives

- Introduce the concept of measurement and scaling in marketing research.
- Briefly discuss the different scales in measurement.
- Introduce the different types of scales used for measuring attitudes.
- Give a description of each of the well-known scales that are used to measure attitudes.
- Provide an approximate heuristic for choosing an attitude scale.
- Discuss the concepts of reliability, validity, and generalizability.

Most questions in marketing research surveys are designed to measure attitudes. For example, each of the following situations involves the measurement of some aspect of a respondent's attitude:

1. An appliance manufacturer wants to know how many potential buyers are aware of a brand name. (What brand names do they think of in connection with dishwashers?)
2. Administrators concerned with formulating an energy policy want to know what proportion of voters agree that car buyers should pay an extra tax of several hundred dollars on cars that get poor gasoline mileage.
3. A food manufacturer is interested in the intentions of a sample of consumers to buy a possible new product after the concept has been described to them.

Marketing Research in Practice 9-1 shows how American Express used customer behavior to improve market share. Common to each of these examples is a need to learn something about the basic orientation or attitude of present or prospective customers. Their attitudes are based on the information they have, their feelings (liking and disliking), and their intended behavior.

What management really wants to understand—and ultimately influence—is behavior. For many reasons, however, they are likely to use attitude measures instead of behavior. First, there is a widely held belief that attitudes are precursors of behavior. If consumers like a brand, they are more likely to choose that brand over one they like less. Second, it is generally more feasible to ask attitude questions than to observe and interpret actual behavior. Attitude measures offer the greatest advantage over

MARKETING RESEARCH IN PRACTICE 9-1

American Express Satisfaction Survey

Researchers at American Express know that customer satisfaction is important to business success. But they rate customer behavior as even more important. Satisfaction research has led the company to a better understanding of what the customer wanted from the Amex cards in their pockets and purses. These studies focused more on improving the internal processes rather than on customer needs. Recently, the company has started focusing more on behavior. Research has concentrated on why the customer used Amex cards for some purchases and some other card for other purchases. This has helped the company identify the most important card attributes for new customer segments, permitting the company to differentiate and target individual card products. Focus on behavior rather than satisfaction has helped Amex increase its market share for the first time in 1996.

Source: Marketing News (May 12 1997), p. 6.

behavior measures in their capacity for diagnosis or explanation. Attitude measures can be used to help researchers learn which features of a new product concept are acceptable or unacceptable, as well as the perceived strengths and weaknesses of competitive alternatives. Insights can be gained into the process by which choice decisions are made: What alternatives are known and considered? Why are some rejected? What problems are encountered with the products or services that are used?

This chapter is concerned primarily with the measurement of attitudes. Some measurement approaches were encountered in earlier chapters. Projective techniques and physiological methods, discussed in Chapter 7, are indirect methods for inferring a person's attitude. By far the most popular approach is the direct self-report, in which the respondent is asked a series of questions. The two previous chapters described the survey methods appropriate for such self-reports. This chapter and the next are devoted specifically to attitude measurements, in recognition of their importance to marketing and of the special problems of specifying and identifying attitudes.

◆ WHAT ARE ATTITUDES?

Attitudes are mental states used by individuals to structure the way they perceive their environment and guide the way they respond to it.

Attitudes are mental states used by individuals to structure the way they perceive their environment and guide the way they respond to it. There are three generally accepted, related components that form an attitude: a cognitive or knowledge component, a liking or affective component, and an intentions or actions component. Each component provides a different insight into a person's attitude.

Attitudes are truly the essence of the "human change agent" that all marketers strive to influence. But without the right tools to effectively measure attitude, attitudinal research has little to offer.[1]

Cognitive or Knowledge Component

The **cognitive** or **knowledge component** represents a person's information about an object. This information includes awareness of the existence of the object, beliefs about the characteristics or attributes of the object, and judgments about the relative importance of each of the attributes.

The **cognitive** or **knowledge component** represents a person's information about an object. This information includes awareness of the existence of the object, beliefs about the characteristics or attributes of the object, and judgments about the relative importance of each of the attributes.

Consider the knowledge people might bring to planning a ski vacation in the Rockies. They might remember the names of several ski areas without prompting: Aspen, Snowmass, Alta, and Park City, for example. This is unaided recall awareness. The names of additional ski areas are likely to be remembered when the travel agent mentions them. This is **aided recall awareness.**

Knowledge of ski areas is not limited to awareness, however. From the experience of friends, brochures, magazine articles, and other sources, a person will have formed beliefs or judgments about the characteristics or attributes of each of these ski areas. These attributes might range from the difficulty of the slopes to the type of social life and the cost of accommodations. Often, these beliefs incorporate explicit comparative judgments within a set, such as which ski area is the most difficult or the cheapest. Another kind of belief is an overall similarity judgment: Are Aspen and Snowmass more similar to each other than Aspen and Alta, for example?

Affective or Liking Component

The **affective** or **liking component** summarizes a person's a overall feelings toward an object, situation, or person, on a scale of *like–dislike* or *favorable–unfavorable*.

The **affective** or **liking component** summarizes a person's overall feelings toward an object, situation, or person, on a scale of like–dislike or favorable–unfavorable. When there are several alternatives to choose among, liking is expressed in terms of preference for one alternative over another. Preferences can be measured by asking which is "most preferred" or the "first choice," the "second choice," and so forth. Affective judgments also can be made about the attributes of an object, such as a ski area. Someone may like all other aspects of an area, but dislike the location because it requires too much traveling.

Intention or Action Component

The **intention** or **action component** refers to a person's expectations of future behavior toward an object. Intentions usually are limited to a distinct time period that depends on buying habits and planning horizons.

The **intention** or **action component** refers to a person's expectations of future behavior toward an object. Is he or she "very," "somewhat," or "not at all" likely to go to Aspen for a ski week next winter? Intentions usually are limited to a distinct time period that depends on buying habits and planning horizons. The great advantage of an intentions question is that it incorporates information about a respondent's ability or willingness to pay for the object, or otherwise take action. One may prefer Aspen over all other ski areas in the Rockies, but have no intention of going next year because of the cost.

◆ THE CONCEPT OF MEASUREMENT AND SCALING

Measurement can be defined as a standardized process of assigning numbers or other symbols to certain characteristics of the objects of interest, according to some prespecified rules.

Measurement can be defined as a standardized process of assigning numbers or other symbols to certain characteristics of the objects of interest, according to some prespecified rules. Measurement often deals with numbers, because mathematical and statistical analyses can be performed only on numbers, and they can be communicated throughout the world in the same form without any translation problems. For a measurement process to be a standardized process of assignment, two characteristics are necessary. First, there must be one-to-one correspondence between the symbol and the characteristic in the object that is being measured. Second, the rules for assignment must be invariant over time and the objects being measured.

Scaling is the process of creating a continuum on which objects are located according to the amount of the measured characteristic they possess. An illustration of a scale that is often used in research is the dichotomous scale for sex. The object with male (or female) characteristics is assigned the number 1 and the object with the opposite characteristics is assigned the number 0. This scale meets the requirements of the measurement process in that the assignment is one to one and it is invariate with respect to time and object. Measurement and scaling are basic tools used in the scientific method and are used in almost every marketing research situation.

◆ PROPERTIES OF MEASUREMENT SCALES

The assignment of numbers is made according to rules that should correspond to the properties of whatever is being measured. The rule may be very simple, as when a bus route is given a number to distinguish it from other routes. Here, the only property is identity, and any comparisons of numbers are meaningless. This is a **nominal scale.** At the other extreme is the **ratio scale,** which has very rigorous properties. In between the extremes are **ordinal scales** and **interval scales,** as shown in Table 9-1.

Attitude variables, such as beliefs, preferences, and intentions, are also measured using rating scales. These scales provide respondents with a set of numbered categories that represent the range of possible judgments or positions. An attitude scale involves measurement in the same sense that a thermometer measures temperature or a ruler measures distance. In each of these cases, measurement means the assignment of numbers to objects or persons to represent quantities of their attributes. For example, the attributes of a person include his or her income, social class, attitude, and so forth. Therefore, it is very important to understand the differences among the types of scales and to be able to identify them in practice, for their properties put significant restrictions on the interpretation and use of the resulting measurements.

Nominal Scale

In a nominal scale, objects are assigned to mutually exclusive, labeled categories, but there are no necessary relationships among the categories; that is, no ordering or spacing is implied. If one entity is assigned the same number as another, they are

TABLE 9-1   Types of Scales and Their Properties

Type of Measurement Scale	Types of Attitude Scales	Rules for Assigning Number	Typical Application	Statistics/ Statistical Tests
Nominal	Dichotomous "yes" or "no" scales	Objects are either identical or different	Classification (by sex, geographic area, social class)	Percentages, mode/chi-square
Ordinal or Rank Order	Comparative, rank order, itemized category, paired comparison	Objects are greater or smaller	Rankings (preference, class standing)	Percentile, median, rank-order correlation/ Friedman ANOVA
Interval	Likert, Thurstone, Stapel, Associative, Semantic-Differential	Intervals between adjacent ranks are equal	Index numbers, temperature scales, attitude measures	Mean, standard deviation, product moment correlations/t-tests, ANOVA, regression, factor analysis
Ratio	Certain scales with special instructions	There is a meaningful zero, so comparison of absolute magnitudes is possible	Sales, incomes, units produced, costs, age	Geometric and harmonic mean, coefficient of variation

In a **nominal scale**, objects are assigned to mutually exclusive, labeled categories, but there are no necessary relationships among the categories; that is, no ordering or spacing is implied.

identical with respect to a nominal variable. Otherwise, they are just different. Sex, geographic location, and marital status are nominally scaled variables. The only arithmetic operation that can be performed on such a scale is a count of each category. Thus, we can count the number of automobile dealers in the state of California or the number of buses seen on a given route in the past hour.

Ordinal Scale

An **ordinal scale** is obtained by ranking objects or arranging them in order with regard to some common variable.

An ordinal scale is obtained by ranking objects or by arranging them in order with regard to some common variable. The question is simply whether each object has more or less of this variable than some other object. The scale provides information as to how much difference there is between the objects.

Because we do not know the amount of difference between objects, the permissible arithmetic operations are limited to statistics such as the median or mode (but not the mean). For example, suppose a sample of 1,000 consumers ranked five brands of frozen mixed vegetables according to quality. The results for Birds-Eye brand were as follows:

Quality Rank	Number of Respondents Giving Ranking to Birds-Eye
Highest	150
Second	300
Third	250
Fourth	200
Lowest	100
Total	1,000

The "second" quality category is the mode; the "third" category is the median. However, it is not possible to compute a mean ranking, because the differences between ordinal scaled values are not necessarily the same. The finishing order in a horse race or class standing illustrates this type of scale. Similarly, brands of frozen vegetables can be ranked according to quality, from highest to lowest.

Interval Scale

In an **interval scale**, the numbers used to rank the objects also represent equal increments of the attribute being measured. This means that the differences can be compared.

In an interval scale, the numbers used to rank the objects also represent equal increments of the attribute being measured. This means that differences can be compared. The difference between 1 and 2 is the same as between 2 and 3, but is only half the difference between 2 and 4. The location of the zero point is not fixed, since zero does not denote the absence of the attribute. Fahrenheit and Celsius temperatures are measured with different interval scales and have different zero points. Interval scales have very desirable properties, because virtually the entire range of statistical operations can be employed to analyze the resulting number, including addition and subtraction. Consequently, it is possible to compute an arithmetic mean from interval-scale measures.

A recurring question regarding most attitude measures is whether or not they are interval scales. Usually it is doubtful that the intervals between categories are exactly equal, but they may not be so unequal as to preclude treating the whole as an interval scale. A good example is a "willingness to buy" scale with 10 categories labeled from 1 to 10. If this were an interval scale, we could say that two people with scores of 2 and 4, respectively, differed by the same degree of "willingness" as two other people with scores of 8 and 10. Further, only ratios of the differences in scale values can be meaningfully interpreted, not ratios of the absolute scale values. For example, the difference between 8 and 10 is twice the difference between 2 and 3, but 6 on the "willingness" scale does not represent three times the value of 2 in terms of the degree of willingness.

Ratio Scale

A ratio scale is a special kind of interval scale that has a meaningful zero point. With such a scale—of weight, market share, or dollars in savings accounts, for example—it is possible to say how many times greater or smaller one object is than another. This is the only type of scale that permits us to make comparisons of absolute magnitude. For example, we can say that an annual income of $80,000 is two times as large as an income of $40,000.

A **ratio scale** is a special kind of interval scale that has a meaningful zero point. With such a scale, it is possible to say how many times greater or smaller one object is than another.

There have been some contemporary efforts to adapt ratio scales to the measurement of social opinion. Some researchers have attempted to use magnitude estimation scales to overcome the loss of information that results when categories arbitrarily constrain the range of opinion. Magnitude scaling of attitudes has been calibrated through numeric estimation. The following is an example of numeric estimation of social opinion:[2]

> I would like to ask your opinion about how serious you think certain crimes are. The first situation is, "A person steals a bicycle parked on the street." This has been given a score of 10 to show its seriousness. Use this situation to judge all others. For example, if you think a situation is 20 times more serious than the bicycle theft, the number you tell me should be around 200, or if you think it is half as serious the number you tell me should be around 5, and so on.
>
> COMPARED TO THE BICYCLE THEFT AT SCORE 10, *how serious is:*
>
> *A parent beats his young child with his fists. The child requires hospitalization.*
>
> *A person plants a bomb in a public building. The bomb explodes and 20 people are killed…*

Magnitude scaling of this type has shown some interesting results, but there are problems with the technique. The researcher must be sure that the respondents have the competence to make these proportional judgments, which means that respondents must be allowed to practice before attempting the actual research questions.

◆ TYPES OF ATTITUDE RATING SCALES

There are many ways to present a respondent with a continuum of numbered categories that represent the range of possible attitude judgments. Figure 9-1 shows one of the ways the various attitudinal scales used in marketing research can be classified. They can be generally classified as single-item scales and multiple-item scales.

Single-Item Scales

As the name itself suggests, single-item scales are those that have only one item to measure a construct. Under the single-item scales, the **itemized-category scale** is the most widely used by marketing researchers. In some situations, **comparative scales, rank-order scales,** or **constant-sum scales** have advantages. Each of these major types of rating scales will be discussed in turn.

An **itemized-category scale** is a kind of single-item scale that measures the consumers' attitudes toward various categories of a variable.

Itemized-Category Scales

The following scale from the Tasty Ice-Cream Case Example (discussed in Chapter 3) is an itemized-category scale. There are four categories from which respondents

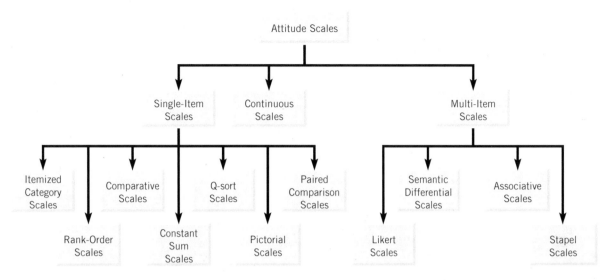

Figure 9-1 Classification of attitude scales.

can choose to indicate their overall level of satisfaction with the present shop they visit:

___ Very satisfied
___ Quite satisfied
___ Somewhat satisfied
___ Not at all satisfied

This satisfaction scale has the following characteristics:

1. All categories are labeled.
2. The respondent is forced to make a choice; there is no provision for neutral opinion or "don't know" responses.
3. There are more favorable than unfavorable categories, so the scale is unbalanced.
4. There is no explicit comparison of the respondents' present shop with other shops.

The design of the satisfaction scale requires decisions along several dimensions, as shown in Figure 9-2. Another feature of this scale is that there is no attempt to

1. Extent of category description	All categories labeled Polar categories labeled
2. Treatment of respondent uncertainty or ignorance	Forced choice (no neutral point) Neutral point Provision of "don't know" category
3. Balance of favorable and unfavorable categories	Equal Unbalanced
4. Comparison judgment required	Yes No

Figure 9-2 Types of itemized-category scales.

make the intervals between categories even approximately the same. A quite different scale would have resulted had the decision been to label only the polar or end categories, balance the favorable and unfavorable categories, and provide an obvious neutral category.

Yet another set of choices is illustrated by the following scale, which was used to ask respondents in the Tasty study about the various ice-cream shops compared to Tasty on a number of attributes, one of which was quality of the product.

Q28: compared to the other ice-cream shops that you have visited, how would you rate Tasty on the following factors? (mark your response)

	Excellent	Very Good	Average	Below Average	Don't Know
Product range	[ ]	[ ]	[ ]	[ ]	[ ]
Product quality	[ ]	[ ]	[ ]	[ ]	[ ]
Price	[ ]	[ ]	[ ]	[ ]	[ ]

The scale used for this question is unbalanced, with all categories labeled and a "don't know" category provided, and implies a comparison with other ice-cream shops. The decision to use an unbalanced scale was based on an assumption of positively skewed attitudes toward all ice-cream shops. In general, a "don't know" category should be provided whenever respondents may have insufficient experience to make a meaningful attitude judgment.

Comparative Scales

Another version of the preceding scale would label the categories "excellent," "very good," "good," "fair," and "poor," thereby eliminating the implicit comparison. The problem with a comparative scale is that the reference point is unclear and different respondents may use different reference points or standards. Is Tasty rated "excellent" or "very good" because it is superior to the existing alternatives, or because they measure up to an ideal form of ice-cream shop? In marketing studies where competitive alternatives are being evaluated, some form of explicit or implicit comparison should be built into the scale; for example:

Compared to other ice-cream shops in the area, Tasty offers ice-creams that are

Very Superior	Neither Superior nor Inferior	Very Inferior
_____	_____	_____

A recent review of research on the question of the appropriate number of response categories concluded:[3]

- Scales with two or three response alternatives generally are inadequate in that they are incapable of transmitting very much information and they tend to frustrate and stifle respondents.
- There is little to be gained from using more than nine categories.
- An odd rather than an even number of categories is preferable when the respondent legitimately can adopt a neutral position.

Rank-Order Scales

Rank-order scales require the respondent to arrange a set of objects with regard to a common criterion: advertisements in terms of interest, product features in terms of importance, or new-product concepts with regard to willingness to buy in the future. The result is an ordinal scale with the inherent limitations of weak scale properties. Ranking is widely used in surveys, however, because it corresponds to the choice process occurring in a shopping environment where a buyer makes direct comparisons among competing alternatives (brands, flavors, product variations, and so on). An example of a rank-order scale is given as follows.

Please rank from 1 to 6 the following characteristics of the cellular phone service (1 is most important and 6 is least important, no ties allowed).

Characteristics	Rank	Characteristics	Rank
Total cost of service	_____	Reliability of service	_____
Reception clarity	_____	24-hour customer service	_____
Low fixed cost of service	_____	Size of local coverage area	_____

Rank-order scales are not without problems. Ranking scales are more difficult than rating scales because they involve comparisons, and hence require more attention and mental effort. The ranking technique may force respondents to make choices they might not otherwise make, which raises the issue of whether the researcher is measuring a real relationship or one that is artificially contrived.

Due to the difficulties of rating, respondents usually cannot meaningfully rank more than five or six objects. The problem is not with the rankings of the first and last objects but with those in the undifferentiated middle. When there are several objects, one solution is to break the ranking task into two stages. With nine objects, for example, the first stage would be to rank the objects into classes: top three, middle three, and bottom three. The next stage would be to rank the three objects within each class.

When using paired comparisons, the objects to be ranked are presented two at a time, and the respondent has to choose between them according to some criterion such as overall preference or willingness to buy. Before a ranking of all objects can be obtained, all possible combinations of pairs have to be presented. This means that for n objects there are $[n(n - 1)/2]$ comparisons. This is very manageable for five objects (10 comparisons), but with more objects the task can get out of hand. With 10 brands, for example, there are 45 paired comparisons. A serious problem, however, is that the comparison of two objects at a time is seldom the way choices are made in the marketplace; thus, an item may do well in a paired-comparison situation but perform poorly in an actual market situation.[4] Despite these limitations, however, rankings still have much to recommend them if a researcher is interested in how consumers rank alternatives.

Q-Sort Scaling

When the number of objects or characteristics that are to be rated or ranked is very large, it becomes rather tedious for the respondent to rank order or do a pairwise comparison. If the respondent is forced to do a rank ordering or a pairwise comparison, a number of problems and biases creep into the study. To deal with such a situation, the **Q-sort scaling process** is used. In Q-sort scaling the respondents are asked to sort the various characteristics or objects that are being compared into various groups, such that the distribution of the number of objects or characteristics in each group follows a normal distribution. For example, let us take the case of a toy manufacturing company such as Toys " Я " Us developing a new product. After a marathon brain-storming session, the new-product team has come up with a hundred different products, each with minor variations in features, and it wants to test and find out from consumers which feature combination is the most preferred and will generate the maximum sales. The best scaling procedure that can be used in this context is Q-sort scaling. The procedure to be adopted is as follows.

In **Q-sort scaling**, the respondents are asked to sort the various characteristics or objects that are being compared into various groups, such that the distribution of the number of objects or characteristics in each group follows a normal distribution.

> Each respondent is handed 100 cards, each containing a product with various features. The respondent is then asked to sort the cards into 12 different piles in such a way that one pile contains what they feel is the most preferred among the products that have been developed, and another pile contains the least preferred of the products that have been developed. The other 10 piles will contain cards with products that vary gradually from those with higher preference to those with lower preference. The number of cards in each pile is normally distributed as shown in Figure 9-3. In this particular case, only five cards can be placed in the most and the least preferred product piles. After placing all the cards in the piles, the respondent is asked to rank-order only those products in the most-preferred pile or in the top few sets of piles.

In Q-sort scaling, a relatively large number of groups or piles should be used (10 or more). This increases the reliability or precision of the results.

Constant-Sum Scales

Constant-sum scales require respondents to allocate a fixed number of rating points (usually 100) among several objects, to reflect the relative preference for each object.[5]

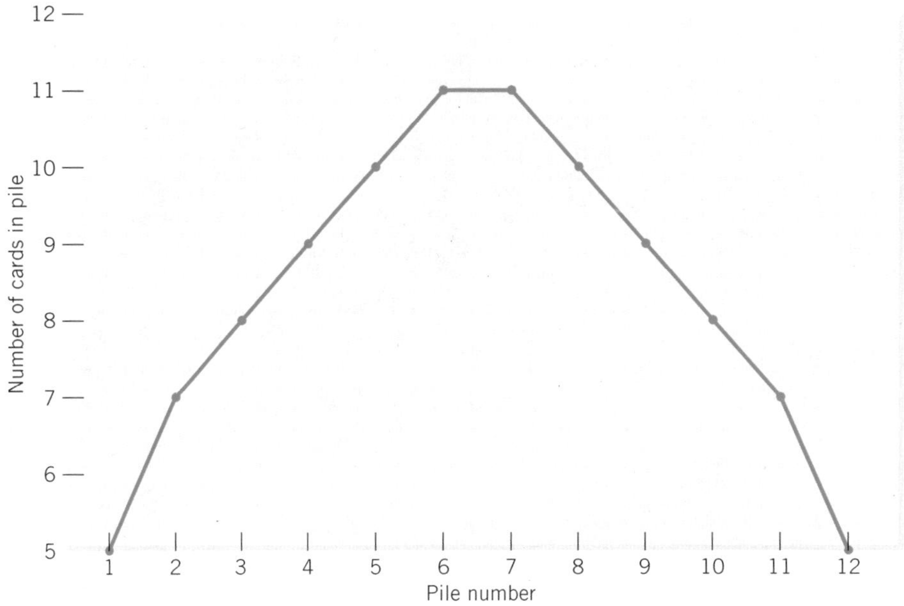

Constant-sum scales require respondents to allocate a fixed number of rating points among several objects, to reflect the relative preference for each object.

Figure 9-3 Plot of number of cards in each pile.

It is widely used to measure the relative importance of attributes, as in the following example.

Please divide 100 points among the following characteristics so the division reflects the relative importance of each characteristic to you in the selection of a health care plan.

Ability to choose a doctor	_____
Extent of coverage provided	_____
Quality of medical care	_____
Monthly cost of the plan	_____
Distance to clinic or doctor from your home	_____
Total	100

The most attractive feature of this scale is the quasi-interval nature of the resulting scale. However, just how close it comes to a true interval scale has not been fully established. The scale is limited in the number of objects or attributes it can address at one time. Respondents sometimes have difficulty allocating points accurately among more than a few categories.

Pictorial Scales

In **pictorial scales,** the various categories of the scale are depicted pictorially. The respondents are shown a concept or read an attitudinal statement and are asked to indicate their degree of agreement or interest by indicating the corresponding position on the pictorial scale. Therefore, in designing a format, it is of prime importance to design one that the respondent will comprehend and that will enable him or her to respond accurately. Commonly used pictorial scales are the **thermometer scale** and the **funny faces scale.** Pictorial scales are used mainly when the respondents are young children or other people who are illiterate.

In **pictorial scales,** the various categories of the scale are depicted pictorially. The respondents are shown a concept or read an attitudinal statement and are asked to indicate their degree of agreement or interest by indicating the corresponding position on the pictorial scale.

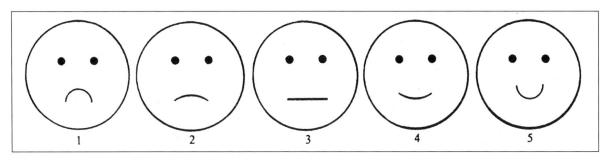

Funny faces scale.
Courtesy James P. Neelankavil.

Paired-Comparison Scales

In **paired-comparison scales,** the brands to be rated are presented two at a time, so that each brand in the category is compared once to every other brand.

The brands to be rated were presented two at a time, so each brand in the category was compared once to every other brand. In each pair the respondents were asked to divide 10 points among the brands, on the basis of how much they liked one compared to the other. A score was then totaled for each brand. Although this scale performs well on the criteria, it is cumbersome to administer. Another possible limitation is that the frame of reference is always the other brands in the set being tested. These brands may change over time.

Several features are shared by all three of the most effective scales:

- They restrict the numbers of highly positive ratings that can be given, either by forcing a choice or by comparing brands directly.
- They provide a limited number of categories that have verbal anchors. Respondents prefer words to numbers, and especially avoid negative numbers. Also, including more than seven categories may actually reduce the scale's power to discriminate.
- The stimulus to the respondent is simple and unambiguous. One of the worst-performing scales presented a picture of a thermometer with 10 categories of liking; each was labeled by a number from 0 to 100, as well as an assortment of verbal anchors. For example, 80 was labeled "like very much," while 50 was "indifferent" and 30 was "not so good."

Although these issues are useful, and should be carefully considered, the best guidance still comes from carefully tailoring the scale to the research objectives, followed by thorough pretesting for comprehension and discrimination.

Issues in Designing Single-Item Scales

Attitude-rating scales are widely used to test the effectiveness of advertising copy or compare the performance of new product concepts and segment markets. Despite years of experience with these applications, the design of the rating scale is usually an ad-hoc judgment based on the researcher's preferences and past experiences in similar situations. The various decisions that a researcher has to make regarding the form and structure of the scale while designing a scale are described briefly here:

1. *Number of scale categories.* Theoretically, the number of rating-scale categories can vary from two to infinity. A continuous rating scale has infinite categories, whereas the number of categories in a discontinuous scale depends on several factors, such as the capabilities of the scalers, the format of the interview, and the nature of the object.[6] For example, if the survey is done by telephone, the number of categories that a scale can have is very limited, because the memory of the respondent is limited.

2. *Types of poles used in the scale.* All rating scales have verbal descriptors or adjectives that serve as end points or anchors. The scale can have a single pole or two poles. An example of a two-pole scale is "sweet … not sweet," and an example of a scale with a single pole is the Stapel scale, which is discussed later. The advantage of the single-pole scale over the scale with double poles is ease of construction, as one need not look for adjectives to achieve bipolarity. The disadvantage is that we do not know what each category represents in a single-pole scale.

3. *Strength of the anchors.* By strength of the anchor we refer to the intensity of the adjective that is used to anchor the scale. A rating-scale anchor could vary from "extremely colorful" to "very colorful" to "colorful." Anchor strength has been found to shape scale-response distributions; the stronger the anchors, the less likely scalers are to use the extreme scale categories, so the resulting scale response distribution will be more peaked.

4. *Labeling of the categories.* Another decision that has to be made while developing scales is whether to label every category of the scale or to label only

the extreme categories. Labeling all categories reduces the scale's ambiguity.[7] Evidence also shows that using such terms as *very* or *somewhat* markedly influences responses to scales.[8]

5. *Balance of the scale.* A related decision is whether category labels should be balanced or unbalanced. A balanced four-category scale to measure the smell of a perfume could be

The smell of Morning Dew is…

_____ Very good   _____ Good   _____ Bad   _____ Very bad

while a corresponding unbalanced scale might be expressed as

_____ Superb   _____ Very good   _____ Good   _____ Average

Generally, a balanced scale is preferred to an unbalanced scale in order to obtain meaningful results.

There is little argument on the criteria a rating scale ideally should satisfy. The results should be reliable and valid, and there should be a sharp discrimination among the objects being rated and a sensitivity to advertising or product stimuli. These criteria are seldom employed in practice. Part of the reason is the sheer variety of rating scales. The real problem is the absence of empirical evidence on the performance of the various rating scales on these criteria. However, one study of different scales did shed some useful light on the subject, and can help us narrow down the set of acceptable scales.[9]

Respondents in the study were given various subsets of the scales, and asked to rate six brands in each of six package-goods categories such as coffee, analgesics, detergents, and toothpaste. Three criteria were used to compare the performance of the scales: (1) response distribution, which is the ability to avoid having responses pile up in the end categories; (2) discrimination among brands in the category; and (3) concurrent validity—how well the ratings related to current brand usage.

Two scales were found to be particularly attractive:

- **Brand Awareness Scale.** This question asked: "When I mention detergents, what brand do you think of? Any others? Have you heard of (interviewer mentions other brands of interest that were not reported)?

  _____ First unaided mention
  _____ Second unaided mention
  _____ Other unaided mention
  _____ Aided recall
  _____ Never heard of

This scale was consistently the best discriminator among brands and had high concurrent validity. By design, it yielded uniform distributions of responses.

- **Verbal Purchase Intent Scale.** The question asked: "What is the chance of your buying (brand) the next time you purchase this product?"

Definitely buy	Probably buy	Might buy	Probably not buy	Definitely not buy
_____	_____	_____	_____	_____

This balanced scale made efficient use of the five categories, distributing the responses quite uniformly. The labels were easy for the respondents to handle. On average it discriminated well.

Multiple-Item Scales

Attitudes toward complex objects such as health plans, automobiles, credit instruments, or transportation modes have many facets. Thus, it is often unrealistic to attempt to capture the full picture with one overall attitude-scale question. For example, the public appears to support the general idea of income tax reform but opposes the elimination of the most popular tax loopholes. While beliefs in any specific issue, aspect, or characteristic are useful indicators of the overall attitude, there may be unusual reasons that make the single belief unrepresentative of the general position.[10] To cope with this problem, a variety of methods have been developed to measure a sample of beliefs toward the attitude objects (such as agreement or disagreement with a number of statements about the attitude object) and combine the set of answers into some form of average score. The most frequently employed **multiple-item scales** are Likert, and semantic-differential scales. An adaptation of these methods, with particular relevance to marketing problems, is associative scaling.

Likert Scales

Likert scales require a respondent to indicate a degree of agreement or disagreement with a variety of statements related to the attitude or object. They are also called **summated scales**, because the scores on the individual items are summed to produce a total score for the respondent.

Likert Scales require a respondent to indicate a degree of agreement or disagreement with a variety of statements related to the attitude or object. They are also called **summated scales,** because the scores on the individual items are summed to produce a total score for the respondent. A Likert scale usually consists of two parts, the item part and the evaluative part. The item part is essentially a statement about a certain product, event, or attitude. The evaluative part is a list of response categories ranging from "strongly agree" to "strongly disagree." An important assumption of this scaling method is that each of the items (statements) measures some aspect of a single common factor; otherwise, the items cannot legitimately be summed. In other words, the resulting scale is unidimensional. The Likert scaling method, then, refers to the several steps in the procedure for cutting out the items that do not belong. The result is a series of 5 to 20 or more statements and questions, of which those given below are illustrative.

	Agree Strongly	Agree Somewhat	Neither Agree nor Disagree	Disagree Somewhat	Disagree Strongly
1. There needs to be much improvement in the health insurance available for people like me.	[ ]	[ ]	[ ]	[ ]	[ ]
2. I have a variety of very good health plans from which to choose.	[ ]	[ ]	[ ]	[ ]	[ ]
3. I haven't heard of a health insurance plan that will protect me against a disastrous illness.	[ ]	[ ]	[ ]	[ ]	[ ]

Semantic-Differential Scales

Semantic-differential scales are used widely to describe the set of beliefs that compromise a person's image of an organization or brand.

Semantic-differential scales are used widely to describe the set of beliefs that comprise a person's image of an organization or brand. The procedure is also insightful for comparing the images of competing brands, stores, or services.[11] Respondents are asked to rate each attitude object on a number of five- or seven-point rating scales, bounded at each end by polar adjectives or phrases. Some researchers prefer unipolar scales, while others use bipolar scales. In either case, the respondent chooses the end point only if that adjective is closely descriptive of that object. However, the midpoint of the scale has two different meanings, depending on the type of scale. With unipolar scales, the midpoint is simply a step on the scale from "sweet" to "not sweet," whereas on a bipolar scale it is a neutral point.

There may be as many as 15 to 25 semantic-differential scales for each attitude object. The scales in Figure 9-4 were used in a beer-brand image study in a U.S. regional market. (Only 6 of a total of 10 scales are shown.) Each of 10 brands were evaluated separetely on the same set of 10 scales, for comparison. However, only 3 brands are shown here. To show what can be done, Figure 9-4 compares the ratings for two well-known national brands of beer and a regional brand, on six of the 10 scales. Even with three brands and only six of 10 attributes, the interpretation of the profiles is not easy. With more brands and attributes, the overall comparisons of brands are even harder to grasp. A second difficulty is that not all attributes are independent; that is, several of the attributes may be measuring approximately the same dimension. For example, to most beer drinkers there is not likely to be much difference in the meaning of the "tangy-smooth" and "bitter-not bitter" scales. This is borne out by the similarity of the scores of the three brands on these two scales in Figure 9-4.

Profile Analysis

Profile analysis is an application of the semantic-differential scale. Visual comparisons of the images of different objects can be aided by plotting the mean ratings for each object on each scale.

Profile analysis is an application of the semantic-differential scale. Visual comparisons of the images of different objects can be aided by plotting the mean ratings for each object on each scale. Fortunately, there are several procedures using multidimensional scaling techniques that can deal effectively with these problems and yield easily interpreted spatial maps that describe the overall image of a brand.

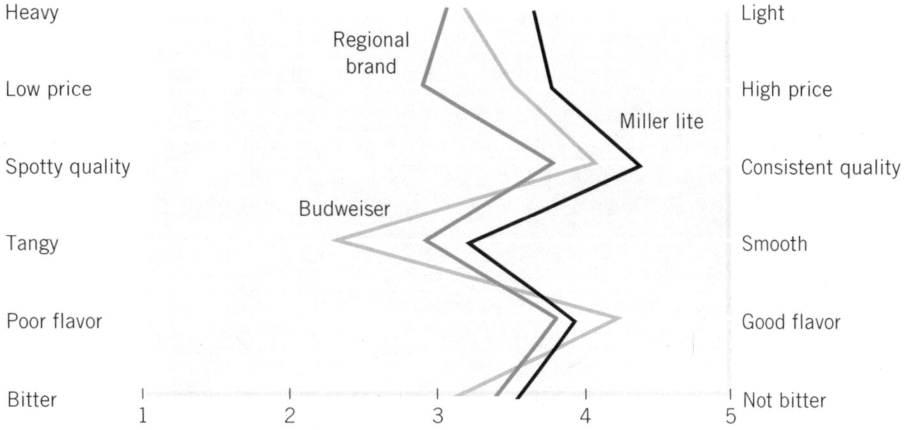

Figure 9-4 Profile analysis of three beer brands.

This set of scales is characteristic of most marketing applications of the semantic differential:

1. The pairs of objects or phrases are selected carefully to be meaningful in the market being studied and often correspond to product or service attributes.[12] Exploratory research generally is required to ensure that important attributes are represented and described in words that are familiar to respondents.[13]

2. The negative or unfavorable pole is sometimes on the right side and sometimes on the left. This rotation is necessary to avoid the *halo effect,* in which the location of previous judgments on the scale affects subsequent judgments because of respondent carelessness.

3. The category increments are treated as interval scales, so group mean values can be computed for each object on each scale. As with Likert scaling, this assumption is controversial, but is adopted because it permits more powerful methods of analysis to be used.

The semantic differential also may be analyzed as a summated rating scale. Each of the seven scale categories is assigned a value from −3 to 3 or 1 to 7, and the scores across all adjective pairs are summed for each respondent. Individuals then can be compared on the basis of their total scores. Summation is not usually advisable, however, for a good deal of specific information is lost in the aggregate score, which may be distorted if there are several scales that measure roughly the same thing.

Stapel Scales

Stapel scales are simplified versions of semantic-differential scales, which use only one pole rather than two. Respondents are asked to indicate the object by selecting a numerical response category. The higher the positive score, the better the adjective describes the object. The main virtue of this scale is that it is easy to administer and construct, because there is no need to provide adjectives or phrases to assure bipolarity.[14]

Associative Scaling

Although the semantic-differential and Stapel scales are used widely for image studies, they have substantial limitations in markets where the average respondent is likely to be knowledgeable only about a small subset among a large number of choice alternatives. They also can be cumbersome and time consuming to administer when there are a number of attributes and alternatives to consider. An alternative approach, **associative scaling,** designed to overcome these limitations, asks the respondent simply to associate one alternative with each question. The questions in Figure 9-5 illustrate how this approach is employed in a telephone survey of retail-store images.

The technique is argued to be particularly appropriate to choice situations that involve a sequential decision process. For example, supermarkets have to be within a reasonable distance to be considered, and within that set the choice is made on the basis of which chain is best in satisfying customers' needs. Of course, the technique does not answer the questions of how consumers make trade-offs when there are several important dimensions and no alternative is superior across the board. Thus, the benefits of low cost and ease of telephone administration are purchased at a possible cost of reduced validity in representing the market structure. For this reason the associative technique is best suited to market tracking, where the emphasis is on understanding shifts in relative competitive positions.

Stapel scales are simplified versions of semantic-differential scales, which use only one pole rather than two. Respondents are asked to indicate the object by selecting a numerical response category. The higher the positive scale, the better the adjective describes the object.

Associative scaling is appropriate to choice situations that involve a sequential decision process. In associative scaling the respondent is asked to associate one alternative with each question.

	Eaton's Store or Catalog	The Bay	Simpsons	Any Other	None DK	More Than One Answer
Which store:						
1. Has the lowest overall prices?	1	2	3	0	B	X
2. Has the highest overall prices?	1	2	3	0	B	X
3. Is the easiest one to get to from your home?	1	2	3	0	B	X
4. Has the most knowledgeable, helpful sales clerks?	1	2	3	0	B	X

Figure 9-5   Retail store image questions (telephone questionnaire). DK = Don't know.

Continuous-Rating Scales

In **continuous-rating scales,** the respondents rate the objects by placing a mark at the appropriate position on a line that runs from one extreme of the criterion variable to the other.[15] They are also referred to as *graphical rating scales.* The main advantage of the continuous-rating scale is that it is easy to construct. However, scoring is cumbersome and unreliable, and these scales do not provide much new information. Hence, continuous-rating scales are not widely used in marketing research.

◆ GENERAL GUIDELINES FOR DEVELOPING A MULTIPLE-ITEM SCALE

Multiple-item scales are often used in social sciences research to measure abstract constructs. The characteristic to be measured is generally referred to as the construct. Most of the well-known scales that measure constructs, such as IQ, consumer confidence, and so on, are multiple-item scales. Developing a multiple-item scale is a complex procedure and requires quite a lot of technical expertise. Figure 9-6 presents the various steps in the development of a multiple-item scale.

◆ INTERPRETING ATTITUDE SCALES

Conclusions obtained from attitude-scale measurements are strictly limited by the properties of the scale that is used. Failure to recognize these limits can lead to serious misinterpretation. The problem was created by assuming a ratio scale where there was really only an interval scale.

◆ CHOOSING AN ATTITUDINAL SCALE

The choice of an appropriate scale is complicated by two problems:

1. There are many different techniques, each with its own strengths and weaknesses.
2. Virtually any technique can be adapted to the measurement of any one of the attitude components.

Although these problems are significant impediments to broad generalizations it is also true that all techniques are not equally suitable for all purposes. Table 9-2 summarizes some useful rules of thumb as to which scale types are likely to be best

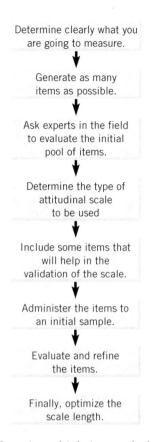

Figure 9-6 Steps in multiple-item scale development.

suited to the various components of attitudes. What is most evident from this table is the versatility of the itemized-category scale, which itself has many variations. Ultimately, the researcher's choice will be shaped by (1) the specific information that is required to satisfy the research objectives, (2) the adaptability of the scale to the data

TABLE 9-2   Appropriate Applications of Various Attitude Scales

	Types of Scales				
Attitude Component	Itemized Category	Rank Order	Constant Sum	Likert	Semantic Differential
Knowledge					
awareness	a				
attribute beliefs	a	b	b	b	a
attribute importance	a	b	a	b	
Affect or liking					
overall preferences	a	b	a	b	b
specific attributes	a	b	b	b	a
Action					
intentions	a	b	a	b	

a—Very appropriate.

b—Sometimes appropriate.

collection method and budget constraints, and (3) the compatibility of the scale with the structure of the respondent's attitude.

◆ ACCURACY OF ATTITUDE MEASUREMENTS

Attitude measures, in common with all measures used in marketing, must be both accurate and useful. In this section, the focus is on those aspects of attitude measures that contribute to accuracy: validity, reliability, and sensitivity.

Validity

An attitude measure has validity if it measures what it is supposed to measure. If this is the case, then differences in attitude scores will reflect differences among the objects or individuals on the characteristic being measured. This is a very troublesome question. For example, how is a researcher to know whether measured differences in the attitudes of managers, consumer activists, and consumers toward marketing practices, regulation, and the contribution of the consumer movement are true differences? There have been three basic approaches to this question of validity assessment.

Face, or **consensus, validity** is invoked when the argument is made that the measurement so self-evidently reflects or represents the various aspects of the phenomenon that there can be little quarrel with it. For instance, buyers' recognition of advertisements is usually accepted at face value as an indication of past ad exposure.

Criterion validity is more defensible, for it is based on empirical evidence that the attitude measure correlates with other "criterion" variables. If the two variables are measured at the same time, **concurrent validity** is established. Better yet, if the attitude measure can predict some future event, then **predictive validity** has been established. A measure of brand preference or buying intentions is valid if it can be shown through sales records to predict future sales. This is the most important type of validity for decision-making purposes, for the very nature of decisions requires predictions of uncertain future events.

Although face, concurrent, and predictive validity provide necessary evidence of overall validity, often they are not sufficient. The characteristic of these three approaches is that they provide evidence on **convergent validity.** That is, an attitude measure can adequately represent a characteristic or variable if it correlates or "converges" with other supposed measures of that variable. Unfortunately, an attitude measure may converge with measures of other variables in addition to the one of interest. Thus, it is also necessary to establish **discriminant validity** through low correlations between the measure of interest and other measures that are supposedly not measuring the same variable or concept. Advertising recognition measures often fail this second test. While they correlate or converge with past ad exposure, which is what we want, they are also correlated with number of magazines read and product interest.

Construct validity can be considered only after discriminant and convergent validity have been established.[16] It is achieved when a logical argument can be advanced to defend a particular measure. The argument aims first to define the concept or construct explicitly and then to show that the measurement, or operational definition, logically connects the empirical phenomenon to the concept. The extreme difficulty of this kind of validation lies in the unobservable nature of many of the constructs (such as social class, personality, or attitudes) used to explain marketing behavior.

Reliability

So far we have been talking about systematic errors between an observed score (X_o) and a true score (X_t), which will determine whether a measure is valid. However, the total error of a measurement consists of this systematic error component (X_s) and a random error component (X_r). Random error is manifested by lack of consistency (unreliability) in repeated or equivalent measures of the same object or person. As a result, any measurement can be expressed as a function of several components:

$$X_o = X_t + X_s + X_r$$

Observed score = true score + systematic error + random error

To interpret this equation, remember that a valid measure is one that reflects the true score. In this situation, $X_o = X_t$ and both X_s and X_r are zero. Thus, if we know the measure is valid, it has to be reliable. The converse is not necessarily true. A measure may be highly reliable, $X_r = 0$, and still have a substantial systematic error that distorts the validity. If the measure is not reliable, then it cannot be valid since at a minimum we are left with $X_o = X_t + X_r$. In brief, reliability is a necessary but not a sufficient condition for validity.

Although **reliability** is less important, it is easier to measure, and so receives relatively more emphasis. The basic methods for establishing reliability can be classified according to whether they measure stability of results over time or internal consistency of items in an attitude scale.[17]

Stability over time is assessed by repeating the measurement with the same instrument and the same respondents at two points in time and correlating the results. To the extent that random fluctuations result in different scores for the two administrations, this correlation and hence the reliability will be lowered. The problems of this *test–retest* method are similar to those encountered during any pretest–posttest measurement of attitudes. The first administration may sensitize the respondent to the subject and lead to attitude change. The likelihood of a true change in attitude (versus a random fluctuation) is increased further if the interval between the test and the retest is too long. For most topics, this would be more than two weeks. If the interval is too short, however, there may be a carryover from the test to the retest: attempts to remember the responses in the first test, boredom or annoyance at the imposition, and so forth. Because of these problems, a very short interval will bias the reliability estimate upward, whereas longer periods will have the opposite effect.

The equivalence approach to assessing reliability is appropriate for attitude scales composed of multiple items that presumably measure the same underlying unidimensional attitude. The *split-half* method assumes that these items can be divided into two equivalent subsets that then can be compared. A number of methods have been devised to divide the items randomly into two halves and compute a measure of similarity of the total scores of the two halves across the sample. An average split-half measure of similarity—coefficient alpha—can be obtained from a procedure that has the effect of comparing every item to every other item.

Sensitivity

The third characteristic of a good attitude measure is **sensitivity,** or the ability to discriminate among meaningful differences in attitudes. Sensitivity is achieved by increasing the number of scale categories; however, the more categories there are, the lower the reliability will be. This is because very coarse response categories, such as yes or no, in response to an attitude question can absorb a great deal of response variability before a change would be noted using the test–retest method. Conversely, the use of a large number of response categories when there are only a few distinct attitude positions would be subject to a considerable, but unwarranted, amount of random fluctuation.

Generalizability

Generalizability refers to the ease of scale administration and interpretation in different research settings and situations.[18] Thus, the generalizability of a multiple-item scale is determined by whether it can be applied in a wide variety of data collection modes, whether it can be used to obtain data from a wide variety of individuals, and under what conditions it can be interpreted. As in the case of reliability and validity, generalizability is not an absolute but rather, is a matter of degree.

Relevancy

Relevancy of a scale refers to how meaningful it is to apply the scale to measure a construct. Mathematically, it is represented as the product of reliability and validity:

$$\text{Relevance} = \text{reliability} \times \text{validity}$$

If reliability and validity are evaluated by means of correlation coefficients, the implications are:

- The relevance of a scale can vary from 0 (no relevance) to 1 (complete relevance).
- If either reliability or validity is low, the scale will possess little relevance.
- Both reliability and validity are necessary for scale relevance.

◆ SCALES IN CROSS-NATIONAL RESEARCH

The previous sections of this chapter discussed the various types of scales that are typically used in domestic marketing research. The question remains whether the same scales can be administered to respondents all over the world.[19] Low educational or literacy levels in some countries must be considered when the decision is made to administer the same scale. Literacy and educational levels influence the response formats of the scales employed. Moreover, the culture in a country can also affect the responses and may induce some cultural biases.

Research has been conducted to find out whether there is a pan-cultural scale. The semantic-differential scale seems to come closest to being a truly pan-cultural scale. It consistently gives similar results in terms of concepts or dimensions that are used to evaluate stimuli, and also accounts for a major portion of the variation in response when it is administered in different countries. An alternative approach that has been attempted is to apply techniques that use a base referent, a self-defined cultural norm. This type of approach is likely to be particularly useful in evaluating attitudinal positions where evidence exists to suggest that these are defined relative to the dominant cultural norm.

Another issue that is important in international research is whether response formats, particularly their calibration, need to be adapted for specific countries and cultures. For example, in France a 20-point scale is commonly used to rate performance in primary and secondary schools. Consequently, it has been suggested that 20-point scales should also be used in marketing research. In general, verbal scales are more effective among less educated respondents, but a more appropriate procedure for illiterate respondents would be scales with pictorial stimuli. For example, in the case of lifestyle, pictures of different lifestyle segments may be shown to the respondents, and they may be asked to indicate how similar they perceive themselves to be to the one in the picture. Some other devices, such as the funny faces and the thermometer scales, are also used among less educated respondents.

END OF CHAPTER MATERIAL

SUMMARY

This chapter has dealt with attitudes, defined as the mental orientation of individuals that structures the way they respond to their environment. This concept is useful to marketers only to the extent that the various components of attitudes can be measured "accurately."

Measurement was defined here as the assignment of numbers to objects or persons to represent quantities of their attributes. The problem is to establish how to assign numbers. This leads to an examination of the properties of different scales of measurement—nominal, ordinal, interval, ratio—and establishes a useful basis for evaluating various attitude scales, including itemized-category, rank-order, semantic-differential, Thurstone, and Likert scales. Each of these methods involves a direct self-report, which means that they should be supplemented with the behavioral and indirect measures discussed in Chapter 7.

To this point we have not been explicit as to what is meant by an "accurate" measurement of any kind. Intuitively, it means freedom from error. More formally, an accurate measure is both valid and reliable.

Video Segment:

Branding

The emphasis of this clip is to reflect on the role of brands and the rise and fall of its pricing strategy. The importance is on measuring the attitudes of consumers toward brands and private labels. As John Steel, senior vice president of Colgate-Palmolive explains, consumers pay more for the extra value that they perceive exists with higher pricing for branded goods. Compared to private labels, which comprise 19 percent of supermarket sales, the remaining 89 percent of the sales attributed to brands would have to try boosting profit levels without inflating prices.

KEY TERMS

attitudes
cognitive/knowledge component
aided recall awareness
affective/liking component

intention/action component
measurement
scaling
nominal scale

ratio scale
ordinal scale
interval scale
itemized-category scales
comparative scales
rank-order scales
Q-sort scaling
constant-sum scales
pictorial scales
thermometer scale
funny faces scale
paired-comparison scales
brand awareness scale
verbal purchase intent scale
Likert scales
summated scales
semantic-differential scales

profile analysis
Stapel scales
associative scaling
continous-rating scales
multiple-item scales
face/consensus validity
criterion validity
concurrent validity
predictive validity
convergent validity
discriminant validity
construct validity
reliability
sensitivity
generalizability
relevancy

MARKETING RESEARCH TOOLBOX
REVIEW POINTS

1. Attitudes are mental states used by individuals to structure the way they perceive their environment and guide the way they respond to it.

2. The three related components that form an attitude are: a cognitive or knowledge component, a liking or affective component, and an intentions or actions component.

3. The cognitive or knowledge component represents a person's information about an object. This information includes awareness of the existence of the object, beliefs about the characteristics or attributes of the object, and judgments about the relative importance of each of the attributes.

4. The affective or liking component summarizes a person's overall feelings toward an object, situation, or person, on a scale of *like–dislike* or *favorable–unfavorable.*

5. The intention or action component refers to a person's expectations of future behavior toward an object. Intentions usually are limited to a distinct time period that depends on buying habits and planning horizons.

6. Measurement can be defined as a standardized process of assigning numbers or other symbols to certain characteristics of the objects of interest, according to some prespecified rules. There must be a one-to-one correspondence between the symbol and the characteristic in the object that is being measured, and the rules for assignment must be invariant over time and the objects being measured.

7. Scaling is the process of creating a continuum on which objects are located according to the amount of the measured characteristic they possess.

8. In a nominal scale, objects are assigned to mutually exclusive, labeled categories, but there are no necessary relationships among the categories; that is, no ordering or spacing is implied.

9. An ordinal scale is obtained by ranking objects or arranging them in order with regard to some common variable. The question is simply whether each object has more or less of this variable than some other object. The scale provides information as to how much difference there is between the objects.

10. In an interval scale, the numbers used to rank the objects also represent equal increments of the attribute being measured. This means that the differences can be compared.

11. A ratio scale is a special kind of interval scale that has a meaningful zero point. With such a scale—of weight, market share, or dollars in savings accounts, for example—it is possible to say how many times greater or smaller one object is than another. This is the only type of scale that permits us to make comparisons of absolute magnitude.

12. An itemized-category scale is a kind of single-item scale that measures the consumers' attitudes toward various categories of a variable. Itemized category scales are differentiated based on the extent of category description, treatment of respondent uncertainty or ignorance, balance of favorable and unfavorable categories, and requirement of comparative judgment.

13. A version of the itemized category scaling is comparative scaling. In comparative scaling the categories are labeled as "excellent," "very good," "good," "fair," and "poor," thereby eliminating the implicit comparison. The problem with a comparative scale is that the reference point is unclear and different respondents may use use different reference points or standards.

14. Rank-order scales require the respondent to arrange a set of objects with regard to a common criterion. The result is an ordinal scale with the inherent limitations of weak scale properties. Ranking scales are more difficult than rating scales because they involve comparisons, and hence require more attention and mental effort.

15. In Q-sort scaling, the respondents are asked to sort the various characteristics or objects that are being compared into various groups, such that the distribution of the number of objects or characteristics in each group follows a normal distribution.

16. Constant-sum scales require respondents to allocate a fixed number of rating points among several objects, to reflect the relative preference for each object. It is widely used to measure the relative importance of attributes. The scale is limited in the number of objects or attributes it can address at one time.

17. In pictorial scales the various categories of the scale are depicted pictorially. The respondents are shown a concept or read an attitudinal statement and are asked to indicate their degree of agreement or interest by indicating the corresponding position on the pictorial scale.

18. In paired-comparison scales the brands to be rated are presented two at a time, so that each brand in the category is compared once to every other brand. In each pair the respondents are asked to divide 10 points among the brands, on the basis of how much they like one compared to the other. A score is then totaled for each brand.

19. Issues in designing single-item scales include deciding on the number of scale categories, the types of poles to be used in the scale, the intensity of the adjective used to anchor the scale, the labeling of the categories, and the balance of the scale.

20. Multiple-item scales are used to overcome the problem of measuring attitudes toward complex objects that have many facets. Multiple-item scales measure a sample of beliefs toward the attitude objects, and the answers are then combined into some form of average score.

21. Likert scales require a respondent to indicate a degree of agreement or disagreement with a variety of statements related to the attitude or object. They are also called *summated scales*, because the scores on the individual items are summed to produce a total score for the respondent.

22. Semantic-differential scales are used widely to describe the set of beliefs that compromise a person's image of an organization for the brand. The procedure is also an insightful procedure for comparing the images of competing brands, stores, or services.

23. Profile analysis is an application of the semantic-differential scale. Visual comparisons of the images of different objects can be aided by plotting the mean ratings for each object on each scale.

24. Stapel scales are simplified versions of semantic-differential scales. They use only one pole rather than two. Respondents are asked to indicate the object by selecting a numerical response category. The higher the positive score, the better the adjective describes the object.

25. Associative scaling is appropriate to choice situations that involve a sequential decision process. In associative scaling the respondent is asked to associate one alternative with each question.

26. In continuous-rating scales, the respondents rate the objects by placing a mark at the appropriate position on a line that runs from one extreme of the criterion variable to the other.

27. The choice of an attitude scale is complicated by two problems: each technique has its own strengths and weaknesses and virtually any technique can be adapted to the measurement of any one of the attitude components.

28. An attitude measure has validity if it measures what it is supposed to measure. Face or consensus validity is invoked when the argument is made that the measurement self-evidently reflects or represents the various aspects of the phenomenon.

29. Criterion validity is more defensible, for it is based on empirical evidence that the attitude measure correlates with other "criterion" variables. If the two variables are measured at the same time, concurrent validity is established. Better yet, if the attitude measure can predict some future event, then predictive validity has been established.

30. Discriminant validity is established through low correlations between the measure of interest and other measures that are supposedly not measuring the same variable or concept. Convergent validity is achieved when a logical argument can be advanced to defend a particular measure.

31. Sensitivity is the ability to discriminate among meaningful differences in attitudes. Sensitivity is achieved by increasing the number of scale categories; however, the more categories there are, the lower the reliability will be.

32. Generalizability refers to the ease of scale administration and interpretation in different research settings and situations.

33. Relevancy of a scale refers to how meaningful it is to apply the scale to measure a construct. Mathematically it is represented as the product of reliability and validity.

QUESTIONS AND PROBLEMS

1. Advertising is an expenditure that ultimately must be justified in terms of its effect on sales and profits, yet most evaluations of advertising are in terms of the effects on attitudes. How do you account for this apparent mismatch?

2. What is measurement? What are the scales of measurement, and what information is provided by each?

3. For each of the following, identify the type of scale and justify your answer.
   a. During which season of the year were you born?

   _____ Winter   _____ Spring   _____ Summer   _____ Fall

   b. How satisfied are you with the Ford Taurus that you bought?

   _____ Very satisfied   _____ Satisfied   _____ Neither satisfied nor dissatisfied
   _____ Dissatisfied   _____ Very dissatisfied

   c. On average, how many cigarettes do you smoke in a day?

   _____ Over 1 pack   _____ 1/2 pack to 1 pack   _____ Less than 1/2 pack

   d. Rank the following according to your preference:

   _____ Tide   _____ Surf   _____ Cheer   _____ Wisk   _____ Bold

4. One trend that is expected to have a large impact on marketing is the aging of the Baby Boom population. This aging will likely result in changing consumer attitudes in a variety of areas. What types of attitude changes would be of most interest or concern to a product manager for a branded food product?

5. How would you select a set of phrases or adjectives for use in a semantic-differential scale to evaluate the image of banks and other consumer financial institutions? Would the procedure differ if you were going to use a Likert scale?

6. Develop a battery of attitude scales to predict whether or not people who currently smoke will try to quit smoking within the next year.

7. Under what circumstances can attitude measures be expected to be good predictors of subsequent behavior? Is there any value to measuring attitudes in situations where attitudes are likely to be poor predictors?

8. Explain the concepts of reliability and validity in your own words. What is the relationship between them?

9. Develop a multiple-item scale to measure students' attitudes toward the current system of grading. How would you assess the reliability and validity of this scale?

10. In March 1977 (during an "energy crisis") the U.S. Federal Energy Administration (FEA) conducted a personal interview survey of a sample of homes where there was a heating load (that is, the outside temperature was below 65°F). The average indoor temperature of these homes, as measured by a calibrated thermometer, was 70°F, plus or minus 2°F, during the day and 69°F, plus or minus 2°F, at night. This represented little or no change from the previous two years; yet, during an independent telephone survey, the FEA found that people said they were keeping their homes at 66°F during the day and 64°F at night.
    a. What are some of the possible hypotheses for this difference between stated and actual temperatures?
    b. What questions would you ask during a telephone survey to clarify the stated house temperature and learn about people's attitudes toward reducing the house temperature?

11. In February 1975, the Gallup poll asked, "Do you approve or disapprove of the way Ford is handling his job as president?" and found that 55 percent approved and 28 percent disapproved. A Harris poll at the same time asked, "How do you rate the job President Ford is doing as president—excellent, pretty good, only fair, or poor?" Forty-six percent gave "positive" responses (excellent or pretty good), and 52 percent were negative (only fair or poor). How do you explain the differences? What are the implications of your explanation for public opinion polls as guides to political leaders?

12. It has been said that for decisional research purposes, the investigator is interested in predictive validity, to the exclusion of reliability or any other kind of validity. Do you agree? Explain.

13. Carter Toys, the U.S.-based manufacturer of the popular PollyDolly, feels that a strong sales potential exists for the doll in foreign markets. The management has identified the selection of suitable foreign country markets as being its first priority. Worldwide Research Corp. has been employed to conduct a survey of the three countries that are currently under consideration: the United Kingdom, Japan, and Kenya.
    a. Can the same questionnaire be used to survey all three countries? Give reasons for your answer.
    b. What factors must be considered in selecting a suitable scale to be used in each country?
    c. Recommend the most suitable scale for use in each country.
    d. Do you think that a semantic scale would have a different interpretation in different countries? How would you go about this? Provide suggestions as to how to standardize your operations across the three countries such that the responses are elicited to similar questions.

14. Ben Gatsby is a jewelry craftsman who specializes in high-quality religious artifacts. Recently, he has received a growing number of requests from customers for nonreligious artifacts and is considering expanding his product line to meet this new demand. Mr. Gatsby has decided to contact a local marketing research company to solicit help in formulating a marketing strategy for the new product development. They inform him that the first task is to establish whether an unmet demand exists for the nonreligious items. They suggest that in order to evaluate consumers' jewelry purchase behavior, an attitudinal study should be undertaken. Mr. Gatsby does not understand why attitudes have to be measured when he is interested only in the consumers' behavior. Imagine you are the marketing research consultant and explain to Mr. Gatsby the rationale behind this research method.

15. How are attitude rating scales most commonly applied in marketing research? What decisions must a researcher make in designing a single-item scale for these purposes?

ENDNOTES

1. Steve E. Ballou, "Effective Research Requires a Good (Measurement of) Attitude," *Marketing News* (September 15 1997), p. 15.

2. M. Lodge, *Magnitude Scaling: Quantitative Measurement of Opinions* (Beverly Hills, CA: Sage, 1981).

3. Eli P. Cox III., "The Optimal Number of Response Alternatives for a Scale: A Review," *Journal of Marketing Research*, 17 (November 1980), pp. 407–22.

4. B. Blankership, "Let's Bury Paired Comparisons," *Journal of Advertising Research*, 6 (March 1966), pp. 13–17.

5. J. P. Guilford, *Psychometric Methods* (New York: McGraw-Hill, 1954).

6. M. M. Givon and Z. Shapira, "Response to Rating Scales: A Theoretical Model and Its Application to the Number of Categories Problem," *Journal of Marketing Research* (November 1984), pp. 410–19; Eli P. Cox, III., "The Optimal Number of Response Alternatives for a Scale: A Review," *Journal of Marketing Research*, 17 (November 1980), pp. 407–22.

7. H. H. Friedman and J. R. Leefer, "Label versus Position in Rating Scales," *Journal of the Academy of Marketing Science* (Spring 1981), pp. 88–92; R. I. Haley and P. B. Case, "Testing Thirteen Attitude Scales for Agreement and Brand Discrimination," *Journal of Marketing* (Fall 1979), pp. 20–32.

8. See, for instance, Norman Bradburn and Carrie Miles, "Vague Quantifiers," *Public Opinion Quarterly* (Spring 1979), pp. 92–101.

9. Russell I. Haley and Peter B. Case, "Testing Thirteen Attitude Scales for Agreement and Brand Discrimination," *Journal of Marketing*, 43 (Fall 1979), pp. 20–32.

10. C. A. Moser and G. Kalton, *Survey Method in Social Investigation*, 2nd ed. (London: Heinemann, 1971).

11. Naresh K. Malhotra, "A Scale to Measure Self-Concepts, Person Concepts and Product Concepts," *Journal of Marketing Research*, 18 (November 1981), pp. 456–64.

12. The scale was developed originally by Osgood et al. as a method for measuring the meaning of an object to an individual. They explored a wide variety of adjective pairs that were sufficiently general to be applicable to diverse concepts and objects. From their results they identified three dominant dimensions along which judgments are made, and labeled them the evaluative, potency, and activity dimensions.

13. Several methods for eliciting attribute descriptors are described by John Dickson and Gerald Albaum, "A Method for Developing Tailor-Made Semantic Differentials for Specific Marketing Content Areas," *Journal of Marketing Research*, 14 (February 1977), pp. 87–91.

14. Dennis Menezes and Nobert F. Elbert, "Alternative Semantic Scaling Formats for Measuring Store Image: An Evaluation," *Journal of Marketing Research*, 16 (February 1979), pp. 80–87.

15. C. L. Narayana, "Graphic Positioning Scale: An Economical Instrument for Surveys," *Journal of Marketing Research*, 14 (February 1977), pp. 118–22; S. I. Lampert, "The Attitude Pollimeter: A New Attitude Scaling Device," *Journal of Marketing Research* (November 1979), pp. 578–82.

16. F. M. Andrews, "Construct Validity and Error Components of Survey Measures," *Public Opinion Quarterly* (Summer 1984), p. 432.

17. J. Paul Peter, "Reliability: A Review of Psychometric Basis and Recent Marketing Practices," *Journal of Marketing Research*, 16 (February 1979), pp. 6–17.

18. For a discussion of generalizability theory and its applications in marketing research, see Joseph O. Rentz, "Generalizability Theory: A Comprehensive Method for Assessing and Improving the Dependability of Marketing Measures," *Journal of Marketing Research*, 24 (February 1987), pp. 19–28.

19. Most international research studies conducted use different kinds of scales in their research. A few recent examples are Daniel C. Fieldman and David C. Thomas, "Career Management Issues Facing Expatriates," *Journal of Business Studies* (Second Quarter 1992); Earl Naumann, "Organizational Predictors of Expatriate Job Satisfaction," *Journal of Business Studies* (First Quarter 1993), pp. 61–81.

CASES

For detailed descriptions of the below cases please visit www.wiley.com/college/kumar.

Case 9-1: Wine Horizons
Case 9-2: National Kitchens

Designing the Questionnaire

Learning Objectives

- Introduce the concept of questionnaire design.
- Become familiar with the process of questionnaire design.
- Learn to recognize the characteristics of a good questionnaire.
- Learn how to deal with sensitive questions.
- Discuss the issues of questionnaire design in an international context.

Questionnaire construction is properly regarded as a very imperfect art. There are no established procedures that will lead consistently to a "good" questionnaire. One consequence is that the range of potential error contributed by ambiguous questions may be as much as 20 or 30 percentage points.[1] Fortunately, such extreme errors can be reduced sharply by common sense and insights from the experience of other researchers. A major objective of this chapter is to present systematically the "rules of thumb" that have been acquired with experience.

A good questionnaire accomplishes the research's objectives. Surveys must be custom-built to the specification of given research purposes, and they are much more than a collection of unambiguous questions. A number of constraints are imposed on the development of an appropriate questionnaire. For example, the number, form, and ordering of the specific questions are partly determined by the data collection method. The respondent's willingness and ability to answer, discussed in Chapter 8, also influences the final questionnaire format. The wording and sequence of questions can facilitate recall and motivate more accurate responses.

Although each questionnaire must be designed with the specific research objectives in mind, there is a sequence of logical steps that every researcher must follow to develop a good questionnaire:

1. Plan what to measure.
2. Formulate questions to obtain the needed information.
3. Decide on the order and wording of questions and on the layout of the questionnaire.
4. Using a small sample, test the questionnaire for omissions and ambiguity.
5. Correct the problems (and pretest again, if necessary).

We will use this sequence to organize the remainder of this chapter. Figure 10-1 gives a flowchart for this process.

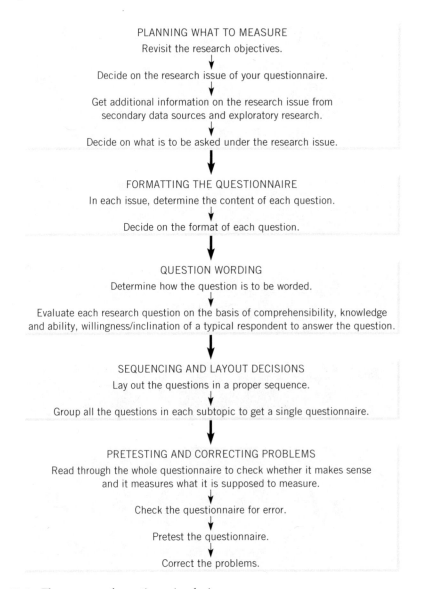

Figure 10-1 The process of questionnaire design.

◆ PLANNING WHAT TO MEASURE

The most difficult step is specifying exactly what information is to be collected from each respondent. Poor judgment and lack of thought at this stage may mean that the results are not relevant to the research purpose or that they are incomplete. Both problems are expensive and may seriously diminish the value of the study.

To combat the lack-of-relevance problem, it is necessary to ask constantly, "How will this information be used?" and ultimately to anticipate the specific analyses that will be made. It is also important to have a clear idea of the target population. Questions that are appropriate for college students may not be appropriate for homemakers. Barrett noted that ratings may differ markedly, depending on whether respondents are primarily buyers or primarily users of the product studied. And it's important to know whether you are talking to the user (who has direct experience with product performance) or the buyer (who may or may not have direct experience). It makes a difference, and the choice depends on the underlying purposes of research.[2] Understanding is related to respondent socioeconomic characteristics.[3]

When a questionnaire is sent into the field and it is incomplete in important aspects, the error is irreversible. To avoid this awful situation, careful thought is required; this is facilitated by

1. Clear research objectives, which describe as fully as possible the kind of information the decision maker needs, the hypotheses, and the scope of the research

2. Exploratory research, which will suggest further relevant variables, and help the researcher absorb the vocabulary and point of view of the typical respondent

3. Experience with similar studies

4. Pretesting of preliminary versions of the questionnaire

◆ TRANSLATING RESEARCH OBJECTIVES INTO INFORMATION REQUIREMENTS

At the end of Chapter 4 we saw how the research objectives for the Tasty Ice-Cream study were established. These objectives are summarized in Table 10-1. Before individual questionnaire items can be written, these objectives have to be translated into specific information requirements. Here is where the hypotheses play an especially important role. Since hypotheses suggest possible answers to the questions implied by the research objectives, there must be questionnaire items that could elicit those possible answers. From the information requirements specified on the right-hand side of Table 10-1, one can see how the process advances.

Formatting the Question

Before specific questions can be phrased, you must decide the degree of freedom to be given to respondents in answering the question. The alternatives are (1) open-ended with no classification, where the interviewer tries to record the response verbatim; (2) open-ended, where the interviewer uses precoded classifications to record the response; or (3) the closed, or structured, format, in which a question or supplementary

TABLE 10-1   Research Objectives for the Tasty Study

Research Objectives	Information Requirements
1. What are the consumption habits of ice cream and coffee by Tasty customers and competition?	General attitudes and preferences of customers of Tasty and strengths and weaknesses of Tasty with respect to competition.
2. Develop demographic and lifestyle profile of the customers of Tasty and customers of competition.	The demographic details such as age, number of family members, and income. Lifestyle activities of customers such as hobbies.
3. Identify relevant strategies for growth of Tasty.	The strengths and weaknesses of Tasty with respect to competition, the preferences of customers and trends in the industry.

card presents the responses the respondent may consider.[4] These options can be illustrated by the following brief sequence of questions from a personal interview survey:

Q10 Is there any particular type of information about life insurance that you would like to have, that you do not now have, or don't know enough about?

Q11 What kind of information?

PROBE What else?

The first question uses a precoded classification, since a yes or no answer is strongly implied. The second question is completely open-ended, and the goal is to achieve an exact transcription. Only 20 percent of a national sample said yes to question 10, and 44 percent of these responded only in very general terms to the follow-up question. This meant that only 11 percent of the total sample said they had a need for specific information, such as rate, or family benefits in case of disability or accident. It is likely that different results would have been obtained if either Q10 or Q11 had been converted to a closed-ended response, such that respondents were handed a card describing many different kinds of information and asked to indicate which they would like to have or didn't know enough about.

Open-Response Questions

There are advantages and disadvantages to **open-response** (or unstructured) **questions.** The advantages stem from the wide range of responses that can be obtained, and the lack of influence in the responses from prespecified categories. Respondents often appreciate this freedom, as illustrated by the surprising frequency with which people write marginal comments in mail surveys when they don't think the response categories capture their feelings adequately. Because of these advantages, open-ended questions are useful in the following circumstances:

- As an introduction to a survey or to a topic. A question such as, "In general, how do you feel about [color TV, this neighborhood, the bus service in this area]," will acquaint the respondent with the subject of the survey, open the way for more specific questions, and make the respondent more comfortable with the questioning process.

- When it is important to measure the salience of an issue to a respondent. Asking "What do you think is the most important problem facing this country today?" for example, will give some insight into what currently is bothering the respondent.

- When there are too many possible responses to be listed, or they cannot be foreseen. For example, you might ask, "What were some of the reasons why you decided to pay cash (for a major appliance purchase?)" or "What do you especially like about living in this neighborhood?"

- When verbatim responses are desired to give the flavor of people's answers or to cite as examples in a report.

- When the behavior to be measured is sensitive or disapproved (such as estimates of drinking or sexual activities). Reported frequencies are higher on an open format where there are no prespecified response categories. When respondents are given a choice of a low-frequency category on a closed format, they are less willing to admit to higher frequencies.[5]

The disadvantages of open-response or open-ended questions are numerous. The major problem is that variability in the clarity and depth of responses depends to a great extent on (1) the articulateness of the respondent in an interview situation, or the willingness to compose a written answer to a mail survey, and (2) the personal or telephone interviewer's ability to record the verbatim answers quickly—or to summarize accurately—and to probe effectively. A third area arose in Chapter 8, where we saw that the interviewer's expectations will influence what is selected for recording or when to stop probing. Open-ended questions are also time consuming, both during the interview and during tabulation. Classifications must be established to summarize the responses, and each answer must be assigned to one or more categories. This involves subjective judgments that are prone to error. To minimize this source of error it may be desirable to have two editors independently categorize the responses and compare their results. This adds further to the cost.

Another problem that occurs frequently in an open-ended question is that the answer given to it expands or contracts, depending on the space or time available for it. When students are given a full page for a question, they have a tendency to fill up the whole page. If only half a page is left, they will write the answer in the space available. Open-ended questions must be designed so that the available answer space and time coincide with question importance. ·

In addition, respondents may not always use the same frame of reference when answering an open-ended question, and these different frames of reference may not be readily discernible by the researcher. This problem is illustrated in the results of an experiment on work values that compared the following two questions:[6]

Q1 *People look for different things in a job. What would you most prefer in a job?*

Q2 *People look for different things in a job. Which one of the following five things would you most prefer in a job?*

1. Work that pays well
2. Work that gives a sense of accomplishment
3. Work where there is not too much supervision and you make most decisions by yourself
4. Work that is pleasant and where the other people are nice to work with
5. Work that is steady with little chance of being laid off

In the open-response format, many respondents said that pay was the most important aspect of a job. There was evidence that some of them meant "high pay," whereas others meant "steady pay." Since both answers were expressed in the same words, it was impossible to separate the two different frames of reference. Answers to the closed-response format did not have this problem, since "work that pays well" and "work that is steady" were two distinct options. Open-response questions run the risk that the researcher may not always be able to tap differences among respondents accurately.

In view of the disadvantages and the lack of convincing evidence that open-ended questions provide more meaningful, relevant, and nonrepetitive responses, it is advisable to close up as many questions as possible in large-scale surveys.

Closed-Response Questions

There are two basic formats for **closed-response** (or **structured) questions.** The first asks respondents to make one or more choices from a list of possible responses. The second is a rating scale where the respondent is given a continuum of labeled categories that represents the range of responses. The following sample of ad testing questions illustrates what can be done.

Choice from a List of Responses

Which one of the following words or phrases best describes the kind of person you feel would be most likely to use this product, based on what you saw and heard in this commercial?

_____ Young	_____ Single
_____ Old	_____ Married
_____ Modern	_____ Homemaker
_____ Old-fashioned	_____ Career woman

Appropriate Single-Choice Rating on a Scale

Please tell us your overall reaction to this commercial.

_____ A great commercial, would like to see it again
_____ A pretty good commercial
_____ Just so-so, like a million others
_____ Another bad commercial

Based on what you saw and heard in this commercial, how interested do you feel you would be in buying the product?

_____ Definitely would buy	_____ Probably would buy
_____ May or may not buy	_____ Probably would not buy
_____ Definitely would not buy	

Regardless of the type of closed-response format, the advantages are the same. Such questions are easier to answer, in both an interview and a mail survey; they require less effort by the interviewer; and they make tabulation and analysis easier. There is less potential error due to differences in the way questions are asked and responses recorded. Normally, a closed-response question takes less time than an equivalent open-ended question. Perhaps the most significant advantage of these

Which commercial is more appealing? The Rold Gold on the left or the Doritos on the right?
Gamma Liaison.

questions in large-scale surveys is that the answers are directly comparable from respondent to respondent (assuming each interprets the words the same way). Comparability of respondents is an essential prelude to the use of any analytical methods.

There are significant limitations to closed-response questions. There is considerable disagreement among researchers on the type of response categories that should be listed. One area of controversy is whether middle alternatives should be included in the questions. It is not unusual for 20 percent of respondents to choose a middle alternative when it is offered, although they would not have volunteered this answer had it not been mentioned. Hence, if one wants to design questions that will help make a clear, actionable decision, it is best not to include the neutral category in the question.

One way of handling this problem is to include the "don't know" alternative, so that respondents are not forced to choose one opinion. Another way of handling this distortion of responses is by providing a scale that captures intensity of a respondent's feeling about a particular question.[7] The measurement of intensity is useful not only as a follow-up for items with logical middle positions but for attitude questions generally. Strength of feeling has been shown to predict both attitude stability and attitude consistency. Two of the most commonly used intensity indicators are the Likert and semantic-differential scales.

Another potential limitation of the closed-response question arises from the fact that an answer will be received for a question, no matter how irrelevant the question is in that context.[8] Hence, if a large number of categories are included in the closed-response question, all the categories will receive a certain percentage of responses. This may not produce meaningful results. Therefore, care should be taken to include only relevant categories.

An extreme form of the closed-ended question is the dichotomous question. A dichotomous question has only two response categories. For example,

Sex:

_____ Male   _____ Female

Dichotomous questions are used mainly to collect demographic and behavioral data when only two answers logically exist. They are not used to collect psychological data because they tend to provide oversimplified, often forced, answers. Dichotomous questions are also prone to a large amount of measurement errors; because alternatives are polarized, the wide range of possible choices between the poles is omitted.

A researcher must constantly strive to overcome the many limitations of closed-response questions. Good questions are hard to develop, and exploratory work is necessary to ensure that all potentially important response alternatives are included. The list of alternative response categories provides answers that respondents might not have considered. In this situation, the respondent might choose a "responsible" alternative. The respondent may also try to avoid a difficult choice or judgment by selecting the easiest alternative, such as "don't know." Where there is a distinct possibility of such biasing occurring in a personal or telephone interview survey, it may be desirable to precede the closed-response question with an open-response question. This is done often in brand-name-awareness studies. The respondent is first asked what brands are associated with the product (unaided recall), and is then given a list of brands and asked to choose those that are known (aided recall).

Number of Response Categories. The number of categories can range from a two-point scale all the way to a 100-point scale. Some questions admit only two possible answers: Did you purchase a new car in the past year? Did you vote in the last election? However, in most situations a dichotomous question will yield misleading results. Sometimes an either/or choice is not possible, and the correct answer may be both. Attitudinal questions invariably have intermediate positions. A simple question such as "Are you considering changing your present health insurance plan?" revealed that 70 percent were not, 8 percent definitely were, and the remaining 22 percent were uncertain or might consider a change in the future. These subtleties are very important in interpreting such a question.

As a general rule, the range of opinion on most issues can be best captured with five or seven categories. Five categories are probably the minimum needed to discriminate effectively among individuals. One popular five-point scale is the Likert scale. This number of categories can be read by the interviewer and understood by the respondent. A seven-or nine-category scale is more precise but cannot be read to respondents with the assurance that they won't get confused.

Multiple-choice questions present special problems. Ideally, the response categories provided for such questions should be mutually exclusive and should exhaust the possibilities. Sometimes it is neither possible nor desirable to include all the possible alternatives since this may prove to be impractical, only the top five or six are listed, and the rest are consigned to an "other" category, which is accompanied by a "please specify" request and a space to enter the brand name.

Order of Response Categories. The order of presentation of categories to respondents in personal or telephone interview situations sometimes can have a big influence on results. A classic study in 1974 provided clear evidence for this. One way of asking a person's income over the telephone is to start by asking "Is your income more than $2,000?" and increasing the figure in increments of $2,000 until the first "no" response. Alternatively, one can start with the highest income category and drop the figure until the first "yes" response. The study found that the median income when the first category was $2,000 was $12,711; however, when the income question started with the high category, $17,184 was the median income.[9] One explanation for this remarkable difference is that respondents find the question threatening and try to get it out of the way by making a premature terminal response. A much better approach is to begin with the median income figure and use a series of branching questions, such as, "Is it over (the median income)?" and if the answer is "no," then asking, "Is it under (half the median income)?" and so forth. This gives a relatively unbiased measure of income and the lowest proportion of refusals.

Another ordering problem is encountered with mail survey questions, in which respondents tend to select categories that are in the middle position of a range of values. This is especially prevalent with questions of fact, such as the number of checkouts at a local store. Respondents who do not know the answer will choose the center position as a safe guess. This also can happen with questions about information that is unique to the respondent, such as the distance to the nearest department store. When the question is constructed with multiple categories, with the middle category representing an estimate of the average distance, the natural tendency to choose the middle position may lead to inaccurate responses. One solution is to place the average or expected distance at various positions in the sequence of categories.[10]

Handling Uncertainty and Ignorance. One awkward question concerns the handling of "don't know" and neutral responses. There are many reasons why respondents do not know the answer to a question, such as forgetting, or an inability to articulate. If an explicit "don't know" response category is provided, it is an easy option for those in the latter group. But often "don't know" is a legitimate response and may yield very important insights. Thus, the option always should be provided as a response to questions about knowledge or opinions when there is some likelihood of ignorance or forgetting. Sometimes this response category is used by those who are unwilling to answer a question. In personal and telephone interviews, it may be advisable to provide the interviewer with an additional "no answer" category to identify these people correctly. A neutral response category such as "not sure" or "neither like nor dislike" also may be desirable for those people who genuinely can't make a choice among specific opinion statements.

If there is likelihood of both ambivalence and ignorance, then both a neutral category and a "don't know" category are appropriate.

Using Both Open-Response and Closed-Response Questions

The choice between open- and closed-response questions, is not necessarily an either/or distinction. Open-response questions can be used in conjunction with closed-response questions to provide additional information. Using an open-response question to follow up a closed-response question is called a **probe.** Probes can efficiently combine some advantages of both open and closed questions. They can be used for specific prechosen questions or to obtain additional information from only a subset of people who respond to previous questions in a certain way. A common example of the latter is to ask respondents who choose "none of the above" a follow-up question to expand on their answer.

There are two general purposes for the use of probes in a questionnaire. The first is to pinpoint questions that were particularly difficult for respondents. Adequate pretesting of questions reduces this need to use probes. The second purpose is to aid researcher interpretation of respondent answers. Answers to open-response follow-ups can provide valuable guidance in the analysis of closed-response questions.

◆ QUESTION WORDING: A PROBLEM OF COMMUNICATION

The wording of particular questions can have a large impact on how a respondent interprets them. Even small changes in **question wording** can shift respondent answers, but it is difficult to know in advance whether a wording change will have such an effect. The following guidelines are of greatest value in critically evaluating and improving an existing question.

1. *Is the vocabulary simple, direct, and familiar to all respondents?*
   The challenge is to choose words that can be understood by all respondents, regardless of education level, but that do not sound patronizing. The most common pitfall is to use technical jargon or specialized terms. Special care must be taken to avoid words that have different meanings for different groups. This can be readily appreciated in cross-cultural studies, where translation problems are profound, but it also is applicable within a culture.

2. *Do any words have vague or ambiguous meanings?*
   A common error is not giving the respondent an adequate frame of reference, in time and space, for interpreting the question. Words such as "often," "occasionally," and "usually" lack an appropriate time referent, so

respondents choose their own, with the result that answers are not comparable. Similarly, the appropriate space or locale often is not specified. Does the question, "How long have you lived here?" refer to this state, county, city, neighborhood, or particular house or apartment?

3. *Are any questions "double-barreled"?*
There are questions in which a respondent can agree with one part of the question but not the other, or cannot answer at all without accepting a particular assumption. In either case, the answers cannot be interpreted. For example, what can be learned from such questions as, "Do you plan to leave your job and look for another one during the coming year?"

4. *Are any questions leading or loaded?*
A leading question is one that clearly suggests the answer or reveals the researcher's (or interviewer's) opinion. This can be done easily by adding "don't you agree?" or "wouldn't you say?" to a desired statement. A loaded question introduces a more subtle bias. A common type of loading of possible responses is through failure to provide a full range of alternatives, for example, by asking, "How do you generally spend your free time—watching television, or what?" Another way to load a question is to provide the respondent with a reason for one of the alternatives: "Should we increase taxes in order to get more housing and better schools, or should we keep them about the same?" A second form of loading results from the use of emotionally charged words. These are words or phrases such as "fair profits," "radical," or "luxury items," which have such strong positive or negative overtones that they overshadow the specific content of the question. Organizations and groups also have emotional associations, and using them to endorse a proposition will certainly bias the response: "A committee of experts has suggested…; Do you approve of this, or do you disagree?" For this reason it is also risky to reveal the sponsor of the study. If one brand or company is identified as the sponsor, the respondents will tend to exaggerate their positive feelings toward the brand.

5. *Questions that involve appeals or threats to the respondent's self-esteem may also be loaded.*[11] A question on occupations usually will produce more "executives" if the respondent chooses from one of a small number of occupational categories rather than being asked for a specific job title.

6. *Are the instructions potentially confusing?* Sheatsley[12] counsels against lengthy questions that explain a complicated situation to a respondent and then ask for an opinion. In his experience, "If the respondent is not aware of these facts, you have probably confused or biased him more than you have enlightened him, and his opinion won't mean much in either case." The question should be directed more toward measuring the respondent's knowledge or interest in the subject.

7. *Is the question applicable to all respondents?* Respondents may try to answer a question even though they don't qualify to do so or may lack an opinion. Examples of such questions are "What is your present occupation?" (assumes respondent is working) or "For whom did you vote in the last election?" (assumes that respondent voted). The solution to this is to ask a qualifying or filter question and limit further questioning to those who qualify.

8. *Split-ballot technique.* Whenever there is doubt as to the appropriate wording, it is desirable to test several alternatives. For instance, the responses to

a question may vary with the degree of personalization. The question, "Do you think there should be government-run off-track betting in this state?" is different from "Is it desirable to have government-run off-track betting in this state?" Sometimes the choice can be resolved by the purpose of the study; the impersonal form being preferred if the study aims at measuring the general tenor of public sentiment. Where the choice is not obvious, the best solution is to use one version in half of the questionnaire and the second version in the remaining half. Any significant differences in the results can be helpful in interpreting the meaning of the question.

9. *Are the questions of an appropriate length?* It is not always the case that shorter questions are better, although one common rule of thumb is to keep the number of words in any question under 20. Under certain circumstances, a question may have to be long in order to avoid ambiguity, but this should be the exception rather than the rule. A questionnaire filled with long questions is more fatiguing to answer and more difficult to understand.

Asking Sensitive Questions

A variety of approaches can be used to attempt to get honest answers. For example, long, open-ended questions with familiar wording have been found effective when asking threatening questions that require quantified responses. The only limit is the creativity of the researcher. Alan Barton made this point best when in 1958 he composed a parody on ways to ask the question, "Did you kill your wife?"[13] His approach has been adapted to a different situation. Here the respondent is a responsible adult who is being questioned about his or her consumption of Kellogg's Frosted Flakes (a potentially embarrassing situation).

1. *The casual approach:* "Have you eaten Frosted Flakes within the last week?"

2. *The numbered card:* "Would you please read off the number on this card that corresponds to what you had eaten for breakfast in the last week?"
(Hand card to respondent.)
   a. Pancakes
   b. Frosted Flakes
   c. Other (what)?
(GET CARD BACK FROM RESPONDENT BEFORE PROCEEDING!)

3. *The everybody approach:* "As you know, many people have been eating Frosted Flakes for breakfast. Do you eat Frosted Flakes?"

4. *The "other people" approach:*
   a. "Do you know of any adult who eats Frosted Flakes?"
   b. "How about yourself?"

5. *The sealed ballot technique:* In this version you explain that the survey respects people's right to anonymity with respect to their eating habits, and that they themselves are to answer the questionnaire, seal it in an envelope, and drop it in a box conspicuously labeled "sealed ballot box" that is carried by the interviewer.

6. *The Kinsey technique:* Stare firmly into respondent's eyes and ask in simple, clear-cut language such as that to which the respondent is accustomed, and with an air of assuming that everyone has done everything, "Do you eat Frosted Flakes for breakfast?"

Hornik, Zaig, and Shadmon report high rates of refusal to answer questions about sexual behavior, personal income, use of drugs, criminal behavior, and so on. It is suggested that the foot-in-the-door (FITD) technique and the low-ball (LB) technique are both effective in enhancing compliance to requests for information about sensitive topics. However, a combination of these two techniques is more effective than either alone. In the combined technique, subjects first commit to responding to a survey (LB), and then are asked, "While we are on the phone, could you please respond to three short questions concerning personal matters?" (FITD).[14]

◆ SEQUENCE AND LAYOUT DECISIONS

The order, or **sequence,** of questions will be determined initially by the need to gain and maintain the respondent's cooperation and make the questionnaire as easy as possible for the interviewer to administer. Once these considerations are satisfied, attention must be given to the problem of **order bias**—the possibility that prior questions will influence answers to subsequent questions.

The basic guidelines for sequencing a questionnaire to make it interesting and logical to both interviewer and respondent are straightforward.

1. Open the interview with an easy and nonthreatening question. This helps to establish rapport and builds the confidence of the respondent in his or her ability to answer.[15]

2. The questionnaire should flow smoothly and logically from one topic to the next. Sudden shifts in topic are to be avoided, as they tend to confuse respondents and cause indecision.

3. For most topics it is better to proceed from broad, general questions to the more specific.

4. Sensitive or difficult questions dealing with income status, ability, and so forth, should not be placed at the beginning of the questionnaire. Rather, they should be introduced at a point where the respondent has developed some trust and confidence in the interviewer and the study.

The physical **layout** of the questionnaire will also influence whether the questionnaire is interesting and easy to administer. For self-administered questionnaires, the quality of the paper, the clarity of reproduction, and the appearance of crowding are important variables. Similarly, the job of the interviewer is considerably eased if the questionnaire is not crowded, if precise instructions are provided, and if flow diagrams with arrows and boxes are used to guide the interviewer through filter questions. The manner in which a typical questionnaire is organized is given in Table 10-2.

Order Bias: Does the Question Create the Answer?

Order bias is the possibility that prior questions will influence answers to subsequent questions.

We have indicated already that it is usually preferable to ease a respondent into a subject by beginning with some general, orienting questions. However, when the topic is unfamiliar to the respondents—or their involvement with the subject is low or little—the nature of the early questions will significantly affect subsequent answers.

A new-product concept test is the most prevalent example of research on an unfamiliar subject. Respondents typically are given a description of the new product and are asked to express their degree of buying interest. As one study showed, how-

TABLE 10-2   Organization of a Typical Questionnaire

Location	Type	Function	Example
Starting questions	Broad, general questions	To break the ice and establish a rapport with the respondent	Do you own a VCR?
Next few questions	Simple and direct questions	To reassure the respondent that the survey is simple and easy to answer	What brands of VCR did you consider when you bought it?
Questions up to a third of the questionnaire	Focused questions	Relate more to the research objectives and convey to the respondent the area of research	What attributes did you consider when you purchased your VCR?
Major portion of the questionnaire	Focused questions; some may be difficult and complicated	To obtain most of the information required for the research	Rank the following attributes of a VCR based on their importance to you.
Last few questions	Personal questions that may be perceived by the respondent as sensitive	To get classification and demographic information about the respondent	What is the highest level of education you have attained?

ever, this interest will depend on the sequence of the preceding questions.[16] The new product was described as a combination pen-and-pencil selling for 29 cents. Four different types of questions were asked of four matched sets of respondents before the buying-interest question was asked:

Questions Preceding Buying Interest Question	Percentage of Respondents "Very Much Interested" in Buying New Product
1. No question asked	2.8
2. Asked only about advantages	16.7
3. Asked only about disadvantages	0.0
4. Asked about both advantages and disadvantages	5.7

The nature of the preceding questions definitely establishes the frame of reference to be used by the respondent. The issue for the questionnaire designer, is to decide which is the most valid frame of reference—that is, which corresponds most closely to the type of thinking that would precede an actual purchase decision in this product category. The same problem confronts survey researchers dealing with social issues that are not of immediate relevance to the respondent. The "cautionary tale" by Charles Raymond in Marketing Research in Practice 10-1 shows how questions create answers in these settings.

Order bias is also a concern when the answer to one question has an obvious implication for the answer to another. Thus, fewer people say their taxes are too high after being asked a series of questions about whether government spending should be increased in various areas.[17] This may be explained in a number of different ways. Respondents may attempt to maintain consistency in their answers. Another explanation is that earlier questions may make some experiences or judgments more

MARKETING RESEARCH IN PRACTICE 10-1

When Questions Create Answers

Suppose I were to call you on the telephone as follows: "Hello, this is Charles Raymond of the XYZ Poll. We are trying to find out what people think about certain issues. Do you watch television?"

Whatever your answer, the next question is, "Some people say that oil tankers are spilling oil and killing the fish and want to pass a law against this; do you agree or disagree?" Your answer is duly recorded and the next question is, "Have you ever read or heard anything about this?"

Again, your answer is recorded, and finally I ask, "Do you think anyone should do anything about this? Who? What?"

And now the main question, "I'd like you to rate some companies on a scale from minus five to plus five—minus five if you totally dislike the company, plus five if you totally like it, and zero if you are in between or indifferent. First, U.S. Steel." You give a number and I say, "The gas company." You give another number and I say, "Exxon."

You see what is happening. Or do you? Suppose I now tell you that this form of questioning is given only to a random half of a large sample called the experimental group. To the control group, the interview is as follows: "Hello, this is Charles Raymond from XYZ Poll. We are trying to find out what people think about certain things. Do you ever watch TV?" You answer and then I ask, "Now I'd like you to rate some companies on a scale from minus five to plus five…" And the difference in the average rating between the experimental and control group can be attributed to them having thought about tankers spilling oil and killing the fish, for that is the only difference in the way the two groups were treated.

Questions Shape the Attitudes

I think you can see for yourselves, merely by following this interview pattern, how you might very well rate companies differently after having rehearsed your "attitude" toward oil pollution than without having done so. In case it is difficult for you to imagine how you would respond under these two conditions, I can assure you that random halves of well-drawn samples of certain elite publics rated large companies very differently, depending on whether they were in the experimental or control group. They did so in survey after survey, consistently over time, thereby showing the reliability of the phenomenon.

Source: Charles Raymond, "When Questions Create Answers," Speech to the Annual Meeting, Advertising Research Foundation, New York, May 1977.

salient to the respondent than they would otherwise be. For example, in a study dealing with pricing questions, it is observed that greater price sensitivity is found when individuals are asked to respond to a low price first, followed by successively higher prices. In contrast, the reverse order (i.e., high price to low) results in considerably less price sensitivity. This effect has been seen with all popular data collection modes.

The difficulty with this type of order bias is that even where context is shown to have an effect, it is frequently unclear that one order is better than another. Instead, each order may reveal a different facet of the issue being studied.

Pretesting and Correcting Problems

The purpose of a **pretest** is to ensure that the questionnaire meets the researcher's expectations in terms of the information that will be obtained. First drafts of questionnaires tend to be too long, often lack important variables, and are subject to all the hazards of ambiguous, ill-defined, loaded, or double-barreled questions. The objective of the questionnaire pretest is to identify and correct these deficiencies.

Effective pretesting demands that the researcher be open to criticism and be willing to pursue the deficiencies. Thus, a good starting point for the researcher is to take the respondent's point of view and try to answer the questions.

Pretest Design

Because a pretest is a pilot run, the respondents should be reasonably representative of the sample population. However, they should not all be "typical," for much can be learned from those at the extremes of the sample. Will the questions work with those who have a limited education, strong negative opinions, or little understanding of the subject? Only small samples are necessary—15 is sufficient for a short and straightforward questionnaire, whereas 25 may be needed if the questionnaire is long and complex, with many branches and multiple options. Even when the field survey will be done by mail, the pretest should be done with a personal or telephone interview to get direct feedback on problems. Only the best, most insightful, and experienced interviewers should be used for this work.

Pretesting Specific Questions

There are some very specific reasons for pretest questions. Four common reasons are as follows:[18]

1. *Variation.* The researcher is on the lookout for items showing greater variability than will be useful in detecting subgroups of people. Very skewed distributions from a pretest can serve as a warning signal that the question is not tapping the intended construct.

2. *Meaning.* The intended meaning of the questions for the investigators may not be the meaning the respondents interpret it to be, for two important reasons. The first is that respondents may not necessarily hear or even see every word in a question. This can result in a distortion of the meaning of the question, as when, for example, the *"im"* is missed from the word "impossible." The second reason for problems with meaning is that a respondent is likely to modify a difficult question in a way that makes it easier for him or her to respond.

3. *Task difficulty.* A meaningful and clear question can still be difficult to answer if the question requires that a respondent make connections or put together information in unfamiliar ways. A question such as "How many pounds of laundry detergent have you consumed this past year?" is likely to be too difficult for most respondents to answer, since they probably do not total up their consumption of laundry detergent by the pound or even by the year.

4. *Respondent interest and attention.* This is an area of pretesting that is often overlooked by researchers. Excessive repetition within a question or use of the same format within a question can reduce the amount of attention paid to questions by respondents.

Pretesting the Questionnaire

Some research concerns about the questionnaire as a whole, such as the order of questions, have already been mentioned. Other concerns that should be pretested are the following.

1. *Flow of the questionnaire.* Testing the "flow" of the questionnaire is often a matter of intuitive judgment. Transitions from one topic to another must be pretested to ensure that they are clear and logical.

2. *Skip patterns.* Many questionnaires have instructions on what questions to skip, depending on the answer to a previous question. Whether the skip patterns are to be followed by the respondent (as in a mail survey) or by the interviewer (as in a personal interview), they must be clear and well laid out.

3. *Length.* Each section of the questionnaire should be timed to ensure that none of them is too long. Unless the length is pretested, the research may experience problems with respondent fatigue, interview break-off, and initial refusal if respondents know in advance the expected length.

4. *Respondent interest and attention.* Capturing and maintaining the interest of a respondent throughout the entire questionnaire is a major design challenge. Often the answering task is varied throughout the questionnaire, to engage a respondent's active attention. The extent to which this is successful can and should be pretested.

Role of the Pretest

There are limits to how well a pretest can detect errors. One study found that pretest respondents were virtually unable to detect loaded questions, and most did not recognize when response alternatives were missing or questions were ambiguous.[19] For example, less than 10 percent of a pretest sample pointed out the ambiguity of the following question: "Do you think things will be better or worse next summer than they are now?" Five response options were provided, ranging from much better to much worse.

Although it requires only one perceptive or confused respondent to identify problems or improvements, respondents are not the only source of insights. Interviewers are equally important to the pretesting process. Once the interviewers have reported their experiences, they also should be asked for their suggestions. There is a danger that some interviewers will make changes in the field on their own initiative if they believe it will make their job easier. This can create serious problems if some interviewers make the change and others do not.

Finally, the pretest analysis should return to the first step in the design process. Each question should be reviewed once again and asked to justify its place in the questionnaire. How will the answer be used in the analysis? Is the pattern of answers from the pretest sensible, or difficult to interpret? Does the question add substantial new information, or unnecessarily duplicate the results from another question? Of course, the last step in the process may be another pretest, if far-reaching changes have been necessary.

◆ QUESTIONNAIRE DESIGN FOR INTERNATIONAL RESEARCH

Choosing the Question Format for Cross-National Research

The issue of question format is an important one when constructing a questionnaire for cross-cultural or cross-national research.[20] The researcher may lack experience with purchasing behavior or relevant determinants of response in another country or cultural context. Use of open-ended questions may thus be desirable in a number of situations. Since they do not impose any structure or response categories, open-ended questions avoid the imposition of cultural bias by the researcher. Furthermore, they do not require familiarity with all the respondents' possible responses.

In addition, differences in levels of literacy may affect the appropriateness of using open-ended questions as opposed to closed questions. Since open-ended questions require the respondent to answer on his or her own terms, they also require a moderate level of sophistication and comprehension of the topic on the part of the respondent; otherwise, responses will not be meaningful. Open-ended questions must therefore be used with care in cross-cultural and cross-national research, in order to ensure that bias does not occur as a result of differences in levels of education.

Another consideration is whether direct or indirect questions should be utilized. Direct questions avoid any ambiguity concerning question content and meaning. On the other hand, respondents may be reluctant to answer certain types of questions. Similarly, they may tend to provide responses perceived as socially desirable or those they think are desired by the interviewer. Use of indirect questions may aid in by-passing such biases. In this case, rather than being stated directly, the question is posed in an indirect form.

For example, respondents might be asked to indicate, rather than their own preferences, those they would anticipate from the majority of respondents, neighbors, or other relevant reference groups. Thus, the decision to use a direct or an indirect format for a particular question depends on the respondent's perception of the topic. If the topic is perceived as sensitive by the respondent, then it is better to use an indirect format than a direct one. The sensitivity of a topic may vary from culture to culture. Hence, a direct question in one country may have to be asked as an indirect one in a different country.

Another important consideration in instrument design is the extent to which nonverbal, as opposed to verbal, stimuli are utilized in order to facilitate respondent comprehension. Particularly where research is conducted in countries or cultures with high levels of illiteracy—as, for example, Africa and the Far East—it is often desirable to use nonverbal stimuli such as show cards. Questionnaires can be administered orally by an interviewer, but respondent comprehension will be facilitated if pictures of products, concepts, or test packs are provided.

Various types of nonverbal stimuli may be used in conjunction with questionnaires, including show cards, product samples, or pictures. It should be noted that nonverbal stimuli are often used in other data collection techniques. The main focus here, however, is on their use in surveys in order to ensure that respondents understand verbal questions, relevant products, and product concepts.

Problems Faced in Wording Questions for International Research

When conducting cross-national research, the wording of questions has to be changed according to the country in which the questionnaire is being administered. Certain categories, such as sex and age, are the same in all countries or cultures, and hence, equivalent questions can be posed. Somewhat greater difficulties may be encountered with regard to other categories, such as income, education, occupation, or the dwelling unit, since these are not always exactly comparable from one culture or country to another. In addition to the fact that in some countries men may have several wives, querying marital status can present problems, depending on how the question is put. The growing number of cohabitating couples, especially those who are divorced, creates a particular problem in this regard. What is included in the category of income may vary from country to country, and incomes vary considerably within countries.

Similarly, with regard to education, types of schools, colleges, or universities are not always comparable from one country to another. Also, certain occupational categories may not be comparable from one country to another. In general, however, the major distinctions or broad categories tend to be the same—that is, farm workers, industrial workers, blue-collar workers, office or white-collar workers, self-employed persons, lower and upper management, and professionals. Alternatively, comparable social hierarchies can be identified. Another category where differences may occur is in the dwelling unit. In the major Western societies, dwelling units are primarily apartments or multistory houses. In African countries, however, dwelling units may be huts, whereas in Far Eastern countries many homes are one-story units.

In developing questions related to purchase behavior and consumption or usage behavior, and to specific product markets, two important issues need to be considered. The first concerns the extent to which such behavior is conditioned by a specific sociocultural or economic environment and hence is likely to vary from one country or cultural context to another. Each culture, society, or social group has its own particular conventions, rituals, and practices relating to behavior in social situations, such as entertaining family or friends on festive occasions—for example, graduation or Christmas. Rules relating to the exchange of gifts and products are, for example, governed by local cultural conventions. Thus, in some cultures wine may be an appropriate gift for a dinner host or hostess, whereas in others, flowers are preferred. Consequently, questions relating to the gift market, and products positioned as gifts, will need to be tailored to these specific behavior patterns. Significant differences

MARKETING RESEARCH IN PRACTICE 10-2

An Example of Questionnaire Construction in International Research

A study was conducted to find out the influence of the role of stress on industrial sales people's work outcomes in the United States, Japan, and Korea. The brief discussion that follows tells us how the questionnaire was constructed and the difficulties faced in constructing the questionnaire.

When conducting comparative studies, each version of the questionnaire should be equivalent across countries: that is, the terms in each version of the survey instrument should be relevant to the specific country surveyed. To maintain equivalence, a questionnaire that is translated from one language to another needs to be back-translated into the original language. Those doing the back-translation should be familiar with the different languages, the different cultures, and the usage of the concepts and their meanings in the different countries. Following the above guidelines, in this study the English version of the questionnaire was translated into Japanese and Korean and back-translated into English by Japanese and Korean nationals, respectively. Despite the care that was taken to preserve the meaning and intent of the scale items across the three questionnaires, there is a chance that questionnaire equivalence was not achieved, and even if this had occurred its degree cannot be assessed. The questionnaire items used to assess the key constructs had been employed in previous research. These scales originally were developed using U.S.-based samples: admittedly, then, their substantive meaning, derived from work in the United States, may not be portable to samples in other countries.

Source: Alan J. Dubinsky, Ronald E. Michaels, Masaaki Kotabe, Chae Un Lim, and Hee Cheol Moon, "Influence of the Role of Stress on Industrial Sales People's Work Outcomes in the U.S., Japan and Korea," *Journal of International Business Studies,* 23 (First Quarter, 1992).

also occur in the retail distribution network. In many developing countries, for example, there are few self-service outlets or supermarkets, except in major cities, and most purchases are made in small Mom-and-Pop-type stores. Such shopping patterns affect the formulation of questions relating to the location and timing of purchasing, as well as the importance of investigating the salesperson's influence on purchase decisions.

In addition to such differences in usage and purchase behavior, relevant product class boundaries or competing and substitute products vary from one country to another. For example, washing machines and other household appliances may be competing with domestic help and professional washerwomen, as well as with other brands of washing machines.

The most significant problems in drawing up questions in multicountry research are likely to occur in relation to attitudinal, psychographic, and lifestyle data. Here, as has already been pointed out, it is not always clear that comparable or equivalent attitudinal or personality constructs—such as aggressiveness, respect for authority, and honor—are relevant in all countries and cultures. Even where similar constructs exist, it is far from clear whether they are most effectively tapped by the same question or attitude statement. Problems that were encountered in conducting an actual cross-cultural research project are described in Marketing Research in Practice 10-2 .

END OF CHAPTER MATERIAL

SUMMARY

As with most steps in the research process, the design of the questionnaire is highly iterative. Because it is an integral part of the research design, the objective is to seek consistency with the other elements of the design, notably the research purpose, the budget, and the methods of analysis. Additional constraints are imposed by the data collection method and the respondent's ability and willingness to answer questions about the subject.

Within these constraints the questionnaire writer practices this art through the adroit choice of wording, response format, sequencing of questions, and layout of the questionnaire. Success in this activity comes from experience, an ability to look at the subject and the wording of the questions from the respondent's perspective, and a good understanding of the objectives of the research.

The difficulties in designing a good questionnaire have encouraged researchers to use previously published survey questions wherever possible. There are many published compilations of survey questions that can be consulted to save time and effort. This does not mean, however, that only previously published questions can or should be used, since it is the specific research purpose that ultimately determines the questionnaire design.

Guidelines for writing and organizing questionnaires have been presented here. Since they are a distillation of the experience of many researchers, adherence to these principles will narrow the range of problems. Ultimately, a good questionnaire is one that has been thoroughly pretested. There can be no substitute for this step in the process.

Even though the process of designing questionnaires for international research is essentially the same, there are certain key differences that have been discussed earlier. A classic trade-off situation exists with respect to the use of closed- versus open-response format in international research. While closed-response questions will lead to an imposition of the researcher's cultural biases on the respondent, open-response questions require a certain level of education and familiarity with the subject, which may not be present among respondents in many countries. Another area where a researcher is likely to encounter problems in cross-cultural research is in question wording. Words that represent a construct in one culture may turn out to be totally different in another culture when they are translated—or, worse, a particular construct may not have a word at all in the language of that culture. A researcher conducting cross-cultural research has to overcome many such problems in questionnaire design.

KEY TERMS

open-response questions	layout
closed-response questions	order bias
question wording	probe
sequence	pretest

MARKETING RESEARCH TOOLBOX
REVIEW POINTS

1. The sequence of logical steps to be followed while developing a good questionnaire are planning what to measure, formatting the questionnaire, wording questions, deciding on sequence and layout, and pretesting and correcting problems.

2. Poor judgment and lack of thought in the planning stage may mean that the results are not relevant to the research purpose or that they are incomplete. Both problems are expensive, and may seriously diminish the value of the study.

3. The relevance problem can be overcome by clear research objectives, exploratory research, experience from similar studies, and pretesting of preliminary versions of the questionnaire.

4. Hypotheses play an important role in translating research questions into information requirements. Since hypotheses suggest possible answers to the questions implied by the research objectives, there must be questionnaire items that could elicit those possible answers.

5. Before specific questions can be phrased, a decision has to be made as to the degree of freedom to be given to the respondents in answering the question. The alternatives are open-ended questions with no classification, open-ended questions, and closed or structured format questions.

6. The advantages of open-response questions stem from the wide range of questions that can be obtained and the lack of influence in the responses from prespecified categories. The major disadvantage of open-response questions is the variability in the clarity and depth of responses. The variability depends on the articulateness of the respondent in an interview situation, or the willingness to compose a written answer to a mail survey, and the personal and telephone interviewer's ability to record the verbatim answers quickly—or to summarize accurately—and to probe effectively.

7. There are two basic formats for closed-ended (or structured) questions. The first asks respondents to make one or more choices from a list of possible responses. The second is a rating scale where the respondent is given a continuum of labeled categories that represents the range of responses.

8. Closed-response questions are easier to answer, in both an interview and a mail survey; they require less effort by the interviewer; and they make tabulation and analysis easier. There is less potential error due to differences in the way questions are asked and responses are recorded.

9. Using an open-response question to follow up a closed-response question is called a probe. Probes can efficiently combine some advantages of both open and closed response questions.

10. The guidelines to be followed in critically evaluating and improving an existing question include using simple, direct, and familiar vocabulary, avoiding words having vague or ambiguous meanings, avoiding double-barreled questions and leading or loaded questions, avoiding confusing instructions, using questions applicable to all respondents, and avoiding long questions.

11. Order bias is the possibility that prior questions will influence answers to subsequent questions. The basic guidelines for avoiding order bias are opening the interview with an easy and nonthreatening question, ensuring smooth and logical flow from one topic to another, proceeding from broad, general questions to more specific ones, and placing sensitive or difficult questions dealing with income status, ability, and so forth at the end of the questionnaire.

12. The purpose of a pretest is to ensure that the questionnaire meets the researcher's expectations in terms of information that will be obtained.

13. The four common tests for pretesting specific questions are variation, meaning, task difficulty, and respondent interest and attention.

14. Research concerns that should be pretested are flow of the questionnaire, skip patterns, length of the questionnaire, and respondent interest and attention.

15. Concerns regarding questionnaires in international marketing research include (1) lack of experience with purchasing behavior or relevant determinants of response in another country or cultural context, (2) differences in the levels of literacy may affect the appropriateness of using open-ended questions as opposed to closed questions, (3) deciding whether to use direct or indirect questions, and (4) deciding whether to use verbal or nonverbal stimuli.

16. When conducting cross-national research, the wording of questions has to be changed according to the country in which the questionnaire is being administered.

QUESTIONS AND PROBLEMS

1. A researcher investigating the general happiness of respondents in a particular age and socioeconomic group is considering using the following two questions in a questionnaire:
   a. All things considered, how happy would you say you were these days? Would you say that you were very happy, pretty happy, or not too happy?
   b. All things considered, how would you describe your marriage? Would you say your marriage is very happy, pretty happy, or not too happy? What are some concerns you might have about the order in which these questions might be asked? Which order would you suggest?

2. "As long as a question pertains to at least one of the research objectives, it must be included in the questionnaire." Do you agree or disagree with this statement? Explain your answer.

3. Open-response questions sometimes are used to establish the salience or importance of issues such as irritation from clutter due to excessive advertisements and station announcements during TV programs. Why would you want to use this type of response format rather than a closed-response question?

4. How do the responses from an unaided-recall question on brand awareness compare to those from an aided-recall question?

5. What can a researcher do to make the request for information seem legitimate?

6. Evaluate the following questions and suggest improvements.
   a. Please check the following activities in which you participate as a private citizen interested in politics.
      ____ Read books and articles on the subject
      ____ Belong to political party
      ____ Attend political rallies
      ____ Write letters to legislators, newspapers, or government officials
      ____ Other (please specify)

    b.   When you eat dinner out, do you sometimes eat at the same place?

        ____ Yes   ____ No

    c.   Is the current level of government regulation on environmental protection adequate or inadequate?

        ____ Adequate   ____ Inadequate

    d.   Where do you buy most of your clothes?

    e.   Do you think that Con Edison is doing everything possible to reduce air pollution from their electricity-generating stations?

        ____ Yes   ____ No

    f.   Please indicate how much of an average issue of *Sunset* magazine you usually read:

        ____ 1. Less than 1/3   ____ 2. 1/3 to 1/2   ____ 3. Over 1/2

    g.   List the magazines you read regularly ("read" means read or look at; "regularly" means almost as often as the magazine is published).

    h.   What kind of hobbies do you have?

    i.   Everybody knows that teenagers and their parents have lots of arguments. What are some of the things you and your parents have argued about lately?

7.   A large automobile manufacturer has asked you to develop a questionnaire to measure owners' satisfaction with the servicing of their vehicles. One sequence of questions will deal with satisfaction with the design, construction, operating costs, performance, and amount of service required. In order to interpret these results, it has been decided to ask further questions to isolate the responsibility for car problems. That is, do car owners tend to blame the manufacturers, the service work by the dealer, or poor upkeep and driving habits of car owners? What kind of questions would you ask to determine this information?

8.   Develop three double-barreled questions related to eating habits and restaurant preferences. Also develop correct versions of each question.

9.   What are some recommended ways by which one can ask sensitive information? Where in the questionnaire should one ask for sensitive information?

10.   A research company has decided to pretest a personal interview questionnaire prior to collecting the actual data. Interviewers will conduct the pretest interviews. Design a separate questionnaire containing from 5 to 10 questions that you think the interviewer should fill out after each pretest interview. The objective of this separate questionnaire is to provide the research company with sufficient information to evaluate any problems with the personal interview questionnaire.

11.   The Student Disciplinary Committee of Clint State University is extremely concerned about the increasing incidence of cheating in both in-class and out-of-class student assignments. They have approached a marketing research class to conduct a survey of Clint State students. They wish to know:

(i)   How predominant this behavior is campus-wide

(ii)   Whether it occurs most frequently among freshmen, sophomores, juniors, or seniors

(iii)   Some of the reasons for this behavior

(iv)   Possible solutions to the problem

    a.   What are the information requirements for the study?

    b.   How should the questions be formatted? (*Hint:* consider the topic of the study.) Give reasons for your answer.

    c.   How could order bias affect the results of this survey?

    d.   It has been decided that the questionnaire should be pretested. What are the reasons for pretesting a questionnaire? Suggest a suitable group of respondents for the pretest.

As part of its assimilation in the current global environment, the marketing research class is paying close attention to research techniques for international markets. To meet this objective, the professor has instructed the students to undertake a similar study among students of a university in France.

    e. What is the most appropriate question format for this research?

    f. What are the possible problems that may be encountered by the class in the international research project?

12. The finance committee of St. Dunstan's Church has reported a fall in the level of donations to the church at Sunday services, despite the fact that attendance has not declined. In an effort to boost donations, the committee has decided to conduct personal interviews of all church members in their homes to determine each member's habits regarding donations to the church.

    a. How might this survey method bias the results of the study? Each member of the committee has been given a questionnaire from which to conduct the personal interviews. The first four questions are as follows:

      (i) How often do you attend Sunday services per year?

      (ii) Do you realize that the church's only form of income is the donations from its members?

      (iii) Do you donate to the church every Sunday?

      (iv) How much, on average, do you donate?

    b. How would the following factors affect the results of this study?

      (i) Question order

      (ii) Question wording

      (iii) Subject matter

      (iv) Interviewer's affiliation to the church

13. Two consumers were considering buying a lawnmower. Bill's wife suggested brand B, and after shopping for a good price, Bill bought brand B at a discount store. Jake, however, consulted *Consumer Reports* and found repair trouble reported with brands A, C, D, F, and H, and unwanted features in brands M, E, end G. Therefore, he decided on brand B as well. Jake can respond accurately to the question of why he did not buy brand M. Bill cannot because he had no reason for not buying brand M, and may not even have been aware of the product. Both, however, can easily explain why they bought brand B.

Meanwhile, at Markmix Co., the owner pondered over the low sales record for heavily promoted brand M and decided to conduct a survey to find out why his product was not being bought. However, if this question were asked directly in a survey, a problem of focus would appear. Company M's focus is on the product, but the consumer's is not. In Bill's case, the reason for not buying brand M does not concern brand M, or brands A, C, D, E, F, G, and H, for that matter. There was no decision to buy brand M, only a positive reason to buy brand B.

Design a questionnaire (10 questions) that will open doors to the reasons for not buying Markmix Co.'s brand. Consider carefully the process described in Figure 10-1. [*Hint:* How would you approach: (1) the question regarding the reason for buying the product, (2) the uncertainty and ignorance of the respondent, and (3) the buying-interest question—indirectly or directly?][21]

ENDNOTES

1. Stanley L. Payne, *The Art of Asking Questions* (Princeton, NJ: Princeton University Press, 1951).

2. Thomas T. Semon, "Buyers, Users May Have Different Viewpoints," *Marketing News* (November 10 1997), p. 16.

3. Jagdip Singh, Roy D. Howell, and Gary K. Rhoads, "Adaptive Designs for Likert-Type Data: An Approach for Implementing Market Surveys," *Journal of Marketing Research,* 27 (August 1990), pp. 304–21.

4. Gregory J. Spagna, "Questionnaires: Which Approach Do You Use?" *Journal of Advertising Research*, 24 (February–March 1984), pp. 67–70.

5. J. M. Converse and Stanley Presser, *Survey Questions, Handcrafting the Standardized Questionnaire*, Sage University Paper, Series on Quantitative Applications in the Social Sciences, 07–063, (Beverly Hills, CA: Sage, 1986).

6. H. Schuman and S. Presser, *Questions and Answers in Attitude Surveys: Experiments in Question Form, Wording and Context* (New York: Academic Free Press, 1981).

7. George F. Bishop, "Experiments with the Middle Response Alternatives in Survey Questions," *Public Opinion Quarterly* (Summer 1987), pp. 220–32.

8. George F. Bishop, Alfred J. Tuchfarber, and Robert W. Oldendick, "Opinions on Fictitious Issues: The Pressure to Answer Survey Questions," *Public Opinion Quarterly* (Summer 1986), pp. 240–50.

9. W. B. Locander and J. P. Burton, "The Effect of Question Form on Gathering Income Data by Telephone," *Journal of Marketing Research*, 13 (May 1976), pp. 189–92.

10. Niels J. Blunch, "Position Bias in Multiple-Choice Questions," *Journal of Marketing Research*, 21 (May 1984), pp. 216–20, has argued that position bias in multiple-choice questions cannot be eliminated by rotating the order of the categories.

11. Such questions are vulnerable to the prestige seeking and social-desirability-response bias discussed in Chapter 8.

12. Paul B. Sheatsley, *Questionnaire Design and Wording* (Chicago: National Opinion Research Corporation, 1969).

13. A. J. Barton, "Asking the Embarrassing Question," *Public Opinion Quarterly* (Spring 1958), pp. 67–68.

14. J. Hornik, T. Zaig, and D. Shadmon, "Reducing Refusals in Telephone Surveys on Sensitive Topics," *Journal of Advertising Research*, 31 (1991), pp. 49–56.

15. R. L. Kahn and C. F. Cannell, *The Dynamics of Interviewing* (New York: John Wiley, 1957).

16. Edwin J. Gross, "The Effect of Question Sequence on Measures of Buying Interest," *Journal of Advertising Research*, 4 (September 1964), p. 41.

17. C. F. Turner and K. Krauss, "Fallible Indicators of the Subjective State of the Nation," *American Psychologist*, 33 (September 1978), pp. 456–70.

18. J. M. Converse and Stanley Presser, *Survey Questions, Handcrafting the Standardized Questionnaire*, Sage University Paper, Series on Quantitative Applications in the Social Sciences, 07–063 (Beverly Hills, CA: Sage, 1986).

19. Shelby Hunt, Richard D. Sparkman, and James B. Wilcox, "The Pretest in Survey Research: Issues and Preliminary Findings," *Journal of Marketing Research* (May 1982), pp. 269–73.

20. E. D. Jaffe and I. D. Nebenzahl, "Alternative Questionnaire Formats for Country Image Studies," *Journal of Marketing Research* (November 1984), pp. 463–71.

21. Thomas T. Semon, "Why Didn't You Buy Brand C?" *Marketing News* (July 1, 1996), p. 13.

CASES

For detailed descriptions of the below cases please visit www.wiley.com/college/kumar.

Case 10-1: Smith's Clothing
Case 10-2: Compact Lemon

Sampling Fundamentals

Learning Objectives

- Distinguish between a census and a sample.
- Know the differences between sampling and nonsampling errors.
- Learn the concepts of the sampling process.
- Describe probability and nonprobability sampling procedures.
- Determine sample size with ad hoc methods.
- Learn to deal with nonresponse problems.
- Understand sampling in the international context.

Marketing research often involves the estimation of a characteristic of some population of interest. For instance, the average level of usage of a park by community residents might be of interest; or information might be needed on the attitudes of a student body toward a proposed intramural facility. In either case, it would be unlikely that all members of the population would be surveyed. Contacting the entire population—that is, the entire census list—simply would not be worthwhile from a cost–benefit viewpoint. It would be both costly and, in nearly all cases, unnecessary, since a sample usually is sufficiently reliable. Further, it often would be less accurate, since nonsampling errors, such as nonresponse, cheating, and data coding errors, are more difficult to control. A **population** can be defined as the set of all objects that possess some common set of characteristics with respect to a marketing research problem.

> A **population** can be defined as the set of all objects that possess some common set of characteristics with respect to a marketing research problem.

◆ SAMPLE OR CENSUS

A researcher typically is interested in the characteristics of a population. For example, if the proportion of people in a city watching a television show has to be determined, then the information can be obtained by asking every household in that city. If all the respondents in a population are asked to provide information, such a survey is called a **census.** The proportion of television viewers generated from a census is known as the **parameter.** On the other hand, a subset of all the households may be chosen and the relevant information could be obtained from that. Information obtained from a subset of the households is known as the *statistic* (from sample). Researchers then attempt to make an inference about the population parameter with the knowledge of the relevant sample statistic. A critical assumption in the process of

> If all the respondents in a population are asked to provide information, such a survey is called a **census**.

inference is that the sample chosen is representative of the population. Estimation procedures and hypotheses tests are the types of inferences that link sample statistics and the corresponding population parameters.

When a Census Is Appropriate

A census is appropriate if the population size itself is quite small. For example, a researcher may be interested in contacting all the firms in the petroleum industry to obtain information on the use of a particular software. A census also is conducted if information is needed from every individual or object in the population. For example, if the researcher is interested in determining the number of foreign students enrolled in a university, it is necessary to get information from all the departments in the university because of possible variations within each department. Further, if the cost of making an incorrect decision is high or if sampling errors are high, then a census may be more appropriate than a sample.

When a Sample Is Appropriate

Sampling may be useful if the population size is large and if both the cost and time associated with obtaining information from the population is high. Further, the opportunity to make a quick decision may be lost if a large population must be surveyed. Also, with sampling, in a given time period, more time can be spent on each interview (personal), thereby increasing the response quality. Additionally, it is easy to manage surveys of smaller samples and still exercise quality control in the interview process.

Sampling may be sufficient in many instances. For example, if a company is interested in obtaining reactions to installing a check-cashing operation within the premises, a sample of employees may be adequate. If the population being dealt with is homogeneous, then sampling is fine. Finally, if taking a census is not possible, then sampling is the only alternative. For example, if a researcher is interested in obtaining consumer response from all over the world to a new advertising theme for Coca-Cola, a census is not possible.

Error in Sampling

Execution of a research project always introduces some error in the study. As stated in Chapter 4, the total error in a research study is the difference between the true value (in the population) of the variable of interest and the observed value (in the sample). The total error in the study has two major components: sampling and nonsampling errors. If the difference in value (error) between the population parameter and the sample statistic is only because of sampling, then the error is known as **sampling error.** If a population is surveyed and error is observed, this error is known as a **nonsampling error.** Nonsampling errors can be observed in both a census and a sample.[1] Some of the common sources of nonsampling errors include measurement error, data-recording error, data analysis error, and nonresponse error. The sources of nonsampling errors are discussed in Chapter 4.

> If the difference in value (error) between the population parameter and the sample statistic is only because of sampling, then the error is known as **sampling error.** If a population is surveyed and error is observed, this error is known as a **nonsampling error.**

Because of their nature, sampling errors can be minimized by increasing the sample size. However, as sample size is increased, the quality control of the research study may become more difficult. Consequently, nonsampling errors can increase (e.g., the number of nonresponses can go up), thereby setting up a classic trade-off between sampling and nonsampling errors. Since nonsampling errors can occur from various sources, it is difficult to identify and control them. Therefore, more attention should be given to reducing them.

◆ SAMPLING PROCESS

When a decision is made to use a sample, a number of factors must be taken into consideration. The various steps involved in the sampling process are given in Figure 11-1. The major activities associated with the sampling process are (1) identifying the target population, (2) determining the sampling frame, (3) resolving the differences, (4) selecting a sampling procedure, (5) determining the relevant sample size, (6) obtaining information from respondents, (7) dealing with the nonresponse public, and (8) generating the information for decision-making purposes.

Determining the Target Population

Sampling is intended to gain information about a population. Thus it is critical at the outset to identify the population properly and accurately. If the population is defined improperly, the research probably will answer the wrong question.

A target population for a toy store can be defined as "all households with children living in Houston." The ambiguities with this definition are many:

- How do you define children? Are they below 10 years, 13 years, or 16 years?
- How do you define Houston? Does it include only the metropolitan area, or are suburbs also included?
- Who in the household is going to provide the information?

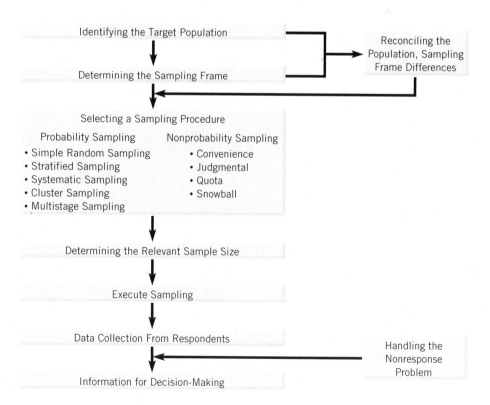

Figure 11-1   The sampling process.

Therefore, the definition of a target population should contain information on sampling elements (children or parent), sampling units (households with children), and area of coverage (Standard Metropolitan Statistical Area [SMSA] or greater Houston).

Devoting effort to identifying the **target population** usually will pay off. The following guidelines should be considered.

Look to the Research Objectives

If the research objectives are well thought out, the target population definition will be clear as well. Recall from Chapter 3 that the research objectives include the research question, the research hypothesis, and a statement of the research boundaries. Each of these elements contributes to refining the definition of the target population.

Consider Alternatives

It is rare to find a study for which there are no alternative, reasonable target population definitions. The task really is to identify and evaluate several of the alternatives instead of simply assuming that the first one mentioned is appropriate. The choice will depend on the research objectives, and the key point is to recognize that alternative definitions exist.

Know Your Market

If the research objective is to learn about the market response to some element of the marketing program, it is necessary to know something about the market. One might hope that some previous research will provide this type of information. Without it, the population definition will have to be unnecessarily broad and, therefore, will lead to an unnecessary increase in research expenses.

Consider the Appropriate Sampling Unit

The target population consists of sampling units. A **sampling unit** may contain people, stores, households, organization transactions, products, or whatever. One task is to specify which sampling unit is appropriate. Should a study of banking activity or of leisure-time activities use individuals or households? The choice will depend on the purpose of the study and perhaps on some judgments about consumer behavior.

Clearly Specify What Is Excluded

The specification of the target population should make clear what is excluded. A study of voting intentions on certain candidates and issues might restrict the sampling population to those of voting age and even to those who intend to vote or to those who voted in the last election.

Don't Overdefine

The population, of course, should be compatible with the study purpose and the research questions; however, the researcher should not arbitrarily overdefine the population. For example, a population of working wives between the ages of 25 and 30, earning more than $15,000, may be artificially restrictive. Such a restrictive population can generate a very costly design, because so many people need to be screened out to obtain the desired sample.

Should Be Reproducible

The population definition should be not so restrictive that it might not be reproducible at a later point in time. For example, if a researcher defines population as "all households living in the Kleine school district as of June 4, 2001," it would be hard to reproduce at a later date because of the time factor in the population definition.

Consider Convenience

When there is a choice, preference should be given to populations that are convenient to sample. Suppose that the population was to include those who are bothered by airplane noise. One population compatible with the research purpose might be those who live within one mile of an airport. This population would be easy and convenient to sample.

Determining the Sampling Frame

The **sampling frame** usually is a list of population members used to obtain a sample.

It is important to distinguish between the population and the sampling frame. The **sampling frame** usually is a list of population members used to obtain a sample. It might be a list of magazine subscribers, retail hardware stores, or college students; even a map can serve as a list.[2] Actually, the description of a sampling frame does not have to enumerate all population members. It may be sufficient to specify the procedure by which each sampling unit can be located. For instance, a member of a probability sample of school children could be obtained by randomly selecting a school district, a school, a classroom, and, finally, a pupil. The probability of picking any given pupil could be determined, even if a physical list were not created that included all students in the population.

Creating Lists

The biggest problem in simple random sampling is obtaining appropriate lists. R. R. Donnelley Company maintains a list drawn from telephone directories and automobile registrations that contains around 88 percent of U.S. households. Such a list can be used to obtain a national sample for a mail survey. Within a community, the local utility company will have a fairly complete list of households.

The problem, of course, is that lists do not exist for specialized populations. A solution for this problem that is usually unsatisfactory is just to use a convenient list. When lists that do not match the population are used, biases are introduced. A list of residents of a given community will not include new arrivals or people living in dwellings built since the list was created. Thus, whole new subdivisions can be omitted. If such omissions are important, it can be worthwhile to identify areas of new construction and design a separate sampling plan for them.

Sometimes several lists are combined in the hope of obtaining a more complete representation of the population. This approach, however, introduces the problem of duplication. Those appearing on several lists will have an increased chance of being selected. Removing duplication can be expensive and must be balanced against the bias that is introduced.

Another problem with lists is simply that of keeping them current. Many industrial firms maintain lists of those who have expressed interest in their products, and these are used in part for the mailing of promotional material. Similarly, many organizations, such as charities, symphony orchestras, and art galleries, have lists of various types, but these lists can become outdated quickly as people move and change jobs within an organization.

Many special populations, such as ethnic and religious groups or high-income households, are not spread evenly across the United States, but are found in a limited number of geographic areas. Therefore, if traditional sampling procedures are employed in such cases, large numbers of contacts in many segments are made that yield no eligible respondents. If these segments (with no special populations) can be determined in advance from Census data or other sources, and can be eliminated from the sample, substantial cost savings are possible. If those segments are not known in advance, it is still possible to make substantial savings by the use of a modified *Waksberg procedure.* This procedure requires that initially a single member be screened (usually by telephone) within a geographic segment. If that member belongs to a special population, additional screenings are conducted in the segment until a predetermined segment size is reached. If that member does not belong to the special population, no additional screenings are made. This eliminates all the segments with no special population, after a single call.

Creating Lists for Telephone Interviewing

As might be expected, telephone directories are used extensively as a basis for generating a sample. The concern with the use of directories is that population members may be omitted because they have changed residences, requested an unlisted number, or simply do not have a telephone.[3]

The incidence of unlisted numbers is extensive and varies dramatically from area to area. The percentage of unlisted phones in the major metropolitan areas ranges from 10.9 percent in West Palm Beach, Florida, to 59.8 percent in Las Vegas, Nevada, according to a study done by Survey Sampling, a firm that provides telephone samples for the market research industry.[4] Table 11-1 lists the 25 metropolitan areas with the highest levels of unlisted numbers. Nationally, 28.5 percent of phones were unlisted in 1996, up from 21.8 percent in 1984 and 10 percent in 1965.

Those with unlisted numbers differ from other telephone subscribers. Demographically, these households tend to be younger, more urban, and less likely to own single-family dwelling units. Households that are unlisted by choice tend to have a higher-than-average income. Households that are unlisted by circumstance tend to be lower-income. Lower-income households own fewer automobiles, are less educated, and tend to be nonwhite.

One way to reach unlisted numbers, dialing numbers randomly, can be very costly, because many of the numbers will be unassigned or will be business numbers.[5] The working phone rate (WPR) of random-digit-dialing (RDD) samples has dropped to a national average of 61.4 percent, according to a recent SSI analysis. Many factors cause the WPR to drop. The main problem is the demand for more telephone numbers for modems, faxes, and second and third lines. New area codes and blocks are introduced to accommodate volume. Because blocks are being completely filled, there are fewer residences in working blocks (the first two digits in the last four digits of a telephone number that has at least one listed number).

Another approach is to buy lists from magazines, credit-card firms, mail-order firms, or other such sources. One problem is that each such list has its own type of biases.

Sometimes it is possible to define the population to match the sampling frame exactly. Usually, however, an exact match is not possible and the task is to consider what portions of the population are excluded by the sampling frame and what biases are therefore created.

Dealing with Population Sampling Frame Differences

When a sampling frame does not coincide with a population definition, three types of problems arise: the **subset problem,** the **superset problem,** and the **intersection**

TABLE 11-1   Top 25 Unlisted Markets (of the top 100 metropolitan areas)

MSA Rank Based on Percent Unlisted Households	MSA Name	Total MSA Households	Percent Households with Phone	Percent Households Estimated Phone Unlisted
1	Sacramento, CA PMSA	563,000	97.6	71.6
2	Oakland, CA PMSA	822,700	98.0	71.4
3	Fresno, CA	284,300	95.8	71.1
4	Los Angeles-Long Beach, CA PMSA	3,023,300	96.7	69.8
5	San Diego, CA	940,100	97.8	68.9
6	San Jose, CA PMSA	540,500	98.8	68.9
7	Orange County, CA PMSA	875,300	98.5	67.0
8	Riverside-San Bernardino, CA PMSA	987,200	96.0	65.5
9	Bakersfield, CA	203,400	94.7	64.8
10	San Francisco, CA PMSA	665,100	98.3	64.4
11	Ventura, CA PMSA	228,000	98.4	63.5
12	Las Vegas, NV-AZ	465,100	96.2	59.8
13	Portland-Vancouver, OR-WA PMSA	668,100	97.2	44.9
14	Tacoma, WA PMSA	239,700	97.1	44.4
15	Honolulu, HI	283,800	98.0	42.6
16	Jersey City, NJ PMSA	205,100	93.3	42.0
17	Tucson, AZ	301,700	94.5	40.1
18	El Paso, TX	205,200	91.9	39.5
19	Seattle-Bellevue-Everett, WA PMSA	880,100	98.2	38.8
20	San Antonio, TX	510,900	93.4	38.4
21	Detroit, MI PMSA	1,607,000	96.6	38.1
22	Phoenix-Mesa, AZ	986,000	94.7	36.8
23	Chicago, IL PMSA	2,774,200	96.1	35.9
24	Miami, FL PMSA	718,600	95.2	33.6
25	Houston, TX PMSA	1,328,900	93.7	33.0

Source: "U.S. Areas with Most Households Not Listed in Telephone Directories, by metropolitan statistical area (MSA)," http://www.worldopinion.com. Copyright Survey Sampling Inc. (1996–2000). PMSA = Primary metropolitan statistical area.

A **subset problem** occurs when the sampling frame is smaller than the population.

problem. A subset problem occurs when the sampling frame is smaller than the population. In other words, some of the elements in the population will not be present in the sampling frame. For example, if a researcher is using the Dun & Bradstreet small business list for contacting all firms with less than 1,000 employees, then a subset problem occurs. The D&B small business list contains names of firms with less than 500 employees. To deal with the subset problem, a researcher may have to redefine the population in terms of sampling frame or get information from other sources to match up with population.

A **superset problem** occurs when the sampling frame is larger than the population but contains all the elements of the population.

A superset problem occurs when the sampling frame is larger than the population but contains all the elements of the population. For example, a researcher may be interested in contacting the buyers of Revlon lipstick. However, if the sampling frame contains a list of buyers of all Revlon cosmetics, then a superset problem occurs. To deal with a superset problem, a researcher may pose a filter question such as "Do you buy Revlon lipsticks?"; if yes, that person will be included in the sample.

An **intersection problem** occurs when some elements of the population are omitted from the sampling frame and when the sampling frame contains more elements than the population.

Finally, the most serious of these types of problems, an intersection problem, occurs when some elements of the population are omitted from the sampling frame, and when the sampling frame contains more elements than the population. Assume a researcher is interested in contacting small business owners with at least $4 million in sales. If the researcher uses the American Business list, which contains all businesses (not strictly small businesses) with more than $5 million in sales, an intersection problem results. To deal with such problems, a researcher may not only have to redefine the population but also may have to pose a better question.

Selecting a Sampling Procedure

There are many ways of obtaining a sample and many decisions associated with generating a sample. A researcher should first choose between using a Bayesian procedure and a traditional sampling procedure. Next, a decision is made to sample with or without replacement. Most marketing research projects employ a traditional sampling method without replacement, because a respondent is not contacted twice to obtain the same information. Among traditional sampling procedures, some are informal or even casual. Passers-by may be queried as to their opinions about a new product. If the response of everyone in the population is uniform—they all either love it or hate it—such an approach may be satisfactory. If you want to determine whether the water in a swimming pool is too cold, it is not necessary to take a random sample; you just have to test the water at any one place, because the temperature will be constant throughout.

In most cases, however, the situation is more complex. There are several questions to be answered and a wide variability in responses. It is then necessary to obtain a representative sample of the population consisting of more than a handful of units. It is possible, even necessary in some cases, to obtain a sample representative of the population just by using judgment and common sense. The preferred approach, however, is to use probability sampling (where some randomization process is used) to obtain a representative sample. In probability sampling, all population members have a known probability of being in the sample. In most probability sampling procedures, a sampling frame is needed and information on objects/sampling units is necessary prior to employing the sampling process.

Probability sampling has several advantages over nonprobability sampling. First, it permits the researcher to demonstrate the sample's representativeness. Second, it allows an explicit statement as to how much variation is introduced, because a sample is used instead of a census of the population. Finally, it makes possible the more explicit identification of possible biases.

In the next two sections, probability sampling will be described first, followed by a description and comparison of nonprobability sampling methods.

◆ PROBABILITY SAMPLING

Probability sampling involves four considerations. First, the target population—the group about which information is being sought—must be specified. Second, the method for selecting the sample needs to be developed. Third, the sample size must be determined. The sample size will depend on the accuracy needs, the variation within the population, and the cost. Finally, the nonresponse problem must be addressed.

Selecting the Probability Sample

Various methods can be used to select a probability sample. The simplest, conceptually, is termed simple random sampling. It not only has practical value, it is a good vehicle for gaining intuitive understanding of the logic and power of random sampling.

Simple Random Sampling

Simple random sampling is an approach in which each population member, and thus each possible sample, has an equal probability of being selected. The implementation is straightforward. Put the name of each person in the population on a tag and place the tags in a large bowl. Mix the contents of the bowl thoroughly and then draw out the desired number for the sample. Such a method, using birth dates, was in fact used to select the order in which men would be drafted for military service during the Vietnam War. Despite the fact that the bowl was well mixed, the early drawings revealed a much higher number of December dates than January dates, indicating that the randomizing process can be more involved than it seems. The apparent reason was that the December tags were put in last, and the mixing was not sufficient to create a random draw. The solution was to randomize the order in which the dates were placed in the bowl.[6]

The use of a table of random numbers usually is much more practical than the use of a large bowl. A **random-number table** is a long list of numbers, each of which is computer generated by randomly selecting a number from 0 to 9. It has the property that knowledge of a string of 10 numbers gives no information about what the eleventh number will be. Suppose that a sample is desired from a list of 5,000 opera season-ticket holders. A random-number table such as that shown in Table 11-2 might provide the following set of numbers:

7659/0783/4710/3749/7741/2960/0016/9347

Using these numbers, a sample of five would be created that would include these ticket holders:

0783/4710/3749/2960/0016

TABLE 11-2   A Set of Random Numbers

55	38	32	99	55	62	70	92	44	32
87	63	93	95	17	81	83	83	04	49
11	59	44	39	58	81	09	62	08	66
82	93	67	50	45	60	33	01	07	98
31	40	45	33	12	36	23	47	11	85
24	38	77	63	99	89	85	29	53	93
57	68	48	78	37	87	06	43	97	48
44	84	11	59	73	56	45	65	99	24
65	60	59	52	06	03	04	79	88	44
98	24	05	10	07	88	81	76	22	71
59	67	80	91	41	63	18	63	13	34
76	59	07	83	47	10	37	49	54	91
77	41	29	60	00	16	93	47	54	91
28	04	61	59	37	31	66	59	97	38

The numbers above 5,000 are disregarded, because there are no season-ticket holders associated with them.

The researcher can start anywhere in the random-number table, as long as the choice is made before looking at the numbers. It is not fair to discard some numbers from the table because "they don't look random" or because they are not "convenient" for some reason or other.

If the original list of season-ticket holders were randomly arranged, a result equivalent to the computer-generated list could be obtained by taking the first ticket holders in the list. However, there is always the danger that the list may have some subtle deviations from random order. Perhaps it was prepared according to the order in which the tickets were purchased; thus, the more interested and organized patrons would be early on the list. The use of random numbers eliminates such concerns.

Accuracy–Cost Trade-off

The trade-off between the cost of employing a probability sampling procedure and the resulting accuracy can best be described by the term **sampling efficiency,** or **efficiency of sampling,** which is defined as the ratio of accuracy over cost. In general, the higher the cost, the higher is the accuracy. The simple random sampling process has some sampling efficiency associated with it. Researchers are always interested in increasing the sampling efficiency, and the various attempts to increase it have resulted in different probability sampling techniques. The feasible ways to increase the sampling efficiency include: (1) holding the accuracy constant and decreasing the cost, (2) holding the cost constant and increasing the accuracy, (3) increasing the accuracy at a faster rate than the rate of cost increase, and (4) decreasing the accuracy at a slower rate than the rate of cost decrease. The subsequent probability sampling procedures are the result of the attempts to increase the sampling efficiency in the previously described ways.

Stratified Sampling

In simple random sampling, a random sample is taken from a list (or sampling frame) representing the population. Often, some information about subgroups within the sample frame can be used to improve the efficiency of sampling. **Stratified**

Reprinted courtesy of Beta Research,
© 1987, 1988 Robert Leighton

sampling improves the sampling efficiency by increasing the accuracy at a faster rate than the cost increase. The rate of increase of both accuracy and cost depends on the variable(s) used to form the groups and the strength of association between the measure of interest (e.g., attitudes) and the variable(s) used to form the groups.

Suppose that information is needed on the attitudes of students toward a proposed new intramural athletic facility. Let us assume that there are three groups of students in the school: off-campus students, dormitory dwellers, and those living in fraternity and sorority houses. Assume, further, that those living in fraternities and sororities have very homogeneous attitudes toward the proposed facility; that is, the variation, or variance, in their attitudes is very low. Suppose also that the dormitory dwellers are less homogeneous and that the off-campus students vary widely in their opinions. In such a situation, instead of allowing the sample to come from all three groups randomly, it will be more sensible to take fewer members from the fraternity/sorority group and draw more from the off-campus group. We would separate the student-body list into the three groups and draw a simple random sample from each of the three groups, resulting in stratified sampling.

The sample size of the three groups will depend on two factors. First, it will depend on the amount of attitude variation in each group. The larger the variation, the larger the sample. Second, the sample size will tend to be inversely proportional to the cost of sampling. The smaller the cost, the larger the sample size that can be justified.

In developing a sample plan, it is wise to look for natural subgroups that will be more homogeneous than the total population. Such subgroups are called *strata.* Thus, there will be more homogeneity within the strata compared to between the strata. In fact, the accuracy of stratified sampling is increased if there are dissimilarities between the groups, and similarities within the groups, with respect to the measure of interest.

The major difference among the different types of stratified sampling processes is in the selection of sample sizes within each group. The different types of stratified sampling are described as follows.

Proportional Stratified Sampling

In this type of sampling procedure the number of objects or sampling units chosen from each group is proportional to the number in the population. **Proportional stratified sampling** can further be classified as **directly proportional** and **inversely proportional stratified sampling.** Examples of both types of proportional stratified sampling are provided here.

Directly Proportional Stratified Sampling. Assume that a researcher is evaluating customer satisfaction for a beverage that is consumed by a total of 600 people. Among the 600 people, 400 are brand-loyal and 200 are variety-seeking. Past research indicates that the level of customer satisfaction is related to consumer characteristics, such as being either brand-loyal or variety-seeking. Therefore, it should be beneficial to divide the total population of 600 consumers into two groups of 400 and 200 each, and randomly sample from within each of the two groups. If a sample size of 60 is desired, then a 10 percent directly proportional stratified sampling is employed.

Consumer type	Group size	10 Percent directly proportional stratified sample size
Brand-loyal	400	40
Variety-seeking	200	20
Total	600	60

Inversely Proportional Stratified Sampling. Assume, now, that among the 600 consumers in the population, 200 are heavy drinkers and 400 are light drinkers. If a researcher values the opinion of the heavy drinkers more than that of the light drinkers, more people will have to be sampled from the heavy drinkers group. In such instances, one can use an inversely proportional stratified sampling. If a sample size of 60 is desired, a 10 percent inversely proportional stratified sampling is employed.

In inversely proportional stratified sampling, the selection probabilities are computed as follows:

Denominator	→	$600/200 + 600/400 = 3 + 1.5 = 4.5$
Heavy drinkers proportional and sample size	→	$3/4.5 = 0.667; 0.667 \times 60 = 40$
Light drinkers proportional and sample size	→	$1.5/4.5 = 0.333; 0.333 \times 60 = 20$

Disproportional Stratified Sampling

In stratified sampling, when the sample size in each group is not proportional to the respective group sizes, it is known as **disproportional stratified sampling.** When multiple groups are compared and their respective group sizes are small, a proportional stratified sampling will not yield a sample size large enough for meaningful comparisons, and disproportional stratified sampling is used. One way of selecting sample sizes within each group is to have equal group sizes in the sample. In the example of heavy and light drinkers, a researcher could select 30 people from each of the two groups.

In general, stratified sampling is employed in many research projects, because it is easy to understand and execute.

Cluster Sampling

In **cluster sampling,** the sampling efficiency is improved by decreasing cost at a faster rate than accuracy. Like stratified sampling, cluster sampling is a two-step process. Unlike stratified sampling, the process of cluster sampling involves dividing the population into subgroups, here termed clusters instead of strata. This time, however, a random sample of subgroups or clusters is selected and all members of the subgroups are interviewed. Even though cluster sampling is very cost effective, it has its limitations. Cluster sampling results in relatively imprecise samples, and it is difficult to form heterogeneous clusters because, for example, households in a block tend to be similar rather than dissimilar.[7]

Cluster sampling is useful when subgroups that are representative of the whole population can be identified.

Suppose a sample of high school sophomores who took an English class is needed in a Midwestern city. There are 200 English classes, each of which contains a fairly representative sample with respect to student opinions on rock groups, the subject of the study. A cluster sample randomly selects a number of classrooms, say 15, and includes all members of those classrooms in the sample. The big advantage of cluster sampling is lower cost. The subgroups or clusters are selected so that the cost of obtaining the desired information within the cluster is much smaller than if a simple random sample were obtained. If the average English class has 30 students, a sample of 450 can be obtained by contacting only 15 classes. If a simple random sample of 450 students across all English classes were obtained, the cost probably would be significantly greater. The big question, of course, is whether the classes are representative of the population. If the classes from upper-income areas have different opinions about rock groups than classes with more lower-income students, then the assumption underlying the approach will not hold. The differences between stratified sampling and cluster sampling are striking. A comparison between the stratified sampling process and the cluster sampling process is given in Table 11-3.

Systematic Sampling

Another approach, termed **systematic sampling,** involves systematically spreading the sample through the list of population members (e.g., telephone directory, small business owners list). Thus, if the population contains 10,000 (= N) people and a sample size of 1,000 (= n) is desired, every tenth (= I, sampling interval) person is selected for the sample. A starting point could be randomly chosen between the first name and the Ith name initially, and then every Ith name is chosen. Although in nearly all practical examples such a procedure will generate a sample equivalent to a simple random sample, the researcher should be aware of regularities in the list. Suppose, for example, that a list of couples in a dance club routinely places the female's name first. Then selecting every tenth name will result in a sample of all males.

In general, the sampling efficiency of systematic sampling is improved by lowering costs while maintaining accuracy relative to simple random sampling. However, the sampling efficiency of systematic sampling depends on the ordering of the list.

If the list of elements in the sampling frame is arranged in a random order (say, alphabetical), then the accuracy of systematic sampling may be equal to that of simple random sampling. If the elements (firms) are arranged in a monotonic order (say, increasing sales revenues), then the accuracy of systematic sampling will exceed that of a simple random sampling, because the sample will be representative (include firms from low to high sales revenues) of the population. Finally, if the elements are arranged in a cyclical order (say, days of the week) and a sampling interval of 7 is selected, then a researcher studying consumer visits to a theater will be collecting data from the same day of the week, resulting in a lower accuracy than simple random sampling.

One situation in which systematic sampling is risky is the sampling of time periods. Suppose the task is to estimate the weekly traffic flow on a certain street. If every twelfth 10-minute period is selected, then the sampling point will be the same each day; and periods of peak travel or low usage easily could be missed.

Figure 11-2 gives an illustration of the various sampling methods.

Multistage Design

It is often appropriate to use a **multistage design** in developing a sample. Perhaps the most common example is in the case of area samples, in which a sample of some area such as the United States or the state of California is desired.

Suppose the need is to sample the state of California. The first step is to develop a cluster sample of counties in the state. Each county has a probability of being in the cluster sample proportionate to its population. Thus, the largest county—Los Angeles

TABLE 11-3   A Comparison of Stratified and Cluster Sampling Processes

Stratified sampling	Cluster sampling
Homogeneity within group	Homogeneity between groups
Heterogeneity between groups	Heterogeneity within groups
All groups are included	Random selection of groups
Sampling efficiency improved by increasing accuracy at a faster rate than cost	Sampling efficiency improved by decreasing cost at a faster rate than accuracy

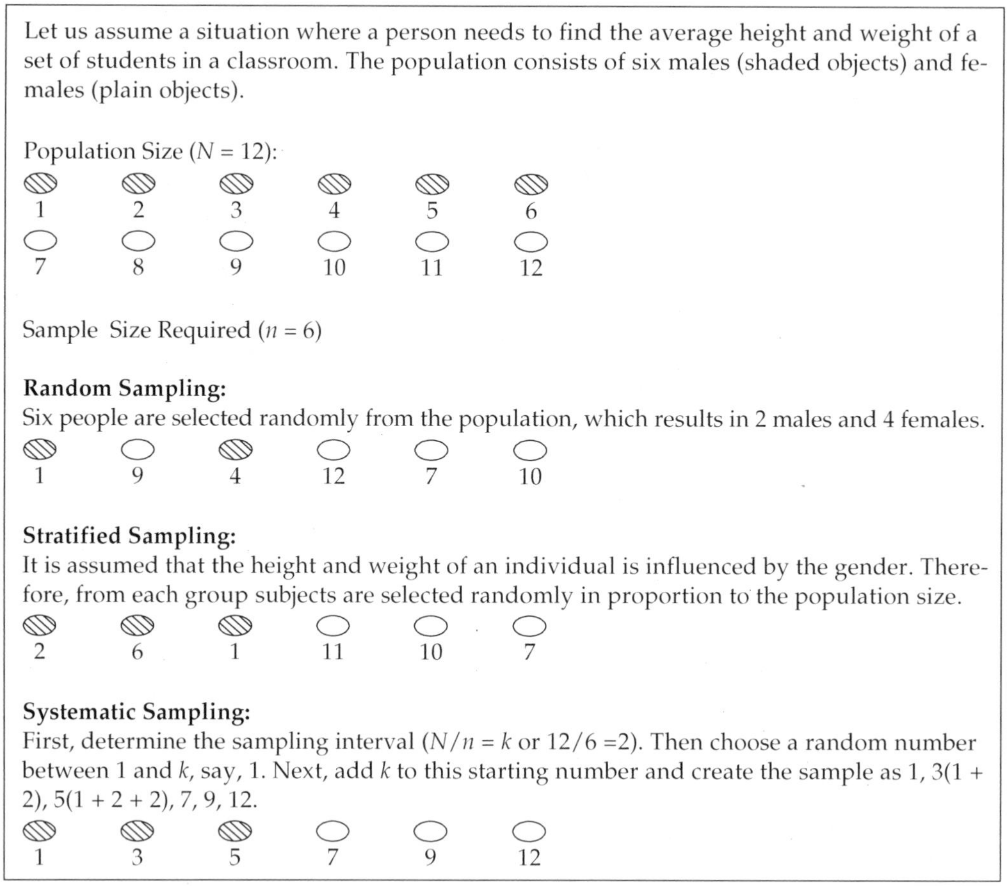

Let us assume a situation where a person needs to find the average height and weight of a set of students in a classroom. The population consists of six males (shaded objects) and females (plain objects).

Population Size ($N = 12$):

Sample Size Required ($n = 6$)

Random Sampling:
Six people are selected randomly from the population, which results in 2 males and 4 females.

Stratified Sampling:
It is assumed that the height and weight of an individual is influenced by the gender. Therefore, from each group subjects are selected randomly in proportion to the population size.

Systematic Sampling:
First, determine the sampling interval ($N/n = k$ or $12/6 = 2$). Then choose a random number between 1 and k, say, 1. Next, add k to this starting number and create the sample as 1, 3(1 + 2), 5(1 + 2 + 2), 7, 9, 12.

Figure 11-2 Illustration of sampling methods.

County—will much more likely be in the sample than a rural county. The second step is to obtain a cluster sample of cities from each county selected. Again, each city is selected with a probability proportionate to its size. The third step is to select a cluster sample of blocks from each city, again weighing each block by the number of dwellings in it. Finally, a systematic sample of dwellings from each block is selected, and a random sample of members of each dwelling is obtained. The result is a random sample of the area, in which each dwelling has an equal chance of being in the sample. Note that individuals living alone will have a greater chance of being in the sample than individuals living in dwellings with other people.

◆ NONPROBABILITY SAMPLING

In probability sampling, the theory of probability allows the researcher to calculate the nature and extent of any biases in the estimate and to determine what variation in the estimate is due to the sampling procedure. It requires a sampling frame—a list of sampling units or a procedure to reach respondents with a known probability. In **nonprobability sampling,** the costs and trouble of developing a sampling frame are eliminated, but so is the precision with which the resulting information can be presented. In fact, the results can contain hidden biases and uncertainties that make them worse

"And don't waste your time canvasssing the whole building,
young man. We think alike."

James Stevenson © 1980 from The *New Yorker Collection.*
All rights reserved/The Cartoon Bank, Inc.

than no information at all. These problems, it should be noted, are not alleviated by increasing the sample size. For this reason, statisticians prefer to avoid nonprobability sampling designs; however, they often are used legitimately and effectively.

Nonprobability sampling typically is used in situations such as (1) the exploratory stages of a research project, (2) pretesting a questionnaire, (3) dealing with a homogeneous population, (4) when a researcher lacks statistical knowledge, and (5) when operational ease is required. It is worthwhile to distinguish among four types of nonprobability sampling procedures: judgmental, snowball, convenience, and quota sampling.

Judgmental Sampling

In judgmental sampling an "expert" uses judgment to identify representative samples. For example, patrons of a shopping center might serve to represent the residents of a city, or several cities might be selected to represent a country.

Judgmental sampling usually is associated with a variety of obvious and not-so-obvious biases. For example, shopping center intercept interviewing can over-sample those who shop frequently, who appear friendly, and who have extra time. Worse, there is no way of really quantifying the resulting bias and uncertainty, because the sampling frame is unknown and the sampling procedure is not well specified.

There are situations where judgmental sampling is useful and even advisable. First, there are times when probability sampling is either not feasible or prohibitively expensive. For example, a list of sidewalk vendors might be impossible to obtain, and a judgmental sample might be appropriate in that case.

Second, if the sample size is to be very small—say, under 10—a judgmental sample usually will be more reliable and representative than a probability sample. Suppose one or two cities of medium size are to be used to represent 200 such cities. Then it would be appropriate to pick judgmentally two cities that appeared to be most representative with respect to such external criteria as demographics, media habits, and shopping characteristics. The process of randomly selecting two cities could very well generate a highly nonrepresentative set. If a focus-group interview of eight or nine people is needed, again, a judgmental sample might be a highly appropriate way to proceed.

Third, sometimes it is useful to obtain a deliberately biased sample. If, for example, a product or service modification is to be evaluated, it might be possible to identify, a group that, by its very nature, should be disposed toward the modification. If it is found that they do not like it, then it can be assumed that the rest of the population will be at least as negative. If they like it, of course, more research probably is required.

Snowball Sampling

Snowball sampling is a form of judgmental sampling that is very appropriate when it is necessary to reach small, specialized populations. Suppose a long-range planning group wants to sample people who are very knowledgeable about a specialized new technology, such as the use of lasers in construction. Even specialized magazines would have a small percentage of readers in this category. Further, the target group may be employed by diverse organizations, such as the government, universities, research organizations, and industrial firms. Under a snowball design, each respondent, after being interviewed, is asked to identify one or more others in the field. The result can be a very useful sample. This design can be used to reach any small population, such as deep-sea divers, people confined to wheelchairs, owners of dunebuggies, families with triplets, and so on. One problem is that those who are socially visible are more likely to be selected.

Convenience Sampling

To obtain information quickly and inexpensively, a **convenience sample** may be employed. The procedure is simply to contact sampling units that are convenient—a church activity group, a classroom of students, women at a shopping center on a particular day, the first 50 recipients of mail questionnaires, or a few friends and neighbors. Such procedures seem indefensible, and, in an absolute sense, they are. The reader should recall, however, that information must be evaluated not "absolutely," but in the context of a decision. If a quick reaction to a preliminary service concept is desired to determine if it is worthwhile to develop it further, a convenience sample may be appropriate. It obviously would be foolish to rely on it in any context where a biased result could have serious economic consequences, unless the biases can be identified. A convenience sample often is used to pretest a questionnaire.

Quota Sampling

Quota sampling is judgmental sampling with the constraint that the sample includes a minimum number from each specified subgroup in the population. Suppose that a 1,000-person sample of a city is desired and it is known how the population of the city is distributed geographically. The interviewers might be asked to obtain 100 interviews on the east side, 300 on the north side, and so on.

Quota sampling often is based on such demographic data as geographic location, age, sex, education, and income. As a result, the researcher knows that the sample "matches" the population with respect to these demographic characteristics. This fact is reassuring and does eliminate some gross biases that could be part of a judgmental sample; however, there are often serious biases that are not controlled by the quota sampling approach. The interviewers will contact those most accessible, at home, with time, with acceptable appearance, and so forth. Biases will result. Of course, a random sample with a 15 to 25 percent or more nonresponse rate will have many of the same biases. Thus, quota sampling and other judgmental approaches, which are faster and cheaper, should not always be discarded as inferior.

In order to meet the quotas, researchers using quota sampling sometimes overlook the problems associated with adhering to the quotas. For example, the researcher may match the marginal frequencies but not the joint frequencies. Assume that an oil company is interested in finding out if women assume responsibility for vehicle maintenance. The company is interested in interviewing women aged below 35 and with age equal to and above 35, as well as working women and nonworking women. Suppose the distribution of the population of women in a city ($N = 1,000$) is as follows:

Population Characteristics

	Less than 35 years	35 years and above	Total	Percentage
Working women	300	200	500	50
Nonworking women	200	300	500	50
Total	500	500	1,000	100

Assume that the researcher is interested in interviewing 100 women from this city and develops a quota system such that 50 percent of the sample should be working women and 50 percent of the sample should also be under 35 years old. A quota matrix can be developed for a sample size of 100.

Sample Characteristics

	Less than 35 years	35 years and above	Total	Percentage
Working women	50	0	50	50
Nonworking women	0	50	50	50
Total	50	50	100	100
Percentage	50	50		

In this illustration, although the marginal frequencies (50 percent and 50 percent) in the sample match those of the population, the joint frequencies (in each cell, 30 percent, 20 percent, 20 percent, 30 percent) do not match. Researchers should take precautions to avoid making such errors when using quota sampling.

◆ SAMPLE SIZE: EFFECT OF SAMPLE SIZE ON SAMPLING DISTRIBUTIONS

Estimating the mean useful life of refrigerators, the mean monthly sales for cellular phones in a big city, and the mean breaking strength of a new plastic are practical problems with something in common. In each, we are interested in making an inference about the **mean,** μ, of some population. Because many practical business problems involve estimating μ, it is particularly important to have a sample statistic that is a good estimator of μ. The mean and standard deviation of the sampling distribution of this useful statistic are related to the mean, μ, and standard deviation, σ, of the sampled population as described next.

Regardless of the shape of the population relative frequency distribution,

1. The mean of the sampling distribution of $\overline{X}$ will equal μ, the mean of the sampled population; i.e., $\mu_{\overline{X}} = \mu$.

2. The standard deviation of the sampling distribution of $\overline{X}$ will equal σ, the standard deviation of the sampled population, divided by the square root of the sample size, n; i.e., and the standard deviation of $\overline{X}$ is inversely to the (square root of the) sample size.

$$\sigma_{\overline{X}} = \frac{\sigma}{\sqrt{n}}$$

The standard deviation $\sigma_{\overline{X}}$ is often referred to as the **standard error of the mean.**

Thus, $\overline{X}$ is an unbiased estimator of the population mean μ (i.e., $E(\overline{X}) = \mu$), and the standard deviation of $\overline{X}$ is inversely proportional to the (square root of the) sample size.

If a random sample of n observations is selected from a population (any population), then, when n is sufficiently large, the sampling distribution of $\overline{X}$ will be approximately a normal distribution. The larger the sample size, n, the better will be the normal approximation to the sampling distribution of $\overline{X}$.

Thus, for sufficiently large samples, the sampling distribution of $\overline{X}$ will be approximately normal. How large must the sample size, n, be so that X has a normal sampling distribution? The answer depends on the shape of the relative frequency distribution of the sampled population.

Generally speaking, the greater the skewness of the distribution of the sampled population, the larger the sample size must be to obtain an adequate normal approximation to the sampling distribution of $\overline{X}$. But for some populations, particularly those with symmetric distributions, n may be fairly small and the sampling distribution of $\overline{X}$ will be approximately normal. Thus, a random sampling process with a larger sample size in general can yield a more accurate estimate ($\overline{X}$) of the mean (μ).

◆ DETERMINING THE SAMPLE SIZE: AD HOC METHODS

The size of a sample can be determined either by using statistical techniques or through some ad hoc methods. Ad hoc methods are used when a person knows from experience what sample size to adopt or when there are some constraints, such as budgetary constraints, that dictate the sample size. This section discusses a few common ad hoc methods for determining sample size.

Rules of Thumb

One approach is to use some rules of thumb. Sudman suggests that the sample should be large enough so that when it is divided into groups, each group will have a minimum sample size of 100 or more.[8]

Suppose that the opinions of citizens regarding municipal parks are desired. In particular, an estimation is to be made of the percentage who felt that tennis courts are needed. Suppose, further, that a comparison is desired among those who (1) use parks frequently, (2) use parks occasionally, and (3) never use parks. Thus, the sample size should be such that each of these groups has at least 100 people. If the frequent park users, the smallest group, are thought to be about 10 percent of the population, then under simple random sampling a sample size of 1,000 would be needed to generate a group of 100 subjects.

In almost every study, a comparison between groups provides useful information and is often the motivating reason for the study. It is therefore necessary to consider the smallest group and to make sure that it is of sufficient size to provide the needed reliability.

In addition to considering comparisons between major groups, the analysis might consider subgroups. For example, there might be an interest in breaking down the group of frequent park users by age, and comparing the usage by teenagers, young adults, middle-aged persons, and senior citizens. Sudman suggests that for such minor breakdowns the minimum sample size in each subgroup should be 20 to 50.[9] The assumption is that less accuracy is needed for the subgroups. Suppose that the smallest subgroup of frequent park users, the senior citizens, is about 1 percent of the population and it is desired to have 20 in each subgroup. Under simple random sampling, a sample size of about 2,000 might be recommended in this case.

If one of the groups or subgroups of the population is a relatively small percentage of the population, then it is sensible to use disproportionate sampling. Suppose that only 10 percent of the population watches educational television, and the opinions of this group are to be compared with those of others in the population. If telephone interviewing is involved, people might be contacted randomly until 100 people who do not watch educational television are identified. The interviewing then would continue, but all respondents would be screened, and only those who watch educational television would be interviewed. The result would be a sample of 200, half of whom watch educational television.

Budget Constraints

Often there is a strict **budget constraint.** A museum director might be able to spare only $500 for a study, and no more. If data analysis will require $100 and a respondent interview is $5, then the maximum affordable sample size is 80. The question then becomes whether a sample size of 80 is worthwhile, or if the study should be changed or simply not conducted.

Comparable Studies

Another approach is to find similar studies and use their sample sizes as a guide. The studies should be *comparable* in terms of the number of groups into which the sample is divided for comparison purposes. They also should have achieved a satisfactory level of reliability.

Table 11-4 which is based on a summary of several hundred studies, provides a very rough idea of typical sample size. Note that the typical sample size tends to be larger for national studies than for regional studies. A possible reason is that national studies generally address issues with more financial impact and therefore require a bit more accuracy. Note, also, that samples involving institutions tend to be smaller

TABLE 11-4   Typical Sample Sizes for Studies of Human and Institutional Populations

Number of Subgroup Analyses	People or Households		Institutions	
	National	Regional or Special	National	Regional or Special
None or few	1,000–1,500	200–500	200–500	50–200
Average	1,500–2,500	500–1,000	500–1,000	200–500
Many	2,500+	1,000+	1,000+	500+

Source: Seymour Sudman, *Applied Sampling* (New York: Academic Press, 1976), p. 87.

than those involving people or households. The reason is probably that institutions are more costly to sample than people.

Factors Determining Sample Size

Sample size really depends on four factors. The first is the number of groups and subgroups within the sample that will be analyzed. The second is the value of the information in the study in general, and the accuracy required of the results in particular. At one extreme, the research need not be conducted if the study is of little importance. The third factor is the cost of the sample. A cost-benefit analysis must be considered. A larger sample size can be justified if sampling costs are low than if sampling costs are high. The final factor is the variability of the population. If all members of the population have identical opinions on an issue, a sample of one is satisfactory. As the variability within the population increases, the sample size also will need to be larger.

◆ POPULATION CHARACTERISTICS/PARAMETERS

Let us assume that we are interested in the attitudes of symphony season-ticket holders toward changing the starting time of weekday performances from 8:00 P.M. to 7:30 P.M. The population comprises the 10,000 symphony season-ticket holders. Their response to the proposal is shown in Figure 11-3. Of these ticket holders, 3,000 respond "definitely yes" (which is coded as +2). Another 2,000 would "prefer yes" (coded as +1), and so on. The needed information is the average, or *mean*, response of the population (the 10,000 season-ticket holders), which is termed μ:

$$\mu = \text{population mean} = 0.3$$

This population mean is one population characteristic of interest. Normally, it is unknown, and our goal is to determine its value as closely as possible, by taking a sample from the population.

Population variance is the degree to which a response differs from the population average response μ. This difference is squared and averaged across responses.

Another population characteristic of interest is the population **variance, σ^2**, and its square root, the population **standard deviation, σ**. The population variance is a measure of the population dispersion, the degree to which the different season-ticket holders differ from one another in terms of their attitude. It is based on the degree to which a response differs from the population average response, μ. This difference is squared (making all values positive) and averaged across all responses.[10] In our example, the population variance is

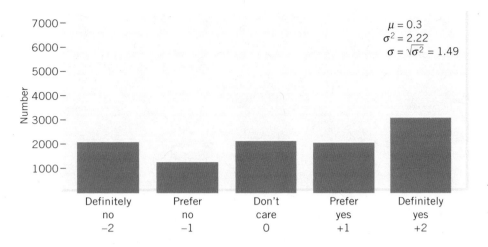

Figure 11-3   The population opinion on symphony starting time (7:30 on weekdays).

$$\sigma^2 = \text{population variance} = 2.22$$

and

$$\sigma = \text{population standard deviation} = 1.49$$

◆ SAMPLE CHARACTERISTICS/STATISTICS

The problem is that the population mean is not known but must be estimated from a sample. Assume that a simple random sample size of 10 is taken from the population. The 10 people selected and their respective attitudes are shown in Figure 11-4.

$$\bar{X} = \frac{1}{10} \sum_{j=1}^{10} X_j = 0.5$$

$$s^2 = \frac{1}{n-1} \sum_{j=1}^{n} (X_j - \bar{X})^2 = \frac{14.50}{9} = 1.61$$

$$s = \sqrt{s^2} = 1.27$$

		Attitude
1.	John T.	$X_1 = +1$
2.	Lois M.	$X_2 = +2$
3.	Steve K.	$X_3 = +2$
4.	Paul A.	$X_4 = 0$
5.	Carol Z.	$X_5 = +1$
6.	Judy D.	$X_6 = +1$
7.	Tom E.	$X_7 = -1$
8.	Sharon P.	$X_8 = +1$
9.	Jan K.	$X_9 = -2$
10.	Ed J.	$X_{10} = 0$

Figure 11-4   A sample of symphony season-ticket holders.

Just as the population has a set of characteristics, each sample also has a set of characteristics. One sample characteristic is the sample average, or mean:

$$\bar{X} = \frac{1}{n}\sum_{j=1}^{n} X_j = 0.5$$

Two means now have been introduced, and it is important to keep them separate. One is the population mean (μ), a population characteristic. The second is the sample mean ($\bar{X}$), a sample characteristic. Because $\bar{X}$ is a sample characteristic, it will change if a new sample is obtained. The sample mean ($\bar{X}$) is used to estimate the unknown population mean (μ).

Another sample characteristic or statistic is the sample variance (s^2), which can be used to estimate the population variance (s^2). Under simple random sampling, the sample variance is

$$s^2 = \text{sample variance} = \frac{1}{n-1}\sum_{j=1}^{n}(X_j - \bar{X})^2 = 1.61$$

Note that s^2 will be small if the sample responses are similar, and large if they are spread out. The corresponding sample standard deviation is simply.[11]

$$S = \text{sample standard deviation} = \sqrt{s^2} = 1.27$$

Again, it is important to make a distinction between the population variance (σ^2) and the sample variance (s^2).

◆ SAMPLE RELIABILITY

Of course, all samples will not generate the same value of $\bar{X}$ (or s). If another simple random sample size of 10 were taken from the population, $\bar{X}$ might be 0.3 or 1.2 or 0.4, or whatever. The point is that $\bar{X}$ will vary from sample to sample. Intuitively, it is reasonable to believe that the variation in $\bar{X}$ will be larger as the variance in the population σ^2 is larger. At one extreme, if there is no variation in the population, there will be no variation in $\bar{X}$. It also is reasonable to believe that as the size of the sample increases, the variation in $\bar{X}$ will decrease. When the sample is small, it takes only one or two extreme scores to substantially affect the sample mean, thus generating a relatively large or small $\bar{X}$. As the sample size increases, these extreme values will have less impact when they do appear, because they will be averaged with more values. The variation in $\bar{X}$ is measured by its standard error,[12] which is

$$\sigma_{\bar{X}} = \text{standard error of } \bar{X} = \sigma_X / \sqrt{n} = 1.49/\sqrt{10} = 0.47$$

($\sigma_{\bar{X}}$ can be written simply as σ). Note that the standard error of $\bar{X}$ depends on n, the sample size. If n is altered, the standard error will change accordingly, as Table 11–5 shows.

◆ SAMPLE SIZE QUESTION

Based on Statistical Theory

Now we are finally ready to use these concepts to help determine sample size. To proceed, the analyst must specify

TABLE 11-5   Increasing Sample Size

Sample Size	σ	$\sigma_{\bar{x}} = \sigma_x/\sqrt{n}$
10	1.49	0.470
40	1.49	0.235
100	1.49	0.149
500	1.49	0.067

1. Size of the sampling error that is desired
2. Confidence level; for example, the 95 percent confidence level

This specification will depend on a trade-off between the value of more accurate information and the cost of an increased sample size. For a given confidence level, a smaller sampling error will "cost" in terms of a larger sample size. Similarly, for a given sampling error, a higher confidence level will "cost" in terms of a larger sample size. These statements will become more tangible in the context of some examples. (See Table 11-5.)

Using the general formula for the interval estimate (recall that s and s_x are the same),

$$\bar{X} \pm \text{sampling error, or } \bar{X} \pm z\sigma_x/\sqrt{n}$$

We know that

$$\text{Sampling error} = z\sigma/\sqrt{n}$$

Dividing through by the sampling error and multiplying by n

$$\sqrt{n} = z\sigma/(\text{sampling error})$$

and squaring both sides, we get an expression for sample size:

$$n = z^2\sigma^2/(\text{sampling error})^2$$

Thus, if we know the required confidence level, and therefore z, and also know the allowed sampling error, then the needed sample size is specified by the formula. Let us assume that we need to have a 95 percent confidence level and that our sampling error in estimating the population mean does not exceed 0.3. In this case, sampling error = 0.3, and, since the confidence level is 95 percent, $z = 2$. In our example from Figure 11-3, the population standard deviation is 1.49, so the sample size should be

$$n = 2^2(1.49)^2/(0.3)^2 = 98.7 \approx 99$$

◆ NONRESPONSE PROBLEMS

The object of sampling is to obtain a body of data that are representative of the population. Unfortunately, some sample members become nonrespondents because they (1) refuse to respond, (2) lack the ability to respond, (3) are not at home, or (4) are inaccessible.

Nonresponse can be a serious problem. It means, of course, that the sample size has to be large enough to allow for nonresponse. If a sample size of 1,000 is needed and only a 50 percent response rate is expected, then 2,000 people will need to be identified as possible sample members. Second, and more serious, is the possibility that those who respond differ from nonrespondents in a meaningful way, thereby creating biases.

The seriousness of **nonresponse bias** depends on the extent of the nonresponse. If the percentage involved is small, the bias is small. Unfortunately, however, as the discussion in Chapter 8 made clear, the percentage can be significant. For example, a review of 182 telephone studies found a refusal rate of 28 percent.[13] Further, this level is likely to increase with the increase in the use of telemarketing, and the problem is generally more severe in home personal interviews and worse in mail surveys, where nonresponse of 90 percent is not uncommon.

The nonresponse problem depends on how the nonrespondents differ from the respondents, particularly on the key questions of interest. The problem is that the very act of being a nonrespondent often implies a meaningful difference. Nonrespondents to in-home interviews tend to be urban dwellers, single or divorced, employed, and from the higher social classes. A comparison of 100 nonrespondents to a telephone interview with 100 respondents revealed that responses were associated with older age, lower income, nonparticipation in the work force, interest in the question, and concern with invasion of privacy.[14] Clearly, the nonresponse problem can be substantial and significant in many studies, although its impact will depend on the context.

What can be done about the nonresponse problem? A natural tendency is to replace each nonrespondent with a "matched" member of the sample. For example, if a home is included in the sample but the resident is not at home, a neighbor may be substituted. The difficulty is that the replacement cannot be matched easily on the characteristic that prompted the nonresponse, such as being employed or being a frequent traveler. Three more defensible approaches are (1) to improve the research design to reduce the number of nonresponses, (2) to repeat the contact one or more times (call-backs) to try to reduce nonresponses, and (3) to attempt to estimate the nonresponse bias.

Estimating the Effects of Nonresponse

One approach is to make an extra effort to interview a subsample of the nonrespondents. In the case of a mail survey, the subsample might be interviewed by telephone. In a telephone or personal survey, an attractive incentive, such as a worth-while gift, might be employed to entice a sample of the nonrespondents to cooperate. Often, only some of the critical questions thought to be sensitive to a nonresponse bias are employed in this stage.

The Politz approach is based on the fact that not-at-homes can be predicted from a knowledge of respondents' frequency of being away from home.[15] The respondents are asked how many evenings they are usually at home (if the interviewing is to be done in the evening). This information serves to categorize them into groups that can serve to represent the not-at-home respondents. For instance, if a respondent usually is at home only one night a week, it might be assumed that there are six more similar ones among the nonrespondents. On any given night, there would be only one chance in seven of finding one home. Thus, on the average, six homes with people with this tendency to be away would have to be contacted to find one person at home. This respondent is therefore assumed to represent six of the non-respondents.

There are uncertainties introduced by this approach, but it does provide a way to proceed, especially when call-backs are costly.

◆ SAMPLING IN THE INTERNATIONAL CONTEXT

Sampling in the international context requires certain special care and is seldom an easy task. The major problems here are the absence of information on sampling frames in other countries, and one of sampling equivalence. The procedure to be followed when sampling for an international research is described briefly.

Selecting the Sampling Frame

In domestic research, in order to determine the sampling frame, one has to first decide on the target population. Once the target population has been determined, the availability of a list of population elements from which the sample may be drawn should be assessed. In the international context, this frequently presents difficulties because of the paucity of information available in other countries. Even when sampling frames such as municipal lists, directories, and telephone books are available, they do not provide adequate coverage, particularly in less developed countries, and hence give rise to frame error.

Another point of difference between sampling in the domestic and international contexts is that sampling in the international context may take place at a number of geographic levels. The most aggregate level is the world, the next being regions such as the Pacific Rim or Europe, following which are the country level units and then the subunits within each country. The level at which the sample is drawn will depend to a large extent on the specific product market, the research objectives, and the availability of lists at each level. Table 11-6 gives a few examples of lists for different levels of the sampling frame.

TABLE 11-6   The Different Levels of Sampling Frames

Levels	Examples of Sampling Lists
World	Compass International
	Kelly's Manufacturer's and Merchant's Directory
	Financial Times, International Business and Company Yearbook
Regions	Latin American Trade Organization
	Directory of Regional Associations
	Regional Yearbooks
Countries	Professional Associations
	Trade Associations
States	State Owned Business List
	Telephone Listing
	Private Corporations List
Cities	Municipal Lists
	Non-Profit Organizations
	City Owned Organizations

Source: V. Kumar, *International Marketing Research* (Englewood Cliffs, NJ: Prentice-Hall, 2000).

Once the sampling frame has been determined, the next step is to determine the specific respondents to be interviewed. The specific respondents in each country have to be identified, as they may vary from country to country. For example, in some cultures (such as the Oriental cultures), parents buy toys without even consulting the children, whereas in some other cultures (Western cultures), the child is the decider. Hence, when conducting research about toys, in some countries the respondent will be adults, whereas in some it will be children.

Sampling Procedure

The next step in the sampling process is to determine the appropriate sampling procedure. In international research, the first decision that has to be taken in this context is whether research has to be conducted in all countries or whether results and findings are generalizable from one country to another. Ideally, it is best if research is conducted in all the countries where marketing operations are planned. Given the high costs of multicountry research, however, there is a trade-off between the number of countries in which the research can be conducted and the cost of the research project. In many cases, findings in one country can be used as a proxy for findings in another. For example, the market response pattern in Denmark will be similar to that in the other Scandinavian countries.

Once the number of countries or other sample units and the sequence in which they are to be investigated have been determined, the next step is selecting the appropriate sampling technique. The most appropriate sampling technique for domestic research is that of random or probabilistic sampling, but this may not always be true in the international context. Random sampling is a good technique only if there are comprehensive lists available of the target population. If such information does not exist, then conducting random sampling will lead to errors in sampling. Hence, probabilistic sampling techniques may not be best for international research.

Researchers facing a paucity of information have two options open to them. Either they can obtain the required information themselves and construct a sampling list from which they can randomly sample, or they can adopt a nonprobability sampling technique. In the international context, nonprobability sampling techniques are used more frequently than probability sampling techniques because of lack of information. Techniques such as convenience sampling, judgmental sampling, and quota sampling are used. One technique that is very popular in international research is the snowball sampling technique. In this technique, the initial respondents are selected at random and additional respondents are selected based on information given by the initial respondents. Two-phase sampling procedures also are frequently employed to reduce costs. In two-phase sampling, the data collection process is done in two stages. In the first phase, data is collected from the customers on certain characteristics such as purchase behavior, demographic variables, and so forth. Based on this information, a sampling frame is developed, and then a second sample is drawn from this frame.

A related issue that a researcher in the international context faces is whether to use the same sampling procedure across countries. Sampling procedures vary in reliability across countries. Therefore, instead of using a single sampling procedure in all the countries, it may be preferable to use different methods or procedures that have equivalent levels of accuracy or reliability. Further, costs of different sampling procedures may also differ from country to country. Hence, cost savings can be achieved by choosing the cheapest method in that country. Cost savings also can be achieved by using the same method in many countries, so that the cost of analysis, coding, and so on may be reduced because of economies of scale. Hence, the researcher has to weigh all these issues and make a decision.

Another important decision facing an international researcher concerns sample size. Given a fixed budget, the researcher has to decide on the number of countries to sample, and also on the number of respondents in each country. To estimate sample sizes statistically, some measure of population variance is required. Since this may not be available, in many instances the researcher determines the sample size on an ad hoc basis.

END OF CHAPTER MATERIAL

SUMMARY

There are two methods by which one can obtain information on the population of interest. Census is the process of obtaining information about the population by contacting every member in the population. Sampling is the process of estimating a population parameter by contacting only a subset of the population. Sampling is adopted because of the limitations of time and money. In some cases a census may not be possible and sampling may be the only alternative.

The first step in the sampling process is to define the target population. The target population has to be defined in such a manner that it contains information on sampling elements, sampling units, and the area of coverage. In order to define the target population, certain simple rules of thumb should be adopted, such as looking to the research objectives, reproducibility, and convenience.

The next step is to determine the sampling frame. The sampling frame is usually a convenient list of population members that is used to obtain a sample. A number of biases will result if the sampling frame is not representative of the population. Hence, care should be taken to choose an appropriate list. There is extensive use of telephone directories as a basis for generating lists, but problems such as changed residences, unlisted numbers, and so forth introduce biases in the sample.

Next, the mechanism for selecting the sample needs to be determined. There are essentially two different methodologies for sample selection. In probability sampling, probability theory is used to determine the appropriate sample. Simple random sampling, cluster sampling, stratified sampling, systematic sampling, and multistage designs are among the various available choices in probability sampling.

Nonprobability sampling methods, such as judgmental sampling, snowball sampling, and quota sampling, are appropriate in the right context, even though they can be biased and lack precise estimates of sampling variation. Shopping center sampling is used widely, in part because it is relatively inexpensive. Biases in shopping center samples can be reduced by adjusting the samples to reflect shopping center characteristics, the location of the shoppers within the shopping center, the time period of the interviewing, and the frequency of shopping.

The fourth consideration in the process is determining the sample size. This chapter examines the various approaches to determining sample size.

The final consideration is nonresponse bias. Nonresponse bias can be reduced by improving the research design to reduce refusals and by using call-backs. Sometimes the best approach is to estimate the amount of bias and adjust the interpretation accordingly.

Sampling in international research poses some special problems. The absence of reliable sampling lists brings a number of biases into the study. Moreover, adopting the same sampling method in different countries may not yield the best results. Even if one adopts the same sampling procedure across all countries, sampling equivalence will not necessarily be achieved.

KEY TERMS

population	cluster sampling
census	systematic sampling
sampling error	multistage design
nonsampling error	nonprobability sampling
target population	judgmental sampling
sampling unit	snowball sampling
sampling frame	convenience sampling
superset problem	quota sampling
subset problem	nonresponse bias
intersection problem	parameter
probability sampling	directly proportional stratified sampling
simple random sampling	inversely proportional stratified sampling
random-number table	standard error of the mean
stratified sampling	budget constraint
proportional stratified sampling	mean
sampling efficiency	variance
disproportional stratified sampling	standard deviation

MARKETING RESEARCH TOOLBOX
REVIEW POINTS

1. A population can be defined as the set of all objects that possess some common set of characteristics with respect to a marketing research problem.

2. If all the respondents in a population are asked to provide information, such a survey is called a census. A census is appropriate if the population size itself is quite small. Sampling may be useful if the population size is large and if both the cost and time associated with obtaining information from the population is high.

3. If the difference in value (error) between the population parameter and the sample statistic is only because of sampling, then the error is known as sampling error. If a population is surveyed and error is observed, this error is known as a nonsampling error.

4. The major activities associated with the sampling process are identifying the target population, determining the sampling frame, resolving the differences, selecting a sampling procedure, determining the relevant sample size, obtaining information from respondents, dealing with the nonresponse public, and generating the information for decision-making purposes.

5. Steps for deciding target population include clear definition of research objectives, consideration of several alternative target populations, and gathering knowledge of market, deciding on the appropriate sampling unit, clearly defining what is excluded. Also, the target population should be reproducible and convenient to access.

6. The sampling frame usually is a list of population members used to obtain a sample.

7. The biggest problem in simple random sampling is obtaining appropriate lists. Lists do not exist for specialized populations. Another problem with lists is keeping them current.

8. Telephone directories are used extensively as a basis for generating a sample. The concern with the use of directories is that population members may be omitted because they have changed residences, requested an unlisted number, or simply do not have a telephone.

9. One way to reach unlisted numbers, dialing numbers randomly, can be very costly, because many of the numbers will be unassigned or will be business numbers. Another approach is to buy lists from magazines, credit-card firms, mail-order firms, or other such sources. One problem is that each such list has its own type of biases.

10. When a sampling frame does not coincide with a population definition, three types of problems arise: the subset problem, the superset problem, and the intersection problem.

11. A subset problem occurs when the sampling frame is smaller than the population. A superset problem occurs when the sampling frame is larger than the population but contains all the elements of the population. An intersection problem occurs when some elements of the population are omitted from the sampling frame, and when the sampling frame contains more elements than the population.

12. Probability sampling has several advantages over nonprobability sampling. First, it permits the researcher to demonstrate the sample's representativeness. Second, it allows an explicit statement as to how much variation is introduced, because a sample is used instead of a census of the population. Finally, it makes possible the more explicit identification of possible biases.

13. Probability sampling involves four considerations. First, the target population—the group about which information is being sought—must be specified. Second, the method for selecting the sample needs to be developed. Third, the sample size must be determined. The sample size will depend on the accuracy needs, the variation within the population, and the cost. Finally, the nonresponse problem must be addressed.

14. Simple random sampling is an approach in which each population member, and thus each possible sample, has an equal probability of being selected.

15. The trade-off between the cost of employing a probability sampling procedure and the resulting accuracy can best be described by the term *sampling efficiency,* or efficiency of sampling, which is defined as the ratio of accuracy over cost. In general, the higher the cost, the higher is the accuracy.

16. In proportional stratified sampling the number of objects or sampling units chosen from each group is proportional to the number in the population.

17. In stratified sampling, when the sample size in each group is not proportional to the respective group sizes, it is known as disproportional stratified sampling.

18. Cluster sampling involves dividing the population into subgroups, here termed clusters. A random sample of subgroups or clusters is selected and all members of the subgroups are interviewed. Cluster sampling is useful when subgroups that are representative of the whole population can be identified.

19. Systematic sampling involves systematically spreading the sample through the list of population members. In general, the sampling efficiency of systematic sampling is improved by lowering costs while maintaining accuracy relative to simple random sampling. However, the sampling efficiency of systematic sampling depends on the ordering of the list.

20. In nonprobability sampling, the costs and trouble of developing a sampling frame are eliminated, but so is the precision with which the resulting information can be presented. In fact, the results can contain hidden biases and uncertainties that make them worse than no information at all.

21. Nonprobability sampling typically is used in situations such as the exploratory stages of a research project, pretesting a questionnaire, dealing with a homogeneous population, when a researcher lacks statistical knowledge, and when operational ease is required.

22. In judgmental sampling an "expert" uses judgment to identify representative samples. There are situations where judgmental sampling is useful and even advisable. First, there are times when probability sampling is either not feasible or prohibitively expensive. Second, if the sample size is to be very samll—say, under 10—a judgmental sample usually will be more reliable and representative than a probability sample. Third, sometimes it is useful to obtain a deliberately biased sample.

23. Snowball sampling is a form of judgmental sampling that is appropriate when it is necessary to reach small, specialized populations. Under a snowball design, each respondent,

after being interviewed, is asked to identify one or more others in the field. The result can be a very useful sample. This design can be used to reach any small population.

24. To obtain information quickly and inexpensively, a convenience sample may be employed. The procedure is simply to contact sampling units that are convenient—a church activity group, a classroom of students, women at a shopping center on a particular day, the first 50 recipients of mail questionnaires, or a few friends and neighbors.

25. Quota sampling is judgmental sampling with the constraint that the sample includes a minimum number from each specified subgroup in the population.

26. The object of sampling is to obtain a body of data that are representative of the population. Unfortunately, some sample members become nonrespondents because they refuse to respond, lack the ability to respond, are not at home, or are inaccessible.

27. Three more defensible approaches to avoid nonresponse are to improve the research design to reduce the number of nonresponses, to repeat the contact one or more times (call-backs) to try to reduce nonresponses, and to attempt to estimate the nonresponse bias.

28. In the international context, sampling frame problems frequently present difficulties because of the paucity of information available in other countries. Even when sampling frames such as municipal lists, directories, and telephone books are available, they do not provide adequate coverage, particularly in less developed countries, and hence give rise to frame error.

29. Given the high costs of multicountry research, however, there is a trade-off between the number of countries in which the research can be conducted and the cost of the research project. In many cases, findings in one country can be used as a proxy for findings in another.

30. Random sampling is a good technique only if there are comprehensive lists available of the target population. If such information does not exist, then conducting random sampling will lead to sampling errors. Hence, probabilistic sampling techniques may not be best for international research.

31. An issue that researchers face in the international context is whether to use the same sampling procedure across countries. Sampling procedures vary in reliability across countries. Therefore, instead of using a single sampling procedure in all the countries, it may be preferable to use different methods or procedures that have equivalent levels of accuracy or reliability.

QUESTIONS AND PROBLEMS

1. A town planning group is concerned about the low usage of a library by its citizens. To determine how the library could increase its patronage, they plan to sample all library-card holders. What do you think would be an effective sampling method given the diversity of the reading population?

2. Assume that you have a list of 80 managers of research and development departments, who are numbered from 1 to 80. Further, you want to talk to a random sample of seven of them. Use the following random numbers to draw a sample of seven. Draw four additional samples. Calculate the average number in each case.

   60311428243730443968059455937559496 7

   763914506080850417657944447441288200

3. A concept for a new microcomputer designed for use in the home is to be tested. Because a demonstration is required, a personal interview is necessary. Thus, it has been decided to bring a product demonstrator into the home. The city of Sacramento has been selected for the test. The metropolitan area map has been divided into a grid of 22,500 squares, 100 of which have been selected randomly. Interviewers have been sent out to call on homes within

the selected square until five interviews are completed. Comment on the design. Would you make any changes? Do you think that this sampling method would be accurate?

4. Discuss the differences between stratified sampling and cluster sampling.

5. Briefly describe the concept of sampling efficiency and discuss the ways in which it could be improved.

6. The sampling efficiency of systematic sampling can be greater than, less than, or equal to single random sampling. Discuss.

7. Identify a situation where you would be in favor of using a nonprobability method over a probability sampling method.

8. Discuss the differences between proportionate and disproportionate stratified sampling.

9. Pete Thames, the general manager of the Winona Wildcats, a minor league baseball team, is concerned about the declining level of attendance at the team's games in the past two seasons. He is unsure whether the decline is due to a national decrease in the popularity of baseball or to factors that are specific to the Wildcats. Having worked in the marketing research department of the team's major league affiliate, the New Jersey Lights, Thames is prepared to conduct a study on the subject. However, because it is a small organization, limited financial resources are available for the project. Fortunately, the Wildcats have a large group of volunteers who can be used to implement the survey. The study's primary objective is to discover the reasons why Winona residents are not attending games. A list of 1,200 names, which includes all attendees for the past two seasons, is available as a mailing list.
    a. What is the target population for this study?
    b. Which kind of sample would provide the most efficient sampling?
    c. Why would this method of sampling be the most efficient in this situation?

10. Jane Walker is the founder and CEO of Sport Style, a sporting goods manufacturing company based in Louisville, Kentucky, that specializes in leather goods. The company currently is under contract as exclusive supplier of Sport Style accessories for one of the leading sporting goods companies. This large multinational company markets the products under its own label as part of its "Made in the USA" promotional campaign. Sport Style has expanded its product line to include golf gloves; premium quality leather grips for tennis, squash, racquetball, and badminton rackets; and sports bags. The contract for exclusive supply will expire within the next year.

    Ms. Walker has recently wondered whether Sport Style specialized products are best served by this method of distribution, and she thinks that her company's sales revenue could be increased drastically if Sport Style were to market its goods under its own label as specialty goods. This would allow the company to eliminate the intermediary and its portion of the selling price. The specialty goods could be offered at the same prices as are currently being asked, but without the intermediary Sport Style would get a larger proportion of the final retail sales price. Ms. Walker has decided to undertake a marketing research study to determine whether a market exists among retail outlets and sporting goods distributors for these specialty items, under the Sport Style brand name.

    a. Define the target population for this study.
    b. Recommend a sampling procedure for this study and support your answer.

11. a. How does the sampling procedure employed in an international environment differ from that used domestically?
    b. What issues are relevant to a researcher's decision to use the same sampling procedure across countries?

12. When selling to a developing country such as India, what do you think are some of the shortcomings? Especially in a market where the income levels and corresponding buyer levels are extremely polarized, what are the steps that you would take in sampling in an international market?

ENDNOTES

1. Assael and J. Keon, "Non Sampling Vs. Sampling Errors in Sampling Research," *Journal of Marketing* (Spring 1982), pp. 114–123.

2. Edward Blair, "Sampling Issues in Trade Area Maps Drawn from Shopper Surveys," *Journal of Marketing*, 47 (Winter 1983), pp. 98–106.

3. For a comparison of directory-based sampling with other methods of sampling, see R. Czaja, J. Blair, and J. P. Sebestik, "Respondent Selection in a Telephone Survey: A Comparison of Three Techniques," *Journal of Marketing Research* (August 1982), pp. 381–85.

4. "U.S. Areas with Most Households Not Listed in Telephone Directories (by metropolitan statistical area (MSA))," http://www.worldopinion.com/reference.taf?f=refi&id=1253(October 2000).

5. Clyde L. Rich, "Is Random Digit Dialing Really Necessary?" *Journal of Marketing Research*, 14 (August 1977), pp. 301–304.

6. S. Sudman, *Applied Sampling* (New York: Academic Press, 1976), p. 50.

7. Geographic clustering of rare populations, however, can be an advantage. See Seymour Sudman, "Efficient Screening Methods for the Sampling of Geographically Clustered Special Populations," *Journal of Marketing Research*, 22 (February 1985), pp. 20–29.

8. Sudman, *Applied Sampling*.

9. Ibid., p. 30.

10. Here follows one method for calculating the population mean and variance. Note the responses are weighted by the response frequency (f). Thus, the response + 1 is weighted by 0.20, because it occurs 0.20 of the time in the population. For further discussion, see any introductory statistics book.

11. The term $n - 1$ appears in the expression for the sample variance so that s^2 will be an unbiased estimate of the population variance. The reader need not be concerned about this fact; it has little practical significance. If the population size, termed N, is small relative to the sample size, n, a "finite population correction factor" of $N - n/N - 1$ should be added. Thus, if N is 1,000 and n is 100, the correction factor would be 0.9. If N is more than 10 times the sample size, the correction factor is rarely significant.

12. We also could use the term *population standard error* of x. The word "population" is omitted in this context to make the discussion less cumbersome.

13. Frederick Wiseman and Philip McDonald, *The Nonresponse Problem in Consumer Telephone Surveys* (Cambridge, MA: Marketing Science Institute, 1978).

14. Jolene M. Struebbe, Jerome B. Kernan, and Thomas J. Grogan, "The Refusal Problem in Telephone Surveys," *Journal of Advertising Research* (June/July 1986), pp. 29–37.

15. Alfred N. Politz and Willard R. Simmons, "An Attempt to Get 'Not-At-Homes' into the Sample Without Callbacks," *Journal of the American Statistical Association*, 44 (March 1949), pp. 9–31, and 45 (March 1950), pp. 136–37.

Determining Sample Statistics

Changing the Confidence Level

If the confidence level is changed from 95 percent to 90 percent, the sample size can be reduced, because we do not have to be as certain of the resulting estimate. The z term is then 5/3 and the sample size is

$$n = (z\sigma)^2/(\text{sampling error})^2 = (5/3)^2 \, (1.49)^2/(0.3)^2 = 68.5 \approx 69$$

Changing the Allowed Error

If the allowed error is increased, the sample size will also decrease, even if a 95 percent confidence level is retained. In our example, if the allowed error is increased to 0.5, then the sample size is

$$n = (z\sigma)^2/(\text{sampling error})^2 = 4(1.49)^2/(0.5)^2 = 35.5 \approx 36$$

Population Size

It should be noted that the sample size calculation is independent of the size of the population. A common misconception is that a "good" sample should include a relatively high percentage of the sampling frame. Actually, the size of the sample will be determined in the same manner, whether the population is 1,000 or 1,000,000. There should be no concern that the sample contain a reasonable percentage of the population. Of course, if the population is small, the sample size can be reduced.[16] Obviously, the sample size should not exceed the population.

Determining the Population Standard Deviation

The procedure just displayed assumes that the population standard deviation is known. In most practical situations it is not known, and it must be estimated by using one of several available approaches.

One method is to use a sample standard deviation obtained from a previous comparable survey or from a pilot survey. Another approach is to estimate s subjectively. Suppose the task is to estimate the income of a community. It might be possible to say that 95 percent of the people will have a monthly income of between $4,000 and $20,000. Assuming a normal distribution, there will be four population standard deviations between the two figures, so that one population standard deviation will be equal to $4,000.

Another approach is to take a "worst-case" situation. In our example, the largest population variance would occur if half the population would respond with a +2 and the other half with a –2. The population variance would then be 4, and the recommended sample size, at a 95 percent confidence level and a 0.3 allowable error, would be 178. Note that the sample size would be larger than desired, and thus the desired accuracy would be exceeded. The logic is that it is acceptable to err on the side of being too accurate.

◆ PROPORTIONS

When proportions are to be estimated (the proportion of people with negative feelings about a change in the symphony's starting time, for example), the procedure is to use the sample proportion to estimate the unknown population proportion, π. Because this estimate is based on a sample, it has a population variance, namely,

$$\sigma^2_p = \pi(1 - \pi)/n$$

where

π = population proportion

p = sample proportion (corresponding to X), used to estimate the unknown

σ^2_p = population variance of p

The formula for sample size is then

$$n = z^2 \, \pi(1 - \pi)/(\text{sampling error})^2$$

As figure 11-5 shows, the worst case (where the population variance is at its maximum) occurs when the population proportion is equal to 0.50:

$$\pi(1 - \pi) = 0.25$$
$$\pi = 0.50$$

Because the population proportion is unknown, a common procedure is to assume the worst case. The formula for sample size then simplifies to

$$n = z^2 \, (0.25)/(\text{sampling error})^2$$

Thus, if the population proportion is to be estimated within an error of 0.05 (or 5 percentage points) at a 95 percent confidence level, the needed sample size is

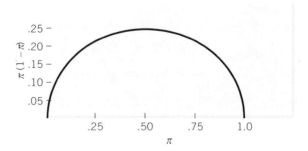

Figure 11–5 A Graph of $\pi(1-\pi)$.

In general,

Sample size = $n = z^2\sigma^2/(\text{sampling error})^2$

where

$z = 2$ for a 95 percent confidence level

$z = 5/3$ for a 90 percent confidence level

σ = population standard deviation

and

sampling error = allowed sampling error

For proportions,

Sample size = $n = z^2(0.25) \div (\text{sampling error})^2$

Figure 11–6 Some useful sample size formulas.

$$n = 2^2 (0.25)/(0.05)^2 = 400$$

since z equals 2, corresponding to a 95 percent confidence level, and the allowed sampling error equals 0.05. Figure 11-6 summarizes the two sample size formulas.

Sampling error (also known as *accuracy* or *precision error*) can be defined in relative rather than absolute terms. In other words, a researcher might require that the sample estimate be within plus or minus G percentage points of the population value. Therefore,

$$D = G\mu$$

The sample size formula may be written as

$$n = \sigma^2 z^2/(\text{sampling error})^2$$
$$= \sigma^2 z^2/D^2$$
$$= c^2 z^2/G^2$$

where

$c = (\sigma/\mu)$

which is known as the *coefficient of variation.*

If a researcher has information on the coeffecient of variation, the required confidence level, and the desired precision accuracy level, then the estimation of sample size can be readily obtained from the chart in Exhibit 11-1. One has to locate a number corresponding to the desired information level and read the sample size. For example, if $c = 0.30$, the confidence level = 95 percent and the desired precision = 0.034, then the required sample size, n, is equal to 300.

Several Questions

A survey instrument or an experiment usually will not be based on just one question. Sometimes hundreds can be involved. It usually will not be worthwhile to go through such a process for all questions. A reasonable approach is to pick a few representative questions and determine the sample size from them. The most crucial ones with the highest expected variance should be included.

EXHIBIT 11-1

Calculation of Sample Size

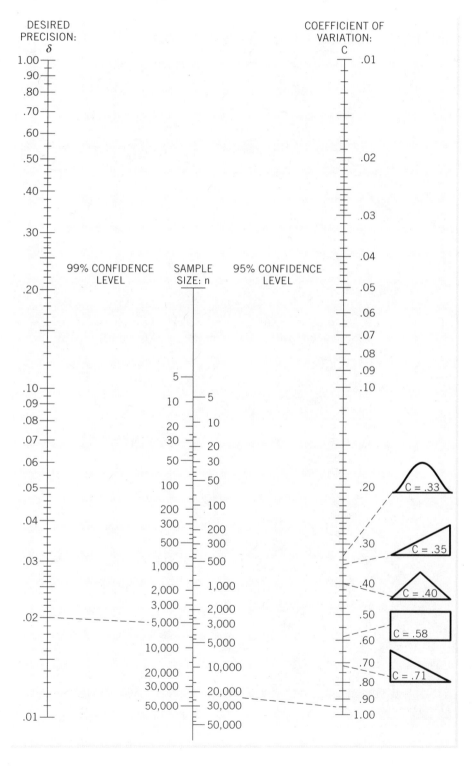

Shopping Center Sampling

Shopping center studies in which shoppers are intercepted present some difficult sampling problems. As noted in Chapter 9, well over 20 percent of all questionnaires completed or interviews granted were store-intercept interviews.[17] One limitation with shopping center surveys is the bias introduced by the methods used to select the sample. In particular, biases that are potentially damaging to a study can be caused by the selection of the shopping center, the part of the shopping center from which the respondents are drawn, the time of day, and the fact that more frequent shoppers will be more likely to be selected. Sudman suggests approaches to minimize these problems and, in doing so, clarifies the nature of these biases.[18]

Shopping Center Selection

A shopping center sample usually will reflect primarily those families who live in the area. Obviously, there can be great differences between people living in a low-income neighborhood and those in a high-income, professional neighborhood. It is usually good policy to use several shopping centers in different neighborhoods, so that differences between them can be observed. Another concern is how representative are the cities used. When possible, several diverse cities should be used.

Sample Locations within a Center

The goal usually is to obtain a random sample of shopping center visits. Because of traffic routes and parking, one entrance may draw from very different neighborhoods than another. A solution is to stratify by entrance location and to take a separate sample from each entrance. To obtain an overall average, the resulting strata averages need to be combined by weighting them to reflect the relative traffic that is associated with each entrance.

Suppose that a survey is employed to determine the average purchase during a shopping trip. Assume that there are two shopping mall entrances. Entrance A, which draws from a working-class neighborhood, averages 200 shoppers per hour; while entrance B, which draws from a professional suburb, averages 100 shoppers per hour. Thus, 67 percent of shoppers use entrance A and 33 percent of shoppers use entrance B. Assume further that the entrance A shoppers spend $60 on the average, while the entrance B shoppers average $36. These statistics are tabulated as follows.

The estimate of the average dollar amount of the purchase made by a shopping center visitor is the entrance A average purchase plus the entrance B average purchase, weighted by the proportion of shoppers represented, or

$$(0.67 * 60) + (0.33 * 36) = \$52$$

Sometimes it is necessary to sample within a shopping center, because the entrances are inappropriate places to intercept respondents. The location used to intercept shoppers can affect the sample. A cluster of exclusive women's stores will attract a very different shopper than the Sears store at the other end of the mall. A solution is to select several "representative" locations, determine from traffic counts about how many shoppers pass by each location, and then weight the results accordingly.

A major problem is that refusals can increase if respondents are asked to walk a specific distance to an interviewing facility. The cost of increasing nonresponse may outweigh any increase in the sample's representativeness.

Time Sampling

Another issue is the time period. For example, people who work usually shop during the evening, on weekends, or during lunch hours. Thus, it is reasonable to stratify by time segments—such as weekdays, weekday evenings, and weekends—and interview during each segment. Again, traffic counts can provide estimates of the proportion of shoppers that will be in each stratum, so the final results can be weighted appropriately.

Sampling People versus Shopping Visits

Obviously, some people shop more frequently than others and will be more likely to be selected in a shopping center sample. If the interest is in sampling shopping center visits, then it is appropriate to oversample those who shop more. If the goal is to develop a sample that represents the total population, however, it becomes important to adjust the sample so that it reflects the infrequent as well as the frequent shoppers.

One approach is to ask respondents how many times they visited the shopping center during a specified time period, such as the last four weeks. Those whose current visit was the only one during the time period would receive a weight of 1. Those who visited two times would have a weight of 1/2; those who visited three times would have a weight of 1/3; and so on.

One industry researcher measured the effect of weighting results by the frequency of visiting a shopping center on the analysis of four commercial studies.[19] He found that the weighting procedure did not affect either the demographic profiles or the values of the key questions in each study. He concluded that a frequent-shopper bias should be a problem warranting the use of a weighting procedure only where there is some reason to suspect that the bias will affect a key question. For example, if a test of a Sears commercial is conducted in a mall with a Sears store, there could be a problem.

Another approach is to use quotas, which serve to reduce the biases to levels that may be acceptable. One obvious factor to control is respondents' sex, since women shop more than men. The interviewers can be instructed simply to sample an equal proportion of men and women. Another factor to control is age, as those aged 25 to 45 tend to make more visits to shopping centers than do either younger or older shoppers.[20] Still another is employment status, as unemployed people spend more time shopping than do those who are employed.[21] The quotas would be set up so that the number sampled is proportional to the number of the population. If 55 percent of the people are employed, then the quota should ensure that 55 percent of the sample is employed.

ENDNOTES

16. When sampling with relatively small populations, the standard error of x is

$$(\sigma/\sqrt{n}) \sqrt{\frac{N-n}{N-1}}$$

   where N is the size of the population. If the sample size is a meaningful percentage of N (such as 30 to 50 percent), then it might be worthwhile to reduce the sample size.

17. "Shoppers Grant 91 Million Interviews Yearly," *Survey Sampling Frame* (Spring 1978), p. 1.

18. Seymour Sudman, "Improving the Quality of Shopping Center Sampling," *Journal of Marketing Research,* 17 (November 1980), pp. 423–431.

19. Thomas D. DuPont, "Do Frequent Shoppers Distort Mall-Intercept Results?," *Journal of Advertising Research* (August/September 1987), pp. 45–51.

20. Seymour Sudman, "Improving the Quality of Shoping Center Sampling," p. 430.

21. Ibid.

CASES

For a detailed description of the below cases please visit www.wiley.com/college/kumar.

   Case 11.1: Exercises in Sample Design
   Case 11.2: Talbot Razor Products Company

CASES AND PRACTICAL EXERCISES FOR PART II

CASE STUDY

II-1

Pacific Gas & Electric (A)[1]

Pacific Gas & Electric (PG&E) was interested in determining what could be done to encourage the installation of solar water heaters. As a first step it was decided that some exploratory marketing research should be conducted. As a result, a research proposal for a telephone survey to determine homeowners' knowledge, attitudes, and intentions toward solar water heaters was on the desk of John Glenning, a marketing research analyst of PG&E. John needed to decide whether the methodology, including the sampling plan and the questionnaire, was sound. He further needed to decide whether a telephone interview was the appropriate research approach. Focus-group interviews had been very helpful in developing a home insulation program several years earlier, and he thought that a real alternative was to commission several focus groups.

Solar Water Heaters

Solar water heaters have been in use for a long time. In fact, they were very popular in Florida during the early 1930s. They are extremely simple, as Exhibit II-1 illustrates. Cold water is pumped onto the roof of a

EXHIBIT II-1

Solar Hot-Water Heating System

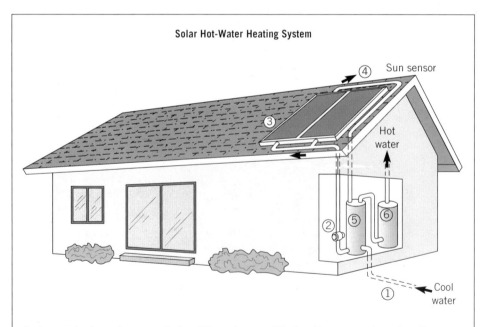

Cool water is drawn from supply line (1), and pump (2) circulates water through collector panels (3). Hot water leaving panels (4) is transferred to storage tank (5). Preheated water circulates to backup heater (6) for additional heating, if necessary, before distribution through hot-water outlets

CASES AND PRACTICAL EXERCISES FOR PART II (*continued*)

house, where it circulates through "collector panels" that are heated by the sun. Hot water then returns to a storage tank. A conventional gas or electric water heater will raise the water temperature, if necessary, on cloudy days. The water heater application of solar energy is attractive because solar water heaters are much more economical than solar space (house) heaters and because the market potential for solar swimming-pool heaters is limited.

The rate of return that a homeowner can expect from the installation of a solar water heater will depend on a set of assumptions about how the unit is financed and what energy source it will replace. Generally, the investment is unattractive if gas currently is used, but it can be attractive if water is now heated with electricity. If a utility were to install and lease units to homeowners, the investment's attractiveness might improve, since the payments could be stretched out and since the utility probably would have lower installment costs than a conventional dealer. One possibility to be explored is whether PG&E should be involved in leasing and installing solar water heaters.

PG&E's Solar Program

PG&E's solar program, budgeted at over half a million dollars, had two primary objectives. The first was to gather and analyze information on available solar energy systems' cost-effectiveness, dependability, and acceptability to PG&E customers. The second was to inform customers of the information obtained.

Projects undertaken toward these objectives included solar demonstration homes, monitoring of other solar installations, product testing, and customer information programs. Three demonstration solar houses were built, and five more were planned. A part of PG&E advertising had been devoted to solar applications. An energy conservation trailer was displayed at fairs and shopping centers. Over 90,000 copies of a booklet entitled *Sun Energy* were distributed.

Two approaches toward encouraging homeowner installation of solar water heaters had been proposed. The first, now under active consideration by PG&E, was the use of advertising and other customer information programs to communicate information regarding solar water heaters and to get homeowners to consider installing them. One purpose of the proposed research was thus to determine who should be the target audience, what their characteristics and their information needs were, and what appeals would be most effective. The second approach was to involve PG&E

in the solar heating business. This involvement could take a variety of forms. One possibilty was to develop a pilot program in which PG&E would install and lease solar water heaters to homeowners. Another purpose of the research was to evaluate the practicality of such a pilot program. At the time, the only known solar leasing program was operated by the Municipal Utility of Santa Clara, which installed plastic solar swimming-pool heaters for a $200 installation fee and a monthly fee payable during the six-month swimming season.

Research Objectives

Several specific types of research information were desired. First, a knowledge of homeowners' awareness, attitudes, and intentions concerning residential applications of solar energy, particularly water heaters, was needed to determine appropriate objectives of customer information programs. Second, knowing what information was desired by consumers and from what sources would guide customer information programs. Third, an estimate of the effect on intentions of alternative financing methods in general and a PG&E leasing program in particular had to be developed. Fourth, descriptions of the different customer groups on the basis of awareness, knowledge, attitudes, and intentions were required.

Several specific hypotheses were developed, based in part on some marketing research conducted by the San Diego Gas and Electric Company. The hypotheses were intended to make the issues represented by the research questions more specific and to summarize current thinking about customers' positions toward solar energy.

1. Interest in and general awareness of solar energy is high, but knowledge of specific applications, including solar water heaters, is rather low.
2. Solar energy is regarded as expensive and not yet fully perfected.
3. Attractions of solar energy include saving money, conserving energy, helping the environment, and being innovative. Cost payback is a very important consideration in any solar energy decision.
4. Utilities are generally perceived as reliable sources of information and equipment.
5. Solar leasing by utilities will be attractive to one segment because less investment is required and because a utility company would be trusted to assure performance. Another segment will be

opposed to utility involvement with solar programs.

6. There should be a positive association between knowledge and intention, because information should influence intentions and because interested people seek out information.

7. People interested in installing solar water heaters tend to be young, affluent, well-educated, concerned about energy, "handy" people who enjoy trying new things, and owners or friends of owners of swimming pools.

These hypotheses, together with other opinions, served as the basis for a tentative model of the decision process associated with solar water heaters. This model is shown in Exhibit II-2.

Methodology

The research approach was a telephone interview of a sample of 200 homeowners in the San Francisco Bay Area. The questionnaire is shown in the next section. A telephone survey was selected because it is relatively free of bias and is economical and fast.

The target population for the survey was all PG&E customers in the San Francisco Bay Area who own their own detached homes. The sample was obtained from the telephone directories of the six Bay Area counties. Thus, there were to be 70 respondents in the largest county and 14 in the smallest. Within each county a sample was drawn by systematically sampling from the telephone directory. If a telephone interviewer needed 25 respondents and the directory allocated to her or him contained 250 pages, then one respondent would be obtained from every tenth page. On each selected page the interviewer would measure a fixed amount, such as 3 inches from the top of the first column. The interviewer would then begin calling people starting at that point and continue until a completed interview was obtained.

EXHIBIT II-2

Hypothesized Model

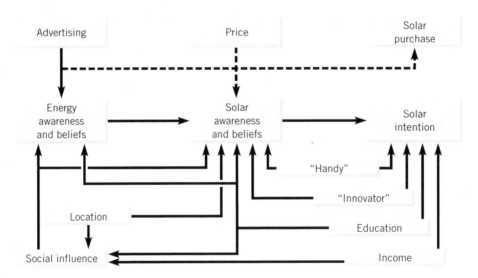

Telephone Interview Format

Responder: No. _____ (1–3)
City _____ (4)

SOLAR ENERGY SURVEY

Hello, I'm _____ from Drexel Research Corporation, a national consumer research firm. We're taking a survey in your area about home energy use and would like to ask you a few questions. May I please speak to the head of the household? *(IF THE HEAD OF THE HOUSEHOLD IS NOT AVAILABLE, THANK THE PERSON ON THE PHONE AND TERMINATE THE INTERVIEW. IF THE HEAD OF THE HOUSEHOLD IS REACHED, REINTRODUCE YOURSELF AND PROCEED.)*

1. Do you own or rent the home in which you live?

Own _____ (CONTINUE) _____ ☐
Rent _____ (TERMINATE)

1a. Is that home a single family dwelling?

Yes _____ (CONTINUE) _____ ☐
No _____ (TERMINATE)

2. I'm going to read you a few statements about energy conservation and for each one I'd like you to tell me whether you agree or disagree with it. (READ STATEMENTS BELOW)

(FOR EACH STATEMENT "AGREE" WITH, ASK:) Do you agree completely or somewhat?
(FOR EACH STATEMENT "DISAGREE" WITH, ASK:) Do you disagree somewhat or completely?

	AGREE		DISAGREE		
	Completely	Somewhat	Somewhat	Completely	
a. It is important for the United States to have an energy conservation program.	_____ 1	_____ 2	_____ 3	_____ 4	(6)
b. What an individual consumer does or does *not* do to save energy has a meaningful effect on the energy shortage.	_____ 1	_____ 2	_____ 3	_____ 4	(7)
c. New supplies of natural gas will be discovered before any serious shortages develop.	_____ 1	_____ 2	_____ 3	_____ 4	(8)

3. I'd like to know how well the following statements describe you. Please tell me whether you agree completely, agree somewhat, disagree somewhat, or disagree completely with … (READ LIST)

	Agree Completely	Agree Somewhat	Disagree Somewhat	Disagree Completely	
I generally like to try new ideas at work and in my life.	_____ 1	_____ 2	_____ 3	_____ 4	(9)
I like to experiment with new ways of doing things.	_____ 1	_____ 2	_____ 3	_____ 4	(10)
I like to build things for my house.	_____ 1	_____ 2	_____ 3	_____ 4	(11)
I like to fix things around the house.	_____ 1	_____ 2	_____ 3	_____ 4	(12)
I wait for new things to be proven before trying them.	_____ 1	_____ 2	_____ 3	_____ 4	(13)

CASES AND PRACTICAL EXERCISES FOR PART II (continued)

4. Now I'd like to talk about solar energy. Please tell me all the ways that you can think of that solar energy can be used in the home. (PROBE and CLARIFY)

_____ (14)

_____ (15)

_____ (16)

_____ (17)

5a. Have you seen any advertisements or brochures about solar energy devices recently?

Yes _____ (CONTINUE) _____ 1   (18)

No _____ (SKIP TO Q. 5c) _____ 2

5b. Whom was the advertisement or brochure from?

_____ (19)

_____

5c. Have you read any articles about solar energy recently in magazines or newspapers?

Yes _____ 1   (20)

No _____ 2

6a. Have you seen any displays of solar ?

Yes _____ (CONTINUE) _____ 1   (21)

No _____ (SKIP TO Q. 7a) _____ 2

6b. Where did you see this display?

_____ (22)

7a. Have you ever seen a solar heating unit on a house or building?

Yes _____ (CONTINUE) _____ 1   (23)

No _____ (SKIP TO Q. 8) _____ 2

7b. Where was that?

_____ (24)

_____

8. Have you ever discussed solar energy with your friends?

Yes _____ 1   (25)

No _____ 2

9a. Have you ever considered buying a solar water heater for your home?

Yes _____ (CONTINUE) _____ 1   (26)

No _____ (SKIP TO Q. 10) _____ 2

9b. What kind was that? (PROBE AND CLARIFY)

_____ (27)

_____

_____ (28)

10a. What would be the main _advantage_ of having a solar water heater in your home? (PROBE) What other advantages?

_____ (29)

_____

_____ (30)

CASES AND PRACTICAL EXERCISES FOR PART II *(continued)*

10b. And what would be the main *disadvantage* of having a solar water heater? (PROBE)
What other disadvantages?

_____ (31)

_____
_____ (32)

11a. About how much would you estimate your average monthly utility bill is for gas and electricity?

$ _____ (33)

11b. About how much per month do you think you might save on your gas and electricity bill if you had a
solar water heater?

$ _____ (34)

12a. As you may know, water in a solar water heater is pumped through solar collector panels and the roof and
stored in a tank. This water is then heated additionally by the existing water heater if it isn't hot enough—
say on a cloudy day. A solar water heater costs about $1500 installed, and can save $4 to $5 per month on
your gas bill. How interested do you think you might be in buying and installing a solar water heater in
your home? Would you say you would be … (READ LIST)

Definitely interested in buying one _____ (CONTINUE) _____ 1 (35)
Somewhat interested in buying one _____ (SKIP TO Q. 13a) _____ 2
Not at all interested in buying one _____ (SKIP TO Q. 13a) _____ 3

12b. If you did purchase a solar water heater, would you pay cash for it or finance it?

Pay cash _____ 1 (36)
Finance _____ 2

13a. Have you heard that you can deduct 10 percent of the cost of any solar equipment you buy from your
state income tax?

Yes _____ 1 (37)
No _____ 2

13b. Would this tax deduction make you more likely to buy a solar water heater, less likely to buy one, or
wouldn't make any difference one way or the other?

More likely _____ 1 (38)
Less likely _____ 2
No difference _____ 3

14a. If you could lease a water heater for a lower monthly charge than a loan payment, would you rather lease
one than buy one?

Yes _____ (CONTINUE) _____ 1 (39)

No _____ | SKIP TO | _____ 2
No difference _____ | Q. 15a | _____ 3

14b. Who would you prefer to lease a solar water heater from … (READ LIST)

Utility company _____ (ASK Q. 14c, THEN SKIP TO Q. 15a) 1 (40)

Government _____ | SKIP TO | _____ 2
Some other company _____ | Q. 14d | _____ 3

CASES AND PRACTICAL EXERCISES FOR PART II (*continued*)

14c. Why would you prefer to lease from a utility company? (PROBE AND CLARIFY)

_____ (41)

_____

_____ (42)

14d. Why wouldn't you want to lease it from a utility company? (PROBE AND CLARIFY)

_____ (43)

_____

_____ (44)

15a. What information would you need to have before deciding on buying a solar water heater? (PROBE AND CLARIFY)

_____ (45)

_____

_____ (46)

15b. Which of the following would you consider to be the most reliable source of information on solar water heaters ... (READ LIST)

Solar heater company _____ 1   (47)
Government _____ 2
Utility company _____ 3

16a. Do you have a swimming pool?

Yes _____ (CONTINUE) _____ 1   (48)
No _____ (SKIP TO Q. 17) _____ 2

16b. Is your pool heated?

Yes _____ (CONTINUE) _____ 1   (49)
No _____ (SKIP TO Q. 16d) _____ 2

16c. How is your pool heated?

Gas heater _____ 1   (50)
Solar heater _____ 2
Other (specify) _____ x

16d. Do you have a pool cover?

Yes _____ 1   (51)
No _____ 2

Now I need to ask some questions about you and your home so we can classify your answers with those of the others on this survey.

17. What is the total number of rooms in your home, excluding bathrooms? # _____ (52)

18. Approximately how old is your home? (DO NOT READ LIST)

Years   (53)
1 or less _____
1
2 _____ 2
3 _____ 3
4–7 _____ 4
8–10 _____ 5

11–15 _____	6
16–20 _____	7
Over 25 _____	8
Don't know _____	9

19. How many people are living in your home, including yourself?   # _____ (54)

20. Are you—(READ LIST)

Married _____ 1   (55)
Single, widowed, or divorced _____ 2

21. Are there any children under the age of 18 living at home with you?

Yes _____ 1   (56)
No _____ 2

22. Into which of the following groups does your age fall? (READ LIST)

Under 25 _____ 1   (57)
25–35 _____ 2
36–49 _____ 3
50–64 _____ 4
65 and over _____ 5
(DO NOT READ) Refused _____ 0

23. Which of the following best describes the amount of formal education you had the opportunity to complete? (READ LIST)

Grade school _____ 1   (58)
Some high school _____ 2
Graduate high school _____ 3
Some college _____ 4
Graduated college _____ 5

24. Which of the following categories best describes the approximate market value of your home? (READ LIST)

Under $25,000 _____ 1   (59)
$25,000–$34,999 _____ 2
$35,000–$49,999 _____ 3
$50,000–$59,999 _____ 4
$60,000–$75,000 _____ 5
Over $75,000 _____ 6
(DO NOT READ)→ ⌈Don't know _____ 0
⌊Refused _____ 0

25. Which of the following groups best represents your total annual family income before taxes? (READ LIST)

Under $10,000 _____ 1   (60)
$10,000–$14,999 _____ 2
$15,000–$19,999 _____ 3

CASES AND PRACTICAL EXERCISES FOR PART II (*continued*)

$20,000–$24,999 _____ 4	
$25,000–$35,000 _____ 5	
Over $35,000 _____ 6	
(DO NOT READ) Refused _____ 0	

26. (RECORD ONLY:) Sex

Male _____ 1   (61)
Female _____ 2

---

[1] Written by Darrell R. Clarke and David A. Aaker as a basis for class discussion.

CASE STUDY

II-2

Currency Concepts International[1]

Dr. Karen Anderson, Manager of Planning for Century Bank of Los Angeles, settled down for an unexpected evening of work in her small beach apartment. It seemed that every research project Century had commissioned in the last year had been completed during her 10-day trip to Taiwan. She had brought three research reports home that evening to try to catch up before meeting with the bank's Executive Planning Committee the next day.

Possibly because the currency-exchange facilities had been closed at the Taiwan Airport when she first arrived, Dr. Anderson's attention turned first to a report on a project currently under consideration by one of Century Bank's wholly owned subsidiaries, Currency Concepts International (CCI). The project concerned the manufacture and installation of currency-exchange automatic teller machines (ATMs) in major foreign airports.

CCI had been responsible for the development of Century Bank's very popular ATM ("money machine"), now installed in numerous branches of the bank, as well as in its main location in downtown Los Angeles. The current project was a small part of CCI and Century Bank's plan to expand electronic banking services worldwide.

As she started to review the marketing research effort of Information Resources, Inc., she wondered what she would be able to recommend to the Executive Planning Committee the next day regarding the currency-exchange project. She liked her recommendations to be backed by solid evidence, and she looked forward to reviewing results of the research performed to date.

Activities of Information Resources, Inc.

Personnel of Information Resources, Inc., had decided to follow three different approaches in investigating the problem presented to them: (1) review secondary statistical data; (2) interview companies that currently engage in currency exchange; and (3) conduct an exploratory consumer survey of a convenience sample.

Secondary Data

The review of secondary data had three objectives:

1. To determine whether the number of persons flying abroad constitutes a market potentially large enough to merit automated currency exchange

2. To isolate any trends in the numbers of people flying abroad

3. To determine whether the amount of money that these travelers spend abroad is sizable enough to provide a potential market for automated currency exchange

CASES AND PRACTICAL EXERCISES FOR PART II *(continued)*

The U.S. Department of Transportation monitors the number of people traveling from U.S. airports to foreign airports. These statistics are maintained and categorized as follows: citizen and noncitizen passengers, and civilian and military passengers. Since this study was concerned only with Americans who travel abroad, only citizen categories were considered. Furthermore, since American military flights do not utilize the same foreign airport facilities as civilian passenger flights, the military category was also excluded. The prospect that non-Americans might also use these facilities causes the statistics to be somewhat conservative. The figures, for 1988, were summed for each foreign airport; the results by geographic area are shown in Exhibit II-3. The top 10 gateway cities from all American ports are shown in Exhibit II-4.

EXHIBIT II-3

American Citizens Flying Abroad in 1988 to Foreign Ports of Entry with over 25,000 Arrivals[a]

Europe	3,725,952
Caribbean	1,930,756
Central America	1,356,496
South America	301,347
Far East	516,861
Oceania	133,584

[a] Sources are given only for informative purposes. The actual numbers have been modified.

Note: Included in these area totals are all ports of entry that receive more than 25,000 passengers annually (68 per day). Ports of entry with a lower through-put rate were excluded.

Source: U.S. Department of Transportation, *United States International Air Travel Statistics,* Washington, DC, 1988.

EXHIBIT II-4

Most Frequented Foreign Ports of Entry from All American Ports

	Port	Passengers
1.	London, England	1,420,285
2.	Mexico City, Mexico	641,054
3.	Frankfurt, Germany	446,166
4.	Hamilton, Bermuda	378,897
5.	Nassau, Bahamas	361,791
6.	Tokyo, Japan	320,827
7.	Freeport, Bahamas	309,288
8.	Paris, France	295,823
9.	Rome, Italy	272,186
10.	Acapulco, Mexico	226,120

Source: Based on data provided in U.S. Department of Transportation, *United States International Air Travel Statistics,* Washington, DC, 1988.

CASES AND PRACTICAL EXERCISES FOR PART II *(continued)*

The second objective, to determine any growth trends in air travel, was addressed by studying the number of Americans flying abroad in the last five years. Exhibit II-5 shows the number of American travelers flying to various geographic areas and the associated growth rates in each of those areas. Europe clearly has the greatest number of travelers; and, although it did not show the greatest percentage growth in 1988, it does have the largest growth in absolute numbers. Generally, growth rates in overseas air travel have been good for the last four years; at this time, these trends appear to be positive from the standpoint of a potential market. However, there are also some potential problems on the horizon. As the world's energy situation increasingly worsens, there is the possibility of significant decreases in international travel.

In order to address the third objective, whether the amount of money spent by American travelers abroad constitutes a potential market, per-capita spending was examined. Exhibit II-6 shows per-capita spending, by geographic area, for the last five years as well as yearly percentages of growth. The category that includes the Far East, "other areas," shows the highest per-capita spending. This may be the result of the relatively low prices found in the Far East.

Europe shows the second-highest figures for per-capita spending; this area also exhibited strong growth in the last year. These figures indicate that Americans

EXHIBIT II-5

Growth in Number of Americans Flying Abroad, 1984–1988 (Thousands)

	1984	Percent Change	1985	Percent Change	1986	Percent Change	1987	Percent Change	1988
European and Mediterranean	3,325	(4.2)	3,185	10.6	3,523	11.3	3,920	5.2	4,105
Western Europe	3,118	(4.1)	2,990	10.0	3,245	11.2	3,663	6.9	3,914
Caribbean and Central America	2,147	(3.8)	2,065	6.6	2,201	—	2,203	7.4	2,365
South America	423	5.7	447	(2.5)	436	10.8	483	6.6	515
Other areas	572	14.9	657	12.2	737	6.4	784	2.7	805
Total	9,585	8.5	9,344	36.9	10,142	39.7	11,053	28.8	11,704

Source: U.S. Department of Commerce, *Survey of Current Business,* June 1989, Washington, DC.

EXHIBIT II-6

Per-Capita Spending by Americans Traveling Abroad, 1984–1988

	1984	Percent Change	1985	Percent Change	1986	Percent Change	1987	Percent Change	1988
Europe	542	11.1	602	1.3	610	—	612	17.2	717
Caribbean and Central America	319	19.4	381	(6.6)	356	—	359	4.5	375
South America	494	9.5	541	(1.7)	532	(1.1)	525	12.9	594
Other Areas	786	1.9	802	0.9	809	3.7	839	20.0	1,007
All Areas	486	12.6	547	—	545	1.8	555	14.6	635

Source: U.S. Department of Commerce, *Survey of Current Business,* June 1989, Washington, DC.

are spending increasing amounts of money abroad; even when inflation is taken into consideration, these figures are positive.

Information Resources, Inc., concluded, therefore, that Europe holds the greatest market potential for the new system. As Dick Knowlton, coordinator of the research team, said, "Not only are all of the statistics for Europe high, but the short geographic distances between countries can be expected to provide a good deal of intra-area travel."

Company Interviews

In an attempt to better understand the current operations of currency exchange in airports, four major firms engaged in these activities were contacted. While some firms were naturally reluctant to provide information on some areas of their operations, several were quite cooperative. These firms, and a number of knowledgeable individuals whose names surfaced in initial interviews, provided the information that follows.

In both New York and Los Angeles, there is only one bank engaged in airport currency exchange: Deak-Perera. American Express, Bank of America, and Citibank, as well as Deak-Perera, are engaged in airport currency exchange in a variety of foreign locations. Approval of permits to engage in airport currency exchange activity rests with the municipal body that governs the airport, and is highly controlled, It appears that foreign currency exchange is a highly profitable venture. Banks make most of their profits on the spread in exchange rates, which are posted daily.

Both Citibank and Bank of America indicated that they attempt to ensure their facilities' availability to all flights. The more profitable flights were found to be those that were regularly scheduled, rather than chartered. The person more likely to use the facilities was the vacationer rather than the businessperson. Neither bank could give an exact figure for the average transaction size; estimates ranged from $85 to $100.

It was the opinion of bank Deak employees, who dealt with travelers on a daily basis, that the average traveler was somewhat uncomfortable changing money in a foreign country. They also believed it to be particularly helpful if clerks at the exchange counter converse with travelers in their own language. A number of years ago Deak attempted to use a type of vending machine to dispense money at Kennedy Airport. This venture failed; industry observers felt that the absence of human conversation and assurance contributed to its lack of success.

Most of the exchanges performed the same types of services, including the sale of foreign currency and the sale of travelers checks. The actual brand of travelers checks sold varies with the vendors.

American Express has recently placed automated unmanned travelers check dispensers in various American airports. This service is available to American Express card holders and the only charge is 1 percent of the face value of the purchase checks; the purchase is charged directly to the customer's checking account. As yet, the machines have not enjoyed a great deal of use, although American Express has been successful in enrolling its customers as potential users.

Methods of payment for currency purchases are similar at all exchanges. Accepted forms of payment include: actual cash, travelers checks, cashier checks drawn on local banks, and MasterCard or Visa cards. When using a credit card to pay for currency purchases, there is a service charge added to the customer's bill, as with any cash advance.

Traveler Interviews

To supplement and complement the statistical foundation gained by reviewing secondary data sources, the consumer interview portion of the study was purposefully designed to elicit qualitative information about travelers' feelings toward current and future forms of exchanging currency. Approximately sixty American travelers were interviewed at both the San Francisco and Los Angeles International Airports, due to the accessibility of these locations to Information Resources' sole location. An unstructured, undisguised questionnaire was developed to assist in channeling the interview toward specific topics (see Appendix A). Questions were not fixed and the question order was dependent on the respondent's answers. Basically, the guide served to force the interview conversation around the central foreign currency exchange theme. The interviews were conducted primarily in the arrival/departure lobbies of international carriers and spanned over four weeks, beginning in mid-December 1989. A deliberate attempt was made to include as many arriving as departing passengers to neutralize the effect of increasing holiday traffic. Additionally, to reduce interviewer bias, three different interviewers were used. Interviews were intentionally kept informal. And Dick Knowlton cautioned the interviewers to remain objective and "not let your excitement over the product concept spill over into the interview and bias the responses."

The interviews were divided almost evenly between those who favored the concept and those who did not. Those who did perceive value in the concept tended also to support other innovations such as the automated teller machine and charging foreign currency on credit cards. Those who would not use the currency exchange terminals wanted more human interaction and generally did not favor automation in any form; a fair proportion also had had previous problems exchanging foreign currency. However, even those who did not favor the currency exchange idea did seem to prefer the system of having twenty-four-hour availability of the machines, and of using credit cards to get cash under emergency situations.

The respondents represent a diverse group of individuals ranging in age from 18 to 80 years, holding such different positions as oil executive, photographer, housewife, and customs officer. Primarily bound for Europe, Canada, and Mexico, the interviewees were mainly split between pleasure-seekers and those on business. Only three individuals interviewed were part of tour groups, and of these three, only one had previously traveled abroad. The majority of the others had been out of the United States before and had exchanged currency in at least one other country. Many had exchanged currency in remote parts of the world, including Morocco, Brazil, Australia, Japan, Tanzania, and Russia. Only five individuals had not exchanged money in airports at one time or another. The majority had obtained foreign currency in airports and exchanged money in airports primarily in small denominations for use in taxi cab fares, bus fares, phones, and airport gift shops, as well as for food, tips, and drinks. Most respondents agreed a prime motive for exchanging money in airports was the security of having local currency.

Exchanging currency can become a trying ordeal for some individuals. They fear being cheated on the exchange rate; they cannot convert the foreign currency into tangible concepts (for example, "how many yen should a loaf of bread cost?"); they dislike lines and associated red tape; and many cannot understand the rates as posted in percentages. Most individuals exchange money in airports, hotels, or banks, but sometimes there are no convenient facilities at all for exchanging currency.

People like to deal with well-known bank branches, especially in airports, because they feel more confident about the rate they are receiving. However, major fears of individuals are that money exchange personnel will not understand English and that they will be cheated in the transaction. Furthermore, a few people mentioned poor documentation when they exchange currency in foreign airports.

The travelers were divided as to whether they exchange currency before or after they arrive in the foreign country, but a few said that the decision depended on what country they were entering. If a currency, such as English pounds, could easily be obtained from a local bank before leaving the United States, they were more likely to exchange before leaving. However, in no case would the traveler arrange for currency beyond a week in advance. Most preferred to obtain the foreign currency on relatively short notice—less than three days before the trip. Of the individuals on tours, none planned to obtain currency in the foreign airport. Apparently, the tour guide had previously arranged for the necessary transportation from the airport to the hotels, and there would be only enough time to gather one's luggage and find the bus before it would depart, leaving no time to enjoy the facilities of the airport that required foreign currency. All three tour individuals did mention that they planned to obtain foreign currency once they arrived at the hotel. All individuals mentioned that they had secured their own foreign currency, but a few of the wives who were traveling with their husbands conceded that their spouses usually converted the currency in the foreign airport.

Very few of the interviewees had actually used an automated teller machine, but the majority had heard of or seen the teller machines on television. Those who had used the automated machines preferred their convenience and were generally satisfied with the terminal's performance. Many of those who had not used the automated teller machines mistrusted the machine and possible loss of control over their finances. Concerns about security and problems with the machines breaking down were also expressed. One woman described the teller machines as being "convenient, but cold." Apparently, many people prefer having human interaction when their money is concerned.

As noted earlier, approximately thirty of the respondents would favor the exchange terminals over their normal airport currency exchange routine, while the same number would have nothing to do with the machines. However, the majority of potential users qualified their use by such features as competitive rates, knowing the precise charges, or knowing they could get help if something went wrong. Individuals who indicated no preference were included in the favorable category, simply because they would not refuse to try the machine. Most of the indifferent people seemed to indicate they would try such a machine if some type of introductory promotional offer was included, such as travel information, currency tips, or a better rate.

With virtually unanimity, the respondents felt that 24-hour availability made the currency exchange machines more attractive, yet that alone would not persuade the dissenters to use the terminals. Some individuals felt that a machine simply could not give the travel advice that could be obtained at the currency exchange booths.

The opportunity to charge foreign currency against a major credit card, such as MasterCard or Visa, was a definite plus in the minds of most respondents. One individual clearly resented the idea, however, feeling that he would "overspend" if given such a convenient way to obtain cash. Respondents offered a number of suggestions concerning implementations of the product concept and a number of specific product features:

1. Add information about the country.
2. Provide small denominations and include coins.
3. Have it communicate in English.
4. Put in travelers checks to get cash.
5. Put in cash to get foreign currency.
6. Post rates daily.
7. Keep rates competitive and post charges.
8. Have television screen with person to describe procedure.
9. Place the machines in hotels and banks.
10. Have a change machine nearby that can convert paper money.
11. Place machine near existing currency exchange facilities for convenience when normal lines become long.
12. Demonstrate how to use the machine.
13. Use all bank credit cards.

Appendix A

Interview Guide for International Travelers (U.S. Citizens)

These interviews should remain as informal as possible. The object is not to obtain statistically reliable results, but to get ideas that will help to stimulate research. These questions are not fixed; the order, however, is sometimes dependent on answers the respondents give.

Introduce yourself.

1. Are you going to be traveling to a foreign country? Arriving from a foreign country? A United States resident?
2. Where is/was your final destination?
3. Why are you traveling (business, pleasure, a tour)?
4. How often do you travel outside of the United States?
5. Have you ever exchanged currency in a foreign country? (If no, go to #6). Where? Does anything in particular stand out in your mind when you exchanged currency?
6. Have you ever changed money in an airport?
7. Where do you plan to exchange currency on this trip?
8. Where do you change money normally?
9. Have you ever had any problems changing currencies? Explain circumstances.
10. Normally, would you change money before entering a country or after you arrive? If before, how long in advance? Where? (Probe.)
11. Are you familiar with automated teller machines that banks are using? (If not, explain.) Have you used one of these machines?
12. What are your feelings toward these machines?
13. If a currency exchange terminal, similar to an automated teller machine, was placed in your destination airport, would you use the machine or follow your normal routine?
14. Would 24-hour availability make the currency exchange machines more attractive? Would you use the terminals at night?
15. None of the currency exchange machines currently exists. What features or services could be provided so that you might choose to use a terminal rather than other currency exchange facilities?
16. If you could charge the foreign currency received to a major credit card, such as MasterCard or Visa, would you be more likely to use the machine?
17. Demographics—Age range (visual) Occupation? Sex? Traveling alone?

[1] This case is printed with permission of the author, Grady D. Bruce of the California State University, Fullerton.

◆ PRACTICAL EXERCISES

Q1.   ABC Enterprises plans to introduce a detergent that is an extension of its current product line. The company would like to position this product such that it does not erode into the current products. What secondary sources would you look into prior to conducting your own research? Conduct a market analysis that includes analyzing the market for the new detergent, the competition as well as the available data that you can use. What are the other areas that you believe may not be covered by the existing secondary data?

Q2.   Assume Post Cereal is planning to introduce a low-fat version of its Almond Nut Crunch cornflakes. What are the threats to the introduction of such a product? How would you go about testing the current market for breakfast cereal? Do you think that secondary data would suffice?

Go to the supermarket and observe at least 10 consumers buying cereal. How many bought a low-fat version? Based on observation, project the demand for the entire market. How reliable an estimate would this be to gauging demand in the market? Is there a niche to be filled? Also, if you survey the stores nearer the university, do you think this would affect the projection onto the whole market? Give reasons.

Q3.   The Sales and Marketing Management Survey of Buying Power is an important secondary source to obtain a profile of the average consumer. Using this as a guide, find information on the country in which you live. Assuming that a frozen dinners' manufacturer were to plan to sell to your local market, what critical pieces of information would you have to obtain prior to introducing this product? What other sources might you consult for this purpose?

Q4.   In order to assess the interest of shoppers in natural beauty products (such as those products by Body Shop and Bath and Body Works), a mall-intercept survey has been chosen as the most appropriate method. What issues would you address in the questionnaire to obtain as much information as possible? Given that several interviewers are to be employed for this task, incorporate into your questionnaire the process of selecting the "right" respondent. What sample size would you recommend to deduce valid inferences in this study? What kind of scales would you use to measure the attitude of your respondents? Develop a questionnaire and obtain the relevant information from the sample that you have chosen.

Q5.   Choose a local radio station and identify what its target audience is. Develop ways by which you would conduct research. Also, construct a questionnaire that addresses listener habits and that would allow you to get feedback regarding the areas by which the radio station can increase its listener base. Conduct the survey on a selected portion of the population. Use the Internet to collect the data for these studies—do you see any differences in your finding?

DATA ANALYSIS

Fundamentals of Data Analysis

Learning Objectives

- Become familiar with the fundamental concepts of data analysis.
- Understand the need for preliminary data preparation techniques such as data editing, coding, and statistically adjusting the data where required.
- Describe the various statistical techniques for adjusting the data.
- Discuss the significance of data tabulation.
- Identify the factors that influence the selection of an appropriate data analysis strategy.
- Become familiar with the various statistical techniques available for data analysis.
- Explain the need for a brief explanation of the various multivariate techniques.

An understanding of the principles of data analysis is useful for several reasons. First, it can lead the researcher to information and insights that otherwise would not be available. Second, it can help avoid erroneous judgments and conclusions. Third, it can provide a background to help interpret and understand analysis conducted by others. Finally, a knowledge of the power of data analysis techniques can constructively influence research objectives and research design.

Although data analysis can be a powerful aid to gaining useful knowledge, it cannot rescue a badly conceived marketing research study. If the research purpose is not well conceived, if the research questions are irrelevant, or if the hypothesis is nonviable or uninteresting, the research will require an abundance of good fortune to be useful. Further, data analysis rarely can compensate for a bad question, an inadequate sampling procedure, or sloppy fieldwork.

Data analysis has the potential to ruin a well-designed study. Inappropriate or misused data analysis can suggest judgments and conclusions that are at best unclear and incomplete, and at worst erroneous. Thus, it can lead to decisions inferior to those that would have been made without the benefit of the research. One important reason for studying data analysis therefore, is to avoid the pitfalls associated with it.

The purpose of Part III of this book is to describe data analysis techniques, so that when the appropriate situation arises, the researcher can draw on them. Another goal is to provide an understanding of the limitations of the various techniques, to minimize the likelihood that they will be misused or misinterpreted. The techniques and approaches revealed in this chapter are used routinely in nearly all descriptive and causal research. It is therefore important for the reader to understand them.

The type of data analysis required will be unique to each study; however, nearly all studies involving data analysis will require the editing and coding of data, will use one or more data analysis techniques, and will have to be concerned with presenting the results effectively.

In this chapter some preliminary data preparation techniques, such as data editing, coding, and statistically adjusting the data for further analysis, will be discussed. Basic ways to tabulate individual questions from a questionnaire (one-way tabulation) then will be developed. The discussion on tabulation will also include graphical representation of tabulated data. Next, the focus will turn to the question of tabulation among sample subgroups (cross-tabulation). Further, we will provide a discussion of the various factors that influence the selection of an appropriate data analysis strategy. This chapter will also present an overview of the various statistical techniques that a researcher can use in analyzing data.

◆ PREPARING THE DATA FOR ANALYSIS

The raw data obtained from the questionnaires must undergo preliminary preparation before they can be analyzed using statistical techniques. The quality of the results obtained from the statistical techniques and their subsequent interpretation depend to a great degree on how well the data were prepared and converted into a form suitable for analysis. The major data preparation techniques include (1) data editing, (2) coding, and (3) statistically adjusting the data (if required).

Data Editing

The role of **data editing** is to identify omissions, ambiguities, and errors in the responses. It should be conducted in the field by the interviewer and field supervisor, as well as by the analyst, just prior to data analysis. Among the problems to be identified are the following.

Interviewer error	Interviewers might not be giving the respondent the correct instructions.
Omissions	Respondents often fail to answer a single question or a section of the questionnaire, either deliberately or inadvertently.
Ambiguity	A response might not be legible or it might be unclear (e.g., which of two boxes is checked in a multiple-response system).
Inconsistencies	Sometimes two responses can be logically inconsistent. For example, a respondent who is a lawyer might have checked a box indicating that he or she did not complete high school.
Lack of cooperation	In a long questionnaire with hundreds of attitude or image questions, a respondent might rebel and check the same response (in an agree—disagree scale, for example) for each question in a long list of questions.
Ineligible respondent	An inappropriate respondent might be included in the sample. For example, if a sample is supposed to include only women over 18, others should be excluded.

When such problems are identified, several alternatives are available.[1] The preferred alternative, where practical, is to contact the respondent again. This is often quite feasible and should be done by the interviewer if the questions involved are important enough to warrant the effort. Another alternative, to throw out the whole questionnaire as not usable, might be appropriate if it is clear that the respondent either did not understand the survey or was not cooperating. A less extreme alternative is to throw out only the problem questions and retain the balance of the questions. Some respondents will bypass questions such as income or age, for example, and cooperate fully with the other questions. In the parts of the analysis involving income or age, only those respondents who answered those questions will be included, but in the rest of the analysis all respondents could be included. Still another alternative is to code illegible or missing answers into a category such as "don't know" or "no opinion." Such an approach may simplify the data analysis without materially distorting the interpretation. Alternatively, for any respondent one can input missing values for certain variables through the use of mean profile values, or infer the values by matching the respondent's profile to that of another, similar respondent.

A byproduct of the editing process is that it helps in evaluating and guiding the interviewers; an interviewer's tendency to allow a certain type of error to occur should be detected by the editing process.

Coding

Coding the closed-ended questions is fairly straightforward. In this process, we specify exactly how the responses are to be entered. Figure 12-1 is an example of an auto maintenance questionnaire, and Figure 12-2 illustrates the corresponding coding mechanism. The survey was mailed to 500 participants, and 150 responded.

As shown in Figure 12-2, the first three columns are used for identifying the respondents. The column reference is synonymous with variable identification; the questionnaire number is also indicated to provide a direct link between the question number, the variable identification, and the column numbers. Each question is described briefly in a separate column, and the range of permissible values provides the key information of the value to be entered for the particular type of response.

Once the response values are entered into a computer file, a statistical software program can be employed to generate diagnostic information. However, before any data analysis is performed, the data have to be checked for any error that might have come from the process of data entry. Once the data are error free, statistical adjustments to the data can be made.

Coding for open-ended questions is much more difficult. Usually a lengthy list of possible responses is generated, and then each response is placed into one of the list items. Often the assignment of a response involves a judgment decision if the response does not match a list item exactly. For example, a question such as "Why did you select your instrument from Ajax Electronics?" might elicit literally hundreds of different responses, such as *price, delivery, accuracy, reliability, familiarity, does not break down, can get it repaired, features, includes spare parts, a good manual, appearance, size,* and *shape.* Decisions must be made about the response categories. Should "reliability" and "does not break down" be in the same category, or do they represent two different responses? The difficulty of coding and analyzing open-ended responses provide a reason to avoid them in the questionnaire whenever possible.[2]

Directions: Please answer the questions below by placing a check mark (✓) in the appropriate boxes or, where applicable, by writing your response in the space provided.

1. Are you solely responsible for taking care of your automotive maintenance needs?

   ☐ Yes   ☐ No

   If you answered no to question No. 1, who is and what is that person's relation to you?

2. Do you perform simple auto maintenance yourself? *(e.g., tire pressure, change wiper blades, change air filter, etc.)*

   ☐ Yes   ☐ No

3. If you answered no to question No. 2, where do you take your car for servicing?

   _____

4. How often do you either perform maintenance on your automobile or have it serviced?
   ☐ Once per month
   ☐ Once every three months
   ☐ Once every six months
   ☐ Once per year
   ☐ Once *(please specify)* _____

5. When do you handle maintenance related automobile problems?
   ☐ Through scheduled maintenance
   ☐ As problems arise
   ☐ Postpone as long as possible
   ☐ Other *(please specify)* _____
   ☐ I do not keep track of it

6. If scheduled maintenance is done on your automobile, how do you keep track of what has been done?
   ☐ Auto dealer or mechanic's records
   ☐ Personal records
   ☐ Mental recollection
   ☐ Other *(please specify)*
   ☐ I do not keep track of it

7. Please rank the following list of car maintenance activities in order of importance. *(1 = most important; 2 = second most important; 3 = third most important; etc.)*
   _____ Tire maintenance
   _____ Oil change
   _____ Brake maintenance
   _____ Check belts and hoses
   _____ Check spark plugs

8. Are there any other maintenance activities that should be included in the above list?

   _____

   _____

AUTO MAINTENANCE QUESTIONNAIRE

Figure 12-1   Auto Maintenance Questionnaire.

Statistically Adjusting the Data

Many adjustments can be made to the data in order to enhance its quality for data analysis. The most common procedures for statistically adjusting data are as follows.

Weighting

Weighting is a procedure by which each response in the database is assigned a number according to some prespecified rule. Most often, weighting is done to make the

Column Number	Column Ref.	Question Number	Question Description	Range of Permissible Values
1–3	A		ID No. of Questionnaire	001–150
4	B	1	Responsible for maintenance	0 = no, 1 = yes, 9 = blank
5	C	1	Who is responsible	0 = husband, 1 = boyfriend, 2 = father, 3 = mother, 4 = relative, 5 = friend, 6 = other, 9 = blank
6	D	2	Perform simple maintenance	0 = no, 1 = yes, 9 = blank
7	E	3	Where for service	
8	F	4	How often is maintenance performed	Once per: 0 = month, 1 = three months, 2 = six months, 3 = year, 4 = other, 9 = blank
9	G	4	Other for "how often"	
10	H	5	When are problems handled	0 = scheduled maintenance, 1 = as problems arise, 2 = postpone as long as possible, 3 = other, 9 = blank
11	I	5	Other for "when problems handled"	
12	J	6	How maintenance is tracked	0 = not tracked, 1 = auto dealer/ mechanics' records, 2 = personal records, 3 = mental recollection, 4 = other, 5 = doesn't keep track, 9 = blank
13	K	6	Other for "how maintenance is tracked"	
14	L	7	Rank in order of importance: tire	0 = blank, 1 = most important, 2 = second most important, 3 = third, 4 = fourth, 5 = fifth
15	M	7	Rank in order of importance: oil	0 = blank, 1 = most important, 2 = second most important, 3 = third, 4 = fourth, 5 = fifth
16	N	7	Rank in order of importance: brake	0 = blank, 1 = most important, 2 = second most important, 3 = third, 4 = fourth, 5 = fifth
17	O	7	Rank in order of importance: belts	0 = blank, 1 = most important, 2 = second most important, 3 = third, 4 = fourth, 5 = fifth
18	P	7	Rank in order of importance: plugs	0 = blank, 1 = most important, 2 = second most important, 3 = third, 4 = fourth, 5 = fifth
19	Q	8	Any that should be included in No. 7	

Figure 12-2   Coding instructions for the Auto Maintenance Questionnaire.

Weighting is a procedure by which each response in the database is assigned a number according to some pre-specified rule, usually to make the sample data more representative of a target population on specific characteristics.

sample data more representative of a target population on specific characteristics. Categories underrepresented in the sample are given higher weights, while overrepresented categories are given lower weights. Weighting also is done to increase or decrease the number of cases in the sample that possess certain characteristics.

Weighting may also be used for adjusting the sample so that greater importance is attached to respondents with certain characteristics. For example, if a study is conducted to determine the market potential of a new sports drink, the researcher might want to attach greater weight to the opinions of the younger people in the market, who will be the heavy users of the product. This could be accomplished by assigning weights of 2.0 to persons in the sample who are under age 30 and 1.0 to respondents over 30. Weighting should be applied with caution, and the weighting procedure should be documented and made a part of the project report.[3]

Variable Respecification

Variable respecification is a procedure in which the existing data are modified to create new variables, or in which a large number of variables are collapsed into fewer variables. The purpose of this procedure is to create variables that are consistent with the study's objectives. For example, suppose the original variable represented the reasons for purchasing a car, with 10 response categories. These might be collapsed into four categories: performance, price, appearance, and service. Respecification also includes taking the ratio of two variables to create a new variable, taking square root and log transformations, and using dummy variables.

Dummy variables are used extensively for respecifying categorical variables. They are also called **binary, dichotomous, instrumental,** or **qualitative** variables. The general rule is that if there are m levels of the qualitative variable, we use $m - 1$ dummy variables to specify them. The reason for using only $m - 1$ dummy variables is that only $m - 1$ levels (or categories) are independent, and the information pertaining to the mth level can be obtained from the existing $m - 1$ dummy variables. A product could have been purchased in either the first half or the second half of the year (a qualitative variable with two levels). The purchase time could be represented by a single dummy variable[4] that will take a value of 1 if it was bought in the first half of the year and 0 if it was bought in the second half.

Scale Transformation

Yet another common procedure for statistically adjusting data is scale transformation. **Scale transformation** involves the manipulation of scale values to ensure comparability with other scales. In the same study, different scales may be empolyed for measuring different variables. Therefore, it would not be meaningful to make comparisons across the measurement scales for any respondent. Even if the same scale is employed for all the variables, different respondents may use the scale differently. Some respondents may consistently use the lower end of a rating scale, whereas others may consistently use the upper end. These differences can be corrected by appropriately transforming the data.[5]

One of the most common scale tranformation procedures is standardization. **Standardization** allows the researcher to compare variables that have been measured using different types of scales. For example, if sales are measured in actual dollars, and price is measured in cents, then the actual value of the variance for the sales variable will be higher compared to price, because of the units of measurement. To compare the variances, both variables can be brought down to a common unit of measurement. This can be achieved by forcing the variables, by standardization, to have a mean of zero and a standard deviation of one. Mathematically, this is done by first subtracting the mean, $\bar{X}$, from each score and then dividing by the standard deviation, s_x. Standardization can be done only on interval or ratio-scaled data. The formula for standardized score, z_i, is

$$z_i = (X_i - \bar{X})/s_x$$

Variable respecification is a procedure in which the existing data are modified to create new variables, or in which a large number of variables are collapsed into fewer variables to be consistent with the study's objectives.

Scale transformation involves the manipulation of scale values to ensure comparability with other scales.

Standardization allows the researcher to compare variables that have been measured using different types of scales by forcing the variables into a common unit of measure.

◆ STRATEGY FOR DATA ANALYSIS

Usually the first step in data analysis, after data preparation, is to analyze each question or measure by itself. This is done by tabulating the data. Tabulation consists simply of counting the number of cases that fall into the various categories. Other than aiding in "data cleaning" aspects, such as identifying the degree of omissions, ambiguities, and errors in the responses, the primary use of tabulation is in (1) determining the empirical distribution (frequency distribution) of the variable in question and (2) calculating the descriptive (summary) statistics, particularly the mean or percentages.

Next, the data are subjected to cross-tabulations to assess if any association is present between two (typically) nominal variables. If the variables are measured as interval or ratio, they are transformed to nominally scaled variables for the purpose of cross-tabulation. For example, the income of a household can be rescaled to less than $30,000 and greater than or equal to $30,000 to cross-tab with another nominally scaled variable. For analyzing relationships between two or more variables, *multivariate analysis* (discussed later) can be performed.

Tabulation: Frequency Distribution

A **frequency distribution** reports the number of responses that each question received, and is the simplest way of determining the empirical distribution of the variable.

A **frequency distribution** simply reports the number of responses that each question received, and is the simplest way of determining the empirical distribution of the variable. A frequency distribution organizes data into **classes,** or groups of values, and shows the number of observations from the data set that falls into each of the classes. Figure 12-3 provides a frequency distribution for one of the questions from the Tasty study. A key question is the likelihood-of-revisit question, in which the respondents are asked if they would revisit the shop. The number of people in each response category is shown. Thus, 24 responded, "I will revisit definitely." Figure 12-3 shows two other methods of presenting the frequency distribution. One is the percentage breakdown of the various categories; the percentage often is easier to interpret than the actual numbers (rounding errors cause the percentage total to differ from 100 percent). The other is a visual bar-graph presentation known as a histogram.

A **histogram** is a series of rectangles, each proportional in width to the range of values within a class and proportional in height to the number of items falling in the class. If the classes we use in the frequency distribution are of equal width, the verti-

Likelihood of Revisit	Number	Percent
Definitely	24	19.2
Probably	11	8.8
Maybe	76	60.8
Probably Not	04	3.2
Definitely Not	10	8.0

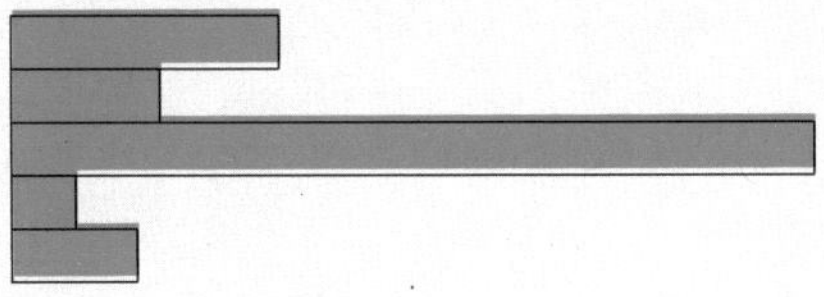

Figure 12-3 Frequency distribution.

A **histrogram** is a series of rectangles, each proportional in width to the range of values within a class and proportional in length to the number of items falling in the class.

cal bars in the histograms are also of equal width. The height of the bar for each class corresponds to the number of items in the class. The actual distribution of the variable can be visualized easily through the histogram. The actual distribution can then be compared to some theoretical distribution to determine whether the data are consistent with some a priori model.

For many questions it is useful to combine some of the question categories. For example, in Figure 12-3 the revisit question could have been shown with three of the responses combined into an "uncertain or uninterested" category. The logic is that a response of "I am not sure now" probably means that the respondent will not revisit. Responses to a new concept usually need to be discounted somewhat to correct for initial curiosity and a desire to please the survey sponsor. Decisions to combine categories should be supported by some kind of logic or theory. The resulting combinations also should result in categories that contain a worthwhile number of respondents. Usually, it is not useful to work with categories with only a few respondents. In fact, one purpose of combining categories is to develop larger respondent groups. Note that the two lowest income categories had relatively small respondent groups before they were combined.

Why not start with only three categories in each case? The questionnaire then would be shorter and easier to complete. One reason for not doing so is that before the study is conducted there may be no knowledge as to how the respondents are distributed. If too few categories are planned, all the respondents may end up in one of them and none in the others. Furthermore, extra categories might make responses more realistic. In the revisit question in Figure 12-3, if there were not five responses available, people might have a greater tendency to check the "I would probably revisit" category.

Tabulation: Descriptive Statistics

Descriptive statistics are statistics normally associated with a frequency distribution that helps summarize the information presented in the frequency table. These include (1) measures of central tendency (mean, median, and mode), (2) measures of dispersion (range, standard deviation, and coefficient of variation), and (3) measures of shape (skewness and kurtosis).[6] Here we restrict our discussion to the more commonly used statistics, the mean and the percentage.

Means and Percentages

In some situations it is desirable to use a single number to describe the responses to a question. In such circumstances, the **sample mean** or **percentage** is used. The sample mean is simply the average number, obtained by dividing the sum of the responses to a question by the sample size (the number of respondents to that question). The percentage is the proportion who answered a question a certain way, multiplied by 100.

Table 12-1 illustrates a study of the reaction of members of a community to a transit system. As part of the study, four lifestyle and attitude questions were asked, using a seven-point, agree-disagree scale. The first column of Table 12-1 gives the mean or average score among the 62 respondents. They indicate that the sample in general is concerned with gasoline costs and is not excited about jogging. When the response is based on two alternatives, or when a single alternative is the focus of the analysis, the percentage is used. For example, Question 5 in Table 12-1 reports that 36

TABLE 12-1   Rapid Transit User

	Mean Score	Transit System		Difference Between Sample Means
		User[a] $\bar{X}_u$	Nonuser[b] $\bar{X}_H$	$\bar{X}_u - \bar{X}_H$
Agreement on a seven-point scale (7 is strongly agree; 1 is strongly disagree) to the statements:				
1. I dislike driving.	3.7	4.3	2.9	1.4
2. I like to jog.	3.9	3.8	4.0	–0.2
3. I am concerned about gasoline costs.	5.3	6.1	4.4	1.7[c]
4. I am concerned about air pollution.	4.6	4.6	3.9	0.7
Percentage who answer affirmatively to the question:				
5. Do you live within 3 miles of a transit station?	36%	50%	25%	25%[d]
Sample size	62	28	34	

[a] Average score over the 28 respondents using the transit system.

[b] Average score over the 34 respondents not using the transit system.

[c] Significant at the 0.01 level.

[d] Significant at the 0.10 level.

percent of the shoppers live close to a transit station. The balance of Table 12-1 will be discussed shortly.

When to Use What

Descriptive statistics can provide accurate, simple, and meaningful figures by summarizing information in a large set of data. The summary measures can sometimes communicate the information in an entire distribution. There is an obvious trade-off between the use of the frequency distribution and the use of a single number. The frequency distribution can be unwieldy but does provide more information. For example, Table 12-2 shows the response to an attitude question. The average response indicates that the sample is fairly neutral about abstract art. Underlying that mean response, however, is the frequency distribution that indicates that a substantial group likes abstract art, a larger group dislikes it, and, in fact, very few people actually are neutral. In situations where the population is not likely to be clustered around the mean, the frequency distribution can be useful.

TABLE 12-2   A Question Response[a]

		Response	Frequency	Percentage
	Disagree	–3	300	30
		–2	120	12
I prefer abstract art exhibitions to nonabstract art exhibitions.		–1	50	5
		0	50	5
		+1	100	10
		+2	300	30
	Agree	+3	80	8

[a] Mean response = –0.3.

When nominal scales are involved, frequency distributions must be employed. Recall that a *nominal scale* is one in which numbers merely label or identify categories of objects. For example, suppose respondents were asked if they lived in an urban area, a suburban area, or a rural area. There would be no way to determine an average number to represent that sample (although the percentage who live in rural areas could be used).

Difference between Means or Percentages

The second step in most data analysis procedures is to repeat the analysis of a single question for various subgroups of the population. Thus, the interest might be in the heavy user, and the analysis would be done for this group. More likely, it would be done for the heavy user, the light user, and the nonuser; then the results would be compared. Responses often are more meaningful and useful when a comparison is involved. For instance, in this case it might be of interest to determine how those who use the transit system differ from those who do not use it.

Table 12-1 presents the sample means of the five questions for the users and the nonusers. The sample percentages answering positively to the location question are also presented for each group. The differences between the responses for the two groups provide some interesting insights. The difference between the sample means for Question 1, for example, indicates that the transit user tends to dislike driving more than the transit nonuser. The Question 2 difference indicates that the nonuser shows only a small tendency to enjoy jogging more than the users. The other comparisons suggest that the user is more concerned about gasoline costs and air pollution and lives closer to a transit station.

The difference between means is concerned with the association between two questions, the question defining the groups (transit usage in this case) and another question (Question 1, on disliking driving, for example). In terms of the scale definitions, the question defining the groups would be considered a **nominally scaled question** and the question on which the means are based would be considered an **intervally scaled question.** Of course, the analysis could use three, four, or more groups instead of just two. For example, comparisons could be made among nonusers of the transit system, light users, medium users, and heavy users. Other variables besides usage can be used to identify subgroups of interest. For example, in a segmentation study we might focus on

- Loyal buyers versus nonloyal buyers
- Those interested in abstract art versus those not interested
- Customers of a competing store versus others
- Those aware of our art gallery versus others
- High-income versus moderate-income versus low-income groups

If our initial analysis involved means (or percentages), the focus would turn to the difference between means (or percentages). If the initial analysis involved frequency distributions, then cross-tabulation, the subject of the next section, would be the focus.

◆ CROSS-TABULATIONS

The appropriate statistical analysis technique for studying the relationships among and between nominal variables is termed **cross-tabulation.** It also is called crosstabs, cross-classification, and **contingency table analysis.** In cross-tabulation, the sample is divided into subgroups in order to learn how the dependent variable varies from subgroup to subgroup. Cross-tabulation tables require fewer assumptions to construct, and they serve as the basis of several statistical techniques such as chi-square and log-linear analysis. Percentages are computed on each cell basis or by rows or columns. When the computations are by rows or columns, cross-tabulation tables usually are referred to as contingency tables, because the percentages are basically contingent on the row or column totals.

Figure 12-4 illustrates cross-tabulation with two examples from the Tasty study. The focus here is on the question of revisit intentions. Often, a usage or intentions question is the key question in a study.

We wish to determine if various income groups differ in their intentions. One way to define groups is by using the income question, or variable. The top of Figure 12-4 shows an intentions-by-income cross-tabulation. It presents the frequency distribution breakdown for the degree of intentions within each of three income groups. If the three groups were similar, each of their frequency distributions should be expected to be similar to that of the total sample (marginal frequencies shown in the last column). The results do not support this view. In fact, the higher-income people are less likely to be interested than the middle-income groups, and the low-income group is the most interested. More than 20 percent of the low-income group was classified as "most interested," as contrasted with only 7.6 percent of the high-income group. When the intentions-by-income cross-tabulated data are subjected to statistical analysis to evaluate the association between income groups and degree of intentions, the results indicate that there are differences among the three income groups in the degree of intentions to enroll.

The bottom of Figure 12-4 shows the intentions-by-age cross-tabulation. Again, the frequency distribution within each of the subgroups must be compared to the frequency distribution for the total sample, shown in the last column. The youngest group has somewhat more interest than the middle group, and both have considerably more interest than the older group.

Cross-tabulation is the analysis of association between two variables that are nominally scaled. Of course, any interval-scaled variable can be used to define

Likelihood to Revisit, by Income.			
	Less than $14,999	$15,000–$29,999	$30,000–$49,000	
Definitely	20.4%	11.6%	7.6%	11.3%
Probably	19.4%	11.9%	17.9%	16.0%
Maybe	60.2%	76.5%	74.5%	72.5%
	100%	100%	100%	100%

Likelihood to Revisit, by Age.			
	Under 18 Years	19–24 Years	25–34 Years	
Definitely	14.0%	12.5%	6.6%	11.1%
Probably	21.9%	20.0%	14.5%	18.9%
Maybe	64.1%	67.5%	78.9%	70.0%
	100%	100%	100%	100%

Figure 12-4 Cross-tabulations.

groups and therefore form a nominally scaled variable. For example, income and age are **intervally scaled** (actually, ratio scaled), but in the context of Figure 12-4 they are used to define categories and thus are nominally scaled. Most marketing research studies go no further than cross-tabulation, and even those studies that do use more sophisticated analytical methods still use cross-tabulation as an important component. Hence, along with the data-preparation techniques, understanding, developing, and interpreting cross-tabulation are the fundamental needs of data analysis.[7]

Chapters 13 and 14 will discuss in detail the various statistical tests and techniques that can be used to analyze the data obtained from questionnaires. Before we launch a formal discussion of these statistical techniques, it will be beneficial to discuss the various factors that influence the choice of an analysis technique. This will help us to identify the appropriate technique(s), based on our needs. Finally, we will end this chapter with an overview of the various statistical techniques that are available to the researcher and a brief discussion on how these techniques are classified.

◆ FACTORS INFLUENCING THE CHOICE OF A STATISTICAL TECHNIQUE

Data analysis is not an end in itself. Its purpose is to produce information that will help to address the problem at hand. Several factors influence the selection of the appropriate technique for data analysis. These include: (1) type of data, (2) research design, and (3) assumptions underlying the test statistic and related considerations.[8]

For discussion on type of data and research design, refer to the appendix in Chapter 4 and to Chapter 9.

Assumptions Underlying the Test Statistic

The assumptions underlying the test statistic also affect the choice of a statistical method of analysis. For example, the assumptions of a two-sample t-test are as follows:

1. The samples are independent.
2. The characteristics of interest in each population have normal distribution.
3. The two populations have equal variances.

The t-test is more sensitive to certain violations of these assumptions than others. For example, it still works well with respect to violations of the normality assumption, but is quite sensitive to violations of the equal-variance assumption. When the violation is too severe, the conclusions drawn are inappropriate. Hence, if the assumptions on which a statistical test is based are violated or are not met, those tests should not be performed, because they will give meaningless results. If the samples are not independent or have unequal variances, a modified t-test can still be employed. Ultimately, the researcher's knowledge about statistical techniques does matter in the selection of the technique for data analysis.

◆ AN OVERVIEW OF STATISTICAL TECHNIQUES

The entire gamut of statistical techniques can be broadly classified as univariate and multivariate techniques based on the nature of the problem. **Univariate techniques** are appropriate when there is a single measurement of each of the n sample objects, or when there are several measurements of each of the n observations but each variable is analyzed in isolation. On the other hand, **multivariate techniques** are

Univariate techniques are appropriate when there is a single measurement of each of the n sample objects, or when there are several measurements of each of the n observations, but each variable is analyzed in isolation.

Multivariate techniques are appropriate for analyzing data when there are two or more measurements of each observation and the variables are to be analyzed simultaneously.

Multivariate statistical techniques can be broadly defined as "a collection of procedures for analyzing the association between two or more sets of measurements that were made on each object in one or more samples of objects."

appropriate for analyzing data when there are two or more measurements of each observation and the variables are to be analyzed simultaneously.

Univariate techniques can be further classified based on the type of data—whether they are nonmetric or metric. As mentioned earlier, **nonmetric data** are measured on a nominal or ordinal scale, whereas metric data are measured on an interval or ratio scale. Nonparametric statistical tests can be used to analyze nonmetric data. Nonparametric tests do not require any assumptions regarding the distribution of data.

For both nonmetric and metric data, the next level of classification involves determining whether a single sample or multiple samples are involved. Further, in the case of multiple samples, the appropriate statistical test depends on whether the samples are independent or dependent. Figure 12-5 provides an overview of the univariate analysis techniques.

For metric data, t-tests and z-tests can be used for one or two samples. For more than two samples, the **analysis of variance (ANOVA)** is used. For nonmetric data, with a single sample, chi-square, Kolmogorov–Smirnov (K–S), and RUN tests can be used. For two or more independent samples, chi-square, rank sum tests, K–S, and ANOVA (Kruskal–Wallis ANOVA) should be used. For two or more dependent samples, sign test, Wilcoxon test, McNemar, and Cochran Q-tests can be used. A detailed discussion of nonparametric statistics is beyond the scope of this book.[9]

Multivariate statistical techniques can be broadly defined as *a collection of procedures for analyzing the association between two or more sets of measurements that were made on each object in one or more samples of objects.* If only two sets of measurements are involved, the data typically are referred to as *bivariate.*[10] The multivariate techniques can be classified based on the following logic.

- Can the data be partitioned into dependent and independent variable sets? If so, classify according to the number of variables in each set. If not, classify the technique as an interdependence technique.

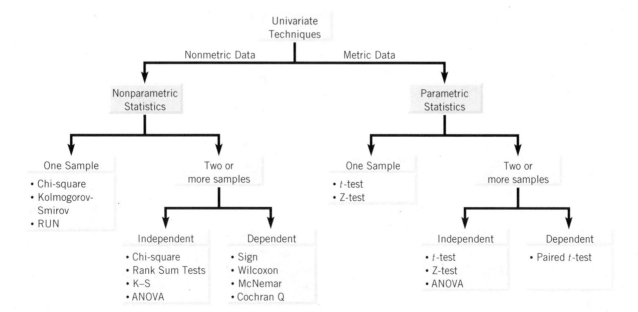

Figure 12-5 Classification of univariate statistical techniques.

- In the case of interdependence techniques, classification is done based on the principal focus of the analysis. Is the focus on the object (person/thing/event) or is it on the variable?

Based on the first factor, the multivariate techniques can be broadly classified as **dependence techniques** or **interdependence techniques.** Dependence techniques are appropriate when one or more variables can be identified as dependent variables, with the remaining as independent variables such as in multiple regression and analysis of variance (ANOVA).

In interdependence techniques, the variables are not classified as dependent or independent; rather, the whole set of interdependent relationships is examined. For example, association between 2 variables can be measured using correlation analysis. Subsequent chapters will discuss the commonly used techniques represented in Figure 12-5 and correlation regression in ANOVA. The chi-square tests for independence and goodness-of-fit, hypothesis testing (t-test and z-test), and the analysis of variance will be discussed in Chapter 13. Chapter 14 will focus on correlation and regression analysis. The appendix in Chapter 14 will very briefly describe the various multivariate techniques that are available to the marketing researcher.

Why use multivariate analysis, anyway? Clearly, substantial information can be obtained without using such complex techniques; however, there are several reasons why multivariate analysis is useful, which are beyond the scope of this textbook.

Presenting the Results

Eventually, the researcher must develop some conclusions from the data analysis and must present the results. The presentation, whether oral, written, or both, can be critical to the ultimate ability of the research to influence decisions. We will address this in Chapter 15 where we provide several guidelines that will lead to effective presentations and where we also offer some special tips for making written and oral presentations.

Choice of a Statistical Package

SAS and SPSS are the two commonly used statistical packages for marketing research analysis. Additional information on these can be found at the respective web sites listed here.

SAS:

http://www.sas.com

SPSS:

http://www.spss.com

TASTY ICE-CREAM: A CASE EXAMPLE OF MARKETING INTELLIGENCE (*continued*)

Figures A, B, C, D show the results of the data analysis of the Tasty study. Figure A shows the frequencies and percents obtained about the age of people visiting Tasty. It can be seen that more than 70 percent of the respondents lie within the 19–34 age group. This implies that Tasty's customer base is predominantly young and that the atmospherics inside Tasty and the menu should reflect the young generation's preferences. It can also be seen from Figure B that Tasty has a very high female patronage. This can be due to factors such as the location of Tasty and its cleanliness. Figure C shows that a majority of the customers are very satisfied with the product range and the product quality of Tasty. However, the figure also indicates that the customers are not happy about the price of Tasty Ice-Cream. Location, room for dine-in, and waiting time are also areas of concern.

Figure D shows the cross-tabulations of the intentions of the customers to revisit and the age and income of the respondents, respectively. It can be seen that the people in the age group of 19–34 are the ones more likely to revisit. Also, it can be seen that people with higher income have indicated higher likelihood of revisit. These facts enable Tasty to plan its future course of action. It can either lower its prices and cater to everyone, or it can improve its service and locations and cater to its niche audience.

		Age		
Age (Years)	Frequency	Percent	Cumulative Frequency	Cumulative Percent
<18	7	13.5	7	13.5
19–24	24	46.2	31	59.6
25–34	14	26.9	45	86.5
35–44	2	3.8	47	90.4
45–64	5	9.6	52	100.0
		Frequency Missing = 1		

Figure A

		Gender		
Gender	Frequency	Percent	Cumulative Frequency	Cumulative Percent
Male	27	52.9	27	52.9
Female	24	47.1	51	100.0
		Frequency Missing = 2		

Figure B

		Rating of Tasty on Product Range		
Satisfaction Level	Frequency	Percent	Cumulative Frequency	Cumulative Percent
2	4	7.7	4	7.7
3	22	42.3	26	50.0
4	26	50.0	52	100.0
		Frequency Missing = 1		

Figure C

Rating of Tasty on Product Quality

Satisfaction Level	Frequency	Percent	Cumulative Frequency	Cumulative Percent
2	1	1.9	1	1.9
3	17	32.7	18	34.6
4	34	65.4	52	100.0

Frequency Missing = 1

Rating of Tasty on Price

Satisfaction Level	Frequency	Percent	Cumulative Frequency	Cumulative Percent
1	4	8.2	4	8.2
2	13	26.5	17	34.7
3	21	42.9	38	77.6
4	11	22.4	49	100.0

Frequency Missing = 4

Rating of Tasty on Location

Satisfaction Level	Frequency	Percent	Cumulative Frequency	Cumulative Percent
1	3	5.9	3	5.9
2	4	7.8	7	13.7
3	16	31.4	23	45.1
4	28	54.9	51	100.0

Frequency Missing = 2

Rating of Tasty on Room for Dine-in

Satisfaction Level	Frequency	Percent	Cumulative Frequency	Cumulative Percent
1	1	2.0	1	2.0
2	6	12.2	7	14.3
3	22	44.9	29	59.2
4	20	40.8	49	100.0

Frequency Missing = 4

Rating of Tasty on Waiting Time

Satisfaction Level	Frequency	Percent	Cumulative Frequency	Cumulative Percent
2	6	11.8	6	11.8
3	13	25.5	19	37.3
4	32	62.7	51	100.0

Frequency Missing = 2

Figure C   *(continued)*

Rating of Tasty on Clean Atmosphere

Satisfaction Level	Frequency	Percent	Cumulative Frequency	Cumulative Percent
1	2	4.0	2	4.0
2	4	8.0	6	12.0
3	7	14.0	13	26.0
4	37	74.0	50	100.0

Frequency Missing = 3

4—Very Satisfied
3—Quite Satisfied
2—Somewhat Satisfied
1—Not Satisfied

Figure C *(continued)*

Table of Revisit Intention (Q8) by Age (Q20)

Q8 Frequency Percent	1	2	3	4	5	Total
1	0 / 0.00	1 / 1.96	0 / 0.00	0 / 0.00	0 / 0.00	1 / 1.96
2	0 / 0.00	0 / 0.00	1 / 1.96	0 / 0.00	0 / 0.00	1 / 1.96
3	0 / 0.00	1 / 1.96	0 / 0.00	0 / 0.00	0 / 0.00	1 / 1.96
5	7 / 13.73	21 / 41.18	13 / 25.49	2 / 3.92	5 / 9.80	48 / 94.12
Total	7 / 13.73	23 / 45.10	14 / 27.45	2 / 3.92	5 / 9.80	51 / 100.00

Frequency Missing = 2

Table of Revisit Intention (Q8) by Gender (Q21)

Q8 Frequency Percent	1	2	Total
1	1 / 2.00	0 / 0.00	1 / 2.00

Figure D

Frequency Percent	1	2	Total
2	0	1	1
	0.00	2.00	2.00
3	0	1	1
	0.00	2.00	2.00
5	26	21	47
	52.00	42.00	94.00
Total	27	23	50
	54.00	46.00	100.00
Frequency Missing = 3			

Figure D   *(continued)*

END OF CHAPTER MATERIAL

SUMMARY

The first phase in data analysis involves editing, coding, and statistically preparing the data for analysis. Editing involves identifying omissions, ambiguities, inconsistencies, lack of cooperation, and ineligible respondents. Coding involves deciding how the responses are going to be entered. Several techniques can be used to statistically adjust the data. These include (1) weighting. (2) variable respecification, and (3) scale transformation.

A variety of data analysis techniques are available. The most basic is to analyze each question by itself. A frequency distribution provides the most complete information and often leads to decisions to combine response categories. Several descriptive statistics such as the mean, median, mode, standard deviation, and variance can be obtained from these distributions. In most marketing research applications, only the sample means and/or percentages are reported.

Responses at times are much more meaningful and useful when a comparison is made. The usual step is to tabulate questions among subgroups, and this involves two of the questions from the questionnaire. Thus, the sample mean or the frequency distribution is obtained for subgroups such as transit users and transit nonusers, and they are compared to identify the differences. Guidelines are developed for selecting the appropriate statistical techniques. A discussion on the overview of statistical analysis is provided.

KEY TERMS

data editing	standardization
coding	frequency distribution
weighting	sample mean percentages
variable respecification	histogram
dummy variables	nominally scaled question
scale transformation	intervally scaled question

cross-tabulation
contingency table analysis
ordinal scale
nominal scale
interval and ratio-scaled data
metric data
variable control
univariate technique
median

mode
multivariate techniques
nonmetric data
multivariate statistical techniques
dependence techniques
interdependence techniques
multiple linear regression
analysis of variance (ANOVA)

MARKETING RESEARCH TOOLBOX
REVIEW POINTS

1. The raw data obtained from the questionnaires must undergo preliminary preparation before they can be analyzed using statistical techniques. The major data preparation techniques include data editing, coding, and statistically adjusting the data (if required).

2. The role of the editing process is to identify omissions, ambiguities, and errors in the responses. It should be conducted in the field by the interviewer and field supervisor, as well as by the analyst, just prior to data analysis.

3. A byproduct of the editing process is that it helps in evaluating and guiding the interviewers; an interviewer's tendency to allow a certain type of error to occur should be detected by the editing process.

4. Coding the closed-ended questions is fairly straightforward. In this process, we specify exactly how the responses are to be entered.

5. Coding for open-ended questions is much more difficult. Usually a lengthy list of possible responses is generated and then each response is placed into one of the list items. Often the assignment of a response involves a judgment decision if the response does not match a list item exactly.

6. Many adjustments can be made to the data in order to enhance its quality for data analysis. The most common procedures for statistically adjusting data are weighting, variable respecification, and scale transformation.

7. Weighting is a procedure by which each response in the database is assigned a number according to some prespecified rule. Most often, weighting is done to make the sample data more representative of a target population on specific characteristics.

8. Variable respecification is a procedure in which the existing data are modified to create new variables, or in which a large number of variables are collapsed into fewer variables. The purpose of this procedure is to create variables that are consistent with the study's objectives.

9. Scale transformation involves the manipulation of scale values to ensure comparability with other scales. In the same study, different scales may be employed for measuring different variables. Therefore, it would not be meaningful to make comparisons across the measurement scales for any respondent.

10. One of the most common scale transformation procedures is standardization. Standardization allows the researcher to compare variables that have been measured using different types of scales.

11. The primary use of tabulation is in determining the empirical distribution (frequency distribution) of the variable in question, and calculating the descriptive (summary) statistics, particularly the mean or percentages.

12. A frequency distribution simply reports the number of responses that each question received, and is the simplest way of determining the empirical distribution of the vari-

able. A frequency distribution organizes data into classes, or groups of values, and shows the number of observations from the data set that falls into each of the classes.

13. A histogram is a series of rectangles, each proportional in width to the range of values within a class and proportional in height to the number of items falling in the class.

14. Descriptive statistics are statistics normally associated with a frequency distribution that helps summarize the information presented in the frequency table. These include measures of central tendency (mean, median, and mode), measures of dispersion (range, standard deviation, and coefficient of variation), and measures of shape (skewness and kurtosis).

15. In some situations it is desirable to use a single number to describe the responses to a question. In such circumstances, the sample mean or percentage is used. The sample mean is simply the average number, obtained by dividing the sum of the responses to a question by the sample size (the number of respondents to that question). The percentage is the proportion who answered a question a certain way, multiplied by 100.

16. If the initial analysis involved means (or percentages), the focus would turn to the difference between means (or percentages). If the initial analysis involved frequency distributions, then cross-tabulation would be the focus.

17. The appropriate statistical analysis technique for studying the relationships among and between nominal variables is termed cross-tabulation. In cross-tabulation, the sample is divided into subgroups in order to learn how the dependent variable varies from subgroup to subgroup.

18. Several factors influence the selection of the appropriate technique for data analysis. These include: type of data, research design, and assumptions underlying the test statistic and related considerations.

19. The entire gamut of statistical techniques can be broadly classified as univariate and multivariate techniques, based on the nature of the problem.

20. Univariate techniques are appropriate when there is a single measurement of each of the n sample objects, or when there are several measurements of each of the n observations but each variable is analyzed in isolation.

21. Multivariate techniques are appropriate for analyzing data when there are two or more measurements of each observation and the variables are to be analyzed simultaneously.

22. Univariate techniques can be further classified based on the type of data—whether they are nonmetric or metric. Nonmetric data are measured on a nominal or ordinal scale, whereas metric data are measured on an interval or ratio scale.

23. Multivariate statistical techniques can be broadly defined as "a collection of procedures for analyzing the association between two or more sets of measurements that were made on each object in one or more samples of objects."

24. Multivariate techniques can be broadly classified as dependence techniques or interdependence techniques. Dependence techniques are appropriate when one or more variables can be identified as dependent variables and the remaining as independent variables. The appropriate choice of dependence techniques further depends on whether there are one or more dependent variables involved in the analysis.

QUESTIONS AND PROBLEMS

1. A poll of just over 1,000 Californians selected by an area sampling plan were asked early in Governor Jerry Brown's tenure whether they thought that Governor Brown was doing a good, fair, or poor job as governor. They were then asked why they held those opinions. The results were coded into 35 response categories. Each respondent's answer was coded in from one to six of the categories. A total of 1,351 responses were coded. The most fre-

quently used categories (besides "No answer," given by 135 of the respondents) were the following:

(i)   Not bad or good; OK so far; Too soon to tell (253)
(ii)   Doing his best (123)
(iii)   Trying to help people; cares about people (105)
(iv)   Cutting down government expenses (88)
(v)   Like or agree with his ideas (69)
(vi)   Not afraid to take a stand (61)

Do you think the responses are being analyzed properly? A respondent who gives a lengthy reply that includes as many as six coded responses will have more weight than a respondent who gives a short direct response that is coded into only one category. Is that appropriate? Are there any alternatives? Code the following responses based on the categories listed, and into others you think are appropriate.

a.   I like his position on welfare. It's probably the most critical problem facing the state. On the other hand he is not helping the business climate. All the regulations are making it impossible to bring in industry. It's really too soon to make a judgment, however.

b.   He's reducing unemployment, improving the economy. I like his ideas about welfare and cutting down government expense. However, I don't like his position on the smog device bill. On balance, he's doing okay.

c.   He's too much of a politician. He will swing with the political currents. He has started some needed government reorganization, however.

d.   I dislike his stand on education. He is really not interested in education, perhaps because he has no children. He's young and immature. He takes strong stands without getting his facts straight.

e.   He's concerned about the farm workers. He's doing a good job. I like him.

2.   Do you think that such coding is an accurate means of interpreting and analyzing responses? What would some of the problems be if these same set of responses were coded by others? Would there be a necessity for guidelines?

3.   Analyze Figure 12-4. What conclusions can you draw? What are the implications? What additional data analysis would you recommend, given your conclusions?

4.   Consider the PG&E (A) case at the end of Part II. Plan an analysis strategy. What cross-tabulations would you run? What difference-between-means calculations? What correlations would be useful? Identify some questions for which you would use means (or percentages) and others for which you might consider the entire frequency distribution in your analysis. Using the case data, identify two key questions and determine the frequency distribution.

ENDNOTES

1.   See Naresh K. Malhotra, "Analyzing Marketing Research Data with Incomplete Information on the Dependent Variable," *Journal of Marketing Research,* 24 (February 1987), pp. 74–84.

2.   For a more detailed discussion on coding, see Philip S. Sidel, "Coding," in Robert Ferber (ed.), *Handbook of Marketing Research* (New York: McGraw-Hill, 1974); Pamela L. Alreck and Robert B. Settle, *The Survey Research Handbook* (Homewood, IL: Richard D. Irwin, 1985), pp. 254–86; J. Pope, *Practical Marketing Research* (New York: AMACOM, 1981), pp. 89–90.

3.   For more information on weighting, see Trevor Sharot, "Weighting Survey Results," *Journal of the Marketing Research Society,* 28 (July 1986), pp. 269–84.

4.   See L. Bruce Bowerman and Richard T. O'Connell, *Linear Statistical Models: An Applied Approach* (Boston: PWS-Kent, 1990).

5.   See Ronald E. Frank, "Use of Transformations," *Journal of Marketing Research* (August 1966), pp. 247–53.

6. The biggest advantage of the standard deviation is that it enables us to determine, with a great deal of accuracy, where the values of a frequency distribution are located in relation to the mean. This can be done using Chebyshev's theorem, which states that regardless of the shape of the distribution, at least 75 percent of the values will fall within plus and minus two standard deviations from the mean of the distribution, and at least 89 percent of the values will lie within plus and minus three standard deviations from the mean. If the distribution is a symmetrical, bell-shaped curve, then, using Chebyshev's theorem, we can say that:

   - About 68 percent of the values in the population will fall within plus and minus one standard deviation from the mean.

   - About 95 percent of the values will fall within plus and minus two standard deviations from the mean.

   - About 99 percent of the values will fall within plus and minus three standard deviations from the mean.

   - For a detailed discussion on fundamental statistics, see Richard I. Levin, *Statistics for Management* (Englewood Cliffs, NJ: Prentice-Hall, 1987), or any business statistics textbook.

7. See O. Hellevik, *Introduction to Causal Analysis: Exploring Survey Data by Crosstabulation* (Beverly Hills, CA: Sage, 1984).

8. Adapted from Gilbert A. Churchill, Jr., *Marketing Research: Methodological Foundations* (Orlando, FL: Dryden Press, 1991).

9. For a detailed discussion of nonparametric tests, refer to Wayne W. Daniel, *Applied Nonparametric Statistics* (Boston: PWS-Kent, 1990).

10. Aaker, Kumar and Day, *Marketing Research*, seventh edition, (New York, NY: John Wiley and Sons, Inc., 2001).

Hypothesis Testing

Learning Objectives

- Understand the logic behind hypothesis testing.
- Become familiar with the concepts basic to the hypothesis-testing procedure.
- Describe the steps involved in testing a hypothesis.
- Interpret the significance level of a test.
- Understand the difference between Type I and Type II errors.
- Describe the chi-square test of independence and the chi-square goodness-of-fit test.
- Discuss the purpose of measuring the strength of association.
- Be exposed to the more commonly used hypothesis tests in marketing research—tests of means and proportions.
- Understand the relationship between confidence interval and hypothesis testing.
- Describe the effect of sample size on hypothesis testing.
- Discuss the use of the analysis of variance technique.
- Describe one-way and n-way analysis of variance.

When an interesting, relevant, empirical finding emerges from data analysis based on a sample, a simple, yet penetrating, hypothesis test question should occur to every manager and researcher as a matter of course: Does the empirical finding represent only a sampling accident? For example, suppose that a study is made of wine consumption. Data analysis reveals that a random sample of 100 California residents consumes more wine per family than a random sample of 100 New York residents. It could be that the observed difference was caused only by a sampling error; in actuality, there may be no difference between the two populations. If the difference found in the two samples could be caused by sampling fluctuations, it makes little sense to spend additional time on the results or to base decisions on it. If, on the other hand, the results are not caused simply by sampling variations, there is a reason to consider the results further.

Hypothesis testing begins with an assumption, called a **hypothesis,** that is made about a population parameter. Then, data from an appropriate sample are collected, and the information obtained from the sample (sample statistics) is used to decide how likely it is that the hypothesized population parameter is correct. The hypothesis test question is thus a screening question. Empirical results should pass this test before the researcher spends much effort considering them further.

Hypothesis testing
begins with an assumption, called a **hypothesis**, that is made about a population parameter. Then, data from an appropriate sample are collected, and the information obtained from the sample (sample statistics) is used to decide how likely it is that the hypothesized population parameter is correct.

The purpose of hypothesis testing is not to question the computed value of the sample statistic but to make a judgment about the difference between two sample statistics or the sample statistic and a hypothesized population parameter. For example, in many marketing research situations the need arises to test an assumption regarding a certain value for the population mean. To test the assumption's validity, data from a sample are gathered and the sample mean is calculated. Then the difference between the sample mean and the hypothesized value of the population mean is calculated. The smaller the difference is, the greater is the likelihood that the hypothesized value for the population mean is correct. The larger the difference is, the smaller is the likelihood.

Unfortunately, the difference between the hypothesized population parameter and the actual sample statistic is more often neither so large that the hypothesis automatically is rejected nor so small that it is not rejected just as quickly. In hypothesis testing, as in most significant real-life decisions, clear-cut solutions are the exception, not the rule. The mechanism that is adopted to make an objective decision regarding the hypothesized parameter forms the core of hypothesis testing.

A primary objective of this chapter is to provide a real understanding of the logic of hypothesis testing. The hope is that the reader will become conditioned to asking whether the result was an accident. Just thinking of the question at the appropriate time is winning half the battle. Further, an effort will be made to help the reader think in terms of a model or set of assumptions (such as that there is no difference between California and New York in per-capita wine consumption) in very specific terms. Hypothesis testing provides an excellent opportunity to be rigorous and precise in thinking and in presenting results.

In the first section, the logic of hypothesis testing is developed in the context of an example. This is followed by sections describing the steps in the hypothesis-testing process and the concepts basic to the hypothesis-testing procedure. The final section presents the hypothesis tests used in cross-tabulations. Here the chi-square statistic, which is useful in interpreting a cross-tabulation table, is developed. Also, the two major applications of the chi-square test—as a goodness-of-fit measure and as a test of independence—are discussed.

◆ THE LOGIC OF HYPOTHESIS TESTING: AN ILLUSTRATIVE EXAMPLE

To guide the development and control of wilderness areas and national parks, a large-scale survey was conducted. A total of nearly 10,000 people participated and answered a series of questions about their usage of wilderness areas and their opinions on public policy alternatives regarding them. One key question was how to control the number of people asking to use some of the popular rafting rivers. At one extreme, a very restrictive policy was proposed, using a permit system that would preserve the wilderness character of the parks but that would also deprive many people of the opportunity to use them as a national resource. At the other extreme, there would be unrestricted access. One question asked for opinions about this policy spectrum as it applied to several wilderness areas. The scale was as follows:

Highly restrictive									No restrictions
0	1	2	3	4	5	6	7	8	9

The average response of the 10,000 respondents was 5.6.

The researcher who conducted this survey wanted to test the theory that those who did white-water rafting would favor fewer restrictions. To test this hypothesis, 35 such people were identified in the study, which had an average response rate of 6.1. Thus, the evidence supports the contention that those engaging in white-water rafting did tend to support a no-restrictions policy more than did the rest of the population.

But how convincing is the evidence? After all, the opinions of a sample of only 35 rafters is known. The difference between 5.6 (the 10,000 respondent average) and 6.1 (the white-water rafters' average) might be more a case of luck than proof that the white-water rafters had different opinions. The extent to which the statement about the population is believable depends on whether the sample from which the information was generated is large or small (other things being equal). If the average response rate of the 35 white-water rafters was, say, 8.6, then the hypothesis that those who did white-water rafting favor fewer restrictions cannot be rejected. On the other hand, if the average response of rafters was 2.7, then without any hesitation, the hypothesis can be rejected. With an average response rate of 6.1, however, we can neither accept nor reject the hypothesis with absolute certainty; a decision about the hypothesis has to be based not on intuition, but on some objective measure. To what extent the statement about the population parameter is believable depends on whether the information generated from the sample is a result of few or many observations. In other words, evidence has to be evaluated statistically before arriving at a conclusion regarding the hypothesis. This is the logic behind hypothesis testing.

◆ STEPS IN HYPOTHESIS TESTING

The steps involved in the process of hypothesis testing are illustrated in Figure 13-1. As shown in the figure, problem definition leads to the generation of hypotheses. The relevant probability distribution is then chosen. The corresponding critical value is determined from the information on the significance level, degrees of freedom, and one- or two-tailed test. The appropriate test statistic (calculated from the sample data) is then compared with the relevant critical value, and if the test statistic falls in the critical region (i.e., in general, when the test statistic equals or exceeds the critical value), the null hypothesis is rejected.

◆ BASIC CONCEPTS OF HYPOTHESIS TESTING

The Null and Alternative Hypotheses

Let us continue with the wilderness survey example. To test the theory that people who did white-water rafting would be in favor of fewer restrictions, the researcher has to formulate—just for argument—the **null hypothesis**[1] that the opinions of white-water rafters do not differ from those of the general population (the 10,000 respondents); and that if all the white-water rafters were contacted, their average response would be 5.6 instead of 6.1. This null hypothesis (represented mathematically as H_o) will be tested against the **alternative hypothesis** (represented mathematically as H_a); that is, the contention that people who did white-water rafting would favor fewer restrictions.

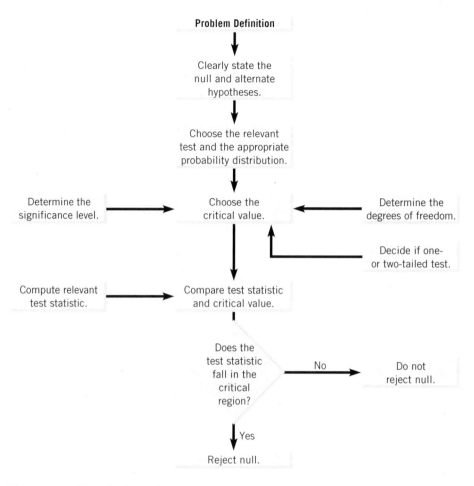

Figure 13-1 Hypothesis-testing process.

As mentioned earlier, the purpose of hypothesis testing is not to question the computed value of the sample statistic but (for example) to make a judgment about the difference between that sample statistic and the hypothesized population parameter.

Choosing the Relevant Statistical Test and the Appropriate Probability Distribution

The next step in hypothesis testing is selecting the appropriate probability distribution. The choice of an appropriate probability distribution depends on the purpose of the hypothesis test. The purpose could vary, from comparing sample and population to comparing two sample characteristics such as means, proportions, variances, and so on. Table 13-1 provides the conditions under which various statistical tests can be used for different purposes. For a given purpose, a particular form of a statistical test may or may not be appropriate, depending on the sample size and whether the population standard deviation is known. In marketing research applications, typically, we deal with large samples ($n \geq 30$), which allows us to draw valid conclusions.

Hence, the next logical step, after stating the null and alternative hypotheses, is to decide upon the criteria (for choosing the critical or the table values for a statistical

TABLE 13-1   Hypothesis Testing and Associated Statistical Tests

Hypothesis Testing	No. of Groups/ Samples	Purpose	Statistical Test	Assumptions/Comments
Frequency distributions	one	Goodness of fit	χ^2	
	two	Tests of independence	χ^2	
Proportions	one	Comparing sample and populations proportions	Z	If σ is known, and for large samples
		Comparing sample and populations proportions	t	If σ is unknown, and for small samples
	two	Comparing two sample proportions	Z	If σ is known
		Comparing two sample proportions	t	If σ is unknown
Means	one	Comparing sample and population mean	Z	If σ is known
		Comparing sample and population mean		
	two	Comparing two sample means	Z	If σ is known
		Comparing two sample means (from independent samples)	t	If σ is unknown
		Comparing two sample means (from related samples)	t	If σ is unknown
	two or more	Comparing multiple sample means	F	Using analysis of variance framework (discussed in next chapter)
Variance	one	Comparing sample and population variances	χ^2	
	two	Comparing sample variances	F	

Legend: σ = population standard deviation

test) to use for making the decision whether to accept or reject the null hypothesis. (Strictly speaking, one should use the terminology "not reject" instead of "accept"; however, for simplicity's sake, we use the term "accept.") The three criteria referred to are (1) the significance level, (2) the number of degrees of freedom, and (3) one- or two-tail test.

Choosing the Critical Value

Significance Level

Say that the hypothesis is to be tested at the 10 percent level of significance. This means that the null hypothesis will be rejected if the difference between the sample statistic and the hypothesized population parameter is so large that this or a larger difference would occur, on the average, only 10 or fewer times in every 100 samples (assuming the hypothesized population parameter is correct). In other words, assuming the hypothesis to be true, the **significance level** indicates the percentage of *sample means that is outside the cutoff limits,* also called the *critical value.*[2]

There is no single rule for selecting a significance level, called *alpha* (α). The most commonly chosen levels in academic research are the 1-percent level, the 5-percent level, and the 10-percent level. Although it is possible to test a hypothesis at any level of significance, bear in mind that the significance level selected is also the risk assumed of rejecting a null hypothesis when it is true. The *higher the significance level*

Assuming the hypothesis to be true, the **significance level** indicates the percentage of sample means that is outside the cutoff limits, also called the critical value.

used for testing a hypothesis, the greater is the probability of rejecting a null hypothesis when it is true. This is called *Type I error.*

Alternately, accepting a null hypothesis when it is false is called *Type II error,* and its probability is represented as *beta (β).* Whenever a choice of the significance level for a test of hypothesis is made, there is an inherent trade-off between these two types of errors. The probability of making one type of error can be reduced only if the manager or researcher is willing to increase the probability of making the other type of error.

Figure 13-2 provides a graphical illustration of this concept.[3] From this figure it can be seen that as the significance level increases, the acceptance region becomes quite small (.50 of the area under the curve in Figure 13-2c). With an acceptance region this small, rarely will a null hypothesis be accepted when it is not true; but at a cost of being this sure, the probability that a null hypothesis will be rejected when it is true will increase.

To deal with this trade-off, researchers decide the appropriate level of significance by examining the costs or penalties attached to both types of errors. For example, if making a Type I error (rejecting a null hypothesis when it is true) involves taking the time and trouble to reexamine the batch of packaged-food products that should have been accepted, but making a Type II error (accepting a null hypothesis when it is false) means taking a chance that the consumers purchasing the product may suffer from food poisoning, obviously the company management will prefer a Type I error to a Type II error. As a result, it will set high levels of significance in its testing. Likewise, if the cost of committing a Type I error is overwhelming when compared to the cost of committing a Type II error, the researcher will go for low values of α.

The Power of a Hypothesis Test

Ideally, a good test of a hypothesis ought to reject a null hypothesis when it is false. In other words, β (the probability of accepting a null hypothesis when it is false) should be as low as possible, or $1 - \beta$ should be as high a value as possible (preferably close to 1.0). A high value of $1 - \beta$ indicates that the hypothesis test is working very well. Since the value of $1 - \beta$ provides a measure of how well the test works, it is also known as the **power of the hypothesis test.**

A high value of $1 - \beta$ (where β is the probability of accepting a null hypothesis when it is false) indicates that the hypothesis test is working well. Since the value of $1 - \beta$ provides a measure of how well the test works, it is also known as the **power of the hypothesis test.**

Thus, the power of a statistical test of a null hypothesis is the probability that it will lead to the rejection of the null hypothesis; that is, the probability that it will result in the conclusion that the phenomenon exists. The power of a statistical test depends on three parameters: the significance level of the test, the reliability of the sample results, and the "effect size" (that is, the degree to which the phenomenon exists).[4] The following table gives a summary of the possible data analysis outcomes.

Type of Errors in Hypothesis Testing

Data Analysis Conclusion	Null Hypothesis in Population is	
	True	False
Do not reject H_0	Correct Decision Probability = $1 - \alpha$ Confidence level	Type II Error Probability = β
Reject H_0	Type I error Probability = α Significance level	Correct Decision Probability = $1 - \beta$ Power of Test

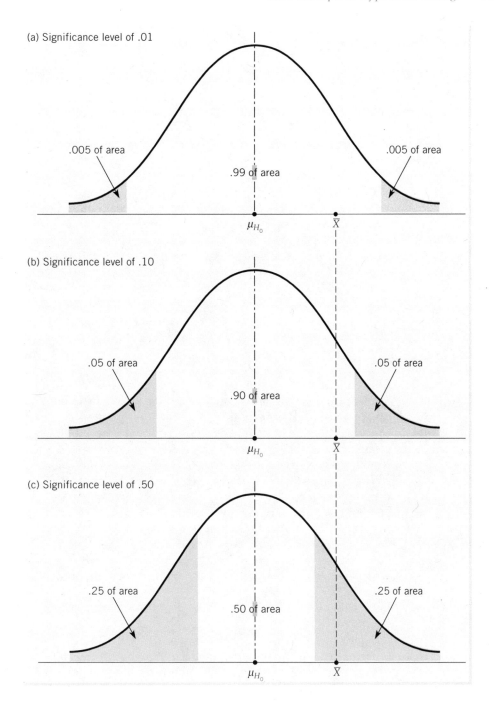

(a) Significance level of .01

.005 of area

.99 of area

.005 of area

μ_{H_0} $\overline{X}$

(b) Significance level of .10

.05 of area

.90 of area

.05 of area

μ_{H_0} $\overline{X}$

(c) Significance level of .50

.25 of area

.50 of area

.25 of area

μ_{H_0} $\overline{X}$

Figure 13-2   Relationship between Type I and Type II errors.

Degrees of Freedom

Degrees of freedom (df) refers to the number or bits of "free" or unconstrained data used in calculating a sample statistic or test statistic. Degrees of freedom is traditionally represented as $n - k$, where n is the total number of information bits available and k is the number of linear constraints or restrictions required when calculating a sample statistic or test statistic. In a simple random sample of n observations, there

Degrees of freedom (df) refers to the number or bits of "free" or unconstrained data used in calculating a sample statistic or test statistic.

are n degrees of freedom if no restrictions are placed on the sample. A sample mean $\bar{X}$ has n degrees of freedom, since there are no constraints or restrictions applied to the sample when calculating its value. However, there are $(n-1)$ degrees of freedom associated with a sample variance, because 1 degree of freedom is "lost" due to the restriction that it is necessary to calculate a mean before calculating the variance. Stated somewhat differently, the first $n-1$ observations in a sample can be selected freely, but the nth value must be chosen so that the constraint of an identical mean value is satisfied. In general, the more degrees of freedom there are, the greater is the likelihood of observing differences or relationships among variables.

One- or Two-Tailed Test

When conducting a one-sided hypothesis test, a **one-tailed test,** the researcher determines whether a particular population parameter is larger or smaller than some predefined value. In this case, only one critical value (and region) of a test statistic is used. In a two-sided hypothesis test, called a **two-tailed test,** the researcher determines the likelihood that a population parameter is within certain upper and lower bounds. Depending on the statistical technique applied, one or two critical values may be used.

The next section discusses the statistical test used to measure associations.

◆ CROSS-TABULATION AND CHI-SQUARE

Chapter 12 presented the data analysis technique of cross-tabulating two questions. Recollect that the Figure 12-4 illustrated cross-tabulation with the focus on the intention-to-revisit question. In this case, the appropriate null hypothesis would be that there was no relationship between the respondents' intention to revisit and the age group to which they belong. Such a hypothesis can be tested based on a measure of the relationship between the questions of the cross-tabulation table, termed the **chi-square statistic.** This section discusses the chi-square and its associated test. Typically, in marketing research applications, the chi-square statistic is employed either as a test of independence or as a test of goodness of fit.

A test of **statistical independence** is used when the manager or the researcher wants to know whether there are associations between two or more variables in a given study. On the other hand, in situations where the manager needs to know whether there is a significant difference between an observed frequency distribution and a theoretical frequency distribution, the **goodness-of-fit test** is used. In this section we will discuss each of these applications of the chi-square statistic in detail.

Before introducing the chi-square statistic as a test of independence, however, it is useful to develop and illustrate the notion of statistical independence. The concept of independence is really central not only to the chi-square statistic, but to all association measures.

A test of **statistical independence** is used when the manager or the researcher wants to know whether there are associations between two or more variables in a given study.

The **goodness-of-fit test** is used when the manager needs to know whether there is a significant difference between an observed frequency distribution and a theoretical frequency distribution.

The Concept of Statistical Independence

Two variables are *statistically independent* if knowledge of one would offer no information as to the identity of the other. Consider the following experiment, illustrated in Table 13-2. Suppose that in a repeated-choice task conducted in New York City, a product was preferred in such a manner that it would yield a choice share of .40 (4 of 10 individuals would choose the product). Suppose, further, that a group of con-

TABLE 13-2   An Experiment and Its Expected Outcome

| | | Choice Task in New York | | Outcomes Expected | Probability |
		Choose	Not Choose		
	Loyal	$E_1 = 16^a$	$E_2 = 24$	40	0.20
	Deal prone	$E_3 = 40$	$E_4 = 60$	100	0.50
Drawing a customer in Los Angeles	Variety seekers	$E_5 = 24$	$E_6 = 36$	60	0.30
	Outcome expected	80	120	200	
	Probability	0.40	0.60		

[a] E_1 = expected cell size under independence

sumers in Los Angeles consists of 20 percent loyals, 30 percent variety seekers, and the rest deal-prone consumers. The experiment executes the choice task and draws a consumer from the group. The outcome of the choice task is independent of the draw from the group of consumers. Before the experiment begins, the chance of getting a loyal consumer is .20. After the choice task, the probability of getting a loyal is still .20. The knowledge of the outcome of the choice task does not affect our information as to the outcome of the consumer draw; therefore, the choice task is statistically independent of the consumer draw.

Expected Value

If the previous experiment were repeated many times, we would expect 20 percent of the outcomes to include a loyal consumer. The number of "loyal" outcomes that we would expect would be $.20n$, where n is the number of experiments conducted. In each experiment we would expect 40 percent of consumers to choose the product, and 60 percent not to choose the product. Then the number of experiments resulting in drawing a loyal consumer and choosing the product would be "expected" to be $[(.40) \times (.20n)]$.

If n is equal to 200 and E_i is the number of outcomes expected in cell i, then for cells 1, 2, and 3 we have

$$E_1 = (.40) \times (.20n) = 16$$
$$E_2 = (.60) \times (.20n) = 24$$
$$E_3 = (.40) \times (.50n) = 40$$

The reader should determine E_4, E_5, and E_6. The **expected value** of outcomes in cell i, E_i, is the number that would be expected, on average, if the experiments involving independent variables were repeated many times. Of course, cell 1 will not have 16 entries; sometimes it will have more and sometimes fewer. However, on average, it will have 16.

Chi-Square as a Test of Independence

Consider Table 13-3, which shows the results of a survey of 200 opera patrons who were asked how frequently they attended the symphony in a neighboring city. The frequency of attendance was partitioned into the categories of never, occasionally, and often; thus, it became a nominally scaled variable. The respondents also were asked whether they regarded the location of the symphony as convenient or incon-

TABLE 13-3   A Cross-Tabulation of Opera Patrons

| | | Location (L) | | | |
		Convenient	Not Convenient	Row Total	P_A
		1	2		
	Often (more than 6 times a season)	27.5%	15%	20%	.20
		$O_1 = 22$	$O_2 = 18$	(40)	
		3	4		
Attendance at symphony (A)	Occasionally	60%	43.3%	50%	.50
		$O_3 = 48$	$O_4 = 52$	(100)	
		5	6		
	Never	12.5%	41.7%	30%	.30
		$O_5 = 10$	$O_6 = 50$	(60)	
				100%	1.00
	Column total	100% (80)	100% (120)	(200)	
	P_L	.40	.60	1.00	

$$\chi^2 = \sum \frac{(O_i - E_i)^2}{E_i} = 20$$

Note: E_i equals the expected cell values and O_i equals the observed cell values.

venient. The resulting cross-tabulation shows the percentage breakdown of attendance in each location category. The observed number of respondents in cell i, termed O_1, also is shown. Thus, 22 people in cell 1 attended the symphony often and thought that the location was convenient ($O_1 = 22$).

The row totals and column totals and the proportions (P_A and P_L) are tabulated in the margin. Note that they are the frequency distribution for the respective variables. For example, the column total indicates that 80 respondents (.40 of all the respondents) thought the location was convenient and 120 (.60 of all the respondents) thought it was inconvenient.

The null hypothesis associated with this test is that the two (nominally scaled) variables are statistically independent. The alternative hypothesis is that the two variables are not independent. Formally,

Null hypothesis H_0: attendance at symphony is independent of the location
Alternative hypothesis H_a: attendance at symphony is dependent on the location

The Chi-Square Distribution

If the variables are statistically independent—that is, if the null hypothesis is true—then the sampling distribution of the chi-square statistic can be closely approximated by a continuous curve known as a **chi-square distribution.** The chi-square distribution is a probability distribution and, therefore, the total area under the curve in each chi-square distribution is 1.0. As in the case of the t-distribution, different chi-square distributions are associated with different degrees of freedom. The chi-square distribution is one of the statistical distributions that is completely determined by its degree of freedom. The mean of the distribution is equal to v, the number of degrees of freedom, and the variance of the chi-square distribution is equal to $2v$. The chi-

*If the variables are statistically independent, then the sampling distribution of the chi-square statistic can be closely approximated by a continuous curve known as a **chi-square distribution.** The total area under the curve is 1.0.*

square values based on the distribution are given in Table 13-4 in the case study at the end of the chapter.

The number of degrees of freedom, v, for the chi-square test of independence is obtained using the formula $v = (r - 1) \times (c - 1)$, where r is the number of rows in the contingency table and c is the number of columns. For large values of v, the distribution is approximately normal.

The Chi-Square Statistic

The chi-square statistic (χ^2) is a measure of the difference between the actual numbers observed in cell i, termed O_i, and the number expected if the null hypothesis were true, that is, under the assumption of statistical independence, E_i. The chi-square statistic is defined as

$$\chi^2 = \sum_{i=1}^{k} \frac{(O_i - E_i)^2}{E_i}$$

with $(r - 1)(c - 1)$ degrees of freedom, *where*

O_i = observed number in cell i

E_i = number in cell i expected under independence

r = number of rows

c = number of columns

k = number of cells

If the two variables (location and attendance) are independent, then the expected frequencies in each cell will be

$$E_i = P_L \times P_A \times n$$

where P_L and P_A are proportions defined in Table 13-3. Thus, for the data in Table 13-2,

$$E_i = .40 \times .20 \times 200 = 16$$

The appropriate χ^2 statistic is computed as

$$\chi^2 = \frac{(22 - 16)^2}{16} + \frac{(18 - 24)^2}{24} + \frac{(48 - 40)^2}{40} + \frac{(52 - 60)^2}{60} + \frac{(10 - 24)^2}{24} + \frac{(50 - 36)^2}{36} = 20.03$$

The number of degrees of freedom in this case is given by $(r - 1) \times (c - 1)$, which is $(3 - 1) \times (2 - 1) = 2$, and if the test is done at a significance level $\beta = 0.05$, the table value of χ^2 can be found to be 5.99. Since the calculated value of χ^2 (20.03) is greater than the table value (5.99), the *null hypothesis is rejected*. The researcher can thus conclude that the attendance at the symphony is dependent on the location of the symphony. Figure 13-3 shows a graphical description of the chi-square test.

Interpreting the Chi-Square Test of Independence

The chi-square test of independence is valid only if the sample size is large enough to guarantee the similarity between the theoretically correct distribution and the χ^2 sampling distribution. If the expected frequencies are too small, the value of χ^2 will be overestimated and will result in too many rejections of the null hypothesis. As a

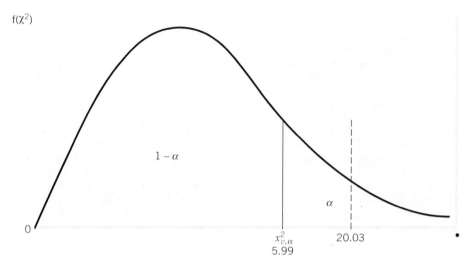

Figure 13-3 Cutoff points of the chi-square distribution function.

general rule, the results of the *chi-square test are valid only if the value of expected frequency in each cell of the contingency table is at least 5*. If the table contains more than one cell with an expected frequency of less than 5, the chi-square test can still be used by combining these in order to get an expected frequency of 5 or more. In doing this, however, the number of degrees of freedom is reduced and thus will yield less information from the contingency table.

Although the rejection rule in a chi-square hypothesis test is to reject the null hypothesis if the computed chi-square value is greater than the table value and vice versa, if the computed chi-square value is zero, we should be careful to question whether *absolutely no difference* exists between observed and expected frequencies. If the manager or researcher has reasons to believe that some difference ought to exist, he or she should examine either the way the data were collected or the manner in which measurements were taken, or both, to be certain that existing differences had not been obscured or missed in collecting sample data.

Strength of Association

The **strength of association** can be measured by the contingency coefficient (*C*). This index is also related to chi-square, as follows:

$$C = \sqrt{\frac{\chi^2}{\chi^2 + n}}$$

The contingency coefficient varies between 0 and 1. The 0 value occurs in the case of no association (that is, the variables are statistically independent), but the maximum value of 1 is never achieved. Rather, the maximum value of the contingency coefficient depends on the size of the table (number of rows and number of columns). For this reason it should be used only to compare tables of the same size. The value of the contingency coefficient for our example is

$$C = \sqrt{\frac{20.03}{20.03 + 200}}$$

$$= .30$$

Limitations as an Association Measure

The chi-square statistic provides a measure of association between two variables, but it has several limitations. First, it is basically proportional to the sample size, which makes it difficult to interpret in an absolute sense (free from the effect of sample size) and to compare cross-tabulations with different sample sizes. However, in a given analysis it is often necessary to compare different cross-tabulations with the same sample size. Second, it has no upper bound; thus, it is difficult to obtain a feel for its value. Furthermore, the chi-square value does not indicate how the two variables are related. A further discussion of the use of chi-square as an association measure and some alternatives are presented next. Chapter 14 presents a detailed discussion of the more commonly used measures of association, such as the correlation and regression analysis.

Measures Based on Chi-Square

The most obvious flaw of chi-square is that the value is directly proportional to the sample size. If the sample were 2,000 rather than 200, and if the distribution of responses were the same (that is, all cells were 10 times as large), the chi-square would be 200 rather than 20. Two measures have been proposed to overcome this problem; they are the contingency coefficient (C), which was discussed earlier, and phi-squared (φ^2).

$$\text{phi-squared: } \varphi^2 = \frac{\chi^2}{n} = \frac{20.03}{200} = .10$$

Other measures include Cramer's V, which is a modified version of the phi-squared coefficient and is used for larger tables (greater than 2×2).

$$V = \sqrt{\frac{\varphi^2}{\min(r-1)(c-1)}}$$

$$= \sqrt{\frac{\chi^2/n}{\min(r-1)(c-1)}}$$

$$= \sqrt{\frac{.10}{2}}$$

$$= .223$$

Although the phi-squared correlation has no upper limit for larger tables, Cramer's V adjusts φ^2 by the minimum of the number of columns or rows in the table. This adjustment results in V ranging from 0 to 1, and a higher value indicates a stronger association. For a 2×2 table, Cramer's V is identical to the coefficient phi (φ).

Both measures are easy to calculate but, unfortunately, are hard to interpret. On the one hand, when there is no association they are both zero. When there is an association between the two variables, there is no upper limit against which to compare the calculated value. In a special case, when the cross-tabulation has the same number of rows r and columns c, an upper limit of the contingency efficient can be computed for two perfectly correlated variables as $(r-1)/r$.

The Chi-Square Goodness-of-Fit Test

In marketing, there are situations when the manager or researcher is interested in determining whether a population distribution corresponds to a particular form such as a normal or a Poisson distribution. Also, there are situations where the manager wants to know whether some observed pattern of frequencies corresponds to an "expected" pattern. In such situations, the chi-square test can be used as a goodness-of-fit test to investigate how well the observed pattern fits the expected pattern.

For example, an automobile manufacturer, planning the production schedule for the next model year, is interested in knowing how many different colors of the car should be produced, and how many in each of the various shades. Past data indicate that red, green, black, and white are the fast-moving shades and that, for every 100 cars, 30 red, 25 each of green and black, and 20 white cars are sold. Also, of the 2,500 current-year model cars sold to date, 680 were red, 520 were green, 675 were black, and the remaining 625 were white. Based on this sample of 2,500 cars, the production manager thinks there has been a substantial shift in consumer preference for color and that the next model year production should not follow the 30:25:25:20 ratio of the previous years. The manager wants to test this hypothesis at a level of .05. The purchases are independent and fall into 4 (= k) mutually exclusive categories. Therefore, the chi-square goodness-of-fit test can be employed to test this hypothesis. Formally,

H_o: The observed color preference coincides with the expected pattern.

H_a: The observed color preference does not coincide with the expected pattern.

$\alpha = $ .05.

The number of degrees of freedom for this test is determined to be $v = (k - 1) = 3$. The expected value for each category is calculated using $E_i = p_i \times n$. For the case of the red cars this will be $0.3 \times 2,500 = 750$. Hence, the chi-square statistic can be calculated to be

$$\chi^2 = (680 - 750)^2/750 + (520 - 625)^2/625 + (675 - 625)^2/625 + (625 - 500)^2/500 = 59.42$$

The chi-square at $\alpha = .05$ for 3 degrees of freedom is obtained from the tables as 7.81. Since the calculated value of χ^2 (59.42) is greater than the table value (7.81), the null hypothesis is rejected. The production manager can thus conclude that consumer preference for colors has definitely changed.

As mentioned earlier, the results of the chi-square goodness-of-fit test are valid only if the expected number of cases in each category is five or more, although this value can be less for some cells. Also, in the case of problems where the researcher is interested in determining whether the population distribution corresponds to either a normal or Poisson or binomial distribution, certain additional restrictions might be imposed on the calculations of the degrees of freedom. For example, if we have six categories, v is calculated to be $6 - 1 = 5$. If, however, the sample mean is to be used as an estimate for the population mean, an additional degree of freedom has to be sacrificed. Also, if the sample standard deviation is to be used as an estimate for the population standard deviation, another degree of freedom has to be sacrificed. In this case v will be equal to 3. The rule of thumb to determine the degrees of freedom for the goodness-of-fit test is first to employ the $(k - 1)$ rule and then subtract an additional degree of freedom for each population parameter that has to be estimated from the sample data.

◆ MEANS AND PROPORTIONS

Testing Hypothesis About a Single Mean

One of the most commonly occurring problems in marketing research is the need to make some judgment about the population mean. This can be done by testing the hypothesized value of the population mean. A discussion on the hypothesis test of the mean will not be complete until we clarify a few issues pertaining to the test. Table 13-1 describes the factors that influence the choice of the appropriate probability distribution. Broadly speaking, the choice of the distribution depends on (1) the purpose of hypothesis testing, (2) the size of the sample, and (3) whether the population standard deviation is known. When the population standard deviation is known, the sample size does not really matter, because the normal distribution and the associated Z-tables can be used for either of the cases. When the population standard deviation is not known, the size of the sample dictates the choice of the probability standard distribution. Hence, this section discusses applications pertaining to both the Z- and the t-distributions. Also, it was mentioned earlier that the test could be either a two-tailed test or a one-tailed test, depending on the nature of the hypothesis. Examples of both tests will be presented in this section.

Samples with Known σ

Two-tailed Test

Superior Shields, a manufacturer of automobile windshields, is faced with a problem. The company has to manufacture windshields that can obtain a quality rating of 5,000 points (the average of the competition). But any further increase in the ratings raises production costs significantly and will result in a competitive disadvantage. Based on past experience, the manufacturer knows that the standard deviation of the quality rating is 250. To check whether this company's windshields meet the competitive standards for quality, the management picks a random sample of 100 industrial customers and finds that the mean quality rating from the sample is 4,960. Based on this sample, the management of Superior Shields wants to know whether its product meets the competitive standards and is neither higher nor lower. Management wants to test its hypothesis at a .05 level of significance.

Statistically, the data in this case can be presented as follows:

Null hypothesis	H_o: $\mu = 5,000$	Hypothesized value of the population mean (competitive standards)
Alternative hypothesis	H_a: $\mu \neq 5,000$	The true mean value is not 5,000
Sample size	$n = 100$	
Sample mean	$\bar{X} = 4,960$	
Population standard deviation	$\sigma = 250$	
Significance level	$\alpha = .05$	

Since the population standard deviation is known, and the size of the sample is large enough to be treated as infinite, the normal distribution can be used. The first step, then, is to calculate the standard error of the mean. This is done using the formula

$$\text{Standard error of mean } \sigma_{\bar{X}} = \sigma/\sqrt{n}$$

Because this is a two-tailed test with a significance level α of .05, using the normal distribution table (found in Appendix A-1 at the end of this book), the Z-value for .975 [1 − (0.05/2)] of the area under the curve is found to be 1.96. The calculated Z-score is

$$Z = \bar{X} - \mu = \frac{(4,960 - 5,000)}{25} = -1.6$$
$$\quad \sigma_{\bar{X}}$$

Figure 13-4 provides a graphical description of the hypothesis test. The rejection rule is to reject the null hypothesis in favor of the alternative hypothesis if $|Z_{calc}| > Z_{\alpha/2}$. Because 1.6 < 1.96, the management of Superior Shields is convinced that its windshields meet the competitive standards of a quality rating of 5,000 points.

One-tail Test

Mr. James Ginter, the purchase manager of a big automobile manufacturer, wants to buy windshields that have quality ratings of *at least* 5,000 points, and he doesn't mind paying the price for a good-quality windshield. But Mr. Ginter is skeptical about the claims of Superior Shields that its windshields meet the competitive level. To convince Mr. Ginter, Superior Shields offers to pay for the survey of a sample of 50 consumers. The quality ratings from the sample reveal a mean of 4,970 points. The problem facing Mr. Ginter now is whether to accept the claims of Superior Shields based on the sample mean. Also, Mr. Ginter wants the probability of a Type II error occurring (accepting the null hypothesis when it is false) to be as low as possible; hence, he wants the test to be done at a .01 level of significance.

Statistically, the new data can be presented as follows:

Null hypothesis	$H_0: \mu \geq 5{,}000$	Hypothesized value of the population mean
Alternative hypothesis	$H_a: \mu < 5{,}000$	The true mean value is less than 5,000
Sample size	$n = 50$	
Sample mean	$\bar{X} = 4{,}970$	
Population standard deviation	$\sigma = 250$	
Significance level	$\alpha = .01$	
Standard error of mean	$\sigma_{\bar{X}} = \sigma/\sqrt{n}$	
	$= 250/7.07 = 35.36$	

Since this is now a one-tailed test (left-tailed test) with a significance level of .01, using the normal distribution table, the Z-value for .990 (1 − .01) of the area under the left or right tail of the curve can be found to be 2.33. The calculated Z-score is

$$Z = \frac{\bar{X} - \mu}{\sigma_{\bar{X}}} = \frac{(4{,}970 - 5{,}000)}{35.36} = -0.85$$

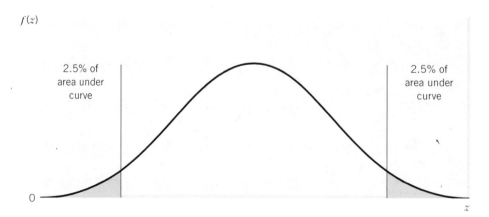

Figure 13-4 The normal distribution.

Figure 13-5 provides an illustration of this test. The rejection rule for a left-tailed test is to reject the null hypothesis in favor of the alternative hypothesis if $Z_{calc} < -Z_\alpha$. Since $-0.85 > -2.33$, we fail to reject the null hypothesis.

Samples with σ Not Known

Now assume that Superior Shields provided Mr. Ginter with a sample of only 25 consumers for the previous example, and that the mean quality ratings from the sample were 4,962 points. Also, assume that Superior Shields did not have prior knowledge of the population standard deviation, and the sample standard deviation was found to be 245.

Statistically, the data can now be presented as follows:

Null hypothesis	H_o: μ ≥ 5,000	Hypothesized value of the population mean
Alternative hypothesis	H_a: μ < 5,000	The true mean value is less than 5,000
Sample size	$n = 25$	
Sample mean	$\bar{X} = 4,962$	
Sample standard deviation	$s = 245$	
Significance level	$\alpha = .01$	

Because the population standard deviation is not known, the sample standard deviation can be used as an estimate of the population standard deviation. Also, since an estimate for the population standard deviation is being used, the standard error of the mean will also be an estimate, given by

$$S_{\bar{X}} = \frac{s}{\sqrt{n}} = \frac{245}{\sqrt{5}} = 49$$

As discussed earlier, if **σ** is not known, the appropriate probability distribution will be the *t*-distribution. The appropriate *t*-distribution will have $n - 1$ (in our case 24) degrees of freedom. The table value can be obtained by looking at the *t*-table under the .01 column for the 24 degrees of freedom row. The *t*-value thus obtained is 2.492. The calculated *t*-value is given by

$$t_{calc} = (\bar{x} - \mu)/S_{\bar{X}} = \frac{(4,962 - 5,000)}{49} = -0.78$$

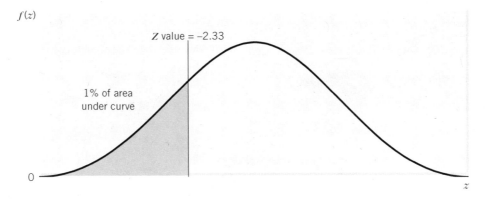

Figure 13-5 The normal distribution.

The rejection rule for a left-tailed t-test is to reject the null hypothesis in favor of the alternative hypothesis if $t_{calc} < -t^{\alpha}_{n-1}$. Here, $-0.78 > -2.492$; hence, Mr. Ginter again will fail to reject the null hypothesis that the mean quality rating of Superior Shields' windshields is greater than or equal to 5,000 points.

Hypothesis Testing for Differences between Means

The mayor of a city wants to test whether the daily wages received by the male and female employees of large organizations in that city are the same for the same job description. To test this hypothesis, a random sample of 400 male and 576 female employees is selected and the average wages are recorded. The mean and standard deviation of the wages for the males are $105.70 and $5.00, respectively, whereas for the females the corresponding numbers are $112.80 and $4.80. A significance level of .01 is desired. The hypothesis testing procedure for differences in means differs depending on whether the samples are obtained from unrelated or related samples.

The logic behind the hypothesis tests and the basic concepts of the tests remain the same for this condition. What varies is the statistical formula used to compute the standard error of the difference between the means. Also, for small sample sizes in the testing of means and proportions, the t-distribution is used.

Case 1: Unrelated (Independent) Samples Test. In the salary comparison example, the null hypothesis will be that the mean salary of male employees is equal to the mean salary of the female employees of the same job description. Hence, in this case $\mu_1 - \mu_2 = 0$. Thus, the null hypothesis will be

$$H_o: \mu_1 - \mu_2 = c(= 0)$$

For a two-tailed test, the alternative hypothesis will be

$$H_a: \mu_1 - \mu_2 \neq c$$
$$\text{Reject } H_o \text{ if } |Z_{calc}| > Z_{\alpha/2}$$

If one has to use the sample standard deviation, then a t-test can be used with the degree of freedom equal to $(n_1 + n_2 - 2)$. Since we use large sample sizes, we can adopt the approximation of using the sample standard deviation instead of the population standard deviation. The standard error of difference in means

$$S_{\bar{X}_1 - \bar{X}_2} = \sqrt{\frac{s_1^2}{n_1} + \frac{s_2^2}{n_2}} = \sqrt{\frac{(5.00)^2}{400} + \frac{(4.80)^2}{576}} = \$0.32$$

where

s_1 = standard deviation of sample 1

s_2 = standard deviation of sample 2

n_1 = size of sample 1

n_2 = size of sample 2

and the calculated value of Z is

$$\bar{Z}_{calc} = ((\bar{X}_1 - \bar{X}_2) - (\mu_1 - \mu_2))/S_{\bar{X}_1 - \bar{X}_2} = ((105.70 - 112.80) - 0)/0.32 = -22.19$$

where

$(\bar{X}_1 - \bar{X}_2)$ = difference between sample means

$(\mu_1 - \mu_2)$ = difference between the population means

For $\alpha = .01$ and a two-tailed test, the Z-table value is 2.58. Since the $|Z_{calc}|$ is greater than $Z_{\alpha/2}$, the null hypothesis is rejected. This means that the mean daily wages of males and females are not equal.

If the null hypothesis is H_o: $\mu_1 \geq \mu_2$, the alternative hypothesis will be

$$H_a: \mu_1 - \mu_2 > c$$
$$\text{Reject } H_o \text{ if } Z_{calc} > Z_\alpha$$

If the null hypothesis is H_o: $\mu_1 < \mu_2$, the alternative hypothesis will be

$$H_a: \mu_1 - \mu_2 < c$$
$$\text{Reject } H_o \text{ if } Z_{calc} < -Z_\alpha$$

For unknown α, whether or not it is assumed to be equal across the two samples, the *t*-distribution is used.

Case 2: Related (Dependent) Samples Test. Instant Fit, a health club, advertises that on average its clientele lose at least 20 pounds within the first 30 days of joining the club. A health-conscious chief executive of an organization wants to provide his employees with free memberships to Instant Fit as part of the organization's employee benefit program, but the chief finance officer is rather skeptical about Instant Fit's advertising claims. In an effort to satisfy the finance officer, Instant Fit provides him with "before and after" weight data for 10 of its clients. The finance officer wants to test the claim at a significance level of .05. Formally, the data can be presented as

Null hypothesis	H_o: $\mu_1 - \mu_2 \geq 20$
Alternative hypothesis	H_a: $\mu_1 - \mu_2 < 20$
Significance level	$\alpha = .05$

In this case, the *t*-test for differences between means is not appropriate because the test assumes that the samples are independent. Conceptually, Instant Fit has not provided two independent samples of before and after weights, inasmuch as the weights of the same 10 persons were recorded twice. The appropriate procedure for this case is to obtain the mean and standard deviation of the "difference"; that is, the data have to be viewed as one sample of weight losses.

This can be done by defining a variable D, which is the difference between the before and after weights of each individual in the sample. Assume that the data provided by Instant Fit are as follows:

Before:	237	135	183	225	147	146	214	157	157	144
After:	153	114	181	186	134	166	189	113	188	111
Then D:	84	21	2	39	13	–20	25	44	–31	33

Let $\bar{D}$ be the mean of the difference variable D and let $s_{\bar{D}}$ be the standard deviation of the difference. Now:

Null hypothesis $\qquad H_0: \bar{D} \geq 20$

Alternative hypothesis $\qquad H_a: \bar{D} < 20$

The appropriate test statistic is

$$t = \frac{\bar{D} - d}{s_{\bar{D}}/\sqrt{n}}$$

where

d = hypothesized valued difference; in our case, $d = 20$

n = sample size (10)

Then

$$\bar{D} = \frac{1}{n} \sum_{i=1}^{n} D_i = \frac{210}{10} = 21$$

$$s_{\bar{D}}^2 = \frac{1}{n-1} \left(\sum_{i=1}^{n} D_i^2 - n\bar{D}^2 \right) = \frac{1}{9}[14{,}202 - 10(21)^2] = 1{,}088$$

$$s_{\bar{D}} = 32.98$$

Thus,

$$t = \frac{21 - 20}{32.98/\sqrt{10}} = 0.096$$

The rejection rule is the same as before.

If $\alpha = .05$, for 9 (i.e., $n - 1$) degrees of freedom and a one-tail test, the critical *t*-value is -1.833. Because the calculated *t*-value of $0.096 \geq -1.833$, the null hypothesis is not rejected. Therefore, Instant Fit's claim is valid.

Hypothesis Testing of Proportions

There are instances in marketing research where the management is concerned not with the mean but with proportions. Consider, for example, the quality assurance department of a light bulb manufacturing company. The manager of the department, based on his experience, claims that 95 percent of the bulbs manufactured by the company are defect-free. The CEO of the company, a quality-conscious person, checks a random sample of 225 bulbs and finds only 87 percent of the bulbs to be defect-free. The CEO now wants to test the hypothesis (at the .05 level of significance) that 95 percent of the bulbs manufactured by the company are defect-free.[5]

The data for this test can be described statistically as

$p_0 = .95$: hypothesized value of the proportion of defect-free bulbs

$q_0 = .05$: hypothesized value of the proportion of defective bulbs

$p = .87$: sample proportion of defect-free bulbs

$q = .13$: sample proportion of defective bulbs

Null hypothesis	$H_0: p = 0.95$
Alternative hypothesis	$H_a: p \neq 0.95$
Sample size	$n = 225$
Significance level	$\alpha = 0.05$

The first step in the hypothesis test of proportions is to calculate the standard error of the proportion using the hypothesized value of defect-free and defective bulbs; that is,

$$\sigma_p = \sqrt{\frac{p_0 q_0}{n}} = \sqrt{\frac{.95 \times .05}{225}} = .0145$$

The two-tailed test of proportions is graphically illustrated in Figure 13-6. Since np and nq are each larger than 5, the normal approximation of the binomial distribution can be used. Hence, the appropriate Z-value for .975 of the area under the curve can be obtained from the Z-tables as 1.96. Thus, the limits of the acceptance region are

$$\rho_0 \pm 1.96 \sigma_p = .95 \pm (1.96 \times .0145) = (.922, .978)$$

In as much as the sample proportion of defect-free bulbs, .87, does not fall within the acceptance region, the CEO should reject the quality assurance manager's claims (the null hypothesis). A one-tailed test of hypothesis of proportions can be performed similarly.

Hypothesis Testing of Differences between Proportions

John and Linda, sales executives for a big computer company, have been short-listed as the finalists in their company's annual sales competition. John and Linda have identical track records, and the winner of the competition will be selected based on his or her "conversion ratio" (i.e., the number of prospects converted into sales). The sales manager randomly picks 100 of John's prospects and finds that 84 of them have been converted to customers. In Linda's case, 82 of her sample of 100 prospects have been converted. The sales manager needs to know (at $\alpha = .05$) whether there is a difference in the conversion ratio, based on the sample proportions. Statistically, the data in this case can be represented as

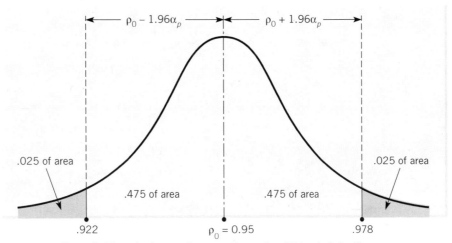

Two-tailed hypothesis test of a proportion at the .05 level of significance

Figure 13-6   The normal distribution.

$p_J = .84 =$ John's conversion ratio based on this sample of prospects

$q_J = .16 =$ Proportion that John failed to convert

$n_1 = 100 =$ John's prospect sample size

$p_L = .82 =$ Linda's conversion ratio based on her sample of prospects

$q_L = .18 =$ Proportion that Linda failed to convert

$n_2 = 100 =$ Linda's prospect sample size

Null hypothesis	$H_o: p_J = p_L$
Alternative hypothesis	$H_a: p_J \neq p_L$
Significance level	$\alpha = .05$

As in the case of the pooled variance estimate of difference in means, the best estimate of p (the proportion of success), if the two proportions are hypothesized to be equal, is

$$p = \frac{\text{total number of successes in the two samples weighted by the respective sample sizes}}{\text{total number of observations in the two samples}}$$

$$q = 1 - p$$

In this example,

$$p = [(n_1 p_J) + (n_2 p_L)]/(n_1 + n_2)] = [(100 \times .84) + (100 \times .82)]/200 = .83$$
$$q = .17$$

Now an estimate of $\sigma_{p_J - p_L}$ can be obtained using

$$\sigma_{p_J - p_L} = \sqrt{\frac{pq}{n_1} + \frac{pq}{n_2}}$$

$$= \sqrt{\frac{(.83)(.17)}{100} + \frac{(.83)(.17)}{100}}$$

$$= .053$$

The Z-value can be calculated using

$$Z_{calc} = [(p_J - p_L) - 0]/\sigma_{p_J - p_L} = \frac{.02}{.053} = .38$$

The Z-value obtained from the table is 1.96 (for $\alpha = .05$). Hence, we fail to reject the null hypothesis.

◆ RELATIONSHIP BETWEEN CONFIDENCE INTERVAL AND HYPOTHESIS TESTING

In the white-water rafter example, can one determine whether the white-water rafters' average response of 6.1, which will be termed X-bar (the sample mean, $\bar{X}$), is the same as the population mean response of 5.6?

$$H_0: \mu = 5.6$$

$$H_a: \mu \neq 5.6$$

To answer this question, an estimate of the sample standard error of X has to be obtained using the formula

$$s_{\bar{X}} = s/\sqrt{n} = 2.5/\sqrt{35} = 0.42$$

where s, the standard deviation of the sample, was determined to be 2.5 in this example. Although, the population standard deviation is not known, the normal distribution can be used, because we have an estimate based on the sample standard deviation. The appropriate Z-value for $\alpha = .05$ can be obtained from the Z-table (Appendix A-1), and is found to be 1.96. Now the critical values or the cutoff limits can be calculated using the formula

$$\mu_0 \pm 1.96s_{\bar{X}} = 5.6 \pm (1.96 \times 0.42) = (4.78, 6.42)$$

Because 6.1 falls within the limits, we fail to reject the null hypothesis. Figure 13.7 provides a graphical illustration of the hypothesis test. From the Z-table, it can be determined that 95 percent of all the area under the curve is included in the interval extending 1.96 $\sigma_{\bar{X}}$ on either side of the hypothesized mean. In 95 percent of the area, then, there is no significant difference between the sample statistic and the hypothesized population parameter. If the sample statistic falls into the shaded area under the curve, representing 5 percent of the total area (2.5 percent in each tail), then we would reject the null hypothesis.

The term *fail to reject* is used instead of *accept* because even though the sample statistic falls within the critical values, this does not prove that the null hypothesis is true; it *simply does not provide statistical evidence to reject it.*

Alternatively, acceptance or rejection of the hypothesis can be done without the need for calculating the critical values. This is done by calculating the Z-statistic. The Z-statistic is obtained using the formula

$$Z = \frac{\bar{X} - \mu}{s_{\bar{X}}} = \frac{6.1 - 5.6}{0.42} = 1.19$$

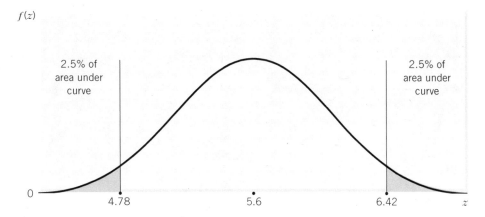

Figure 13-7 The normal distribution.

Then one should apply the rejection rule, which states: For a two-tailed test (for which the alternative hypothesis would be H_a: $\mu \neq c$, the hypothesized value), the rejection rule is to reject the null hypothesis if $|Z_{calc}| > Z_{\alpha/2}$; for a right-tailed test of hypothesis, reject the null hypothesis if $Z_{calc} > Z_\alpha$ (where Z_α is obtained from the Z-tables). There are similar rules for a left-tailed test: For a left-tailed test (for which the alternative hypothesis would be H_a: $\mu < c$, the hypothesized value), the rejection rule is to reject the null hypothesis if $Z_{calc} < -Z_\alpha$.

◆ ANALYSIS OF VARIANCE (ANOVA)

Consider the following pricing experiment. Three prices are under consideration for a new product: 39 cents, 44 cents, and 49 cents. To determine the influence the various price levels will have on sales, three samples of five supermarkets are randomly selected from the geographic area of interest. Each sample is assigned one of the three price levels. Figure 13-8 shows the resulting sales levels in both graphic and tabular form. The 39-cent stores, the first row, had sales of 8, 12, 10, 9, and 11, with an average of 10 units. The 44-cent stores, the second row, averaged 8 units; and the 49-cent stores, the third row, averaged 7 units. Obviously, determining the optimal price will require an extensive analysis involving a host of considerations. However, before the analysis begins, it is appropriate to consider the basic concepts of experiment analysis.

In experimental design, the dependent variable is called the *response variable* and the independent variables are called *factors*. The different levels of a factor are called

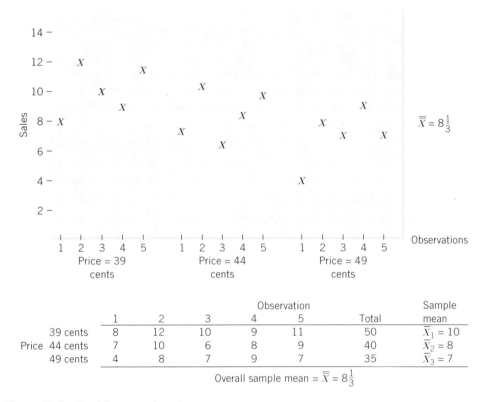

	Observation						Sample
	1	2	3	4	5	Total	mean
39 cents	8	12	10	9	11	50	$\bar{X}_1 = 10$
Price 44 cents	7	10	6	8	9	40	$\bar{X}_2 = 8$
49 cents	4	8	7	9	7	35	$\bar{X}_3 = 7$

Overall sample mean $= \bar{\bar{X}} = 8\frac{1}{3}$

Figure 13-8 A pricing experiment.

treatments. The purpose of most statistical experiments is to (1) determine whether the effects of the various treatments on the response variable are different, and (2) if so, to estimate how different they are. In our pricing experiment, the response variable is sales, the factor being the price, and the treatment being the three levels of the price—39 cents, 44 cents, and 49 cents.

One-Factor Analysis of Variance

Suppose that we wish to study one qualitative factor with levels 1, 2, ..., r. (In the case of the pricing experiment, the number of levels is 3.) That is, we wish to study the effects of these r treatments on a response variable (in this case, sales). The ANOVA of a one-factor model is sometimes called a one-way analysis of variance. As a preliminary step in one-way ANOVA, we wish to determine whether or not there are any statistically significant differences between the treatment means $\mu_1, \mu_2, \mu_3, ..., \mu_r$ (μ_r being the mean value of the population of all possible values of the response variable that could potentially be observed using treatment r.) To do this we test the null hypothesis,

$$H_0: \mu_1 = \mu_2 = \mu_3 = ... = \mu_r$$

(This hypothesis says that all treatments have the same effect on the mean response.) against the alternative hypothesis,

$$H_1: \text{at least 2 of } \mu_1, \mu_2, ..., \mu_r \text{ are different}$$

(This hypothesis says that at least two treatments have different effects on the mean response.)

Essentially, in the case of the pricing experiment, the null hypothesis will be that the price levels have no effect on sales. The differences between sample means could be caused by the fact that a sample of only five was employed for each price level. The alternative hypothesis is that there is a price effect—sales would not be the same for each of the price levels if they were applied to all stores.

To test these hypotheses, we need to compute the ratio between the "between-treatment" variance and "within-treatment" variance. Here, we define *between-treatment variance* as the variance in the response variable for different treatments. On the other hand, *within-treatment variance* is defined as the variance in the response variable for a given treatment. If we can show that "between" variance is significantly larger than the "within" variance, then we can reject the null hypothesis.

Variation among Price Levels

Consider the pricing experiment illustrated in Figure 13-8. To test the null hypothesis, first focus on the variation among price levels ($X_1 = 10$, $X_2 = 8$, and $X_3 = 7$). Then consider the variation within price levels (for example, the stores with the 39-cent price level had sales of 8, 12, 10, 9, and 11). Under the null hypothesis that price levels have no effect on sales, each of these estimates should be similar. If the estimate based on variation among stores of different price levels is inflated, doubt will be cast on the null hypothesis.

The "between" variance estimate is based on the variation between the sample mean values of each row (price level), which is calculated using the formula

$$SS_r = \sum_{p=1}^{r} n_p \left(\bar{X}_p - \bar{\bar{X}} \right)^2$$

where

SS_r = sum of squares between price levels (rows), also called the treatment sum of squares or the variation explained by the price level.

$\bar{X}_p$ = mean sales at price level p (e.g., $X_1 = 10$)

$\bar{\bar{X}}$ = overall mean (in this case = 25/3)

n = number of observations at each price level ($n = 5$)

p = treatment or price level ($p = 1,2,3$)

r = number of treatments or price levels ($r = 3$)

Hence, in this example, the treatment sum of squares can be calculated to be

$$SS_r = 5[(10 - 25/3)^2 + (8 - 25/3)^2 + (7 - 25/3)^2] = 23.3$$

Clearly, as the difference between means gets larger, so will the treatment sum of squares. The "between" variance estimate is termed MSS_r (the mean sum of squares between price levels and is an estimate of the variance among stores), and is obtained by dividing the SS_r by its associated degree of freedom (df), which here is the number of treatments (rows) less one. Thus,

$$MSS_r = \frac{SS_r}{r-1} = \frac{23.3}{2} = 11.65$$

Variation within Price Levels

The "within" variance estimate is based on the variation within each price level (row), which is calculated using the formula

$$SS_u = \sum_{i=1}^{n_p} \sum_{p=1}^{r} (X_{ip} - \bar{X})^2$$

where

SS_u = sum of squares unexplained by the price level (row), also called the error sum of squares or the variation within the price levels.

X_{ip} = sales of observations (stores) i at price level p

n_p = number of observations at each price level ($n_p = 5$ for all p's)

p = treatment or price level ($p = 1, 2, 3$)

r = number of treatments or price levels ($r = 3$)

Hence, in this example, the error sum of squares (or unexplained variations) can be calculated to be

$$SS_u = (8 - 10)^2 + (12 - 10)^2 + \ldots + (7 - 7)^2$$
$$= 34$$

The "within" variance estimate is termed MSS_u (the mean sum of squares unexplained by the price level, an estimate of the variance within stores) and is generated by dividing SS_u by its associated degrees of freedom,[6] which is here equal to $r(n-1)$ when the group sizes are equal, or 12 [also equal to total sample size (N) minus the total number of treatment levels (r) for unequal and equal group sizes]. Thus,

$$\text{MSS}_u = \frac{\text{SS}_u}{N - r} = \frac{34}{12} = 2.8$$

Having calculated the variation explained by the treatment (price level) and the variation unexplained by it, an addition of these two factors would give the total variation or the sum of squares total (SS_t). Thus,

$$\text{SS}_t = \text{SS}_r + \text{SS}_u$$
$$= 23.3 + 34 = 57.3$$

ANOVA Table

The expressions just derived are summarized in Table 13-5, which presents an *analysis of variance* and is termed an *ANOVA* table. The ANOVA table is a conventional way to present a hypothesis test regarding the difference between several means. The table indicates, at the left, the source to the variation. The first row summarizes the determination of MSS_r, which is based on the variation between rows (the explained variation, or the variation explained by the price level). The second row summarizes the determination of MSS_u, which is based on the within-row variation (variation unexplained by the price levels). The third row represents the total variation based on the deviations of the individual sales results from the overall mean. All the variation is thus accounted for.[7]

F-Statistic

We now consider the ratio of the two estimates of the variance (the "between" and "within") of the store sales. This ratio is termed an *F-ratio* or *F-statistic*:

$$F = \text{MSS}_r / \text{MSS}_u$$
$$= 11.65 / 2.8 = 4.16$$

If the null hypothesis that price levels have no effect on sales is true, then our variance estimates using the difference between the sample means, MSS_r, should be the

TABLE 13-5   Price Experiment ANOVA Table

Source of Variation	Variation, Sum of Squares (SS)	Degrees of Freedom (df)	Variance Estimate, Mean Sum of Squares (MSS)	F-ratio
Between price levels explained variation	$SS_r = \sum_{p=1}^{r} n_p(\bar{X}_p - \bar{\bar{X}})^2$ $= 23.3$	$r - 1 = 2$	$MSS_r = \frac{SS_r}{2} = 11.65$	$\frac{MSS_r}{MSS_u} = 4.16$
Within price levels unexplained variation	$SS_u = \sum_{i=1}^{5}\sum_{p=1}^{3}(X_{ip} - \bar{X}_p)^2$ $= 34$	$N - r = 12$	$MSS_u = \frac{SS_u}{12} = 2.8$	
Total	$SS_t = \sum_{i=1}^{5}\sum_{p=1}^{3}(X_{ip} - \bar{\bar{X}})^2$ $= 57.3$	$N - 1 = 14$		

same as those based on the within-row (price-level) variations. The F-ratio should then be close to 1. If, however, the hypothesis is not true and the different price levels generate different sales levels, the MSS_r term will have two components. One component will reflect the variance among stores; the other will reflect the different price effects. As a result, the F-ratio will tend to become large.

Strength of Association

A good descriptive statistic for measuring the strength of association is to compute ρ (rho), the ratio of the sums of squares for the treatment (SS_r) to the total sums of squares (SS_t). Rho is a measure of the proportion of variance accounted for in the sample data. In our example, $\rho = 23.3/57.3 = .407$. In other words, 40.7 percent of the total variation in the data is explained by the treatment (price levels). However, since the sample value (ρ) tends to be upward-biased, it is useful to have an estimate of the population strength of association ($\bar{\omega}^2$, omega squared) between the treatment and the dependent variable. A sample estimate of this population value can be computed as

$$\bar{\omega}^2 = \frac{SS_r - (r - 1)MSS_u}{SS_r + MSS_u} = \frac{23.3 - 2(2.8)}{57.3 + 2.8} = .295$$

In other words, 29.5 percent of the total variation in the data is accounted for by the treatment.

END OF CHAPTER MATERIAL

SUMMARY

Hypothesis testing begins with an assumption, called a hypothesis, that is made about a population parameter. Then data from an appropriate sample are collected, and the information obtained from the sample (sample statistics) is used to decide how likely it is that the hypothesized population parameter is correct. The purpose of hypothesis testing is not to question the computed value of the sample statistic but to make a judgment about the difference between (1) the sample statistics, and (2) the sample statistic and a hypothesized population parameter. There are several points worth remembering about hypothesis testing.

1. Hypothesis testing is a screening test. If the evidence does not pass this test, it may not be worth much attention. If it does pass this test, then it might at least be worth further analysis.
2. Hypothesis testing really measures the effect of sample size. A large sample has a tendency to always yield "statistically significant" results, whereas a small sample will not. Thus, the test really does no more than provide a measure of sample size.
3. Hypothesis testing does not establish whether the null hypothesis is true or false; it only quantifies how persuasive the evidence is against it.

It is common to test a hypothesis concerning a single mean or proportion and the difference between means (or proportions) in data analysis, particularly when experimentation is involved. The hypothesis-testing procedure for differences in means differs, depending on the following criteria:

1. Whether the samples are obtained from different or related samples
2. Whether the population standard deviation is known or not known

3. If the population standard deviation is not known, whether they can be assumed to be equal

4. Whether it is a large sample (n ≥ 30)

A cross-tabulation has associated with it a chi-square test of the relationship between the two variables. A goodness-of-fit test can also be performed with the chi-square analysis.

The more commonly used hypothesis testing of means and proportions was discussed. The chapter proposed the use of various statistical tests, depending on factors such as whether one or two groups are involved and whether the population or sample standard deviation is used. The probability value approach to hypothesis testing and the relationship between confidence interval and hypothesis testing was also discussed. Finally, for comparison of multiple group means, an analysis of variance framework was proposed.

The goal of one-factor ANOVA is to estimate and compare the effects of the different treatments on the response variable. The purpose of most statistical experiments is to (1) determine whether the effects of the various treatments on the response variable are different, and (2) if so, to estimate how different they are. The ANOVA table can be expanded to accommodate *n*-factor or *n*-way analysis of variance.

KEY TERMS

<table>
<tr><td>hypothesis testing</td><td>statistical independence</td></tr>
<tr><td>null hypothesis</td><td>goodness-of-fit test</td></tr>
<tr><td>alternative hypothesis</td><td>expected value</td></tr>
<tr><td>significance level</td><td>chi-square distribution</td></tr>
<tr><td>degrees of freedom</td><td>chi-square statistic</td></tr>
<tr><td>one- or two tail tests</td><td>strength of association</td></tr>
<tr><td>power of the hypothesis test</td><td></td></tr>
</table>

MARKETING RESEARCH TOOLBOX
REVIEW POINTS

1. Hypothesis testing begins with an assumption, called a hypothesis, that is made about a population parameter. Then, data from an appropriate sample are collected, and the information obtained from the sample (sample statistics) is used to decide how likely it is that the hypothesized population parameter is correct.

2. The purpose of hypothesis testing is not to question the computed value of the sample statistic but to make a judgment about the difference between two sample statistics or the sample statistic and a hypothesized population parameter.

3. The criteria used to make decisions on accepting or rejecting the null hypothesis are the significance level, the number of degrees of freedom, and the one- or two-tail test.

4. Assuming the hypothesis to be true, the significance level indicates the percentage of sample means that is outside the cutoff limits, also called the critical value.

5. The higher the significance level used for testing the hypothesis, the greater the probability of rejecting a null hypothesis when it is true. This is called Type I error. Alternately, accepting a null hypothesis when it is false is called Type II error.

6. A high value of $1-\beta$ (where β is the probability of accepting a null hypothesis when it is false) indicates that the hypothesis test is working well. Since the value of $1-\beta$ provides a measure of how well the test works, it is also known as the power of the hypothesis test.

7. Degrees of freedom (df) refers to the number or bits of "free" or unconstrained data used in calculating a sample statistic or test statistic.

8. When conducting a one-sided hypothesis test, the researcher determines whether a particular population parameter is larger or smaller than some predefined value. In this case, only one critical value (and region) of a test statistic is used. In a two-sided hypothesis test, the researcher determines the likelihood that a population parameter is within certain upper and lower bounds.

9. A test of statistical independence is employed when the manager or the researcher wants to know whether there are associations between two or more variables in a given study.

10. In situations where the manager needs to know whether there is a significant difference between an observed frequency distribution and a theoretical frequency distribution, the goodness-of-fit test is employed.

11. If the variables are statistically independent—that is, if the null hypothesis is true—then the sampling distribution of the chi-square statistic can be closely approximated by a continuous curve known as a chi-square distribution. The chi-square distribution is a probability distribution and, therefore, the total area under the curve in each chi-square distribution is 1.0.

12. The chi-square statistic (χ^2) is a measure of the difference between the actual numbers observed in cell i, termed O_i, and the number expected if the null hypothesis were true.

13. The chi-square test of independence is valid only if the sample size is large enough to guarantee the similarity between the theoretically correct distribution and the χ^2 sampling distribution. If the expected frequencies are too small, the value of χ^2 will be overestimated and will result in too many rejections of the null hypothesis.

14. The chi-square statistic provides a measure of association between two variables, but it has several limitations. First, it is basically proportional to the sample size, which makes it difficult to interpret in an absolute sense (free from the effect of sample size) and to compare cross-tabulations with different sample sizes. Second, it has no upper bound; thus, it is difficult to obtain a feel for its value.

15. The rule of thumb to determine the degrees of freedom for the goodness-of-fit test is first to employ the $(k - 1)$ rule and then subtract an additional degree of freedom for each population parameter that has to be estimated from the sample data.

QUESTIONS AND PROBLEMS

1. A study was conducted to determine the relationship between usage of a library and age of users. A sample of 400 was polled and the following cross-tabulation was generated. The numbers in parentheses are the observed cell sizes (O_1).

Age of Library Users

		Under 25	25 to 45	Over 45	Raw Total	Prop.
Library Usage	Heavy	26.2% (21)/E_1 = 17.8	19.5% (41)/E_4 =	24.5% (27)/E_7 =	22.3% (89)	.223
	Medium	32.5% (26)/E_2 =	18.1% (38)/E_5 =	31.8% (35)/E_8 =		
	Light	41.3% (33)/E_3 =	62.4% (131)/E_6 =	43.6% (48)/E_9		
	Column	100% (80)			100% (400)	1.00
	Total Proportion	.20			1.00	

a. Complete the table.
b. Interpret the term $E_1 = 17.8$.
c. Calculate the χ^2 value.
d. Is the χ^2 value significant? At what level? What exactly is the null hypothesis?
e. This data set proves that the usage of the library differs by age: True or false? Why?

2. P&G sampled 400 people to determine their cereal purchase behavior on a particular trip to the store. The results of the study are as follows:

Brand

Purchaser	A	B	C	D
Buys the brand	45	50	45	60
Doesn't buy the brand	55	50	55	40

Are preferences and brands related?

3. It is known that on a particular high school campus, 62 percent of all students are juniors, 23 percent are seniors, and 15 percent are freshmen and sophomores. A sample of 80 students attending a concert was taken. Of these sample members, 74 percent were juniors, 17 percent were seniors, and 9 percent were freshmen and sophomores. Test the null hypothesis that the distribution of students attending the concert was the same as the distribution of students on campus.

4. An admissions dean has noted that, historically, 70 percent of all applications for a college program are from in-state, 20 percent are from neighboring states, and 10 percent are from other states. For a random sample of 100 applicants for the current year, 75 were from in-state, 15 were from neighboring states, and 9 were from other states. Test the null hypothesis that applications in the current year follow the usual pattern. What would you think are some of the factors which would contribute to the deviation from the null hypothesis?

5. The accompanying table shows, for independent random samples of boys and girls, the numbers who play for more or less than 2.5 hours per day. Test at the 10 percent level the null hypothesis of no relationship between a child's sex and the hours of play.

Number of Hours of Play per Day

	Less than 2.5	2.5 or More
Boys	18	10
Girls	17	13

6. A new product was tested in Fresno with a 25-cent coupon and in Tulsa with a 50-cent coupon. A sample of 100 people was contacted in each test city. A total of 40 percent of those contacted in Tulsa had tried the new product, whereas only 30 percent of those contacted in Fresno had tried it, a 10 percent difference. Prior to making the decision as to which coupon to use in the marketing program, a hypothesis was suggested.
   a. What should the null hypothesis be?
   b. What should the alternative hypothesis be?
   c. Is the result significant at the .10 level? At the .05 level? Would you reject the null hypothesis at the .10 level? At the .05 level?
   d. Does the hypothesis show that there will be more trials with a 50-cent coupon? Do you feel that a 50-cent coupon should be used?
   e. How would you account for differences between the audiences? What would the differences in geographical preferences be equal to when tabulating the effectiveness of the test?

7. A manufacturer claims that through the use of a fuel additive, automobiles should achieve, on average, an additional 5 miles per gallon of gas. A random sample of 100 automobiles was used to evaluate this claim. The sample mean increase in miles per gallon achieved was 4.4, and the sample standard deviation was 1.8 miles per gallon. Test the null hypothesis that the population mean is at least 5 miles per gallon.

8. A beer distributer claims that a new display, featuring a life-size picture of a well-known athlete, will increase product sales in supermarkets by an average of 40 cases a week. For a random sample of 25 supermarkets, the average sales increase was 31.3 cases and the sample standard deviation was 12.2 cases. Test, at the 5 percent level, the null hypothesis that the population mean sales increase is at least 40 cases, stating any assumption you make.

9. Of a sample of 361 owners of retail service and business firms which had gone into bankruptcy, 105 reported having no business experience prior to opening the business. Test the null hypothesis that at most 25 percent of all members of this population had no business experience before opening the business.

10. In a random sample of 400 people purchasing state lottery tickets, 172 sample members were women. Test the null hypothesis that half of all purchasers are women.

11. A random sample of 200 members of the American Marketing Association was asked which continuing professional education course had most appeal. Of these sample members, 70 opted for international marketing research–related courses. Test the null hypothesis that 45 percent of all members of the association hold this view against the alternative that the true percentage is lower.

12. A questionnaire was designed to compare the level of students' familiarity with two types of product. For a random sample of 120 students, the mean familiarity level with burglar alarms was found to be 3.355, and the sample standard deviation was 2.03. In an independent random sample of 100 students, the mean familiarity level for television was 9.5, and the sample standard deviation was 2.1. Assuming that the two population distributions are normal and have the same variance, test the null hypothesis that the population means are equal.

13. A random sample of consumers is taken, and their mean preference for visiting a sports event is found to be 5.1 (on a 1 to 7 scale, where 7 denotes most preferred). In the previous surveys, the mean preference has always been 5.0. Has the mean preference changed now? (Use $a = .10$ and $s = .1$.)

14. In a test-marketing study, the average sales for a new brand of shampoo in 9 stores is 1.95 units (each unit is 100 bottles). The retail management was expecting to sell on the average 2.0 units. Was the management's expectation realized? (Use $a = .05$ and $s = .06$.)

15. An experiment was conducted to determine which of three advertisements to use in introducing a new personal computer. A total of 120 people who were thinking of buying a personal computer was split randomly into three groups of 40 each. Each group was shown a different advertisement and each person was asked his or her likelihood of buying the advertised brand. A scale of 1 (very unlikely) to 7 (very likely) was used. The results showed that the average likelihood of purchase was

Advertisement A: 5.5

Advertisement B: 5.8

Advertisement C: 5.2

The ANOVA table was as follows:

Source of Variation	SS	df	MSS	F-Ratio	p-Value
Due to advertisements	12	2	6.0		
Unexplained	234	117	2.0		
Total	246	119			

a. What is the appropriate null hypothesis? The alternative hypothesis?
b. What is the F-ratio?
c. Is the result significant at the .10 level? the .05 level? the .01 level?
d. Are there any differences among the impacts of the three advertisements?

ENDNOTES

1. The term *null hypothesis* arises from earlier agricultural and medical applications of statistics. In order to test the effectiveness of a new fertilizer or drug, the tested hypothesis (the null hypothesis) was that it had no effect; that is, there was no difference between treated and untreated samples.

2. For a more detailed description of significance tests, see Alan G. Sawyer and Paul J. Peter, "The Significance of Statistical Significance Tests in Marketing Research," *Journal of Marketing Research* (May 1982), pp. 122–131.

3. See Richard I. Levin, *Statistics for Management* (Englewood Cliffs, NJ: Prentice-Hall, 1987).

4. For a more detailed discussion on the power of a test, see "The Concept of Power Analysis," Chapter 1, pp. 1–16, of J. Cohen, *Statistical Power for the Behavioral Sciences* (New York: Academic Press, 1969).

5. Companies practicing total quality management (discussed in Chapter 25) usually go for zero defects, or six sigma quality, rather than the 5 percent defects used in this example.

6. For a more detailed description of the analysis technique, see Geoffrey Kepel, *Design and Analysis: A Researcher's Handbook* (Englewood Cliffs, NJ: Prentice-Hall, 1973).

7. The reader also might note that the total degrees of freedom, which is the total sample size of 15 less one, or 14, is equal to the sum of the degrees of freedom associated with the first two rows of the ANOVA table.

$$t = \frac{(\bar{X} - u)}{s_{\bar{X}}/\sqrt{n}} = \frac{(5.8 - 5.6)}{2.5/\sqrt{900}} = 2.4$$

CASES

For a detailed description of the cases please visit www.wiley.com/college/kumar.

Case 13-1: Medical Systems Associates: Measuring Patient Satisfaction
Case 13-2: American Conservatory Theater

Correlation Analysis and Regression Analysis

Learning Objectives

- Understand the use of correlation as a measure of association.
- Distinguish between simple correlation and partial correlation.
- Discuss the objectives of regression analysis.
- Explain the procedure adopted to estimate the regression parameters.
- Interpret the meaning of the parameter estimates.
- Discuss the applications of regression analysis.
- Understand the concept and use of multiple regression.

Oftentimes in business research, the researcher is interested in determining whether there is any association (relationship) between two or more variables and, if so, the researcher would like to know the strength of the association and the nature of the relationship. In the previous chapter we discussed the chi-square goodness-of-fit test as a measure of association. We also discussed the limitations of the chi-square test as an association measure. In this chapter we will discuss the more commonly used measure of association—the correlation coefficient. Correlation analysis involves measuring the strength of the relationship between two variables. For example, the *correlation coefficient* provides a measure of the degree to which there is an association between two variables (X and Y).

Regression analysis is a statistical technique that is used to relate two or more variables. Here, a variable of interest, the dependent or response variable (Y) is related to one or more independent or predictor variables $(X's)$. The objective in regression analysis is to build a regression model or a prediction equation relating the dependent variable to one or more independent variables. The model can then be used to describe, predict, and control the variable of interest on the basis of the independent variables. For example, when a new product or concept is being explored, one of the key variables of interest is usually the respondent's attitude or intentions toward it. Is it something that the respondent would consider buying or using? The goal may be to predict the ultimate usage of the product or concept under a variety of conditions. Another goal might be to understand what causes high intentions to purchase so that when the product does emerge, the marketing program can be adjusted to improve the success probability.

In this chapter, we will discuss in detail the most simple form of regression analysis, the *bivariate analysis*. We will study how, in the bivariate analysis, the variable of interest is related to one independent variable. Regression analysis that involves more than one independent variable is called *multiple regression analysis*.

◆ CORRELATION ANALYSIS

The **Pearson correlation coefficient** measures the degree to which there is a linear association between two intervally scaled variables. A positive correlation reflects a tendency for a high value in one variable to be associated with a high value in the second. A negative correlation reflects an association between a high value in one variable and a low value in the second variable. If the database includes an entire population, such as all adults in California, the measure is termed the **population correlation** (ρ). If it is based on a sample, it is termed **sample correlation** (r).

> The **Pearson correlation coefficient** measures the degree to which there is a linear association between two intervally scaled variables. A positive correlation reflects a tendency for a high value in one variable to be associated with a high value in the second. A negative correlation reflects an association between a high value in one variable and a low value in the second variable.

If two variables are plotted on a two-dimensional graph, called a **scatter diagram,** the sample correlation reflects the tendency for the points to cluster systematically about a straight line rising or falling from left to right. The sample correlation r always lies between -1 and 1. An r of 1 indicates a perfect positive linear association between the two variables, whereas if r is -1 there is perfect negative linear association. A zero correlation coefficient reflects the absence of any linear association.

> If two variables are plotted on a two-dimensional graph, called a **scatter diagram**, the sample correlation reflects the tendency for the points to cluster systematically about a straight line rising or falling from left to right.

Figure 14-1 illustrates five scatter diagrams. In Figure 14-1a there is a rather strong tendency for a small Y to be associated with a large X. The sample correlation is .80. In Figure 14-1b the pattern slopes from the lower left to the upper right, and thus the sample correlation is .80. Figure 14-1c is an example of a sample correlation of 1. It is a straight line running from the lower left to the upper right. Figure 14-1d is an example in which there is no relationship between X and Y. Figure 14-1e shows a plot in which there is a clear relationship between the two variables, but it is not a linear or straight-line relationship. Thus, the sample correlation is zero.

Simple Correlation Coefficient

The concept of simple or bivariate correlation can be best understood by following the methodology for calculating it. First, the points are plotted in a scatter diagram. In the sample shown in Figure 14-2, the Y-axis indicates the sales in thousands of dollars per day of six stores in a retail chain, and the X axis indicates the distance in travel time to the nearest competing store corresponding to each of the six stores. Six stores are located on the scatter diagram. A reasonable measure of association between the two variables is the covariance between the two variables:

$$\text{Cov}(x, y) = \Sigma(X_i - \bar{X}) * (Y_i - \bar{Y})$$

Points in quadrants I and III suggest a positive association, so large values of X will be associated with large values of Y. For store E, for example, the $(X_i - \bar{X}) * (Y_i - \bar{Y})$ term equals 5 times 6, or 30. Table 14-1 provides a summary of this calculation.

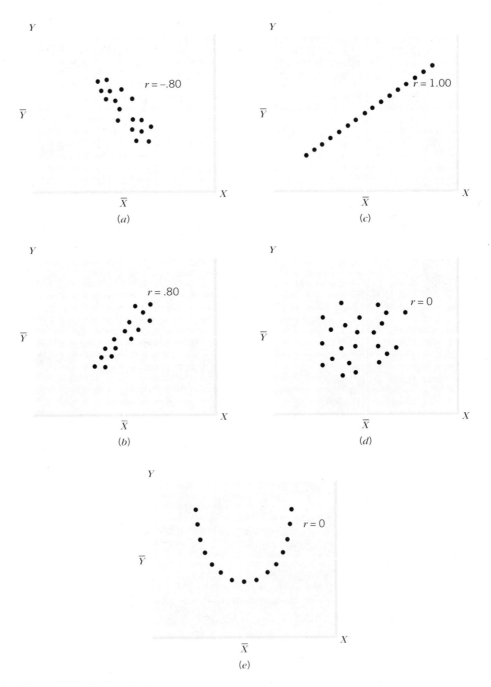

Figure 14-1 Scatter plots.

If the data point had been higher (farther away from $\overline{Y}$) or farther to the right (farther from $\overline{X}$), then the value of the $(X_i - \overline{X}) * (Y_i - \overline{Y})$ term for store E would have been greater. On the other hand, a point near one of the dotted axes would contribute little to the association measure. Store D is located on the X-axis and, as shown in Table 14-1, contributes zero to the association measure. Similarly, points in quadrants

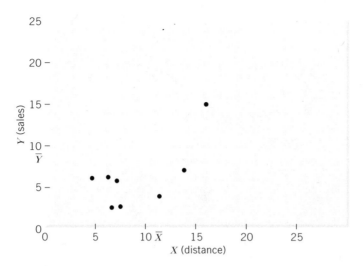

Figure 14-2 Store sales versus distance.

II and IV suggest a negative association. Thus, store B, which is in quadrant II, has a negative contribution to the association measure. Table 14-1 shows this contribution to be −2.

The second step of the method for calculating the sample correlation is to divide the association expression by the sample size:

TABLE 14-1   Determining the Sample Correlation Coefficient

	Daily Sales (thousands), Y_i	$Y_i - \bar{Y}$	Distance to Nearest Competing Store (min), X_i	$X_i - \bar{X}$	$(X_i - \bar{X})(Y_i - \bar{Y})$
Store A	3	−6	7	−4	24
Store B	8	−1	13	2	−2
Store C	17	8	13	2	16
Store D	4	−5	11	0	0
Store E	15	6	16	5	30
Store F	7	−2	6	−5	10
Total	54	0	66	0	$78 = \sum_i (X_i - \bar{X})(Y_i - \bar{Y})$
Average	$\bar{Y} = 9$		$\bar{X} = 11$		$15.6 = \dfrac{1}{n-1}\sum_i (X_i - \bar{X})(Y_i - \bar{Y})$

$$r_{yx} = \frac{1}{n-1}\frac{\sum(X_i - \bar{X})(Y_i - \bar{Y})}{S_x S_y} = \frac{78}{5(3.85)(5.76)} = .70$$

$$S_x = 3.85 = \sqrt{\frac{1}{n-1}\sum_i (X_i - \bar{X})^2}$$

$$S_y = 5.76 = \sqrt{\frac{1}{n-1}\sum_i (Y_i - \bar{Y})^2}$$

$$\frac{1}{(n-1)} * \sum (X_i - \bar{X}) * (Y_i - \bar{Y})$$

To ensure that the measure does not increase simply by increasing the sample size (one of the limitations associated with the use of chi-square as an association measure), it is divided by the sample size. The association between retail store sales volume and distance to competitive stores should not get larger simply because the association measure is calculated using data from 20 stores instead of 10. Thus, we divide by the sample size [strictly speaking, by $(n - 1)$]. Table 14-1 shows that this association measure would then be 15.6. This expression is called the *sample covariance*. Thus, the covariance between X and Y (denoted Cov_{XY}), measures the extent to which X and Y are related.

The size of the covariance measure could be changed simply by changing the units of one of the variables. For example, if sales are measured in dollars instead of thousands of dollars, then the association measure is 15.6 million instead of 15.6. Such a dependence on the units of measure makes the measure difficult to interpret. The solution is to divide the measure by the sample standard deviations for X and Y.[1] The result is the sample correlation coefficient, which will not be affected by a change in the measurement units of one or both of the variables:

$$r_{xy} = \frac{1}{(n-1)} * \sum \frac{(X_i - \bar{X})}{S_x} * \frac{(Y_i - \bar{Y})}{S_y}$$

$$r_{xy} = \frac{Cov_{XY}}{S_x * S_y}$$

This expression for the sample correlation coefficient (*r*) is called the **Pearson product-moment correlation coefficient.** If the correlation coefficient is calculated for the entire population, it is denoted by ρ, the population correlation coefficient. Like the case of the sample mean being an estimator of the population mean, the sample correlation coefficient r is an estimate of the population correlation coefficient ρ.

The product-moment correlation coefficient has several important properties. First, as the methodology has demonstrated, it is independent of sample size and units of measurement. Second, it lies between −1 and +1. Thus, the interpretation is intuitively reasonable. Further, when regression analysis is discussed later in this chapter, a rather useful interpretation of the square of the sample correlation (r^2) will be presented that will provide additional insights into its interpretation.

Here it should be stressed that, even though the correlation coefficient (r) provides a measure of association between two variables, *it does not imply any causal relationship* between the variables. A correlation analysis or, for that matter, even a regression analysis, can measure only the nature and degree of association (or covariation) between variables; it cannot imply causation. Statements of causality must spring from underlying knowledge and theories about the phenomenon under investigation and not from mathematical measures of association.[2] Further, the sample correlation coefficient can be seriously affected by outliers or extreme observations.

The correlation coefficient provides a measure of the relationship between two questions or variables. The underlying assumption is that *the variables are intervally scaled,* such as age or income. At issue is to what extent a variable must satisfy that criterion. Does a seven-point agree-disagree scale qualify? The answer depends in part on the researcher's judgment about the scale. Is the difference between −2 and −1 the same as the difference between +2 and +3? If so, it qualifies. If not, a correlation analysis may still be useful, but the results should be tempered with the knowledge that one or both of the scales may not be intervally scaled.

Testing the Significance of the Correlation Coefficient

As discussed earlier, the calculation of the correlation coefficient r assumes that the variables, whose relationship is being tested, are metric. If this assumption is not met either partially or completely, it affects the value of ρ. A simple test of hypothesis can be performed to check the significance of the relationship between two variables, measured by r. This involves testing the null hypothesis H_o: $\rho = 0$ against the alternative hypothesis H_a: $\rho \neq 0$.

Consider the example presented in Table 14-1. Here, the relationship between the sales per day of stores in a retail chain and the distance in travel time to the nearest competing store is determined using the sample correlation coefficient r, and is calculated to be .70. To test the significance of this relationship, the test statistic t can be computed using

$$t = r \sqrt{\frac{n-2}{1-r^2}}$$

In our example, $n = 6$ and $r = .70$. Hence,

$$t = .70 \sqrt{\frac{6-2}{1-0.70^2}} = 1.96$$

If the test is done at $\alpha = .05$ with $n - 2 = 4$ degrees of freedom, then the critical value of t can be obtained from the tables to be 2.78. Since $1.96 < 2.78$, we fail to reject the null hypothesis.

What does this mean? The statistical test of significance reveals that the value of the sample correlation r (found to be .70) is not significantly different from zero. In other words, the strength of the relationship between store sales and the distance from competing stores at best can be attributed to a chance occurrence. If the same value of r (.70) had been obtained from a larger sample (say, $n = 50$), then one could possibly conclude that there is a systematic association between the variables.

As an exercise, retest the hypothesis that $\rho = 0$, assuming that the value of $r = .70$ was obtained from a sample size of 50. Do you still fail to reject the null hypothesis? Why not?

Partial Correlation Coefficient

The **partial correlation coefficient** provides a measure of association between two variables after controlling for the effects of one or more additional variables.

The Pearson correlation coefficient provides a measure of linear association between two variables. When there are more than two variables involved in the relationship, partial correlation analysis is used. The **partial correlation coefficient** provides a measure of association between two variables after controlling for the effects of one or more additional variables. For example, the relationship between the advertising expenditures and sales of a brand is influenced by several other variables. For the sake of simplicity, let us assume that the relationship is affected by a third variable, the use of coupons. If the brand manager is interested in measuring the relationship between the dollar amount spent on advertisements (X) and the associated sales of the brand (Y), the manager has to control for the effect of coupons (Z). The partial correlation coefficient can thus be expressed as

$$r_{XY,Z} = \frac{r_{XY} - r_{XZ} * r_{YZ}}{\sqrt{(1 - r^2{}_{XY})} * \sqrt{(1 - r^2{}_{YZ})}}$$

Although the correlation analysis provides a measure of the strength of the association between two variables, it tells us little or nothing about the nature of the relationship. Hence, *regression analysis is used to understand the nature of the relationship between two or more variables.*

Measures of Association of Ordinal Variables

The **Spearman rank correlation coefficient** is an index of the correlation between two rank-order variables. The correlation between the ranks tells us very little about the degree of the linear relationship between the underlying variables. Furthermore, the square of the rank correlation coefficient is not to be interpreted as similar to the population coefficient of determination. Thus, we cannot say it is the proportion of the total variation in Y explained by its association with the variation in X.

Let's consider an example. Assume two respondents A and B rank-ordered 10 brands of cereals in terms of their preferences. The ranking data for the two respondents are provided here. The question of interest is whether the two respondents have similar preferences. It is possible to answer this question by computing the rank-order correlation between the two sets of ranks.

Brand	1	2	3	4	5	6	7	8	9	10
Respondent A	6	9	1	3	4	5	8	7	2	10
Respondent B	5	10	4	7	2	6	8	3	1	9

For the rank correlation, ranks enter into the calculation of the coefficient. Thus, we have a very simple computational form when no ties exist, as shown here,

$$r_s = 1 - \frac{6\left(\sum_i D_i^2\right)}{n(n^2 - 1)}$$

where D_i is defined as the difference between the ranks associated with the particular brand i and n is the number of brands evaluated.

The Spearman rank correlation is a simple value to compute. All we need to know are the number n of objects (i.e., brands ranked) and the difference in the rankings of each individual, D_i. The term r_s is a correlation coefficient computed for the ranks. We now illustrate the computation of this coefficient.

Brand i	Respondent A	Respondent B	Difference D_i	Squares of Difference, D_i^2
1	6	5	1	1
2	9	10	−1	1
3	1	4	−3	9

4	3	7	−4	16
5	4	2	2	4
6	5	6	−1	1
7	8	8	0	0
8	7	3	4	16
9	2	1	1	1
10	10	9	1	1
				$\Sigma D_i^2 = 50$

Now, we can substitue values into the equation for r_s. We have $n = 10$ and $\Sigma D_i^2 = 50$. So

$$r_s = 1 - \frac{6(50)}{10(10^2 - 1)} = 1 - (300/990) = 1 - .303 = .697$$

The Spearman correlation is 0.697, which can be considered to be on the higher side.

If a tie occurs in the rankings, we can still use the Spearman correlation equation. However, the means and variances of the ranks no longer have the simple relationship to n, as in the case where no ties exist. If ties occur, the simplest procedure is to assign mean ranks to sets of tied measurements. When two or more items are tied in order, each item is assigned the mean of the ranks they would otherwise occupy.

◆ REGRESSION ANALYSIS[3]

Regression analysis is a statistical technique that is used to relate two or more variables. Here, a variable of interest, the dependent or response variable (Y) is related to one or more independent or predictor variables (X's).

As mentioned earlier, **regression analysis** is a statistical technique that is used to relate two or more variables. Here, a variable of interest, the *dependent* or response variable *(Y)* is related to one or more independent or predictor variables *(X's)*. The objective in regression analysis is to build a regression model or a prediction equation relating the dependent variable to one or more independent variables. The model can then be used to *describe, predict, and control* the variable of interest on the basis of the independent variables.

Prediction is not the only reason that knowledge of the relationship between intentions and other variables are useful. Another motivation is to gain an understanding of the relationship so that the marketing program can be adjusted. If the relationship between the preferences toward different products and the age of the consumers is known, then a decision as to the age group toward whom the marketing program should be focused can be made intelligently. It makes little sense to expend marketing effort on groups with little potential. Further, if the relationship between the features that consumers consider while deciding which shop to visit and the ratings of the features of competitors' shop that consumers currently visit is known, it is possible to change the marketing strategy to suit the customers of competition. Such features as providing parking space and a large dine-in area could be improved and features such as a wide product range and good product quality could be emphasized in the marketing strategy.

Regression analysis provides a tool that can quantify such relationships. Further, unlike cross-tabulations and other association measures, which deal only with two variables, regression analysis can integrate the relationship of intentions with two, three, or more variables simultaneously. Regression analysis not only quantifies individual relationships, it also provides statistical control.

Simple Linear Regression Model

The construction of a simple linear regression model usually starts with the specification of the dependent variable and the independent variable. Suppose that our organization, Midwest Stereo, has 200 retail stores that sell hi-fi and related equipment. Our goal is to determine the effect of advertising on store traffic, that is, the number of people who come into the store as a result of the advertising. More specifically, we are concerned with the number of people entering the store on a Saturday as a result of advertising placed the day before. The following regression model might be hypothesized:

$$Y_i = \beta_0 + \beta_1 X_i + \varepsilon_i$$

where

Y = the number of people entering the store on Saturday (dependent variable)

X = the amount of money the store spent on advertising on Friday (independent variable)

β_0 = a model parameter that represents the mean value of the dependent variable (Y) when the value of the independent variable X is zero (It is also called the Y-intercept.)

β_1 = a model parameter that represents the slope that measures the change in the value of the independent variable associated with a one-unit increase in the value of the independent variable

ε_i = an error term that describes the effects on Y_i of all factors other than the value of X_i

Several aspects of the model are worth emphasizing. First, the hypothesized relationship is linear; it represents a straight line, as shown in Figure 14-3. Such an assumption is not as restrictive as might first appear. Even if the actual relationship is curved, as illustrated by the dotted arc in Figure 14-3, the relationship still may be close to linear in the range of advertising expenditures of interest. Thus, a linear relationship still may be entirely adequate.[4]

The error term is central to the model. In reality, store traffic is affected by variables other than advertising expenditures; it also is affected by store size and location, the weather, the nature of what is advertised, whether the advertising is in newspapers or on radio, and other factors. Thus, even if advertising expenditures are known, and our hypothesized linear relationship between advertising expenditures and store traffic is correct, it will be impossible to predict store traffic exactly. There still will be a margin of error. The error term reflects the error explicitly. Several assumptions surrounding the error term are made when estimating the parameters of the model and during significance testing. These are called the **assumptions of the regression model.**

Assumptions of the Regression Model

There are five major assumptions associated with the simple linear regression model.[5]

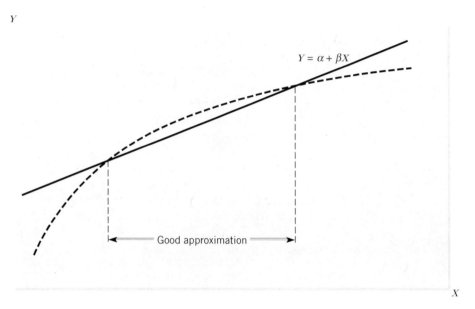

Figure 14-3 The linear approximation.

- The error term is normally distributed (i.e., for each value of X, the distribution of Y is normal).
- The mean or average value of the error term is zero $[E(\varepsilon_i) = 0]$.
- The variance of the error term is a constant and is independent of the values of X.
- The error terms are independent of each other (the observations are drawn independently).
- The values of the independent variable X are fixed (for example, by an experimenter).

Figure 14-4 provides an illustration of the model.

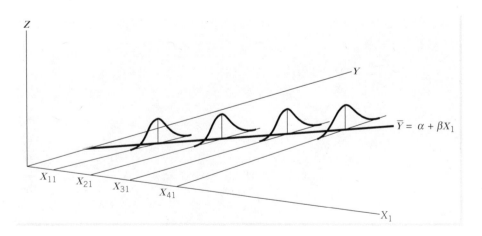

Figure 14-4 Simple linear regression model-A graphical illustration.

Estimating the Model Parameters

The parameters, β_0 and β_1, that characterize the relationship between X and Y are of prime interest. One of the goals of the regression analysis is to determine what they are. Although we do not know the true values of the parameters β_0 and β_1, we can calculate point estimate b_0 and b_1 of β_0 and β_1. The procedure is used to obtain a random sample of stores and to use the information from it to estimate β_0 and β_1. For example, assume that a random sample of 20 stores was selected. For each store in the sample, the number of people entering the store on a given Saturday is determined. Further, for each store the amount spent on advertising for the previous day is recorded. Table 14-2 presents the data for the 20 stores in our sample. The results are plotted in Figure 14-5.

The next step is to obtain a line that has the best "fit" to these points. Of course, a line could be drawn freehand; in practice, however, a computer program is used. The computer program generates a line with the property that the squared vertical deviations from the line are minimized. Such a line is termed a *least-squares* line and is denoted by the following expression:

$$\hat{Y}_i = b_0 + b_1 X_i$$

where $\hat{Y}_i$ is called the predicted value of Y_i.

The values of the least-squares estimates b_0 and b_1 are calculated using the formulas

TABLE 14-2 Advertising vs. Store Traffic Data

Number of Stores	Store Traffic Y_i	Advertising Dollars X_i	$X_i * Y_i$	X_i^2
1	90	40	3,600	1,600
2	125	75	9,375	5,625
3	320	100	32,000	10,000
4	200	110	22,000	12,100
5	600	190	114,000	36,100
6	450	200	90,000	40,000
7	400	300	120,000	90,000
8	700	310	217,000	96,100
9	800	380	304,000	144,400
10	810	410	332,100	168,100
11	1,000	480	480,000	230,400
12	1,170	500	585,000	250,000
13	1,200	520	624,000	270,400
14	1,500	550	825,000	302,500
15	1,000	560	560,000	313,600
16	900	580	522,000	336,400
17	700	690	483,000	476,100
18	1,000	700	700,000	490,000
19	1,300	710	923,000	504,100
20	1,350	800	1,080,000	640,000
Mean	780.75	410.25		
Sum	15,615	8,205	8,026,075	4,417,525

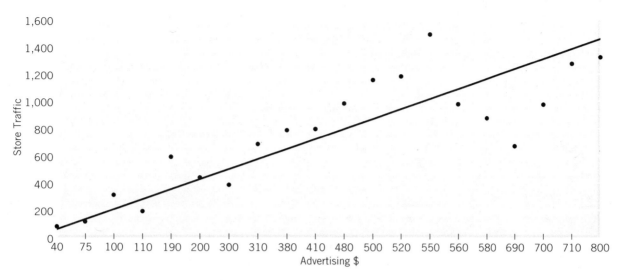

Figure 14-5 Advertising vs. store traffic.

$$b_1 = \frac{n\sum X_i Y_i - \left(\sum X_i\right)\left(\sum Y_i\right)}{n\sum X_i^2 - \left(\sum X_i\right)^2}$$

and

$$b_0 = \overline{Y} - b_1\overline{X}$$

where

$$\overline{Y} = \sum Y_i/n$$
$$\overline{X} = \sum X_i/n$$

In this case, from Table 14-2, we can calculate b_0 and b_1 to be 148.64 and 1.54, respectively. In the case of the simple linear regression model involving one dependent and one independent variable, the parameter estimates and other model values can be easily hand-calculated. As the number of independent variables increases, however, the model becomes large, and hand computation is no longer feasible. In such situations, statistical packages such as SAS and SPSS normally are used. Subsequent sections and chapters, dealing with multiple regression analysis and other advanced multivariate techniques, provide the relevant SAS outputs along with the interpretations.

The value b_0 (148.64) is an estimate of the parameter β_0, and the value b_1 (1.54) is an estimate of the parameter β_1. These estimates are termed **regression coefficients** and are based on the random sample. The term $\hat{Y}$ (read "Y-hat") indicates the points on the line, and is an estimate of store traffic based on the regression model. For example, when X is 600, then $\hat{Y} = 148.64 + 1.54 \times 600 = 1,073$ (approx). Thus, if advertising expenditures of 600 are planned, our estimated store traffic will be 1,073. In contrast, Y is the actual sales level. For example, for one store the advertising expenditure (X) was

500, the store traffic (Y) was 1,170, and the store traffic estimate $(\hat{Y})$ was calculated to be 919. The difference between the actual and predicted values is called the **residual** and is an estimate of the error in the population, represented by e.

If another random sample of 20 stores were to be obtained, undoubtedly it would contain different stores. As a result, the plot of X and Y would differ from Figure 14-5 and the regression coefficients, b_0 and b_1, would be different. Every random sample would have associated with it a different b_0 and b_1. In general, if any particular values of b_0 and b_1 are good point estimates of β_0 and β_1, they will, for $i = 1, 2, \ldots, n$, make β_i fairly close to Y_i. Therefore, the ith residual,

$$e_i = Y_i - \hat{Y}_i$$
$$= Y_i - (b_0 + b_1 X_i)$$

will be fairly small.

The regression coefficients can be estimated using a number of statistical techniques. Each of the techniques is based on some criterion to get the best measure of the population coefficients from the sample. One of the most commonly used techniques to estimate these coefficients is based on the **least-squares criterion.** According to this criterion, the regression coefficients are calculated so as to minimize the residual sum of squares. In mathematical form, this can be represented as

$$\text{Minimize: SSE} = \sum e_i^2 = \left[\sum (Y_i - \hat{Y}_i)\right]^2$$
$$= \sum \left[Y_i - (b_0 + b_1 X_i)\right]^2$$

Thus, the point estimates, b_0 and b_1, *minimize the residual or error* sum of squares (SSE). Hence, these estimates are called the **least-square estimates.**

Standard Error of Estimate

An examination of Figure 14-5 reveals that, although the least-squares regression line provides a reasonable fit of the data points, there are some deviations in the sample data about the line. An estimate of the population variation about the regression line provides a reasonable measure of goodness-of-fit of the model (called **the mean square error, MSE**), and can be calculated using the formula

$$s^2_{y/x} = \frac{\text{SSE}}{n-2} = \frac{\sum e_i^2}{n-2} = \frac{(Y_i - \bar{Y}_i)^2}{n-2}$$

The square root of mean square error given by $s_{y/x}$ (more commonly denoted simply as s) is called the **standard error of the estimate.** In our example, the standard error can be calculated to be 218.40.

The standard error of the estimate (s) is interpreted to mean that, for any given value of the independent variable X_i, the dependent variable tends to be distributed about the predicted value $\hat{Y}_i$, with a standard deviation equal to the standard error of the estimate. Hence, the smaller the standard error of the estimate, the better the fit. Further, the standard error of the estimate is the same for any given value of the independent variable. In other words, as the value of the independent variable X_i changes, the predicted value of $\hat{Y}_i$ will also change, but the standard deviation of the distribution of Y_i about $\hat{Y}_i$ remains a constant.

Interpretation of the Parameter Estimates

The parameter estimates have a very precise meaning. The parameter β_1 indicates that if the variable X is changed by one unit, the variable Y will change by β_1 units. Thus, if $1 is added to the advertising budget, regardless of the level at which the budget is set, an extra b_1 customers will be expected to visit the store. Similarly, the parameter β_0 reflects the number of customers expected, on average, if no advertising is run the previous day. When understanding the phenomenon of interest is the motivation behind the data analysis, the prime interest is in b_1, the estimate of the β_1 parameter. The size of b_1 will be a reflection of the influence of advertising on store traffic.

Testing the Significance of the Independent Variables

If β_1 is zero, there will be no effect of advertising on store traffic, and hence the model specified does not serve any purpose. Before using the model, it is useful to consider the hypothesis that β_1 is zero. If the evidence that β_1 is zero (namely, a nonzero estimate b_1) is impressive, we may want to discard the model.

As indicated previously, the estimate b_1 has a variation associated with it (measured by s_{b_1}) because it is based on a sample of stores. Thus, it could happen that b_1 is nonzero even if the parameter β_1 is zero. In fact, it would be highly likely that, even if there were no relationship between advertising (X) and store traffic (Y), any given random sample would produce a nonzero value for b_1. One way to evaluate the magnitude of b_1, taking into account its variation (measured by the standard error), is to use a statistical hypothesis test. In this example, the standard error of b_0 and b_1 can be calculated to be 100.10 and 0.21, respectively. The null hypothesis is that there is no linear relationship between the dependent and the independent variables. The hypothesis test can be represented formally as

$$\text{Null hypothesis} \qquad H_o: \beta_1 = 0$$
$$\text{Alternative hypothesis} \qquad H_a: \beta_1 \neq 0$$

The test statistic is given by

$$t = \frac{b_1 - \beta_1}{s_{b_1}} = \frac{1.54 - 0}{.21} = 7.33$$

The calculated test statistic has a t-distribution. Hence, if we fix α as .05, the table value of t corresponding to df = $n - 2 = 18$ degrees of freedom is 2.10. Applying the rejection rule for a two-tailed test of hypothesis, we reject the null hypothesis that there is no linear relationship between the dependent and independent variables (since $t_{\text{calc}} > t_{\text{table}}$). Therefore, one can conclude that advertising expenditure affects store traffic.

In this example, the test of hypothesis resulted in the rejection of the null hypothesis. If it had resulted otherwise—that is, if the hypothesis test had failed to reject the null—this does not immediately indicate that the independent variable is not significant. It is perfectly possible that the dependent and independent variables are in fact related, albeit in a nonlinear manner. Also, before any hasty decision is made regarding the significance of the independent variable, the researcher needs to ascertain that a Type II error is not being committed.

The rejection rule is then: Reject H_o: $\beta_1 = 0$ if $\alpha >$ p-value. In our case, the p-value (computed by SAS) was found to be .0001, resulting in the rejection of the null hypothesis. Hence, the smaller the p-value, the stronger is the evidence to reject H_o.

Predicting the Dependent

The regression model can also be used as a predictive tool. Given an advertising expenditure, the model will predict how much store traffic will be generated. For example, if an advertising expenditure level of $200 is proposed, a model-based estimated store traffic is

$$\hat{Y} = b_0 + b_1 X_{01} = 148.64 + (1.54 \times 200) = 457$$

Two cautionary comments: First, prediction using extreme values of the independent variable (such as $X = 2{,}000$ in our example) can be risky. Recall Figure 14-3, which illustrates that the linearity assumption may be appropriate for only a limited range of the independent variables. Further, the random sample provides no information about extreme values of advertising. Second, if the market environment changes, such as if a competitive chain opens a series of stores, the model parameters probably will be affected. The data from the random sample were obtained under a set of environmental conditions; if they change, the model may well be affected.

How Good Is the Prediction?

A natural question is, "How well does the model predict?" Assume that we have n observed values of the dependent variable, but we do not have the n observed values of the independent variable X with which to predict Y_i. In such a case the only reasonable prediction of Y_i is

$$\hat{Y} = \Sigma \, Y_i / n$$

The error of prediction is then $Y_i - \hat{Y}$.

While adopting the simple linear regression model, we predict Y_i using the formula $\hat{Y}_i = b_0 + b_i X_i$. The error of prediction here is $Y_i - \hat{Y}_i$. Therefore, by using the independent variable, the error of prediction has decreased by an amount equal to

$$(Y_i - \bar{Y}) - (Y_i - \hat{Y}_i) = (\hat{Y}_i - \bar{Y})$$

It can be shown that, in general,

$$\sum (Y_i - \bar{Y})^2 - \sum (Y_i - \hat{Y}_i)^2 = \sum (\hat{Y}_i - \bar{Y})^2$$

Or by rearranging, it can be shown that the total variation = explained variation + unexplained variation:

$$\sum (Y_i - \bar{Y})^2 = \sum (\hat{Y}_i - \bar{Y}_i)^2 + \sum (Y_i - \hat{Y})^2$$

where

Total variation (SST) = sum of squared prediction error that would be obtained if we do not use X to predict Y.

Unexplained variation (SSE) = sum of squared prediction error that is obtained when we use X to predict Y.

Explained variation (SSM) = reduction in the sum of squared prediction errors that has been accomplished by using X in predicting Y.

That is, the explained variation measures the amount of the total variation that can be explained by the simple linear regression model.

The measure of the regression model's ability to predict is called the **coefficient of determination** (r^2) and is the ratio of the explained variation to the total variation,

$$r^2 = (SST - SSE)/SST = SSM/SST$$

For our example, r^2 is equal to .74. Thus, 74 percent of the total variation of Y is explained or accounted for by X. The variation in Y was reduced by 74 percent by using X and applying the regression model.

The r^2 term is the square of the correlation between X and Y. Thus, it lies between 0 and +1. It is 0 if there is no linear relationship between X and Y. It will be 1 if a plot of X and Y points generates a perfect straight line. Another way to interpret r, the sample correlation, is to interpret r^2 instead. A reduction or increase in r^2 can be interpreted as the percentage of reduction or increase in the explained variation.

So far, we have discussed the concepts and issues related to the simple linear regression model. When more than one independent variable is included in a single linear regression model, we get a **multiple regression** model.

END OF CHAPTER MATERIAL

SUMMARY

In this chapter we discussed two of the more commonly used data analysis techniques in business research, correlation analysis and regression analysis.

Correlation analysis involves measuring the strength of the relationship between two or more variables. Regression analysis is used (1) to predict the dependent variable, given knowledge of independent variable, and (2) to gain an understanding of the relationship between the dependent variable and independent variables.

Applications. Regression analysis is used (1) to predict the dependent variable, given knowledge of independent variable values, and (2) to gain an understanding of the relationship between the dependent variable and independent variables.

Inputs. The model inputs required are the variable values for the dependent variable and the independent variables.

Outputs. The regression model will output regression coefficients—and their associated beta coefficient and t-values—which can be used to evaluate the strength of the relationship between the respective independent variable and the dependent variable. The model automatically controls statistically for the other independent variables. Thus, a regression coefficient represents the effect of one independent variable when the other independent variables are held constant. Another output is the R^2 value, which provides a measure of the predictive ability of the model.

Statistical Tests. The hypothesis that a regression parameter obtained from the sample evidence is zero is based on the t-value.

Assumptions. The most important assumption is that the selected independent variables do, in fact, explain or predict the dependent variable, and that no important variables have been omitted. In creating and evaluating regression models the following questions are appropriate: Do these independent variables influence the dependent variable? Do any lack logical justification for being in the model? Are any variables omitted that logically should be in the model? A second assumption is that the relationship between the independent variables and the dependent variable is linear and additive. A third assumption is that there is a "random" error term that absorbs the effects of measurement error and the influences of variables not included in the regression equation.

Limitations. First, a knowledge of a regression coefficient and its t-value can suggest the extent of association or influence that an independent variable has on the dependent variable. However, if an omitted variable is correlated with the independent variable, the regression coefficient will reflect the impact of the omitted variables on the dependent variables. A second limitation is that the model is based on collected data that represent certain environmental conditions. If those conditions change, the model may no longer reflect the current situations and can lead to erroneous judgments. Third, the ability of the model to predict, as reflected by R^2, can become significantly reduced if the prediction is based on values of the independent variables that are extreme in comparison to the independent variable values used to estimate the model parameters. Fourth, the model is limited by the methodology associated with the data collection, including the sample size and measures used.

KEY TERMS

Pearson correlation coefficient	regression coefficient
population correlation	residual
sample correlation	least-squares criterion
scatter diagram	least-squares estimates
Pearson product-moment correlation coefficient	the mean square error (MSE)
	standard error of the estimate
Spearman rank correlation coefficient	coefficient of determination
partial correlation coefficient	multiple regression
regression analysis	stepwise regression
assumptions of the regression model	

MARKETING RESEARCH TOOLBOX
REVIEW POINTS

1. The Pearson correlation coefficient measures the degree to which there is a linear association between two intervally scaled variables. A positive correlation reflects a tendency for a high value in one variable to be associated with a high value in the second. A negative correlation coefficient reflects an association between a high value in one variable and a low value in the second variable.

2. The Pearson correlation coefficient provides a measure of linear association between two variables. When there are more than two variables involved in the relationship, partial correlation analysis is used. The partial correlation coefficient provides a measure of association between two variables after controlling for the effects of one or more additional variables.

3. Regression analysis is a statistical technique that is used to relate two or more variables. A variable of interest, the dependent or response variable (Y) is related to one or more independent or predictor variables $(X's)$. The objective in regression analysis is to build a regression model or a prediction equation relating the dependent variable to one or more independent variables.

4. An estimate of the population variation about the regression line provides a reasonable measure of the goodness-of-fit of the model (called the mean square error, MSE).

5. The measure of the regression model's ability to predict is called the coefficient of determination (r^2).

6. The Spearman rank correlation coefficient is an index of the correlation between two rank-order variables.

7. A multiple regression model is used when there is more than one independent variable in a single linear regression model.

8. The relative importance of the independent variables on the dependent variable can be found using two methods. In the first method the t-values of the various coefficients are compared. In the second approach the size of the regression coefficients are examined. The coefficients are converted into "beta coefficients" before comparing. The larger the beta coefficient is, the larger is the impact of that variable on the dependent variable.

9. A residual is the difference between the observed value Y_I and the value predicted ($\hat{Y}_I$) by the regression equation. Residuals are used in the calculation of several statistics associated with regression.

QUESTIONS AND PROBLEMS

1. A random sample of eight introductory marketing texts yielded the figures shown in the table for annual sales (in thousands) and price (in dollars):

Sales	00.0	00.0	00.0	00.0	00.0	00.0	00.0	00.0
Price	29.2	30.5	29.7	31.3	30.8	29.9	27.8	27.0

a. Determine the sample correlation between sales and price.
b. Test at the 5 percent level that the population correlation coefficient is zero.

2. A college administers a student evaluation questionnaire for all its courses. For a random sample of 12 courses, the accompanying table shows both the instructor's average student ratings (on a scale from 1 to 5), and the average grades that the students expected (on a scale from A = 4 to E = 0).

Instructor rating	2.8	3.7	4.4	3.6	4.7	3.5
Expected grade	2.6	2.9	3.3	3.2	3.1	2.8
Instructor rating	4.1	3.2	4.9	4.2	3.8	3.3
Expected grade	2.7	2.4	3.5	3.0	3.4	2.5

a. Find the sample correlation between the instructor ratings and expected grades.
b. At the 10 percent significance level, test the hypothesis that the population correlation coefficient is zero against the alternative that it is positive.

3. Some regression models are used to predict, some to gain understanding, and some to do both. Consider a product manager for Betty Crocker cake mix: Give an example of each of the three types of models in the context of this product manager.

4. If an estimated regression model $Y = a + bX$ yielded an r^2 of .64, we could say (choose one):
a. 64 percent of the variation in the dependent variable was explained by the independent variable.
b. The sample correlation between Y and X was 0.80.
c. 64 percent of the data points lie on the regression line.
d. a and b only.
e. None of the above.

5. A company sets different prices for a pool table in eight different regions of the country. The accompanying table shows the numbers of units sold and the corresponding prices (in hundreds of dollars).

Sales	420	380	350	400	440	380	450	420
Price	5.5	6.0	6.5	6.0	5.0	6.5	4.5	5.0

    a. Plot these data, and estimate the linear regression of sales on price.
    b. What effect would you expect a $150 increase in price to have on sales?

6. An attempt was made to evaluate the forward rate as a predictor of the spot rate in the Spanish treasury bill market. For a sample of 79 quarterly observations, the estimated linear regression,

$$\bar{Y} = .00027 + .7916X$$

was obtained, where

    $\bar{Y}$ = actual change in the spot rate
    X = change in the spot rate predicted by the forward rate
The coefficient of determination was .1, and the estimated standard deviation of the estimator of the slope of the population regression line was .27.

    a. Interpret the slope of the estimated regression line.
    b. Interpret the coefficient of determination.
    c. Test the null hypothesis that the slope of the population regression line is 0 against the alternative that the true slope is positive, and interpret your result.
    d. Test the null hypothesis that the slope of the population regression line is +1, and interpret your result.

7. An analyst for an oil company has developed a formal linear regression model to predict the sales of 50 of their filling stations. The estimated model is

$$\bar{Y} = b_0 + b_1 X_1$$

where

    $\bar{Y}$ = average monthly sales in gallons
    X = square foot area of station property
    $X_1 = X - \bar{X}$ (difference from the mean)
Some empirical results were

Variable	Mean	Range of Data	Reg. Coefficient	t-Value	r^2
Y		5,000–80,000 gal	$b_0 = 10,000$		
X	10,000	3,000–20,000 sq ft	$b_1 = 3.1$	2	.3

    a. What does r^2 mean?
    b. Interpret the parameter estimates b_0 and b_1.
    c. Is the X_1 variable significant? At what level?
    d. A new station is proposed with 30,000 sq. ft. What would you predict sales to be?
    e. What assumptions underlie the estimate?

8. Consider the problem of predicting sales for each store in a chain of 220 bookstores. The model will have two functions. First, it will be used to generate norms that will be used to evaluate store managers. Second, it will be used to evaluate new site locations. What independent variables would you include in the model? How would you measure them?

9. Refer to Question 7. If two additional variables are now added to the model in that question, then

$$Y = b_0 + b_1X_1 + b_2 X_2 + b_3X_3$$

where

X_2 = average daily traffic flow, cars

X_3 = number of competing filling stations

The empirical results now are

Variable	Variable Mean	Variable Range	Regression Coefficient	t-Value
Y	10,000			
X	10,000	3,000–20,000	$b_1 = 4.0$	1.3
X_2	6,000	2,500–12,500	$b_2 = 4.0$	1.0
X_3	12	0–25	$b_3 = -1,000$	1.0
$r^2 = .45$			$b_0 = 10,000$	

a. Which independent variable seems now to be the most significant predictor?
b. Are X_1, X_2, and X_3 significant at the .05 level?
c. How might you explain why b_1 is now larger?
d. Interpret b_2.
e. Provide a prediction of sales given the following inputs:

$$X_1 = 5,000$$
$$X_2 = 2,000$$
$$X_3 = 0$$

How might you qualify that prediction? What model assumptions may be violated?

f. A skeptic in upper management claims that your model is lousy and cites as evidence a station in Crosby, North Dakota, where

$$X_1 = 5,000$$
$$X_2 = 2,000$$
$$X_3 = 0$$

Yet sales are 50,000, which is far more than predicted by the model. How would you answer this attack?

10. The following regression model was estimated to explain the annual sales from a direct marketing campaign:

$$S_t = 55 + 1.5P_t + 6.0M_t + 0.25C_t \qquad R^2 = 0.92$$
$$ (2.1) \quad (0.5) \quad (0.55)$$

where

S_t = $ sales in year t
P_t = $ promotional expenditure in year t
M_t = $ product mailing expenditures in year t
C_t = Number of pamphlets distributed in year t

The estimated standard errors are given (in parentheses) corresponding to the coefficient estimates. The marketing director suggests that we should increase our mailing expenditures next year by sending more shipments first class, rather than via parcel post, since the mailing expenditure coefficient is "significant" in the regression. What would you advise?

ENDNOTES

1. Recollect that the sample standard deviation is obtained using the formula

$$s_X = \sqrt{\frac{\sum (X_i - \bar{X})^2}{(n - 1)}}$$

2. See Gilbert A. Churchill, Jr., *Marketing Research: Methodological Foundations,* 5th ed. (Orlando, FL: Dryden, 1991), pp. 824–825.

3. For a more detailed and comprehensive discussion on regression, see Bruce L. Bowerman and Richard T. O'Connell, *Linear Statistical Models: An Applied Approach* (Boston: PWS-Kent, 1990); or David G. Kleinbaum, Lawrence L. Kupper, and Keith E. Muller, *Applied Regression Analysis and Other Multivariable Methods* (Boston: PWS-Kent, 1988); or any other advanced applied statistical textbook.

4. Further, a simple transformation of the independent variable can change some types of non-linear relationships into linear ones. For example, instead of advertising, we might replace the advertising term with the logarithm of advertising. The result would be a model such as

$$Y_i = \beta_0 + \beta_1 \log X_i + e_i$$

5. Violation of these assumptions can cause serious problems in applying and interpreting the regression model. For a more detailed discussion of the regression assumptions and remedies for violations of model assumptions, see Kmenta, *Elements of Econometrics,* 2nd ed. (New York: Macmillan, 1986).

CASES

For detailed descriptions of the below cases please visit www.wiley.com/college/kumar.

Case 14-1: The Seafood Grotto
Case 14-2: Ajax Advertising Agency
Case 14-3: Election Research, Inc.

CASES AND PRACTICAL EXERCISES FOR PART III

CASE STUDY

III-1

The Vancouver Symphony Orchestra[1]

Daniel Gardiner and Charles Weinberg

At an afternoon meeting at the Vancouver Symphony Orchestra (VSO) offices, three executives, concerned with the marketing of the VSO, were discussing some of the challenges they currently faced.[2]

Ed Oscapella: We've go to do something, and do it fast, to get out of this difficult situation. Time is running out of the 1987/88 season.

Jane Corbett: From my point of view, I've got to find out who wants what: Do subscribers want something different from nonsubscribers? If so, what? We've got all this information that needs analyzing and I'm hoping it will be useful in marketing the 1987/88 season.

E. Douglas Hughes: I've got to decide on an appropriate theme or themes to communicate to the segment(s) we go after. We've got to give the printers sufficient lead time to get our brochures out, so I need to know what to focus on in the promotion.

Armed with the computer data from a recent audience survey completed January 6, 1987 (four weeks earlier), the three knew that they had to sift through all the information very carefully. Within two weeks they had to come up with a set of specific and actionable recommendations. The VSO's Board had already voted to cancel many concerts in June so as to lower its deficit.

All three agreed that perhaps their immediate task was to build ticket sales for the remaining four months of the 1986/87 season. The guest artist and concert schedule from February through June is shown in Exhibit III-1. During this time period, two subscription series were offered. The first was a six-concert "Seagram Pops" series. The second was a five-concert celebration series. In the prior year, a "Musically Speaking" series and "Jubilee" series were both offered.

Background

Situated midway between Asia Pacific countries and the United Kingdom and approximately 40 miles north of the United States, Vancouver is Canada's third largest city. Home to more than 1.3 million people, Vancouver is the largest metropolitan area in western Canada and is an emerging center of international trade and investment.

Vancouver is rated one of the five most beautiful cities in the world, and in addition to varied recreational and sports attractions, Vancouver has many cultural and theatrical attractions as well. These include the Vancouver Museum, the Queen Elizabeth Playhouse, the Arts Club, the Vancouver Art Gallery, the Vancouver Opera Society, and the Vancouver Symphony Orchestra.

The VSO is one of the oldest cultural institutions in Vancouver, with its inaugural concert held in 1897. Regular seasons were offered in the 1930s when the orchestra came under the patronage of Mrs. B. T. Rogers. The orchestra's original repertoire included mostly big band music. Over the years, the repertoire expanded to reflect more classical and romantic symphonic works, changing in response to the tastes of the various musical directors. As well, the regular season was lengthened and the number of scheduled programs and series increased.

The orchestra, among the 10 largest in North America, has been plagued with financial, managerial, and artistic problems over the past two years. Subscription revenue has steadily declined in the last five years, putting pressure on the symphony to emphasize sales of single tickets and to heavily promote each event. With 122 scheduled performances in the 1986/87 season, a 15 percent decrease in regular subscribers (to the "Jubilee" and "Musically Speaking" series), the sluggish economic climate in Vancouver post-Expo '86, and a deficit of $811,000, the Vancouver Symphony Orchestra faced an enormous challenge just to maintain the status quo, let alone reduce its deficit.

[1] Ed Oscapella, Executive Director; Jane Corbett, Director of Marketing; and E. Douglas Hughes, Director of Communications for the Vancouver Symphony Orchestra.

[2] The data for this case are available; see your instructor.

CASES AND PRACTICAL EXERCISES FOR PART III *(continued)*

EXHIBIT III-1

VSO Guest Artist and Concert Schedule February-June 1987

Date	Series	Conductor[a]	Soloist
Feb. 7, 9	CS#1	R. Barshai	I. Kipnis, harpsichord
Feb. 13	Recital		V. Ashkenazy, piano
Feb. 15, 16, 17	J#8	R. Barshai	C-L Lin, violin
Feb. 19, 20, 21, (2)	Bal #2		P. N. Balet
			Vanc-Canata Singers
Feb. 24(2)	School	P. McCoppin	K. Rudolph, pic., E. Volpe, hp.
Feb. 27, 28, Mar. 2, 3	POP#2	S. Dankworth	No soloists
Mar. 8, 9, 10	J#9	H. Holliger	Cond & ob solist
Mar. 12	Recital		M. Perahia, piano
Mar. 14, 16	CS#2	G. Sebastian	B. Tuckwell, hn
Mar. 18	Benefit Concert		M. J. Fox, T. Banks,
			B. Zarankin, piano/E. Northcott
Mar. 19, 20, 21(2)	Bal #3	E. Stafford	Royal Winnipeg Ballet
Mar. 24	SP Bal	P. McCoppin	R. Nureyev and Friends
Mar. 29, 30, 31	J#10	Y. P. Tortelier	W. Klien, piano
April 3, 4, 6, 7	POP#3	R. Hayman	The Cambridge Buskers
April 6	Tea & Trumpets	P. McCoppin	E. Northcott, sop, O. Lowry, host
April 12, 13, 14	J#11	K. Akiyama	L. Lortie, piano
April 18, 20	CS#3	T. Otaka	A. de Larrocha, piano
April 21	SP	P. McCoppin	Visions: Mission Andromeda
		B. Buckley	
Apr. 24, 25, 27, 28	POP#4	M. Miller	No soloists
May 3, 4, 5	J#12	R. Barshai	Bach Choir J. Coop, piano; M. Collins, sop; S. Graham, mezzo; G. Evans, tnr; D. Garrard bass
May 9, 11	CS#4	R. Barshai	E. Mathis, sop
May 22, 23, 25, 26	POP#5	J. Everly and Bach Choir	S. Woods, spo/M. Paris, mezzo D. Eisler, trn/B Hubbard, bari
May 30, June 1	CS#5	K. Akiyama	C. Parkening, guitar-May 30 Norbert Kraaft, guitar-June 2
May 31	F. Pops#3	F. McCoppin	Jarvis Benoit Quartet
June 5, 6, 8, 9	POP#6	K. Akiyama	M. Martin, soprano; B. Zarankin, piano; Y. Guilbert, piano

[a] Rudolf Barshai is Music Director and Principal Conductor and Kazuyoshi Akiyama is Conductor Laureate of the VSO.

Source: VSO files.

CASES AND PRACTICAL EXERCISES FOR PART III *(continued)*

Although small consolation, symphony orchestras throughout North America were going through difficult times (*Newsweek*, January 5, 1987, pp. 54–56). In September 1986, the Oakland Symphony declared bankruptcy and closed its doors; others such as the San Diego Symphony and the one in Halifax, Nova Scotia, had suspended operations for a season or more. The Chicago Symphony, despite playing to a 98 percent capacity, was able to pay back only 62 percent of its $20 million operating budget. On the other hand, the symphonies in Montreal and Hamilton were enjoying record attendance levels and renewed financial support.

Decline in Attendance

At one point in the 1970s, the VSO enjoyed the largest subscription base of any orchestra in North America. However, the number of subscribers has been steadily declining. In 1985/86, subscriptions dropped by 18 percent. In 1986/87, the decrease in subscriptions could approach 20 percent, for an overall decline since 1984/85 of over 30 percent. Plans were being made to revise the subscription packages for the 1987/88 season in order to reverse this trend. However, the program for the current season was set. Single-ticket sales had also been decreasing, but at a slower rate than subscriptions and were becoming relatively more important in terms of total attendance. They accounted for 36,701 tickets sold in the 1985/86 season. In 1984/85, regular subscribers accounted for 79 percent of the total attendance. However, the proportion of subscribers for 1986/87 was projected at only 70 percent of total attendance.

The Free Concert

One of the ways to offset declining revenues may be to focus on nonsubscribers. After a date to make a recording of the VSO was postponed, it was decided in early December that a "free concert" be given in order to obtain "trial" by the nonsubscriber group. This concert was held in the evening on Tuesday Jan-

EXHIBIT III-2

Audience Questionnaire

VANCOUVER SYMPHONY

Audience Questionnaire

Dear Patron,

We at the Vancouver Symphony Orchestra want very much to provide the best possible musical experience for our audiences and the Vancouver community as a whole. In our continuing efforts to improve our performances and make your concert-going as satisfying and enjoyable as possible, we ask that you take a little time to answer the following questions. Your opinions and suggestions are extremely important and will be most useful in helping us to evaluate our programs, as well as our manner of presentation.

When you leave tonight's concert, please be so kind as to place the completed questionnaire in one of the special boxes located near the exits and the VSO Gift Shop. If you do not have time to complete it this evening, we would request that you mail it to us at your convenience. On behalf of the members of the orchestra and the staff, thank you very much for your assistance.

Edward Philip Oscapella
Executive Director
Vancouver Symphony Orchestra

400 East Broadway, Vancouver, B. C., V5T 1×2—875, 1661

CASES AND PRACTICAL EXERCISES FOR PART III *(continued)*

EXHIBIT III-2 *(continued)*

Audience Questionnaire

VANCOUVER SYMPHONY

1.[a] Are you a subscriber (i.e., purchase series tickets) to the VSO.
    19% 1-1 _____ Yes, currently
    29   1-2 _____ No, but formerly
    51   1-3 _____ Never subscribed

2. Have you ever purchased tickets to an individual VSO event?
    22% 2-1 _____ Yes, since September 1986
    51   2-2 _____ Yes, but only before September 1986
    26   2-3 _____ No

3. Since September 1986, how many times have you attended a VSO performance?
    56% 3-1 _____ I haven't attended a VSO performance since September 1986
    18   3-2 _____ Attended once
    12   3-3 _____ Attended 2–3 times
    7   3-4 _____ Attended 4–5 times
    5   3-5 _____ Attended more than 5 times

4. If you have ever attended previous VSO performances, we would like to know why.
    Please indicate the THREE most important reasons from the list below. (1 = Most Im-
    portant, 2 = Second-Most Important, 3 = Third-Most Important). Write 1, 2, or 3 on the
    appropriate lines.

i.[b]	ii.	iii.		
42%[a]	19%	39%	(4-) _____	I wanted to see and hear classical music performed live
2	16	81	(5-) _____	The VSO under Maestro Rudolf Barshai is an excellent orchestra
7	44	49	(6-) _____	I think the Orpheum is an excellent setting for great music
13	31	54	(7-) _____	The choice of music appealed to me
13	37	50	(8-) _____	I wanted to see famous guest artists and conductors

Please list any additional reasons below:

(9-) _____
(10-) _____
(11-) _____

5. Overall, what is your rating of the VSO on the following characteristics? Put a check-
    mark on the appropriate lines.

	EXCELLENT (4)[a]	GOOD (3)	FAIR (2)	POOR (1)	
_____ Performance of Orchestra	65%	33%	1%	0%	(12-)
_____ Guest Artists	43	53	2	2	(13-)
_____ Music Selection	22	59	10	8	(14-)
_____ Acoustics in Orpheum	56	39	3	1	(15-)
_____ Prices of Tickets	13	46	35	6	(16-)
_____ Convenience of Parking	12	41	33	13	(17-)
_____ General Atmosphere of Orpheum	63	34	2	1	(18-)
_____ Service from VTC-CBO	26	57	13	4	(19-)

CASES AND PRACTICAL EXERCISES FOR PART III *(continued)*

EXHIBIT III-2 *(continued)*

Audience Questionnaire

6. Please give us your opinion about the amount of each type of music played by the VSO.

	TOO MUCH (3)	ABOUT RIGHT (2)	TOO LITTLE (1)	
_____ Classical (e.g., Bach, Mozart)	6%[a]	72%	22%	(20-)
_____ 20th century century music (e.g., Debussy, Stravinsky)	14	71	14	(21-)
_____ Pops (e.g., Mantovani, Williams)	20	62	18	(22-)
_____ Canadian (e.g., Schaeffer)	24	60	16	(23-)

7. Below are presented eight pairs of events characterized by reputation of performer, seating arrangements and single ticket prices. Assuming everything else about each pair is identical, please check your preference in each case.

International Performers & $20 price $\frac{44\%^a}{24\text{-}1}$ vs. $\frac{56\%}{24\text{-}2}$ New, Promising Performers & $8 price

Orchestra & $20 price $\frac{26\%}{28\text{-}1}$ vs. $\frac{74\%}{28\text{-}2}$ Balcony & $8 price

Orchestra & $20 price $\frac{30}{25\text{-}1}$ vs. $\frac{70}{25\text{-}2}$ Balcony & $14 price

International Performers & $20 price $\frac{63}{29\text{-}1}$ vs. $\frac{37}{29\text{-}2}$ New, Promising Perfomers & $14 price

International Performers & $14 price $\frac{77}{26\text{-}1}$ vs. $\frac{23}{26\text{-}2}$ New, Promising Performers & $8 price

Orchestra & $14 price $\frac{46}{30\text{-}1}$ vs. $\frac{54}{30\text{-}2}$ Balcony & $8 price

International Performers & Balcony $\frac{67}{27\text{-}1}$ vs. $\frac{33}{27\text{-}2}$ New, Promising Performers & Orchestra

International Performers & Orchestra $\frac{59}{31\text{-}1}$ vs. $\frac{41}{31\text{-}2}$ International Performers & Balcony

8. What concert times do you prefer?

12%[a]	32-1	_____ Matinees (2:30 P.M.)
34	32-2	_____ 7:30 P.M.
55	32-3	_____ 8:00 P.M.
7	32-4	_____ 8:30 P.M.

9. What day of the week do you prefer to attend concerts?

18%[a]	33-1	_____ Sunday
21	33-2	_____ Monday
27	33-3	_____ Tuesday
17	33-4	_____ Wednesday
17	33-5	_____ Thursday
25	33-6	_____ Friday
32	33-7	_____ Saturday

10. From where do you get most of your information about VSO events?

47%[a]	34-1	_____ From VSO mailings
46	34-2	_____ From ads in daily newspapers (e.g., *Sun, Province*)

CASES AND PRACTICAL EXERCISES FOR PART III *(continued)*

EXHIBIT III-2 *(continued)*

Audience Questionnaire

3	34-3	_____ From ads in community newspapers
32	34-4	_____ From radio ads
3	34-5	_____ From television ads
10	34-6	_____ From reviews and feature stories
	34-7	_____ Other-please specify $\frac{\text{word-of-mouth 9%}}{\text{nonword-of-mouth 3}}$

11. Which daily newspaper do you read most often?

71%[a]	35-1	_____ *Vancouver Sun*
24	35-2	_____ *Province*
7	35-3	_____ *Globe and Mail*
6	35-4	_____ Other—*please specify* _____

12. Are you

| 39%[a] | 36-1 | _____ Male |
| 61 | 36-2 | _____ Female |

13. To which age group do you belong?

2%[a]	37-1	_____ Under 18
6	37-2	_____ 18–24
16	37-3	_____ 25–34
17	37-4	_____ 35–44
21	37-5	_____ 45–54
22	37-6	_____ 55–64
19	37-7	_____ 65 and over

14. Please specify your postal code V ___ ___ ___ ___ ___ See EXHIBIT
   38 39 40 41 42

15. If you prefer to purchase tickets to individual events (as opposed to subscription tickets) why is this so? Please indicate below.

_____
_____
_____
_____
_____

[a] Percentage given in questionnaire are for all respondents.

[b] i = most important; ii = second or third most important; iii = not ranked in top three.

16. All things considered, what would it take to get you to attend VSO performances on a regular basis?

uary 6, 1987. People had to go to the VSO's administrative office located three miles away from the Orpheum Theater (where the VSO performed) to pick up tickets. After being heavily promoted on a local FM radio station, the concert was an immediate "sellout" with all 2,761 tickets distributed. So as to obtain information about the concert-goers in a cost-effective manner, a questionnaire was developed and

CASES AND PRACTICAL EXERCISES FOR PART III *(continued)*

given to audience members. Because of time constraints, an initial draft of the questionnaire was pretested only on VSO office employees. A photoreduced copy of the survey is shown in Exhibit III-2, along with relevant response frequencies for each question for the entire sample. Respondents had the choice of dropping off the instrument at various places in the Orpheum or mailing it in later. A total of 614 completed questionnaires from the 2,400 people actually in attendance were returned. Since almost

EXHIBIT III-3

Variable Listing

VARIABLE	REC	START	END	VARIABLE	REC	START	END
SUBSCRBR	1	1	1	MATINEE	1	32	32
INDPURCH	1	2	2	SVNTHRTY	1	33	33
ATTEND	1	3	3	EIGHT	1	34	34
LIVEMUS	1	4	4	EGHTHRTY	1	35	35
VSOGOOD	1	5	5	SUNDAY	1	36	36
ORPGOOD	1	6	6	MONDAY	1	37	37
CHOICE	1	7	7	TUESDAY	1	38	38
FAMOUS	1	8	8	WEDNESDAY	1	39	39
OTHER1	1	9	9	THURSDAY	1	40	40
OTHER2	1	10	10	FRIDAY	1	41	41
OTHER3	1	11	11	SATURDAY	1	42	42
ORCHSTRA	1	12	12	VSOMAIL	1	43	43
GUESTS	1	13	13	PAPERADS	1	44	44
SELETION	1	14	14	COMMPAPR	1	45	45
ACOUSTIC	1	15	15	RADIOADS	1	46	46
PRICES	1	16	16	TVADS	1	47	47
PARKING	1	17	17	STORIES	1	48	48
ATMSPERE	1	18	18	OTHRSRCE	1	49	49
SERVICE	1	19	19	VANCSUN	1	50	50
CLASICAL	1	20	20	PROVINCE	1	51	51
TWENTITH	1	21	21	GLBEMAIL	1	52	52
POPS	1	22	22	OTHRPAPR	1	53	53
CANADIAN	1	23	23	GENDER	1	54	54
PAIR1	1	24	24	AGEGROUP	1	55	55
PAIR2	1	25	25	POSTCOD1	1	56	56
PAIR3	1	26	26	POSTCOD2	1	57	57
PAIR4	1	27	27	POSTCOD3	1	58	58
PAIR5	1	28	28	POSTCOD4	1	59	59
PAIR6	1	29	29	POSTCOD5	1	60	60
PAIR7	1	30	30	RESPID	1	61	61
PAIR8	1	31	31				

CASES AND PRACTICAL EXERCISES FOR PART III (continued)

everyone attended in groups of two or more, this was considered a good response rate by management.

The data from the survey is in a file called VSO. Exhibit III-3 provides a sequential listing of the variables in the file and each variable corresponds to a specific question in the survey. For example, SUBSCRBR is the first variable and corresponds to Question 1 on the questionnaire. POSTCOD5 is the last variable and refers to the sixth digit of the respondent's postal code as asked by Question 14. RESPID refers to respondent identification and was inserted after receiving the research instruments. It is to be noted that no quantitative analysis can readily be performed on Questions 15 and 16.

Given all this information, Ed, Jane, and Doug sat down to analyze it and work on a report for the Board of Directors. They knew that any recommendation(s) they make must be supported by the data.

Questions for Discussion

1. What are the strengths and weaknesses of this market research project?

2. What information can you derive from the data? State specifically the managerial questions you are hoping to resolve and how the data would help you. Make at least one specific recommendation based on the results of this research.

PRACTICAL EXERCISES

Q1. The personnel manager in a company wants to obtain the opinion of employees toward increasing the number of work days from five to five and a half (alternative to this question would be increasing the retirement age from 60 to 65 years). Construct the null hypothesis and the alternative hypothesis.

Q2. The Cues company wants to find out the number of people who purchase its CDs who are within the age ranges of below 18, 18–24, 25–34 and 35 and above. A research study conducted previously determined that 25 percent of its shoppers are below 18 (of a sample of 2000 people), 10 percent are at the age range of 18–24 years, 35 percent from the 25–34 age group, and the remaining from the 35 and above. Determine the hypothesis for the company and substantiate the manager's claim that 35 percent of its shoppers are of the "required" age group (i.e., are from the most viable group for Cues—below 18).

Q3. In order to understand the various segments in the coffee drinkers market, Acorn agency conducted a research study. This resulted in an outcome regarding the growth of the gourmet coffee market. Analyze the potential of this market and the impact on the instant coffee market. The results of a certain study revealed that 10 percent of buyers are interested in switching to gourmet coffees. Construct a null hypothesis and conduct a field study in your area to determine the applicability of the estimated market.

◆ MULTIPLE REGRESSION

Recall from our earlier discussion that the error term includes the effects on the dependent variable of variables other than the independent variable. It may be desirable to explicitly include some of these variables in the model. As predictions, their inclusion will improve the model's ability to predict and will decrease the unexplained variation; in terms of understanding, they will introduce the effect of other variables and therefore elaborate and clarify the relationships. The general form of the multiple regression model can be expressed as

$$Y = \alpha + \beta_1 X_1 + \beta_2 X_2 + \ldots + \beta_i X_i + e$$

where $\beta_1, \beta_2, \ldots, \beta_k$ are regression coefficients associated with the independent variables $X_1, X_2, \ldots, X_k$ and e is the error or residual. The assumptions discussed in relation to simple linear regression apply equally to the case of multiple regression, except that instead of the one X used in the former, more than one X is used in the latter. As was the case in simple linear regression, a solution is sought for the constants (α and the β's) such that the sum of the squared errors of prediction (Σe^2) is minimized, or that the prediction is optimized. It is worth noting that the equations cannot be solved if (1) the sample size, n, is smaller than or equal to the number of independent variables, k; or (2) one independent variable is correlated perfectly with another. The prediction equation in multiple regression analysis is

$$\hat{Y} = \alpha + b_1 X_1 + b_2 X_2 + \ldots + b_k X_k$$

where $\hat{Y}$ is the predicted Y score, and $b_1, \ldots, b_k$ are the partial regression coefficients.

To understand the meaning of a partial regression coefficient, let us consider a case in which there are two independent variables, so that

$$Y = \alpha + b_1 X_1 + b_2 X_2 + \text{error}$$

First, note that the relative magnitude of the partial regression coefficient of an independent variable is, in general, different from that of its bivariate regression coefficient. In other words, the partial regression coefficient, b_1, will be different from the regression coefficient, b_1, obtained by regressing Y on X_1 only. This happens because X_1 and X_2 usually are correlated. In bivariate regression, X_2 was not considered, and any variation in Y that was shared by X_1 and X_2 was attributed to X_1. In the case of multiple independent variables, however, this is no longer true.

The interpretation of the partial regression coefficient, b_1, is that it represents the expected change in Y when X_1 is changed by one unit, keeping X_2 constant or controlling for its effects. Similarly, b_2 represents the expected change in Y for a unit change in

X_2, when X_1 is held constant. Therefore, b_1 and b_2 are called partial regression coefficients. It can also be seen that the combined effects of X_1 and X_2 on Y are additive. In other words, if X_1 and X_2 are each changed by one unit, the expected change in Y will be $(b_1 + b_2)$. Similar interpretation holds good for the case of k variables.

The regression coefficients will be unique to the random sample that happens to be selected. If another random sample were taken, the regression coefficients would be slightly different. This sampling variation in the regression coefficients is measured by the standard error (discussed in the previous chapter) associated with each of them. The procedure installed in most software packages calculates this standard error and provides it as one of the outputs.

Consider the following example, where a researcher did a survey of the CEOs of some small businesses to explore the firms' interest in exporting to foreign markets. The description of the variables and the associated scale values are presented in Table 14-3. Two hundred small businesses received the questionnaire, and 98 were returned. Eight instruments could not be used because of random responding and incomplete information. Of the 90 usable questionnaires (45 percent response rate), data for 60 firms were used for model estimation and the remaining 30 observations were held for model validation (discussed later in this appendix). The information obtained from the survey instrument is given in Table 14-4.

The estimated regression equation is

$$\hat{\text{Will}} = 1.927 + .026 \text{ size (model 1)}$$

where

$\hat{\text{Will}}$ = predicted value for Will

Table 14-5 shows the results of this simple linear regression model (model 1).

The regression coefficient for size is .026 and is significant at the 10 percent level ($a = .10$). The amount of variance in "Will" explained by size is about 5.8 percent ($R^2 = .058$). R^2 cannot decrease as more independent variables are added to the regression equation. Yet diminishing returns set in, so after the first few variables, the additional independent variables do not make much of a contribution. For this reason,

TABLE 14-3   Survey of Small-Business CEOs: Description of Variables

Variable Description		Corresponding Name In the Computer Output	Scale Values
Willingness to export	(Y_1)	Will	1 (definitely not interested) to 5 (definitely interested)
Level of interest in seeking government assistance	(Y_2)	Govt	1 (definitely not interested) to 5 (definitely interested)
Employee size	(X_1)	Size	Greater than zero
Firm revenue	(X_2)	Rev	In millions of dollars
Years of operation in the domestic market	(X_3)	Years	Actual number of years
Number of products currently produced by the firm	(X_4)	Prod	Actual number
Training of employees	(X_5)	Train	0 (no formal program) or 1 (existence of a formal program)
Management experience in international operation	(X_6)	Exp	0 (no experience) or 1 (presence of experience)

TABLE 14-4   Export Data Set for CEO Surveys

Company	Willingness to Export (Y_1)	Level of Interest in Seeking Government Assistance (Y_2)	Employee Size (X_1)	Firm Revenue (million) (X_2)	Years of Operation in the Domestic Market (X_3)	Number of Products (X_4)	Training of Employees (X_5)	Management Experience in International Operations (X_6)
1	5	4	54	4.0	6.5	7	1	1
2	3	4	45	2.0	6.0	6	1	1
3	2	5	44	2.0	5.8	11	1	1
4	4	3	46	1.0	7.0	3	1	0
5	5	4	46	3.0	6.5	8	1	1
6	1	2	37	0.9	5.0	2	0	1
7	2	1	42	0.9	5.0	2	0	1
8	3	3	29	3.6	6.5	3	0	0
9	3	2	46	0.9	6.0	5	0	1
10	2	3	28	0.9	6.0	2	0	1
11	4	1	39	3.6	7.0	3	0	1
12	3	2	31	4.0	7.0	3	1	0
13	4	5	65	1.0	7.0	9	1	1
14	1	4	50	1.0	7.0	9	1	1
15	4	1	30	2.0	7.5	3	1	0
16	5	4	58	1.0	6.0	5	1	1
17	3	4	54	2.0	6.5	4	1	1
18	4	5	58	1.0	7.0	9	1	1
19	2	1	37	1.0	7.0	9	1	0
20	5	1	35	2.0	9.5	5	1	0
21	4	3	49	2.0	8.5	4	1	1
22	3	2	37	2.0	7.0	2	0	1
23	3	4	34	0.9	6.0	5	0	1
24	2	5	66	1.0	5.5	10	1	1
25	5	4	50	0.3	6.5	6	1	1
26	4	3	43	1.0	7.0	3	1	0
27	4	3	54	1.0	7.0	4	1	1
28	3	4	49	1.0	6.5	7	1	1
29	3	2	43	1.8	6.0	2	0	1
30	2	4	52	1.8	5.0	7	0	1
31	4	5	29	0.9	4.5	11	0	1
32	2	3	37	0.9	5.5	2	0	1
33	3	1	27	0.9	7.0	3	0	0
34	2	2	32	0.9	6.5	3	0	0
35	3	2	34	2.7	6.5	2	0	1
36	3	4	48	1.8	5.0	4	0	1
37	4	5	53	0.9	4.5	5	0	0
38	4	3	41	0.9	5.5	2	0	1
39	5	4	47	2.7	5.5	4	0	1
40	1	2	31	1.8	6.0	4	0	0
41	3	2	34	0.9	6.5	3	0	0
42	1	1	28	0.9	7.0	2	0	0

(continued)

TABLE 14-4 *(continued)*

Company	Willingness to Export (Y_1)	Level of Interest in Seeking Government Assistance (Y_2)	Employee Size (X_1)	Firm Revenue (million) (X_2)	Years of Operation in the Domestic Market (X_3)	Number of Products (X_4)	Training of Employees (X_5)	Management Experience in International Operations (X_6)
43	2	3	39	0.9	5.5	2	0	1
44	1	4	45	0.9	5.5	4	0	0
45	2	2	29	1.8	7.0	2	0	0
46	2	3	37	1.8	6.0	3	0	1
47	2	5	49	0.9	4.5	9	0	1
48	2	1	33	0.9	6.5	2	0	1
49	3	1	27	1.8	7.0	3	0	0
50	2	4	49	1.0	5.5	6	1	1
51	4	3	46	1.0	6.5	4	1	1
52	4	5	54	1.0	6.0	7	1	1
53	2	2	31	0.9	6.0	3	0	0
54	3	2	31	3.0	6.0	5	1	0
55	3	4	50	2.0	6.5	7	1	1
56	2	5	69	1.0	5.5	9	1	1
57	5	1	34	1.0	7.0	6	1	1
58	4	5	62	2.0	5.5	7	1	1
59	3	4	49	1.0	7.0	5	1	0
60	4	3	43	2.0	7.5	4	1	1

Table 14-5 Results of Model 1

Model: MODEL1
Dependent Variable: WILL

Analysis of Variance

Source	df	Sum of Squares	Mean Square	F-Value	Prob > F
Model	1	4.601	4.601	3.595	0.0629
Error	58	74.248	1.280		
C Total	59	78.850			
	Root MSE		1.131	R-square	0.058
	Deep Mean		3.050	Adj R-sq	0.041
	C.V.		37.096		

Parameter Estimates

Variable	df	Parameter Estimate	Standard Error	T for H_0: Parameter = 0	Prob > $|T|$	Standardized Estimate
INTERCEPT	1	1.927	0.609	3.161	0.002	0.000
SIZE	1	0.026	0.013	1.896	0.062	0.241

R^2 is adjusted for the number of independent variables and the sample size. The adjusted R^2 (adjusted for the number of degrees of freedom) is .042 in this example and is computed from the following formula:

$$R^2 \text{ (adjusted)} = 1 - [(1 - R^2)\, n - 1]/(n - k - 1)$$
$$= 1 - [(1 - .058)\, (60 - 1)]/(60 - 1 - 1)$$
$$= .042$$

where
  n = number of observations
  k = number of parameters

Since the variation explained is low, the researcher might consider adding a few more independent variables to explain additional variation in the dependent variable. It might be that the researcher considers adding variables X_2, X_3, and X_4 to the original regression equation. The resulting model (model 2) is

$$Y = b_0 + b_1 X_1 + b_2 X_2 + b_3 X_3 + b_4 X_4 + \text{error}$$

◆ PARAMETER INTERPRETATION IN MULTIPLE REGRESSION

When the parameters of model 2 are estimated using the least-squares criterion, the result is

$$\hat{\text{Will}} = -2.153 + 0.032 \text{ size} + 0.344 \text{ Rev} + 0.483 \text{ years} + 0.042 \text{ Prod}$$

Table 14-6 shows the results of model 2.

A major assumption of multiple regression is that the model includes all the important and relevant variables. If an important variable is omitted, the model's predictive power is reduced. Further, if the omitted variable is correlated with an included variable, the estimated coefficient of the included variable will reflect both the included variable and the omitted variable.[6] In our example, the coefficient of size in the simple linear regression model (model 1) is about 0.03, and in the multiple regression model (model 2) it remains around 0.03. This indicates that the additional variables (Rev, Years, and Prod) did not have large correlations with size and that the size coefficient remains unaffected to a large extent. From the results of model 2, one can interpret that the score on a firm's willingness to export would go up by 0.03 units for every one unit increase in the firm's size, keeping other variables (X_2, X_3, and X_4) at a constant/fixed value. Similar interpretations hold true for other variables.

◆ TESTS OF SIGNIFICANCE AND THEIR INTERPRETATIONS

Several tests of significance may be applied to the results of multiple regression analysis. Three of them are presented here: (1) test of R^2, (2) tests of regression coefficients, and (3) tests of increments in the proportion of variance accounted for by a given variable or a set of variables.

Test of R^2

Significance testing involves testing the significance of the overall regression equation as well as specific partial regression coefficients. The null hypothesis for the

Table 14-6   Results of Model 2

Model: MODEL2
Dependent Variable: WILL

Analysis of Variance

Source	df	Sum of Squares		Mean Square	F value	Prob > F
Model	4	25.976		6.494	6.755	0.0002
Error	55	52.873		0.961		
C Total	59	78.850				
		Root MSE	0.980	R-square	0.329	
		Dep Mean	3.050	Adj R-sq	0.280	
		C.V.	32.146			

Parameter Estimates

Variable	df	Parameter Estimate	Standard Error	T for H_0: Parameter = 0	Prob > $|T|$	Standardized Estimate
INTERCEPT	1	−2.153	1.131	−1.903	0.062	0.000
SIZE	1	0.032	0.014	2.215	0.030	0.298
REV	1	0.344	0.140	2.442	0.017	0.279
YEARS	1	0.483	0.146	3.294	0.001	0.385
PROD	1	0.042	0.060	0.690	0.492	0.092

overall test is that the coefficient of multiple determinations in the population, R^2 pop, is zero:

$$H_o: R^2 \text{ pop} = 0$$
$$H_a: R^2 \text{ pop} \neq 0$$

This is equivalent to the following null hypothesis:

$$H_o: \beta_1 = \beta_2 = \beta_3 = \ldots = \beta k = 0$$
$$H_a: \text{not all } \beta\text{'s are equal to zero}$$

The overall test can be conducted by using an F-statistic:

$$F = \frac{R^2/k}{(1 - R^2)(n - k - 1)}$$

with k and $n - k - 1$ degrees of freedom, where k = number of independent variables and n = sample size. For the data of Table 14-6, $R^2 = .329$, $N = 60$.

$$F = \frac{.329/4}{(1 - .329)/(60 - 4 - 1)}$$

$$= .0823/012$$
$$= 6.75$$

with 4 and 55 df, $p < .01$. The results clearly indicate that H_o is rejected, meaning the independent variables do have a systematic association with the dependent variable in the model. If the independent variables are statistically independent (uncorrelated), then R^2 will be the sum of bivariate R^2 of each independent variable with the dependent variable.

◆ TEST OF REGRESSION COEFFICIENTS

If the overall null hypothesis is rejected, one or more population partial regression coefficients has a value different from zero. To determine which specific coefficients (b_i's) are nonzero, additional tests are necessary. Testing for the significance of the b_i's can be done in a manner similar to that in the bivariate case, by using t-tests. The significance of the partial regression coefficient for size may be tested by the following equation:

$$t = b/S_b$$
$$= 0.0320/014$$
$$= 2.215$$

which has a t-distribution with $n - k - 1$ degrees of freedom. If the significance level (α) is 0.05, then this t-value is significant. All the regression coefficients are significant at the 5 percent level, with the exception of p.

◆ EVALUATING THE IMPORTANCE OF INDEPENDENT VARIABLES

When regression analysis is used to gain understanding of the relationships between variables, a natural question is: *Which of the independent variables has the greatest influence on the dependent variable?* One approach is to consider the t-values for the various coefficients. The t-value, already introduced in the single-variable regression case, is used to test the hypothesis that a regression coefficient (i.e., β_i) is equal to zero and a nonzero estimate (i.e., b_i) was simply a sampling phenomenon.[7] The one with the largest t-value can be interpreted as the one that is the least likely to have a zero b parameter.

A second approach is to examine the size of the regression coefficients; however, when each independent variable is in a different unit of measurement (store size, advertising expenditures, and so on), it is difficult to compare their coefficients. One solution is to convert regression coefficients to "beta coefficients." Beta coefficients are simply the regression coefficients multiplied by the ratio of the standard deviations of the corresponding independent variable to the dependent variable.

Standardized $\beta_i = b_i$ (standard deviation of X_i/standard deviation of Y)

The beta coefficients can be compared to each other: the larger the beta coefficient is, the stronger is the impact of that variable on the dependent variable. The beta coefficients are the partial regression coefficients obtained when all the variables ($Y, X_1, X_2, \dots X_k$) have been standardized to a mean of zero and a variance of 1 before estimating the regression equation. In Table 14-6, an analysis of the beta coefficients indicates that years (0.385) and firm size (0.298) have the most explanatory power, the same conclusion that the analysis of t-values showed. Comparing the unstandardized b directly does not achieve this result because of the different units and degrees of variability of the X variables. The regression equation itself should be reported for future use in terms of the unstandardized coefficients, so that prediction can be made directly from the raw X values.

The manager is quite excited about the ability to explain more variation in model 2 with the addition of some variables. In the interest of explaining some more variation, the manager adds the two remaining variables (X_5 and X_6) to the equation and then estimates the model (model 3). Table 14-7 shows the results of the OLS estimation of the model with all the six-predictor variables.

One can also use **stepwise regression** to select, from a large number of predictor variables, a small subset of variables that account for most of the variation in the dependent or criterion variable. Here, the predictor variables enter or are removed from the regression equation one at a time.

Regression with Dummy Variables

Nominal or categorical variables may be used as predictors if they are coded as dummy variables. The concept of dummy variables was introduced in Chapter 13. In that chapter, we explained how a categorical variable with four categories can be coded in terms of three dummy variables, D_1, D_2, and D_3, as shown:

Dummy-Variable Coding

Consumer Types	Original Variable Code	D_1	D_2	D_3
Brand loyalty	1	1	0	0
Variety seeker	2	0	1	0
Impulse buyer	3	0	0	1
Rational buyer	4	0	0	0

Assume that the researcher is interested in running a regression analysis of the effect of consumer types on coupon redemption. The dummy variables D_1, D_2, and D_3 can be used as predictors. A *regression with dummy variables* would then be

TABLE 14–7   **Results of Model 3**

Model: MODEL3
Dependent Variable: WILL

Analysis of Variance

Source	df	Sum of Squares	Mean Square	F-value	Prob > F
Model	6	27.652	4.608	4.771	0.0006
Error	53	51.197	0.966		
C Total	59	78.850			

Root MSE	0.982	R-square	0.350
Dep Mean	3.050	Adj R-sq	0.277
C.V.	32.224		

Parameter Estimates

Variable	df	Parameter Estimate	Standard Error	T for H0: Parameter = 0	Prob > |T|	Standardized Estimate
INTERCEPT	1	−1.824	1.578	−1.156	0.252	0.000
SIZE	1	0.019	0.018	1.062	0.293	0.181
REV	1	0.344	0.155	2.220	0.030	0.257
YEARS	1	0.474	0.193	2.450	0.017	0.377
PROD	1	0.027	0.067	0.400	0.690	0.059
TRAIN	1	0.216	0.417	0.518	0.606	0.094
EXP	1	0.409	0.328	1.248	0.217	0.166

$$Y_i = a + b_1 D_1 + b_2 D_2 + b_3 D_3 + \text{error}$$

Here the "rational buyer" has been chosen as the base level and has not been included directly in the regression equation. However, for the rational buyer group, D_1, D_2, and D_3 assume a value of 0, and the regression equation becomes

$$\bar{Y}_i = a$$

For brand-loyal consumers, $D_1 = 1$, and $D_2 = D_3 = 0$, and the regression equation becomes

$$\bar{Y}_i = a + b_1$$

Thus, the coefficient b_1 is the difference in predicted Y_i for brand-loyal as compared to rational buyers. The coefficients b_2 and b_3 have similar interpretations.

APPENDIX ENDNOTES

6. Adapted from Naresh K. Malhotra, *Marketing Research* (Englewood Cliffs, NJ: Prentice-Hall, 1993); and V. Kumar, A. Ghosh, and G. Tellis, "A Decomposition of Repeat Buying," *Marketing Letters*, 3(4), 1992, pp. 407–417.

7. Three qualifications. First, like any hypothesis test, the *t*-test is sensitive to the sample size. A small but nonzero regression parameter (i.e., b_1) can generate a low "p-level" if the sample size is large enough (and therefore s_b is small enough). Second, if the independent variables are intercorrelated (multicollinearity exists), the model will have a difficult time ascertaining which independent variable is influencing the dependent variable, and small *t*-values will emerge (s_b terms will get large). Thus, small *t*-values can be caused by inter-correlated independent variables. Third, in addition to testing each independent variable using the *t*-test, it is possible to test (using an *F*-test) the hypothesis that all regression parameters are simultaneously zero. If such a hypothesis is not "passed," the entire model might be dismissed.

PART

VI

APPLICATIONS

Presenting the Results

Learning Objectives

- Discuss the fundamentals of research presentation.
- Provide details on preparing the research report.
- Discuss issues related to successful oral presentation.
- Explain the importance of continued relationship with the client.

It is difficult to exaggerate the importance of the role that communication skills play in effective management. Along with the related skill of working with and motivating people, the ability to communicate effectively is undoubtedly the most important attribute a manager can have. There is also little doubt that managers are dissatisfied with the current level of communication skills. Business schools are criticized routinely and justifiably for focusing on techniques and neglecting communication skills. Further, managers frequently make harsh judgments about themselves and their colleagues with respect to communication skills. A senior advertising executive concluded that "advertising people are bright, presentable, usually articulate—but most of them are duds when it comes to making presentations."[1] A special *Business Week* report said, "So appalling is the quality of written reports in some companies that senior executives are sending their managers through writing courses, to try to put some point back into the reports that cross their desks and eliminate the extraneous material that increasingly obscures the point."[2]

Effective communication between research users and research professionals is extremely important to the research process. The formal presentation usually plays a key role in the communication effort. Generally, presentations are made twice during the research process. First, there is the research proposal presentation, discussed in Chapter 4, when the client must decide to accept, change, or reject it. Second, there is the presentation of the research results, when decisions associated with the research purpose are addressed and the advisability of conducting further research often is considered. This chapter will focus on the presentation of research results, but much of the material will apply to the original research proposal presentation as well.

◆ GUIDELINES FOR SUCCESSFUL PRESENTATIONS

The purpose of this chapter is to help readers avoid making presentations that are ineffective because they are dull, confusing, or irrelevant. Have you been exposed lately to any that hit the jackpot—that were all three? Presentations can be written, oral, or both. Later in the chapter, we will offer some tips on making both written and oral presentations. First, however, here are some guidelines that apply to both types of presentations. In general, a presenter should:

1. Communicate to a specific audience.
2. Structure the presentation.
3. Create audience interest.
4. Be specific and visual.
5. Address validity and reliability issues.

Each of these guidelines will be discussed in turn.

Communicate to a Specific Audience

The first step is to know the audience, its background, and its objectives. Most effective presentations seem like conversations, or memos to a particular person, as opposed to an amorphous group. The key to obtaining that feeling is to identify the audience members as precisely as possible.

Audience identification affects presentation decisions such as selecting the material to be included and the level of presentation. Excessive detail or material presented at too low a level can be boring or seem patronizing. However, the audience can become irritated or lost when material perceived as relevant is excluded or the material is presented at too high a level. In an oral presentation, the presenter can ask audience members whether they already know some of the material.

Frequently, a presentation must be addressed to two or more different audiences. There are several ways to deal with such a problem. In a written presentation, an executive summary at the outset can provide an overview of the conclusions for the benefit of those in the audience who are not interested in details. The presentation should respect the audience's time constraints. An appendix also can be used to reach some people selectively, without distracting the others. Sometimes the introduction to a chapter or a section can convey the nature of the contents, which certain audiences may bypass. In an oral presentation, the presence of multiple audiences should be recognized with a statement such as, "I need to provide some information on instrumentation next. You engineers in the audience can help by making sure that I don't miss anything." Such an acknowledgment probably will please the engineers so that they will be helpful rather than bored and restless.

Structure the Presentation

Each piece of the presentation should fit into the whole, just as individual pieces fit into a jigsaw puzzle. The audience should not be muttering, "What on earth is this person talking about?" or "How does this material fit in?" or "I'm lost." The solution is to provide a well-defined structure. As Figure 15-1 illustrates, the structure should include an introduction, a body, and a summary. Further, each of the major sections should be structured similarly. The precept is to tell the audience what you are going to say, say it, and then tell them what you said. Sometimes you want to withhold the conclusion, to create interest. In that case the audience could be told, "The objective here will be to come to a recommendation as to whether this new product should go into test market and, if so, with what type of pricing strategy." Further, use nontechnical definitions as much as possible to present the report in simple language. For

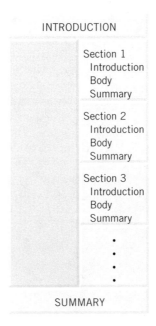

Figure 15-1   The presentation structure.

example, *critical path* could simply be stated as "the list of activities that must be completed on time."

Introduction

The presentation intro-
duction should provide
audience interest, identify
the presentation's central
idea or objective, and
provide a road map to the
rest of the presentation.

The **presentation introduction** should play several roles. First, it should provide audience interest, a task that will be discussed in detail in the next section. A second function is to identify the presentation's central idea or objective. Third, it should provide a road map to the rest of the presentation so that the audience can picture its organization and flow. Sometimes the only way to develop such a road map is to say something like, "This presentation has four parts. The research purpose and objectives will be discussed first. The second section will describe the research design…" However, with a little effort and luck it is sometimes possible to develop and use a flowchart that will convey the structure in a more interesting way. For example, in this book such a structural role was played by Figures 1-1, 3-1, and 4-2 (The reader should attempt to identify other figures so used). When such a device is used, the audience should be clear when each section will be addressed. The label for the section should use identical wording throughout, and the start of the section should be made clear: "Having finished the second section, we now move to the third."

Body

It is usually best to divide
the **body** of the presentation into between two and
five parts. A presentation
can also be structured
using research questions.
Most useful presentations
will include a statement of
implications and recom-
mendations relevant to
the research purpose.

Usually, it is best to divide the **body of the presentation** (or the major section) between two and five parts. The audience will be able to absorb only so much information. If that information can be aggregated into chunks, it will be easier to assimilate. Sometimes the points to be made cannot be combined easily or naturally. In that case, it is sometimes necessary to use a longer list: "There are 12 problems in this new product concept." However, the presentation should never drift through the body with no structure at all.

One way to structure a presentation is by the research questions: "This research was conducted to address four research questions. Each of these will be considered in turn." Another method that is often useful when presenting the research proposal is to base it on the research process, as was illustrated in Chapter 4.

The most useful presentations will include a statement of implications and recommendations relevant to the research purpose. However, when the researcher lacks information about the total situation because the research study addresses only a limited aspect of it, the ability to generate recommendations may be limited.

Summary

The purpose of the **presentation summary** is to identify and underline the important points of the presentation and to provide some repetition of their content. The summary should support the presentation communication objectives by helping the audience to retain the key parts of the content. The audience usually will perk up when they realize the end is near and an overview of the presentation is coming, so the summary section should be signaled clearly. A section summary has the additional task of providing a transition to the next section. The audience should feel that there is a natural flow from one section to the next.

The purpose of the **presentation summary** is to identify and underline the important points of the presentation and to provide some repetition of their content.

Create Audience Interest

The audience should be motivated to read or listen to the presentation's major parts and to the individual elements of each section. Those in the audience should know why the presentation is relevant to them and why each section was included. A section that cannot hold interest probably should be excluded or relegated to appendix status.

The research purpose and objectives are good vehicles to provide motivation. The research purpose should specify decisions to be made and should relate to the research questions. A presentation that focuses on those research questions and their associated hypotheses will naturally be tied to relevant decisions and hold audience interest. In contrast, a presentation that attempts to report on all the questions that were included in the survey and in the cross-tabulations often will be long, uninteresting, and of little value.

The researcher should point out those aspects of the results that are important and interesting. Suppose a chart is used that contains 10 descriptors of customers in 13 different markets. The presenter should circle 3 or so of those 130 numbers and be prepared to say, "Look at this number. We had hypothesized it to be higher than the others and it actually is lower. Let's look at the possible reasons and implications." The presenter should not feel compelled to wade through every detail of the questionnaire and the analysis.

As the analysis proceeds and the presentation is being prepared, the researcher should be on the lookout for results that are exceptionally persuasive, relevant, interesting, and unusual. Sometimes the deviant respondent with the strange answers can provide the most insight if his or her responses are pursued and not discarded. For example, in Figure 12-4, more respondents answered the age question than the income question. Of the 48 respondents who did not answer the income question, almost all of them were "moderately interested" in revisiting. Why? Are there any implications? Sometimes a few or even one deviant respondent can provide useful ideas and insights.

The best way to provide interest is to make the content so relevant that the audience will be interested; however, they may not always be absorbing the content.

Especially in those cases, it is very useful to make the presentation a lively and interesting experience. One way is to interject humor. The best humor is that tied to the subject matter or to the presentation, as opposed to memorized jokes that really do not fit. It is good to reward the audience periodically, however, and humor often works. Another tactic is to change the pace of the presentation. Break up the text with graphs, pictures, or even cartoons. In an oral presentation, try a variety of visual aids and some audience-involvement techniques. For example, the audience may be asked a question periodically and given a chance to talk and become involved.

Be Specific and Visual

Avoid talking or writing in the abstract. If different members of the audience have different or vague understandings of important concepts, there is a potential problem. Terms that are ambiguous or not well known should be defined and illustrated or else omitted. Thus, in a segmentation study, an "active saver" might be unambiguously defined as one who saved at least $500 in each of the last two years.

The most interesting presentations usually use specific stories, anecdotes, studies, or incidents to make points. They will be much more interesting and graphic than a generalization, however accurate and scientific. Instead of "studies have shown that …," it is more effective to say, "In the Topeka test market the 69-cent price had far less trial than the 89-cent price for product X when the bright blue package was used." In other words, give concrete examples. A utility company conducted a focus-group study to learn homeowners' motivations to conserve energy and their attitudes toward adding insulation. The marketing research director, in presenting the results to top management, played a 20-minute edited videotape recording of the focus groups, in which the key segments were illustrated graphically. The impact on the audience was greater than otherwise would have been possible. They actually heard specific customers, representative of the emerged segments, forcefully put forth their views.

The adage "A picture is worth a thousand words" applies to both written and oral presentations. A mass of data often can be communicated clearly with graphs. A wide variety is available, such as bar graphs, line graphs, and pie charts (see Figure 15-2). Color can be employed to add interest, to highlight findings, and to help deal with complexity. Also, use short, "crisp" titles as opposed to longer titles (see Table 15-1).

Presenting a trend graph.
©Jon Feingersh/Corbis Stock Market.

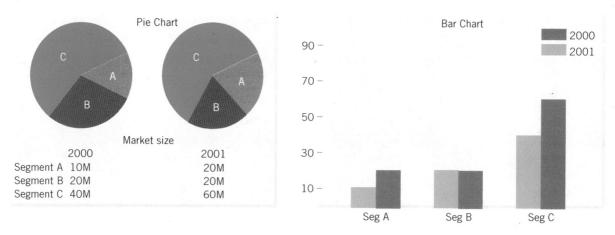

Figure 15-2 Graphically portrayed data.

Address Issues of Validity and Reliability

The presentation should help the audience avoid misinterpreting the results. Throughout Part II of this book, countless potential research design issues were raised that can affect the validity and interpretation of the results. The wording of the questions, the order in which they are asked, and the sampling design are among the design dimensions that can lead to biased results and misinterpretations. The presentation should not include an exhaustive description of all the design considerations. Nobody is interested in a textbook discussion of the advantages of telephone over mail surveys, or how you located homes in an area sampling design. However, when the wording of a question or some other design issue can affect an interpretation and ultimately a research conclusion, that issue should be raised and its possible effect on the interpretation discussed. For example, in a product-concept test, the method of exposing respondents to the concept may be crucial. Some discussion of why the method used was selected and its effect on the interpretation may be very useful. Try to identify those design issues that will affect interpretation and raise them in the context of the interpretation.

TABLE 15-1   Title of Tables/Figures

	Hypothetical, Longer, More Explanatory Titles Typical of Many Presentations	Short, "Crisp" Titles
Example 1	Median incomes for families, by type of community, for 1940 through 1980	Family incomes by area (1940–1980)
Example 2	Projected incomes for families, by type of community, for 2002 through 2032	Income predictions: the next 30 years
Example 3	Critical path analysis, tasks, and slack time for 12-month work program	Next year's work program
Example 4	Effectiveness—cost ratios for alternative development projects for fiscal year 2002–2003	Project recommendations for next year
Example 5	Unemployment rates and frequencies for major industries and communities for six-country area	Regional unemployment statistics

Source: Adapted from Witzling and Greenstreet, *Presenting Statistics* (New York: John Wiley & Sons), 1992, p. 224.

The presentation should include some indication of the reliability of the results. At a minimum, it always should be clear what sample size was involved. The key results should be supported by more precise information in the form of interval estimates or a hypothesis test. The hypothesis test basically indicates, given the sample size, what probability exists that the results were merely an accident of sampling. If the probability (or significance level) of the latter is not low, then the results probably would not be repeated. Do not imply more precision than is warranted. If 15 out of 52 respondents answered positively, do not give the percentage as 28.846. Rather, use 29 percent, or "nearly 30 percent." Consider the following exchange:

Speaker:	27.273 percent favored version B of the product.
Audience Member:	*What was the sample size?*
Speaker:	Around 11.
Audience Member:	*Really? As large as that!*

◆ WRITTEN PRESENTATION

The general guidelines discussed so far are applicable to both written and oral presentations. However, it is important to generate a research report that will be interesting to read. Most researchers are not trained in effective report writing. In their enthusiasm for research, they often overlook the need for a good writing style. In writing a report, long sentences should be reconsidered and the critical main points should stand out. Here are some hints[3] for effective report writing.

- Use main heading and subheadings to communicate the content of the material discussed.
    Main Heading: Probability Sampling
    Subheading: Statistical Issues in Probability Sampling—Systematic Sampling
- Use the present tense as much as possible to communicate information.
    "Most of the consumers prefer Brand A to Brand B"
- Whether the presentation is written or oral, use active voice construction to make it lively and interesting. Passive voice is wordy and dull.
    Active voice: Most consumers prefer Brand A.
    Passive voice: Brand A is preferred by most of the consumers.
- Use computer-generated tables and graphs for effective presentation. Figures 15-3 through 15-7[4] are examples of graphical illustration, and Table 15-2 shows the results for a sample of questions in a table form.
- Use informative headings:
    "Brand Quality is the Key Factor in Product Selection," not
    "Outcomes of Product Selection Analysis."
- Use verbations to communicate respondents' comments. Many times the way a customer expresses himself or herself means a lot to the brand manager.
- Use double-sided presentation if possible. For example, tables or graphs could be presented on the left side of an open report and their descriptions on the right side.

The Organization of the Report

A report can be organized in many ways since no single format is suitable for all purposes. The nature of the topic, the type of study, and the nature of the audience will

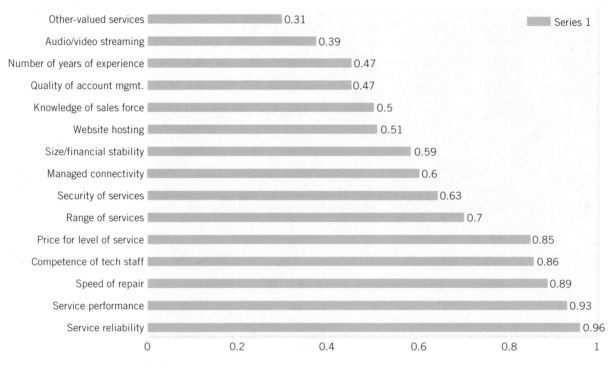

Figure 15-3 Rating the importance of internet service providers' attributes.

dictate the report's format. A general format for presenting a research report is given in Table 15-3.

Cover Page: The cover page should provide information on the title of the study, the date prepared, for whom it is prepared, and the researcher(s)' names and organization.

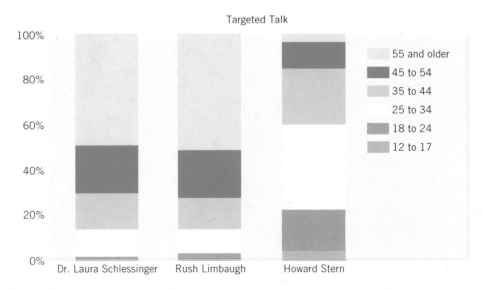

Figure 15-4 Age distribution of listening for selected talk radio shows, 1997.

(percent of husbands and wives who usually wins arguments over selected topics, 1995 and 2000)

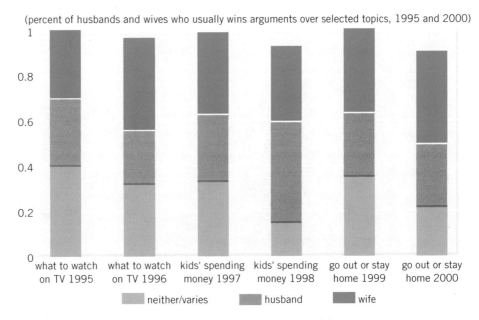

Figure 15-5   Who wins arguments.

Executive Summary: This must be brief, crisp, and informative, since most of the time executives pay attention only to this section. Present the research objectives and goals, findings, conclusions, and recommendations.

Table of Contents: This includes complete details of all the major sections and subsections and gives the associated page numbers. Table 15-4 is an example of a table of contents for a research report.

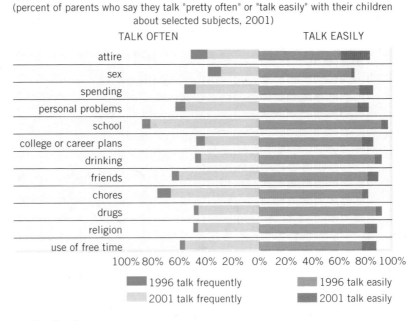

Figure 15-6   Family chats.

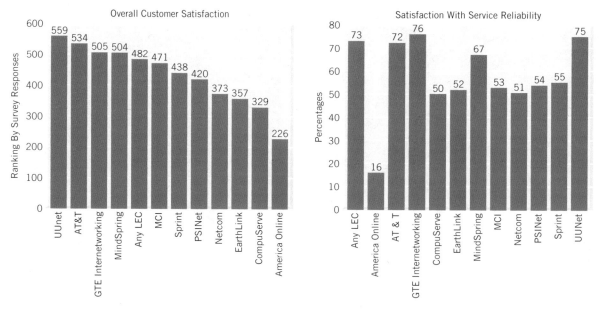

Figure 15-7 Customer satisfaction.

TABLE 15-2 **Descriptive Information on the Responses**

		Statistic				
	Question	Mean	Median	Min	Max	Standard Deviation
M	Need for external marketing research great?[1]	2.68	2.50	1	5	1.04
A	Importance of need for external marketing research[2]	2.50	2.50	1	5	1.18
R	Duration too long?[1]	2.90	3.00	2	5	1.01
K	Duration too short?[1]	2.45	3.00	1	4	0.85
E	Importance of duration[2]	2.09	2.00	1	4	1.06
T	Frequency good?[1]	2.72	3.00	1	4	10.7
I	Importance of Frequency[2]	2.13	2.00	1	4	0.99
N	Price Good?[1]	2.90	3.00	1	5	1.15
G	Importance of Price[2]	2.68	3.00	1	5	1.17
	Results Confidential?[1]	4.04	5.00	2	5	1.55
R	Importance of Confidentiality[2]	3.90	4.00	1	5	1.41
E	Benefits to UH Great?[1]	4.00	4.00	2	5	0.81
S	Importance of UH Benefits[2]	2.45	2.00	1	5	1.14
E	Sponsor time too long?[1]	2.27	2.00	1	4	0.82
A	Sponsor time too short?[1]	2.90	3.00	2	4	0.68
R	Importance of Sponsor time[2]	2.27	2.00	1	4	0.88
C	Value of Project?[1]	3.18	3.00	1	5	1.05
H	Importance of Value[2]	3.50	3.00	1	5	1.10

[1] 1 = Strongly Disagree, 2 = Disagree, 3 = Neither Agree nor Disagree, 4 = Agree, 5 = Strongly Agree

[2] 1 = Of No Importance, 2 = Moderately Important, 3 = Important, 4 = Very Important, 5 = Extremely Important

TABLE 15-3   General Format for a Research Report

    I.   Cover Page
    II.   Executive Summary
    III.   Table of Contents
    IV.   Introduction
    V.   Methodology
    VI.   Findings
    VII.   Limitations
    VIII.   Conclusions and Recommendations
    IX.   Appendixes

TABLE 15-4   Table of Contents of a Research Report

Presenting research results.
©Jose L. Pelaez/Corbis Stock Market.

Introduction: This section should describe the nature of the problem, clearly state the research objectives and research questions, and give an overview of the report's organization.

Methodology: Describe the methodology used to conduct the study. All technical details should be presented in an appendix.

Findings: The results of the study usually occupy the bulk of the report. Describe the findings in detail, along with the necessary tables and graphs. This is the place to give the managerial implications of the study results.

Limitations: Usually assumptions are made while conducting a research study. This section should describe the limitations of the assumptions and any problems that may have arisen during the data collection, sampling, or survey process.

Conclusions and Recommendations: Here, you should clearly state the conclusions of the study and give possible recommendations. These recommendations would involve either suggesting a strategy or presenting ideas for implementing strategies, and so forth.

Appendixes: These contain all the technical details of the study such as copies of questionnaires, coding instructions, data, sampling, plan, and so on.

Finally, you should include a cover letter with the report. This cover letter provides details on the enclosed material—the research report, who is responsible for the project, and which people are receiving copies of the report. It should also communicate that the researcher will be happy to answer any questions that may arise from the report.

◆ ORAL PRESENTATION

The ability to communicate orally is extremely important to effective management in general and to the marketing research functions in particular. What can be done to ensure that the oral presentation is as effective as possible? The following five suggestions will be discussed in this section:

1. Don't read.
2. Use visual aids.
3. Make sure the start is positive.
4. Avoid distracting the audience.
5. Involve the audience.

Don't Read

Not everyone will agree with this first suggestion; however, we firmly believe that the risks and disadvantages of reading outweigh the advantages. The biggest problem with reading is that it usually is boring for the reader and for the audience. Very few can make a script sound interesting, and those few usually do even better without a script. Further, it is necessary to develop the ability to communicate orally in front of a group without a script, to prepare for those occasions when there is no time to prepare a script or when the presenter must adapt to new developments in the middle of a presentation. If you rely too heavily on a script and use it in what may be limited opportunities to give presentations, you will not develop this important capability.

The advantages of reading from a written report are that the time of the presentation and the choice of words are not left to chance, and you are protected from an attack of stage fright. The alternative is good preparation, a set of notes, and rehearsal. The notes should provide (1) an outline so that the proper flow is maintained, and (2) a list of items that should be included. You may want to consult the notes occasionally to make sure you have not omitted anything. More detailed notes can be consulted more frequently. To avoid distraction, keep the notes on a lectern or on cards or a clipboard, positioned so that you can manage them easily with one hand. Especially when the length of the presentation needs to be carefully controlled, rehearsal is essential. Often, five or more rehearsals can be worthwhile. It is even better if feedback is available in the form of a practice audience or a videotape. You can combat stage fright with deep breathing, pauses, and experience. There is no substitute for experience.

Use Visual Aids

Visual aids perform several functions. First, they give impact to the information and focus attention on important points. Second, ideas that are extremely difficult to express in words often can be communicated easily with visual aids. Finally, they help to give the presentation variety. Visual aids include computer-assisted (e.g., Powerpoint) presentations, transparencies, charts, hand-outs, slides, videotapes, films, samples, demonstrations, and role-playing. Transparencies, charts, slides, and hand-outs are probably the most widely used. However, computer-assisted presentations are increasingly being used when appropriate facilities are available.

Computer-assisted presentations provide many advantages, including high-quality pictures, ability to focus on a point-by-point basis (bullet method), the ease of going forward/backward during the presentation, and opportunity to tie-in with the

Internet. This method of presentation requires computer hardware and appropriate software (e.g., Powerpoint, Corel), along with a projector. Portable devices are expensive and therefore the use of this method is not very common. Since most medium to large-size companies have the required material, it is becoming the norm to use the computer-assisted presentation method when dealing with these companies.

Transparencies are easy to make and can be carried in a folder. They have the advantage of controlling the audience's attention. The transparency can be exposed one line at a time by covering the rest with a piece of paper. The audience thus focuses on what is being uncovered at the moment and does not wander ahead of the presentation. You can write on the transparency to make a point during the presentation. The key to successful use of transparencies is using readable, large type, and minimizing the number of words or numbers used. Experienced and skilled users of transparencies often use only five or fewer lines per transparency, with each line containing only a few words or numbers. One rule of thumb is that a single transparency should contain no more then 30 words or items of data.

Similar guidelines apply to charts and slides, which share most of the characteristics of transparencies. Charts are more versatile than transparencies but are less convenient to make and carry. Slides are better for large audiences, since they can be seen more easily, but they require time to prepare and are not easily modified. Thus, they are not suitable for a presentation that is still being developed and refined.

The use of hand-outs provides the audience with something to take notes on and to take with them. As a result, the audience burden of taking notes is greatly reduced. Sometimes, when transparencies are used, the audience's note-taking task is so difficult that it becomes distracting. Hand-outs free listeners to attend to and participate more fully in the presentation. Their disadvantages are that they must be prepared beforehand and the audience is tempted to look ahead. Further, there is always the distraction of making sure everyone is on the right page, although numbering the pages helps.

Make Sure the Start Is Positive

The start should be positive in tone, confident, and involving. Sometimes a period of silence can be used effectively to get attention. It is useful to stimulate and involve the audience immediately, perhaps by a provocative question or statement. Absolutely never apologize at the outset, even in jest. If you tell the audience you are nervous, unprepared, or unknowledgeable, even in the context of a humorous line, the audience will tend to believe you.

Avoid Distracting the Audience

The presenter needs to be aware that the audience is easily distracted. The following do's and don'ts address some common causes of distraction.

1. Take everything out of your pockets and make sure there is nothing on the lectern other than your notes. Remove pens, pointers, keys, clips—everything. It often happens, without your even being aware of it, that you will pick up objects and manipulate them until the audience is severely distracted, if not driven bananas.

2. Try to avoid the extremes of either obvious pacing or hiding behind a lectern. It can be as distracting to see a speaker clutch a lectern for support as to see someone pace back and forth. The speaker's movements should be purposeful and natural, such as stepping aside to point to a chart, standing

or sitting beside the lectern, or moving closer to the audience for a short portion of the presentation.

3. Maintain good eye contact. This allows audience feedback, stimulates trust and confidence in what you are saying, and involves the audience. A speaker who avoids eye contact by looking up or down or somewhere else risks distracting the audience.

4. Be concerned about the sound of your voice. Listen to a tape of your presentation if possible. A presentation can be distracting if it is too soft, loud, fast, slow, or monotoned. Be sure to use pauses to break up the presentation and to allow the audience time to digest the material.

Involve the Audience

An involved audience will be more interested. An effective technique is to intersperse questions throughout. If time does not permit a discussion, a pause at least gives the audience members a chance to reflect. Sometimes it is useful to ask each person to write down his or her opinion on a piece of paper—for example, a personal judgment on a key value in the data analysis. Another technique is to refer to the ideas of people in the audience, saying, for example, "As John mentioned last week…"

The question-and-answer part of the presentation is particularly important. This often concludes the talk, but it can be permitted to occur during the presentation. Pause and make sure that the question is understood. Then, if possible, give a short positive or negative response and as compact an explanation as possible. If you do not know, say so, adding (if appropriate) that you will get the answer by the next day. A good technique is to write the question down so you do not forget it. Equally important, those in the audience see that you are taking them seriously. Anticipate questions beforehand, and rehearse the answers. Sometimes it is even effective to leave things out of the presentation if they can be covered more effectively during the question-and-answer period.

◆ RELATIONSHIP WITH THE CLIENT

It is important to work with the client or at least be available to clarify or interpret the research results when the findings are implemented. This continued relationship not only helps researchers to evaluate the project's usefulness, it gives them a sense of confidence about the quality of their work. Since most marketing research projects are obtained through word-of-mouth referrals, not through advertising, it is important to satisfy the client. It may be useful for the researcher to sit with the client and get feedback on various aspects of the research project.

END OF CHAPTER MATERIAL

SUMMARY

Communication skills are important to the marketing research process; this includes the presentation of both the research proposal and the research results. An effective presentation involves several elements. The audience should be clearly identified so that the presentation will be on target. It should include an introduction with an overview of the presentation structure, a body, and a summary. Motivation can be provided by relating the presentation to the research objectives and purpose, by focusing on the most interesting findings, and by having an interesting presentation style. The use of specific examples and visual material can help you communicate more effectively and interestingly. You should discuss those elements of methodology that affect interpretation.

Several guidelines can help improve both written and oral presentation. Reading a report tends to be boring and should be avoided. Visual aids such as computer-assisted presentations, transparencies, and hand-outs can add punch and improve communication. Make sure the start is positive. Try to involve the audience, and avoid distracting mannerisms.

KEY TERMS

presentation introduction
body of the presentation

presentation summary

MARKETING RESEARCH TOOLBOX
REVIEW POINTS

1. In general, irrespective of the type of the presentation, the presenter should communicate to a specific audience, structure the presentation, create audience interest, be specific and visual, and address validity and reliability issues.

2. The introduction in a presentation should provide audience interest, identify the presentation's central idea or objective, and provide a road map to the rest of the presentation.

3. It is usually best to divide the body of the presentation into between two and five parts. A presentation can also be structured using research questions. Most useful presentations will include a statement of implications and recommendations relevant to the research purpose.

4. The purpose of the presentation summary is to identify and underline the important points of the presentation and to provide some repetition of their content.

5. The research purpose and objectives are good vehicles to provide motivation. The research purpose should specify decisions to be made and should relate to the research questions. A presentation that focuses on those research questions and their associated hypotheses will naturally be tied to relevant decisions and hold audience interest.

6. The most interesting presentations usually use specific stories, anecdotes, studies, or incidents to make points. They will be much more interesting and graphic than a generalization, however accurate and scientific.

7. The presentation should help the audience avoid misinterpreting the results. When the wording of a question or some other design issue can affect an interpretation and ultimately a research conclusion, that issue should be raised and its possible effect on the interpretation should be discussed. The presentation should include some indication of the reliability of the results.

8. Suggestions for making an oral presentation effective include avoiding reading from a written report, using visual aids, making a positive start, avoiding distracting the audience, and involving the audience.

9. It is important to work with the client or at least be available to clarify or interpret the research results when the findings are implemented. This continued relationship not only helps researchers to evaluate the project's usefulness, it gives them a sense of confidence about the quality of their work.

QUESTIONS AND PROBLEMS

1. By what criteria would you evaluate a written presentation? Develop an evaluation form. Would it differ depending on whether the research proposal or the research results were being presented?

2. By what criteria would you evaluate an oral presentation? Develop an evaluation form.

3. Observe three specific oral presentations outside of class. Consider the following:
   a. Were there any distracting mannerisms?
   b. What did the presenters do with their hands?
   c. How was the audience involved, if at all?
   d. Evaluate the visual aids used. Would you recommend the use of other visual aids?
   e. Did you ever become confused or bored? Was there anything the presenter could have done differently to counteract that tendency?

ENDNOTES

1. Ron Hoff, "What's Your Presentation Quotient?" *Advertising Age* (January 16, 1978), p. 93.

2. "Teaching the Boss to Write," *Business Week* (October 25, 1976), p. 56.

3. Adapted from H. L. Gordon, "Eight Ways to Dress a Research Report," *Advertising Age* (October 20, 1980), p. S–37.

4. "Kaleidoscope: A Swiftly Changing Scene," *American Demographics* (February 1998), p. 34–41.

Applications of Marketing Research

Learning Objectives

- Introduce the major applications of marketing research.
- Discuss the information requirements for new-product, pricing, distribution, advertising, and promotion research.
- Provide discussion on the various techniques used for concept generation, product evaluation and development, and pretest and test marketing.
- Introduce the applications of marketing research in pricing of a product.
- Introduce the various distribution decisions that require marketing research inputs.
- Describe the techniques used in the actual industry to obtain the measures used to evaluate advertisements.
- Briefly mention the methods used to obtain information for other media decisions.
- Introduce the agenda for marketing research in the nineties.
- Discuss the concept of competitive advantage and the various ways of measuring it.
- Discuss brand equity and the various techniques used to measure it.
- Discuss customer satisfaction and the different methods of operationalizing it.
- Describe the concept and methodologies used to measure the different dimensions of total quality management.
- Introduce the concept of database marketing research.
- Discuss the marketing research needs for constructing a database.
- Discuss the key elements of building a customer database.
- Briefly discuss the role of marketing research in relationship marketing.

Now that we have considered the various steps in the marketing research process in detail, let's think about what to do with it. In this chapter, we talk briefly about the various applications of marketing research, which can be applied to every stage of the marketing process. Traditionally, marketing decisions have been divided into 4Ps—product, price, promotion, and place (henceforth, distribution) decisions. This chapter has been divided into three sections. In the first section of this chapter, we discuss the information needs for the 4P decisions and the various techniques available in the industry to obtain that information. The next section deals with marketing research applications for contemporary issues such as total quality management, brand equity, and customer satisfaction. The last section focuses on the use of marketing research for emerging applications such as direct marketing, database marketing and relationship marketing, along with some discussion of forecasting methods.

The first section deals with product, price, distribution, and promotion decisions. The main product decisions to be considered are the physical design of the product and its demand potential. The various information requirements and techniques used for this purpose are covered in the section called "New-Product Research." The other major decision regarding new products is how to forecast sales potential. Once the product is available, its price must be determined. We also discuss two methods of pricing and their informational requirements. The distribution decisions that are discussed here are (1) the number and location of warehouses and retail outlets, and (2) the number and location of salespersons (territory allocation decisions). The section on promotional research briefly discusses sales promotion research. Then, various methods of copy testing and the research required for other media decisions are described.

This second section discusses various new methods of operationalizing well-established constructs such as competitive advantage, brand equity, customer satisfaction, and emerging strategy in the field of marketing such as **Total Quality Management.** Then it enumerates the informational requirements to implement this strategy. This section also briefly touches upon various techniques and methods that marketing research companies use to satisfy these informational requirements.

The third section discusses the emerging applications of marketing research. The creation of customers is only a first step in building a successful business. The next—and more important—step is to manage and retain these customers. Mail-order firms, faced with high up-front costs of printing and circulation, long ago adopted the concept of lifetime value of a customer (LTV) to guide marketing decision making. In the past, the nurturing of customer relationships has been difficult,

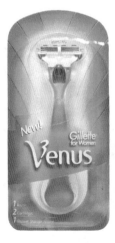

Courtesy Gillette Company.

because of not knowing which customers came or went or why. Database technology has changed all that. Through database technology, an organization can at last identify its loyal customers, its repeat purchasers, and its one-time-only "triers," especially within well-defined market segments.

The power of database technology ties these three characteristics together. The database collects and analyzes customer information; it is able to target specific benefits to specific customers and it provides the means for accurately measuring results. With the advent of customer lists, direct marketing came into prominence. The last section discusses these emerging applications of marketing research.

◆ SECTION I: TRADITIONAL APPLICATIONS OF MARKETING RESEARCH: PRODUCT, PRICE, DISTRIBUTION, AND PROMOTION

New Product Research

New product development is critical to the life of most organizations as they adapt to their changing environment. Since, by definition, new products contain unfamiliar aspects for the organization, there will be uncertainty associated with them. Thus, it is not surprising that a large proportion of marketing research is for the purpose of reducing the uncertainty associated with new products.

New-product research can be divided into four stages, as shown in Figure 16-1. The first stage is generating new-product concepts; the second is evaluating and developing those concepts; the third is evaluating and developing the actual products; finally, the product is tested in a marketing program.

New products launched.
A. Ramey/PhotoEdit.

Concept Generation

There are two types of concept generation research. The first might be termed *need identification research*. The emphasis in need research is on identifying unfilled needs in the market. The second is termed *concept identification*. Here, an effort is made to determine concepts that might fill an identified need.

Need Identification. Marketing research can identify needs in various ways. Some are qualitative and others, such as segmentation studies, can be quantitative. Following are some examples:

- Perceptual maps, in which products are positioned along the dimensions by which users perceive and evaluate, can suggest gaps into which new products might fit. Multidimensional scaling typically is used to generate these perceptual maps.
- Social and environmental trends can be analyzed.
- An approach termed *benefit structure analysis* has product users identify the benefits desired and the extent to which the product delivers those benefits, for specific applications. The result is an identification of benefits sought that current products do not deliver.[1]
- Product users might be asked to keep a diary of a relevant portion of their activities. Analyzing such diaries can provide an understanding of unsolved problems associated with a particular task.
- In focus-group interviews, product users might discuss problems associated with product-use situations.
- In lead user analysis, instead of just asking users what they have done, their solutions are collected more formally. First, lead users are identified. Lead users are the first to face needs that later will be general in a marketplace; they are positioned to benefit significantly by solving problems associated with these needs. Once a lead user is identified, the concepts that company or person generates are tested.

Figure 16-1 Phases in new-product research.

Concept Identification. There are various ways to identify concepts. Some are neither user-based nor follow from identification of unfilled needs. One role of marketing research is to monitor the environment systematically to learn of technological or competitive developments that may suggest new concepts.

During the new-product development process there is usually a point where a concept is formed but there is no tangible usable product that can be tested. The concept should be defined well enough so that it is communicable. There may be simply a verbal description, or there may be a rough idea for a name, a package, or an advertising approach. The role of marketing research at this stage is to determine if the concept warrants further development and to provide guidance on how it might be improved and refined.

Some approaches to concept testing do not involve obtaining reactions from relevant people. One is to attempt to identify a set of similar products and to learn what the market response to them has been. Most concept testing, however, involves exposing people to the concept and getting their reactions.

There will always be a trade-off between the timing of the concept test and the development of the marketing program. The whole point of concept testing is to determine if it is worthwhile to develop a marketing program, so it is not realistic to hold off concept testing until a marketing program exists. Still, there is always the danger that a missing element in the final marketing program could distort the test. Usually, the concept test will explore several versions of a concept or several product concepts that respond to a user need.

Researchers must interpret the results cautiously, particularly when they are encouraging, since the exposure, even if presented in a relatively neutral way, will sensitize the respondent to the product. The result actually is then an exaggerated tendency to indicate that the respondent will buy the product.

Concept testing is particularly important for durable goods and many industrial products, because they rarely employ testing or test markets. The conventional approach to concept testing can be subject to various problems:

- Respondents may read the concept statements without considering the environment in which the new product will be used.
- Participants are usually presented with only a small amount of information.
- For some new products, consumers prefer to learn through trial rather than reading.

These limitations can be restrictive when testing really new products. Since different people follow different information-processing strategies, concept statements to some extent constrain respondents' information search and processing. To overcome these problems, the *information acceleration (IA)* technique was developed.[2] Respondents are placed in a virtual buying environment in which they are first accelerated into a future time period and then allowed to choose information sources they wish to use to evaluate a new product.[3]

Product Evaluation and Development

Product evaluation and development, or product testing, is very similar to concept testing, in terms of both the objectives and the techniques. The aim is still to predict market response to determine whether the product should be carried forward.

Use Testing. The simplest form of use testing gives users the product, and, after a reasonable amount of time, asks their reactions to it, including their intentions to buy it. Now market researchers can use the latest in computer technology and can do virtual product testing, which is explained in Marketing Research in Practice 16-1. IA and Visionary Shopper are product-oriented techniques that do not take account of the fact that it is difficult to evaluate a service until it is consumed. Thus, when testing services, another virtual reality model, SERVASSOR, is more appropriate.[4]

Problems associated with use tests are:

- Because of unclear instructions, a misunderstanding, or lack of cooperation, respondents may not use the product correctly and may therefore report a negative opinion. Or they may not use it at all and simply fabricate an opinion.

MARKETING RESEARCH IN PRACTICE 16-1

Virtual Testing

MarketWare Corp. believes it has captured real marketing research on consumer behavior in its new software, Visionary Shopper. The suburban Atlanta-based firm, already a leader in pegboard-display product space management software with its Pegman product, now is trying to take its technology into the rest of the store with its new virtual reality-based software. The system, which runs on PCs, allows consumers to stroll through store aisles on a computer screen, allowing examination of packages as though the shelf was really in front of them. MarketWare believes a multitude of marketing variables can be measured in impact through the process, which for most brands and categories runs about 30 minutes per consumer.

Most significantly, though, according to MarketWare's Stephen Needel, who directs the firm's simulation efforts, "it feels like fun" for the consumer. "We can extend the time we have them in there" doing the testing because of the appeal of the three-dimensional presentation and real-shelf look. Consumers can actually remove products easily from a shelf, examine labels, study prices and other product options, and react to shelf-layout changes or promotional and pricing considerations—all without setting foot in a store. And for consumers sensitized to batteries of direct marketing and marketing research mail and phone calls, the system is a pleasant break, because "it's not survey work," said Needel, "It's virtual reality."

Consumers are recruited through store and mall intercepts and given about five minutes' training on the software. Then MarketWare personnel leave them alone to do their shopping so that they'll rely on themselves rather than a proctor to walk through the virtual store aisles. The anonymity also helps boost real consumer responses to the variables being tested. Literally, the software gives consumers a grocery-store look, allowing for zoom-ins on shelves and packages, and real handling of packages to study labels, right down to rotating the package, seemingly by hand. Prompts allow the consumers to place the package in their grocery carts for purchase and/or replace it on the shelf. If designated for purchase, it appears in the cart with other purchased items, while the hole it created in being removed from the shelf appears on the computer screen image of that shelf.

In combination with the firm's market-leading Pegman software, shelf rearrangement and different marketing variable examinations are rapidly and easily done. "We can test as many variables at the same time as you want," said Needel. Needel also believes the system will get beyond some consumer responses that otherwise might not be accurately attained. For instance, the amount of beer a consumer might remove from a shelf in such a virtual reality test might be more in line with reality than what the consumer might say in survey research to avoid presenting an image of drinking too much.

Source: Howard Schlossberg, "Shoppers Virtually Stroll through Store Aisles to Examine Packages," *Marketing News* (June 7, 1993), p. 2.

- The fact that they were given a free sample and are participating in a test may distort their impressions.

- Even when repurchase opportunities are made available, such decisions may be quite different than when they are made in a more realistic store situation with special displays presenting the new brand and those of its competitors.

- There is the issue of whether the users will accept the product over a long time period. This problem is especially acute when repurchase data cannot be or are not obtained.

- They may inflate their intention to buy. Consumers may say that they will buy the product but may end up not doing so.[5]

A particular type of use test is the blind-use test, which is most appropriate just after the product emerges from the R & D laboratory. Even though a product may be proved superior in the laboratory, the consumer may not perceive it to be superior. The blind taste tests used for New Coke, described in Marketing Research in Practice 16-2, are a classic example of how these tests can lead to false results.

Predicting Trial Purchase. Several models have been developed to predict trial levels of new, frequently purchased consumer products.[6] The model called ESP (estimating

MARKETING RESEARCH IN PRACTICE 16-2

The Introduction of New Coke

During the early 1980s, Pepsi gained share at the expense of Coca-Cola in part because Pepsi had a sweeter, smoother taste. Pepsi ads show that in "Pepsi Challenge" blind taste tests, people actually did prefer Pepsi over Coke. As a result, Coca-Cola ran tests of a new cola formula that involved 190,000 consumers in 35 cities, costing more than $4 million. They found that with brands not identified, the new Coke flavor was preferred to the original Coke by 55 percent to 45 percent. When the same consumers were told what they were tasting, their preference for the new flavor was 61 percent. The new flavor was preferred to Pepsi by as much as 56 percent to 44 percent.

Encouraged by this market research, Coca-Cola on May 9, 1985, replaced the Coca-Cola drink with "New Coke." It was a disaster. Coke users rebelled and demanded that the original Coke be returned. By July, a poll found that 60 percent of those who tried New Coke thought that the now unavailable original Coke tasted better. On July 10, 1985, Coca-Cola reintroduced the original product as "Classic Coke" and just a few months later Classic Coke was outperforming New Coke by as much as nine to one in some markets. In 1986 New Coke fell to a 2.3 percent share.

How did the research go so wrong? In retrospect, it seems clear that consumer reaction to the withdrawal of Coca-Cola should have been examined. New Coke was tested, but not as a replacement to the original Coke. In the market introduction of New Coke, the original Coke was no longer available, and thus, consumers no longer had the freedom to choose. The fact that a choice was imposed was clearly resented and affected the acceptance and, in fact, the perceived taste of the product.

The Coke experience illustrates that it is very tenuous to use an attitude measure for an object in one context to predict the opinions in another context.

Source: Debra Jones Ringold, "Consumer Response to Product Withdrawal: The Reformulation of Coca-Cola," *Psychology and Marketing* (Fall 1988), pp. 189–210.

sales potential) is typical.[7] Data from 45 new-product introductions were obtained and used to estimate the model. Trial levels (the percentage of a sample of consumers who had purchased the product at least once within 12 months after launch) were predicted on the basis of three variables:

- *Product class penetration (PCP):* the percentage of households purchasing at least one item in the product class within one year[8]
- *Promotional expenditures:* total consumer-directed promotional expenditures on the product
- *Distribution of the product:* percentage of stores stocking the product (weighted by the store's total sales volume)

Knowledge of these three variables enabled ESP to predict trial levels of the 45 new products extremely accurately. Trial also can be estimated directly using controlled shopping experience.

Pretest Marketing. ASSESOR is one of the popular models used for **pretest marketing.** Two approaches are used to predict the new brand's market share. The first is based on the preference judgments. The preference data are used to predict the proportion of purchases of the new brand that respondents will make given that the new brand is in their response set. These estimates for the respondents in the study are coupled with an estimate of the proportion of all people who will have the new brand in their response set, to provide an estimate of market share. A useful byproduct of this approach is an analysis of the concomitant market share losses of the other brands.

The second approach involves estimating trial and repeat purchase levels based on the respondent's purchase decisions and intentions-to-buy judgments. A trial estimate is based on the percentage of respondents who purchase the product in the laboratory, plus an estimate of the product's distribution, advertising (which will create product awareness), and the number of free samples to be given away. The repeat-purchase rate is based on the proportion of respondents who make a mail-order repurchase of the new brand and the buying-intentions judgments of those who elected not to make a mail-order repurchase. The product of the trial estimate and the repeat purchase estimate become a second estimate of market share.

The method has a host of limiting assumptions and other limitations. Perhaps the most critical assumption is that the preference data and the purchase and repurchase decisions are valid predictors of what actually would happen in the marketplace. The artificiality of the product exposure and such surrogates for purchase decisions in the marketplace is a problem common to all laboratory approaches. Another problem is related to the convenience-sampling approach and the fact that there will be attrition from the original sample.[10]

Laboratory tests have a number of advantages, too.

- Compared with test markets, they are fast, relatively cheap, confidential, and flexible.
- For a relatively modest incremental cost, a laboratory test market can evaluate alternative executions of elements in the marketing program such as packaging, price, advertising, product features, and location within the store.

Test Marketing

Test marketing allows the researcher to test the impact of the total marketing program, with all its interdependencies, in a market context as opposed to the artificial context associated with the concept and product tests that have been discussed.

Test marketing has two primary functions. The first is to gain information and experience with the marketing program before making a total commitment to it. The second is to predict the program's outcome when it is applied to the total market.

There are really two types of test markets: the sell-in test market and the controlled-distribution scanner market. Sell-in test markets are cities in which the product is sold just as it would be in a national launch. In particular, the product has to gain distribution space. Controlled-distribution scanner markets are cities for which distribution is prearranged and the purchases of a panel of customers are monitored using scanner data.

Really New Products

Really new products normally take a long time (sometimes 15 to 20 years) from conception to national introduction. Table 16-1 enumerates what really new products (RNPs)[11] are and the role that marketing research plays in getting ideas for such products.

Pricing Research

Research may be used to evaluate alternative price approaches for new products before launch or for proposed changes in products already on the market. As in the case of test marketing, the question of "reality" applies, and it has been found that the sales response to products at different prices in actual stores produces far more discriminating results than the sales response in an artificial store.

There are two general approaches to pricing research. The first is the well-established Gabor and Grainger method.[12] In this method, different prices for a product are presented to respondents (often by using test-priced packs), who then are asked if they would buy. A "buy-response" curve of different prices, with the corresponding number of affirmative purchase intentions, is produced. In a second approach, respondents are shown different sets of brands in the same product category, at different prices, and are asked which they would buy. This multibrand-choice method allows respondents to take into account competitors' brands, as they normally

TABLE 16-1   **Really New Products and Role of Marketing Research in Idea Generation**

What Are Really New Products	Role of Marketing Research in Idea Generation
1. Create or expand a new category, thereby making cross-category competition the key (e.g., fruit teas versus soft drinks)	1. Asking (or listening to) dissatisfied customers
	2. Asking nonrepresentative customers
2. Are new to customers, for whom substantial learning is often required (i.e., what it can be used for, what it competes with, why it is useful)	3. Using open-ended, qualitative (versus structured survey) procedures
	4. Involving customers as co-developers (especially for industrial products)
3. Raise broad issues such as appropriate channels of distribution and organizational responsibility	5. Listening to scientists and newcomers rather than engineers and experts
4. Create (sometimes) a need for infrastructure, software, and add-ons	6. Scanning the literature (especially the technical literature) for interesting possibilities

would outside such a test. As such, this technique represents a form of simulation of the point of sale.

Either of two general pricing strategies can be followed. The first is a skimming strategy, in which the objective is to generate as much profit as possible in the current period. The other is a share-penetration strategy, whose objective is to capture an increasingly larger market share by offering a lower price. Pricing research for the two different approaches differs substantially in terms of the information sought.

Research for Skimming Pricing

The **skimming pricing** strategy is based on the concept of pricing the product at the point at which profits will be the greatest until market conditions change or supply costs dictate a price change. Under this strategy, the optimal price is the one that results in the greatest positive difference between total revenues and total costs. This implies that the researcher's major tasks are to forecast the costs and the revenues over the relevant range of alternative prices.

Research for Penetration Pricing

Penetration pricing is a strategy based on the concept that average unit production costs continue to go down as cumulative output increases. Potential profits in the early stages of the product life cycle are sacrificed in the expectation that higher volumes in later periods will generate sufficiently greater profits to result in overall profit for the product over its life. For some products, this reduction takes the form of an experience curve.

The pricing pattern that is adopted for increasing market share is to:

1. Offer a lower price (even below cost) when entering the market.
2. Hold that price constant until unit costs produce a desired percentage markup.
3. Reduce price as costs fall to maintain markup at the same desired percentage of costs.

The pricing pattern is illustrated in Figure 16-2. A simple typology of the various pricing strategies that are followed in practice and the informational requirements for these strategies are given in Table 16-2.[13]

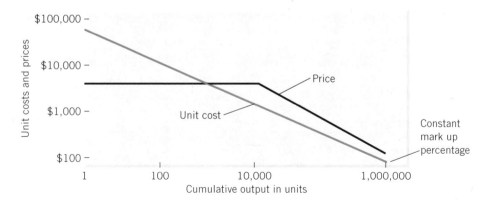

Figure 16-2 Share-oriented penetration pricing.

TABLE 16-2 Informational Requirements for Pricing Strategies

Strategy	Description	Information Requirements	Sources of Information
Random discounting	If some consumers have heterogeneous search costs, firms discount their prices in a random manner to take advantage of those consumers. These consumers buy at the undiscounted price instead of searching for the lowest price, whereas consumers with low search costs will buy at the low price.	Knowledge of consumer segments in the market Characteristics of consumers (their search costs, etc.) Product and cost information Information on legal constraints	Demographic consumer data Analysis of scanner data Internal records Legal data
Second-market discounting	If distinct markets exist and if the consumers in one market incur transaction costs to buy in another, the firm can discount its price in the other markets to below its average cost. In the international context this is called dumping.	Knowledge about the different markets and their characteristics Product and cost information Information on the legal aspects of the other markets Information on the transaction cost incurred by the consumer when he or she buys from the different market	Internal records Legal data Secondary data sources that give the demographic profile of the markets
Periodic discounting	When some consumers in the market have differential reservation prices, firms can start at high prices and periodically discount them in order to draw consumers with lower reservation prices.	Information about consumers' reservation prices Product and cost information	Internal records Survey research to determine the consumers' reservation price Legal data
Price signaling	When consumers in the market are willing to pay more for a product despite lack of knowledge regarding its quality, then price signaling can be used. Essentially the strategy is to produce an inferior product and sell it at the same price as the better-quality product another firm produces, in the belief that consumers will assume that the product is of high quality and buy it because of its high price.	Information about your competitor's prices and costs Information about the legal constraints of price signaling Product and cost information	Internal records Secondary data on competitor prices Legal data Inferential information on competitor costs
Penetration pricing	Penetration pricing is used in situations similar to that in periodic discounting, except in this case competitors are also free to enter at the same price. Hence, the threat of competitive entry and price-sensitive consumers force the firm to price its products at a low price.	Product and cost information Information about competitor's prices and costs	Secondary data and inferential information on competitor's prices and costs Internal records

(Continued)

Table 16-2 (continued)

Strategy	Description	Information Requirements	Sources of Information
Geographic pricing	Geographic pricing strategies are used by firms that sell in markets that are separated geographically. The difference in pricing is due to transportation costs rather than reservation prices or transaction costs.	Information on the characteristics of the different markets Product and cost information Information on the transportation costs and about any legal aspects that may hinder this particular type of pricing strategy	Internal records Secondary data and inferential information on competitor prices and costs
Premium pricing	This strategy and price signaling are very similar. The difference stems from the fact that in price signaling the firm produces only the inferior product and prices it high, whereas here the firm produces both the inferior and the better product and sells them at the same price to exploit the joint economies of scale.	Product and cost information Information on the competitor's prices and costs Information on the characteristics of the consumers (like the maximum price they are willing to pay for this product)	Secondary sources of legal data Internal records Secondary sources of information on markets and transportation costs
Price bundling	Bundling strategy is adopted when the products are nonsubstitutable, perishable, and there is an assymetric demand structure for them. An example of this strategy is selling a car with the maximum number of options. The perishability in the case of durables is with regard to the purchase occasion.	Information on the demand characteristics for the various components of the bundle Product and cost information Information on the consumer preferences for the various combinations of the bundle	Internal records Survey data on consumer characteristics and preferences Secondary sources of information on competitor costs and prices
Complementary pricing	Complementary pricing is the strategy used by firms to price complementary products. They usually price the main product at a low price while the price of the complement is high. The classic example is Japanese pricing of their cars and the spare parts.	Product and cost information	Internal records

Distribution Research[14]

Traditionally, the distribution decisions in marketing strategy involve the number and location of salespersons, retail outlets, warehouses, and the size of discount to be offered. The discount to be offered to the members in the channel of distribution usually is determined by what is being offered by existing or similar products, and also whether the firm wants to follow a "push" or a "pull" strategy. Marketing research, however, plays an important role in decisions about numbers and locations.

Warehouse and Retail Location Research

The essential questions to be answered before a location decision is made are: "What costs and delivery times would result if we choose one location over another?" Simulation of scenarios is used to answer these questions. The simulation can be a relatively simple, paper-and-pencil exercise for the location of a single warehouse in a limited geographic area, or it can be a complex, computerized simulation of a warehousing system for a regional or national market. Table 16-3 enumerates the methods used and the typical information needed.

Number and Location of Sales Representatives

How many sales representatives should there be in a given territory? There are three general research methods for answering this question. The first, the sales effort approach, is applicable when the product line is first introduced and there is no operating history to provide sales data. The second involves the statistical analysis of sales data and can be used after the sales program is underway. The third involves a field experiment and is also applicable only after the sales program has begun.

Sales Effort Approach. A simple approach to estimating the number of sales representatives required for a given territory is as follows:

1. Estimate the number of sales calls required to sell to, and to service, prospective customers in an area for a year.
2. Estimate the average number of sales calls per representative that can be made in that territory in a year.
3. Divide the estimate in step 1 by the estimate in step 2 to obtain the number of sales representatives required.

Once a sales history is available from each territory, an analysis can be made to determine if the appropriate number of sales representatives is being used in each territory.

Field Experiments. Experimenting with the number of calls made is another method of determining the number and location of sales representatives. This may be done in two ways: (1) making more frequent calls on some prospects or customers and less frequent calls on others in order to see the effect on overall sales (in this method the number of sales representatives remains unchanged); and (2) increasing the number of representatives in some territories and decreasing them in others to determine the sales effect.

The design of the experiment(s), and the advantages and limitations of conducting them for determining the appropriate number of sales representatives for each territory, are very similar to those for conducting other experiments.

Computerized Models of Sales Force Size and Allocation by Market and by Product Line. A number of computerized models, spreadsheet and others, can be used for

TABLE 16-3 Warehouse and Retail Location Research

Method	Explanation	Typical Information Requirement
Center-of-Gravity Simulation	The center-of-gravity method of simulation is used to locate a single warehouse or retail site	Data that describe the customer characteristics (location of plants, potential warehouse and retail sites) and distribution costs (costs per mile by volume shipped, fixed and variable costs of operating each warehouse, the effect of shipping delays on customer demand)
Computerized Simulation Models	A computer simulation approach is required to work on multiple warehouse location problems	
Trade Area Analysis	Formal models have been developed that can be used to predict the trading area of a given shopping center or retail outlet based on relative size, travel time, and image.[15]	An analysis of the addresses of credit card customers or the license plates of the cars (by plotting the addresses of the car owners) can provide a useful estimate of the trading area. Check-clearance data can be used to supplement this information. The best, but also the most expensive, way of establishing trading-area boundaries is to conduct surveys to determine them. Shopping-center intercept surveys are commonly conducted for this purpose. When information on market potential and market penetration is desired, the shopping-center intercept survey needs to be supplemented by a survey of nonshoppers at the shopping center or store. The nonshopper surveys are often conducted by telephone, with screening to eliminate shoppers. To avoid selection bias when merging the two samples, appropriate weightings based on shopping frequencies must be used.[16]
Outlet Location Research	This method is used for selecting specific store sites	Three general methods are in use for selecting specific store sites. 1. The analogous location method which involves plotting the area surrounding the potential site in terms of residential neighborhoods, income levels, and competitive stores. 2. Multiple regression models can be used to generate a relationship between store sales and a range of store, population, and competitor characteristics. 3. Gravity theory holds that more people will travel from a particular origin to a given destination than will travel to a more distant destination of the same type and size.

determining sales force size and for allocating the sales force by market and by product line. When management is considering using a formal model to assist in making sales-force-related decisions, marketing research often becomes involved in many ways:

1. Determining what models are available and recommending which, if any, should be adopted

2. Developing the data needed to operate the model selected (market potential) by product and by market, desirable call frequencies by class of customer, and so on

3. Operating the model

The model selected should be valid and should require data that can be obtained at a reasonable cost. An approach to testing the validity of a model is to run analyses with it under different conditions and see how it performs.

Promotion Research

This subsection focuses on the decisions that are commonly made when designing a promotion strategy. The decisions for the promotion part of a marketing strategy can be divided into (1) advertising and (2) sales promotion. Sales promotion affects the company in the short term, whereas advertising decisions have long-term effects. Companies spend more time and resources on advertising research than on sales promotion research because of the greater risk and uncertainty in advertising research. We first discuss the use of marketing research in advertising decisions, and then talk briefly about the use of marketing research in sales promotion.

Advertising Research

Most promotion research companies concentrate on advertising because advertising decisions are more costly and risky than sales promotion decisions. Advertising research typically involves generating information for making decisions in the awareness, recognition, preference, and purchasing stages. Most often, advertising research decisions are about advertising copy. Marketing research helps to determine how effective the advertisement will be.

Criteria. The criteria for an effective advertisement will depend, of course, on the brand involved and its advertising objective. However, four basic categories of responses are used in advertising research in general and copy testing in particular: (1) advertisement recognition, (2) recall of the commercial and its contents, (3) the measure of commercial persuasion, and (4) the impact on purchase behavior.

Recognition. One level of testing recognition is whether respondents can recognize the advertisement as one they have seen before. An example of recognition testing is the Bruzzone Research Company (BRC) tests of television commercials.

Recall. The **day-after recall** (DAR) measure of a television commercial, first used in the early 1940s by George Gallup, then by Young & Rubicam, is closely associated with Burke Marketing Research.[17] DAR is the percent of those in the commercial audience who were watching the show, before and after the commercial was shown, who remembered something specific about it, such as the sales message, the story line, the plot, or some visual or audio element.

The DAR is an "on-air" test in that the commercial exposure occurs in a natural, realistic, in-home setting. It is well established and has developed extensive norms over the years. Gallup as well as Robinson, Mapes, and Ross provide a similar measure for print media.

DAR scores have many limitations. First, their reliability is suspect. Extremely low test-retest correlations (below .30) have been found when commercials from the same product class are studied. Second, DAR scores are unduly affected by the nature of the program and whether viewers like the particular program. Third, of eight relevant studies, seven found practically no association between recall and the measure of persuasion it generated.

Persuasion. The forced-exposure, brand-preference change test measures the change in brand preference after watching an advertisement in a theater. Theater testing, pioneered by Horace Schwerin and Paul Lazarsfeld in the 1950s, is now done by McCollum/Spielman, ASI, and ARS.[18]

Customized Measures of Communication/Attitude. Standardized-copy test measures are useful because they come with norms, sometimes based on thousands of past tests. Thus, the interpretation of a test becomes more meaningful. Some objectives, particularly communication objectives, necessarily are unique to a brand, and may require questions tailored to that brand. Customized measures of communication or attitude have to be developed for such applications.

On-Air Brand-Preference Change Tests. In the Mapes and Ross on-air test, commercials are aired on a radio station in a preselected prime-time position in each of three major markets. Prior to the test, a sample of 200 viewers (150 if the target audience is all male) are contacted by phone and asked to participate in a survey and a cash-award drawing that requires viewing the test program. During the telephone interview, respondents provide unaided brand-name awareness and are questioned about their brand preferences for a number of different product categories. The day following the commercial exposure, the respondents again answer brand-preference questions, as well as DAR questions. The key Mapes and Ross measure is pre- and post-brand-preference change. There are also other measures of brand-preference change, such as the one done by ASI Apex System, which differs slightly from the Mapes and Ross test.[19] A sample proposal for a Mapes and Ross on-air test is provided on the website.

Purchase Behavior

Coupon-Stimulated Purchasing. In the Tele-Research approach, 600 shoppers are intercepted in a shopping center location, usually in Los Angeles, and randomly assigned to test or control groups. The test group is exposed to five television or radio commercials or six print ads. About 250 subjects in the test group complete a questionnaire on the commercial. Both groups are given a customer code number and a packet of coupons, including one for the test brand, which can be redeemed in a nearby cooperating drugstore or supermarket, depending on the product. The selling-effectiveness score is the ratio of purchases by viewer shoppers divided by the purchases by control shoppers. Purchases are tracked by scanner data. Although the exposure context is highly artificial, the purchase choice is relatively realistic in that real money is spent in a real store.

Split-Cable Tests. Information Resources, Inc.'s (IRI) BehaviorScan is one of several **split-cable testing** operations (Burke and Nielsen being two others). BehaviorScan was described in part in Chapter 5. BehaviorScan monitors the purchases of panel members as well as in-store information such as special prices, features, and displays.

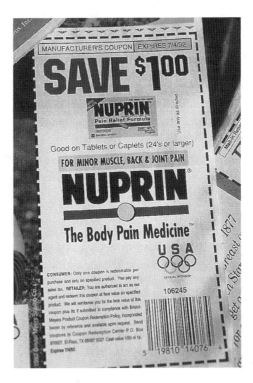

Nuprin coupon.
Gwyn M. Kibbe/Stock, Boston.

An additional capability of split-cable testing makes it extremely important in advertising research. Panelists have a device connected to their TV sets that not only allows the channel selection to be monitored, but also allows the advertiser to substitute one advertisement for another in what are called "cut-ins." Thus, a host of tests can be conducted, such as the effect of specific commercials, sets of commercials, advertising budget levels, the time of day or the program in which the ad appears, the commerical length, or the interaction with promotion programs.

Tracking Studies

When a campaign is running, its impact often is monitored via a **tracking study.** Periodic sampling of the target audience provides a time trend of measures of interest. The purpose is to evaluate and reassess the advertising campaign, and perhaps also to understand why it is or is not working. Among the measures that often are traced are advertisement awareness, awareness of elements of the advertisement, brand awareness, beliefs about brand attributes, brand image, occasions of use, and brand preference. Of particular interest is knowing how the campaign is affecting the brand, as opposed to how the advertisement is communicating the message. Table 16-4 gives a comprehensive view of the measures of advertisement effectiveness and the various tests the industry uses to obtain them.

Diagnostic Testing

A whole category of advertising research methods is designed primarily not to test the impact of a total ad but rather, to help creative people understand how the parts of the ad contribute to its impact. Which are weak, and how do they interact? Most of

TABLE 16-4   **Measures and Tests of Ad Effectiveness**

Measure of Advertising Effectiveness	Test Used in the Industry
Recognition	1. BRC tests of television commercials
	2. Communicus recognition measures of radio and television advertisements
	3. Starch Scores
Recall	1. DAR measure by Young and Rubicam
	2. Gallup & Robinson and Mapes and Ross provide similar measure for the print media
Persuasion	1. Forced exposure brand preference change tests done by McCollum/Spielman, ASI and ARS
	2. On-air tests of brand preference change done by Mapes and Ross and ASI Apex system
	3. Customized measures
Purchase behavior	1. Coupon-stimulated purchasing done by Tele-Research
	2. Split-cable testing by IRI (BehaviorScan)
Tracking studies	1. Customized studies
	2. Eric Marder's TEC audit

these approaches can be applied to mock-ups of proposed ads as well as finished ads.

Copy Test Validity

Copy test validity refers to the ability to predict advertising response. Figure 16-3 is an overview of some of the important ways in which copy tests can differ. Each dimension involves validity issues and trade-offs with cost. Hence, each of these issues has to be considered carefully before a copy test can be designed.

Qualitative Research.   Focus-group research is widely used at the front end of the development of an advertising campaign. In such groups, people will discuss their opinions about the product and the brand, their use experiences, and their reaction to potential advertisement concepts and actual advertisements.[20]

Audience Impressions of the Ad.   Many copy test approaches append a set of ope-nended questions designed to tap the audience's impressions of what the ad was about, what ideas were presented, interest in the ideas, and so on. One goal is to detect potential misperceptions. Another is to uncover unintended associations that may have been created. If too many negative comments are elicited, there may be cause for concern.

Adjective Checklist.   The BRC mail questionnaire includes an adjective checklist that allows the advertiser to determine how warm, amusing, irritating, or informative the respondent thinks the ad is. Several of the phrases tap an empathy dimension: "I can see myself doing that," "I can relate to that," and so on. Some believe that unless advertisements can achieve a degree of empathy, they will not perform well.

Eye Movement.   Eye movement devices, such as those used by Perception Research and Burke, record the point on a print ad or package where the eye focuses, 60 times

Advertisement used
  Mock-up
  Finished advertisement
Frequency of exposure
  Single-exposure test
  Multiple-exposure test
How it's shown
  Isolated
  In a cluster
  In a program or magazine
Where the exposure occurs
  In a shopping center facility
  At home on TV
  At home through the mail
  In a theater
How respondents are obtained
  Prerecruited forced exposure
  Not prerecruited/natural exposure
Geographic scope
  One city
  Several cities
  Nationwide
Alternative measures of persuasion
  Pre/post measures of attitudes or behavior
  (i.e., pre/post attitude or behavior shifts)
  Multiple measures
  (i.e., recall/involvement/buying commitment)
  After-only questions to measure persuasion
  (i.e., constant sum brand preference)
  Test market sales measures
  (i.e., using scanner panels)
Bases of comparison and evaluation
  Comparing test results to norms
  Using a control group

Figure 16-3 Alternative methods of copy testing.

each second. An analysis can determine what the reader saw, what he or she "returned to" for reexamination, what point was "fixed on."

Physiological Measurement. Of particular interest in advertisements that are intended to precipitate emotional responses is the use of measures that reflect physiological arousal that the respondent normally cannot control. Among the measures used are galvanic skin response (GSR), skin resistance, heart beat, facial expressions, muscle movement, and voice pitch analysis.

Budget Decision

Arriving at analytical, research-based judgments as to the optimal advertising budget is surprisingly difficult. However, there are research inputs that can be helpful. Tracking studies that show advertising is either surpassing or failing to reach communication objectives can suggest that the budget should be either reduced or increased. Forced-exposure testing of multiple exposures can suggest the optimal number of exposures per month for an audience member. Such a number can help guide advertising budget expenditures. More direct approaches include regression analysis of internal sales and advertising data, field experimentation, and split-cable experimentation.

Media Research

In evaluating a particular media alternative such as *Time* magazine or *Suddenly Susan* (TV sitcom), it is necessary to know how many advertising exposures it will deliver and what will be the characteristics of the audience. A first cut of the vehicle's value is the cost per thousand (circulation), the advertisement insertion cost divided by the size of the audience.

Measuring Print-Vehicle Audiences. Print-vehicle circulation data are easily obtained, but they neglect pass-along readers both inside and outside the home. Thus, to measure a vehicle's audience, it is necessary to apply approaches such as recent-reading, reading-habit, and through-the-book methods to a randomly selected sample.

In the *recent-reading method,* respondents are asked whether they looked at a copy of a weekly publication within the past week, or during the last month if it is a monthly publication.[21] The *reading-habit method,* which asks respondents how many issues out of the last four they personally read or looked at, is also sensitive to memory difficulties. In particular, it is difficult to discriminate between reading the same issue several times and reading several issues. The *through-the-book* method attempts to reduce the problem resulting from faulty memory. Respondents' readership is ascertained only after they are shown a specific issue of a magazine, asked whether they read several articles, and if they were interesting. The approach, which requires an expensive personal interview, is sensitive to the age of the issue.

Measuring Broadcast-Vehicle Audiences. Television audience size is estimated by a peoplemeter and a diary. The peoplemeter is attached to a television set and monitors the set's activity 24 hours a day, recording any change or activity that lasts over 30 seconds. Nielsen, in its national ratings estimates, supplements the peoplemeter with a matched-sample diary panel. A diary household notes viewing activity, including who is doing the watching.

Sales Promotion Research

There are three major types of sales promotion: consumer promotions, retailer promotions, and trade promotions. Figure 16-4 depicts the major agents involved in sales promotion. In general, the consumer, or end user, is the ultimate target of all sales promotion activities. In consumer promotion, manufacturers offer promotions directly to consumers, whereas retail promotions involve promotions by retailers to consumers. Trade promotions involve manufacturers offering promotions to retailers or other trade entities. Trade entities can also promote to each other. For example, a distributor can offer a steep temporary price cut to retailers in order to sell excess inventory. We call these **trade promotions,** since the recipient of the promotion is a marketing intermediary.

Sometimes several manufacturers or several retailers combine in one promotion. These are called **cooperative promotions** or **promotion partnerships.** Partnership

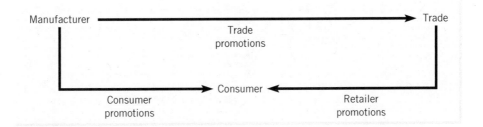

Figure 16-4 A schematic framework of the major types of sales promotion.

promotions often "tie in" a sample or other promotion for one product with the purchase of another.

Strategically, trade promotions and the resultant retailer promotions are elements of the "push" component of a manufacturer's marketing effort, whereas consumer promotions are part of the "pull" effort. It is important that the push and pull elements of sales promotion strategy work hand in hand with the push and pull elements of a firm's marketing strategy. Table 16-5 lists some specific retailer, trade, and consumer promotions. This list is by no means exhaustive.

Unfortunately, much of the research on sales promotion has concentrated on only a few types or has considered promotion only more generically. For example, couponing by far is the most researched form of consumer promotion. In one sense this is appropriate, since coupons are clearly the most important consumer promotion for packaged-goods marketers.[22] However, contests and sweepstakes, continuity offers, price packs, and premiums are clearly underresearched. Rebates, which are the durable-goods analog of couponing, have received very little attention. The use of premiums and financing incentives in a durable-goods context is also vastly under-researched. With scanner data so easily and widely available, most of the information requirements for decisions on sales promotions can be readily acquired.

TABLE 16-5 Specific Sales Promotional Tools

Retailer Promotions	Trade Promotions	Consumer Promotions
Price cuts	Case allowances	Couponing
Displays	Advertising allowances	Sampling
Feature advertising	Display allowances	Price packs
Free goods	Trade coupons	Value packs
Retailer coupons	"Spiffs"	Refunds
Contests/premiums	Financing incentives	Continuity programs
	Contests	Financing incentives
		Bonus packs
		Special events
		Sweepstakes
		Contests
		Premiums
		Tie-ins

◆ SECTION II: CONTEMPORARY APPLICATIONS OF MARKETING RESEARCH

Competitive Advantage

The notion that achieving superior performance requires a business to gain and hold an advantage over competitors is central to contemporary strategic thinking. Businesses seeking advantage are exhorted to develop distinctive competencies at the lowest delivered cost or to achieve differentiation through superior value. The promised payoff is market share dominance and above-average profitability. Michael Porter's pioneering text on competitive strategy changed the way many companies think about their competition.[23] Porter identified five forces that shape competition: current competitors, the threat of new entrants, the threat of new substitutes, the bargaining power of customers, and the bargaining power of suppliers.

Assessing Competitive Advantage[24]

Assessing competitive advantage can be done in a number of ways. The methods can be broadly classified as market-based assessment and process-based assessment. **Market-based assessment** is direct comparison with a few target competitors, whereas **process-based assessment** is a comparison of the methods employed by the competitors in achieving their distinctive advantage. The different methods of assessing competitive advantage are given in Table 16-6.

Market-Based Assessment

Here the firm is interested in ascertaining market share, recall share, R&D share, and ad share of their own brand as well as that of the competition.

Process-Based Assessment

Here the firm conducts a marketing skills audit, compares relative costs, compares winning versus losing competitors and attempts to identify high-leverage phenomena.

Brand Equity

Brand equity is defined as a set of assets and liabilities linked to a brand that adds to or subtracts from the value of a product or service to a company and/or its customers.[25] The assets or liabilities that underlie brand equity must be linked to the name and/or symbol of the brand. The assets and liabilities on which brand equity is based will differ from context to context. However, they can be usefully grouped into five categories:

1. Brand loyalty
2. Name awareness

TABLE 16-6 Methods of Assessing Competitive Advantage

Market-based	Process-based
Market share	Marketing skills audit
Recall share	Comparison of relative costs
Advertising share	Comparison of winning versus losing competitors
R & D share	Identifying high-leverage phenomena

3. Perceived quality
4. Brand associations in addition to perceived quality
5. Other proprietary brand assets: patents, trademarks, channel relationships, etc.

The concept of brand equity is summarized in Figure 16-5, which shows the five categories of assets that are the basis of brand equity. The figure also shows that brand equity creates value for both the customer and the firm.

Research Questions Under Brand Equity

An appraisal of the brand based on the five dimensions involves addressing and obtaining answers to the following questions. Marketing research can help to answer these questions.

Brand loyalty: What are the brand-loyalty levels, by segment? Are customers satisfied? What do "exit interviews" suggest? Why are customers leaving? What is causing dissatisfaction? What do customers say are their problems with buying or using the brand? What are the market share and sales trends?

Awareness: How valuable an asset is brand awareness in this market? What is the company's brand awareness level as compared to that of competitors? What are the trends? Is the brand being considered? Is brand awareness a problem? What can be done to improve brand awareness?

Perceived quality: What drives perceived quality? What is important to the customer? What signals quality? Is perceived quality valued—or is the market

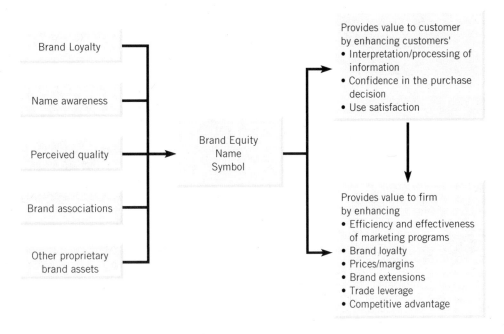

Figure 16-5   Brand equity.

Source: David A. Aaker, *Managing Brand Equity* (New York: The Free Press, 1994).

Nike building brand equity.
Courtesy Nike, Inc.

moving toward a commodity business? Are prices and margins eroding? If so, can the movement be slowed or reversed? How do competitors stack up with respect to perceived quality? Are there any changes? In blind-use tests, what is our brand name worth? Has it changed over time?

Brand associations: What mental image, if any, does the brand stimulate? Is that image a competitive advantage? Does it have a slogan or symbol that is a differentiating asset? How are the brand and its competitors positioned? Evaluate each position with respect to its value or relevance to customers and how protected or vulnerable it is to competitors.

Other brand assets: Are sustainable competitive advantages attached to the brand name that are not reflected in the other four equity dimensions? Is there a patent or trademark that is important? Are there channel relationships that provide barriers to competitors?

Typically, marketing research is used to obtain answers to these questions. Marketing Research in Practice 16-3 provides an example of how McDonald's builds brand equity.

MARKETING RESEARCH IN PRACTICE 16-3

The Golden Arches of Convenience

Marketing research must be linked to business results in order to gain management commitment and significantly change the way research is conducted. McDonald's Corp. relies on the theory of world-class research, which is defined as answering questions before they are posed; synthesizing data and insights rather than processing information; understanding results before options are considered; and compiling strategies and priorities in order to process needs.

McDonald's brand equity is strengthened by defining and managing value, which, by their philosophy, translates into convenience. The restaurant started the breakfast push with the Egg McMuffin in 1979. McDonald's now accounts for 30 percent of fast-food restaurant breakfasts in the United States.

What used to be only a hamburger joint trademarked by "golden arches" in the sixties has blossomed into a multinational, multi-item menu, fast-food chain. In the sixties, the company brought in about $170 million per year domestically and nothing internationally. Now, the company brings in $170 million worldwide in two days of business.

Source: "McDonald's Execs Outline Research Philosophy," *Marketing News* (October 23, 1995), p. 37.

Measuring Brand Equity

It is important to develop approaches that place a value on a brand, for several reasons. First, since brands are bought and sold, a value must be assessed by both buyers and sellers. Which approach makes the most sense? Second, investments to enhance brand equity need to be justified, as there always are competing uses for funds. A bottom-line justification is that the investment will enhance the value of the brand. Thus, some "feel" for how a brand should be valued may help managers address such decisions. Third, the valuation question provides additional insight into the brand-equity concept.

What is the value of a brand name? Consider Compaq, Boeing, Betty Crocker, Ford, Weight Watchers, Budweiser, and Wells Fargo. What would happen to those firms if they lost their brand name but retained the other assets associated with the business? How much would they have to spend to avoid damage to their business if the name were lost? Could any expenditure avoid a loss of business, perhaps permanently?

At least four general approaches have been proposed to assess the value of brand equity. One is based on the excess price that the name can command in the marketplace. The second looks at how much it would cost to replace the brand with a new one. The third is based on the stock price. The fourth focuses on a brand's earning power. Many other methods have also been proposed to measure brand equity.[26] We shall now consider these in the order listed.

Excess-Price Approach. Brand-equity assets such as name awareness, perceived quality, associations, and loyalty all have the potential to provide a brand with a price premium. The resulting extra revenue can be used (for example) to enhance profits, or to reinvest in building more equity.

Observation. One way to measure the excess price a brand can support is simply to observe the price levels in the market. What are the differences, and how are they associated with different brands? For example, what are the price levels of comparable automobiles? How much are the different brands depreciating each year? How responsive is the brand to a firm's own price changes, or to competitors' price changes?

Customer Research. Price premiums can also be measured through customer research. Customers can be asked what they would pay for various features and characteristics of a product (one characteristic would be the brand name).[27] Termed a *dollarmetric scale,* this survey provides a direct measure of the brand name's value.

Obtaining buyer-preference or purchase-likelihood measures for different price levels furnishes additional insight. Such studies can gauge buyer resistance to competitors' price decreases, and determine consumer response to one's own company's decrease in price. A high-equity brand will lose little share to a competitor's lower price, and (up to a point) can gain share when its own relative price is decreased.

Trade-off Analysis. Trade-off (conjoint) analysis is another approach. Here, respondents are asked to make trade-off judgments about brand attributes.

The output of trade-off analysis is a dollar value associated with each attribute alternative. The dollar value of the brand name is thus created in the context of making judgments relative to other relevant attributes of the product class. Given that a price premium can be obtained, the value of the brand name in a given year is that price differential multiplied by the unit sales volume. Discounting these cash flows over a reasonable time is one approach to valuing the brand.

Impact on Customer Evaluation. Considering the price premium for a brand may not be the best way to quantify brand equity, especially for product classes such as cigarettes and air travel, for which prices are fairly similar. An alternative is to consider the impact of the brand name of the customer evaluation of the brand, as measured by preference, attitude, or intent to purchase. What does the brand name do to the evaluation? The value of the brand is then the marginal value of the extra sales (or market share) that the brand name supports.

The size of any price premium and the preference rating of a brand can both be measured and tracked over time using survey research. However, this approach is static, in that it looks at the brand's current position—a view that does not necessarily take into account the future impact of changes (such as improvements in quality).

Replacement-Cost Approach. Another perspective is the cost of establishing a comparable product that can bring in the same amount of business.

Stock-Price Approach. Another approach, suggested by financial theory, is to use stock price as a basis on which to evaluate the value of a firm's brand equities.[28] The argument is that the stock market will adjust the price of a firm to reflect the future prospects of its brands.

The problem with this approach is that if a firm has more than one brand, it is difficult to evaluate the value of each brand to the firm. The internal records of the company are sufficient to evaluate brand equity by this method.

Future-Earnings Approach. The best measure of brand equity would be the discounted present value of future earnings attributable to brand-equity assets.[29] The problem is how to provide such an estimate.

Discounting the Future Profit Stream

One approach is simply to discount the profit stream that is projected for the brand. Such a plan should take into account brand strengths and their impact on the competitive environment.

Applying an Earnings Multiplier

Another approach that researchers can use, even when a brand profit plan is unavailable or unsuitable, is to estimate current earnings and apply an earnings multiplier. The earnings multiplier provides a way to estimate and place a value on future earnings.

Evaluation of Brand Extensions

It is difficult to estimate the earnings streams from brand extensions (the use of the brand name to enter new product classes—for example, Kellogg's bread products, or Hershey's ice cream). Usually, the value of potential brand extensions has to be estimated separately. The methodology followed by *Financial World* to measure the brand equity of Coca-Cola during its annual evaluation of global brands is given in Marketing Research in Practice 16-4.

Customer Satisfaction

The measurement of customer satisfaction and its link to product/service attributes is the vehicle for developing a market-driven quality approach.[30]

Customer satisfaction research has been around for a long time, but it has become a fixture at most large corporations only in recent years. The growth in the popularity of customer satisfaction research is, of course, a corollary to the quality

MARKETING RESEARCH IN PRACTICE 16-4

Estimation of Brand Equity of Coke

Financial World (FW) determined, for example, that the Coca-Cola brand family had 1992 worldwide sales of $49 billion. According to the best estimates of consultants and beverage experts, Coke enjoys an operating margin of around 30 percent, so operating profits for the Coke brand were $2.8 billion.

Coke's elaborate bottling and distribution system generated another $27 billion in revenues and operating profits of $3 billion. But *FW* did not take these numbers into consideration in valuing the Coca-Cola name, because to some extent that would be an overvaluation. We include only the value added by Coke directly, not the value added by the bottlers or distributors. "It is important to recognize that not all of the profitability attributed to a brand should be used in the calculation of brand value to avoid overvaluation and double counting," says Noel Penrose, executive vice president of the Interbrand Group.

Even if Coca-Cola's bottling and distribution network does contribute to brand image, it will be reflected in higher sales and margins of the product itself. The value of the distribution system, though significant, is not the value of the brand. Were we to include the bottling and distribution system, we would have added another $40 billion to our value of Coca-Cola.

Which brings us to the next step: Once product-related profits have been determined, we deduct from a brand's operating profit an amount equal to what would be earned on a basic, unbranded, or generic version of the product. To do this, we estimate the amount of capital it takes to generate a brand's sales. On average, analysts believe that it requires 60 cents worth of capital, which is generally a little higher than net property, plant, and equipment plus net-working capital, to produce each dollar of sales. Using that yardstick, the capital used in production in Coke's case comes to $5.5 billion. Second, we assume that a 5 percent net return on employed capital after inflation can be expected from a similar nonbranded product. So we deduct 5 percent of Coke's capital employed ($273 million) from the $2.7 billion in operating profits to obtain the profit attributable to the brand name alone.

For coke, that leaves an adjusted operating profit figure of $2.4 billion. We then make a provision for taxes, and the remainder is deemed to the net brand-related profits. Finally, we assign a multiple based on brand strength as having seven components: leadership, or the brand's ability to influence its market; stability, the ability of the brand to survive; market, the brand's trade environment; internationality, the ability of the brand to cross geographic and culture borders; trend, the ongoing direction; support, effectiveness of the brand's communications; and protection, the brand owner's legal title. Obviously, the stronger the brand, the higher the multiple applied to earnings. This year, we used multiples ranging from 9 to 20. Coke was assigned the highest multiple, which results in a brand value of $33.4 billion.

Source: Alexandra Ourusoff, "How the Brand Values Were Assigned," *Brand Week* (August 1993), p. 27.

movement in American business. The idea that the customer defines quality should not be new to marketers. However, its recognition in the Malcom Baldrige criteria has given this idea a credibility that was previously lacking.

Satisfaction research, like advertising tracking research, should be conducted at planned intervals so as to track satisfaction over time. Thus, satisfaction research can be put in the context of an interrupted, time-series, quasi-experimental design.

This approach requires a sequential research design that uses the results from each research phase to build and enhance the value of subsequent efforts. During this process, it is imperative to study customers who were lost, to determine why they left. This issue must be addressed early in the system design.

A sequential design provides some level of comfort, because it allows for the luxury of making critical decisions after you have sufficient data to reduce the risk of error inherent in establishing a customer satisfaction system.

Customer Satisfaction Measurement Process

It is believed that 96 percent of dissatisfied customers never complain; 60 to 90 percent of these "silent" dissatisfied customers will not buy from you again; 90 percent of those who do complain will not buy from you again. Therefore, it is important that every firm should have a customer satisfaction program. Table 16-7 enumerates the steps involved in a "no frills" customer satisfaction program.[31]

Issues in Questionnaire Design and Scaling in Satisfaction Research

Each customer-satisfaction study utilizes questions that are, to some degree, unique. However, as in the two other types of studies discussed in this chapter, certain general types of information are collected in most customer-satisfaction studies and these are discussed briefly in Table 16-8.

To measure satisfaction with a service encounter, instruments such as SERVQUAL can be used. This can be modified and adapted to retailing and other settings.

TABLE 16-7   Steps in a "No Frills" Customer Satisfaction Program

1. Define goals and how information will be used.

Key parts of a company must be involved in setting objectives for customer satisfaction measurement and management. This helps to clarify the needs of various users of the information, creates a sense of ownership of the process, and identifies how various levels of a company may have to cooperate to plan action.

Equally important is determining how the information will be used once it is developed. Careful analysis of strategic and tactical organizational applications will ensure that issues of design, sample, analysis, reporting, and deployment are structured to provide customer-focused information that can be acted on most effectively.

2. Discover what is important to customers and employees.

This discovery phase of data collection is intended to identify, in customer's and employees' own language, the attributes that compose their perceptions and expectations for quality and satisfaction. The research will generate a comprehensive list of everything that customers and employees consider important.

3. Measure critical needs.

Measuring the relative importance of the attributes identified in qualitative discovery and a company's competitive performance on those attributes is accomplished through critical-needs assessment. Using trade-off techniques, instead of traditional importance scaling, provides improved discrimination on the relative importance of attributes.

4. Act on the information.

Action planning organizes activity to improve customer satisfaction by operationally defining and functionally deploying customer requirements.

5. Measure performance over time.

Periodic measurement of how a company and its competitors perform on the key drivers of satisfaction reveals the rate at which customer satisfaction is improving or declining.

TABLE 16-8   General Types of Information Collected in Customer Satisfaction Studies

- **Screening questions.** The study begins with screening questions to make sure that the person contacted falls into the target group.
- **Overall ratings.** Some experts argue that it is important to get an overall satisfaction rating from respondents very early in the interview.
- **Performance ratings.** The researchers are interested in measuring customer perceptions of a firm's performance on a number of specific aspects of the product or service. The specific aspects are the key satisfaction factors discussed previously. The researcher will use a numerical rating scale to gauge the satisfaction with each element.
- **Intent to use or purchase product or service in the future.** Satisfaction surveys usually include some measurement of customer likelihood to do business with the firm in the future. This provides a basis for determining whether to purchase or use the product or service. The researcher would hypothesize that the higher the satisfaction level, the higher the likelihood to do business with the organization in the future.
- **Category or brand usage information.** This information will be used for classification purposes in cross-tabulation analysis.
- **Demographic and lifestyle information.** This information is used for classification purposes. The researcher often is interested in determining whether any particular demographic or lifestyle group is more or less satisfied than the business's average customer.

◆ SECTION III: EMERGING APPLICATIONS OF MARKETING RESEARCH: DATABASE MARKETING AND RELATIONSHIP MARKETING

What Is a Database?

A database is a customer list to which has been added information about the characteristics and the transactions of these customers. Businesses use it to cultivate customers and develop statistical profiles of prospects most like their present customers—as they seek new customers. Marketing Research in Practice 16-5 shows the rate at which databases are growing and how e-commerce is facilitating data collection. Increasing size of the databases illustrates the importance they hold for the companies.

MARKETING RESEARCH IN PRACTICE 16-5

Increasing Database Size

A database is just information, not yet knowledge. Companies are collecting more data than ever but are not getting the full value of their efforts. In the networked economy, companies are able to collect more information than ever before about their customers and suppliers. E-commerce is continuously driving the data explosion, and companies are able to collect more information from transactions and also from click streams. Multimedia has made it clear that a large, robust, and scalable data warehouse is a *must* and not a luxury.

In 1996, NCR (www.ncr.com) showed an 11-terabyte database system. At the same time, Wal-Mart had a 6-terabyte system; now Wal-Mart has 100 terabytes. The average size of a database system today is about one terabyte and is expected to be in the 6-terabyte range in about three years. Predicting the requirements for size and scalability is one of the biggest challenges database experts face today.

Source: An interview with Lars Nyberg, *Interactive*, 7,5 (February 7, 2000).

The Need for Databases

A database is, of course, important. A database provides the means for research to support decisions. It enables profiling of customers by searching for prospects who are similar to existing customers. It provides the means for implementation of profitable programs of repeat business and cross-selling. It assists in marketing planning and forecasting. Further, a database (with the use of marketing models) can:[32]

- Match products or services to customers' wants and needs
- Help select new lists or use new media that fit the profile of existing customers
- Maximize personalization of all offers to each customer
- Provide for ongoing interaction with customers and prospects
- Pinpoint ideal timing and frequency for promotions
- Measure response and be accountable for results
- Help create the offers most likely to elicit responses from customers
- Help achieve a unique selling proposition (USP), targeted to appeal to your customers
- Integrate direct-response communication with other forms of advertising
- Demonstrate that customers are valuable assets

Marketing Research in Practice 16-6, provides illustrations of how some companies target their customers.

Elements of a Database

A database should attempt to create:[33]

- A unique identifier such as an ID or match code
- Name and title of individual and/or organization

MARKETING RESEARCH IN PRACTICE 16-6

Targeting Customers

Kraft General Foods, Inc. (KGF), has amassed a list of more than 30 million users of its products who have provided their names when sending in coupons or responding to some other KGF promotion. Based on the interests they've expressed in surveys, it regularly sends them tips on such things as nutrition and exercise—as well as recipes and coupons for specific brands. The company figures that the more information consumers have about a product, the more they are likely to use it (for example, use Miracle Whip instead of butter for grilling sandwiches). KGF constantly refines its database by sending surveys to the names on its list.

Facing increasing restrictions on advertising, Philip Morris Cos. and RJR have assembled a huge database of smokers they can reach directly. For example, by requiring consumers who respond for offers of free shirts, sleeping bags, or other merchandise to fill out detailed questionnaires, Philip Morris has built a list of some 26 million smokers' names and addresses. The companies use their lists both to market to smokers with coupons and promotions and to enlist grassroots support for their lobbying efforts.

Source: "A Potent New Tool for Selling: Database Marketing," *Business Week* (September 5, 1994).

- Mailing address, including ZIP Code
- Telephone number
- Source of order, inquiry, or referral
- Date and purchase details of first transaction
- Recency/frequency/monetary transaction history by date, dollar amounts (cumulative) of purchase, and products (lines) purchased
- Credit history and rating (scoring)
- Relevant demographic data for consumer buyers, such as age, gender, marital status, family data, education, income, occupation, length of residence at address given, geodemographic cluster information, and similar data of value
- Relevant organization data for industrial buyers, such as standard industrial classification (SIC), size, revenues, number of employees, length of time in business, perhaps information about the area of the organization's economic or social location, and even information about the personality of individual buyers within the organization

Using Marketing Databases for Marketing Intelligence

Your customers may have chosen you over your competitors for any of several reasons or even for a combination of items. Why are they your customers? Your customers may have come to you because they:

- Simply did not know your competitors' existence and/or their similar products and services (perhaps they even thought you and what you sell were unique)
- Found you and your product or service superior in only one respect, but a respect that was important to them
- Did not perceive any significant difference between you and your competitors but chose you by pure chance
- Just found it more convenient to do business with you
- Especially disliked something about your competitors and found you the best of several distasteful choices
- Otherwise do not really know why or how they came to choose you

This is obviously valuable information as input to your marketing planning of strategies and promotions. That the marketing database is a good key to gathering much information should come as no surprise.

Ways to Gather Consumer Data

There are many ways to gather consumer data. You may use such direct means as surveys, questionnaires, and application forms, but you may also get information from secondary sources, such as credit-reporting bureaus and published directories.

For example, the last time you signed onto the Internet, someone could have watched what you did, what you said, or what you bought and then shared the information with a curious marketer who wanted to know. Powerful computers and high-tech scanners now enable marketers to monitor closely how, where, and when you spend your money. These electronic transactions speak much louder than words because they reflect actual behavior. It no longer matters what consumers say they do; marketers can now track what they really do.

Types of Databases

Most firms want to have a customer database and a prospect database. The customer database can categorize customers as active or inactive customers and inquiries.

- *Active customers:* How recently have they purchased? How frequently have they purchased? How much did they spend? What are their product or service preferences? Identifying your most active customers can help you concentrate your resources on the most profitable segment of your customer list.
- *Inactive customers:* How long have prior customers been inactive? How long had they been active? What was their buying pattern while active? What offers have they received since? This information can help you design promotions that re-activate your inactive customers.
- *Inquiries:* From what media source did inquirers come? What was the nature and seriousness of the inquiry? Do you have any demographic or psychographic information on inquirers?

The prospect database is developed based on the characteristics similar to those of the customer database.

The objective of developing customer and prospect databases is to break down customers and the most likely prospects into groups identifiable by the kinds of appeals they find most persuasive. **Database marketing** can prevent marketing disasters, which is as important a consideration or objective as increasing marketing successes.

Modeling customers serves several purposes or objectives:

- It helps us identify our most typical customers and so become more effective in our prospecting.
- It helps us identify our best customers, another aid to prospecting.
- It helps us identify niche markets to add to our marketing universe.
- It helps us develop more effective marketing tools (materials and media).

However, soliciting every member of the database can be quite costly. The breakeven response rate a solicitation needs to be profitable is:

$$\text{Breakeven response rate} = \frac{\text{cost of solicitation}}{\text{expected net revenue from a respondent}}$$

Hence, one rule is to solicit only those segments whose expected response rates are above the breakeven rate.

Value-Added Databases

Database enhancement can substantially increase the amount and quality of information you hold on each customer or prospect.

- In its simplest form, an enhancement might be the addition of age (from a driver's license record) or telephone number (from a directory record). Other possibilities include past transactions; demographic and psychographic data; credit experience, if pertinent; people on the move, evidenced by an address change; significant characteristics of a business; and a multiple of customer behavior and transaction data.

- By overlaying multiple databases, you can eliminate duplication between and among the lists and identify "hotline names" (those who responded most recently) and "multi-buyers" (those who appear on more than one response list).

- Negative screening, such as a credit check, can be used to remove a record from a solicitation database.

- Finally, your database is not just to collect transaction information and segment your list, but also to aid decision making—both in marketing and in overall business planning. Using your database as an analytical tool involves the use of statistical techniques and findings of research as well as the results of testing. It also includes the models you build and the simulations you use to support your decisions.

Identifying Most Profitable Customers

An essential tool for identifying your best customers is the recency/frequency/monetary (R/F/M) formula.[34] The exact R/F/M formulation for each direct marketer will vary according to the relative importance given each of the three variables:

- *Recency of purchase:* How often does the customer buy something from you?
- *Frequency of purchase:* How much does the customer spend on a typical transaction?
- *Monetary value of purchase:* How long has it been since this customer last placed an order with you?

Validating Prospect Profiles

You want to develop a profile that defines the best prospect for what you sell. You have therefore somehow decided what the criteria and characteristics are that identify your customers. That information constitutes a model. If the model is a true representation and you can use it to build a list of prospects that matches the model, your response rate ought to skyrocket. On the other hand, because of this accelerated response rate, your marketing cost, the cost per order, ought to drop drastically. In substance, you will have the model to ensure continued marketing success in your business. You can now examine the characteristics and qualifications of every prospect in your general database to screen out those who do not conform to the model and make a first-priority list of those who do conform. This way, you can build a marketing database that represents a gold mine.[35]

Benefits of Database Marketing

Customers Are Easier to Retain than Acquire

The first reason is that it takes five times the energy and budget to get a new customer as it does to keep an existing one. Also, a disproportionately small number of your customers generate a very large proportion of your income. The old 80/20 rule—that 80 percent of your business comes from 20 percent of your customers—is a remarkably accurate generalization. Therefore, the priority has changed to relationship building with the top 20 percent of your customers and working on the next 25 percent to upgrade them. A smaller effort should go into the following 25 percent, while the final 30 percent are probably not worth bothering about.

Determine Their "Lifetime Value"

How do you assess the lifetime value of $50 for a monthly cellular phone bill? 93 cents for a can of cat food? $1.50 for a private bus fare? $40,000 for a new car? If you can keep the cellular phone customer's loyalty for 10 years, he or she is worth more than $6,000 to you. The cat-food buyer is worth at least $5,000 over the same period. The private-bus passenger, traveling both ways each day has a 10-year value of $7,200. And the car buyer? With a new car every three years, plus servicing, plus at least one second car, that could be $175,000 over 10 years. Once you start valuing your customers along these lines, the worth of each customer becomes an asset. Building a lasting relationship becomes the obvious way to a prosperous and profitable future.

Developing Relationships with Customers

Understanding your customers' tastes and preferences on an individual basis is the foundation for relationship marketing. Relationship marketing combines elements of general advertising, sales promotion, public relations, and direct marketing to create more effective and more efficient ways of reaching consumers.[36] It centers on developing a continuous relationship with consumers across a family of related products and services.

E-Commerce

In 1996, only 8 percent of major retailers were on-line. In 1997, this rose to 20 percent, and by Christmas 1998, over 28 percent of major retailers were taking orders on-line. Although total holiday shopping was up only 3.5 percent from 1997 to 1998, on-line shopping rose 230 percent. Price was the driver for some consumers but convenience was even more important than price.

Time is precious during the holidays. Over 90 percent of on-line shoppers cited the convenience of shopping from home at any time of day as a critical reason for using on-line stores. Selection and available choices drove many other shoppers on-line. Over 58 percent of shoppers cited selection and the "availability of anything I want to buy" as critical reasons to use on-line retailing. Electronic commerce reinforces all aspects of on-line marketing. It provides a close connection between actions and profits. It dramatizes the problems of an organization and areas where improvements are needed. Moreover, it creates pressure to get closer to customers and do a better job of solving their problems.

According to PC Data's *September E-Tailing Report*, the top 20 e-tailers saw a combined total of 4 million buyers in September 1999, and Amazon.com broke the one-million mark for the first time. Fifteen of the top 20 retail sites posted double-digit increases over August 1999 numbers.[37]

To take a closer look at e-commerce, we must define its fundamentals:

- *E-commerce influence* is the impact of the Net on purchases made entirely off-line.
- *E-commerce ordering* captures the orders that are placed on-line but paid for later via telephone or in-store.
- *E-commerce buying* combines ordering and paying on-line.

The entertainment component of e-commerce is less developed than many of its functional aspects. This is partly due to technical reasons; currently most consumers' access speeds are too slow for high-quality video; the Internet will be capable of a much higher entertainment quotient. Pay-per-view movies, interactive simulations, and near video-on-demand will blur the distinction between the Internet, television, and interactive video games. There is one notable exception to the lack of on-line media entertainment for pay. Forrester Research (www.forrester.com) estimated that the adult entertainment websites brought nearly $1 billion in 1998. This is a sizable fraction of consumer-oriented publishing revenue and continues to grow rapidly.

Stores magazine surveyed 1,000 households to find the 100 largest retailers on the Web. They report results regarding on-line shoppers who have actually made purchases in 1998, how much they spent over a 12-month period, and how pleased they were with the experience. This is a treasure trove of data for researchers.[38]

Companies that do embrace electronic commerce must decide on the best channel structure. One method is to shift sales entirely to manufacturer-direct. Some of the most successful companies of the 1990s, such as Dell Computer and Cisco Systems, follow this route. Channel conflict is one of the main concerns of companies as their e-commerce interests increase. Traditional distribution channels are threatened by on-line e-commerce. Threats come from final customers asking for direct extranet links to manufacturers, manufacturers launching e-commerce sites, and new on-line intermediaries with valuable information and innovative business models.

Electronic commerce is the challenge for retailers in the new century. Several responses from retailers are already emerging. Some seek to slow customer adoption of on-line commerce; some seek to differentiate physical retailers even more from on-line competitors; and still others seek to combine on-line efficiency with the benefits of a bricks-and-mortar outlet. Among the retailer responses are:

- Selective price discounts
- Concentrating attention on late adopters of technology
- Creating and staging experiences
- Partially adapting the Internet into a hybrid system

Consumers' adoption of e-commerce will continue to accelerate, as in 1999, 7 million Internet users made their first on-line purchases. By 2004, Forrester predicts that a new type of retailer—the post-Web retailer—will emerge to serve the 49 million U.S. households that will spend more than $184 billion on-line for a variety of good.[39]

Each of these approaches will have some success, and on-line retailers need to be aware of the power of incumbent retailers to learn and respond. A different e-commerce approach is through existing retailers and their websites. As more retailers adopt e-commerce, this strategy will grow in popularity. Some firms convinced of e-commerce benefits are moving their operations on-line and closing their traditional retail outlets.

This was the situation with Egghead Software when it closed its last store and went entirely on-line in February 1998. An on-line move allowed Egghead to stay in business and capitalize on its well-known brand name. It could expand into another region of the computer industry profit pool that was not feasible with a physical setting.

Continuous direct contact with customers is a requirement for effective real-time marketing. *Real-time marketing* is the marketing process of personally customizing goods or services that continuously updates itself to track changing customer needs, without intervention by corporate personnel, and often without conscious or overt input from each customer. As the goal of real-time marketing is customization of the product both before and after the sale, a marketing organization must be able to maintain ongoing feedback with customers.

Building a database of customer wants, needs, and preferences is valuable for several of the most widely used personalization systems. One of the incentives for on-line intermediaries is the ability to build a profile of customer choices based on a much wider array of business than a direct seller would acquire.

Building a customer profile leads to two very different incentives for data-driven intermediaries. These are *customer coalitions,* where customers join with intermediaries that protect their privacy while sharing appropriate knowledge with vendors that can personalize offerings based on data, and *seller scope,* which is how a multiproduct vendor can learn more about customers and use this information across its product categories. Marketing Research in Practice 16-7 is an example of how e-commerce software can help in real-time enhancement of speed and dynamism of a business and how marketing research can benefit from such a powerful software.

MARKETING RESEARCH IN PRACTICE 16-7

An E-Commerce Software: RAMCO VirtualWorks™

The Net is reinventing business and this will continue endlessly. What started essentially as a highway for data traffic has now become a phenomenon that will impose far-reaching and recurring consequences. The Net falls within the basket of the basic needs of society. The Net transcends geography, politics, culture, platforms, protocols, technologies, business, and information systems.

Enterprises are moving from "within-focus" to an environment of extravagated enterprises and the attention is shifting to the "individual customer." The components of the supply chain, such as media, producers, and distributors, movers of the material, and regulatory agencies, are colluding to satisfy and excel the needs of an individual customer as never before.

Questions will continue to prevail: What does the individual customer need? How do we improve the techniques that will unravel the mystery behind individual thinking? Market researchers will use technological advancement, the Net, to quickly understand customers' behaviors. Market research will not only understand the population of netizens on-line, but will also immediately suggest their preferences.

Let us take a closer look at a possibility. Suppose we have a prospective buyer who is surfing. Let us assume that this Mr. Prospect is under "buyer behavior" surveillance. Also, take for granted the availability of a "Research Agent," an advanced and sophisticated technological mechanism that observes and gathers Mr. Prospect's behavior data as they happen, colludes with the "Analyzer Agent" to establish and foretell the needs of Mr. Prospect, and "registers" Mr. Prospect's possible interests/likes—all in near real-time. What next? This information must be acted on, again in near real-time, to do business with Mr. Prospect—the bottom line. This turns our attention to the supporting business application systems that are responsible for delivery.

In the future, speed (near real-time), complexity, and evolving needs will determine the operating environment for business applications systems. A radical surgery is called for to completely destroy the current way of thinking. The time has come to write the next chapter in enterprise applications.

Enterprise Applications—The Next Chapter

To effectively service an end customer using the pervasive Internet, the application software needs to have the power to "think." Applications need to have the ability to abstract the tactical decision-making elements of a business—changing customer preferences in real time.

Enterprise Application Compilers

Enterprise application compilers recognize business requirements made available in the form of models and deploy applications. When business requirements change, organizations need

MARKETING RESEARCH IN PRACTICE 16-7 *(continued)*

An E-Commerce Software: RAMCO VirtualWorks™

to change the definition(s) of business component(s) and invoke the services of the compiler to incorporate the necessary changes. Sooner or later this need would have to be met. A good example for meeting this need is RAMCO VirtualWorks™ from RAMCO Systems. This product is the result of years of research in devising an application architecture that separates fundamental business requirements and their physical implementation. This allows companies to keep the business knowledge content of their applications independent of the underlying technical implementation.

As S. Ramachandran, Ex-CEO of RAMCO Systems, says, "The application should behave as the software needs to respond to business needs. As a new idea 'strikes,' the software should be able to accommodate the changing needs, on the fly."

RAMCO VirtualWorks™ unifies various technologies and methodologies to provide organizations with the capability to adapt to changing business scenarios in near real-time. RAMCO VirtualWorks™ is a new paradigm in enterprise application architecture that allows organizations to change their applications by just redefining the requirements. It is a sustainable technological innovation and a compelling paradigm for enterprises to adopt. It will help organizations to attain and sustain a competitive advantage in an environment of evolving business. The product, which is currently available, addresses the needs of an application compiler. It consists of a suite of software modules called *workbenches*. These workbenches can be used for defining business components, services deployment details, and so on.

Organizations using RAMCO VirtualWorks™ could benefit from:

- Implementing end-to-end application solutions with substantial reduction in effort
- A low-risk method for migrating and conversions
- Deploying configurable integration solutions
- Providing new foundations for business-to-business and back-fulfillment solutions
- Reductions in the dependence on specific skills
- Componentization of all business requirements
- Drastic reduction in time for basic construction or coding

In the near future, RAMCO Systems plans to provide a rich set of standard business components that go along with the above-mentioned application architecture. Thus a company could purchase off-the shelf components (like purchase orders) and then proceed to configure them through the workbenches to suit specific scenarios.

Marketing Research and VirtualWorks™

VirtualWorks™ tremendously increases the scope and power of marketing research and strategy in organizations. Consider the example of a dynamic pricing strategy that a firm wants to adopt during an upcoming holiday season. Implementing the modified pricing strategy in the organization depends upon the flexibility of the information technology (IT) framework in the organization. A typical strategy shift such as this takes about three months to implement because the IT department has to modify each and every part of its framework to reflect this change. The abstraction from mundane programming provided by VirtualWorks™ reduces both the time and cost of implementation. Thus VirtualWorks™ helps organizations in conducting cost-benefit analysis of marketing research and what-if-analyses of different strategies, and greatly improves response time.

For more information on RAMCO Systems visit http://www.ramcobiz.com.

Source: RAMCO Systems Corporation, Addison, Texas.

Relationship Marketing

Marketing Research in Practice 16-8 talks about how Huggies and a few other companies used **relationship marketing** as a successful competitive strategy.

Three Keys to Relationship Marketing

There are strategic opportunities for companies on the leading edge of relationship marketing techniques.[40] Successfully addressing the trend will depend on a three-pronged effort.

Identify and Build Marketing Databases of Present and Potential Purchasers. In the age of relationship marketing, the customer database will be as important a strategic asset for manufacturers as the brand itself. Advertisers will need the capability to use mass media and more targeted media channels as ways of prospecting for customers. Once potential customers have been identified, advertisers must capture their names and information on their lifestyles in a database for future communications.

It is important to keep in mind that not all consumers are appropriate targets for relationship marketing, and not all targets are customers. Consequently, the initial database must be carefully refined and segmented. Designed and developed properly, the marketing database will allow companies to expand their internal capabilities to include relationship marketing.

Deliver Differentiated Messages to Targeted Households. Advertisers must develop the ability to communicate with a defined audience of the existing and potential users of their products. The media choices they make must therefore offer the ability not only to broadcast the message to the entire circulation or audience but

MARKETING RESEARCH IN PRACTICE 16-8

Relationship Marketing in Practice

Huggies has spent more than $10 million to set up a system that provides it with the names of more than 75 percent of mothers in the United States. The names are obtained from doctors, hospitals, and childbirth trainers. During their pregnancies, the mothers-to-be receive personalized magazines and letters with ideas on baby care, thus building a bond between the mothers and Huggies.

When the baby arrives, a coded coupon is delivered, which Huggies can track to know which mothers have tried the product. Later, as new technologies fall into place, Huggies will be able to know which mothers continue to purchase Huggies. In this case, Huggies' parent, Kimberly Clark, is not only building diaper sales but also establishing relationships with mothers, which can be leveraged across other products. The cost of linking the consumer to the brand can be justified, since the per-baby consumption of single-use diapers averages more than $600 annually.

Other innovative programs include Kraft's "Cheese and Macaroni Club," which sends children a packet of goodies; MTV's custom magazine, which viewers get when they respond to MTV's 800 number; and Isuzu's personalized insets in *Time*, which list nearest dealerships and are redeemable for a premium.

Source: Michael J. Wolf, "Relationship Marketing Positioning for the Future," *Journal of Business Strategy* (July/August 1990), pp. 16-21.

also to target precisely defined demographic slices. For advertisers, more precise targeting means greater impact.

Track the Relationship to Make Media Expenditures More Effective and More Measurable. Common wisdom has it that half of all advertising dollars are wasted; the difficulty is knowing which half. The media innovations just described will allow advertisers to pinpoint what works and what doesn't. Consequently, relationship marketing's most important effect will be a shift in the way decisions are made about where to advertise. Traditionally, decisions have been based on various ex ante measures of exposure, such as cost-per-thousand, audience, or circulation. In the future, however, decisions will be made on ex post factors, such as evidence of penetration of the required target audience or even evidence of sales results.

In this new environment, the basis of measurement changes and emphasis will shift from cost-per-thousand to the value of reaching a target market. Advertisers must evaluate the cost of gaining and maintaining a customer relationship over several years. Once again, marketing research will play a significant role in this phase of the relationship marketing strategy. Tracking usually will be done by survey research. The various statistical tools necessary to process the information in the database are discussed in the data analysis chapters.

END OF CHAPTER MATERIAL

SUMMARY

This chapter covers the major applications of marketing research. The concepts covered help the manager launch a new product, price the product, and decide on proper distribution channels. The chapter also discusses emerging marketing trends such as database marketing, relationship marketing, customer satisfaction, and total quality management. New product research can be divided into (1) generating new-product concepts, (2) evaluating and developing those concepts, (3) evaluating and developing the actual products, and (4) product testing in a marketing program. Pricing research may be used to evaluate alternative price approaches for new product launch or for proposed changes in products already on the market. Distribution decisions in marketing involve the number and location of salespeople, retail outlets, warehouses, and the size of discount to be offered. The decisions for the promotion part of marketing strategy can be divided into (1) advertising, and (2) sales promotion. Sales promotion affects the company in the short term, whereas advertising decisions have long-term effects. Achieving superior performance requires a business to gain and hold an advantage over competitors which is central to contemporary strategic thinking. Brand equity is defined as a set of assets and liabilities linked to a brand that adds to or subtracts from the value of a product or service to a company and/or its customers. Total Quality Management (TQM) is a process of managing complex changes in the organization with the aim of improving quality. One of the interesting marketing trends in the nineties is database marketing. It involves using customer profile databases to cultivate customers and develops statistical profiles of prospects most similar to their present customers as they seek new ones. Relationship marketing involves identifying and building a database of current and potential customers. It records and cross-references a wide range of demographic, lifestyle, and purchase information, delivering differential messages through established and new media channels based on the consumers' characteristics and preferences, and tracking each relationship to monitor the cost of acquiring the consumer and the lifetime value of their purchases.[41]

KEY TERMS

use testing
pretest marketing
test marketing
skimming pricing
penetration pricing
field experiments
day-after recall
coupon-stimulated purchasing
split-cable tests
tracking studies
diagnostic testing
copy test validity
promotion partnerships

trade promotions
cooperative promotions
market-based assessment
process-based assessment
brand equity
excess-price approach
replacement-cost approach
stock-price approach
future-earnings approach
Total Quality Management (TQM)
database marketing
value-added databases
relationship marketing

MARKETING RESEARCH TOOLBOX
REVIEW POINTS

1. *New-product research* can be divided into (1) generating new-product concepts, (2) evaluating and developing those concepts, (3) evaluating and developing the actual products, and (4) product testing in a marketing program.

2. The simplest form of *use testing* gives users the product, and, after a reasonable amount of time, asks their reactions to it, including their intentions to buy it.

3. Two approaches are used to predict the new *brand's market share.* The first is based on the preference judgments. The preference data are used to predict the proportion of purchases of the new brand that respondents will make given that the new brand is in their response set. These estimates for the respondents in the study are coupled with an estimate of the proportion of all people who will have the new brand in their response set, to provide an estimate of market share. The second approach involves estimating trial and repeat purchase levels based on the respondent's purchase decisions and intentions-to-buy judgments.

4. *Test marketing* allows the researcher to test the impact of the total marketing program, with all its interdependencies, in a market context as opposed to the artificial context associated with the concept and product tests.

5. *Skimming pricing strategy* is based on the concept of pricing the product at the point at which profits will be the greatest until market conditions change or supply costs dictate a price change. *Penetration pricing* is a strategy based on the concept that average unit production costs continue to go down as cumulative output increases.

6. Competitive advantage can be assessed in a number of ways. The methods can be broadly classified as market-based assessment and process-based assessment. *Market-based assessment* is direct comparison with a few target competitors, whereas *process-based assessment* is a comparison of the methods employed by the competitors in achieving their distinctive advantage.

7. *Brand equity* is defined as a set of assets and liabilities linked to a brand that add to or subtract from the value of a product or service to a company and/or its customers.

8. *Total Quality Management (TQM)* is a process of managing complex changes in the organization with the aim of improving quality.

9. A *database* is a customer list to which has been added information about the characteristic and the transactions of these customers.

QUESTIONS AND PROBLEMS

1. Develop a research design to provide a demand estimate for the following new products:
   a. A plastic disposable toothbrush that comes in a cylinder 5/8 in. in diameter and 3 in. in length. Its unique, patented quality is that the toothpaste already has been applied.
   b. A lemon condiment. Lemon enhances the flavor of many foods, including corn-on-the-cob, fish, and melons. The lemon condiment would be in a crystallized form that would capture the essence of lemon and be served in a "lemon shaker" that would complement the salt and pepper shakers.
   c. A clear plastic umbrella attachment for bicycles, which folds away behind the handlebars when not in use.
   d. A vibrator secretarial chair that contains a gentle vibrator device designed to provide relaxation and blood circulation for people who must sit for long periods of time.
   e. A battery-powered, two-passenger automobile with a top speed of 40 mph and a range of 120 miles.

2. In benefit structure analysis, 500 or so respondents are asked to react to a large number (75–100) of specific product benefits and to many product characteristics. The reactions are in terms of both the desire for and perceived deficiencies in current brands with respect to each benefit and characteristic. The focus is on a specific-use occasion. For example, if a household cleaner were involved, the respondent would focus on a single cleaning occasion. The brand used also would be asked. How would you generate the list of benefits and product characteristics? Develop a sampling plan. What data analysis would you conduct?

3. In evaluating a new product idea, what criteria should be used? What role should marketing research play in evaluating the idea against each of the criteria?

4. How would you find a name for a new brand of soda that is a new "natural drink" made out of carbonated apple juice with some ginger and lemon added?

5. A major airline announced that it was reducing its fares by 30 percent for off-peak travel. (Off-peak travel is defined as travel time between 8:00 P.M. and 8:00 A.M. on weekdays, and all weekend.) Do you consider this as price signaling or second-market discounting?

6. The top management of your company has come up with a concept they think is exciting and has tremendous potential. It wants to find out the demand for this product. It plans to skim the market if the demand is high for the product. You have been given the responsibility to design a prototype and determine the demand. Further you have also been asked to find out whether skimming would be the best pricing strategy to adopt. What information will you require to answer these questions and how will you obtain it?

7. Is DAR widely used? Why? Would you use it if you were the product manager for Lowenbrau? For American Express? Under what circumstances would you use it?

8. Why conduct tracking studies? Why not just observe sales?

9. How will adjective checklists help a creative group? What about eye-movement data?

10. DuPont conducted a field experiment for an improved version of Teflon several years after they first introduced Teflon. Four cities received 10 daytime commercial minutes per week during the fall months, five cities received 5 minutes per week, and four cities (the control group) received no advertising. Cities were randomly assigned to each of the three test conditions. The sales measure was a purchase of Teflon cookware as reported by telephone interviews with 1000 housewives in each of the test cities. The total purchases turned out to be about 30 percent higher in the heavy advertising cities than in those cities with no or low advertising, but there was no real difference between the low and no advertising groups. Critique this test. What validity problems do you see? What changes would you make? Would you conduct the same test if the product change had been out for three years?

11. Mediamark estimated the total adult readers of *Family Circle* magazine as 32.1 million, while Simmons estimated it as 18.3 million. Why the difference? Which is right?

12. In a survey of homemakers, the readership of *Harper's* was exaggerated and the readership of *Modern Romance* seemed much less than circulation figures indicated. Why would respondents incorrectly report their readership in this manner? Can you think of ways to avoid this bias?

13. What are the weaknesses of the audimeter? Of the diary? If cost was not a problem, do you believe a camera in the room would be a reasonable solution? Identify and evaluate other alternatives.

ENDNOTES

1. James H. Meyers, "Benefit Structure Analysis: A New Tool for Product Planning," *Journal of Marketing*, 40 (October 1976), pp. 23–32.

2. Glen L. Urban, Bruce D. Weinberg, and John R. Hanser, "Premarket Forecasting of Really New Products," *Journal of Marketing*, 60,1 (January 1996), pp. 47–60.

3. Philip J. Rosenberger III and Leslie de Chernaltony, "Virtual Reality Techniques in NPD Research," *Journal of the Marketing Research Society*, 37,4 (1995), pp. 345–355.

4. Rosenberger and de Chernaltony, op. cit.

5. James W. Taylor, John J. Houlahan, and Alan C. Gabriel, "The Purchase Intention Question in New Product Development: A Field Test," *Journal of Marketing*, 40 (January 1975), pp. 90–92.

6. Henry J. Claycamp and Lucien E. Liddy, "Prediction of New Product Performance: An Analytical Approach," *Journal of Marketing Research*, 6 (November 1969), pp. 414–420; Gert Assmus, "NEW-PROD: The Design and Implementation of a New Product Model," *Journal of Marketing*, 39 (January 1975), pp. 16–23.

7. Gerald J. Eskin and John Malec, "A Model for Estimating Sales Potential Prior to the Test Market," in *1976 Educators' Proceedings* (Chicago: American Marketing Association, 1976), pp. 230–233.

8. In situations where no definition of the product class exists, a product appeal measure obtained from a concept test is used to estimate the size of the relevant product class for that particular product.

9. As discussed in the appendix of Chapter 4, the symbols O_1, O_2, etc., refer to a measure or observation and X_1, X_2, etc., refer to experimental treatments.

10. Glen L. Urban, J. R. Hauser, and J. H. Roberts, "Prelaunch Forecasting of New Automobiles: Models and Implementation," *Management Science*, 36,4 (April 1990), pp. 401–421; Glen L. Urban, J. S. Hulland, and B. D. Weinberg, "Premarket Forecasting of New Consumer Durables: Modeling Categorization, Elimination, and Consideration Phenimena," *Journal of Marketing*, 5 (April 1993).

11. Donald R. Lehmann and Russell S. Winer, *Product Management* (Chicago: Richard D. Irwin, 1997).

12. A. Gabor and C. Grainger, "Price as an Indicator of Quality," *Economics*, 33 (1966), pp. 43–70.

13. Table 16-1 was adapted from Gerard J. Tellis, "Beyond the Many Faces of Price: An Integration of Pricing Strategies," *Journal of Marketing*, 50,4 (1986), pp. 146–160.

14. J. A. Paris and L. D. Crabtree, "Survey License Plates to Define Retail Trade Area," *Marketing News*, 19 (1985), p. 12.

15. D. L. Huff and R. R. Batsell, "Delimiting the Areal Extent of a Market Area," *Journal of Marketing Research*, 14 (1977), pp. 581–585.

16. E. Blair, "Sampling Issues in Trade Area Maps Drawn from Shoppers' Surveys," *Journal of Marketing*, 14 (1983), pp. 98–106.

17. Donal F. Bruzzone, "The Case for Testing Commericals by Mail," presented at the *25th Annual Conference of the Advertising Research Foundation*, New York (October 23, 1979).

18. Benjamin Lipstein, "An Historical Perspective of Copy Research," *Journal of Advertising Research*, 24 (December 1984), pp. 11–15.

19. Ibid.

20. TEC audit (New York: TEC Measures).

21. William S. Blair, "Observed vs. Reported Behavior in Magazine Reading: An Investigation of the Editorial Interest Method," *Proceedings of the 12th Annual Conference of the Advertising Research Foundation,* New York (1967).

22. Robert C. Blattberg and Scott A. Neslin, *Sales Promotion: Concepts, Methods and Strategies* (Englewood Cliffs, NJ: Prentice Hall, 1990).

23. Michael E. Porter, *Competitive Strategy* (New York: Free Press, 1980).

24. George S. Day and Robin Wensley, "Assessing Advantage: A Framework for Diagnosing Competitive Superiority," *Journal of Marketing,* 52 (April 1988), pp. 1–20.

25. David A. Aaker, *Managing Brand Equity* (New York: Free Press, 1991).

26. Wagner A. Kamakura and Gary J. Russell, "Measuring Brand Value with Scanner Data," *International Journal of Research in Marketing,* 10 (March 1993), pp. 9–22; Joffre Swait, Tulin Erdem, Jordan Louviere, and Chris Dubelaar, "The Equalization Price: A Measure of Consumer-Perceived Brand Equity," *International Journal of Research in Marketing,* 10 (March 1993), pp. 23–45; Kevin Lane Keller, "Conceptualizing, Measuring, and Managing Customer-Based Brand Equity," *Journal of Marketing,* 57 (January 1993), pp. 1–22.

27. Lewis C. Winters, "Brand Equity Measures: Some Recent Advances," *Marketing Research: A Magazine of Management & Applications,* 4 (December 1991), pp. 70–73.

28. Carol J. Simon and Mary W. Sullivan, "The Measurement and Determinants of Brand Equity: A Financial Approach," *Marketing Science,* 12 (Winter 1993), pp. 28–52.

29. B. G. Yovovich, "What Is Your Brand Really Worth?" *Adweek's Marketing Week* (August 8, 1988), pp. 18–24.

30. William Boulding, Ajay Kalra, Richard Staelin, and Valarie A. Zeithaml, "A Dynamic Process Model of Service Quality: From Expectations to Behavioral Intentions," *Journal of Marketing Research,* 30 (February 1993), pp. 7–27.

31. James M. Salter, "The Systematic Approach to Measuring Satisfaction," *Marketing News,* 25 (February 4, 1991), p. 9.

32. Martin Baier, *How to Find and Cultivate Customers through Direct Marketing* (Lincolnwood, IL: NTC Business Books, 1996).

33. Martin Williams, *Interactive Marketing* (Englewood Cliffs, NJ: Prentice-Hall, 1994).

34. Arthur M. Hughes, *The Complete Database Marketer,* 2nd ed. (Chicago: Irwin, 1996).

35. Herman Holtz, *Databased Marketing* (New York: Wiley, 1992).

36. John J. Harrison, "Transforming Data into Relationships," *National Underwriter,* 97 (August 2, 1993), pp. 7, 12; D. Edelman, D. Schultz, and M. Winkleman, "Up Close and Personal," *Journal of Business Strategy,* 14 (July–August 1993), pp. 22–31.

37. See http://www.ecommercetimes.com/news/articles/991011-6.shtml.

38. See http://www.stores.org/99top100int_1.html.

39. See http://www.forrester.com/ER/Press/Release/0,1769,164,FF.html.

40. Regis Mckenna, "Relationship Marketing," *Executive Excellence,* 9 (April 1992), pp. 7–8; Jonathan R. Copulsky and Michael J. Wolf, "Relationship Marketing: Positioning for the Future," *Journal of Business Strategy* (July–August 1990), pp. 16–21.

41. For recent development on lifetime values, please refer to Reinartz, W. and V. Kumar (2000), "On the Profitability of Long Lifetime Customers: An Empirical Investigation and Implications for Marketing," *Journal of Marketing,* Vol. 64 (October), pp. 17–32.

CASES

For detailed descriptions of the below cases please visit www.wiley.com/college/kumar.

Case 16-1: Brown Microwave
Case 16-2: National Chemical Corporation

CASES AND PRACTICAL EXERCISES FOR PART IV

CASE STUDY

Levi Strauss & Co.

Sue Swenson, a member of the research group at Foote, Cone & Belding/Honig, a San Francisco advertising agency, was reviewing four copy testing techniques, all of which cost about $10,000 per commercial (plus media costs where required):

1. Burke DAR (spots are purchased in three markets for the test ads)
2. Mapes and Ross
3. McCollum/Spielman
4. Tele-Research

A meeting was scheduled with the Levi Strauss account group for the next day to decide on which copy test to employ on two new Levi's campaigns. The following week a similar meeting was scheduled involving a campaign for a new bar of soap for another client. In each case the task was to determine which testing approach would be used to help make the final selection of which commercials to use in the campaigns. Swenson knew that she would be expected to contribute to the discussion by pointing out the strengths and limitations of each test and to make her own recommendations.

Levi Strauss & Co. had grown from a firm serving the needs of miners in the Gold Rush era of the mid-1800s to a large, sophisticated clothing company. In 1996 it had sales of over $2 billion, drawn from an international and domestic operation. The domestic company, Levi Strauss USA, included six divisions: Jeanswear, Sportswear, Womenswear, Youthwear, Activewear, and Accessories. In 1996, Levi Strauss was among the 100 largest advertisers, with expenditures of $38.5 million, primarily on television.

Concerning the Levi's campaigns, Swenson recognized that two very different campaigns were involved. The first was a corporate-image campaign. The overall objective was to build and maintain Levi's brand image. The approach was to build around the concepts of "quality" and "heritage," the most meaningful, believable, and universal aspects of the Levi's corporate personality. Unlike competitors who claimed quality as a product feature, Levi's 128-year-heritage advertisements had an important additional dimension. More specifically, the advertising involved the following strategy:

1. Heritage-quality: communicate to male and female consumers, ages 12 to 49, that Levi's makes a wide variety of apparel products, all of which share in the company's 128-year commitment to quality.

2. Variety-quality: communicate to male and female consumers, ages 12 to 49, that Levi's makes a wide variety of quality apparel products for the entire family.

Figure IV-1 shows one of the commercials from the pool that was to be tested for the corporate campaign.

The second campaign was for Levi's action suits. In 1996, the Sportswear division responsible for action suits spent approximately $6 million on network television commercials and co-op newspaper ads to introduce Actionwear slacks, which topped the sales of both leading brands of men's slacks, Haggar and Farah, in that year. The primary segment was middle-aged males, who often suffer from middle-aged spread. Actionwear slacks, a blend of polyester and other fabrics with a stretchable waistline, were presented as a solution to the problem. The advertising objectives for the new campaign were guided by the following:

Focus: Levi's action garments are comfortable dress clothes.

Benefits: Primary—comfortable; secondary—attractive, good-looking, well made, long-wearing.

Reasons why:
1. Levi's Action slacks are comfortable because they have a hidden stretch waistband and expandable shell fabric.
2. Levi's Action suit jacket is comfortable because it has hidden stretch panels that let you move freely without binding.
3. The Levi's name implies quality, well-made clothes.

Brand character: Levi's Action clothing is sensible, good-value menswear manufactured by Levi Strauss & Co., a company dedicated to quality.

Figure IV-2 shows a commercial from the pool for the Levi Action campaign.

CASES AND PRACTICAL EXERCISES FOR PART IV *(continued)*

LEVI'S® "ROUNDUP"

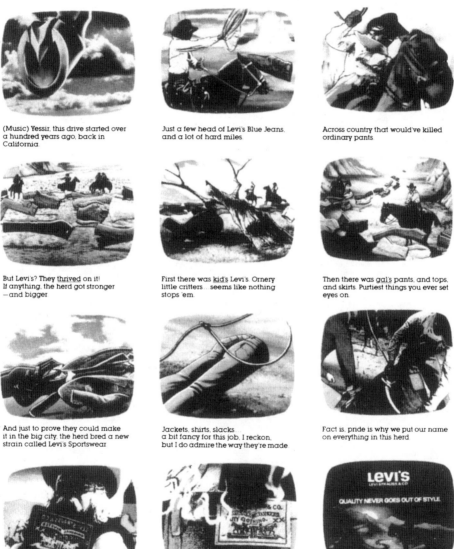

(Music) Yessir, this drive started over a hundred years ago, back in California.

Just a few head of Levi's Blue Jeans, and a lot of hard miles.

Across country that would've killed ordinary pants.

But Levi's? They thrived on it! If anything, the herd got stronger —and bigger

First there was kid's Levi's. Ornery little critters... seems like nothing stops 'em.

Then there was gal's pants, and tops, and skirts. Purtiest things you ever set eyes on.

And just to prove they could make it in the big city, the herd bred a new strain called Levi's Sportswear

Jackets, shirts, slacks... a bit fancy for this job, I reckon, but I do admire the way they're made.

Fact is, pride is why we put our name on everything in this herd.

Tells folks, "This here's ours!" If you like what you got, then c'mon back!

We'll be here. You see, fashions may change...

...but quality never goes out of style!

Figure IV-1 A corporate commercial. (Courtesy Levi Strauss & Co., San Francisco, CA.)

Swenson also knew that previous Levi's commercials had proved exceptionally memorable and effective, owing to their distinctive creative approach. In part, their appeal lies in their ability to challenge the viewer's imagination. The advertising assumes that viewers are thoughtful and appreciate advertising that respects their judgments.

In preparing for the next day's meeting with the Levi account group, she decided to review carefully the four copy testing services. The immediate problem

CASES AND PRACTICAL FOR PART IV (*continued*)

was to decide which of the services to recommend for testing commercials from the two Levi's campaigns. She knew that similar issues would be raised in discussions with another of the agency's clients the following week concerning a national campaign for a bar-soap line extension. Positioning for the bar-soap essentially involved a dual cleanliness–fragrance theme. A demonstration commercial focused on these two copy points.

Questions for Discussion

1. What copy testing service or services should Sue Swenson recommend for testing the two Levi Strauss commercials?
2. What service or services should she recommend for testing the bar-soap commercial?

TV. 30 Sec.
Title: "Action Suit/Bus"

ANNCR: If a man's suit jacket fits
like a straight jacket . . .
WIFE: Hold on, Joe!
JOE: I can't raise my arms.

ANNCR: If his pants fit their worst
around his waist,
WIFE: Sit down.
JOE: I can't—these pants are too
tight.

ANNCR: Then he needs Levi's*
Action Suit . . . perhaps
the most comfortable suit
a man can wear.

ANNCR: The waistband strrrr-
retches to give more room
when you need it.

JOE: Comfortable.
ANNCR: The jacket lets you
move your arms without
binding.

JOE: I can sit.
OLD LADY: Hmmmmmmph!

JOE: I can stand, too.

ANNCR: Levi's Action Suit from
Levi's Sportswear.

Figure IV-2 An action suit commercial. (Courtesy Levi Strauss & Co., San Francisco, CA.)

◆ **PRACTICAL EXERCISES**

Q1.   You have the results of the market research conducted by the Cues Company. The management wants you to present the results at the next board meeting. Prepare a format for a written and oral presentation and list the essential items that need to be included in it.

Q2.   Spring Fresh is a leader in the mouthwash industry, but lately competitors have been eating into its market share. The management believes that introducing a new flavor and in turn a new product can help Spring Fresh regain its lost market share and hence put it back in a comfortable position. As a consultant for Spring Fresh conduct a need/concept identification study in your area to identify a new version of Spring Fresh that is attractive and viable.

Q3.   Create a database of the students in your college/classroom. Based on this database identify the hobbies, interests, and the demographics of each student. Using this information create a personalized direct mail ad-campaign for the upcoming Girl Scout's fund raiser.

Q4.   Jumpin Jucy is a local brand of soft drinks and is immensely popular in your school. Conduct a suitable study to measure the brand equity of Jumpin Jucy among the students.

Tables

TABLE A-1   Standard Normal, Cumulative Probability in Right-Hand Tail for Positive Values of Z; Areas Are Formed by Symmetry

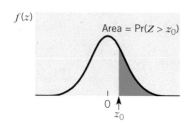

| | | | | | Second Decimal Place of Z_0 | | | | | |
Z_0	.00	.01	.02	.03	.04	.05	.06	.07	.08	.09
0.0	.5000	.4960	.4920	.4880	.4840	.4801	.4761	.4721	.4681	.4641
0.1	.4602	.4562	.4522	.4483	.4443	.4404	.4364	.4325	.4286	.4247
0.2	.4207	.4168	.4129	.4090	.4052	.4013	.3974	.3936	.3897	.3859
0.3	.3821	.3783	.3745	.3707	.3669	.3632	.3594	.3557	.3520	.3483
0.4	.3446	.3409	.3372	.3336	.3300	.3264	.3228	.3192	.3156	.3121
0.5	.3085	.3050	.3015	.2981	.2946	.2912	.2877	.2843	.2810	.2776
0.6	.2743	.2709	.2676	.2643	.2611	.2578	.2546	.2514	.2483	.2451
0.7	.2420	.2389	.2358	.2327	.2296	.2266	.2236	.2206	.2177	.2148
0.8	.2119	.2090	.2061	.2033	.2055	.1977	.1949	.1922	.1894	.1867
0.9	.1841	.1814	.1788	.1762	.1736	.1711	.1685	.1660	.1635	.1611
1.0	.1587	.1562	.1539	.1515	.1492	.1469	.1446	.1423	.1401	.1379
1.1	.1357	.1335	.1314	.1292	.1271	.1251	.1230	.1210	.1190	.1170
1.2	.1151	.1131	.1112	.1093	.1075	.1056	.1038	.1020	.1003	.0985
1.3	.0968	.0951	.0934	.0918	.0901	.0885	.0869	.0853	.0838	.0823
1.4	.0808	.0793	.0778	.0764	.0749	.0735	.0722	.0708	.0694	.0681
1.5	.0668	.0655	.0643	.0630	.0618	.0606	.0594	.0582	.0571	.0559
1.6	.0548	.5037	.0526	.0516	.0505	.0495	.0485	.0475	.0465	.0455
1.7	.0446	.0436	.0427	.0418	.0409	.0401	.0392	.0384	.0375	.0367
1.8	.0359	.0352	.0344	.0336	.0329	.0322	.0314	.0307	.0301	.0294
1.9	.0287	.0281	.0274	.0268	.0262	.0256	.0250	.0244	.0239	.0233
2.0	.0228	.0222	.0217	.0212	.0207	.0202	.0197	.0192	.0188	.0183
2.1	.0179	.0174	.0170	.0166	.0162	.0158	.0154	.0150	.0146	.0143

(continued)

TABLE A-1   *(continued)*

2.2	.1039		.0136	.0132	.0129	.0125	.0122	.0119	.0116	.0113	.0110
2.3	.0107		.0104	.0102	.0099	.0096	.0094	.0091	.0089	.0087	.0084
2.4	.0082		.0080	.0078	.0075	.0073	.0071	.0069	.0068	.0066	.0064
2.5	.0062		.0060	.0059	.0057	.0055	.0054	.0052	.0051	.0049	.0048
2.6	.0047		.0045	.0044	.0043	.0041	.0040	.0039	.0038	.0037	.0036
2.7	.0035		.0034	.0033	.0032	.0031	.0030	.0029	.0028	.0027	.0026
2.8	.0026		.0025	.0023	.0023	.0023	.0022	.0021	.0021	.0020	.0019
2.9	.0019		.0018	.0017	.0017	.0016	.0016	.0015	.0015	.0014	.0014

		Second Decimal Place of Z_0								
Z_0	.00	.01	.02	.03	.04	.05	.06	.07	.08	.09
3.0	.00135									
3.5	.000 233									
4.0	.000 031 7									
4.5	.000 003 40									
5.0	.000 000 287									

TABLE A-2 χ^2 Critical Points

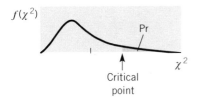

	Pr						
df	.250	.100	.050	.025	.010	.005	.001
1	1.32	2.71	3.84	5.02	6.63	7.88	10.8
2	2.77	4.61	5.99	7.38	9.21	10.6	13.8
3	4.11	6.25	7.81	9.35	11.3	12.8	16.3
4	5.39	7.78	9.49	11.1	13.3	14.9	18.5
5	6.63	9.24	11.1	12.8	15.1	16.7	20.5
6	7.84	10.6	12.6	14.4	16.8	18.5	22.5
7	9.04	12.0	14.1	16.0	18.5	20.3	24.3
8	10.2	13.4	15.5	17.5	20.1	22.0	26.1
9	11.4	14.7	16.9	19.0	21.7	23.6	27.9
10	12.5	16.0	18.8	20.5	23.2	25.2	29.6
11	13.7	17.3	19.7	21.9	24.7	26.8	31.3
12	14.8	18.5	21.0	23.3	26.2	28.3	32.9
13	16.0	19.8	22.4	24.7	27.7	29.8	34.5
14	17.1	21.1	23.7	26.1	29.1	31.3	36.1
15	18.2	22.3	25.0	27.5	30.6	32.8	37.7
16	19.4	23.5	26.3	28.8	32.0	34.3	39.3

(continued)

TABLE A-2 *(continued)*

17	20.5	24.8	27.6	30.2	33.4	35.7	40.8
18	21.6	26.0	28.9	31.5	34.8	37.2	42.3
19	22.7	27.2	30.1	32.9	36.2	38.6	43.8
20	23.8	28.4	31.4	34.2	37.6	40.0	45.3
21	24.9	29.6	32.7	35.5	38.9	41.4	46.8
22	26.0	30.8	33.9	36.8	40.3	42.8	48.3
23	27.1	32.0	35.2	38.1	41.6	44.2	49.7
24	28.2	33.2	36.4	39.4	42.0	45.6	51.2
25	29.3	34.4	37.7	40.6	44.3	46.9	52.6
26	30.4	35.6	38.9	41.9	45.6	48.3	54.1
27	31.5	36.7	40.1	43.2	47.0	49.6	55.5
28	32.6	37.9	41.3	44.5	48.3	51.0	56.9
29	33.7	39.1	42.6	45.7	49.6	52.3	58.3
30	34.8	40.3	43.8	47.0	50.9	53.7	59.7
40	45.6	51.8	55.8	59.3	63.7	66.8	73.4
50	56.3	63.2	67.5	71.4	76.2	79.5	86.7
60	67.0	74.4	79.1	83.3	88.4	92.0	99.6
70	77.6	85.5	90.5	95.0	100	104	112
80	88.1	96.6	102	107	112	116	125
90	98.6	108	113	118	124	128	137
100	109	118	124	130	136	140	149

TABLE A-3 *F* Critical Points

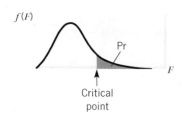

							Degrees of Freedom for Numerator						
		Pr	1	2	3	4	5	6	8	10	20	40	∞
	1	.25	5.83	7.50	8.20	8.58	8.82	8.98	9.19	9.32	9.58	9.71	9.85
		.10	39.9	49.5	53.6	55.8	57.2	58.2	59.4	60.2	61.7	62.5	63.3
		.05	161	200	216	225	230	234	239	242	248	251	254
	2	.25	2.57	3.00	3.15	3.23	3.28	3.31	3.35	3.38	3.43	3.45	3.48
		.10	8.53	9.00	9.16	9.24	9.29	9.33	9.37	9.39	9.44	9.47	9.49
		.05	18.5	19.0	19.2	19.2	19.3	19.3	19.4	19.4	19.4	19.5	19.5
		.01	98.5	99.0	99.2	99.2	99.3	99.3	99.4	99.4	99.4	99.5	99.5
		.001	998	999	999	999	999	999	999	999	999	999	999
	3	.25	2.02	2.28	2.36	2.39	2.41	2.42	2.44	2.44	2.46	2.47	2.47
		.10	5.54	5.46	5.39	5.34	5.31	5.28	5.25	5.23	5.18	5.16	5.13

Degree of Freedom for Denominator

(continued)

TABLE A-3 *(continued)*

| | | \multicolumn{11}{c}{Degrees of Freedom for Numerator} |
	Pr	1	2	3	4	5	6	8	10	20	40	∞
	.05	10.1	9.55	9.28	9.12	9.10	8.94	8.85	8.79	8.66	8.59	8.53
	.01	34.1	30.8	29.5	28.7	28.2	27.9	27.5	27.2	26.7	26.4	26.1
	.001	167	149	141	137	135	133	131	129	126	125	124
4	.25	1.81	2.00	2.05	2.06	2.07	2.08	2.08	2.08	2.08	2.08	2.08
	.10	4.54	4.32	4.19	4.11	4.05	4.01	3.95	3.92	3.84	3.80	3.76
	.05	7.71	6.94	6.59	6.39	6.26	6.16	6.04	5.96	5.80	5.72	5.63
	.01	21.2	18.0	16.7	16.0	15.5	15.2	14.8	14.5	14.0	13.7	13.5
	.001	74.1	61.3	56.2	53.4	51.7	50.5	49.0	48.1	46.1	45.1	44.1
5	.25	1.69	1.85	1.88	1.89	1.89	1.89	1.89	1.89	1.88	1.88	1.87
	.10	4.06	3.78	3.62	3.52	3.45	3.40	3.34	3.30	3.21	3.16	3.10
	.05	6.61	5.79	5.41	5.19	5.05	4.95	4.82	4.74	4.56	4.46	4.36
	.01	16.3	13.3	12.1	11.4	11.0	10.7	10.3	10.1	9.55	9.29	9.02
	.001	47.2	37.1	33.2	31.1	29.8	28.8	27.6	26.9	25.4	24.6	23.8
6	.25	1.62	1.76	1.78	1.79	1.79	1.78	1.77	1.77	1.76	1.75	1.74
	.10	3.78	3.46	3.29	3.18	3.11	3.05	2.98	2.94	2.84	2.78	2.72
	.05	5.99	5.14	4.76	4.53	4.39	4.28	4.15	4.06	3.87	3.77	3.67
	.01	13.7	10.9	9.78	9.15	8.75	8.47	8.10	7.87	7.40	7.14	6.88
	.001	35.5	27.0	23.7	21.9	20.8	20.0	19.0	18.4	17.1	16.4	15.8
7	.25	1.57	1.70	1.72	1.72	1.71	1.71	1.70	1.69	1.67	1.66	1.65
	.10	3.59	3.26	3.07	2.96	2.88	2.83	2.75	2.70	2.59	2.54	2.47
	.05	5.59	4.74	4.35	4.12	3.97	3.87	3.73	3.64	3.44	3.34	3.23
	.01	12.2	9.55	8.45	7.85	7.46	7.19	6.84	6.62	6.16	5.91	5.65
	.001	29.3	21.7	18.8	17.2	16.2	15.5	14.6	14.1	12.9	12.3	11.7
8	.25	1.54	1.66	1.67	1.66	1.66	1.65	1.64	1.64	1.61	1.59	1.58
	.10	3.46	3.11	2.92	2.81	2.73	2.67	2.59	2.54	2.42	2.36	2.29
	.05	5.32	4.46	4.07	3.84	3.69	3.58	3.44	3.35	3.15	3.04	2.93
	.01	11.3	8.65	7.59	7.01	6.63	6.37	6.03	5.81	5.36	5.12	4.86
	.001	25.4	18.5	15.8	14.4	13.5	12.9	12.0	11.5	10.5	9.92	9.33
9	.25	1.51	1.62	1.63	1.63	1.62	1.61	1.60	1.59	1.56	1.55	1.53
	.10	3.36	3.01	2.81	2.69	2.61	2.55	2.47	2.42	2.30	2.23	2.16
	.05	5.12	4.26	3.86	3.63	3.48	3.37	3.23	3.14	2.94	2.83	2.71
	.01	10.6	8.02	6.99	6.42	6.06	5.80	5.47	5.26	4.81	4.57	4.31
	.001	22.9	16.4	13.9	12.6	11.7	11.1	10.4	9.89	8.90	8.37	7.81
10	.25	1.49	1.60	1.60	1.59	1.59	1.58	1.56	1.55	1.52	1.51	1.48
	.10	3.28	2.92	2.73	2.61	2.52	2.46	2.38	2.32	2.20	2.13	2.06
	.05	4.96	4.10	3.71	3.48	3.33	3.22	3.07	2.98	2.77	2.66	2.54
	.01	10.0	7.56	6.55	5.99	5.64	5.39	5.06	4.85	4.41	4.17	3.91
	.001	21.0	14.9	12.6	11.3	10.5	9.92	9.20	8.75	7.80	7.30	6.76
12	.25	1.56	1.56	1.56	1.55	1.54	1.53	1.51	1.50	1.47	1.45	1.42
	.10	3.18	2.81	2.61	2.48	2.39	2.33	2.24	2.19	2.06	1.99	1.90
	.05	4.75	3.89	3.49	3.26	3.11	3.00	2.85	2.75	2.54	2.43	2.30
	.01	9.33	6.93	5.95	5.41	5.06	4.82	4.50	4.30	3.86	3.62	3.36
	.001	18.6	13.0	10.8	9.63	8.89	8.38	7.71	7.29	6.40	5.93	5.42

Degree of Freedom for Denominator

(continued)

TABLE A-3 *(continued)*

						Degrees of Freedom for Numerator							
		Pr	1	2	3	4	5	6	8	10	20	40	∞
14		.25	1.44	1.53	1.53	1.52	1.51	1.50	1.48	1.46	1.43	1.41	1.38
		.10	3.10	2.73	2.52	2.39	2.31	2.24	2.15	2.10	1.96	1.89	1.80
		.05	4.60	3.74	3.34	3.11	2.96	2.85	2.70	2.60	2.39	2.27	2.13
		.01	8.86	5.51	5.56	5.04	4.69	4.46	4.14	3.94	3.51	3.27	3.00
		.001	17.1	11.8	9.73	8.62	7.92	7.43	6.80	6.40	5.56	5.10	4.60
16		.25	1.42	1.51	1.51	1.50	1.48	1.48	1.46	1.45	1.40	1.37	1.34
		.10	3.05	2.67	2.46	2.33	2.24	2.18	2.09	2.03	1.89	1.81	1.72
		.05	4.49	3.63	3.24	3.01	2.85	2.74	2.59	2.49	2.28	2.15	2.01
		.01	8.53	6.23	5.29	4.77	4.44	4.20	3.89	3.69	3.26	3.02	2.75
		.001	16.1	11.0	9.00	7.94	7.27	6.81	6.19	5.81	4.99	4.54	4.06

(Degree of Freedom for Denominator)

TABLE A-4   Cut-off Points for the Student's *t* Distribution

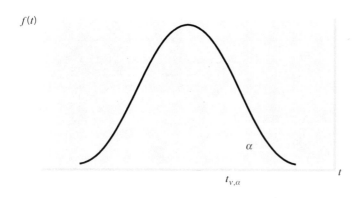

$f(t)$

α

$t_{v,\alpha}$

t

df(v)	.100	.050	α .025	.010	.005
1	3.078	6.314	12.706	31.821	63.657
2	1.886	2.920	4.303	6.965	9.925
3	1.638	2.353	3.182	4.541	5.841
4	1.533	2.132	2.776	3.747	4.604
5	1.476	2.015	2.571	3.365	4.032
6	1.440	1.943	2.447	3.143	3.707
7	1.415	1.895	2.365	2.998	3.499
8	1.397	1.860	2.306	2.896	3.355
9	1.383	1.833	2.262	2.821	3.250
10	1.372	1.812	2.228	2.764	3.169
11	1.363	1.796	2.201	2.718	3.106
12	1.356	1.782	2.179	2.681	3.055
13	1.350	1.771	2.160	2.650	3.012
14	1.345	1.761	2.145	2.624	2.977
15	1.341	1.753	2.131	2.602	2.947

(continued)

TABLE A-4   *(continued)*

df(v)	.100	.050	α .025	.010	.005
16	1.337	1.746	2.120	2.583	2.921
17	1.333	1.740	2.110	2.567	2.898
18	1.330	1.734	2.101	2.552	2.878
19	1.328	1.729	2.093	2.539	2.861
20	1.325	1.725	2.086	2.528	2.845
21	1.323	1.721	2.080	2.518	2.831
22	1.321	1.717	2.074	2.508	2.819
23	1.319	1.714	2.069	2.500	2.807
24	1.318	1.711	2.064	2.492	2.797
25	1.316	1.708	2.060	2.485	2.787
26	1.315	1.706	2.056	2.479	2.779
27	1.314	1.703	2.052	2.473	2.771
28	1.313	1.701	2.048	2.467	2.763
29	1.311	1.699	2.045	2.462	2.756
30	1.310	1.697	2.042	2.457	2.750
40	1.303	1.684	2.021	2.423	2.704
60	1.296	1.671	2.000	2.390	2.660
∞	1.282	1.645	1.960	2.326	2.576

For selected probabilities, α, the table shows the values $t_{v,\alpha}$ such that $P(t_v > t_{v,\alpha} = \alpha$, where t_v is a student's t random variable with v degrees of freedom. For example, the probability is .10 that a student's t random variable with 10 degrees of freedom exceeds 1.372.

◆ PROCEDURES FOR CONDUCTING UNIVARIATE AND MULTIVARIATE ANALYSIS IN SPSS

Univariate Analysis

Chi-Square Tests

Data must be arranged in a special format for performing chi-square tests in SPSS. For example, we want to perform a chi-square test of whether two variables A and B are related to each other. Suppose A has 4 levels and B has 2 levels. The table of data needs to be arranged in a linear form in SPSS. In other words, three columns are necessary for performing the analysis: one column each for A and B, and the frequency of observed cases (say, count) for each combination of A and B. Once the data have been organized in this particular way, follow these steps:

Step 1.   First we have to weight all the variables by the frequency (count). In our case, each level combination of A and B has an observed number of cases. The first step is to weight each unique combination of A and B by the frequency (count): (1) Choose the *Data* option from the main menu. (2) Choose the *Weight Cases* option. (3) Assign the count variable as the frequency variable by which to weight the cases.

Step 2.   Choose *Statistics* from the main menu. Then choose *Summarize→ Crosstabs*. In the Crosstabs window, choose A and B as the row and column variables respectively. Select the chi-square option in the statistics window.

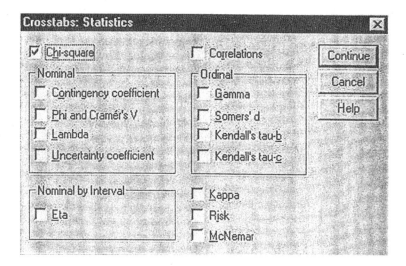

Hypothesis Tests

It is very simple to perform hypothesis tests in SPSS. Choose *Statistics* from the main menu, then choose the *Compare Means* option. Choose the appropriate hypothesis test you want to perform from this menu. Once the hypothesis test to be conducted is chosen, merely provide the variable that is being tested and the value under the null hypothesis.

Multivariate Analysis

Multiple Regression

To perform multiple regression, arrange the dependent (y) and independent (x) variables in columns. From the *Statistics* option in the main menu choose the *regression* option. Choose the linear estimation technique. The regression window will then ask you to specify the dependent and independent variables in the

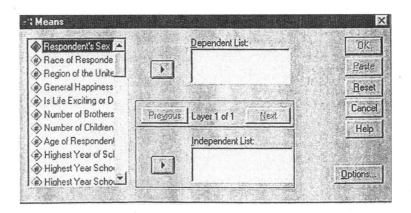

model you want to regress. If you want to include a constant in the model, click on the *Options* button in the regression window. Then check the *Include Constant in Equation* check box. The regression window also lets you decide on the procedure for doing multiple regression (i.e., stepwise, forward step, backward step, enter or remove variables).

Output of Select Tables in SPSS

All of the analysis in this appendix has been performed with the entire export data set (all 120 observations), while the analysis in the book has been performed with

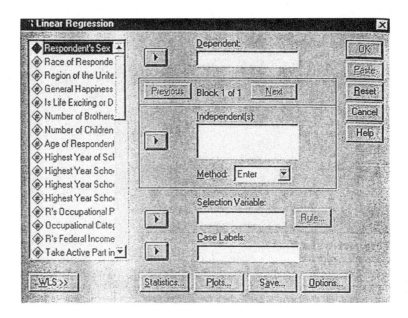

only 60 randomly selected records from the export data set. The export data set along with the other data sets used in the book are available at the web site www.imc-marketing.com/emr2.

REGRESSION

Variables Entered/Removed[b]

Model	Variables Entered	Variables Removed	Method
1	SIZE[a]		Enter

[a] All requested variables entered.
[b] Dependent variable: WILL

Model Summary

Model	R	R Square	Adjusted R Square	Std. Error of the Estimate
1	.743[a]	.552	.548	.8651

[a] Predictors: (Constant), SIZE.

ANOVA[b]

Model		Sum of Squares	df	Mean Square	F	Sig.
1	Regression	108.683	1	108.683	145.226	.000[a]
	Residual	88.308	118	.748		
	Total	196.992	119			

[a] Predictors: (Constant), SIZE.
[b] Dependent variable: WILL.

Coefficients[a]

Model		Unstandardized Coefficients		Standardized Coefficients		
		B	Std. Error	Beta	t	Sig.
1	(Constant)	−.900	.354		−2.542	.012
	SIZE	9.223E-02	.008	.743	12.051	.000

[a] Dependent variable: WILL.

REGRESSION

Variables Entered/Removed[b]

Model	Variables Entered	Variables Removed	Method
1	PRODUCTS, REV, YEARS, SIZE[a]		Enter

[a] All requested variables entered.
[b] Dependent variable: WILL.

Model Summary

Model	R	R Square	Adjusted R Square	Std. Error of the Estimate
1	.850[a]	.723	.714	.6884

[a] Predictors: (Constant), PRODUCTS, REV, YEARS, SIZE.

ANOVA[b]

Model		Sum of Squares	df	Mean Square	F	Sig.
1	Regression	142.493	4	35.623	75.171	.000[a]
	Residual	54.498	115	.474		
	Total	196.992	119			

[a] Predictors: (Constant), PRODUCTS, REV, YEARS, SIZE.
[b] Dependent variable: WILL.

Coefficients[a]

Model		Unstandardized Coefficients		Standardized Coefficients	t	Sig.
		B	Std. Error	Beta		
1	(Constant)	1.792	.605		2.965	.004
	SIZE	6.394E-02	.007	.515	8.566	.000
	REV	.116	.069	.085	1.677	.096
	YEARS	−.395	.076	−.265	−5.167	.000
	PRODUCTS	.174	.031	.342	5.701	.000

[a] Dependent variable: WILL.

REGRESSION

Variables Entered/Removed[b]

Model	Variables Entered	Variables Removed	Method
1	EXP, REV, TRAINING, YEARS, PRODUCTS, SIZE[a]		Enter

[a] All requested variables entered.
[b] Dependent variable: WILL.

Model Summary

Model	R	R Square	Adjusted R Square	Std. Error of the Estimate
1	.851[a]	.724	.709	.6939

[a] Predictors: (Constant), EXP, REV, TRAINING, YEARS, PRODUCTS, SIZE.

ANOVA[b]

Model		Sum of Squares	df	Mean Square	F	Sig.
1	Regression	142.588	6	23.765	49.361	.000[a]
	Residual	54.404	113	.481		
	Total	196.992	119			

[a] Predictors: (Constant), EXP, REV, TRAINING, YEARS, PRODUCTS, SIZE.
[b] Dependent variable: WILL.

Coefficients[a]

Model		Unstandardized Coefficients		Standardized Coefficients	t	Sig.
		B	Std. Error	Beta		
1	(Constant)	1.993	.770		2.590	.011
	SIZE	6.191E-02	.009	.499	6.590	.000
	REV	.111	.071	.082	1.564	.121
	YEARS	−.418	.096	−.280	−4.337	.000
	PRODUCTS	.168	.034	.330	4.995	.000
	TRAINING	9.386E-02	.212	.034	.443	.658
	EXP	1.516E-02	.178	.005	.085	.932

[a] Dependent variable: WILL.

Glossary

Accuracy a criterion used to judge whether a market research study is logical and presents correct information.

Additive causal relationship a causal relationship in which the causal effects of two variables on a third variable are added.

Administering error error that occurs during the administration of a survey instrument to the respondent.

Affective/liking component that part of attitude representing the person's overall feelings of liking or disliking the object, person, or event.

Aided recall a questioning approach that attempts to stimulate a respondent's memory with clues about an object of interest.

American Marketing Association the premier association of marketing practitioners and academicians in the United States, which publishes journals and organizes conferences for the dissemination of marketing knowledge.

Analysis of dependence any multivariate analysis where one or more variables are predicted or explained by other variables.

Analysis of interdependence any multivariate analysis where the interrelationships within a set of variables are examined and no variable is seen to be a dependent variable.

Analysis of value an estimate of the benefits gained by undertaking a market research study.

Analysis of variance (ANOVA) a method of testing a hypothesis regarding the difference between several means.

Artificiality the conditions that differ from the real world in experimental treatment so that projections become difficult and risky.

ASSESSOR a computer model for predicting market share of a new packaged good brand using laboratory test market data.

Associative scaling a scale in which the respondent is asked to associate alternatives with each question.

Attitudes mental states used by individuals to structure the way they perceive their environment and to guide the way in which they respond. A psychological construct comprised of cognitive, affective, and intention components.

Attribute a characteristic or property of an object or person.

Attribute judgment the judgment an individual makes about the numerous characteristics or attributes that are possessed by an object.

Automatic Interaction Detection (AID) a technique for finding interactions in a sample by using nominally scaled independent variables to find subgroups that differ with respect to a dependent variable.

Averaging a memory error whereby something is reported as more like the usual, the expected, or the norm.

Bar graph a graph of bars whose length indicates relative amounts of the variable.

Before-measure effect the alerting of respondents to the fact that they are being studied, due to the presentation of a before measure, causing unnatural responses.

Behavior the past and present overt responses of subjects.

Behavior recording device a mechanical observation method, such as a traffic counter, that continuously monitors behavior, usually unobtrusively.

Benefit segmentation a type of market segmentation based on the benefits that people seek from products.

Bipolar scale a scale bounded at each end by polar adjectives that are antonyms.

Blind use test a use test where consumers are asked to evaluate product alternatives without being aware of brand names.

Blocking a procedure by which a nonmanipulated variable is introduced into the experiment to ensure that the groups are equalized on that variable.

Bottom-up measurement a method of determining market potential that has as its starting point the identification of product use situations or applications.

Brand equity the concept wherein the brand is considered an asset insofar as it can be sold or bought for a price. A powerful brand is said to have high brand equity.

CALLPLAN an interactive model designed to aid a salesperson in his or her call planning process. Its objective is to determine call-frequency norms for each client and prospect.

Canonical correlation analysis an analysis method used in the case of two dependent variables and multiple independent variables. It focuses on the relationship between two sets of interval-scale variables.

Case study a comprehensive description and analysis of a single situation.

Causal relationship a precondition influencing a variable of interest, or, more strictly, a change in one variable that produces a change in another variable.

Causal research research having very specific hypotheses that is usually designed to provide the ultimate level of understanding—a knowledge that one construct under certain conditions causes another construct to occur or to change.

Census tract a group of city blocks having a total population of more than 4000 and generally used to approximate neighborhoods.

Centroid the average value of the objects contained in the cluster on each of the variables making up each object's profile.

Chi-square statistic a measure of association between two nominally scaled variables.

City block the smallest identifiable unit in the U.S. Census, being bounded by four streets or some other physical boundary.

Classification variables used to classify respondents, such as demographic and socioeconomic measures.

Closed-response (or structured) question a question accompanied by the presentation of responses to be considered by the respondent.

Cluster analysis a set of techniques for grouping objects or persons in terms of similarity.

Cluster sampling a sampling method where a random sample of subgroups is selected and all members of the subgroups become part of the sample.

Clutter/awareness the percentage who recalled a brand was advertised when exposed in a "clutter" of seven ads in a McCollum/Speilman test.

Coding the categorization and numbering of responses.

Cognitive/knowledge component that part of attitude representing the information a person knows about an object, person, or event.

Communality the proportion of a variable's variance explained by all of the factors in a factor analysis solution.

Comparative scale a type of scale with some form of explicit or implicit comparison built into the scale.

Compensatory model any multiattribute model in which one attribute compensates for another in the overall preference for an object.

Complementary pricing the pricing strategy used by firms to price complementary products. They usually price the main product at a low price while the complement is charged at a higher price.

Completion test a projective technique in which the respondent is asked to complete a series of sentences.

Compositional approach an attitude measurement approach in which the overall preference judgment for each object is obtained by summing the evaluative rating of each attribute multiplied by the importance of that attribute.

Computer-retrievable databases secondary records accessible by a computer system.

Concept test a test of a product concept where the concept is evaluated by a sample of the target segment.

Concurrent validity criterion validity that is established by correlating the measurement score with the criterion variable, both measured at the same time.

Conjoint analysis a method of obtaining the relative worth or value of each level of several attributes from rank-ordered preferences of attribute combinations.

Consideration/evoked set all the alternatives that potential buyers would consider in their next purchase of the product or service.

Constant sum scale a scale in which the respondent must allocate a fixed number of points among several objects to reflect the relative preference for each object.

Construct a concept, usually psychological, such as attitudes and values, that is not directly observable.

Construct equivalence deals with how the researcher and the subjects of the research see, understand, and code a particular phenomenon.

Construct validity the ability of a measurement instrument to measure a concept or "construct"; construct validity is generally demonstrated by showing both convergent and discriminant validity.

Content analysis a technique used to study written material by breaking it into meaningful units, using carefully applied rules.

Contingency coefficient a chi-square statistic corrected for sample size.

Continuous purchase panel a fixed sample of respondents who are measured on several occasions over a period of time.

Contrived observation an observation method in which people are placed in a contrived situation so that their responses will reveal some aspects of their underlying beliefs, attitudes, and motives; examples are tests of variation in shelf-space, product flavors, and display locations.

Control group the group of subjects not exposed to the experimental treatment.

Controlled Distribution Scanner Markets (CDSM) distribution for new product test is prearranged and results are monitored with scanner data.

Convenience sampling a sampling method in which convenient sampling units are contacted, such as church activity groups or student classes.

Convergent validity the ability of a measurement instrument to correlate or "converge" with other supposed measures of the same variable or construct; the opposite of discriminant validity.

Copy test validity the ability to predict advertising response.

Correlation a number between +1 and 1 that reflects the degree to which two variables have a linear relationship.

Correspondence analysis a technique for producing perceptual maps using binary data.

Criterion/empirical validity the validity of a measurement instrument as determined by empirical evidence that correlates the measurement instrument with other "criterion" variables.

Cross-tabulation/contingency table analysis the determination of a frequency distribution for subgroups.

Cyclical indexes a representation of the effects of business cycle fluctuations in making a forecast.

Data unassimilated facts about the market.

Data analysis error errors that arise due to the faulty procedures employed in coding, editing, analyzing, and interpreting data.

Database an organized store of data, usually within a computer.

Day-after-recall (DAR) the percentage of the audience who can recall something specific about the commercial the next day.

Decision support system (DSS) a collection of rules, procedures, and models for retrieving data from a database, transforming it into usable information, and disseminating it to users so that they can make decisions.

Decompositional approach attitude measurement approach in which the utilities of each attribute are obtained from the overall preference judgment for each object.

Delphi approach a group judgment method where each member makes an individual judgment and then each member is given an opportunity to revise his or her judgment after seeing the others' initial judgments, until, after several iterations, the group members reach their conclusion.

Demographic shifts changes in physical and socioeconomic characteristics of a population such as age, ethnicity, income, and so on.

Descriptive research research that usually is designed to provide a summary of some aspects of the environment when the hypotheses are tentative and speculative in nature.

DETAILER a decision calculus model for determining the sales force allocation by market and by product line.

Diary panel the basic data-gathering instrument for local TV and radio ratings.

Direct observation an observation method in which the researcher directly observes the person or behavior in question.

Discriminant analysis a statistical technique for developing a set of independent variables to classify people or objects into one or more groups.

Discriminant function the linear combination of variables developed by discriminant analysis for the purpose of classifying people or objects into one or more groups.

Discriminant validity the ability of a measurement instrument not to correlate with supposed measures of other variables or constructs; the opposite of convergent validity.

Drop-off approach the hand delivery of a questionnaire to sampling points.

Dummy variable a variable taking on the values of either 0 or 1, which is used to denote characteristics that are not quantifiable.

Efficiency a criterion used to judge whether a market research study produces the maximum amount and quality of information for the minimum expenditure of time and money.

E-mail a major communication path that allows one to send and receive computer messages around the world.

Expected value the value obtained by multiplying each consequence by the probability of that consequence occurring and summing the products.

Experimental control the control of extraneous variables through experimental procedures such as randomization or block designs.

Experimental error error that arises due to the improper design of the experiment.

Experimental group the group of subjects exposed to the experimental treatment.

Experimental treatments alternative manipulations of the independent variable being investigated.

Experiments studies that require the intervention by the observer beyond that required for measurement.

Exploratory research research that usually is designed to generate ideas when the hypotheses are vague or ill-defined.

Exponential smoothing in time-series extrapolations, the weighting of historical data so that the more recent data are weighted more heavily than are less recent data, by exponentially decreasing sets of weights.

External source a marketing data source found outside of the organization.

External validity the applicability of experimental results to situations external to the actual experimental context.

Extraneous variable variables other than the manipulated variable that affect the response of the test units and hence the results of the experiment. Also known as the confounding variables.

Face/consensus validity the validity of a measurement instrument as determined entirely by subjective argument or judgment.

Factor an underlying construct defined by a linear combination of variables.

Factor analysis a set of techniques for the study of interrelationships among variables, usually for the purposes of data reduction and the discovery of underlying constructs or latent dimensions.

Factorial design an experimental design in which two or more experimental variables are considered simultaneously by applying each combination of the experimental treatment levels to randomly selected groups.

Factor loading the correlation (or sometimes the regression weight) of a variable with a factor.

Factor rotation the generation of several factor analysis solutions (factor loadings and scores) from the same data set.

Factor scores a respondent's score or value on a factor.

Field experiments experiments in which the experimental treatment is introduced in a completely natural setting.

File transfer protocol (FTP) used in order to send and retrieve files to/from other locations.

Focus group a group discussion focused on a series of topics introduced by a discussion leader; the group members are encouraged to express their own views on each topic and to elaborate on or react to the views of each other.

Forced exposure respondents are exposed to an ad in a facility as opposed to an "on-air" test in the home.

Foreign market opportunity analysis acquisition of information that would help the management to narrow the possibilities for international marketing activities. The aim of such an exercise is to gather information to aid in managerial decision making.

Frequency distribution a report of the number of responses that a question has received.

F-statistic the statistic used in the analysis of variance to test for differences in groups.

Full-profile approach a method of collecting data for trade-off analysis in which respondents are given cards that describe complete product or service configurations.

Genotypic sources of refusal these pertain to why survey respondents refuse to participate on account of their inherent characteristics such as age, sex, occupation, and so on.

Goodman and Kruskall's tau a measure of association for nominally scaled variables based on a proportional reduction in error.

Hierarchical clustering a method of cluster analysis that starts with each object in its own (single-object) cluster and systematically combines clusters until all objects are in one cluster.

History effect any influence on subjects, external to an experiment, that may affect the results of the experiment.

Hold-out sample a sample used to test a model developed from another sample.

Home audit a method of collecting continuous purchase panel data in which the panel members agree to permit an auditor to check their household stocks of certain product categories at regular intervals.

Humanistic inquiry a method in which the researcher is immersed in the group or system under study.

HyperText Mark-up Language (HTML) the coding language used to create Hypertext documents for use on the World Wide Web.

Hypothesis possible answer to the research question.

Ideal object the object the respondent would prefer over all others, including objects that can be conceptualized but do not actually exist; it is a combination of all the respondent's preferred attribute levels.

Independence in statistics, the property that the knowledge of one variable or event offers no information as to the identity of another variable or event.

Individual depth interview a qualitative research method designed to explore the hidden (deep) feelings, values, and motives of the respondent through a face-to-face interview with the researcher.

Industrial market a market for goods and services composed of industrial firms, other businesses, government agencies, and organizations in general, rather than individual consumers.

Information data that have been transformed into answers for specific questions of the decision makers.

Information system a system containing marketing data and marketing intelligence.

Instrumentation effect the effect of changes in the measuring instrument on the experimental results.

Integrated marketing communications a concept of marketing communications planning that recognizes the added value of a comprehensive plan that evaluates the strategic roles of a variety of communication disciplines and combines these disciplines to provide clarity, consistency, and maximum communication impact through the seamless integration of discrete messages.

Integrated Services Digital Network (ISDN) a way of moving more data over regular telephone lines. ISDN lines can provide speeds of up to 128 Kbps.

Intelligent agent an intelligent software that can keep an eye on topics and sites of individual importance.

Intention/action component the part of an attitude that represents the person's expectations of future behavior toward the object, person, or event.

Interactive effect the case where the effect of one variable on another variable depends on the level of a third variable.

Interference error error that occurs due to the failure of the interviewer to adhere to the exact procedure while collecting the data.

Internal records a marketing data source found within the organization.

Internal validity the ability of an experiment to show relationships unambiguously.

Internet a worldwide network of computers that have the ability to talk to each other.

Interval estimation the estimation of the interval in which an unknown population characteristic is judged to lie, for a given level of confidence.

Interval scale a scale with the property that units have the same width throughout the scale (i.e., thermometer).

Intervening variable any variable positioned between two other variables in a causal path.

Interviewer error a source of error in personal interviews due to the impression the respondent has of the interviewer and the way the interviewer asks questions, follows up partial answers, and records the responses.

Itemized category scale a scale in which the respondent chooses among one of several response options or categories.

Judgmental sampling a nonprobability sampling method in which an "expert" uses judgment to identify representative samples.

Jury of executive opinion an efficient and timely qualitative research approach that combines the judgments of a group of managers about forecasts, most commonly used in consumer products and service companies.

Laboratory experiment an experiment in which the experimental treatment is introduced in an artificial or laboratory setting.

Laboratory test market a procedure whereby shoppers are exposed to an ad for a new product and then taken on a simulated shopping trip in a laboratory facility.

Latin square design an experimental design that reduces the number of groups involved when interactions between the treatment levels and the control variables can be considered relatively unimportant.

Leading indicators a variable that tends to predict the future direction of an object to be forecast.

Lifetime value of a customer the total revenue stream that an individual customer generates for a company over his or her tenure with the company.

Likert scale a scale developed by the Likert method in which the subject must indicate his or her degree of agreement or disagreement with a variety of statements related to the attitude object and which then are summed over all statements to provide a total score.

Lockbox approach the delivery by mail of a small, locked metal box containing a questionnaire and other interviewing exhibits.

Magnitude scaling a technique for measuring opinions using a ratio scale instead of an interval scale.

Mail diary method a method of collecting continuous purchase panel data in which panel members record the details of each purchase in certain categories and return a completed mail diary at regular intervals.

Mail panel a representative national sample of people who have agreed to participate in a limited number of mail surveys each year.

Mail survey the mailing of questionnaires and their return by mail by the designated respondents.

Manipulation the creation of different levels of the independent variable is known as manipulating the variable.

Marketing intelligence a form of business intelligence where legal, ethical collection of data and information will be analyzed and transformed for use in strategic planning and problem solving.

Marketing planning and information system a system of strategic and tactical plans and marketing data and intelligence that provides overall direction and coordination to the organization.

Marketing program development the stage of the market planning process that deals with segmentation decisions, product decisions, distribution decisions, advertising and promotion decisions, personal selling decisions, and pricing decisions.

Marketing research the specification, gathering, analyzing, and interpretation of information that links the organization with its market environment.

Market potential the sales for the product or service that would result if the market were fully developed.

Market segmentation the development and pursuit of marketing programs directed at subgroups or segments of the population that the organization could possibly serve.

Matching a procedure for the assignment of subjects to groups that ensures each group of respondents is matched on the basis of the pertinent characteristics.

Maturation during a research study, changes within respondents that are a consequence of time.

Mean the number obtained by summing all elements in a set and dividing by the number of elements.

Measurement the assignment of numbers by rules to objects in order to reflect quantities of properties.

Measurement equivalence deals with the methods and procedures used by the researcher to collect and categorize essential data and information.

Measurement error error that occurs due to the variation between the information sought by the researcher and the information generated by a particular procedure employed by the researcher.

Monopolar scale a scale bounded at each end by polar adjectives or phrases, one of which is the negation of the other.

Mortality effect the effect on the experimental results of respondents dropping out of an experiment.

Moving average using the moving average of the last n data points (e.g., the monthly averages for a year) to forecast.

Multiattribute model any model linking attribute judgments with overall liking or affect.

Multidimensional scaling a set of techniques for developing perceptual maps.

Multistage designs a sampling procedure that consists of several sampling methods used sequentially.

Multivariate analysis the simultaneous study of two or more measures on a sample of objects.

Need a want, an urge, a wish, or any motivational force directing behavior toward a goal.

Need research/identification a type of concept generation research with the emphasis placed on the identification of unfulfilled needs that exist in the market.

New-product research process a sequential four-stage process consisting of concept generation, concept evaluation and development, product evaluation and development, and product testing.

Nielsen Retail Index a retail store audit conducted by A. C. Nielsen for four major groups of stores: grocery products, drugs, mass merchandisers, and alcoholic beverages.

Nominal scale a measurement that assigns only an identification or label to an object or set of objects.

Nondirective interview a type of individual indepth interview in which the respondent is given maximum freedom to respond, within the bounds of topics of interest to the interviewer.

Nonparametric procedures analysis techniques that are applicable only if the data are nonmetric (nominal or ordinal).

Nonprobability sampling any sampling method where the probability of any population element's inclusion is unknown, such as judgmental or convenience sampling.

Nonresponse bias an error due to the inability to elicit information from some respondents in a sample, often due to refusals.

Nonresponse error error that occurs due to nonparticipation of some eligible respondents in the study. This could be due to the unwillingness of the respondents to participate in the study or the inability of the interviewer to contact the respondents.

Observation a data collection method where the relevant behaviors are recorded; examples are direct observation, contrived observation, physical trace measures, and behavior recording devices.

Omission a memory error where a respondent leaves out an event or some aspect of it.

Omnibus survey a regularly scheduled personal interview survey comprised of questions from several separate firms.

On-air test a test ad that is shown on a channel viewed at home.

On-line telephone interview an interview where the interviewer (1) reads the questions from an on-line cathode-ray-tube (CRT) terminal that is linked directly to a computer and (2) records the answers on a keyboard for entry to the computer.

Open-response/unstructured question a question with either no classification of responses or precoded classification of responses.

Optimizing *(in cluster analysis)* a nonhierarchical method of clustering wherein the objects can later be reassigned to clusters on the basis of optimizing some overall criterion measure.

Order bias the bias of question responses due to the order of question presentation.

Ordinal scale a measurement that assigns only a rank order (i.e., "less than or greater than") to a set of objects.

Paired comparison a scale in which the objects to be ranked are presented two at a time so that the respondent has to choose between them according to some criterion.

Parallel threshold a nonhierarchical clustering method wherein several cluster centers are selected simultaneously and objects within the threshold level are assigned to the nearest center. Threshold levels can be adjusted to admit fewer or more objects to the cluster.

Parameter a number constant in each model considered, but varying in different models.

Parametric procedures analysis techniques that are applicable only if the data are metric (interval or ratio).

Partial correlation coefficient examining the association between a dependent and independent variable after satisfactorily factoring out the effect of other independent variables.

Part-worth utilities utilities associated with particular product or brand attributes that are added together to obtain an overall utility for a product or brand alternative in conjoint analysis.

Past turning point a point in time where a substantial change in growth rate can be identified by an environmental change; a forecast can be based on data since that point.

Perceptual map/reduced space a spatial representation of the perceived relationships among objects in a set, where the objects could be brands, products, or services.

Periodic discounting the strategy adopted by the firm wherein the firms can start at a high price and periodically discount their prices in order to draw consumers with lower reservation prices. This is useful when markets have consumers with differential reservation prices.

Personal interview a face-to-face interview between the respondent and the interviewer.

Phenotypic sources of refusal these pertain to why survey respondents refuse to participate on account of the characteristics of the data collection procedure such as which questions are asked, how they are asked, length of the interview, and so on.

Phi-squared a chi-square statistic corrected for sample size.

Physical trace measures an observation method, such as a home audit, in which the natural "residue" or physical trace of the behavior is recorded.

Picture interpretation a projective technique based on the Thematic Apperception Test (TAT), in which the respondent is asked to tell a story on the presentation of a series of pictures.

Population specification error error that occurs when an inappropriate population is chosen for the study.

Potential Rating Index Zip Markets (PRIZM) the classification and grouping of residents of zip code areas based on demographic and lifestyle data derived from the census.

Predictive validity criterion validity that is established by correlating the measurement score with a future criterion variable.

Pretest the presentation of a questionnaire in a pilot study to a representative sample of the respondent population in order to discover any problems with the questionnaire prior to full-scale use.

Price bundling the pricing strategy adopted to products that are nonsubstitutable, are perishable, and have an asymmetric demand structure. An example is pricing a car that includes many options.

Price signaling the pricing strategy adopted when the consumers in the market are willing to pay more for a product despite lack of knowledge regarding a product's quality. The firm produces an inferior product and sells it at the same price as the better quality product produced by another firm, in the hope that customers will associate high quality with high price.

Primary data data collected to address a specific research objective (as opposed to secondary data).

Principal components/principal factor analysis a type of factor analysis that seeks to explain the greatest amount of variance in a data set, thus providing data reduction.

Probability sampling any sampling method where the probability of any population element's inclusion is known and is greater than zero.

Problem or opportunity definition a process of understanding the causes and predicting the consequences of problems or a process of exploring the size and nature of opportunities; the second phase of marketing program development.

Profile analysis the comparison of evaluations of the alternatives in a consideration set, on the important and determinant attributes.

Projective techniques a set of presentation methods of ambiguous, unstructured objects, activities, or persons for which a respondent is asked to give interpretation and find meaning; the more ambiguous the stimulus, the more the respondent has to project him or herself into the task, thereby revealing hidden feelings, values, and needs; examples are word association, role playing, completion tests, and picture interpretation.

Purchase interception technique a consumer survey technique for collecting data through personal interviews by in-store observation of purchase behavior and then interception of consumers in the shopping environment to determine the reasons behind that behavior.

Qualitative research research designed primarily for exploratory purposes, such as getting oriented to the range and complexity of consumer activity, clarifying the problem, and identifying likely methodological problems; examples are individual and group interviews, projective techniques, and case studies.

Quick clustering   one method of cluster analysis.

Quota sampling   a judgmental sampling method that is constrained to include a minimum from each specified subgroup in the population.

Random error   measurement error due to changing aspects of the respondent or measurement situation.

Randomization   a procedure in which the assignment of subjects and treatments to groups is based on chance. Randomization ensures control over the extraneous variables and increases the reliability of the experiment.

Randomized block design   an experimental design in which the test units first are grouped into homogeneous groups along some prespecified criterion and then are assigned randomly to different treatments within each block.

Rank-order scale   a scale in which the respondent is required to order a set of objects with regard to a common criterion.

Ratio scale   a measurement that has a true or meaningful zero point, allowing for the specification of absolute magnitudes of objects.

Reading-habit method   measuring print media exposure by asking how many issues of the last four you have read.

Recent-reading method   measuring print media exposure by asking whether someone looked at a copy in the past week for a weekly or in the past month for a monthly.

Recording error   error that occurs due to the improper recording of the respondents' answers.

Refusal rate   a measure of any data collection method's ability to induce contacted respondents to participate in the study.

Refusals   a source of nonsampling error caused by a respondent's refusing to participate in the study.

Regression analysis   a statistical technique that develops an equation that relates a dependent variable to one or more independent (predictor, explanatory) variables.

Relationship marketing   establishing, developing, and maintaining long-term, trusting relational exchanges with valued customers, distributors, suppliers, and dealers by promising and delivering high-quality services and products to the parties over time.

Relative market potential   the market potential of one segment relative to other segments.

Relevance   a criterion used to judge whether a market research study acts to support strategic and tactical planning activities.

Reliability   the random error component of a measurement instrument.

Research approach   one of the following six sources of data—the information system, secondary and standardized data sources, qualitative research, surveys, observations, and experiments.

Research boundary   a delineation of the scope of the research study in terms of items such as population characteristics, locations, and product markets.

Research objectives   a precise statement of what information is needed, consisting of the research question, the hypotheses, and the scope or boundaries of the research.

Research process   the series of stages or steps underlying the design and implementation of a marketing research project, including the establishment of the research purpose and objectives, information value estimation, research design, and implementation.

Research proposal   a plan for conducting and controlling a research project.

Research purpose   the shared understanding between the manager and the researcher regarding the decision alternatives, the problems and opportunities to be studied, and who the users of the results shall be.

Research question   the statement(s) of what specific information is required for progress toward the achievement of the research purpose.

Research tactics   the development of the specific details of the research, including the research approach, sampling plan, and choice of research supplier.

Response bias   the tendency of respondents to distort their answers systematically for a variety of reasons, such as social desirability and prestige seeking.

Response error   error that occurs due to the respondents providing inaccurate information (intentionally or unintentionally). This might be due to the inability of the respondent to comprehend the question or misunderstanding the question due to fatigue or boredom.

Response style   the systematic tendency of respondents to select particular categories of responses regardless of the content of the questions.

Retail store audits   audit data collected by research firms whose employees visit a sample of stores at fixed intervals for the purpose of counting stock and recording deliveries to estimate retail sales.

Role-playing   a projective technique in which the respondent assumes the role or behavior of another person so that the respondent may reveal attitudes by projecting him- or herself fully into the role.

Sample a subset of elements from a population.

Sampling equivalence deals with the question of identifying and operationalizing two comparable populations and selecting samples that are representative of other populations and that are comparable across countries.

Sampling frame a listing of population members that is used to create a random sample.

Sampling frame error error that occurs when the sample is drawn from an inaccurate sampling frame.

Sampling unit any type of element that makes up a sample, such as people, stores, and products.

Scale transformation manipulation of scale values to ensure comparability with other scales.

Scanner data the scanner is a device that reads the universal product code from a package as it is processed at a retailer's checkout stand. Scanner data include data on all transactions including size, price, and flavor. It also normally includes in-store information such as special displays.

Scatter diagram a two-dimensional plot of two variables.

Screening sample a representative sample of the population being studied that is used to develop or pretest measurement instruments.

Search engines systems that allow Internet users to search for clickable links to sites of their interest.

Seasonal index a representation of the seasonal forecast.

Secondary data data collected for some purpose other than the present research purpose.

Second market discounting the pricing strategy adapted wherein the firm discounts its prices in the other markets below its average cost.

Selection bias differences among subjects, prior to an experiment, that affect the experimental results.

Selection error error that occurs in a nonprobability sampling method when a sample obtained is not representative of the population.

Sell-in test market the new product being tested must be sold to the retailer. Shelf space is not pre-arranged.

Semantic differential scale a scale in which the respondent is asked to rate each attitude object in turn on a five- or seven-point rating scale bounded at each end by polar adjectives or phrases.

Semistructured/focused individual interview a type of individual indepth interview in which the interviewer attempts to cover a specific list of topics or subareas.

Sensitivity the ability of a measurement instrument to discriminate among meaningful differences in the variable being measured.

Sequential sampling a sampling method in which an initial modest sample is taken and analyzed, following which, based on the results, a decision is made regarding the necessity of further sampling and analysis; this continues until enough data are collected.

Sequential threshold a nonhierarchical clustering method wherein a cluster center is selected and all objects within a prespecified threshold value are grouped. Then a new cluster center is selected and the process is repeated. Once objects enter a cluster they are removed from further processing.

Significance level the probability of obtaining the evidence if the null hypothesis were true.

Similarity/judgment the judgment an individual makes about whether two objects are similar or different without specifying specific attributes.

Simple random sampling a sampling method in which each population member has an equal chance of being selected.

Single-source data data on product purchases and causal factors such as media exposure, promotion influence, and consumer characteristics that come from the same households as a result of advances in scanner and information technology.

Situation analysis the stage of the market planning process that deals with understanding the environment and the market, identifying opportunities and threats, and assessing the firm's competitive position.

Snowball design a judgmental sampling method in which each respondent is asked to identify one or more other sample members.

Social indicators statistical series that describe trends in social rather than economic variables.

Split-ballot technique the inclusion of more than one version of a question in a questionnaire.

Split-cable testing exposing two or more groups of a cable system to different ads and monitoring their purchases.

Spurious association an inappropriate causal interpretation of association due to an unmeasured variable influencing both variables.

Standard deviation the square root of the variance.

Standard error of estimate in regression analysis, the standard deviation of the sampling distribution of the regression model parameter estimates.

Standard Industrial Classification (SIC) System a uniform numbering system developed by the U.S. Government for classifying industrial establishments according to their economic activities.

Standard Metropolitan Statistical Area (SMSA) census tracts that are combined in counties containing a central city with a population of at least 50,000.

Standardized marketing data sources external sources of marketing data collected by outside organizations for several information users who have common information needs.

Stapel scale a 10-category, unipolar rating scale with categories numbered from −5 to +5. It modifies the semantic differential by having the respondent rate how close and in what direction a descriptor adjective fits a given concept.

Statistic any of several characteristics of a sample.

Statistical control the control of extraneous variables through statistical methods.

Strategic plans plans that focus on strategic decisions of resource allocation with long-run performance implications, usually having time horizons of more than one year.

Stratified sampling a sampling method that uses natural subgroups or strata that are more homogeneous than the total population.

Surrogate information error error that occurs due to the difference between the information that is required for a marketing research study and the information being sought by the researcher.

Survey method a method of data collection, such as a telephone or personal interview, a mail survey, or any combination thereof.

Syndicated services services from firms such as A. C. Nielsen, Information Resources Inc., and SAMI/Burke who make available standardized and recurrent marketing research reports to subscribers, usually manufacturers of frequently purchased consumer packaged goods.

Systematic error the measurement error due to constant aspects of the person or measurement situation.

TELNET a program that enables a user to log in to a remote host site.

Test marketing the introduction of the new product in selected test cities that represent the typical market, so that the results of the performance in these markets can be projected on a national basis.

Third person techniques a technique of ascertaining the respondents' views by asking them to answer for a third person.

Through-the-book measurement of exposure to print media by asking respondents if they recognized articles in an issue.

Thurstone/Equal-Appearing Interval Scale a scale developed by first having a group of judges categorize a set of items and then selecting those items that were similarly categorized; the scale is administered by having respondents choose those statements with which they agree.

Time-series forecasting data collected over time, such as weekly sales data for three years, especially effective for short-term forecasting.

Top-down/chain-ratio approach a method of determining market potential that has as its starting point the identification of the total and available markets.

Total quality management (TQM) the concept of creation of value to the consumer through enhanced product and service quality, thereby enhancing customer satisfaction.

Tracking studies monitoring the performance of advertising by regular surveys of the audience.

Trade-off approach a method of collecting data for trade-off analysis in which the respondent is asked to rank each combination of levels of two attributes from most preferred to least preferred.

Transmission Control Protocol/Internet Protocol (TCI/IP) a suite of protocols that defines the Internet.

Unaided recall a questioning approach in which the respondent is asked to remember an object of interest without the assistance of clues from the researcher.

Uniform Product Code (UPC) a standard code assigned to each manufacturer's brand and pack size so that its purchases can be tracked through a store scanner system.

U.S. Bureau of the Census the federal agency that conducts the U.S. Census once every 10 years and compiles demographic statistics on the population. It also conducts one-shot surveys for other federal agencies.

USENET a worldwide system of discussion groups.

Use test a type of product evaluation where the product is given to consumers; after a reasonable period of time, the consumers are asked for their reactions to it.

Utility in trade-off analysis, the worth or value of each level of each attribute relative to the other levels.

Validity the ability of a measurement instrument to measure what it is supposed to measure.

Values and Lifestyles Survey (VALS) a survey conducted by the Stanford Research Institute, which classifies the U.S. population into nine lifestyle segments based on individual values and lifestyles of survey respondents.

Variable respecification a procedure by which existing data are modified to create new variables or a large number of variables are collapsed into fewer variables.

Variance a measure of dispersion based on the degree to which elements of a sample or population differ from the average element.

Varimax rotation a rotation method that searches for simple structure, a pattern of factor loadings where some loadings are close to one, and some loadings are close to zero.

Warehouse withdrawal services syndicated services offered by firms such as SAMI/Burke in which periodic audits are done at the warehouse or wholesale level and reports are produced on product shipments made to retail stores served by those warehouses.

Weighting a procedure by which each response in the database is assigned to a number according to some prespecified rule.

Word association a projective technique in which the respondent is asked to give the first word that comes to mind on the presentation of another word.

World Wide Web a graphical environment that provides point-and-click access to the Internet through a network of World Wide Web servers.

Index